ATLAS
OF
DOG BREEDS
OF THE WORLD

Bonnie Wilcox, DVM,
and
Chris Walkowicz

H-1091

Distributed in the UNITED STATES to the Pet Trade by T.F.H. Publications, Inc., One T.F.H. Plaza, Neptune City, NJ 07753; distributed in the UNITED STATES to the Bookstore and Library Trade by National Book Network, Inc. 4720 Boston Way, Lanham MD 20706; in CANADA to the Pet Trade by H & L Pet Supplies Inc., 27 Kingston Crescent, Kitchener, Ontario N2B 2T6; Rolf C. Hagen Ltd., 3225 Sartelon Street, Montreal 382 Quebec; in CANADA to the Book Trade by Vanwell Publishing Ltd., 1 Northrup Crescent, St. Catharines, Ontario L2M 6P5 ; in ENGLAND by T.F.H. Publications, PO Box 15, Waterlooville PO7 6BQ; in AUSTRALIA AND THE SOUTH PACIFIC by T.F.H. (Australia), Pty. Ltd., Box 149, Brookvale 2100 N.S.W., Australia; in NEW ZEALAND by Brooklands Aquarium Ltd. 5 McGiven Drive, New Plymouth, RD1 New Zealand; in Japan by T.F.H. Publications, Japan—Jiro Tsuda, 10-12-3 Ohjidai, Sakura, Chiba 285, Japan; in SOUTH AFRICA by Lopis (Pty) Ltd., P.O. Box 39127, Booysens, 2016, Johannesburg, South Africa. Published by T.F.H. Publications, Inc.
MANUFACTURED IN THE UNITED STATES OF AMERICA
BY T.F.H. PUBLICATIONS, INC.

ATLAS

OF

DOG BREEDS

OF THE WORLD

Bonnie Wilcox, DVM,
and
Chris Walkowicz

Fifth Edition

About the Authors

Bonnie Wilcox, D.V.M., and Chris Walkowicz, each having established distinguished careers in the dog fancy, combine their talents and experience to bring forth *The Atlas of Dog Breeds of the World*. This volume, the product of four years of research and writing, is the third book co-authored by this team. *Successful Dog Breeding* (1985) and *The Complete Question and Answer Book on Dogs* (1988) have both received recognition by the Dog Writers Association of America, the former being chosen as the Best Dog Book of the Year 1985. The authors have also established themselves as monthly columnists for international dog magazines. Dr. Wilcox, a practicing veterinarian for over 20 years, pens "Tell Me Why," for *Dog Fancy*, while Ms. Walkowicz writes "Breeders Forum" for *Pure-Bred Dogs/American Kennel Gazette*. Ms. Walkowicz, a full-time freelance writer and editor, has authored over 200 published articles as well as two breed books: *The Bearded Collie* (1987) and *Your German Shepherd Dog*. Dr. Wilcox, also a breeder of German Shorthaired Pointers, received her B.S. and D.V.M. degrees from the University of Illinois School of Veterinary Medicine. Both authors, whose association with pure-bred dogs as owners and breeders extends some 20 years, live with their husbands, children and dogs in Illinois.

To Rebecca, Clayton and Amy Wilcox
Dean, Teresa, Michael and Josh Walkowicz
who understand that Moms can be more than cookie bakers.

May you, sometime in your life,
know the love of a very
special dog.

Acknowledgments

A big thank you to our correspondents, who have contributed their time, knowledge and photos of their chosen breeds. Without you, we would have had no direct source of correct information on some of these breeds, particularly in countries outside the United States.

To Isabelle Francais, who supplied many of the marvelous photos from all over the world, and added color to this kaleidoscope of dogs.

To John R. Quinn, who rendered the dog illustrations used to make this volume complete. Mr. Quinn was able to recreate, with enviable accuracy, many of the extremely rare and possibly extinct breeds for which photographs were not available. Much gratitude for his talent and dedication to this project.

To the Quad City branch of the National League of American Pen Women, especially Willetta Balla, Judie Gulley, Betty Klaas, Rhonda Krahl, Connie Heckert, Delores Kuenning, Jan Oliver and Sidney Jeanne Seward, who (thankfully) have been ruthless in their critiquing sessions.

To our translators who have come to our rescue and untwisted our English tongues. They have made it possible for us to ask our questions and to understand the answers we received.

Contents

Authors' Preface

"But the poor dog, in life the firmest friend,
The first to welcome, foremost to defend,
Whose honest heart is still his master's own,
Who labours, fights, lives, breathes for him alone."

Lord Byron

Although most dog owners already recognize—and appreciate—these attributes, it is difficult for us to truly understand our own dogs and their history without a general knowledge about evolution of the human/dog relationship, its roots and transformation.

The authors believe, as do most animal behaviorists, that if more pets were chosen through knowledge rather than seduction by a pair of deep, soulful eyes, fewer pets would end their existence at an animal shelter. . . or worse. An understanding of the individual breeds can best be attained by a study of the parent groups and their accompanying predispositions/inclinations/proclivities. Only after such research should a pet be chosen to fill and complete a family and its individual lifestyle.

Our intent is for this book to help all dog enthusiasts more fully appreciate their own breed choice. These insights will help dog owners see what causes the pleasing characteristics—as well as the ones that irritate them. Ingrained breed nature instills the sweetness, intelligence, loyalty, sturdiness, working and protective qualities that we desire in the various breeds. This very nature also motivates digging, yapping terriers; chasing, yelping herding dogs; aggressive, barking flock guards and mastiffs; straying, howling gun dogs and hounds; and independent, aloof sighthounds and pariahs.

Most people, however, have deep feelings for their pets and, according to surveys, consider them an important part of the family. For these dog lovers, it is interesting to discover and to share what makes their dogs "tick." We intend to unfold a world of dogs—and their roots—hoping to further strengthen this bond between people and their pets. The information and photographs from owners all over the world demonstrate that the love between masters and their dogs transcends the boundaries, tensions and stone walls between countries.

Frequently, people tend to focus on the world of dogs from the narrow viewpoint of their favorite breed, as if it were an isolated phenomenon. Even the professional breeder or exhibitor may attend a kennel club show and watch the Pomeranians, Schipperkes and Norwegian Elkhounds, all in different group divisions, and be unaware that these breeds share a close common background. Through this volume, dog lovers will have the opportunity to look at the great diversity of dogs through a wide-angle lens.

Many people do not realize that more than 400 breeds of dogs share our world with us. Some of them are common in their homelands; others are unknown even to the people who share their native countries. Yet all of these breeds have carved a niche and a relationship with humankind. Moreover, every one was created for a specific purpose. These are truly "Dogs For All Reasons."

—B.W./C.W.

How to Use This *Atlas*

In undertaking this volume that intends to survey the breeds of dog known to man, we, as authors, were pleased to hit upon the notion of "Dogs For All Reasons" to guide us through the immense and fascinating world of dogs. Therefore, each breed of dog in this volume is categorized according to its stem group, original purpose and geographical development. The traditional groupings employed by the major registering bodies have not been used here. Our pursuit of "Dogs For All Reasons" has produced eight categories, into which all 400+ dog breeds fall: Flock Guards, Mastiffs, Scenthounds (referred to in the text simply as Hounds), Gun Dogs, Northern Breeds, Herding Dogs, Terriers, and Southern Dogs. For instance, the Chow Chow, which the American Kennel Club groups as Non-Sporting and the Kennel Club of Great Britain groups as Utility, has here been placed among the Northern Breeds due to its place of origin and traditional purpose. This includes even the breeds which are considered "Toys" in most registries.

A chapter devoted to each of the eight categories of dogs describes the group's general characteristics and gives the reader an historical perspective on the group's evolution. Complete lists of the breeds in the group are included at the end of this chapter.

The next section, "The Dogs of the World," is a collection of articles arranged alphabetically. Inasmuch as some breeds are very similar in historical origins and characteristics, we have combined some related breeds into single articles. The Breed Name Cross-Reference list will show the reader where in the alphabetical section these breeds can be found.

When the information is available, ranges for height and weight are given for each breed, from the smallest female to the largest male. Height is rounded up to the nearest half-inch, and weight is given in pounds. Registry is noted for the Federation Cynologique Internationale (FCI) world registry; the two main registering bodies of the United States: the American Kennel Club (AKC) and the United Kennel Club (UKC); The Kennel Club of England (TKC); and the Canadian Kennel Club (CKC). In addition to the notations in this volume, however, many of the breeds are registered by their own country's kennel clubs, by private registries, or by specialty clubs. The country listed is not always the country of origin, but is that which most cynologists credit with breed development and promotion.

Personal communications from correspondents are included in the body of the text without footnotes; additionally, all other references have been incorporated into the text for smooth and easy reading. Complete lists of sources, contributors, and owners of the dogs portrayed in the book are included at the back of the volume.

Throughout this work, *breed names* are capitalized; however, words referring to *types* of dogs are lowercased (e.g., the American Foxhound is one breed of foxhound).

Breed Name Cross-Reference

Since this list is designed to help the reader locate the dog breeds mentioned in the alphabetically arranged articles in "The Dogs of the World," it does not, of course, contain the titles of all the articles found there. The column on the left states the breed name; the column in the center is the title of the article in which the dog is discussed, and the column on the right indicates the page number.

Because dogs have different names in different lands, this list will aid the reader in locating the name of the article that pertains to the breed in question. To illustrate: the Pyrenean Mountain Dog, as the breed is known in Great Britain, is known more commonly in the United States as the Great Pyrenees; in France, its native land, it is called the Chien de Montagne des Pyrenees. Thus, the reader is able to look up the British or the French name to find the name employed in this atlas (in this case, Great Pyrenees).

Articles that combine two or more breeds of similar origins and characteristics are also covered in this list. For example the article entitled "Elkhounds" treats the Norwegian Elkhound and its two closest relations, the Black Norwegian Elkhound and the Jämthund. Looking up any of these three breed names will direct the reader to the article entitled "Elkhounds."

BREED NAME	ARTICLE TITLE	PAGE
African Lion Hound	Rhodesian Ridgeback	717
Aidi	Chien de l'Atlas	280
Ainu-Ken	Ainu Dog	82
Akita Inu	Akita	88
Alpenlandischer Dachsbracke	Alpine Dachsbracke	96
Alsatian	German Shepherd Dog	423
American Pit Bull	American Pit Bull Terrier	117
AmerToy	Toy Fox Terrier	840
Anatolian Karabash Dog	Anatolian Shepherd Dog	123
Anglo-Francais de Moyen Venerie	Anglos-Francaises	125
Anglo-Francais de Petite Venerie	Anglos-Francaises	125
Appenzell Mountain Dog	Appenzeller	128
Appenzeller Sennenhund	Appenzeller	128
Arabian Greyhound	Sloughi	796
Arctic Husky	Siberian Husky	785
Ardennes Cattle Dog	Bouvier de Ardennes	218
Argentinian Mastiff	Dogo Argentino	340
Ariége Pointer	Braque d'Ariége	226
Artesian Norman Basset	Basset Artésien Normand	150
Atlas Sheepdog	Chien de l'Atlas	280
Australian Greyhound	Kangaroo Dog	530
Australian Native Dog	Dingo	332
Australian Queensland Heeler	Australian Cattle Dog	132
Australian Silky Terrier	Silky Terrier	793
Austrian Smoothhaired Hound	Austrian Brandlbracke	140
Auvergne Pointer	Braque d'Auvergne	227
Balkan Hound	Yugoslavian Hounds	885
Balkanski Gonič	Yugoslavian Hounds	885
Barb	Australian Kelpie	133
Barbone	Poodles	688
Bas Rouge	Berger de Beauce	180
Basset Bleu de Gascogne	Bleus de Gascogne	198
Basset Fauve de Bretagne	Fauves de Bretagne	394
Bayrischer Gebirgsschweisshund	Bavarian Mountain Hound	156

Dogs For All Reasons

Although many beasts have served humanity throughout time, only one serves by choice. Only one animal is willing to forsake its own kind and follow us. Dogs have always been and remain "man's best friend"—and mankind, occasionally, is dog's.

Cynologists and archeologists have found evidence of the canine/human relationship existing almost as early as the species of *Homo sapiens*. Dogs served the hunter, the shepherd and the warrior. They were guardians of the home, beasts of burden and companions on the journey of life. Dogs have long fed human need, their souls—even their bellies. Although few civilizations now incorporate dogs in their menus, dogs still assist their masters in all the ancient ways and in many new ones.

How did this relationship come to exist between people and dogs? What caused the development of so many diverse breeds?

The answer to this special bond can best be explained by studying the wolf. Wolves are the most social of all mammals: cooperating in the hunt, mating for life, sharing in puppy care, playing with and teaching their young. The dog has a built-in capacity to love and serve his "pack" or family. Cynologist John McLoughlin, in his history of dogs, *The Canine Clan, A New Look at Man's Best Friend*, summed up the phenomenon best when he said, "The dog can love us, not because we are so lovable, but because their wild wolf ancestors had such a mighty devotion for one another."

Each breed, each individual dog is valued by someone or by a group of people. It serves a purpose, even if its destination is "only" to stave off loneliness.

Oft-quoted legends portray this special relationship:

God summoned a beast from the field
and He said,
"Behold man, created in my image.
Therefore, adore him.

You shall protect him in the wilderness,
shepherd his flocks,
watch over his children, accompany him
wherever he may go,
even unto civilization. You shall be his
ally, his slave
and his companion.

"To do these things," God said, "I
endow you with these instincts
uncommon to other beasts: faithfulness,
devotion, and understanding surpassing
those of man himself.
Lest it impair your loyalty, you shall be
blind to the faults of man.
Lest it impair your understanding, you
are denied the power of words. Let no
fault of language cleave an accord
beyond that of man with any other beast
or even man with man. Speak to your
master only with your mind and through
honest eyes.
Walk by his side, sleep in his doorway,
forage for him, ward off his enemies,
carry his burdens, share his afflictions,
love him and comfort him.
And in return for this, man will fulfill
your needs and wants which shall be
only food, shelter and affection.
"So be silent, and be a friend to man.
Guide him through the perils along the
way to the land that I have promised
him.
This shall be your destiny and your
immortality."
So spake the Lord.
And the dog heard and was content.

* * *

At the creation of the world, an
earthquake carved a huge chasm,
leaving man on one side, and animals on
the other. Man called to the beasts for
companionship. As the dog saw man on

Like no other creature, dog serves man by choice. The Collie, which serves man as a herder, protector and companion, is one of the world's most famous canines.

the other side alone, he paced up and down the great divide, whining. When man called, "Come!", the dog leaped, narrowly missing and barely hanging onto the edge. Man leaned over and pulled him to safety, and thus began the closest relationship between man and beast.

★ ★ ★

Bible lore credits the dogs with Noah as using their noses to plug the holes which sprang in the Ark. This is why their noses are so cold!

★ ★ ★

A Spanish legend says the Three Wise Men were each accompanied by a dog to welcome the Christ Child. These dogs were Cubillon, Melampo and Lubino, and it is said that any dog that bears one of these names is blessed.

Dog & Man, by Sloan and Farquar

Although the early relatives of dogs and humans were certainly less sentimental than the forego-ing legends, the human-dog relationship was the

The evolution of the dog is closely linked to the history of man—where man has gone, dog has followed, to the North Pole, into the desert, into the woods, and through the prairie. These two American Cocker Spaniels live a contented life on the farm with their owner.

first of all the beasts. When families lived in caves, it is certain canine types were utilized—as scavengers and for hunting; as playmates for the cavekids and for warming cold toes; probably even on the cave menu.

Eventually the relationship grew closer and the dog prototype was looked on as a friend, rather than just a means to a comfy life.

A parallel history exists between *Homo sapiens* and dog. When society was pastoral, flock dogs were developed. When hunters needed assistance, sporting breeds answered the call. When civilizations moved to war, mighty dogs accompanied them, and the diversification of the breeds began.

Many anthropologists believe that the "thinking human" first developed in the area somewhere between northern India and northern Iran. This is also the geographical location that is believed to be the site of the oldest domesticated canines. From this background, it is possible to imagine either a single or twofold origin for the dog and to envision how the animal changed and spread throughout the world.

Human's first success at domestication was the dog. For centuries, the pattern persisted—primitive hunters and their dogs stalked and cut animals out of wild herds, sharing the bounty.

The first domesticated dog probably performed mainly as a herder. The herding progenitor retained many characteristics of the wolf: small, upright ears; foxy (wedge-shaped) faces; a stand-off coat; and the square, athletic body, built for endurance rather than speed. The neotanous (infantile) trait of the curled tail was purposely selected, along with the infantile temperament, i.e., more trusting and companionable than the adult wolf.

Geologists have found cave drawings and other proof of close association occurring during the Stone Age—50,000 years ago. In the United States, remains of dogs (dating to 9,000 years ago) were discovered in the Jaguar Cave, situated in the Beaverhead Mountains of east-central Idaho. Bones of two classes were found: one a small Beagle size, and another closer to the size of a modern-day retriever. Other burial sites in late Mesolithic and Neolithic settlements, circa 600 BC in Denmark, and lake settlements of Switzerland and Austria have disclosed the re-

Dogs have evolved for specific functions: to hunt, to herd, to guide, to defend. Despite a breed's particular original function, it can learn to perform a variety of tasks; this English Setter, a member of the gun dog group, does a fine job of keeping an eye on the farm livestock.

mains of sheepdogs, hunting dogs and miniature dogs. Artwork that depicted dogs was used to decorate stoneware, pottery and paintings from early Egypt, Assyria and Greece, as early as 3200 BC. Canine paw prints appear in a clay brick from Ur (ca. 2100 BC).

In Neolithic times, the Finno-Ugrian peoples first migrated from Tibet westward into Europe, then north to populate the great northern plains. They became Lapps, Samoyeds and other northern tribes. Later still, these nomads crossed the land bridge to populate the North and South American continents. With them, to all points of the world, came dogs of northern type, selected and molded for a variety of tasks.

Meanwhile, civilized Tibetans were selecting dogs for other traits. Smaller and shaggier dogs were used for herding. Others—larger and, eventually, giant—were selected for guardian chores. These became the stem breeds of the eastern herding dogs, as well as the fount of

flock guards and mastiffs. As migrations moved west into Europe and east to the Orient, these varieties moved with them—still retaining the tail curled over the back.

As civilization traveled south into the warm Fertile Crescent, it became more efficient to have a smaller and smoother coated pariah type dog. Within native populations of pariahs in the Middle East, a natural variation occurred and still exists: from the large flock-guard type, to the medium husky size and the collie type, and the svelte racing variety. This pattern indicates that these tendencies traveled with them from other parts of the world.

Nature influenced the development of breed types—when the dog lived in a cold clime, he grew a thick, warm coat. When he ran the hot desert sands, tufts of hair protected his feet.

His owner, too, helped to dictate his transformation. Breeders selectively bred for larger, faster, stronger, tinier—leaner or meaner.

19

Taxes and other impositions dictated canine fashion. In parts of the world, long-tailed dogs were taxed, and it became more economical to own a dog with a short stump or none at all. When genes didn't cooperate by transmuting this expensive appendage into short stubs, many a dog lost his tail to the knife—or even to teeth. For a fee, the whelps were nipped by the town's tail-biting "specialist."

Dogs of the nobility were pampered pets, or favored hunting companions, that enjoyed luxuries most of the populace could not imagine. The dogs of the poor, however, endured suffering and existed mainly to help their masters put food in their mouths or to ease their workloads.

The nobility further protected their advantages with cruel laws designed to prevent a royal hare stewing in a peasant's pot. The poor paid dearly for the luxury of their poverty, and so did their dogs. To prevent poaching by the commoners, their dogs' knee tendons were cut, so they could not run down a hare or deer on royal land. Expeditation, cutting off the toes from one foot, accomplished the same purpose. The "dog gauge," a ring of 7 inches x 5 inches, through which the dog must fit to escape mutilation, separated the fortunate toed from those who would soon be de-toed.

It's a miracle dogs (or their masters) survived to modern times! Treatments for various diseases (human and canine) called for mixtures of ox dung and vinegar; quicksilver, brimstone, nettlefeed and sewet [sic]; new pressed wine or egg white in the ear; a nail or needle to pull out worms. These methods were prescribed to cure everything from infertility or rabies to acne.

To the pharaohs in Egypt, the dog was a symbol of fidelity and a guardian. Anubis, the Egyptian god of death, who enfolded the dying in his arms, had the body of a man and the head of a dog. Even the Dog Star, Sirius, heralded the overflow of the Nile, and the shepherds moved their flocks to higher levels when the guardian star appeared.

Since these times, and even earlier, a wide variety of sizes and types bred true. The definition of a breed is "a race of animals from the same stock, kind or sort." The individual breeds recognized by the various world registries have bred true for many generations. Registry organizations, such as the Federation Cynologique Internationale (FCI), American Kennel Club (AKC), Canadian Kennel Club (CKC), The Kennel Club of Great Britain (TKC), and United Kennel Club (UKC), and those of various countries throughout the world, demand that newly recognized breeds be purebred and that their owners maintain stud books which list matings prior to the time of application for recognition. Many of these dogs boast pedigrees fancier than their masters' family trees. Pedigree is derived from the French *Pied de Grue*, meaning foot of the crane.

The Shih Tzu as a breed has made quite a stir in the dog fancy today—it was indeed one of the nobility's pampered pets centuries ago.

Bred in the Middle Ages by monks, the Basset Hound comes to modern man as a keen trailer of rabbit and hare. The breed's sluggish, sad-eyed expression is no indicator of this scenthound's abilities—it has been also known to work coon, squirrel and opossum.

In Roman times, however, before pedigrees or registrations became important, the earliest listing classified dogs as House, Shepherd, Sporting, Pugnacious or War, Dogs Which Ran By Scent and Swift Dogs Which Ran On Sight. The first breed "catalog" was attributed to Juliana Barnes (Berners), the prioress of Sopwell nunnery, in the 1486 *Boke of St. Albans*: "Greyhound, Bastard, Mengrell, Mastif, Lemor, Raches, Kenettys, Terroures, Butcher's Houndes, Dunghill Dogges, Tryndeltaylles, Prycheryd Currys, [and] Small Ladyes Poppees That Bere Awaye The Flees."

These translate into our current sighthounds, mongrels, mastiffs, Bloodhounds, Beagles, Bulldogs, terriers, long-tailed shepherd dogs, pariahs and toys of today—all of which still occasionally "bere flees."

While the "Small Ladyes Poppees" and the hounds of the hunt enjoyed sumptuous quarters, foods cooked especially for them, and personal servants, the dogs of the underclass scratched for their existence. No wonder certain breeds carry themselves with regal bearing,

while others are scrappy, feisty and independent! Dog expert Edward C. Ash noted: "The dog of well-educated people somehow or other collects some of their education, habits and manners, and the dog of a man who lives by his wits appears verily to vie with his master, behaving with the greatest cunning, sometimes with more wisdom than its biped companion."

Throughout time, individuals have shown their bond to dogs even unto death. Egyptian masters mourned the loss of their pets by shaving all the hair of their heads and bodies. They erected tombs in miniature for their beloved pets, and even fitted their dogs with golden masks, similar to those placed on esteemed personages. The Toltec Indians felt the most perfect, unselfish love was that of a dog for its master. When its owner died, the pet was buried with the master. The selfless beast's devotion carried through life unto death, when the dog interceded with the god of death, relating the master's good deeds. Some cultures fitted deceased dogs with glass eyes so they could see in the afterworld.

The Shar-Pei, a breed of ancient China, has a mastiffy appearance and a respective dominant temperament, but belongs to the northern group as its genes are traced to Nordic, Chow-type dogs. Trained properly, the Shar-Pei is affectionate and personable.

The largest funeral for a dog was hosted by Emperor Norton I of the U.S., Protector of Mexico. Ten thousand people mourned the death of the Emperor's mongrel, "Lazaras."

Concern of masters for their pets in the afterlife has been chronicled by anthropologists who have found evidence of cave dwellers, and later Indians, and their dogs buried together. In the ruins of Pompeii were the remains of an elderly person. Cradled in the skeletal hand was a pet dog, comforting and being comforted to the fiery end. A dog cemetery from 700 BC has been unearthed in Israel. All the skeletons appear to be of sighthound type.

Even today, true dog lovers take it upon themselves to ensure their pet a peaceful departure from life and arrange a burial or memorial of their companions. Pet cemeteries and cremations are common, as are the accoutrements of death: caskets, stone markers and memorial donations.

In some societies, the bond was so strong that dogs were actually chosen over humans. The Fulgian Indian Dog, which guarded the camp and aided in hunting otters and birds, was crucial to the tribe's welfare. The oldest women were assigned to care for these dogs. When food was scarce, these women would be cannibalized, but never the dogs. A tribesman was quoted, "Dogs catch otters . . . old women are good for nothing."

In more modern times, however, the odds leaned to the humans. Wars were hard on dogs, as well as people. Breeds suffered decimation, some to extinction, others to minimal numbers. People were occupied with keeping themselves alive, rather than concerned with breeding pure-bred dogs or even feeding them. Later, with care and nurturing, several endangered breeds again flourished.

In our modern world, as communications expand and walls between countries come down, we learn more and more about other nations, the people and their canine companions. Currently, FCI recognizes nearly 400 dog breeds and varieties worldwide. Those that are unknown in the United States are often termed "rare breeds," which some are, indeed. Others are common-place in their homeland, but still relatively unheard of in some areas of the world. The popularity of many lesser known breeds is increasing, however, in their native lands and the United States.

Most dogs fit neatly within one of the following genres: flock guard, mastiff, scenthound, gun dog, terrier, northern, herding or southern dog. Some of our modern breeds, however, could have their family tree traced back to two or more of these groups through various ancestral crossbreedings.

In this book we have categorized the individual breeds according to the group of their stem breeds, original purpose and/or geographical development. The toy breeds are also classified according to their stem breed.

One of the largest of the flock guards, the Great Pyrenees is surely a people-dog. The flock guardians are as courageous and industrious as they are loyal and beguiling.

The Flock Guards
Keepers of Their Kingdoms

About 8,000 years ago in what is now the Middle East, primitive people evolved into the true modern *Homo sapiens*. This new "thinking" person domesticated herbivores and swine, undertook crude agriculture, molded pottery and conceived the idea of community living. The domesticated flocks represented their wealth, a continual and reproducible food supply.

However, the domesticated plant eater was at constant risk. Carnivores—wolves, bears, and lions—found them easy prey. And, of course, shepherds fought the threat of raids from neighboring villages.

Early herdsmen noted the natural protective qualities of some dogs. Selective breeding began, the largest specimens being chosen to confront a hungry bear or a 125-pound wolf.

Mass alone was not enough, for the job demanded agility as well as power. A flock guardian (not to be confused with a herding dog) needed courage and watchfulness, as well as wholehearted loyalty to his charges. He would stay with the flock all year, facing the same climatic extremes. Food was not always plentiful, yet vigilance had to be maintained. Even facing starvation, he could never turn to the flock for food. Thus the group became "easy keepers," able to survive and keep their large bodies strong with minimal food. They had to earn their keep, or they were eliminated. Flock guarding had stringent job requirements—size, dedication and toughness.

Historians tell us that Neolithic tribes migrated from the high plateaus of Turkey and Iran about 6,000 years ago. They spread in all directions, to Africa, Europe and the East. Accompanying them were dogs of an ancient type (called *ku-assa*, or the horse dog) used to guard their vast herd/flock wealths. Soon throughout the Neolithic world, primitive villages and shepherds used large dogs to help keep their food supplies safe.

Canine protection proved most beneficial in the mountainous regions. The largest and boldest predators roamed the mountains. The forest, rocks and crevices, as well as the distances between pastures and from the village, made keeping track of the entire flock difficult work for shepherds.

Crop cultivation spread through the fertile flat ground. Domestic flocks and herds were often relegated to the poorer pastures and high mountains.

From the great high plains of Turkey and the Caucasus Mountains of southern Russia, to the rugged Carpathians of eastern Europe, through the Balkans, the high Alps, the Pyrenees range of Spain, Portugal's Estrela Mountains, even the low Atlas chain of northern Africa—all have their flock-guarding type, bred true for four or five millenia.

Despite thousands of years and miles separation, all the breeds are amazingly similar in type. They are always large (the higher the mountains, often the larger the specimen), ranging from an economical 60 pounds to a robust 140 pounds.

These flock-guarding dogs were the stem type from which all the mastiff-type dogs developed. They were valued for their ferocity and watchfulness, independent thinking, hardiness, devotion to duty and loyalty to master. Flock guards possessed courage, speed, agility, craftiness, endurance, and stamina. They were free from wanderlust and the hunt or chase urge, attacking only when their property was threatened.

The dogs belonged to the village, sleeping here and there, and feeding on scraps. They guarded their entire territory.

They were then, as well as now, great, imposing beasts—tall, muscular and large-boned. Many have rear dewclaws, which are sometimes retained. The body is balanced, with a long tail carried low. The body might be a bit longer

The Italian contribution to the flock guards, the Maremma Sheepdog, is a fine example of the group. The Maremma spends his nights with the flock, protecting and guarding it, while the shepherd goes home to sleep.

than tall, with very little tuck-up. Although large, they are not ponderous and heavy skinned like the mastiffs. The flat head, with a tendency to a deep median groove, is generous and strong, yet more refined. The stop is pronounced, accompanied by a slightly tapering muzzle. The small drop ears are in distinct opposition to dog's enemy, the wolf.

In their native lands, the ears of working dogs were often cropped short. Sometimes tails were partially docked. The dogs were left outdoors year round, and grooming was not on the shepherds' agenda. Docking and cropping eliminated matting and problems of sanitation. Cropping increased the visibility of the dog's reactions when his ears raised at the base during an alert. This practice is dying out, however, and many exhibited dogs must remain natural.

An ample coat protects them from the elements—the closer coats of the Turkish plains and northern African hills, to the heavy-corded rugs in the high cold peaks. Coats are moderate in length, with thick underwool and, occasionally, a slight wave to the hair. Although the dun or tan/gray color has been accepted by breeders in a few lower elevations, white is the preferred color for many reasons. White distinguishes them from the wolf and allows them acceptance into the flock, as well as making them visible from distances when apart from the sheep.

They are almost indistinguishable from sheep in the middle of the flock. Studies show most guarding "sheep dogs are sheep-sized, sheep-colored, sheep-shaped."

As civilization creeps into areas where the shepherd and his flock guardian have toiled secluded for centuries, the working specimens become fewer and fewer. Fortunately, the breeds are being preserved. Many countries and breed clubs have fostered an interest in saving these magnificent dogs. Through difficult times, wars and poverty, the aristocracy of Turkey protected their purebred dogs. The Veterinary School at Brno has fostered the rebirth of the Czechoslovakian version, and several have gained recognition by the American and English Kennel Clubs.

Although the breeds have long served their native lands, they have achieved the admiration of American shepherds and cattle owners only recently. The wolf is disappearing in Europe and Asia, but it still exists in America and plagues stock, along with its cousin the coyote,

Known in its native Poland as an outstanding mountain worker, the Owczarek Podhalanski is extremely attentive and alert.

causing serious financial and breeding program deprivation. The U.S. government spends many millions a year in an attempt to control this destruction, with annual losses still totaling over a million sheep. Several of the breeds have been imported to the United States for development as flock guardians.

Biologists at Hampshire College in Amherst, Massachusetts, have a study program using these dogs. In their first year they procured ten pups of three different breeds of European and Asian working stock. They bred and raised the first generations, noting behavior, and placed them all on farms and ranches.

Ray and Lorna Coppinger of the college note they brought: "two screaming, quarreling, Russian-type Ovcharka [sic] pups from eastern Turkey to Ankara by bus, while we cut at miles of red tape with dull scissors in Budapest, trying to get four Shar Planinetz [sic] pups we'd bought in southwestern Yugoslavia onto a direct flight to Boston. In Italy, we dickered in millions of lire for the great white Maremmano-Abruzzese sheepdog."

The Livestock Dog Project at Hampshire College has monitored Great Pyrenees, Maremmas, Russian Owtcharkas, Anatolian Shepherds, Sarplaninacs, Tibetan Mastiffs, and Castro Laboreiros. The U.S. Sheep Experiment Station in Dubois, Idaho, has also researched and trained guarding dogs against predators, using Great Pyrenees, Komondors and Akbash Dogs.

The training programs begin when pups are eight weeks old. A shelter is erected near the sheep, where the pup can see its future wards, but not harm them or be harmed.

Youngsters are not left in charge of sheep until they reach about one year of age, although there are exceptions. A future flock guard must be a natural guardian and exhibit proper behavior: nonaggression and attentiveness to sheep, as well as defense of the flock. They should never use their teeth on the sheep. These dogs are protectors rather than herders. When young, the pups tend to play with the sheep. Care must be taken to stop rowdy galloping, harmful to both sheep and dogs. The pup may be injured, and the sheep may lose wool, suffer torn ears or be chased to death.

However, if it's the sheep that reacts aggres-

Spanish shepherds carrying baby lambs with Spanish Mastiff following closely behind. The Spanish Mastiff shares a similar history to other flock-guarding canines from Portugal and Spain and can still be found on hills of Spain close by its well-protected flocks.

sively, the dog shows submissive behavior as it would toward its mother: lowering haunches, turning a back knee out, and licking the sheep's face.

Escape routes of the training pen are not blocked, and pups could easily leave the area. Therefore, they are judged by their desire to stay with the sheep. Most of these dogs instinctively perform well. For instance, one male is recorded to have saved a wet, newborn lamb that was isolated from its mother, curling up with it to keep it warm.

Charles Darwin, *The Zoology of The Voyage of H.M.S. Beagle*, told about these dogs: "It has no wish to leave the flock, and just as another dog will defend its master, man, so will these the sheep. It is amusing to observe, when approaching a flock, how the dog immediately advances barking, and the sheep all close in his rear [*sic*], as if round the oldest ram."

As Darwin wrote in 1833 about the dogs' stringent training in their country of origin: "The method of education consists in separating the puppy, while very young, from the bitch,

and in accustoming it to its future companions. An ewe is held three or four times a day for the little thing to suck, and a nest of wool is made for it in the sheep-pen; at no time is it allowed to associate with other dogs, or with the children of the family."

Flock-guarding dogs have been raised to think of the stock as their family. The best ones show total dedication to their charges, not to their fellow dogs, nor even to their master or master's family unless trained for that chore. Flock guards often are raised among the sheep they will grow to protect. The dogs begin to interact, even to the point of suckling on ewes and performing sexual play as they normally would with their own kind.

As a group, the dogs are difficult to breed. First heats usually occur between one and two years. The bitch is sometimes not receptive in the first heat, and if bred, pseudopregnancy is common. They rarely have a litter until their second heat. The bitch may actually be antagonistic, so that the interested male becomes submissive. Libido in males is low, complicating matters.

Shepherds in various European countries allow their pups to get acquainted with the flock at a very early age. Some owners relay that their flock guards think they are sheep themselves. This Sarplaninac pup seems to get on fine with his woolly pals.

The flock-guarding breeds are much more interested in the sheep or their other charges than in propagating their own species. Once in whelp, however, they become good mothers. In fact, non-breeding females sometimes allow young of other species to nurse.

It is interesting to note a case where Border Collies were raised with flock guards. Though environment was identical, the herding dogs were quicker to respond to commands and the guardians slower; the Collies "eyed" and stalked, where the guards did not. The guarding dogs were non-retrieving and not as responsive to directions. The Collies eagerly did both. As they grew older, the guardians preferred the sheep to playing with their "littermates." Each was growing up exactly as nature intended.

The guarding characteristics of various breeds and individuals range from mild resistance to hostility against intruders. The most aggressive dogs are assigned to remote pastures with flocks suffering high losses. Even then, posting signs and showing the dog its boundaries are suggested. Some dogs insist on guarding adjacent areas; however, they may guard the neighbor's sheep as well!

As guarding maturity is reached, males—even some females—raise legs to urinate rather than squat, and scent marking becomes more deliberate, placed around boundaries. Barking becomes an alarm, rather than puppy yapping. They are active for longer periods and sleep less. The dogs display more interest in the sheep than their handler. Patroling escalates and dogs stay on the job around the clock, taking advantage of any shelter when necessary.

A high-pitched, crisis bark, charging at the trespasser and tail held high in warning are indicative of typical guard behavior. While observing the dogs and collecting choice pups in Yugoslavia, the Coppingers reported that one of their group tested a guard by approaching the flock. The huge dog casually rose, approached, and gave alert signs of lowered head. He meant business, and no further challenge was given.

Records show that the dogs are achieving favor with the New World stock breeders. Most canid predators will not approach when there are multiple guards or one of a larger size. Even though confrontations were not always observed, statistics show fewer casualties to the flocks. In more than one case, the dog had to be removed from the flock for a period of time (such as for a veterinary visit), and kills occurred while it was away.

These dogs have shown amazing success in trial situations, winning the enthusiastic praise of stockmen! They are an attractive alternative to expensive, harmful and unappealing methods, such as poisons, traps, fences, chemicals or special guns.

FLOCK GUARDS

Akbash Dog	Turkey
Caucasian Owtcharka	USSR
Middle Asian Owtcharka	USSR
Kangal Dog	Turkey
Anatolian Shepherd Dog	Turkey
Greek Sheepdog	Greece
Sarplaninac	Yugoslavia
Karst Shepherd	Yugoslavia
Rumanian Sheepdog	Rumania
South Russian Owtcharka	USSR
Komondor	Hungary
Kuvasz	Hungary
Slovak Cuvac	Czechoslovakia
Owczarek Podhalanski	Poland
Maremma Sheepdog	Italy
Great Pyrenees	France
Pyrenean Mastiff	Spain
Spanish Mastiff	Spain
Perro de Pastor Mallorquin	Spain
Estrela Mountain Dog	Portugal
Cão de Castro Laboreiro	Portugal
Rafeiro do Alentejo	Portugal
Chien de l'Atlas	Morocco

Above: Flock guards must be agile and attentive. The Estrela Mountain Dog of Portugal is a cousin to the Spanish Mastiff of Spain and a lively guardian. **Below:** Maremma Sheepdog pups getting acquainted with the family lambs.

The Mastiffs
Let Slip the Dogs of War

Somewhere in Tibet or northern India, about seventy centuries ago, a giant trod the earth. This was not just another "big dog," but a true giant, the mastiff prototype. One in every 10,000 births is a giant, in humans as well as dogs.

Flock-guarding dogs in the 100-pound-plus range were already well-established in human settlements. As humans became more civilized, they began to manipulate animal and plant breeding. The rare giant pups were selected by these early breeders and the type was soon fixed.

Acromegalic traits in dogs are as distinct as those in humans and often correlate similar features. The giants are massive due to substantially increased bone growth. The growth hormone further causes an increased size in the distal extremities, resulting in huge paws and bulky skull with heavy jaw and brows. Overgrowth and thickening of the skin produces the wrinkled, scowling expression, heavy flew and dewlaps, large drop ears, and a tendency to an abundance of skin on the body. (One might imprudently assume he is slow and clumsy.) Sadly, like his human giant counterparts, the acromegalic dog also is predisposed to heart trouble, back, hip, and gastro-intestinal problems, and a generally shortened life span.

The classic mastiff has a deep, abrupt stop and a muzzle that is strong but proportionately shorter than the capacious back skull. Generally the type is smooth-coated—allowing no grasping—and carries its tail low. The mastiff has a superior power of scent and a strong sense of territory, with no tendency to chase or herd—all gifts from flock-guarding ancestors.

The colors originated as sable (red), fawn, black/tan, or brindle without white markings. The rare dilution factors that produce the chocolate, blue, or pale gray hues were present even then. Originally, these frightening behemoths were used to guard flocks—later, home and property. As selective breeding continued with

the most fierce and aggressive, they were adapted to warfare and combat. From this prototype came all of the European mastiff types of today, most of the world's fighting breeds, and other modern dog giants. But this mastiff was also the progenitor of the true hounds, and later the gun dogs. Since the scenthounds and the mastiffs are so closely related genetically, ancient references to "hounds" were often actually describing the lighter bodied mastiff.

From his start in Tibet, the warlike leviathan traveled with tribes as they migrated into other parts of the world, from the Himalayas to the Pyrenees. This mastiff migration followed two major routes, one west through the Middle East and the Mediterranean, and the other northwest via China and Russia. The progress of the northern mastiff parallels the migration of a variety of fierce, nomadic people originally from the Turkistan areas of southern Russia. During the millenia before Christ these nomads migrated east into western China, conquering as they went.

Their mastiffs were lighter in body, perhaps because the wandering lifestyle required a nomadic dog. The most distinct trait of the northern dog was the first appearance of the brachycephalic (undershot) jaw. Whether this was a spontaneous trait (a mutation) or came from crosses with Chinese dogs is unknown. There is reference to a huge, fierce, short-faced "hound," called the Shejos, in China as early as 600 BC.

As the political winds changed, the nomads migrated back to the West. A group called the Alans arrived in eastern Europe five or six centuries BC to settle what is now Albania, and others arrived in waves around 400 AD. Thus the brachycephalic eastern mastiff was possibly the first of his type to arrive in Europe, and he certainly predated the Christian era. The Germanic tribes especially welcomed this canine's toughness and incorporated it into their dog

Used to guard flocks and property, the early relatives of today's mastiff breeds were adapted for fighting and combat. Breeders focused on the traits they considered to be paramount: strength, aggressiveness, and size. This vocal, able-bodied mastiff is an American Bulldog.

populations. Romans wrote of the "broad-mouthed" fighting dogs found on the British island when the Romans arrived in the early centuries AD.

By the Middle Ages the racier, undershot "mastiffs" were known throughout Europe as Alaunts or Alains. This name may have referred to the nomadic Alans, or perhaps came from the word *Allemanni* for people of Germanic origin.

The southern branch of the mastiff family followed the spread of civilization from Tibet, south and east through the Fertile Crescent. The Sumerian, Babylonian, Assyrian and Phoenician cultures all used mammoth war dogs, the fiercest being the "molossian," supposedly from the Greek island of Molossus.

Dogs were heavily utilized—as tools—in warfare. Both Greek and Assyrian armies sent dogs ahead of their men to draw fire and disclose the whereabouts of the enemy. The dogs sometimes wore collars fitted with huge curved blades or fiery torches. Leading the charge into enemy cavalry, the war dogs slashed, burned and spooked the horses. Another ploy was to have the warrior-master go ahead into battle while his war dog, clad in full armor, was forcefully restrained by a slave. As the warrior became engaged in hand-to-hand combat with an enemy, the enraged dog was released to go to the rescue of his master.

These fearsome canines defended their masters to the death and beyond, as shown by Aelian, a Greek cynologist of the early third century AD: "When Darius, the last of the Persian kings, was killed by Bessus in his battle with Alexander, and lay dead, all the men left the

Like human giants, mastiffs have oversized heads, huge feet, and a superabundance of wrinkles (flews). The Dogue de Bordeaux epitomizes these giant features.

The dogs spread to other lands, aided by the seafaring Phoenicians, who may have also introduced this type to England centuries before Christ. After his trip to the Far East, Marco Polo told of the Kubla Khan's vast kennel of 5,000 war mastiffs.

In Rome, the molossian dog found popularity—not only in the army—but also in the pit against bears, lions, and even men in the arena as entertainment. His skill and ferocity in mortal combat were legendary. Romans so depended on these dogs as guards that when some failed to bark as Gaul soldiers scaled the capitol, they were crucified.

"Let slip the dogs of war," a Latin phrase, was an appropriate cry for the Roman tradition. As the Roman legionnaires moved north in their conquest of Europe, the molossian went with them. Through this southern route, the heavier bodied mastiff with a conventional head was introduced to Europe. Many of the modern mastiff breeds trace their ancestry to a combination of the northern Alaunt as well as southern Molossus blood wedded in Europe.

By the Middle Ages, modern warfare had made the war mastiff obsolete. But new tasks were assumed by the great dogs. The molossian was adapted as an estate guardian. The terms bandog and *acathena* refer to the fact that the mastiff was tied during the day and allowed loose at night to roust poachers or intruders. Originally, these canine terrors were believed to be bred from bears and wolves. Little wonder that Cerberus, the canine guard to the gates of Hades, is proclaimed to be a mastiff.

Johannes Caius, writing *Of Englishe Dogges* in 1576, describes the Bandogge as "vaste, stubborne, ougly,...of a burthenous body,...terrible and frightful to behold." Besides describing their use as a guard, he tells of their formal training to fight bears, apes, and other beasts or even "men with pikestaffs and clubs."

Estate-owning nobility became so paranoid about poachers, they feared even their groundskeeper's dogs might be after their game. Thus, for hundreds of years it was illegal to own a large dog unless he had three toes on the front feet chopped off. If the lucky dog fit through the gauge, he was determined too small to harm game and kept his toes. King's men performed

corpse behind but the dog alone he had bred remained faithful. The dog belonging to King Lysimachus chose to die by the same fate as his master, although he could, had he so wished, have saved himself. Again, when there was civil war in Rome, a Roman citizen called Calvus was killed. Many of his enemies strove in rivalry to accomplish the glorious deed of cutting off his head, but none could do so until they had killed the dog who stood by his side."

A parade in Alexandria staged by Pharaoh Ptolemy II displayed a regiment of 2,400 war dogs. These warring beasts, described as "large dogs, the size of asses, and fierce as lions," were led by several soldiers, holding them back with chains. The dogs were arrayed in satin cloth and silver collars, which had iron points. When ancient kings sent military aid to their allies, it often included hundreds of dogs equipped with iron collars and armor plates.

In Japan, dog fighting has been an unrelenting passion—the Tosa Inu, Japan's contribution to the mastiff group, has fulfilled its nation's passion head-on.

the inspection and carried out their grim duty with chisel and mallet. The animals did not give up their toes easily, however. Some of the larger and fiercer dogs chewed up the inspectors!

In Spain and elsewhere, dogs were employed to help control bulls when they were brought into town to market. The Alaunt was touted as well adapted to this job of butcher's dog. If a bull got out of line, the dog grabbed him by the ear and held him helpless until the men could gain control. Hence, another bloodthirsty sport was born for medieval spectators—organized bull-baiting.

By the 15th century, a distinctive bull-baiting breed had been developed. Perhaps through crosses of Alaunt, mastiff, and other unknown brachycephalic dogs, the first bulldog (often called *bullenbeisser*, German for bullbaiter) was created. The genes for white markings were probably introduced with these crosses. The bulldog was low-stationed with an undershot jaw, allowing him to grab and hang on without his upper jaw being in the way. He pinned the bull by grasping the vulnerable nose instead of the ear. If the dog let go or failed to clasp the nose, he would be gored, and if the bull raised his head, the dog would be thrown. Spectators

held blankets between them to catch the dogs on the fly. To win—in fact, to survive—the dog had to quickly gain hold, maintain the grip and lower the bull's head to pin him. The popularity of the sport in England was expressed by Queen Elizabeth I's decree that no plays or other entertainment should be offered on Thursday evenings, so that everyone, including Her Majesty, could go to the bull-baiting.

The trait of holding on to the nose and gamely never letting go was highly prized. Mutilation of a dog's feet when he had a grip on the bull's nose, to prove tenacity despite pain, was said to greatly increase the value of his pups. Ash, writing in 1939, describes a famous bulldog of his time. The dog was "descended from Bratten's 'Peter' who pinned the bull on his raw stumps after his feet had been cut off one by one by his owner for a wager." One unproven legend tells of a determined bitch, mutilated bit by

Above: An American Pit Bull Terrier demonstrating the breed's strength and coordination. **Below:** Argentina's bulldog, the Dogo Argentino, is a manmade breed which has performed a variety of tasks: guard dog, guide dog, sled dog, and hunter.

These Bulldog pups reveal a number of traits specific to the mastiff group: excessive wrinkles, large heads (relative toward bodies) and a fearless, aggressive tendency with their own kind.

bit, limb by limb, until only her jaws remained firmly clenched on the bull.

Bull-baiting proponents claimed the bloody sport made the meat more tender. Whether for juicy roasts or juicy fights, the craze continued for 700 years until the advent of British humane laws in 1835 that finally stopped it.

Unfortunately for the dogs, as bull-baiting waned, other blood sports were introduced. The "humane" laws protected the bull, but the dog who had been humanity's companion since the canine evolution stayed in the pits. Dog-fighting reached its peak in 18th-and 19th-century England, with matches advertized in the papers and huge wagers being made. Again special breeds were developed for the purpose, the mastiff and/or bulldog being crossed with smooth, game, terrier types (called Bull and Terrier) to increase quickness and agility. Since many of these terriers were all white, the blending of the breeds generated more white markings or even all-white coloring in the mastiffs.

Not every mastiff was developed for an evil purpose. Selecting for more benign personalities, many European countries developed draft dogs, rescue workers, and genial companions from these original mastiffs. During the European Renaissance, the Great Butcher Dog was common. This more placid mastiff helped drive cattle to market, guarding the livestock as well as the owners, and often carrying the sales money home around his neck! Few highwaymen challenged such a beast. Also employed as the serf's "horse" in carting and hauling, the dog with a more mellow temperament was desired. This dog had less loose skin, but the same square, bulky, muscular body, and his tail was sometimes docked.

By choosing and crossing with dwarf varieties, breeders even created "miniature" giants. The mastiff group has much greater variation than the flock guards for two reasons. The mastiff was not isolated in rural areas and was allowed opportunity to meet and mate with a variety of dogs, drawing from other gene pools. In addition, the double origin initially provided a greater variety of genes. Despite the wide variation, each individual breed goes back in whole or in part to the common gigantic ancestor from Tibet.

Above: The American Staffordshire Terrier *(left)* and the Staffordshire Bull Terrier *(right)* share similar origins. Notice that the Staffordshire Bull Terrier has uncropped ears and is somewhat smaller than its American counterpart. **Below:** The Rottweiler can be counted among the mastiff breeds which were traditionally used to work cattle; today it more commonly performs as a guard and police dog.

Above: The Entelbucher, one of Switzerland's four mountain dogs, is a territorial herder, protective but not aggressive. **Below:** The Great Dane is one of the tallest of the mastiff group, as this Harlequin attempts to display.

MASTIFF

Mastiff

Tibetan Mastiff	Tibet
Aryan Molossus	Afghanistan
Mastiff	Great Britain
Great Dane	Germany
Saint Bernard	Switzerland
Moscow Watchdog	USSR
Newfoundland	Canada
Landseer	Scandinavia
Tosa Inu	Japan
Fila Brasileiro	Brazil
Leonberger	Germany
Doberman Pinscher	Germany
Danish Broholmer	Denmark

Draft/Cattle

Rottweiler	Germany
Appenzeller	Switzerland
Greater Swiss Mountain Dog	Switzerland
Bernese Mountain Dog	Switzerland
Entelbucher	Switzerland
Belgian Mastiff	Belgium

Bulldog

Neapolitan Mastiff	Italy
Bulldog	Great Britain
Bullmastiff	Great Britain
Dogue de Bordeaux	France
Boxer	Germany
Dogo Argentino	Argentina
Staffordshire Bull Terrier	Great Britain
American Staffordshire Terrier	USA
American Pit Bull Terrier	USA
Bull Terrier	Great Britain
Miniature Bull Terrier	Great Britain
Perro de Presa Mallorquin	Spain
Perro de Presa Canario	Spain
American Bulldog	USA
French Bulldog	France
Pug	China
Boston Terrier	USA

The Scenthounds
In Full Cry

Long before the Christian era, dog breeders created, from existing mastiff stock, the first hounds to hunt by scent. They selected for the mastiff's sensitive nose and tenacity. Breeders retained the dogs' hanging ears and loose, heavy skin while exchanging some of the bulk for speed and endurance. Over the years, the ferocious temperament of the original dogs was mellowed into a sweeter, more benign attitude that allowed for control during the hunt. Unfortunately, many of the larger hounds still retain their mastiff ancestor's tendency for hip and intestinal disorders.

The scenthounds stem mainly from their European ancestors, originating from Celtic breeding. The Celts were a tribal people that lived during the centuries before the rise of Rome.

Mastiffs of the Alaunt type were owned and bred by Celtic clans and used in their warfare. Before 500 BC the Celts were principally in southern Germany, but they soon spread throughout western Europe and all the British Isles, their mastiffs and hounds by their sides. As the Romans, and later barbarian invaders, overtook Europe, the Celts were destroyed or absorbed by other cultures. Eventually only the tribes in Ireland, Britain and Brittany remained. Today, their majestic hounds and the distinctive Celtic languages of Irish, Highland Scottish, Welsh and Breton are their legacy to modern society.

It is these great huntsmen who probably first used the mastiff for hunting by scent. The old-style scenthounds, of the mastiff type, were seeded throughout the Celtic travels. Some remained in pure form while other types, especially those in areas accessible to the Phoenician hound trade, were crossed with sighthounds. Before the discovery of gunpowder, the hound searched out and chased game until the hunter could kill it with spear or arrow, or until the dogs themselves could close in for the kill.

Scenthounds themselves existed many centuries before the first concerted breeding programs to establish types had begun during the Middle Ages. The St. Hubert Hound was the first breed brought to prominence during the sixth century. St. Hubert, a pagan huntsman, was converted to Christianity while out on a Sunday hunt, when he saw a vision of a stag with a gleaming cross rising between its antlers. He later became the Bishop of Liege and achieved sainthood, and the monastery in the Ardennes region of Belgium was named for him. These monks developed and bred a strain of scenthound called the St. Hubert Hound, using Celtic dogs originally from Gaul (France).

Always black and tan, the monks' dogs were medium sized, heavily built with body a bit longer than high, having heavy heads with deep flews. Although slow and methodical, they were noted for their melodious "voice" and incomparable scenting ability. The breed is the direct ancestor to today's Bloodhound, which is still referred to as a St. Hubert in his native Belgium. These hounds became well known throughout Europe and were the basis of many other hound breeds.

By the eighth century, several variations of the St. Hubert had appeared. A variety that was nearly all white (tricolored with a majority of body white) became known as the Southern Hound. Although now extinct, the breed was commonplace through the 16th century and used in England for hunting hare while on foot. The Southern Hound was heavy, slow, and possessed long ears and heavy flews as did the St. Hubert progenitor. Also known for his deep bass bay and exquisite sense of smell, the Southern Hound was the basis for many of the European hound breeds as well.

Emerging in the eighth century was the Talbot Hound, a pied or liver variation of the St. Hubert. Early Dalmatians were often referred to as Talbots, so the term may be a reference to the color variety rather than type.

The 13th century marks the initial rage in Great Britain of fox hunting. Dogs smaller and faster than the St. Hubert Hound with good voice were desired to trail the cunning and elusive fox.

Because many types of hounds were developed to hunt in packs and were kenneled in large groups, they were selected for their nonquarrelsome behavior. It was necessary for the dogs to be amiable with pack members, orderly and mannerly for the hunter to manage in the fields as well as in the kennel. These dogs were, however, independent of spirit, since the pack was often sent to hunt alone for hours without direction from their master. A brand was often shaved into the side of the hound's coat, to enable the Hunt Master to make identification quickly at the end of the day.

The dog continued to be malleable according to the wishes and needs of its master. Each country has developed its own breed(s) of scenthound, usually following a general type, but in great variation, depending on the game sought and the method of following the hounds. Some have become lighter of body for faster and for mounted hunting; various crosses with gaze-hounds have produced even greater speed. Yet others have maintained the heavier body for methodical tracking. Some types were bred for shorter legs to slow the dog's work. While many are smooth-coated, most countries have a few rough or wire-coated scenthounds. The scenthound family has become the most numerous in dogdom for recognized breeds; these are best discussed by country of origin.

France is *the* country of the scenthound; it spawned the genre and boasts the most breeds.

In America, dogs were needed to hunt raccoon. The coonhounds basically developed from the foxhounds in the late 18th century. The first of these coonhounds was the American Black and Tan, illustrated here treeing with a Redbone Coonhound—in full cry!

In fact, in France this family usually does not use the word "hound" in breed names—assuming that, if it's French, it's a scenthound. For many centuries after the Middle Ages, France was not a unified country but a collection of feudal estates, each run by a powerful nobleman. These aristocrats had nearly as much power as the king. Hunting was a passion with the nobility as well as royalty and many kept extensive kennels, developing their own strains of hound.

Although horseracing may be dubbed the "sport of kings," the companionship of dogs and their considered importance fell not far behind. During the reign of Charles I of Lorraine in the 15th century, 70 forests and nearly 800 royal parks were confiscated for the sole purpose of raising and training the king's dogs. Louis IX, of the 1450s, planned all of his wars for summer and fall, leaving his winter free for boar and stag hunting and the spring for hunting with falcons, accompanied, of course, by his hounds.

Originally, most of the early types of hounds were bred to hunt wolves as well as wild boar. These dogs hunted in large packs, sometimes as many as a thousand or more, and had to have great tenacity, courage, and stamina as well as the prerequisite fine nose. The quality of the voice on the trail was of prime importance as well, and strains were selected for the tonal quality and the carrying ability of their bay. While the peasants—without even two pieces of crockery that matched—often went hungry, the royal packs were not only well fed, but were selected for their matching pitch, among other abilities. These early types used on large game are often referred to collectively as the *Grand Chiens Courant*, the Great Hounds of the Chase. Other strains were used to hunt stag, roe deer and fox, for which they needed more speed. Smaller or short-legged varieties were produced to do slower work in heavy cover or for following on foot, especially for rabbit and hare.

The cost of raising and caring for the huge kennels was staggering, and they could not be maintained after the fall of the nobility. While dozens and dozens of breeds were lost after the French Revolution several remained in smaller numbers or have been brought back from the brink of extinction and still exist today.

Above: These three Black Mouth Curs pictured with their day's catch—two wild boars.

Below: Short, crooked legs allow the Basset Hound to keep his nose low to the ground. The breed is certainly of British fame but is closely related to the French bassets.

The general characteristic of all French hounds is one of great grace and beauty. Although Gaul was the source of the pure scenthounds that were the progenitor of the St. Hubert, the French coast was also one of the stops of the Phoenicians. The hounds of France have a definite hint of sighthound in their background. They have a long, lean and chiseled head, not as heavy as the St. Hubert Hound, yet not as slim and pointed as the pure sighthound. Their ears are set very low and are often unusually long and folded; yet the head and neck lack the heavy flews and wrinkles of the St. Hubert type. They are up on leg, being racier and lighter in bone. Although in no way weedy or lacking in strength, they weigh considerably less for their height than English or German hounds. Many of the French hounds have both wire-coated (called *griffon*) and/or short-legged (called *basset*) varieties. Their names are often descriptive and, hence, easily translatable, usually referring to the province where the breed originated, as well as the size, coat and color.

Beagles, like many of the scenthounds, are versatile and enthusiastic hunters. Although usually associated with hunting rabbit or squirrel, this Beagle has cornered this coon well.

HOUNDS

Griffon Nivernais	France
Griffon Vendeen, Grand	France
Griffon Vendeen, Briquet	France
Basset Griffon Vendeen, Grand	France
Basset Griffon Vendeen, Petit	France
Grand Bleu de Gascogne	France
Griffon Bleu de Gascogne, Petit	France
Basset Bleu de Gascogne	France
Poitevin	France
Gascon Saintongeois, Grand	France
Gascon Saintongeois, Petit	France
Griffon Fauve de Bretagne	France
Basset Fauve de Bretagne	France
Chien d'Artois	France
Basset Artésien Normand	France
Billy	France
Levesque	France
Ariégeois	France
Porcelaine	France
Beagle Harrier	France
Chien Francais Blanc et Noir	France
Chien Francais Blanc et Orange	France
Chien Francais Tricolore	France
Anglo-Francais, Grand	France
Anglo-Francais, Moyen	France
Anglo-Francais, Petit	France
Sabueso Español de Monte	Spain
Sabueso Español Lebrero	Spain
Segugio Italiano a Pelo Raso	Italy
Segugio Italiano a Pelo Forte	Italy
Istrian Hound, Wirehaired	Yugoslavia
Istrian Hound, Smoothhaired	Yugoslavia
Posavac Hound	Yugoslavia
Bosnian Roughhaired Hound	Yugoslavia
Balkan Hound	Yugoslavia
Yugoslavian Mountain Hound	Yugoslavia
Yugoslavian Tricolored Hound	Yugoslavia
Greek Harehound	Greece
Transylvanian Hound, Tall	Hungary
Transylvanian Hound, Short	Hungary
Black Forest Hound	Czechoslovakia
Polish Hound	Poland
Deutsche Bracke	Germany
Dachsbracke, Westphalian	Germany
Hanoverian Hound	Germany
Bavarian Mountain Hound	Germany
Dachshund, Standard	Germany
Dachshund, Miniature	Germany

Switzerland, where the scenthound is known as the laufhund, contributes nine individual breeds to this group. Essentially, all these hounds are similar, barring variations of size and color.

Bloodhound	Belgium	Beagle	Great Britain
Austrian Brandlebracke	Austria	Harrier	Great Britain
Styrian Roughhaired Mountain Hound	Austria	Basset Hound	Great Britain
		Otter Hound	Great Britain
Tyroler Bracke	Austria	Kerry Beagle	Ireland
Dachsbracke, Alpine	Austria	American Foxhound	USA
Schweizer Laufhund	Switzerland	American Black and Tan Coonhound	USA
Schweizer Niederlaufhund	Switzerland		
Bruno Jura Laufhund	Switzerland	Redbone Coonhound	USA
St. Hubert Jura Laufhund	Switzerland	English Coonhound	USA
Jura Niederlaufhund	Switzerland	Bluetick Coonhound	USA
Berner Laufhund	Switzerland	Treeing Walker Coonhound	USA
Berner Niederlaufhund	Switzerland	American Blue Gascon Hound	USA
Luzerner Laufhund	Switzerland	Majestic Tree Hound	USA
Luzerner Niederlaufhund	Switzerland	Plott Hound	USA
Strellufstöver	Denmark	Leopard Cur	USA
Finnish Hound	Finland	Mountain Cur	USA
Drever	Sweden	Treeing Tennessee Brindle	USA
Schillerstövare	Sweden	Stephens Stock	USA
Hamiltonstövare	Sweden	Black Mouth Cur	USA
Smalandsstövare	Sweden	Russian Hound	USSR
Haldenstövare	Norway	Russian Harlequin Hound	USSR
Hygenhund	Norway	Estonian Hound	USSR
Dunker	Norway	Latvian Hound	USSR
English Foxhound	Great Britain	Lithuanian Hound	USSR

Gun Dogs
Ready, Willing and Able

Hunting dogs are the equivalent of the melting pot in the canine world. Grouped for their skills, they have diverse backgrounds and varied physical appearances. Even the term "gun dog" is a modern appellation. Long before the invention of firearms, these dogs accompanied hunters who used nets, falcons and bows. At that time they were exclusively "bird dogs," any larger prey being the quarry of hounds.

Many years later with the discovery of gunpowder, firearm use widened the scope of these dogs to finding or retrieving furred and hooved game. Today, they are subdivided into four broad, sometimes overlapping groups: the pointers, the land retrievers, the shaggy water dogs and the setters/spaniels.

The pointers are the most closely related to the scenthounds and are descended directly from them. They are, for the most part, smooth-coated, of basic hound body and head type, and predominantly white with spotting or ticking. They, like their ancestors, also can possess a wire coat.

Even their names become enmeshed. The German word *bracke* and the French *briquet* refer to scenthounds, while *braque* in France and *bracco* in Italian identifies their gun dogs. *Griffon* can mean either a hound or a gun dog (or even a ten-pound toy!) as long as his coat is coarse and shaggy.

While the pointers have inherited the fine nose and strong desire to hunt from the hounds, they differ in their intense desire to please, which was selected in breeding programs. Pointers instinctively look to their masters for direction. The added traits of retrieving and hesitation upon scent of game fine-tuned these breeds for gun work.

Although most Americans think of the English Pointer when this group is named, this one is perhaps the "odd man out" in the dozens of European pointing types. The English developed specialist dogs; the pointer found and

pointed the game, the retriever was brought up to retrieve the shot bird, and the water retrievers were reserved for water work.

Contrarily, the Continental ideal was a dog who could assist in all phases of the hunt. Europeans wanted their "pointers" to work the cover to find game, of course, but also relied upon them to perform well after the shot. They were expected to retrieve shot birds, trail wounded running birds, track wounded ducks on water, retrieve from the water, retrieve furred game if necessary, and even be willing to bloodtrail wounded game. Some of these all-purpose dogs started out very heavy-boned, methodical and houndlike, while the English version of the pointer was racy-bodied and fast.

The pointers in a particular geographical area tended to follow the type of the hounds, due to the available gene pool. In places where a heavier hound was favored, the resulting gun dog was heavy and slow. Where faster, lighter hounds were the root stock, the pointer was of the same type. Later in their development, some of these heavier types were refined with crosses to the elegant English prototype.

Many of the pointer and spaniel breeds have the tail docked at birth, not as short as that of the Doberman and Boxer, but about half the tail's length. The dogs wag their tails vigorously when on the scent, often incurring tail-end injuries which are notoriously hard to heal properly. Poodles, which were originally bred as water retrievers, are also docked. However, the fashion for most setters and retrievers is to leave the tail intact.

Dewclaws, even in the front, are generally clipped off. Removal was for the practical prevention of injury. When the dog hunted in heavy cover, his dewclaws snagged and ripped. These injuries developed into infections and eventual death before the days of antibiotics and veterinary surgeons. Therefore, removal was the customary "ounce of prevention."

The Gordon Setter has been known in its native Scotland since the early 17th century. Setting dogs are traced back to Celtic origin and were found wherever the Celts traveled.

A mystery concerning this group is the preponderance of the liver (brown with brown nose) color. We know this was a common gene carried by the mastiff group, and the liver gene color has been present since the eighth century in the hounds called Talbots.

Nevertheless, it was a color that never gained prominence in any of our current hound breeds, appearing in only a few. Yet the majority of the pointer types, as well as many of the spaniels and water dogs from Europe, have the brown nose and the liver color, at least in spots. If brown were a dominant gene, a "single dog origin " might be assumed, with its influence spreading throughout Europe. However, since the gene for brown is recessive to black, any cross of brown to black eliminates the brown. Thus we know that the color had to be purposely selected, with brown bred to brown by choice in diverse and remote areas. A plausible explanation might be that the gene for brown was closely associated with the genes for crack

gun dog performance, as opposed to the hound's, and early pragmatic breeders found that breeding brown dogs produced superior gun dogs. Another reason for the brown may be that the camouflage effect of that color was desirable for hunting dogs working in the autumn.

The land retrievers, most of British origin, are mastifflike in type. Well-known breeds such as the Labrador and Golden Retrievers are heavy bodied and a bit low on leg. They have the heavier, wide bracoid head (long with square muzzle and median groove), along with a higher incidence of hip dysplasia, as do their mastiff progenitors.

The water dogs' history is more clouded, but they probably are related most closely to the shaggy herding dogs that came originally from the Orient. These sheep dogs were most likely crossed with hunting dogs to create the new group. They show up very early, being commonplace by the Christian era, around the Mediterranean and into Europe. Sporting a shaggy single coat, the hair covered the body and was curly or corded.

The cutting of water dogs' curly coats in a pattern was described by the 1500s. A mass of curly dog wool is not only odorous when wet, but very heavy. Thus a large portion of the coat was sheared off, with only that over the ribs and joints left long. (The thinking of the day was that cover over those areas would prevent the pneumonia and arthritis, often suffered from working long hours in cold water.) This coat pattern gave birth to the coiffure of our modern show Poodle, as well as that of the Portuguese Water Dog.

Water retrievers/dogs were specialized for a host of chores. Used most frequently for waterfowl shooting, they were also adept at flushing and retrieving on shore. Some were used on boats as aids to the fishing communities. The water dogs, or their shaggy progenitors, may have been the source of the rough coat in the wirehaired griffon-type hounds of Europe. As early as the first century AD, efforts were made to miniaturize these water dogs. The diminutive

form yielded the charming family of shaggy bichons, which are popular companions today.

By medieval times in Europe, setting dogs—an old gun dog type with a fringed coat—began to appear, accompanying falconers. A tapestry made in 1400 depicts a falconer's beautifully constructed white dog with long fringed tail, feathering on legs and belly; only the small flat drop ear is free of long coat.

The Greek historian Xenophon, writing in the sixth century BC, tells of hounds that paused upon the scent of game instead of giving chase. Although this was considered an abomination in the hound, this obviates that the genes for "setting" have been around since early times.

The exact origin of the setting dog (also called Èpagneul or Spaniel) is a mystery, probably a great mixture that will never be sorted. The coat, fringed on the ears, legs and tail, is reminiscent of the flock guarders, rather than the shaggy sheep and water dogs. Their passion for the hunt and their superb noses speak of the hound, or the pointing dogs that came from these hounds. Perhaps they were combinations

Few dog lovers would deny that the gun dog group contains many of the world's most intelligent canines. Perched on the shore, these Nova Scotia Duck Tolling Retrievers prepare to outfox an approaching flock of ducks.

Pointers have inherited much of their fine nose and hunting desire from the hounds; they were developed to perform a specific function: to point. Demonstrating its pointing ability is Portugal's only pointer, the Perdigueiro Portugueso.

of the two types, both of which owe their genes originally to the mastiff.

Setting dogs were seeded wherever the Celts migrated: France, southern Germany, the Netherlands, as well as Ireland and Scotland. Since the history of the Celts and hounds are tied together inextricably, the setting dog may have a parallel Celtic background. The much repeated deduction that the spaniel originated in Spain because of his name is probably erroneous. They were known throughout central and northern Europe, particularly France, as well as the British Isles, and seemed to follow the general route of the Celts. Although traded between the capitals of Europe by kings and noblemen courting favors, there is no indication that Spain was the fount of this type. The French verb *espanir* means to crouch or flatten oneself, and seems a more plausible source of the name since it so accurately describes the spaniel's early hunting style.

These early dogs—called "couchers," "setters" and, later, "spaniels"—would slow, crouch and creep in upon scent of the birds. This characterization allowed the hunters with their falcons to approach closer before putting the game birds to flight. The falcons were then released to capture the birds. Another hunting ploy was to have the dogs indicate a covey by creeping in and lying motionless, as the hunters drew their nets over canine and fowl, catching many birds at a time. These setting dogs developed into all of our modern setters and spaniels. What is called a spaniel in Europe is, in reality, a setter that points its game. Later, the English created the flushing spaniels from these couching setters.

Shorter hair appears on the face, body and leg fronts, with fringing of the ears, tail, belly and back of legs. Miniature varieties of the spaniels have been around ever since their beginning as pampered pets and "sleeve" dogs.

Above: In both Great Britain and America, the Labrador Retriever has acquired a fine reputation as a duck dog and hunter. **Below:** The Weimaraner is an ancient gun dog of Germanic origin—in the early 17th century, the breed was used to hunt large game: boars, bears and wolves.

Above: Setters have been well known throughout Europe for many years; most of today's setter breeds have developed from similar stock. Illustrated here are the Irish Setter, Gordon Setter, and English Setter. **Below:** Since the 19th century, the English Cocker Spaniel has been popular in Great Britain. Both the English Cocker Spaniel and its cousin, the American Cocker Spaniel, are categorized as flushing spaniels because they spring or "cock" the game for the net.

GUN DOGS

Water Dogs

Barbet	France
Poodle, Standard	France
Poodle, Miniature	France
Poodle, Toy	France
Irish Water Spaniel	Ireland
Curly-Coated Retriever	Great Britain
Wetterhoun	Netherlands
American Water Spaniel	USA
Portuguese Water Dog	Portugal
Maltese	Malta
Bichon Frise	France/Belgium
Löwchen	France
Bolognese	Italy
Havanese	Cuba
Coton de Tulear	Madagascar

Pointers

Belgian Shorthaired Pointer	Belgium
Wirehaired Pointing Griffon	France
Braque d'Auvergne	France
Braque d'Ariége	France
Braque du Bourbonnais	France
Braque Dupuy	France
Braque Francais de Grande Taille	France
Braque Francais de Petite Taille	France
Braque Saint-Germain	France
Pointer	Great Britain
Old Danish Bird Dog	Denmark
Hertha Pointer	Denmark
Česky Fousek	Czechoslovakia
Dalmatian	Yugoslavia
Vizsla	Hungary
Bracco Italiano	Italy
Spinone Italiano	Italy
Perdiguero de Burgos	Spain
Perdiguero Navarro	Spain
Perdigueiro Portugueso	Portugal
German Shorthaired Pointer	Germany
German Wirehaired Pointer	Germany
Stichelhaar	Germany
Weimaraner	Germany
Pudelpointer	Germany

The Grosser (Large) Münsterländer is a black and white setter of Germany which is popular in both its native land and Great Britain. In appearance and type, it is most similar to the German Longhaired Pointer.

The Wetterhoun of the Netherlands was originally an otter dog; today it is used effectively as a gun dog in land and water.

Retrievers

Flat-Coated Retriever	Great Britain
Labrador Retriever	Great Britain
Golden Retriever	Great Britain
Nova Scotia Duck Tolling Retriever	Canada
Kooikerhondje	Netherlands
Chesapeake Bay Retriever	USA

The creation of American duck hunters and recognized by the five major registries, the Chesapeake Bay Retriever hits the water with passion.

Setters

German Longhaired Pointer	Germany
Large Münsterländer	Germany
Small Münsterländer	Germany
English Setter	Great Britain
Gordon Setter	Great Britain
Irish Setter	Ireland
Irish Red and White Setter	Ireland
Stabyhoun	Netherlands
Drentse Patrijshond	Netherlands
Brittany	France
Épagneul Francais	France
Épagneul Picard	France
Épagneul Bleu de Picardie	France
Épagneul Pont-Audemer	France
Deutscher Wachtelhund	Germany

Flushing Spaniels

Sussex Spaniel	Great Britain
Field Spaniel	Great Britain
English Cocker Spaniel	Great Britain
American Cocker Spaniel	USA
English Springer Spaniel	Great Britain
Welsh Springer Spaniel	Great Britain
Clumber Spaniel	Great Britain
Russian Spaniel	USSR
Boykin Spaniel	USA
English Toy Spaniel	Great Britain
Cavalier King Charles Spaniel	Great Britain
Continental Toy Spaniel, Papillon	France/Belgium
Continental Toy Spaniel, Phalene	France/Belgium

The Northern Breeds
The Horsepower of the North

The northern breeds' story begins with the prehistoric wolf, before the first Ice Age, when the Northern Hemisphere was an unending, cold grassland. The vegetation was so abundant and the boundaries so limitless that it supported millions of grazing animals. Vast herds of deer, goats, sheep, cattle and horses thrived on the range. The giant herbivores, the woolly mammoth, the giant sloths, llamas, bison, musk oxen, and rhinoceroses prospered. Their major enemy, the Gray Northern Wolf, grew large with the never-ending food supply.

Wolves were—and still remain—social (cooperative) hunters, working as allies to bring down prey larger than themselves. They creep toward the herd, intently and silently seeking a vulnerable animal—the sick beast, with its head held lower, or the slower aged, young or weak. After a target animal had been selected, the wolves moved in to frighten and stir the entire group. Natural herders with great stamina, they could bide their time, trotting all day if necessary, to keep up with the panicky quarry. Then they actually began to "herd," manipulating and cutting out the target animal. Once it was isolated and beyond the group's protection, they closed in for the kill. This cooperative hunt was unique to wolves.

This spirit extended to their family life. Pairs mated for life; cubs were raised, fed and protected by the entire pack and played with all members.

The cold clime produced a heavy, thick coat of straight medium-length hair that shed ice and provided warmth. The unlimited food supply enabled the wolf to grow large and heavy boned, up to 130 pounds.

Around the time of the Mesolithic era, another—albeit primitive—social hunter appeared on the scene. Early humans had also learned to cooperate in hunting the larger herbivores. While the wolves concentrated on smaller, deer-sized animals, humans pursued the huge, stupid behemoths, often chasing whole herds into pits or stampeding them over cliffs. After our primitive ancestors made use of one or two beasts, scavenger wolves relished the carnage.

Over many thousands of years, the wasteful hunting methods of humans contributed to the extinction of the large herbivores. For the first time, humans and wolves were hunting the same food source. However, since game was plentiful at that time, competition was scarce.

Hunting side by side gave each species the opportunity to observe and become accustomed to the other. *Homo sapiens* admired the canine ability to divide and efficiently cut the herd. Wolves recognized the cave dweller's ability to kill—and that waste was left for scavengers.

Soon wolves lurked nearby during the hunts, waiting for the "leftovers." Over time, these camp followers developed a shorter jaw with smaller teeth than their hunting cousins. (This has been recreated in modern wolves who are bred in captivity and raised on commercial food.) They were then forced to scavenge, since they were no longer efficient at killing their own game. Their herding skills led them to join in the stampede.

After generations of living in proximity, a mutual trust developed and true domestication occurred. Wolf pups were brought into camps and hand raised. These cubs reached maturity and aided in the hunt and in controlling domesticated flocks and herds. Although herding was the first canine skill used by early humans, many other useful qualities were utilized. These early wolf-dogs served as draft animals to pull the sledges. They searched for and located the herds as well as assisting in the kill. In addition, their presence at the campfire was a deterrent to predators. Even at the dawn of history, a furry and live presence in the tent provided companionship and helped keep toes warm.

Today, the northern dog has retained many of the characteristics of his wolf cousins. He has

The ice-ridden landscapes and the brutally harsh weather may have caused man and dog to combine forces for survival. The Greenland Dogs are close cousins of the Nordic hauling huskies and were used on the island as sleigh dogs and hunters. This pack works in "fan hitch."

their small pricked ears and wedge-shaped head framed with a ruff. The body is powerful, lean and square, with strong muscling and trim loin that allows for efficient trotting over vast distances. He is jacketed with a short, plush stand-off coat that protects him from the worst of weather, but needs no special care. Occasionally, the banded hair coloring is present.

Nordic (northern) dogs possess an independent yet social personality. Most of the draft dogs are friendly and affectionate and do not make good guard dogs. Overall, some of them are aggressive with other dogs and livestock.

The Nordic tail, which curves up over the dogs' backs, is the main feature that separates them from the wolf ancestors. Mature wolves always carry their tails low; cubs have high tails. Barking is also a puppy tendency demonstrated by many northern adults. These neotanous (in-fantile) traits likely were selected during primitive breeding and adoption processes—since the more infantile the wolf, the more manageable he remained.

As sheep, cattle and reindeer were domesticated, the dogs originally used for herding/killing were honed into a herding-only dog. The modern Nordic dogs used for herding are probably the closest to the original domesticated dog. Although used extensively throughout the centuries, modern travel and farming methods have reduced these dogs to a few isolated types.

As the demand for herding diminished, these dogs gained ground with their skills in hunting and draft work, and their warmth as companions. Termed Nordic, Northern or spitz, the type remains distinct in many areas all over the world today.

Above: The Norwegian Buhund is an ancient Nordic herding type dog which originated in the Scandinavian countries but did not gain   much recognition until the 20th century. **Below Left:** The Swedes and the Finnish together partake in the origin of this little spitz, the Norbottenspets. **Below Right:** Lorna Demidoff and her Siberian Husky team, pictured on the grounds of the Monadnock Kennels in New Hampshire.

Above: Even in its homeland, the Greenland Dog is not populous. In addition to employment as a sled dog, the breed was used to find seals' breathing holes in the ice. **Below:** The Japanese Spitz, a miniature lap spitz, weighs in at 13 pounds. In appearance, the breed bears a striking resemblance to the Miniature American Eskimo.

55

Above: Perhaps the most striking characteristic of the northern breeds is the full, plush coat. The Chow Chow, a breed which traces its origin to 1000 BC, can have one of the most impressive and beautiful of coats. **Below:** A 20th-century American creation, the Chinook was developed to be a sled dog par excellence.

NORTHERN DOGS

Hunting

Finnish Spitz	Finland
Karelo-Finnish Laika	USSR
Norwegian Elkhound	Norway
Norwegian Elkhound, Black	Norway
Jamthund	Sweden
Karelian Bear Dog	Finland
Russo-European Laika	USSR
Lundehund	Norway
Norbottenspets	Sweden/Finland
West Siberian Laika	USSR
East Siberian Laika	USSR
Akita	Japan
Ainu Dog	Japan
Kishu	Japan
Kai Dog	Japan
Shikoku	Japan

Draft

Alaskan Malamute	USA
Siberian Husky	USSR
Greenland Dog	Scandinavia
Eskimo Dog	Canada
Chinook	USA
Northeasterly Hauling Laika	USSR

Herding

Samoyed	Scandinavia
Nenets Herding Laika	USSR
Norwegian Buhund	Norway
Iceland Dog	Iceland
Swedish Lapphund	Sweden
Finnish Lapphund	Finland

American Eskimos over a snowy terrain.

The Lundehund, also known as the Norwegian Puffin Dog, is perhaps one of the most fascinating of the world's canines.

Companion

German Wolfspitz	Germany
German Spitz, Giant	Germany
German Spitz, Standard	Germany
German Spitz, Small	Germany
German Spitz, Toy	Germany
Keeshond	Netherlands
Pomeranian	Great Britain
Schipperke	Belgium
Eurasian	Germany
Volpino Italiano	Italy
American Eskimo, Standard	USA
American Eskimo, Miniature	USA
American Eskimo, Toy	USA
Shiba Inu	Japan
Sanshu	Japan
Japanese Spitz	Japan
Chow Chow	China
Shar-Pei	China

Herding Dogs
A Labor of Love

Men clad in ancient running gear once gathered sheep from the mountains, according to *A History of British Livestock Husbandry*. Due to various hindrances—lack of speed and stamina (and perhaps no jogging shoes or suits)—the "sheepmen" were pushed aside by sheep dogs in the 1570s.

Most of the pure herding breeds were produced by selection from early Nordic dogs. Like their northern cousins, these flock-gathering breeds were heavily coated (double-coated), manifested their jaunty personality and usually retained the prick or semi-prick ear.

Other herding breeds were derived from ancient sheep dogs of Tibet and the East. This stem had the same curled tail, with the addition of drop ears and an abundant shaggy or corded coat. Brought into eastern Europe during various migrations, these dogs became a second source of the herding shepherds.

In modern times, the high, curled tail is seen in few of the herding dogs. In fact, many of this group's breed standards specifically mention it as a fault, to eliminate any throwback genes. Most carry their long tails low, and, as a signature of their ancestors, they curve at the end like a shepherd's crook. Some breeders chose to dock the appendage at birth to simplify both the tail-set question and sanitation problem in dogs kept out year-round.

Most of these dogs are long in ribbing, enabling them to make sudden turns. Overall they are lithe, supple and graceful. The length of coat varies according to climate and terrain.

Although many herders originated for working with reindeer, most eventually switched to sheep. Some varieties were selected especially for heeling cattle, where dogs with short legs were the preference to avoid injuries from kicks. Today herding dogs are even used on turkey ranches. All professionally trained dogs are taught only for one species, however, since cat-

tle and hog workers would be too aggressive for sheep or turkeys.

Sheep-herding breeds are intelligent and willing to please, responding best to gentle handling. They also tend to possess playful, exuberant personalities which can be channeled into great obedience competitors or family pets.

The herding dog picks up nearly imperceptible hand and whistle signals to move the flock or retrieve stray sheep. Shepherds with large flocks or in vast grazing lands utilize highly pitched dog whistles and shepherd's crooks to wave their signals. Their dogs usually bear short, sharp names that carry well from master to servant—Fly, Cap, Ben, Hemp, Andy. No Percival, Mehitabel or Lorenzo answers the call.

Early cattle and hog farmers wanted a herding dog which demonstrated more toughness and aggression for their not-so-meek stock. (This type supplied the herd owner with a guardian as well.) To create these dogs, herding breeds were crossed with mastiff or flock guard types. This often produced a drop ear (which may be cropped to stand) and a dog with a more robust, muscular build. It also left the tell-tale rear dewclaws, a distinguishing feature of the flock guard/mastiff dogs for many thousands of years. These dogs are often called "shepherd" instead of "sheepdog." Many of this genre also carry the genes of the shaggy eastern herding dogs.

All native Scottish herding dogs are called collies, possibly derived from the Colley, black-faced sheep, that dotted the hills of Scotland. *Coelio*, from the Welsh, is translated as trustworthy and faithful, which certainly is descriptive of all types of collies.

Shepherds throughout the world were not particular about type, and Scottish shepherds were no different, breeding and crossbreeding various dogs proven to be good workers. Depending on preference, some of the "collies" had smooth coats, others rough. Sizes ranged

Compared to its Belgian counterparts, the German Shepherd Dog is a newcomer to the herding group. Belgian Sheepdogs have enthralled shepherds in their homeland with their outstanding herding abilities since the Middle Ages. The Belgian Tervuren *(left)*, the German Shepherd Dog *(center)* and the Belgian Groenendael *(right)* are illustrated here.

from small to large. Some had prick ears, others drop ears, and some ears folded. Nevertheless, the Scotch were adamant about certain attributes: they demanded that their dogs be sturdy, agile, intelligent, able to cope with rough terrain and inclement weather, and trustworthy with family members. In addition, colored dogs were preferred, (as opposed to the flock guards), for visual dominance over sheep and so they would stand out from the "crowd."

Today the dogs herd instinctively in the manner shown many years ago. They "head" the stock by circling them back to their master, or "heel," driving them away. The Scottish sheepherding dogs evidenced two inherent approaches to their flocks: the "huntaway" or heeler, and the "strong-eyed" dog.

The huntaway dog or heelers drive the sheep by circling, barking and nipping at the heels. This type has to perform much of the herding on its own, searching out sheep in the craggy

mountains. While the dog responds to command, it is still an independent worker. Most huntaways "noise," flushing the sheep from brush and narrow crannies. The barking also marks the dog's position. Its counterpart, the strong-eyed dog, is at its best in open range, controlling the herd in silence with its nearly hypnotic stare in a contest of wills. The strong-eyed dog *always* wins.

The shepherd's dogs must be quick and agile, without an excess of substance, for fleet movement and quick dashes around the flocks—a necessity when there's one dog for every 1,000 sheep. These herders are built for short bursts of high speed and can work in any terrain. Most drive the sheep by nipping, barking or darting at the animals. Yet they must not injure or attack the meek and easily harmed sheep.

As the need for an all-purpose farm and herd dog waned, these shepherd dogs have quite naturally become superb guard, military and law enforcement, and personal protection dogs. They can be strong-natured and willful, but with proper training they also make fine obedience and working dogs, demonstrating their intelligence and willingness both to work and to please.

In the canine family, herding dogs remain among those with the closest affinity to humans. These breeds, unlike flock guards, work under the direction of their masters and are more dependent. This trait carries through in the personality of their modern non-working counterparts. They are biddable and obedient, today making some of the best obedience ring workers. These dogs need their people, just as the shepherds and the cattle breeders need *them*.

Bonding and socializing is important with these breeds. Work and play with them, and they will die for you. Ignore them and they will withdraw.

For many years herding dogs were the helpmates of the peasant or working classes, and no records or formal pedigrees were kept. They were in demand by all agricultural communities. Crossbreeding occurred regularly, since all "breeding programs" were based on work ability and convenience only. Because of proximity-enforced inbreeding, types were established in certain areas. Not until dog shows came on the scene was breeding true to "type" encouraged by show enthusiasts.

In addition to the above hodge-podge, translations of breed names and standards often were careless when breeds were introduced outside their native countries. Therefore, the whole area of sheep dogs and shepherds is confusing and hopelessly tangled.

The English Shepherd, once known as the farm shepherd, is a natural driver and heeler. A hard worker and versatile shepherd, this breed is used on cattle as well as sheep, hogs, and even poultry. Early British settlers to the States brought the forebears of the breed which, despite its name, is considered American in origin.

Two of the most popular of the herders, the Collie and the Shetland Sheepdog, are contributions of Great Britain to the dog world. The Sheltie is about half the height of the Collie but is otherwise extremely similar in appearance.

Above: The Belgian Sheepdog Laekenois, the rarest of the four varieties, has been employed as a herder as well as a guardian. Its population is most prominent in Holland. **Below:** Originally utilized in the Pyrenees mountains of France, the Berger de Pyrenees is extraordinarily adaptable to extremes in weather. Pictured here in the snow is the goathaired coat type.

HERDING DOGS

Lapinporokoira	Finland
Belgian Sheepdog, Malinois	Belgium
Belgian Sheepdog, Groenendael	Belgium
Belgian Sheepdog, Tervuren	Belgium
Belgian Sheepdog, Laekenois	Belgium
Bouvier des Flandres	Belgium
Bouvier de Ardennes	Belgium
German Shepherd Dog	Germany
Giant Schnauzer	Germany
German Sheeppoodle	Germany
Hovawart	Germany
East European Shepherd	USSR
Tibetan Terrier	China
Lhasa Apso	China
Shih Tzu	China
Tibetan Spaniel	China
Pekingese	China
Japanese Chin	Japan
Puli	Hungary
Pumi	Hungary
Mudi	Hungary
Croatian Sheepdog	Yugoslavia
Bergamasco	Italy
Cão da Serra de Aires	Portugal
Catalan Sheepdog	Spain
Polski Owczarek Nizinny	Poland
Berger de Picard	France
Briard	France
Berger de Beauce	France
Berger de Pyrenees	France
Berger de Pyrenees, Smooth Muzzled	France
Berger du Languedoc	France
Armant	Egypt
Dutch Shepherd, Longhaired	Netherlands
Dutch Shepherd, Shorthaired	Netherlands
Dutch Shepherd, Roughhaired	Netherlands
Saarlooswolfhond	Netherlands
Schapendoes	Netherlands
Bearded Collie	Great Britain
Border Collie	Great Britain
Collie, Rough	Great Britain
Collie, Smooth	Great Britain
Shetland Sheepdog	Great Britain
Old English Sheepdog	Great Britain
Lancashire Heeler	Great Britain
Welsh Corgi, Cardigan	Great Britain

Along with the Old English Sheepdog, the Bearded Collie, having evolved from the Polski Owczarek Nizinny, is fast becoming one of the most recognizable shaggy sheep dogs.

Welsh Corgi, Pembroke	Great Britain
Vasgotaspets	Sweden
Australian Kelpie	Australia
Australian Cattle Dog	Australia
Stumpy-Tail Cattle Dog	Australia
Australian Shepherd	USA
English Shepherd	USA
Catahoula Leopard Dog	USA
Blue Lacy	USA
Kyi Leo	USA

The Terriers
True Grit

Terriers are mighty dogs in small packages. Admirers call them "small warriors," "tough guys," and "swashbucklers." In their early days, their prey was savage, and the terriers had to be equally tough. Even today, they have a certain dash and pugnacity. They are described variously as hard-bitten, intrepid and audacious.

True terriers are small to medium dogs that were developed mainly for vermin hunting, often going underground after the quarry. Thus "terrier" came from the Latin *terra*, meaning earth.

These small warriors were used to catch and kill rats in the barn, stable and home. Their services rid the farmyards and pastures of pests that plagued the stock, crops and food supplies, and helped reduce vermin in the teeming cities. In the pastures, they searched out the underground lair of the badger or fox and dug in after the animal. Otters and foxes were maneuvered from their hiding places in the rocky cairns. Snakes were easy prey to these quick, agile dogs, and marmots and weasels, too, fell victim. With their tough-guy attitude, terriers also made excellent watchdogs for the home, and guardians—as well as untiring companions—for youngsters.

Unfortunately, the terrier-type dog was also a victim, as one of the combatant choices in dog-fighting. Besides the "sport" of fighting, there were other competitions that made use of this feisty dog. The "poor man's" sport of rat killing earned the fame and fortunes of many early terriers and their owners. The upper class trained them for formal fox hunts. When the fox had hidden in a hole or drain to escape the hounds, the small terriers were put to the ground (these terriers were carried on horseback, as they were too little to keep up). They darted after the fox, rooting him from his hiding place, and the chase was on once again.

They are rarely used in fox hunts in this modern age, but in some places, terriers still hunt live quarry to prove their gameness and courage. Most modern terrier owners who desire competition prefer to prove their dogs' abilities in formal terrier trials. Artificial burrows are created with "prey" placed in a cage and then in the burrow. While the dog actually cannot engage in combat with the animal, the desire, keenness and aggression toward its quarry can be seen.

Many of the dogs called terrier more correctly belong in other groups. The American Staffordshire Terrier, Boston Terrier, Bull Terrier, and Staffordshire Bull Terrier are actually of mastiff derivation. The Tibetan Terrier is a herding-type dog of Oriental spitz extraction. Yet, Dachshunds (although truly hounds) fit the terrier definition of being tough and going to ground. Many of the terrier breeds that started out as true working dogs, such as the Yorkshire Terrier and Toy Manchester Terrier, have been miniaturized and are now rightly referred to as companion dogs—although they still maintain many of their terrier mental characteristics.

Terriers were bred to stay comparatively small, so they would fit in the burrows and to lessen the expense of feeding. They often have a rough, wiry coat that not only protects them from the elements but also minimizes necessary grooming. Even the terriers that have a comparably smooth coat usually sport one that is thicker and rougher than most smoothhaired dogs (i.e., Smooth Fox Terriers, as compared to Dalmatians). A few have long hanging coats.

Terriers were not used merely to find or chase their quarry like the hounds or gun dogs, but were often required to make the actual kill. Even if they didn't join in mortal combat, facing a frightened and cornered wild animal in the dark many feet underground is not for the faint-hearted. This takes a dog with a bold, fearless, confident and pugnacious temperament. The terrier has presence; he is a dog that, even though only 15 or 20 pounds, acts like he is 120!

The traditional ritual of sparring terriers in

Originally bred to hunt fox, the Jack Russell Terrier is exceedingly successful as a raccoon and varmint hunter, with no qualms about going to ground.

the show ring (the only group where this is done) is to prove they have the true temperament. The judge asks the handlers to bring two or three of the dogs at a time on leash into the center of the ring to face one another head-to-head. Whereas the hound might lower the tail peacefully and a gun dog might sniff interestedly, terriers must show they are ready for a contest if the situation should arise. While not nasty or quarrelsome, they should be up on their toes, leaning forward, heads up, looking the opposite dog right in the eye. The ears and tails are in an erect, dominant position. Each should look and rumble a bit, as if to say, "I'm usually a perfect gentleman, but if *you* want to start something then I'm game!"

The terrier is typically lean and long-headed with a square, strong jaw to seat firmly the punishing teeth. To prevent injury, the eyes are set deep in the sockets. Ears are generally pricked or semi-pricked (button ear). Tails, usually carried straight up, are docked, leaving about half or less, depending on the breed. (This left a good handle to extract the dog from underground!) Terriers that work above ground are built with squarer proportions, while the dogs that go to ground tend to be a bit shorter on leg.

Dogs of terrier type have been known in the British Isles since very ancient times. As early as the Middle Ages, European forms were described by writers, storytellers and painters. Like our other modern dogs, terriers are not of a pure or single origin. Whichever dogs best fit the purpose of the owner were those chosen, and looks and shape did not matter. The basic terrier stock was most likely from small spitz/Nordic dogs.

Even in modern times, these dogs share many of their northern predecessors' characteristics, both in type and temperament. They are busy, active and very vocal dogs who naturally chase and alarm.

The erect, or nearly erect, ears and the tail that almost curves over the back also indicate northern influence. There were probably crossbreedings to the smaller mastiff dogs to gain the heavier jaw and aggressive temperament apparent in some of the terriers. Some breeders now feel the wire coats were the result of crosses to water poodle dogs. This may be the case, since Poodles, with their heavy curling coats, create a double wire coat much like the terrier's when crossed with smooth-coated dogs. The Poodle, in turn, goes back to mastiff/herding dogs, so there is a double line to those two types. Other terriers, in part, owe their ancestry to small sighthounds which yielded a racier dog.

The smooth terrier needs very little coat care other than an occasional brushing. The proper wire coat also requires a minimum of fuss. Terriers with correct wire coats have a soft dense undercoat and an outer jacket of very straight, hard, wiry hair. This outer hair grows to a length of only two or three inches and then dies, when it can be pulled or "stripped" with the fingers or a stripping knife. The dead hair is easily removed once or twice a year, and a new wiry coat soon replaces the old. This process prevents matting and shedding and keeps the dog appearing neat and trim. The wire coat is water-resistant—mud simply can be shaken off when it dries—and it provides good protection in the brambles and briars. A true wire coat never grows very long as the hard hair breaks off easily; early wire terriers often were referred to as broken-coated terriers.

Many modern terrier owners prefer to have the coat trimmed with electric clippers. While an abomination to dedicated terrier breeders, the care of such a trim is easier for the pet owner. The new coat, when it grows back after cutting, is softer and silkier and not of proper texture. Nearly all wire-coated terriers exhibited on the bench are hand-stripped, and the proper technique of creating the smart appearance of modern show winners is a definite art.

England is the origin of most terriers; many that developed in other parts of the world used English breeds in their creation. Exceptions are the German pinschers and schnauzers. These dogs, by the definition of terriers as vermin catchers and watchdogs, are included in the terrier group in this book. Early pinschers and schnauzers were likely the same breed type, the former being smooth-coated and the latter having the wirehair. Miniature versions of both the pinscher and the schnauzer have become popular companion dogs.

The Yorkshire Terrier, although once a true working dog, has been miniaturized and is a quality companion.

Above: The Soft-Coated Wheaten Terrier belongs to the family of Irish terriers. History finds the Wheaten in the homes of the Irish farmers as a companion and hunter. **Below:** The American Hairless Terrier resulted from a single hairless female in a litter of Rat Terriers. These two specimens belong to the Scotts of Louisiana, the founders and promoters of this new breed.

Sharing similar histories to the other British terriers, the Cairn Terrier has been around for about 500 years. These terriers were useful in extracting foxes from their hiding places in the cairns, hence the breed name.

TERRIERS

Manchester Terrier	Great Britain
Toy Manchester Terrier	Great Britain
Fox Terrier, Smooth	Great Britain
Fox Terrier, Wire	Great Britain
Jack Russell Terrier	Great Britain
Lakeland Terrier	Great Britain
Patterdale Terrier	Great Britain
Airedale Terrier	Great Britain
Bedlington Terrier	Great Britain
Welsh Terrier	Great Britain
Border Terrier	Great Britain
Dandie Dinmont Terrier	Great Britain
Norwich Terrier	Great Britain
Norfolk Terrier	Great Britain
Sealyham Terrier	Great Britain
Yorkshire Terrier	Great Britain
Cairn Terrier	Great Britain
Skye Terrier	Great Britain
Scottish Terrier	Great Britain
West Highland White Terrier	Great Britain
Irish Terrier	Ireland
Kerry Blue Terrier	Ireland
Soft-Coated Wheaten Terrier	Ireland
Glen of Imaal Terrier	Ireland
German Pinscher	Germany
Harlequin Pinscher	Germany
Miniature Pinscher	Germany
German Hunt Terrier	Germany
Schnauzer, Standard	Germany
Schnauzer, Miniature	Germany
Affenpinscher	Germany
Kromfohrländer	Germany
Austrian Shorthaired Pinscher	Austria
Dutch Smoushond	Netherlands
Brussels Griffon	Belgium
Belgian Griffon	Belgium
Petit Brabancon	Belgium
Czesky Terrier	Czechoslovakia
Australian Terrier	Australia
Silky Terrier	Australia
Rat Terrier	USA
Toy Fox Terrier	USA
American Hairless Terrier	USA
Brazilian Terrier	Brazil
Japanese Terrier	Japan
Black Russian Terrier	USSR
Moscow Longhaired Toy Terrier	USSR

Above: Jack Russell Terriers after a hard catch! **Below:** One of the largest in the terrier group is the Airedale Terrier, pictured here as a pup.

Southern Dogs
Dogs of the Desert Wind

At the dawn of history, the Southern Hemisphere of the world was semi-arid and less than hospitable to herbivores. This, plus the existence of other predators, meant a more limited food supply. The southern wolves, such as the Pale-Footed Asian Wolf, were much smaller and lighter boned than their northern cousins. Forced to share the meager food supply, the southern wolf did not exhibit the strong group cooperation and family ties. Adaptations for the warmer climate such as a short, smooth coat and large, upright ears appeared. Their ears were large with the blood vessels near the surface to dissipate heat. From this early southern predator came the domesticated dog of the South.

Humankind had evolved faster in the south. Perhaps as long as 10,000 years ago, nomadic tribes in Africa and southeast Asia had tamed sheep and goats, as well as dogs to help herd these flocks. These were, by far, the earliest domesticated canines, predating those of the northern varieties by nearly several thousand years. This early southern canine was basically a herding dog with distinctive physical traits.

The southern dogs were of moderate size (around 30–40 pounds) for efficient keep and short coated to withstand the heat. The body was squarish and up on leg; the head was wedge-shaped and sharply angled with the rather large pricked ears that tilted forward, sometimes creating forehead wrinkles. They sometimes retained the wolf traits of once-a-year estrus and infrequence or absence of barking. Some possessed the low tail of the wolf, although others showed the neotanous trait of the tail curled over the back.

This creation of the southern dog is thought to have occurred in what is now northern Iran. From that starting point, early people migrated to all parts of the globe. With them went their dogs. These nomads went north and east to populate Siberia, crossing the land bridge into the Western Hemisphere. From there they spread through North and South America. Some of these migrations took the tribes south and west into Africa. Still others slowly moved east to settle what is now Malaysia, Oceania and across another land bridge into Australia.

In all of these areas, the southern dog was seeded, very often reverting to a feral state. It was in this venue that he earned his name of pariah, scavenging on the fringes of civilization. As a competitor for the limited food sources and, as an eater of garbage and carrion, he generally became detested. The Chinese, Indian, Moslem and Jewish cultures all looked upon this scavenger as unclean and to be avoided.

In more recent times, as these breeds were unearthed, many experts classified them as true wild dogs, separate species from the domesticated dog. Modern research has shown that they *are* the true feral form of the southern dogs domesticated so long ago, altered and adapted for a variety of lifestyles. Despite their "wild" state, they were—and still are—converted back to domestic living.

Although, numerically, these dogs represent the largest group of dogs in the world, they have the fewest known and established breeds, probably because they have been shunned for so long. In fact, many of these dogs, which tended to breed true in an ecological niche untouched by human intervention, are described in this book. Yet others have been tended and selected by people to fill certain needs or crossed with the better known northern dogs to create new breeds.

During the rise and fall of the pariahs, the great ancient civilizations of the Fertile Crescent had developed. These cultures rapidly learned to modify and change nature's products for their own use. They began practicing selective animal breeding.

War mastiffs were in wide use. In ancient Egyptian culture, archaeologists found records of eight specific and distinct types of dogs, in-

Bred by tribes of the southern Sahara, the Azawakh was employed as a camel and goat guardian. Truly "Dogs of the Desert Wind," the Azawakhs are built like fine Arabian horses, possessing a lightfooted, lithesome gait.

cluding mastiffs, small house dogs, pariahs in various forms, medium-sized hounds, and "new" dogs of the chase. The Egyptians and other cultures also used tamed jackals for hunting. As civilization progressed and people enjoyed more leisure, hunting became not just a necessary chore but a pastime developed to an art.

In the hot, arid and treeless areas where early civilizations settled, hunting was accomplished mainly by sighting and running down prey such as gazelle and antelope. To create a dog specialized for this task, the early racy pariahs were se-lected. Traits that increased speed and minimized wind resistance were sought. Soon the pariah dog was longer legged with more angulation, had wider back vertebrae and more loin muscles. This dog had lighter bone and a deeper chest to allow increased lung capacity, which are all adaptations for speed and the double-suspension gallop.

The head was lengthened and narrowed to slice through the wind and to increase the cooling mechanisms of the nasal passages. But he maintained his upright ears and the wedge-shaped head with forehead wrinkles. This prototype sighthound speedster can be seen today in several breeds.

The swiftness of the sighthound brought a sport to dog lovers that has spanned the years, probably since before Ovid's written description at the time of Christ. Humans, being human, have always relished contests and, from the start, delighted in boasting, "My dog's better'n your dog." The most ancient of dog sports certainly was racing, and enthusiasm for the races have continued to this day. Initially, the dogs pursued a hare; nowadays the thrill of the chase must suffice, as the hare has been replaced by a stuffed bunny or other inanimate lure. English coursing events became organized in 1776, eventually resulting in the Waterloo Cup, the Derby of dogdom.

Races draw enthusiasts from the ranks of Irish Wolfhounds, Scottish Deerhounds, Salukis, Afghan Hounds, Whippets, Italian Greyhounds, and of course, the *creme de la creme*—the Greyhound. Racing competitors stand as far apart from their show brothers as do field trialers from bench competitors, occasionally appearing

to be different breeds altogether. Racing dogs are alert to the extreme (sometimes not making them good pets), deep-chested and powerfully built.

Sighthounds that run down prey alone in open country are distinctly different from ancestral wolf cousins which always trotted in groups after their target.

Their relative, the jackal, has a long, narrow head, is lighter built than the wolf and is adapted to withstand heat. Jackals tend to be higher strung and do more solitary hunting. The jackal is not as closely related biologically as the wolf is to the dog, but crosses can and have occurred. Many cynologists believe that some crossbreeding to the jackal occurred in the development of the sighthound. Gazehounds tend to have an aloof and reserved personality, quite different from other types of dogs. If there were crosses, they were very early with the type being set, since there is very little variation in the group as a whole. Later, the heads became even longer and narrower, the ears dropped or folded back to the neck, and the size and tuck-up be-

A strong bond between the Moslem nomads and their Sloughis exists even to this day. A registration is underway at a Moroccan dog show.

The Pharaoh Hound, like all the sighthounds, possesses great speed and agility. The Pharaoh Hound descends from the pariah-type dogs and is able to hunt by sight as well as scent.

came more exaggerated to create the classic sighthound type.

The Phoenician civilization was at its peak during the years of 800 to 2000 BC. These people were great sailors and had trade routes throughout the known world. They sailed around the entire Mediterranean from their main cities, in what is now Lebanon, to Turkey, Greece, Italy and even the Straits of Gibraltar and Spain, to the north and south, to the northern coast of Africa including Egypt, Libya and Morocco. But they also ventured into the Atlantic to Portugal, Brittany and the British Isles. They were commercial traders for nearly everything—metal products, cedar wood, glass, and their famed purple-dyed cloth—at each port of call.

The fleet sighthounds were in high demand. The Phoenician hound trade was known throughout the ancient world. Wherever Phoenicians landed, whatever strange and new society they encountered, the barter for the dogs of the chase overcame language and cultural barriers. Because of this, the sighthound was seeded over a wide area of Europe, the Middle East, and Africa. In some places, like the islands of Sicily and Ibiza, he remained to breed true for many thousands of years. In other areas the sighthound was used in crosses to native types, creating new breeds. Because of these crosses, long and wire coats also were developed.

As the centuries passed, the desert Bedouins kept and bred choice dogs of the desert type. These dogs of the chase were an exception to the "unclean" rule among the Arabs. They were prized by their owners, lived in tents with the tribal chieftains and were given as treasured gifts. The pedigrees were carried only in the memories of their owners, but passed from generation to generation by word of mouth.

The sighthound became the dog of nobility in other areas of the world as well. Several distinct types were created by the upper classes of Russia. Although fallen into disfavor since the Revolution, some of these breeds are making a comeback in the Soviet Union. The rough-coated sighthounds of Ireland and Scotland hunted with—and were loved by—kings and the

Above: Whippets—some believe a cross of English terriers to the Greyhound—are very social dogs, delighting in the company of people and dogs, such as the Basenji, a fellow southern canine. **Below:** The beloved house pet of Peruvian Indians who surrounded their dogs with orchids, the Peruvian Inca Orchid is still bred by natives today.

nobility, with oft told legends to their credit.

A strange mutation occurred at some time along the line of evolvement from pariah to sighthound. Some pups were born hairless, or nearly so, except for sparse tufts on the feet and head. Always on the lookout for the unusual or different, fanciers kept and bred these types.

The exact origin of the first hairless dogs is unknown, but the dominant hairless dogs are all of pariah/sighthound types. This suggests the North African/Middle East areas, where a hairless species called *Canis Africanis* evolved. Breeds once known included the African Sand Dog, African Elephant Dog, Small African Greyhound and the Nubian Dog. Hairless dogs also have been raised in the Middle East, India, China, Mexico and South America: the Turkish Hairless, Indian Rampur, Guatemalan Hairless and Buenos Aires Hairless, besides the more "common" rarities seen today. They were common during the height of Aztec and Incan advanced cultures. They may have emigrated from Asia with the Indians or may have mutated sepa-

Every hairless breed has a "powderpuff" (coated) variety as well. In order to cut the effect of the lethal homozygous gene, the powderpuffs are essential to the propagation of the breed. These are Chinese Cresteds.

rately, but their basic form is similar to hairless dogs elsewhere in the world. In the Aztec culture, the hairless dog was a food source. Raised in pens and grain-fed, they were an important part of the Aztec diet. It was only much later that they became pets.

Hairless dogs of pariah type share many similarities. The hereditary factor that produces the hairless condition is a dominant lethal gene. Dogs carrying the double-dominant die before birth, so there is never a homozygous hairless dog (one that always reproduces the hairless condition). Dogs born hairless are heterozygous for the trait, meaning they can produce both hairless and coated progeny. About one out of three pups born from a hairless-to-hairless mating are double-recessive for normal hair and are called "powderpuffs," with the powderpuff being the original type and the hairless the mutant. Legend has it that the coated pups are born in

every litter to keep their bald siblings warm. Hairless dogs possess a tendency to have missing teeth, with as many as all of the premolars being absent. It was once believed that these breeds also carried a warmer body temperature.

Puppies born of hairless-to-hairless matings often suffer extreme abnormalities. One in four is stillborn or reabsorbed prior to birth. The hairless variety also has the primitive mouth (teeth extending forward, missing premolars and occasionally missing eyeteeth) with less dental enamel. Hard foods can cause problems, and soft, moistened foods are recommended. Bathing to prevent blackheads and protection from the sun are also advised. Knowledgeable breeders realize the importance of utilizing the powderpuff in the breeding program to aid in correcting these problems. A few types of these ancient hairless dogs have evolved into modern breeds.

The elegant and flowing appearance of the Afghan Hound should not be misinterpreted; as a hunter in his native Afghanistan, the breed was used on swift and powerful game, including wolves, foxes, and gazelles. Of course, the breed's hunting abilities by no means detract from its overall beauty.

SOUTHERN DOGS

Pariah

Dingo	Australia
Telomian	Malaysia
New Guinea Singing Dog	New Guinea
Canaan Dog	Israel
Basenji	Zaire
Carolina Dog	USA
Tahltan Bear Dog	Canada
Hawaiian Poi Dog	USA
Pharaoh Hound	Malta
Ibizan Hound	Spain
Cirneco dell'Etna	Italy
Podengo Portugueso, Grande	Portugal
Podengo Portugueso, Medio	Portugal
Podengo Portugueso, Pequeño	Portugal
Chihuahua	Mexico

Sighthound

Sloughi	Morocco
Saluki	Iran
Azawakh	Mali
Greyhound	Great Britain
Whippet	Great Britain
Galgo Español	Spain
Magyar Agar	Hungary
Borzoi	USSR
Chortaj	USSR
Tazy	USSR
Taigan	USSR
South Russian Steppe Hound	USSR
Kangaroo Dog	Australia
Afghan Hound	Afghanistan
Scottish Deerhound	Great Britain
Irish Wolfhound	Ireland
Rhodesian Ridgeback	South Africa
Italian Greyhound	Italy

Hairless

Peruvian Inca Orchid	Peru
Inca Hairless Dog	Peru
Chinese Crested Dog	Africa/China
Xoloitzcuintli	Mexico
Xoloitzcuintli Toy	Mexico

The prototype sighthound has a long, narrowed head to assist it in slicing the desert wind with speed and grace. The Whippet is a fine example of this sleek and pointed body type.

The Dogs of the World

This chapter is divided into specific articles, arranged alphabetically and each concerned with one individual breed or group of closely related breeds. The reader is advised to consult "How to Use This Atlas" for a more detailed explanation of the most effective approach to this chapter.

Affenpinscher, dark gray.

AFFENPINSCHER

COUNTRY: Germany
WEIGHT: 7–8 pounds
HEIGHT: Less than 10 inches
COAT: Medium long, harsh and wiry
COLOR: Black preferred, black/tan, red or dark gray also allowed
REGISTRY: FCI, AKC, TKC, CKC
GROUP: Terrier

A true toy terrier, this breed has been in existence for more than 300 years. His origins are difficult to pinpoint, but he is seen in nearly his present form in 17th-century paintings. He may be a miniature form of the wire terrier prototype which came from Nordic dogs, such as the Schipperke. These, crossed with the little pinschers or with small brachycephalic Puglike dogs from Asia found in Europe, could have created the Affenpinscher. In fact, earlier Affens may have had a longer muzzle, because the Affenpinscher and smooth Miniature Pinscher were at one time considered two coat varieties of the same breed and even occurred in the same litter.

Whatever his ancestry, this quaint little dog has earned the description of "monkey dog." His rather flat, turned-up nose, alert cropped ears, prominent round eyes, bristling eyebrows and bushy mustache and beard all add to this description. The French often call this dog *Diabletin Moustache,* literally the mustached little devil!

Belying his very small size, he is every inch a terrier in personality. He is alert, yet quiet, game and sturdy. The FCI standard translates: " . . . a charming mixture of fearlessness, obstinancy, loyalty and affection which he will show in rapid change from amusing earnestness to raging passion."

Regular brushing and tidying up is all the Affen requires to look neat. The tail is docked short. Although not among the most numerous of dogs, he has his proponents internationally. American and Canadian recognition was granted in 1936 but, perhaps because of the wealth of terrier types already in Britain, he remains virtually unknown there.

Afghan Hound.

AFGHAN HOUND

COUNTRY: Afghanistan
WEIGHT: 50–60 pounds
HEIGHT: 25–27 inches
COAT: Long, straight, thick, silky; short on face
COLOR: Any color; white on head undesirable
OTHER NAMES: Tazi
REGISTRY: FCI, AKC, UKC, TKC, CKC
GROUP: Southern

The history of the Afghan Hound is ancient, though the legend which claims the Afghan as the dog Noah took into the Ark may be a bit exaggerated. Migration of northern African sighthounds into the mountains of Afghanistan included some hounds with longer hair. In the cold mountain air, the heaviest coats were selected and bred from necessity, eventually creating the Afghan. The breed spread into the border areas and even into India and aided both the hunter and the shepherd.

His unique, upright tail with the curled end served as a marker in the heavier underbrush, and his high-set hip bones enabled him greater flexibility in the mountain ranges. The aristocratic, elegant Afghan was no pussycat, hunting big—even tough—game: wolves, foxes and gazelles. In times past, he was a favorite of the Afghani nobility as an adjunct to the sport of falconry.

His old native name is Tazi, and his obvious resemblance to the like-named Tasy of Russia (even to the ring in the tail) indicates similar histories. The proximity of southern Russia and Afghanistan geographically increases the likelihood of close ancestry.

Originally, sale of the national dog to outsiders was prohibited, and the first specimens to arrive in the United States and England did not appear until the turn of the 20th century. An English Captain Banff imported the exciting hound, "Zardin," from Afghanistan around this time. Exhibited at the Crystal Palace Show in 1907, he won spectacularly and started a true interest in the breed. Good breeding programs existed in Britain by the 1920s. AKC and CKC recognition followed in the 30s.

The Afghan coat bears singular requirements: the topknot and the distinct shorthaired saddle on the back which forms as an adult. It is permissible for the dog to display a shorthaired cuff on the feet. Frequent, fastidious combing is a necessity. An ungroomed Afghan is not only unkempt but uncomfortable.

As well as being a highly celebrated show dog today, the Afghan participates in lure coursing. Despite their high numbers as show competitors, they have not achieved the same status as a pet, due to their size, coat care and exercise demands. Their temperament is aloof, though they can be the greatest of clowns at play time. From their origin on Mount Sinai to today's show ring, the Afghans are majesty at its peak. "At a glance, one can see the Eastern inscrutability; the conviction that they are royalty; the certainty that they are above lesser breeds."

Afghan Hound.

Afghan Hound.

AINU DOG

COUNTRY: Japan
HEIGHT: 18½–21½ inches
COAT: Moderately short, thick, stand-off, with undercoat
COLOR: Sesame, brindle, wolf gray, red, brown or white
OTHER NAMES: Hokkaido Dog, Ainu-Ken
REGISTRY: FCI
GROUP: Northern

When the Ainu tribe arrived in Japan nearly 3,000 years ago, they had dogs of Nordic type with them, and these became the Ainu Dog. The Ainus were an ancient people who migrated to and were the first settlers in Japan, ten centuries before Christ. They were a white race of unknown origin, and at one time lived on all the islands of Japan.

The Ainus were slowly pushed out over the centuries by the influx of Yamato (Japanese) people and now live only in their own settlements on the northernmost island of Hokkaido. (They live in their own groups, with their own separate and quite primitive culture.) Their dog has changed little over the centuries. The Ainu Dog is probably the oldest of the Japanese breeds and may have been altered somewhat through crosses with matagi dogs.

The breed is known for its strength and was a draft dog originally, but is used today for hunting and guarding. The Ainu is extremely courageous for his size, willingly attacking a 650-pound bear. He is generally kept in the home.

As is common with most of the Japanese breeds, this dog is clean and mannerly yet quite ready to warn of danger. As a working dog for so long, he tends to be a bit coarser and more primitive than the other Japanese breeds. His character is sharp and fearless. He also differs by having smaller ears, a broader head and a fiercer expression. Also of interest is that, although not particularly desired, these dogs occasionally have the black tongue. This may hint at ties to the Chow Chow and mainland China. If loved and cared for, he is said to be obedient to his master and an irreplaceable friend.

Facing page: Ainu Dog, red.

Airedale Terrier.

AIREDALE TERRIER

COUNTRY: Great Britain
WEIGHT: 44 pounds
HEIGHT: 23 inches for males
COAT: Wiry, hard, dense with a bit of a curl; undercoat
COLOR: Black/tan, saddled
REGISTRY: FCI, AKC, UKC, TKC, CKC
GROUP: Terrier

The extinct black and tan Old English or Broken-haired Terrier is probably the progenitor of the Welsh, Irish, Wire Fox and Airedale Terriers. Sporting Yorkshiremen used Airedales and their crosses for fox, weasel, otter, badger, water rat and small game in the valleys of the rivers Colne, Calder, Warfe, and Aire. They ranged from 17–30 pounds and excelled in agility, eyesight, hearing and courage, but they lacked the nose and swimming ability of the Otterhound used in the same area. The crossing of the terrier and hound formed the stem of the Airedale, a large terrier that would also work in water. By the 1860s, these crosses were standardized and called Working, Waterside or Bingley Terriers. Classes were first offered at agricultural shows in 1879. In fact, the Airedale agricultural show had an extremely large entry of Waterside Terriers and was responsible for giving the breed its current name.

The patriarch of the breed is Ch. Master Briar, 1897–1906. One of his sons was exported to Philadelphia to initiate the breed in the USA. The Airedale boasts many Best In Shows in the USA and England, but loyal fanciers exist throughout the world.

According to *Hutchinson's Dog Encyclopaedia*, "the breed has long been held in high favour by the armies of European and Asiatic countries being easy to train and once trained, showing great determination of character and devotion to duty, and almost superhuman intelligence, chiefly in carrying despatches on the field of battle and finding the wounded. In fact, the dog's intelligence was so high in the latter respect that they became a source of embarrassment to the Japanese victors during the Russo-Japanese War by always finding and directing to the Russians first and the Japanese soldiers last, for the Airedale's power of scent is remarkable."

They are used on large game in Africa, India and Canada, as well as the USA. The breed was chosen as one of the first to be used for police work in Germany and England. During World War I, the breed was enlisted by the British and Russian armies. During that time it aided the Red Cross, locating wounded and carrying messages. A few also served in the Second World War. When trained for defense, these dogs are usually unbeatable for their weight. It is said the Airedale "can do anything any other dog can do—and then lick the other dog."

Their sweet disposition comes from their hound background. Mature dogs have a certain dignified aloofness, both to strangers and to their own kind. Exceptional playmates for children who are old enough for high-spirited play, their disposition can be molded by their masters.

The Airedale coat, which is not only hard and wiry, but sports a bit of a curl, requires consistent regular grooming. The ears have a half drop and the tail is docked.

Airedale Terrier.

AKBASH DOG

COUNTRY: Turkey
WEIGHT: 80–140 pounds
HEIGHT: 28–34 inches
COAT: Smooth or long, both double coat; thick, with fringing on tail and back of legs, and often a slight wave
COLOR: Solid white (a bit of light biscuit around ears is not to be penalized); complete black pigment of eye rims, nose and lips preferred, but dark brown acceptable.
GROUP: Flock Guard

As one of the oldest breeds of the flock-guarding group, the Akbash Dog still carries the same physical and mental traits that characterized these dogs thousands of years ago. They were probably brought to the *yaylas* (mountain pastures) of Turkey with migrations of peoples from the East. Since sighthounds, mastiffs and flock-guard dogs accompanied these Oriental migrations, all could have contributed to the gene pool. Turkey (Asia Minor) was on the migratory routes between West and East, and stories have been told and records kept of these guardians from very early times.

Lucien G.M. Columella, a first-century AD Roman author, wrote: "Sheepherders wish to have white dogs in order to avoid confusing them with wild animals, since, when the wolf attacks in the twilight, it is important that there be a color difference between the dog and the wolf; otherwise the sheepherder might strike his dog, thinking he was killing a wolf."

A Phrygian civilization (Asia Minor, 750-300 BC) graffito shows a large guarding dog wearing a spiked iron collar. Turkish flock-guarding dogs still wear huge iron-spiked collars as added protection for the vulnerable neck area against predators.

The Akbash is a fleet-moving dog, with acute hearing and eyesight. Natural and owner culling has developed strong, sturdy animals. These dogs are bred to be animal-oriented, rather than toward people. Their independence is sometimes misunderstood by the uninformed as stubbornness or stupidity. They are bred to think, rather than obey with robot precision. A strong

Akbash Dog.

Akbash Dog.

tendency to natural suspicion fosters development of the proper guarding attitude.

Proper bonding with sheep requires calm, quiet, steady temperament. Livestock guardian candidates are never brought inside the home or made into pets. They need to be introduced to their future animal at a tender age.

If pups want to play with sheep, trainers cure this by adding an "old cantankerous ewe or feisty ram . . . to discipline the overly exuberant puppy," so they learn not to injure the young lambs in rough play.

In modern society, the Akbash usually accepts other farm animals (i.e., dogs, cats, horses and other domestics), if reared with them from puppyhood, and is sometimes protective of them. When raised with children, the dogs are good with them. Pets should be confined to an area, rather than being chained which intensifies aggression.

Matings are not readily accomplished. Dogs are so attached to the flock that they are not easily sidetracked, even for affairs of the heart. One bitch owner had to rent an entire flock and the shepherd to convince its guard dog to cooperate.

The animal refused to leave his flock!

Double rear dewclaws are often seen on Akbash Dogs and may be removed. In conformation, the smooths, without padding of coat, falsely tend to appear slighter in build than the long coats. Many Akbash Dogs have the ranginess, fleetness and arch to the loin that give just a hint of the running hound in their background. In the past, the ears were cropped like many breeds of this group to diminish the ability of a predator to grip and hold. Thus many imports have the ears lopped off. Ears on modern dogs are usually left natural.

The handsome Akbash has been successful in USA flock-guarding programs, and American breeders are determined to preserve the working qualities. Their active American-based Akbash Dog Association International promotes the breed for guard work, obedience and exhibition at rare breed shows, as well as for livestock protection on farms and ranches. In addition, the Akbash Dog is showing up in more and more activities, such as therapy dogs and independence dogs (aiding the handicapped).

Akitas.

AKITA

COUNTRY: Japan
WEIGHT: 75–110 pounds or more
HEIGHT: 24–28 inches
COAT: Stiff, moderately short; stand-off, with undercoat
COLOR: All colors allowed, including white, pied, or brindle, with or without mask
OTHER NAMES: Akita Inu
REGISTRY: FCI, AKC, TKC, CKC
GROUP: Northern

Most of the native dogs of Japan are of the classic northern type. They have square bodies, wedge-shaped heads, small upright ears, short, thick stand-off coats, and the tail is curled up over the back. The eyes tend to be triangular and recessed, "suggesting the burning spirit within." Their temperaments are always calm and considerate, with great dignity.

The breed differences lie in the sizes, colors, uses and backgrounds, and a few other minor features. In fact, they are so much alike that in Japan, these native breeds are shown in one classification, divided into sub-groups: large (Akita), medium (Kai, Kishu, Ainu, Shikoku) and small (Shiba).

Both the terms *inu* and *ken* translate into the word dog. Many of the Japanese breeds originally carried one of these terms after their names, but modern usage tends to drop the superfluous suffix.

In the late 19th century, when the National Isolation Policy was repealed, other breeds were brought into the country and, naturally, some

Akita, tan.

crossbreeding occurred. The Japanese government became concerned over the impending loss of their native breeds and formed the Society for Preservation of Japanese Dogs, declaring all native breeds as national monuments.

The largest of these breeds is the well-known Akita from the Akita prefecture in northern Japan. The breed traces back many centuries to the polar regions when the spitz group found its way to the northern mountains in Honshu. The largest and most powerful specimens were selected and bred with the type appearing about 300 years ago. Akitas were originally developed as fighting dogs, as popular in the Far East as they were in Europe. As that sport lost favor, the nobility found new uses for this brave breed in their hunts for deer, wild boar or even black bear. This dog has achieved praise as a bold hunter of large game, a guard and a loyal companion.

A huge statue of an Akita stands in the busy Shibuya Station in Tokyo, erected in the 1920s as a tribute to a dog who appeared daily to greet his master as he returned to the station from work, continuing ten years after the master died. The statue is named *Chuken Hachi-ko*, or Loyal Dog Hachi.

The Akita is a tough, robust fellow, needing firm, loving discipline. He can be obstinate and reacts against harsh methods. The breed cannot be forced but, once shown what is desired, he is quite cooperative. The Akita is aggressive with other animals and will defend its territory against all intruders, human or otherwise. Yet he is an affectionate companion to his family. The Japanese say he is "tender in heart and strong in strength."

To preclude boredom and mischief, sufficient exercise is necessary. The Japanese spitz dogs are hardy and can endure extremes of climate.

The breed's popularity continues as a companion and guardian. He is sometimes called *Shishi Inu*, meaning large dog. The breed is a favorite in Japan, and is fairly well known in the USA as well as in England and the European continent. As noted by Fujino Junko, "the characters of these dogs suggest ancient Japanese people—austere, valiant, faithful, good-natured and gentle, highly affectionate and sensitive to the kindness of their masters."

Akitas, black and white.

Akita puppy, with mask.

Alaskan Malamute.

ALASKAN MALAMUTE

COUNTRY: USA
WEIGHT: 75–85 pounds
HEIGHT: 23–25 inches
COAT: Short, stand-off
COLOR: Black or various shades of gray, with lighter mask and underside common
REGISTRY: FCI, AKC, UKC, TKC, CKC
GROUP: Northern

The draft or combination draft/hunting dogs of the North have been an essential part of the northern people's culture since the Stone Age. Because most northern tribes were nomadic, they could not have existed without their dogs to move their belongings from place to place. In the harsh and bitter cold, dogs were the only domestic animals that could survive.

Historians argue whether the ancestors of the northern Eskimo tribes came over a land bridge from Asia or across the North Pole from Scandinavia. But the fact that Nordic-type dogs accompanied these people is without argument. Each tribe or area developed its own type of dog, so perfected that many remain distinct today. The *Mahlemuts* (later spelled Malamute) were an industrious and skilled Inuit people of upperwestern Alaska (across from Siberia). Since they were nomadic, they moved their families to the site of each new kill, relocating when the need for another food source arose.

This lifestyle necessitated dogs strong enough to haul all of the tribe's possessions and to transport goods to and from the trading post. Speed was not vital, however, and a leisurely pace was quite acceptable. The Mahlemut tribe was never mentioned without a reference to their sledge dogs. Early European explorers and Russian whalers of the last century told that the Mahlemuts had dogs of "beauty and endurance," and that they were "fond of their . . . dogs. The dogs work hard and have great endurance.''

During the settling of Alaska by white people, from 1750 to 1900, dogs were used for hauling and transportation in large numbers. These newcomers did not pay much attention to type, as long as the dogs (named after the tribe) could work. In addition the upsurge of dog-sled racing did the Malamute dog no good. In an attempt to create a faster animal, racing drivers crossed them with established speedsters, and the breed was nearly lost.

At that time, however, some Eskimos kept their dogs pure to type. Fortunately, interest in the promotion of the pure Malamute rose among American dog fanciers, and the breed has been maintained. Eva "Short" Seely became interested in sled dogs, obtaining good Malamutes (and Siberians) and breeding them, even sending her stock with Admiral Byrd to Antarctica. World War I had an effect on these northern dogs as well as on European breeds, but in a different manner. Their numbers were depleted by search-and-rescue, the Byrd expeditions and supply-packing work during the War. The stud book was reopened after the War and additional foundation stock was added to those already registered. Once again, the breed thrived.

The Malamute is as distinct from the Siberian Husky as the draft horse is from the horse of the desert. The Malamute is a dog that denotes power rather than quickness. Never so large as to appear clumsy, he must personify substance and strength. The body is slightly longer than its height, moving the center of gravity back, which allows powerful leaning into heavy loads. A clean, quiet, affectionate companion, the Mal needs firm, early handling to understand who is boss.

Raised and exhibited in much of North America and Europe, the Malamute is a popular dog for home sledding. Many owners and their Mals compete in weight-pulling contests. The dogs take to it quite naturally—in fact, enthusiastically—with many capable of shifting one-ton loads over a short distance.

They prefer outdoor living, with sufficient entertainment provided by their people, and are ready to join in almost any athletic activity. If bored, a Mal will express his displeasure by howling and digging to the South Pole!

Alaskan Malamute.

Alaskan Malamute.

Alaskan Malamute.

Alpine Dachsbracke, profile.

A short-legged hound for closer hunting and tracking was developed in Austria, as in other countries. But in the high altitude of the Alps, a larger dachsbracke was necessary, and the Austrian version is slightly bigger than his German cousin, the Westphalian. Like the other dachsbrackes and bassets, this breed has a normal hound body with short but not curved or twisted legs. He was created from the indigenous hounds of Austria.

The Alpine Dachsbracke is solid, robust, and heavily muscled, giving him an athletic and agile appearance. The coat, although not wiry, is harsh and dense. His stern, with a brush of hair, is extremely long, nearly reaching the ground. Unlike the Westphalian, this variety has no white markings. The standard lists solid black (without the tan markings), chocolate or gray-blue as disqualifications.

Mainly a coldtrailing hound on deer tracks, in full voice he is equally useful after rabbit and fox. The official standard of the breed calls him a "multiple utility dog of the Alpine hunter." A real professional at his craft, he has found little following outside of local gamekeepers and hunters.

Alpine Dachsbracke, red with black ticking.

ALPINE DACHSBRACKE

COUNTRY: Austria
WEIGHT: 33–40 pounds
HEIGHT: 13½–16½ inches, ideal 14-14½ inches
COAT: Short, coarse and hard
COLOR: Stag red, red with black ticking or black/tan, any white is undesirable
OTHER NAMES: Alpenlandischer Dachsbracke
REGISTRY: FCI
GROUP: Hound

American Black and Tan Coonhound.

AMERICAN BLACK AND TAN COONHOUND

COUNTRY: USA
HEIGHT: 23–27 inches
COAT: Short and dense
COLOR: Black with tan points
OTHER NAMES: Black and Tan Coonhound
REGISTRY: AKC, UKC, CKC
GROUP: Hound

Famed scouts and Indian fighters, Simon Kenton and the Poe brothers from the Ohio Valley, were among the first to foster the Black and Tan in the late 1700s. From Poe's stock and the later efforts of Simion Shirk and his grandson, Holmes Lingo, in the early 1800s, evolved the Old Glory strain of Black and Tans, the breed's most famous line which lasted in pure form for more than 130 years, until the mid-1940s. Other promoters of the breed, such as the Merritt Brothers of the 19th century and Don Stringer's Ten Oaks line of the 1920s–1940s, contributed to the modern development of the American Black and Tan breed.

American coonhounds were basically developed from foxhounds, with dashes of French, German and Irish dogs for specific needs. In fact, the AKC position early in this century was that these dogs were Foxhounds, and officials refused to register them as coonhounds. Therefore, breeders of these dogs turned to the United Kennel Club, which has sponsored coonhounds and their competitive events ever since.

The Black and Tan was the first "coonhound" to split off from the American Foxhound umbrella and, ironically, is the only one to be accepted by AKC. Black and Tans developed from early methodical, exquisitely cold-nosed "foxhounds." Most cynologists feel that a large percentage (at least) of the Kerry Beagle was in the stem stock.

The raccoon, an animal unknown in Europe, is a native of the Americas. "Coon" hunting became and has remained a passion with Americans, and the development of specific dogs for this sport ensued. The coon, when pursued, will finally climb a tree where the dogs hold it until the hunters arrive. This quarry is nocturnal, so

The original coonhound, the American Black and Tan is possessed of a versatile, buglelike voice and hunts boar and big cat with the same vigor with which it hunts coon.

hunting is done at night. A group of hounds are cast and, when one of them encounters a fresh coon trail, he "opens" or begins to bay.

Since each hound has a distinctive bawl, the handlers can identify which hound has opened on the trail. Then all the other hounds join the leader in following the scent and combine their voices. The hunters can follow the progress of the chase through the dark by the musical sounds of the hounds, heard for many miles as they pursue the quarry. When the dogs finally tree the raccoon, their voice tone changes, and the hunters then head toward the sound. Eavesdroppers on a typical hunt can hear, "There goes Babe. She's on the trail." Or, "Ol' Joker's got 'im treed."

The American Black and Tan is a big, rangy, strongly headed hound with abundant earage. He possesses a beautiful bugle voice and is a methodical hunter that leaves no stone unturned. E.S. Traverse, a knowledgeable houndsman, writes about the classic Black and Tan as "a cold-nosed hound that opened on tracks the other hounds didn't even know were there, with the determination to finish the track even if it led to Hell's backdoor." Because of these attributes, the Black and Tan has trailed boar, big cats and other similar game, as much or more than on raccoon, so that his specific talents can be fully utilized.

Today a few breeders foster the breed on the bench and occasional specimens are seen at AKC shows. The exhibition specimens have tended to become more refined and racy in type, and it would seem a shame to create a breed split in this fine old hound by forgetting its original use, purpose and proud history. Although called American Black and Tan Coonhound by the UKC, which registers 12,000 each year, the 600 registered by the AKC go by the shortened name of Black and Tan Coonhound.

The Black and Tans are calm, affectionate and good with children. They love being with people and are willing to please. Early socialization is suggested to insure confidence. Droopy ears must be kept clean to avoid odor and infections. Like most hounds, when they catch a scent, they're off and running, so owners are well advised to secure the dogs in an enclosure when not being worked.

American Blue Gascon Hound.

AMERICAN BLUE GASCON HOUND

COUNTRY: USA
WEIGHT: 75–105 pounds
HEIGHT: 25–30 inches
COAT: Short, thick and dense
COLOR: Basically white body with tan points and heavy black ticking creating the "blue"; there are allowed natural variations in color including degree of ticking and roaning, amount of solid black spots, absence of tan marks, and sometimes a grizzled appearance
OTHER NAMES: Big 'n Blue
GROUP: Hound

Those hound aficionados favoring the big, strong-voiced, cold-nosed hound of the old "Gascon" type were forced to keep changing their allegiance. It wasn't the breed so much as the preservation of a type that these hunters wanted.

One of the most successful promoters of this type of hound was Wilson "Bluetick Bill" Harshman. For 30 years he hunted, bred, wrote about and organized events for these dogs. In the 1930s, Harshman wrote about the English Coonhound in a magazine, and later was the man most responsible for the bluetick faction breaking away. He wrote a book called *Big 'N' Blue,* a marvelous collection of stories and legends about the Old Line strain. This was how the American Blue Gascon came by its nickname.

In the 1950s, the sport of competitive night hunting was born. This called for the faster, racier, hotter nosed hound without the patience and thoroughness of the old type. Judging was based on the ability to tree the greatest number of raccoons in the shortest period of time, not the individual ability of each hound. The Redbone and Walker Hounds proved to be highly competitive in these events, and many Bluetick breeders began streamlining their hounds to cop the prizes as well. Those who loved the old Gascon type became alarmed and, in 1976, created the new American Blue Gascon Hound Association.

Ups and downs for the breed followed, but

currently there is a strong central organization to sponsor and maintain this type of hound which was never meant to compete with the speed of the streamlined hounds. The Blue Gascons were and still are prized as game-taking hounds; i.e., they are used on real animals in actual hunting situations. Capable of pursuing a wide variety of quarry including fox, badger, coyotes, wolverine and wild boar, the Big 'n Blue dogs are particularly suited to the big-game hunter going for bear, bobcat, jaguar or mountain lion. "They also make splendid coondogs for the man who hunts for the enjoyment of hearing and seeing good hounds work, or to experience that special bond between a man and his hound."

To insure the maintenance of the type, the breed organization requires all dogs to be examined for type, even those of registered parents, before permanent registration can be granted. The group has not sought UKC recognition, fearing loss of type if control escapes the breeders' hands.

This is not a hound for everyone, but he is excellent for specialized needs. His extremely large size and loud voice, which can be heard up to five miles, necessitate large spaces and remote areas. He is best suited to adverse terrain and poor hunting conditions, such as dry canyons, swamps and bayous, high altitudes or where game is quite scarce. The person who appreciates an American Blue Gascon is a sports enthusiast to whom the hunt is more important than the kill.

Stories, both modern and long past, show the heart of these hounds—tales of "Green's Scout," "Blue," and "Sport." Scout and Blue were two well-known hounds of the late 1930s and early 1940s. One day they hit a bear track in the Wasatch Mountains of Utah and were never seen or heard from again. Sport's spectacular leap of 150 feet from a bluff into water won his owner a field trial in the early 1920s. More recently, "Sugar Creek Blue Ben" kept a lion treed for three days during sub-zero weather in the Bitterroot Mountains of Montana.

It is no wonder that the Blue Gascon is admired for its stamina, perseverance, desire and hunting abilities. These are truly dogs of great heart. They are bold with people they know, aloof with strangers and sometimes protective.

AMERICAN BULLDOG

COUNTRY: USA
WEIGHT: 65–105 pounds
HEIGHT: 19–25 inches
COAT: Short, smooth
COLOR: Preferred in following order—red brindle, all other brindles; solid white, red, fawn or fallow; piebald
OTHER NAMES: Old Country Bulldog, Old English White
GROUP: Mastiff

The old-time bull-baiters did more than provide a day's entertainment. One of the excuses given for baiting was to tenderize the meat. Notices of a bull-baiting were considered advertising for a fresh meat sale, long before refrigeration made that commodity available. Dogs were expected to fight until the bull submitted—or their own

American Bulldog.

death. When tossed, the owner would attempt to catch the dog on a leather apron or, amazingly, on a bamboo pole which the dog then slid down. No matter what the injuries—cracked ribs, injured back, ripped or gored hide—if the dog could walk, it was expected to continue its bloody battle. After the bull was called on a technical KO, and before he was killed, the young canine apprentices were allowed to rush the victim for a "taste of blood."

The American Bulldog, as opposed to today's familiar English version, is very similar to the old 17th-century bull-baiter. If that's confusing, it's because the modern English Bulldog has been changed, modified, improved or exaggerated, depending on who's making the statement.

The original "bulldogge" was first brought to American shores in early colonial times. Here he did not undergo the "improvement" of his English cousins and has come down to the present day in his generally original form.

The American Bulldog remains higher on the leg, more agile and swifter than its English counterpart. This dog can leap eight feet into the air and "turn on a dime." He has tenacity, an iron jaw, small flap or rolled ears and, usually, a long, low tail.

The American version is now an all-around dog, used for protecting homes, with some owners hunting raccoons, squirrels and even wild hogs and bears with their Bulldogs. They boast longevity of up to 16 years, and these dogs are still capable of wrestling down a cantankerous bull. Farmers find all these qualities attractive for a working farm dog and companion.

Reputable breeders recount myriad tales showing the heroism of these dogs. They do not wait for a command, but assess the situation themselves and react appropriately. To protect their masters, they have fought wild dogs, bulls and even fire. It is said that "fighting off one of these dogs is like fighting an animal that possesses an alligator's head and a python's body." Yet when called off by their handler, they immediately obey. No wonder they are said to have "true grit, true devotion and true love." This breed genuinely loves children.

Other types of American or "original" Bulldogs are being bred in the USA. While some are merely dogs crossbred in an attempt to produce

American Bulldog.

something that looks like the former dog, others are truly descendants of early dogs. Some of these latter are called Old Country Bulldogs or Old English Whites and are common in the southern states where they are used as boar dogs.

A small underground faction continues to illegally fight these dogs. This activity is not encouraged or promoted by the breed organization or by reputable breeders.

American Bulldogs are registered with the Game American Bulldog Club (GABC). Some recently have been placed on military bases as Marine mascots.

American Cocker Spaniel, buff.

AMERICAN COCKER SPANIEL

COUNTRY: USA
WEIGHT: 24–28 pounds
HEIGHT: 15 inches maximum
COAT: Long and silky, very abundant, especially the feathering
COLOR: Solid black (including black/tan); any solid color other than black (called ASCOB) such as chocolate, red, buff, sable, cream; particolored; not more than a third of the ground color of any of the other allowed colors, including tri
OTHER NAMES: Cocker Spaniel
REGISTRY: FCI, AKC, UKC, TKC, CKC
GROUP: Gun Dog

The American version of the Cocker Spaniel evolved from early spaniel imports. By the 1930s, this Cocker was much smaller than his English ancestors and had other conformation differences, so the breed was given separate status. Not long after that, in the 1940s, he had changed even more dramatically so that he bore almost no resemblance to his English counterpart.

Early AKC spaniel trials included classes for Cockers, and the little spaniel was used frequently for gunning. During the middle of this century, a Cocker served as friend and playmate in many a household during the week and as a working assistant to the hunter on the weekend. For many years, no competitions were held for the Cocker's field ability, but with AKC's new hunting tests for spaniels, owners once again can try their dogs with game. His modern propensity is mainly as a pet and a show dog. In the 1940s, the Cocker rose to first in AKC registrations and remained there for some time. Displaced by the Poodle for a number of years, he has since regained the top spot in AKC registrations.

For a breed to go to the top in registrations and stay there, he must have a lot of good things going for him. The modern American Cocker is a happy, trusting, intelligent, as well as handsome, companion dog.

His head is domed, with a short, deep muzzle and abrupt stop. Short of back and up on leg, his usual dramatic angulation allows tremendous reach and drive in a small package. The luxurious coat, with thick feathering on legs and belly nearly reaching the ground, creates a picture hard to resist by dog show judge and puppy buyer alike. But prospective owners should be aware of the care necessary to keep that lovely coat "in the pink."

Buyers should also seek the merry temperament, avoiding any fear or stand-offishness exhibited by the parents. As so often happens when puppies are in high demand, the unscrupulous and unknowledgeable "backyard" breeders and disreputable puppy millers rush to fill the demand. Conscientious Cocker fanciers have some of the finest tempered animals in all of dogdom. But it is no secret that there are frightened and snappish examples of this breed produced when the sale of puppies is the only goal.

Hunting instincts are still present inside that well-coiffed body. The superabundant coat, however, does make field work difficult. The Cocker is a good obedience worker, because of his happy nature and desire to please. He fits into almost any household, adapting to a variety of age groups and lifestyles.

American Cocker Spaniel, parti-color.

American Cocker Spaniel.

American Cocker Spaniel, chocolate.

American Cocker Spaniel, parti-color.

American Cocker Spaniels.

AMERICAN ESKIMOS

American Eskimo, Standard

COUNTRY: USA
WEIGHT: 18–35 pounds
HEIGHT: 14–19 inches
COAT: Thick, straight spitz type
COLOR: Pure white preferred, white with biscuit or cream permissible
REGISTRY: UKC
GROUP: Northern

American Eskimo, Miniature

COUNTRY: USA
WEIGHT: 10–20 pounds
HEIGHT: 11–15 inches
COAT: Thick, straight spitz type
COLOR: Pure white preferred, white with biscuit or cream permissible
REGISTRY: UKC
GROUP: Northern

American Eskimo, Toy

COUNTRY: USA
WEIGHT: 6–10 pounds
HEIGHT: Males less than 12, females less than 11 inches
COAT: Thick, straight spitz type
COLOR: Pure white preferred, white with biscuit or cream permissible
GROUP: Northern

Standard American Eskimo.

The only spitz breed created and fostered in America, the American Eskimo is probably related to and descended from white German Spitz dogs. In fact, many people still refer to this breed as "spitz," a carry-over from 100 years ago. During their beginnings in America, most of these Nordic beauties were rather large. When they began to be registered by the United Kennel Club in the early part of this century, owners adopted the name "Eskimo" as a tribute to their ancient Nordic ancestry and "American" for their immediate foster home. The Standard and Miniature sizes have been bred since the start of the 20th century. A toy-sized American Eskimo has evolved, and fanciers are working toward gaining acceptance for that miniscule variety in the UKC show ring. Except for size, all three forms of the breed are judged by the identical standard of perfection.

Like all of the European spitz, the American Eskie is noted for being sturdy, hardy, and long-lived. These canines are natural watchdogs, tending to bark if there is something wrong or unusual. With their owners, they are very affectionate and willing to please, making them ideal obedience prospects. Eskies do, however, tend to be reserved with strangers at first, the watchdog instinct impelling them to be sure before allowing a breach in their protection of family and home. They have a need to be near their owners and feel a part of things. Because of the northern heritage, the breed can be a bit stubborn and willful but cheerfully submits to the owner's wishes if taught from the beginning, firmly and consistently. Because of their intelligence, energy and desire to please, they also make outstanding trick dogs, performing in circuses and shows.

The coat, as is true with all of the spitz dogs, is described as self-cleaning, i.e., the harsh-textured, straight hair shakes off dirt or mud when dry. The dense underwool precludes the dog from getting wet to the skin from the environ-

ment. Thus, they have little doggy odor and, even though white, stay "spic and span" clean. But, again, like their cousins from Europe and the North, there is need for routine brushing, especially in the spring when the undercoat is being shed.

True to their species, the Eskies love to be outdoors, using their doghouses rarely, often curling up in a snow bank with their tails covering the tip of their noses. Although a perennial favorite in the United States, the Eskie is unknown elsewhere, probably due to the fact that many countries have developed their own type of white spitz.

American Eskimo puppies.

Above: Toy American Eskimo. **Below:** Standard American Eskimo.

Standard American Eskimos.

American Foxhound, tricolor.

AMERICAN FOXHOUND

COUNTRY: USA
HEIGHT: 21–25 inches
COAT: Close and hard, not too short
COLOR: Any color
REGISTRY: FCI, AKC, UKC, CKC
GROUP: Hound

Because America was a great melting pot for immigrants, it was also a large mixing cauldron for dogs as well. Immigrants from all over the world, if they could afford the passage, brought their dogs with them. Colonial America was a vast wilderness in which hunting was not only a hobby but often a necessity. Hounds from many countries proved most useful in this young land and, in the spirit of democracy, little worry was wasted about pedigree and purity as long as the dogs were good hunters. Thus, the exact development of the American hounds is only generally known with much overlap, conflict and even fabrication of history.

Since so many of the settlers on American shores were British, it is only logical that the majority of the hounds came with them. English Foxhounds formed the general basis for the American version, but there were Irish, French and other additions as well.

One of the first packs was brought to America in 1650 by Robert Brooke of Maryland. They were black and tan and did well on the slower gray fox which went to ground sooner. Often recorded as English hounds, these dogs now are felt by many to be of the Irish Kerry Beagle type because of their color, size and style of working. With the introduction of the speedy English red fox to America in the 1700s, hunters soon wanted a hotter nosed animal with more speed, so dogs with more of an English type were used. Brooke's line became the basis for the Black and Tan Coonhound, which would be developed later.

George Washington was a dedicated fox hunter and maintained a choice breeding program and good records. French hounds given to him by Lafayette were used for their abilities and their beautiful voices. Many other breeders developed their own strains and types over the years, based on how the hounds were to be used.

Pioneers often hunted the fox with one hound and a gun, requiring a methodical dog with great nose and persistence. This type of hound was more akin to the French hounds or the German schweisshunds and was often used later for bigger game such as wild cats, boar, coyote and bear. Others pursued the fox, or *renard*, in a group with a pack of hounds. For the formal style of group hunting, many clubs did (and still do) use purebred English Foxhounds. But others, especially those who liked informal group night hunts, developed their own strains of rangier, leggier foxhounds.

These pack hounds are the closest to what is

American Foxhound.

known by AKC as the American Foxhound. They are taller, a bit lighter boned, and longer eared than their English ancestors, but are close enough to often be mistaken for one another. Other hound fanciers favored competitive events with both night field trials and drag trials being developed. This necessitated the use of hounds that were not only faster and hotter nosed, but were more individualistic and competitive than those who happily cooperated in a pack.

For decades, this whole gamut of early "foxhounds" slowly separated into a variety of breeds and types. Hounds of the slower, individually hunting type developed into the cold-nosed American breeds such as the Black and Tan, the American Blue Gascon and the Majestic Tree Hound, as well as the Plott Hound. From the speedier, competitive dogs came the faster, treeing breeds like the Treeing Walker and the Redbone Coonhound. And from the middle ground, there remained a wide divergence of true Foxhounds.

Various strains of American Foxhounds have persisted over the years. Famous lines such as the Henry Birdsong and July hounds date from the early 1800s, as do the Walker strains from which the Coonhound of that name later developed. Any mixed breed hound that bears the solid tan color is often called a "July." The July-type Foxhound, often of a solid red or tan color, is still used throughout the country for hunting coyote and other game. Colonel Haiden Trigg of Kentucky developed a renowned strain of blueticked, white-collared hounds in the late 1800s based on Walker, Birdsong and July dogs. The Trigg hound is often erroneously referred to as a separate breed. Modern hunts have developed their own strains, such as the currently well-known black/tan Penn Merrydales.

The AKC Foxhound is very small in actual registration numbers, even though the various strains, not registered with any formal body, represent a large population of American practical hunting hounds.

American Hairless Terrier.

AMERICAN HAIRLESS TERRIER

COUNTRY: USA
WEIGHT: 7–14 pounds
HEIGHT: 9–14 inches
COAT: Hairless
COLOR: Pink skin with gray, black, golden or red spots
REGISTRY: None
GROUP: Terrier

In 1972 one entirely hairless female appeared in a litter of medium-sized Rat Terriers. She was normal in every other way and became the beloved pet of Willie and Edwin Scott of Louisiana. They and several acquaintances grew so fond of their pet "Josephine" that they wanted to produce more of the hairless pups. Jo produced one hairless female in her first litter, but through the next several litters, the little terrier failed to whelp any more exhibiting the hairless trait. Finally, at the age of nine years, she

crowned her attempts by having a litter with two hairless pups, one of each sex. These became the foundation of a breeding program to produce and stabilize the breed, which the Scotts named the American Hairless Terrier.

The Scotts, with the help and cooperation of geneticists and veterinarians, are still working toward their goal of establishing this breed. They want to keep the true type and temperament of the Rat Terrier while maintaining the hairless trait. Hairless advantages naturally include no shedding and the complete absence of fleas—both things many owners would covet! The gene responsible for this form of hairlessness has been proven, through careful breeding trials, to be an autosomal recessive. This is distinctively different from the semi-lethal dominant genetic pattern seen in the pariah-type hairless breeds. The recessive hairlessness is not associated with missing teeth and skin problems often seen in the dominant form.

Hairless-to-hairless breedings always produce 100-percent hairless puppies. Hairless-to-coated matings produce variable results, depending on chance and whether the coated dog is a carrier of the hairless trait. Hairless pups are born with a bit of sparse fuzzy hair all over their body. The pup begins to shed this fuzz, starting with the head, proceeding backwards, becoming entirely—and eternally—hairless by the age of six weeks. American Hairless Terriers do not have tufts of hair on the head, feet and end of tail, as do the Chinese Cresteds. They do, however, have normal eyebrows and whiskers.

The breed can be born with short or full-length tails, each being left in its natural state. The only special care required is preventing sunburn and keeping them warm in cold weather. The ears stand in a natural state, and are called bat, similar to the Rat Terrier's. These dogs make excellent companions for anyone, especially children or the elderly.

Right and Below: American Hairless Terrier.

American Pit Bull Terrier, brindle.

AMERICAN PIT BULL TERRIER

COUNTRY: USA
WEIGHT: 50–80 pounds
HEIGHT: 18–22 inches
COAT: Short, smooth
COLOR: All colors
OTHER NAMES: American Pit Bull, Pit Bull Terrier
REGISTRY: UKC
GROUP: Mastiff

The ancient molossus was the root of all fighting dogs, producing the bull-baiting dogs, which later were crossbred with terriers for ratting, badger hunting and dog-fighting. For many years, the term "pit bull" was given to any dog of the fighting pits. The United Kennel Club originally registered these breeds of dogs and, at one time, regulated dog-fighting.

Pit Bulls are still registered with UKC, but dog-fighting is illegal and any that still occurs takes place "underground" without the kennel club's approval. In fact, both AKC and UKC outlaw any dog and/or owner involved in dog-

Above: American Pit Bull Terriers; brindle (left), liver (right). **Below:** American Pit Bull Terrier, fawn.

American Pit Bull Terrier, parti-color.

fighting, and the old "battle scars" are no longer allowable in the show ring. Although fight advocates claim most contests are over in a couple minutes and that few dogs die, some matches continue for as long as two hours. It is a sad, but true, fact that the Commission on Animal Care and Control of Chicago estimates 1,500 dogs die annually due to organized dogfighting. The fights draw gamblers and high stakes, with one raid netting 20 people who had $500,000 along with assorted illegal weapons and drugs.

These dogs have been the victim of a witchhunt in recent years. Because of their instinctive hostility toward other animals, it has been assumed they will attack people. This aggression has been sought, encouraged, and malevolently intensified by some disreputable owners. These people have misdirected the dog's instincts toward all animals *and* people. The breed has received bad press, and legitimate, dedicated owners of Pit Bulls have paid the price, along with their dogs, since the breed has been outlawed in several communities. Other breeds have also been placed on the "most wanted" list. Like all dogs, particularly those originally bred for aggressive purposes, the Pit Bull should be selected from temperamentally sound parents, bought from responsible breeders, socialized from puppyhood, trained and handled properly.

Not all Pit Bulls are bad, but they *are* strong and, when tested, they *do* attack with a bone-crushing, mutilating bite. They are too much dog for the average dog owner, and should only be purchased by people who are willing and strong enough to channel that power into productive areas. Nevertheless, they are loving and protective of their families, and owners report them particularly responsive to training: herding, obedience, schutzhund and weight-pulling. An incredible Pit Bull weighing less than 70 pounds set a record by pulling 2,000 pounds. A host of admirers included Helen Keller, Theodore Roosevelt, Thomas Edison (whose dog, "Nipper," was the RCA model) and Jimmy Carter, who had one as a boy. Actors Michael J. Fox and James Caan are current owners.

Since the early 1900s, the AKC has called the breed American Staffordshire Terriers; UKC registers them as Pit Bulls. Pit Bulls are robust, courageous and stoic, although they are also laid-back and calm. Ears are cropped, and grooming is almost non-existent. The "Pit Bull smile" and humorous play ingratiate them to their masters and others.

AMERICAN STAFFORDSHIRE TERRIER

COUNTRY: USA
WEIGHT: 40–50 pounds
HEIGHT: 17–19 inches
COAT: Smooth
COLOR: Any color—solid, parti or patched, but black/tan, liver or more than 80 percent white not to be encouraged
REGISTRY: FCI, AKC, UKC, CKC
GROUP: Mastiff

The American Staffordshire Terrier's ancestor, the Staffordshire Bull Terrier, was developed in England and brought to the United States in the mid-19th century to compete in the fighting pits. "Cockney" Charlie Lloyd is credited with bringing over "Pilot," "Paddy" and other dogs who figured in the formation of the American strain. Breeders increased the size and height of the British version, and ears were cropped to accentuate the more massive head and to prevent them from being ripped in a fight. Over the years, this dog has been labeled with a variety of

American Staffordshire Terriers, parti-color.

American Staffordshire Terrier, gray.

names: Bull-and-Terrier, Half-and-Half, Pit Dog, Pit Bull Terrier, American Bull Terrier and even Yankee Terrier. While some of their brethren were sentenced to life in the pits, other more fortunate American Staffordshire Terriers guarded the frontier families and homesteads.

In 1900, dog-fighting was generally outlawed in America, and a group of fanciers, who were opposed to any association with the crime, wanted to promote other characteristics of the breed. The American Staffordshire served its country during WWI, with "Stubby" becoming the most decorated war dog and earning the rank of sergeant. It was important to the new breed image to avoid breed names associated with the pits. Breeder Joe Dunn headed the movement to bring together a club, which resulted in the name (and the breed) Staffordshire Terrier being recognized by AKC in 1936. The word American was added, in 1972, to differentiate from AKC's newly recognized Staffordshire Bull Terrier. A modest demand for AmStaffs exists in America, but they are rarely seen in Canada.

During the breed's early years of AKC competition, an engaging group of kids entertained American children. These "Little Rascals," (or "Our Gang") had a constant pal in "Pete," their black-eyed Staff, also claimed as a Pit Bull.

Even at the nadir of dog-fighting, the hostility was toward other dogs, not to people. This dog was specifically chosen for his acceptance of being grasped or restrained by his handler, even during the frenzy of a fight.

The modern version of the breed is affectionate and reliable with people and, in fact, the high tolerance which served them well in the blood sport gives them unusual patience with children. They barely notice an infant chewing on their ear or a toddler playing "horsie." An occasional bump with a crutch or wheelchair is taken with good humor, making them good companions for the handicapped. Despite this amiability with humans, some Staffs retain their terrierlike pugnacity toward other animals, and owners must be capable of maintaining control.

Their coat requires only a couple swipes with the brush to stay neat. The breed has an uncanny ability to discern between friend and foe. All these qualities, plus their robust good health, make them a good choice whether on farms or in apartments.

American Staffordshire Terrier, fawn.

American Water Spaniel.

AMERICAN WATER SPANIEL

COUNTRY: USA
WEIGHT: 25–45 pounds
HEIGHT: 15–18 inches
COAT: Thick, close curls or a marcelled effect all over, except smooth on the head
COLOR: Solid liver or dark chocolate
REGISTRY: FCI, AKC, UKC, CKC
GROUP: Gun Dog

The origin of this All-American has not been recorded. Among his forebears were various forms of water dogs and spaniels which accompanied immigrants and settlers. Originally, the breed was called the Brown Water Spaniel.

Development occurred in the late 1800s, basically along the great Mississippi flyway, where the waterfowl migrated north and south each year. He was used as a jump-shooting retriever especially in northern Minnesota, which is full of small lakes and pot holes (ponds). To get close enough to shoot the ducks feeding at these waterholes, the hunter and his dog had to crawl the last 50 or so yards. The hunter then "jumped" the ducks and shot, the brown spaniel retrieved them whether they fell on land or in water. His small size also made him an easy dog to tote in a skiff for hunting in open water or from a blind. The natural camouflage of his brown jacket matches the fall flora. He hunts small game as well.

As the 20th century progressed, British retrievers became more prevalent, and the little American brown spaniel, as he was known at the time, began to disappear. Doctor F.J. Pfeifer is credited with rescuing the breed from obscurity through the creation of a written standard and promotion with a breed club. His efforts paved the way for AKC recognition; in fact, his own dog, "Curley Pfeifer," was the first AKC registered American Water Spaniel.

Although very few specimens are seen at dog shows, they still enjoy moderate but steady favor among hunters and as family pets. The brown spaniel is a dog of the common folk, and has the great charm and easy trainability of the true spaniel. The parallel waves of "marcelled" hair are the desired coat type, although a tighter curl is also allowed. The ears are covered with profuse curls, as is the tail, and only his face is smooth haired. The body is a bit longer than tall. He is essentially unknown outside of North America.

ANATOLIAN SHEPHERD DOG

COUNTRY: Turkey
WEIGHT: 80–150 pounds
HEIGHT: 27–30 inches
COAT: Short to medium
COLOR: Usually black-masked fawns, some brindles, tricolors, whites and blacks
OTHER NAMES: Anatolian Karabash Dog
REGISTRY: TKC
GROUP: Flock Guard

With a history spanning centuries of breeding and use—without benefit of any recorded pedigrees or even official names—the large Turkish guarding breeds have been named and categorized by Westerners. They are all ancient Turkish guard dogs, but there is argument over whether they should be "split" or "lumped." Some owners have selected stem stock from specific localities in Turkey, where one set of characteristics was fixed, and made individual breeds from each. Other dog buyers came into Turkey and chose representatives of Turkish guard dogs (in Turkish, the generic *çoban kopegi* or shepherd dog) from various locales. This broad approach has created the breed known as the Anatolian.

The Anatolian was once used as a combat dog and for hunting big game (i.e., lions and horses). They stem directly from ancient flock-guarding and mastiff dogs of the Middle East. The breed is now used as the front-line defense for Turkish flocks. His strength and speed are legendary in his homeland, allowing him to take on such formidable opponents as wolves.

The breed is dominant with all other dogs, males asserting influence over females. With wolves their natural enemies, Anatolian Shepherd Dogs tend to be suspicious of all dogs with upright ears.

American Robert C. Ballard remembers his adventurous search for his Anatolian pup: "Finally we were invited outside to see the stud. He was big—about 130 pounds, rather ferocious looking—overall a fine specimen. Most memorable, though, was the chain leash, heavy enough for tractor towing, and the stance of the handler who was braced as if expecting the dog to lurch or lunge at any moment." Ballard brought the

Anatolian Shepherd Dog, black masked fawn.

first examples of this breed to America toward the end of the 1960s.

Turkish lore says that the dog receives his collar after detecting, outrunning and killing his first wolf. Actually, these collars help to protect them against the wolf. While in Turkey, a tourist observed that other dogs respected and did not challenge those with collars. He bought one for his Anatolian, which was then elevated to a level of respect. Local canines and citizens alike assumed the dog had won the collar in mortal combat.

These dogs are loyal to their masters, but suspicious of strangers, and demonstrate guard instincts at an early age. Obedience training and socialization are strongly urged for acclimating the breed to life as a controllable family dog.

The Anatolian is gentle and playful with children of the family. However, it will tolerate no teasing from strangers. Owners stress that these dogs are not "gentle giants." Formal introductions should be protocol with neighbors, friends and the veterinarian. Breeders suggest leaving a note for delivery drivers not to enter an Anatolian's turf.

A fiercely loyal guard dog, the Anatolian is possessive toward family, property and livestock. It is not unusual for an Anatolian to seek a high vantage point—a hill of dirt if necessary—to survey its domain. Highly territorial, a dog with no family or stock to protect will guard even its dirt mound!

Barks or howls greet an intruder. If the challenger is wise enough to retreat, Anatolians do not attack. However, upon provocation, they have offered fair warning and don't run from a fight. In one instance, hounds made a fatal error, taking a direct route through a flock after a raccoon. The guarding dog systematically killed each hound as it came through the fence.

A blunt muzzle and low-set ears show the mastiff influence on the Anatolian. Its structure and movement give a lionlike impression. This is particularly true when the ears are cropped to erect stubs, as they sometimes are in Turkey. The tail is curled over the back when the dog is alert.

Size is impressive, with pups showing rapid growth. Typical records show pups weighing 15 pounds at seven weeks, and 42 pounds just five weeks later. They are sturdy dogs, working into their teens, at home in rugged terrains and extreme climates from 60 degrees below zero to 120 above.

This dog is hardy, an easy keeper and a freethinker. During hot weather, it may dig an underground shelter to reach cooler ground. The breed seems to have a keen sense of smell, as one owner reported his dog pawing eagerly through a stack of papers on a chair. When the dog reached one handled by his breeders, he rested his head on it!

Enthusiasts in the United States are actively promoting the breed, and several Anatolians are participants in flock-guarding programs. Their club members hold specialty shows for the breed and admirers are working diligently toward AKC recognition. The breed is recognized in England, with numerous entries at larger shows, such as Crufts.

Anatolian Karabash Dog Club of Great Britain contends that dogs must have tan with black mask (karabash meaning black head). The Anatolian Shepherd Dog Club of Great Britain and the Anatolian Shepherd Dog Club of America maintain that color variety is normal and predictable.

Anatolian Shepherd Dog, cream.

ANGLOS-FRANCAISES

Grand Anglo-Francais

COUNTRY: France
WEIGHT: 66–71 pounds
HEIGHT: 24–27 inches
COAT: Short and smooth
COLOR: Black and white, orange and white, or tricolor
OTHER NAMES: Large French-English Hound
REGISTRY: FCI
GROUP: Hound

Anglo-Francais de Moyen Venerie

COUNTRY: France
WEIGHT: 49–55 pounds
HEIGHT: 20 inches
COAT: Short and smooth
COLOR: Black and white, orange and white, or tricolor
OTHER NAMES: Middle-sized French-English Hound
GROUP: Hound

Anglo-Francais de Petite Venerie

COUNTRY: France
WEIGHT: 34–44 pounds
HEIGHT: 16–18 inches
COAT: Short and smooth
COLOR: Black and white, orange and white, or tricolor
OTHER NAMES: Small French-English Hound
REGISTRY: FCI
GROUP: Hound

Grand Anglo-Francais.

The bulk of the working packs in France today falls under the category that the survey committee termed Anglo-Francais. Resulting from the crossing of French and English hounds, these dogs are rarely exhibited and are strictly utilitarian.

The Grand is the result of crossing the bigger French hounds with the English Foxhound. He carries more bone and less ear than his pure French cousins. FCI actually recognizes three color variations of Large: the Black/White, the Tricolor and the Orange/White.

Harriers and the medium French hounds, such as the Poitevin and Porcelaine, contributed to the Middle-sized Anglo-Francais. As a fast hound, he is useful for all types of small game over a variety of terrain. Except for size, this type is similar in appearance to the Grand. The Moyen, also, is divided into three color classifications.

The Petite was the result of blending the smaller French hounds, for instance the d'Artois, with the Beagle. Like his larger brothers, the Petite is a good tracker, and packs are useful when hunting rabbit, pheasant or quail.

These smaller dogs were not sufficiently pure to create a standard, but FCI does recognize them. They look much like the large and medium sizes, a mid-type between the hounds of France and England.

The Petite has readily adapted to indoor life, where it has proven to be tranquil and clean. This variety also separates into three color varieties. At one time, there were wire-coated (griffon) versions of all the sizes and colors of the Anglo-Francais, but interest in these variations waned and the wires seem to have disappeared.

Above: Grand Anglo-Francais. **Below:** Anglo-Francais de Petite Venerie, tricolor.

Above: Anglo-Francais de Moyen Venerie, tricolor. **Below:** Anglo-Francais de Petite Venerie, orange and white.

Appenzeller.

APPENZELLER

COUNTRY: Switzerland
WEIGHT: 49–55 pounds
HEIGHT: 19–23 inches
COAT: Short, smooth
COLOR: Black and tan, with white at toes, tail tip, chest, and blaze. The tan always lies between the black and the white.
OTHER NAMES: Appenzell Mountain Dog, Appenzeller Sennenhund
REGISTRY: FCI
GROUP: Mastiff

As Caesar's legions swept into Switzerland through the Mons Jovis (St. Bernard) pass, their dogs accompanied them to guard the stock and encampments. A descendant of these molossus breeds, the Appenzeller is one of the four Swiss sennenhunds, which offer a choice of sizes to please "big men" to "junior petites." The Appenzeller was most likely developed through crossing with the smaller herding dogs like the Puli. The Eastern influence is suspected due to its tail curled over the back, as well as the mental traits of high energy and watchfulness.

As sure-footed in the mountains as the goats they watched, these dogs were valued by farmers for sundry tasks. When market day came, Appenzellers were harnessed to carts and hauled the goat milk and cheese to town.

In modern times, the breed is dependable and alert as an alarm dog. He adapts easily to his family's needs and, in fact, is happiest when working at some chore, side-by-side with his master.

Owners stress the need for more space, and a more active lifestyle than the other three Swiss mountain dogs. When given the opportunity to expend his energy, the Appenzeller is content to stay within home boundaries. The breed's extroverted demeanor is accentuated by its vocal enthusiasm for life.

As well as farm work in his native Switzerland, the Appenzeller serves as a rescue dog in avalanches and other catastrophes. He participates in obedience and schutzhund trials as well. His prowess as a herder and companion, and the pride of his owner, is depicted on the traditional handworked collars which the dogs still wear on special occasions. Brass figures of cattle and hikers decorate the wide leather neckpieces.

All four Swiss sennenhunds have handsome, rich, glossy coats and pleasant personalities. They differ mainly in size, tail characteristics, and coat length.

Ariégeois.

ARIÉGEOIS

COUNTRY: France
WEIGHT: 66 pounds
HEIGHT: 22–24 inches
COAT: Short and smooth
COLOR: Tricolor, with the black and tan mostly on the head; a few body patches allowed, but the body is basically clear white without ticking
REGISTRY: FCI
GROUP: Hound

This comparative newcomer to the world of hounds originated in 1912. Ariége province, for which the breed is named, is in the very south of France on the Spanish border, midway between the Atlantic and the Mediterranean. Breeders used Bleu de Gascogne, Gascon Saintongeois, and Chien d'Artois in the formation of this hound. Hunting in packs, they are hare dogs par excellence, demonstrating skill over all terrain. They have gained little notice outside their own region, perhaps because the locals referred to them as half-blood or bastard hounds (*batards*) due to their recent blending of breeds.

The Gaston Phoebus Club in southwestern France has promoted the breed, since its recent birth, through pack trials at the Ceron Villa. The Ariége hound is a handsome and vigorous dog, serene and affectionate in the home. He looks very similar to the Grand Bleu de Gascogne without the ticking and in a smaller package.

Appenzeller.

Ariégeois.

Armant, black.

ARMANT

COUNTRY: Egypt
WEIGHT: 50–60 pounds
HEIGHT: 22 inches
COAT: Long, shaggy and rough
COLOR: Black, black/tan, gray and grayish yellow
OTHER NAMES: Ermenti, Egyptian Sheepdog
REGISTRY: None
GROUP: Herding

Napoleon's armies brought the Armant's ancestors to Egypt, where these Briard types bred with native dogs. Named after a village in northern Egypt, the Armant was used first as a drover and guardian of the herds. The breed excels as watchdogs, and these dogs are sometimes called *sabe*, Arabic for lion, symbolizing their ferocity and the legend of their leonine descent.

The Armant is a large, square, powerful dog with a strong muzzle. His mask is dark, and the shaggy coat forms a mustache and topknot. The topknot, muzzle and chest are white. The small ears may be drop or prick and the tail long or docked.

With battles erupting in the Middle East, the current status of the breed is unknown. Recent travelers have found examples of this dog, but type varies greatly and the purity of breeding programs is not known. Others may still exist in isolated areas. The FCI has dropped them from their list of recognized breeds.

Armant, black/tan.

ARYAN MOLOSSUS

COUNTRY: Afghanistan
WEIGHT: Up to 200 pounds
HEIGHT: 34 inches
COAT: Short, plush and dense; abundant undercoat
COLOR: Dark sables; very little white
GROUP: Mastiff

Probably closely related to both the Kangal Dog of Turkey and the Tibetan Mastiff, this ancient breed was utilized by primitive tribes to settle land and tribal disputes. When villagers argued over grazing areas, goat herd ownership or other grievances, a dog from each tribe was placed in the pit to fight out the dispute. Owners of the winning dog were declared victorious. . . with no further argument. This primitive prelude to a third-party decision of a jury or judge eliminated warring and unnecessary loss of life.

The canines were bred, raised and trained by "dog specialists" not affiliated with any tribe. When disputes were percolating, tribal leaders, who were astute experts in such matters, went to the "dog man" and dickered for the best animal. The chosen title contender stayed with his breeder until the day of the contest, when he fought in a pit at the dog compound or was delivered to neutral ground. Only the men came to watch the fight. Tails were painted or dyed so that the opponents could be easily identified during the fracas. Dogs often fought to the death; if not, the loser was necessarily destroyed.

These dogs were extremely large and fractious, with their tails held high and loosely curled over the backs. Loose skin hanging on the head and throat protected them during the vicious melee. Nobody but the owner ever handled them—or cared to, due to their fierce reputation, although they were even-tempered with their "promoter."

These dogs have been moved into the highest mountains and hidden from the Russian army recruitment. Because of expense in upkeep, their numbers were always limited, with breeders retaining just a few title contenders. Their current status is endangered by the Russian occupation of the country, which has overturned old tribal customs.

AUSTRALIAN CATTLE DOG

COUNTRY: Australia
WEIGHT: 35–45 pounds
HEIGHT: 17–20 inches
COAT: Medium-short, harsh, straight, dense
COLOR: Blue speckled, with black, blue or tan markings on head; red speckled, with darker red markings on head
OTHER NAMES: Australian Queensland Heeler, Blue Heeler
REGISTRY: FCI, AKC, UKC, TKC, CKC
GROUP: Herding

Australian Cattle Dog

Derived through intensive and careful cross-breeding over a 60–year period, the Australian Cattle Dog was the result of the deliberate introduction of various breeds serving specific purposes. The AuCaDo came into being because imported herding dogs were not capable of controlling the tough cattle on long treks to market. Most existing herding dogs, i.e., the Smithfields or the Black Bobtail, drove by barking and running after the cattle. The Black Bobtail, according to Robert Kaleski, ". . . bit like an alligator and barked like a consumptive," spooking the wilder cattle native to Australia and running the meat off them. The dogs used for driving these cattle had their problems too. All the running and barking on the journeys from the outback wore them out, and they were in as poor shape as the cattle by the time they arrived at market.

A native wild dog, known as the Dingo, was a silent worker that conserved energy, driving herds by biting or nipping at strays. The Dingo performed well in high temperatures, but was naturally aggressive and too wild to train.

During the 1830s the running, biting, barking Smithfield Collie was experimentally crossed with the silent-working Dingo. The offspring were called Timmon's Biters, which eliminated the barking problem, but accentuated the biting.

Later, in 1840, Thomas Hall, a squatter with two blue-merle, smooth-coated Collies, took a daring step by breeding his purebred Scottish imports to the Dingo. The half-breeds were impressive workers, and the best were retained. The red or blue get, called Hall's Heelers, were hardy, silent drovers with prick ears. Further breeding experiments incorporating the Dingo, Timmon's Biters and Hall's Heelers were conducted by others.

Dr. Allen McNiven conducted an extensive breeding program and found that it takes 12 generations to get a good AuCaDo. He noted, "Most of the first generations run off." McNiven had men from the outback follow a Dingo slut for two weeks prior to whelping. When the pups were about two weeks old, a male would be taken from the litter while the dam was away hunting for food. They chose only the heavy-boned Red Deer Dingo because of its good head and intelligence. This male would be bred to one of McNiven's Blue Merle Collies. As Dingoes mate for life, he would breed no other females.

The next breed to be added to the melting pot was the Dalmatian, changing the merle to its current speckle, and adding loyalty to their masters and a rapport with horses. This combination, however, diluted the heeling ability. A drop of Bull Terrier blood was not enthusiastically received, infusing an excess of toughness. Cattle owners bred out the Bull Terrier influence; but a hint of this breed still is seen in the AuCaDo temperament and shape of the head. Still later, another cross brought in the black/tan Kelpie, which revived heeling capabilities. This was the final cross, and the Australian Cattle Dog has been pure since 1893.

An oddity inherited from their Dalmatian progenitor causes them to be born white. Although the pups do not show their true colors until several weeks of age, color may be ascertained by the paw pads. Reddish brown or brown pads indicate a red, and blue or black pads belong to blue speckle pups. The darker the pad, the darker the dog becomes.

The Dingo influence is shown in the breed's speed, keen hearing and sense of smell, as well

Australian Cattle Dog, blue speckled.

as the general hardiness and ability to withstand heat. AuCaDo dams display their wild heritage by attempting to burrow to whelp their litters, and by weaning pups at four weeks.

Owners say the dogs have cast-iron stomachs and will attempt to eat anything. They're described as watchful, sensible and courageous, willing to tackle hard tasks. They take firm, but not harsh discipline. "Don't beat him too hard, or you will break his heart past mending . . . though the more he is knocked about by cattle, the more eager he becomes to bite."

Their silent work enables them to sneak up on stock—in fact, one theory for development of the silent drover was to obtain help in cattle rustling! A current owner's young AuCaDo doesn't partake in such dubious activities, but has worked horses, goats and ducks. "He's so silent in his approach, he's managed to pluck all the ducks."

It was a Queensland Heeler which became the oldest dog on record: 29 years, five months. "Bluey" served his master by working the flocks nearly 20 years!

The breed was approved to compete for AKC championships in 1980. The Australian Cattle Dog Club of America encourages competition in versatility trials.

Australian Cattle Dog

Australian Kelpie, black with tan.

AUSTRALIAN KELPIE

COUNTRY: Australia
WEIGHT: 25–45 pounds
HEIGHT: 17–20 inches
COAT: Short, smooth
COLOR: Black, red, blue or fawn; with or without tan
OTHER NAMES: Kelpie, Barb
REGISTRY: TKC
GROUP: Herding

The harsh, unaccustomed environment of Australia forced settlers from England and Scotland to select working dogs that fit the land's conditions—much larger spaces, great numbers of fractious merino sheep, plus the intense heat. The *mob* (Aussie lingo for a flock of sheep) had to be *folded* (brought into the pens at the ranch or station) each night, in those early days, to protect them from Dingoes, aborigines and straying. This required a real workaholic "mustering" or gathering-style sheep dog, rather than the shepherding type from the old country.

Many counties and even some estates in the British Isles had established their own strain of sheep dog, most bearing the name of the locale or owner. The majority of these strains are lost today, but they were still active during the 1800s when Australian immigration was at its height. Many breeds were brought to Australia, and those that suited the new land were used and crossed with others.

One of the first types that proved ideal for the Australian conditions was the Rutherford strain of North County Collies. These dogs were smoothhaired, prick or semi-prick eared, and black or black/tan, and were described by G.S. Kempe as "stoutly built, bold tempered . . . . with very thick head and jaws."

Several members of the Rutherford family emigrated from Scotland to Australia, and they received a steady supply of these dogs from their relatives back home. Others soon recognized this type's skills and wanted pups from the strain. It is doubtful they were kept 100-percent pure, as pragmatic sheep owners bred their good working sluts (i.e., bitches) to the best working dogs they could find, no matter the background. But the Rutherford strain formed the

Australian Kelpie, red with tan.

For its size, the Australian Kelpie is a solid, capable dog with tremendous working abilities.

base for the breed we know today as the Kelpie.

In the late 1800s, a rancher named Gleason swapped a horse for a black/tan sheep dog pup bred in Victoria of imported parents from the Rutherford strain. He named her "Kelpie," Gaelic for water sprite, and found her to be a fine worker. She became known as "Gleason's Kelpie," and it was her offspring that gave the breed its name. This original Kelpie was bred twice to "Moss," a black Australian dog from the Rutherford strain, and then to "Caesar," a black/tan dog from pure Scottish parentage. From this last litter by Caesar was created the most renowned "Kelpie" of all. A black/tan female, also named "Kelpie," was given to G.T.W. King. His Kelpie (the second) later won the first sheep dog trial held in Australia. This coup created a greater interest in the strain.

The Kelpie breed evolved from this beginning, with crosses to other strains throughout the years. The breed is essentially all English without introduction of the Dingo. Many fine working black dogs resulted from the line created by back crosses to Moss, particularly one named "Barb." For many years, there was a

general belief that the black ones were a separate breed called Barbs. There were other strains known by the names of the best-known dog or its owner, but soon all were combined into a single grouping under Kelpie.

Around the campfire in the outback, the story of the "immortal Coil," as related in *The Australian Kelpie Handbook*, is still spun. Coil was a famed sheep trial champion and working Kelpie who had "all the qualities necessary for such work, very keen and active, with a good eye and forceful when required."

In the 1898 trial at the Sydney showgrounds, he completed the full course in the first round and was awarded an unheard of 100 points, the maximum possible. But he had to compete again the next day to win the title, and that night was run over by a cab, which broke a front leg.

With the permission of the judges and stewards, the next day Coil completed the full course in six minutes and 12 seconds, "with the injured limb swinging to and fro," and received a second maximum 100 points (a record to this day), all before having his leg set! Although difficult for compassionate people to understand, the

135

Australian Kelpie, black.

story illustrates the breed's intense desire to work which blocks out everything else.

An estimated 70,000 to 80,000 Kelpies are in service on Australian ranches today, still the top herding dog in that country, and sheep workers say a good Kelpie is equivalent to two men on horseback. The labor-saving statistics are staggering, and many American ranchers are learning the worth of these dogs. Although a natural header with sheep, the Kelpie can be taught to drive in order to work cattle. Kelpies bred for cattle work are forceful, and many both head and heel. They can be most useful in gathering sheep and bringing them into the pens, forcing them through the dipping vats, loading them into trucks and railcars, and even "backing" them (leaping on their backs) if they get jammed in the loading chutes. A team of Kelpies can be sent out to round up a herd of dairy cows or cattle while the owner waits at the gate. They can assist in running them through the veterinary chutes, loading them and driving them down the road to another pasture.

Kelpies have been used effectively, also, with hogs, horses, goats, poultry and even reindeer.

Although they are friendly and trainable, their high energy and great drive to work make them unsuitable to a house-bound or apartment environment. They bond strongly to one owner and, although loyal and intelligent, they are independent thinkers, which is necessary for their work. Some dog owners may find their independence hard to deal with, although it helped one American family out of a jam. When a Simmental-cross bull got into the lot with yearling cattle, it was impossible for the family to sort out the willful cattle. Rain had turned the lot into 12 to 16 inches of mud. But their three-year-old Kelpie went right to work. He carefully worked the yearlings into the barn, isolating the bull, then drove the animal to his pen.

Workaholics they remain, and tale after tale abound of the breed's prowess despite personal discomfort. Kelpies are registered with the Working Kelpie Council in Australia and in the USA by the National Stock Dog Registry. They are rarely exhibited. They are used in areas other than herding, and are now useful in search-and-rescue, dog guide and drug detection work.

AUSTRALIAN SHEPHERD

COUNTRY: USA
WEIGHT: 35–70 pounds
HEIGHT: 18–23 inches
COAT: Moderate in length and harshness, straight to slightly wavy, with dense undercoat
COLOR: Blue merle, red (liver) merle, black, liver, red, with or without white and/or tan markings
REGISTRY: UKC
GROUP: Herding

The Australian Shepherd is a true herder, an excellent working dog, bred from old herding breeds. The nomenclature "Australian" is deceiving, since the breed is "made in America" and perfected to type in the USA. The Berger de Pyrenees, brought to America by the Basques, is one obvious ancestor. Other herding dogs, such as the Smithfield, Collie and Border Collie, also contributed to its prototype. It is believed the Aussie's immigration to America (in the late 1800s) was not by direct route, but through a detour to Australia, where Basques accumulated flocks of hardy Australian sheep. When the Americans saw dogs working these sheep, they assumed the dogs, also, were Australian. They were received enthusiastically as hard-working stock dogs and sometimes the only companion for an isolated shepherd.

The Australian Shepherd is well known and in demand on American farms and ranches. Aussies have been a fixture around stables and with horse people for many years as well. Northwest Indian tribes hand down tales of "ghost-eyed dogs," an apt description for the breed with its blue eyes. Despite the fact that they have been in America for more than a hundred years, they have not solicited recognition as a show dog and are only recently entering that arena. The Australian Shepherd Club of America is a strong parent organization and emphasizes working abilities, awarding titles to qualified animals. The breed's herding instincts remain strong.

People who wish to have a doormat dog are instructed to consider a stuffed animal or a "pet

Australian Shepherd, blue merle.

Australian Shepherd, black with white and tan markings.

rock" instead of an Australian Shepherd. The breed is intelligent, active and protective, a combination of qualities which require a dominant owner who is willing to take the time to turn these tendencies into attributes. Those "hot-blooded" specimens are the choice for active work and families. More laid-back Aussies suit the family looking only for a companion.

Aussies not only have become entertainers but have attained success in tracking, narcotics detection, search-and-rescue, and as hearing dogs for the deaf. They love all physical activity and are quick to learn such sports as Frisbee™, flyball and obedience.

Eyes may be brown, amber, blue, flecked or even odd-eyed. The tail is naturally or surgically bobbed. The breed tends to be reserved with strangers. Yet its proponents feel there's no other dog like the Aussie. In fact, as noted in *Stodgehill's Animal Research Magazine*, one stockman states he only maintains his sheep as an excuse to continue raising Aussies!

Australian Shepherd, red with white and tan markings.

AUSTRALIAN TERRIER

COUNTRY: Australia
WEIGHT: 12–14 pounds
HEIGHT: 10 inches
COAT: 2½ inches, harsh, straight, dense
COLOR: Blue/tan or clear sandy
REGISTRY: FCI, AKC, UKC, TKC, CKC
GROUP: Terrier

The histories of the two native Australian terriers are tied inextricably—one to the other. Both the Australian Terrier and the Silky Terrier were developed in the 19th century by Australians using various British terrier breeds. Records show that blue and tan broken-coated terriers of about ten pounds were renowned watchdogs around Tasmania, even in the early 1800s. Other terriers of that era in Australia were sandy colored.

The likely descent of the Australian Terrier was from terriers of Scotland and northern England brought to Australia with settlers. The Scottie (or the Cairn) created the hard coat and short leg—with the Skye strengthening the gene for shortness of leg, plus contributing coat abundance and body length. Later crossbreedings added the Dandie's topknot and the Yorkie's blue fading color and small size. Some experts believe that a bit of Irish Terrier was used to set the red color in the sandies, and Manchester crosses occurred much later to improve the depth of the tan in the blue/tans.

Dog shows in the 1800s had classes for both black/tan and blue/tan broken-coated terriers, for under and over seven pounds. These classifications were the early Australian Terriers before they had any official name or standard. The smaller size was often referred to as the Broken-Coated Toy Terrier.

Selection from these early mixtures developed the modern Australian Terrier. He was welcomed for his skills at dispatching the hated rabbit and at killing snakes. The little dog faced his slithery opponent, then leaped high, turning around in the air. As he landed behind the snake, he grabbed it at the back of the head and killed it.

The Aussie was slow to make headway outside Australia, with British approval not coming until 1936. Although Canada recorded registrations

Australian Terrier, blue/tan.

in 1938, it was 20–some years later before the Americans embraced him. He is now recognized internationally.

He is all terrier—though tiny—with the inborn confidence and spirit of his type. Yet he tends to be quiet and affectionate, making a fine house dog. His coat requires the same care as other broken-coated terriers. The breed is eager to please and is a good choice for children, the elderly or handicapped. Although many terriers contributed to his genetic make-up, the twinkle in the Aussie's eye is all his own.

139

AUSTRIAN BRANDLBRACKE

COUNTRY: Austria
WEIGHT: 33–49 pounds
HEIGHT: 18–23 inches
COAT: Short, thick; hard and shining
COLOR: Black and tan, or red; may have limited white marks on neck, chest and feet
OTHER NAMES: Osterreichischer Glatthaariger Bracke, Austrian Smoothhaired Hound
REGISTRY: FCI
GROUP: Hound

The hounds of Austria are the same general type and often of similar origin as the German hounds. They have the same sturdy, unexaggerated body type including the stopless face and high-set, smooth ear. Austrians also appreciate the fine tracking qualities of scenthounds and enlist them for bloodtrailing as well as hunting live game.

The Brandlbracke has the raciest body of the Austrian hounds, being leggier and lighter of bone than the Bavarian dogs to the north. He stems directly from the Celtic brackes of old, and is closely related to both the Belgian St. Hubert and the Jura Hounds of Switzerland. He

Austrian Brandlbracke, black and tan.

Austrian Brandlbracke, black and tan.

has been recognized as a distinct type since 1884. His elegant head, carried high, is straight and wide, crowned with prominent eyebrows, and tapering to the muzzle. There should be no flew or hanging eyelids.

The Brandlbracke is usually of the black and tan pattern, with the tan actually being a rich shade of red. *Brand* is literally fire in German, and the diminutive *Brandl* indicates the little marks of fire red. The sleek, black body with the trace markings of bright red gave the breed its name. A small white ring may be around the neck, with a star on chest and white feet.

The breed dwells exclusively in the hands of hunters, who appreciate it especially for silent trailing. While work on the cold scent is his specialty, he can also be utilized for hunting hare and fox, for which he gives tongue. Prized by Austrian hunters, he is unknown outside his native land.

AUSTRIAN SHORTHAIRED PINSCHER

COUNTRY: Austria
WEIGHT: 26–40 pounds
HEIGHT: 14–20 inches
COAT: Short, smooth
COLOR: Red, brindle or black/tan often with white markings
OTHER NAMES: Osterreichischer Kurzhaariger Pinscher
REGISTRY: FCI
GROUP: Terrier

A sturdy dog with roots similar to the German Pinscher, this terrier is in the same height range, although broader and heavier. The standard demands a chest so wide that he appears wider than tall when viewed from the front.

Left: Austrian Shorthaired Pinscher, black/tan with white markings. **Below:** Austrian Shorthaired Pinscher, red with white markings.

141

Austrian Shorthaired Pinscher.

AZAWAKH

COUNTRY: Mali
WEIGHT: 37–55 pounds
HEIGHT: 23½–29 inches
COAT: Very short, soft
COLOR: Sable (brown, light fawn to dark red) with white markings
OTHER NAMES: Tuareg Sloughi
REGISTRY: FCI
GROUP: Southern

Bred by the nomadic Tuareg tribes of the southern Sahara as hunting and guard dogs for over a thousand years, the Azawakh was developed for the chase and will course any game. The German term "windhound" is descriptive of this breed and its close relatives. The Azawakh is described by a breeder as "fleetfooted enough to catch gazelles, hares and the European mouflon (wild sheep), courageous enough to ward off big predators, untiring like a camel and beautiful like an Arab horse."

These dogs defended goats and camels and vigorously protected the herds against jackals, hyenas and wild dogs. They still carry out these duties in their homeland. Their true value lies in the chase; however, the nomads appreciate their beauty and look upon the Azawakh as a symbol of high standing and wealth.

The dog must never kill the prey, merely curbing its flight. If the game were killed, it would spoil in the desert heat. The Tuareg hunter has no guns nor even bow and arrow—providing food for the encampment only with a knife and a sighthound.

Pups are cultivated from birth for the hunt. They are fed on milk, never on flesh, and continue this diet throughout their lives. As three-month-old babies, they are introduced to their calling by beginning with rats and progressing to hares.

Eventually, at full growth, the Azawakh is taken on horseback to course gazelle. The hound is seated in front of his master on the saddle until the game is sighted and the chase is begun. When the dog is released, he begins his "breathtaking course," which sometimes lasts five to six hours. Finally, the Azawakh hamstrings the quarry, waiting for his master to join

A true terrier who is a likeable and courageous country companion, the Austrian Pinscher does not thrive in city life, unless given plenty of exercise. An urban owner could have a problem with the dog's predisposition to overzealous barking. He is fearless against predators, enthusiastically goes to ground, and is an alert, noisy alarm dog.

The Austrian Pinscher may be tailless or have a tail rolled up on the back. Ears can be pricked, tipped or rosed. The hair, while shortish, tends to have some fringe on the belly and thighs. Despite a long history, he is quite rare today.

Azawakh, light fawn with white markings.

Prized by their nomadic owners, the Azawakh is hailed as having the stamina of a camel and the beauty and agility of an Arabian horse. As this painting illustrates, the breed is used in Mali for hunting and falconry.

An ambassador to the Upper Volta and Ivory Coast, Dr. Pecar earned the title of "Great African Hunter." He much admired the exotic beauty of these hounds, and spent considerable effort and time attempting to obtain a pair to no avail. When it was necessary for him to return to his home country of Yugoslavia, he was presented with a handsome male in admiration for his prowess as a hunter. Later he attempted to arrange a trade of his services for an Azawakh female. Fortunately—for Dr. Pecar and European sighthound fanciers—a bull elephant had been terrorizing a Tuareg tribe. The doctor destroyed the animal and was awarded a half-starved bitch, otherwise destined to die. But she was to become the beginning of the European breed.

The Tuaregs required their dogs to have white markings—the ones without white were considered worthless. Black nails and black eye rim pigmentation surrounding the large dark eyes were also required by the nomads—along with five obligatory warts on the head!

Owners state that to know one is to love the breed. Nevertheless, Azawakhs are not for everyone. They are a proud, even haughty breed that does not take well to harsh discipline. They are artistocratic, "a friend, never a slave." True to their native land, they love sun and warmth and require protection in cold climes. One breeder warns that they love food and will become food thieves, eating themselves into obesity, particularly if not given the opportunity for the necessary long runs.

Their gait is typical of the sighthounds, almost balletlike in movement, lightfooted, floating. They are built similarly to a good Arabian horse, high on leg, short-coupled, with small feet. This is quite different than many other desert hounds. Their speed reaches 43½ mph.

The Azawakh has a solid foundation in Europe and is bred in several countries, including Switzerland, Germany and Yugoslavia. FCI accepted the breed in 1980. It has been considered one of the purest sighthounds, because these dogs were not crossbred by the Tuareg tribes nor were they sold outside the Azawakh Valley and territories of the Oullimiden Tuareg, in what are now the countries of Mali, Upper Volta, Nigeria and Mauritania.

him and complete the kill.

This breed has been the product of strict culling and selection, based on the nomad's stark existence. When a litter was born, only one male was kept for hunting purposes, and, occasionally, a bitch for reproduction. The others were killed. This practice made it nearly impossible for outsiders to obtain an Azawakh. Asking a nomadic huntsman to sell his sighthound was tantamount to asking him to sell his oldest son.

Above: Head study of fawn Azawakh. **Below:** Red Azawakh running. The breed's gait is gazellelike, or more than gazellelike as it is used to course gazelles in its native land.

Barbet, fawn.

BARBET

COUNTRY: France
WEIGHT: 33–55 pounds
HEIGHT: 18–22 inches
COAT: Thick, long, and "tassled"; curly or wavy
COLOR: Black, chestnut, fawn, gray; with or without white markings; white
OTHER NAMES: Griffon d'Arret a Poil Laineux
REGISTRY: FCI
GROUP: Gun Dog

Exact roots of the Barbet are forever lost, but most likely they stem from corded sheep dogs from Asia and, possibly, early griffon hounds. Woolly water dogs were found throughout 14th-century Europe, answering to various names, i.e., the *wasserhund* meaning water dog. Although not the source of all water dogs, the Bar-

bet is very likely closest to the original type. The Barbet is most generic of water dogs, with a woolly sheep-dog coat and hair all over, allowing him to withstand hours in water and chilly marshes. He resembles a pointing dog, but is slower and heavier of body, without the keen nose or sleek beauty. Sixteenth-century cynologist Fouilloux dubbed him the Barbet, from *barbe*, a French designation for beard; his pseudonym, *laineux*, translates into woolly.

Elizabethan references to shaggy-coated water dogs in France and England describe their use for retrieving and their coat care. Dr. Johannes Caius says personalities were "efficient and playful." Perhaps it is their impishness that entices them to muddy, swampy places, giving them the nickname of "Mud Dog."

They not only retrieved ducks and other game in deep water, but recovered the arrows when huntsmen shot and missed, much like the Portuguese Water Dog. They drew favor from the French royalty. Zella Llewellyn writes that both Louis XV and Henri IV hunted with Barbets, and Henri's mistress, Corisande, was reproached by M. de Bellievre, the chancellor of Marie de Medici, for attending mass in the company of "a madman, a monkey and a Barbet." More prosaically, the breed also aided sailors in a similar manner to its look-alikes, the Porties.

Jean-Claude Hermans, president and founder of the Barbet Club in France, credits the Barbet with being the foundation (crossed with other types) that produced the Briard, the Newfoundland and the Poodle. The modern Barbet is an excellent water dog, using his webbed feet to advantage in swimming, never tiring after long

Barbet, black.

Barbets, fawn.

hours. His personality is noted as gay, obedient and intelligent. These qualities and his fidelity make him a valued companion. Although its stamp has come down through the poodles, the various water spaniels, and even the bichon dogs, the Barbet, as a distinct breed, was nearly lost. Hermans tells us, "Despite . . . good qualities, the breed was abandoned during the 19th century, replaced by its direct descendant the Poodle as a companion dog; the sailors chose the Terre-Neuve (Newfoundland), and the hunters the Korthal griffon."

The Barbet's specialization may have been his undoing. Almost unknown outside his native France, the breed is promoted by a few enthusiasts at home. Today there are only about 200 left in all of France.

Basenji, red.

BASENJI

COUNTRY: Zaire
WEIGHT: 22–24 pounds
HEIGHT: 16–16½ inches
COAT: Short, smooth
COLOR: Red, black/tan, black—all with white markings
OTHER NAMES: Congo Dog
REGISTRY: FCI, AKC, UKC, TKC, CKC
GROUP: Southern

Admired by the pharaohs, these ancient dogs stem from the earliest pariahs. They were used as hunting dogs much like their larger relatives, the Pharaoh and Ibizan. As the great Egyptian culture declined, these hunting partners were adopted by tribes throughout the Congo.

The breed's keen nose (a Basenji can scent at 80 yards) and sharp eyesight were useful to the natives, who used the dogs to drive game into nets or to track wounded prey. Because the Basenji hunted silently, he often wore a bell.

Centuries later, the Basenji was found in the bush by British explorers, nearly in its original form. The Englishmen called the breed the African Bush Dog. The breed's independence, resourcefulness and hunting ability had helped the Basenji to survive on its own.

Finally, in 1936, a pair imported from the Congo by a Mrs. Burn, Bongo of Blean and Bokoto of Blean, produced the first English litter. When these pups were exhibited at Crufts in 1937, they created so much interest that special police had to be employed to keep the crowds moving past the Basenji benches. The Basenji was obviously on its way to acceptance. It was Mrs. Burn who gave the breed its current name, *Basenji*, translating to bush thing from the African dialect. The Basenji was recognized by AKC in 1943.

A popular hunting dog for small game in his native land, he is valued for his silent approach. Today the barkless dog is valued for the same attribute in apartment complexes. Nevertheless, he is not totally silent, communicating with a growl when displeased and a singular yodel when happy. The Basenji is exceptionally clean, licking itself in the manner of a cat, adding to his appeal as a pet. Owners note the use of his feet to cling, play and communicate.

Current owners find them happy playmates and avid coursing dogs. They retain many of the characteristics of the pariahs: the aloofness, the wrinkled brow and the cycling once a year. Basenji bitches come into season between August and November (which would be late winter and early spring in Africa) allowing their young to be several months old by cold weather.

These dogs prefer being with their family and, if left to their own resources, may resort to deviltry and destruction for their amusement. Crate training is suggested by breeders.

Basenji.

Basset Artésien Normand, tricolor.

BASSET ARTÉSIEN NORMAND

COUNTRY: France
WEIGHT: 33 pounds
HEIGHT: 10½–14½ inches
COAT: Short and smooth
COLOR: Tricolor or orange/white
OTHER NAMES: Artesian Norman Basset
REGISTRY: FCI
GROUP: Hound

Short-legged dogs were present in northern France for many years where they were generally known as Norman Bassets, although many also came from Artois (Artésien). Frenchman Fauilloux's memoirs from the 17th century mention his use of short-legged dogs from Artois for hunting badger.

By the end of the 19th century, when identification of individual breeds was begun throughout the world, two types of "Norman" bassets existed that were unrelated to one another. The Count Le Coulteux de Canteleu was breeding strong-bodied, straight-legged bassets with particular emphasis on hunting qualities rather than on "classic" appearance. In head type, they were similar to the Chien d'Artois, with the small flat ear. Near Rouen another breeder, Louis Lane, was emphasizing aesthetic characteristics, and his hounds had noble heads with large drooping ears. But they also had less energy, due to the extremely dwarfed front legs, so curved that the dogs were half disabled. Many other breeders of the area, wanting the best of the extremes, crossbred the two types.

By 1898, when the first written standard was adopted, most of these bassets carried characteristics from both types. The man who spearheaded the modern blend was Leon Verrier. In the early years of this century, his hounds dominated the exhibitions, and were the type most sought by the newly formed association for the breed. During the 1920s, his dogs were often referred to as Artois Bassets (Basset d'Artois), despite their double origin. WWI wiped out Verrier's kennels, but he continued his influence as a judge and leader. Under his presidency, the name of Basset Artésien Normand was chosen, which accurately pinpoints their historical origin. After WWII, the breed was reduced to very few pure specimens, but several dedicated breeders, especially Leparoux de Combree des Maine et Loire, saved the Artésian Norman Basset from extinction.

The desired type is an athletic dog, with an elegant head and long, smooth muscles. The muzzle is long, refined and arched. Ears are low-set, thin and curved. Most modern specimens approach the top of the standard or even larger. While not carrying over-abundant skin, some wrinkles appear on the cheeks, and this hound does have a bit of dewlap.

The Artésien Normand is a happy, good-natured dog who is courageous and headstrong in the hunt. He, like so many of his basset cousins, was designed to go into heavy cover. Originally bred for rabbit shooting, he is now adapted to hunt a variety of prey. His additional qualities of kindness, obedience and patience with children have found him a place as a house dog.

Basset Artésien Normand.

Basset Hound.

BASSET HOUND

COUNTRY: Great Britain
WEIGHT: 40–60 pounds
HEIGHT: 14 inches or less, 15 inches disqualifies
COAT: Short and smooth
COLOR: Any hound color
REGISTRY: FCI, AKC, UKC, TKC, CKC
GROUP: Hound

Alix M. Freedman asserts that French noblemen were so "out-of-shape they could only follow a slow hound with short legs and crooked knees."

The Basset was bred by monks in the Middle Ages to hunt in heavy cover, whether for the heavy-bellied nobility or not is conjecture. His short, crooked legs allowed him to hold his nose close to the ground. Like a Dr. Seuss creation, the Basset has the head and bone of a Bloodhound, the coloring of a Foxhound and the legs of a Dachshund.

Basset Hound.

Developed to individual perfection in England, the breed we know simply as the Basset Hound is closely related to the whole family of French Bassets discussed earlier. Bassets of the Normand and d'Artois type have been noted in England at least since Shakespearean times. In *A Midsummer Night's Dream*, the bard has Theseus, the Duke of Athens, saying:

> My hounds are bred out of the Spartan
>   kind;
> So flew'd, so sanded; and their heads are
>   hung
> With ears that sweep away the morning
>   dew;
> Crook-knee'd and dew-lapp'd like
>   Thessalian bulls;
> Slow in pursuit, but match'd in mouth
>   like bells. . . ."
>
> (IV, 1, 118)

Who could doubt the type of dog being described!

But the fostering of a separate, individual breed came several centuries later. In 1866 the Comte de Tournow sent a pair of Basset Normands, "Basset" and "Belle," to Lord Galway of England. A litter bred from this pair went to Lord Onslow, who proceeded to develop an exceptional pack by crossing with further imports from the Coultreux pack of Normandy.

Soon importation ceased, and the English version of the Basset developed on its own. Except for the legs, this hound closely resembles the St. Hubert Hound, with the same superb nose (considered to be the best, next to the bloodhound's) and coldtrailing ability. From England, he was brought to America, where he has been enthusiastically accepted.

A fine trailer of rabbit, hare and even wounded pheasant, his short-statured bulk proves especially useful in heavy, impenetrable cover. He can be taught to tree coon, squirrels and opossum. AKC sponsors field trials (rabbit trailing) throughout the USA for Basset Hounds, and the breed is also well represented in the North American show ring. The Basset, like the Dachshund or Beagle, is one of the few

Basset Hound.

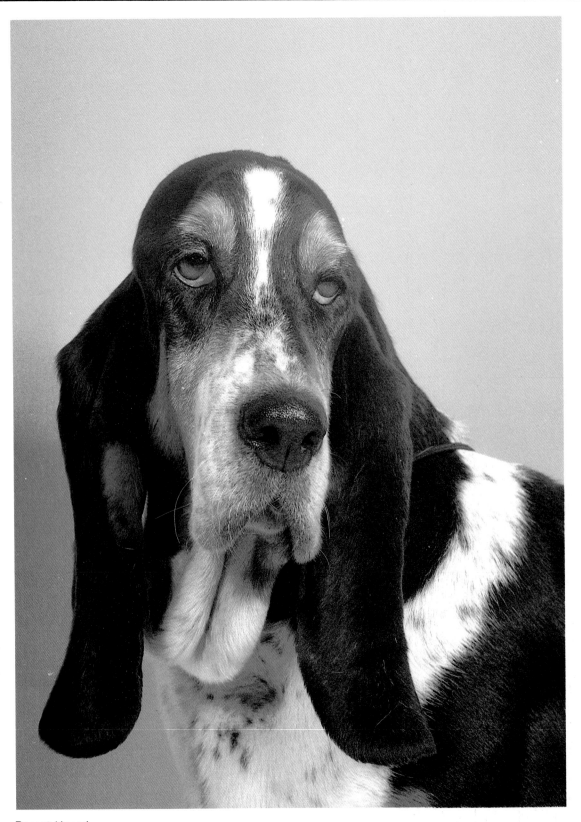

Basset Hound.

hounds that has achieved a fair degree of popularity as a companion dog. This may be due in part to his frequent use in various advertising campaigns. The Hush Puppy™ spokesdog is a Basset, and his soft, sad, appealing face seems to sell a lot of shoes!

In hunting situations, Bassets can be a bit lazy or stubborn, according to some hunt masters, and may get "hung up" on scents—or "go riot" after the scent of a deer. These hounds so love the deer that they cross highways or lose their masters in the woods during a chase. Trailing deer, therefore, is discouraged. But despite the idiosyncracies, true basseters are sold on their breed. As these dogs fill their noses with a bouquet of scents and take off on the trail, their melodious voices blend to create the music of the gods to the basseters. Their slower approach is actually an advantage, as they are less likely to frighten and bolt the game.

Type, in both England and America, is divergent. Like his cousins in Artois and Normandy, there is a variance between hunting type and those bred strictly for appearance. Bassets in formal hunt packs in England and those used for field trialing, or as pets in America, resemble the Coultreux strain with the lighter bone, higher, straighter leg and minimum of hanging skin. Dogs for exhibition, like those originally bred by Louis Lane for their "aesthetics," are massive and extremely low-stationed, with more crooked legs and a super-abundance of wrinkles, flew and dewlap.

Like all hounds, the Basset can be independent in nature, and his baritone musical voice, so loved by connoisseurs of hunting, may be an irritant to neighbors. And, again, in tune with his hound heritage, discipline is a must! Despite these hindrances, the Basset still makes a fine pet. A few in America have proven the critics wrong by winning at the highest level of obedience competition. Many continue to give double service, with the family pet used as a rabbit dog on an occasional weekend hunt.

Pack existence called for a good-humored, sociable dog, and this transfers well to life as a companion. Grooming is minimal. He loves dinner time, but takes the Garfield™ attitude toward exercise, so routine walks must be scheduled to avoid obesity.

Basset Hounds.

Bavarian Mountain Hound.

BAVARIAN MOUNTAIN HOUND

COUNTRY: Germany
WEIGHT: 55–77 pounds
HEIGHT: 20 inches or less
COAT: Short, thick and shiny
COLOR: All shades of black-masked fawn or brindle
OTHER NAMES: Bayrischer Gebirgsschweisshund
REGISTRY: FCI
GROUP: Hound

Schweisshund literally means bloodhound, which is a generic term for a dog, such as the Hanoverian or Bavarian, that follows a bloodtrail. When large game is wounded during a hunt, it may travel many miles in heavy cover only to hide and die a long, slow death. The development of dogs for trailing the wounded animal are common on the Continent. The honor code of the German hunter demands an obligation to find all shot game—dead or wounded. A deer injured with an arrow or bullet may leave only occasional drops of blood many yards apart. The dogs, although brought in even hours later, can follow the cold trail for many miles and lead the hunter to the wounded animal. Sometimes the search goes on for days, but it is never abandoned until the wounded animal is found, dead or alive. This sort of hunting, actually trailing, is not often employed in the USA. It requires a dog with an excellent cold nose and great coldtrailing ability.

Bavaria is a mountainous state in southern Germany near the Austrian and Swiss borders and includes the Bavarian Alps. The hound from this region is a shorter and finer version of the Hanover, probably obtained from crossing the latter with Tyrolean Hounds. The Bavarian is smaller, even shorter on leg, smoother of skin and sharper of temperament, but otherwise very similar to the Hanoverian. He is a tracker par excellence and a fine hunter of the chamois deer, but because he has less size and substance, he can move with more agility in the altitudes of the Bavarian Mountains.

These dogs are calm, quiet, poised and very attached to their master and family. But when hunting, they are "hard, single-minded and persistent." They are highly specialized and must be worked steadily to bring out the best of their talents. Thus, they are not dogs for the casual hunter. Most are owned and utilized by foresters and game wardens.

Bavarian Mountain Hound, black-masked fawn.

Beagle.

BEAGLE

COUNTRY: Great Britain
WEIGHT: 18–30 pounds
HEIGHT: 2 varieties: under 13 inches and 13–15 inches; over 15 inches disqualifies
COAT: Short, smooth and dense
COLOR: Any hound color allowed
REGISTRY: FCI, AKC, TKC, CKC
GROUP: Hound

The history of the Beagle is clouded. Since very early times, small hounds similar to the Beagle have existed for the hunting of hare in the British Isles, particularly in Wales. The original form probably came with the Celts, although certainly crossing with types such as the hounds of Artois or others created this modern breed. Throughout the world, dogs are requisitioned by sporting enthusiasts to be hunted individually or in small packs for squirrel, rabbit and hare, and Beagles are particularly suited for this task. They are determined, keen hunters, and their "music" during a hunt brings goosebumps to neophytes and the oldest pro alike.

During the days of King Henry VIII and his daughter, Elizabeth I, Beagles were sometimes wire-haired. They were also very small, often diminutive enough to be carried to the field in the pocket of a hunt coat. It has even been reported that 10 or 12 couples of Beagles could be carried in saddle baskets! Over the years the size has somewhat increased, but the little "pocket" Beagles still occasionally crop up in a litter. American top size is 15 inches, although in England they allow them up to 16 inches.

Hounds of the Beagle sort were brought into the States throughout the Colonial period, but type varied until further imports from England arrived in the 1880s and 1890s. The Beagle's ability to drill a trail and work the rabbit back around to the waiting hunter have contributed to his demand as a hunting companion. But his small size and happy personality have also been a factor. Needing little grooming, they are easy to maintain and are wonderful playmates for children.

Laboratories traditionally use Beagles in research of diseases, medicines and other medical matters. Large colonies are bred for this pur-

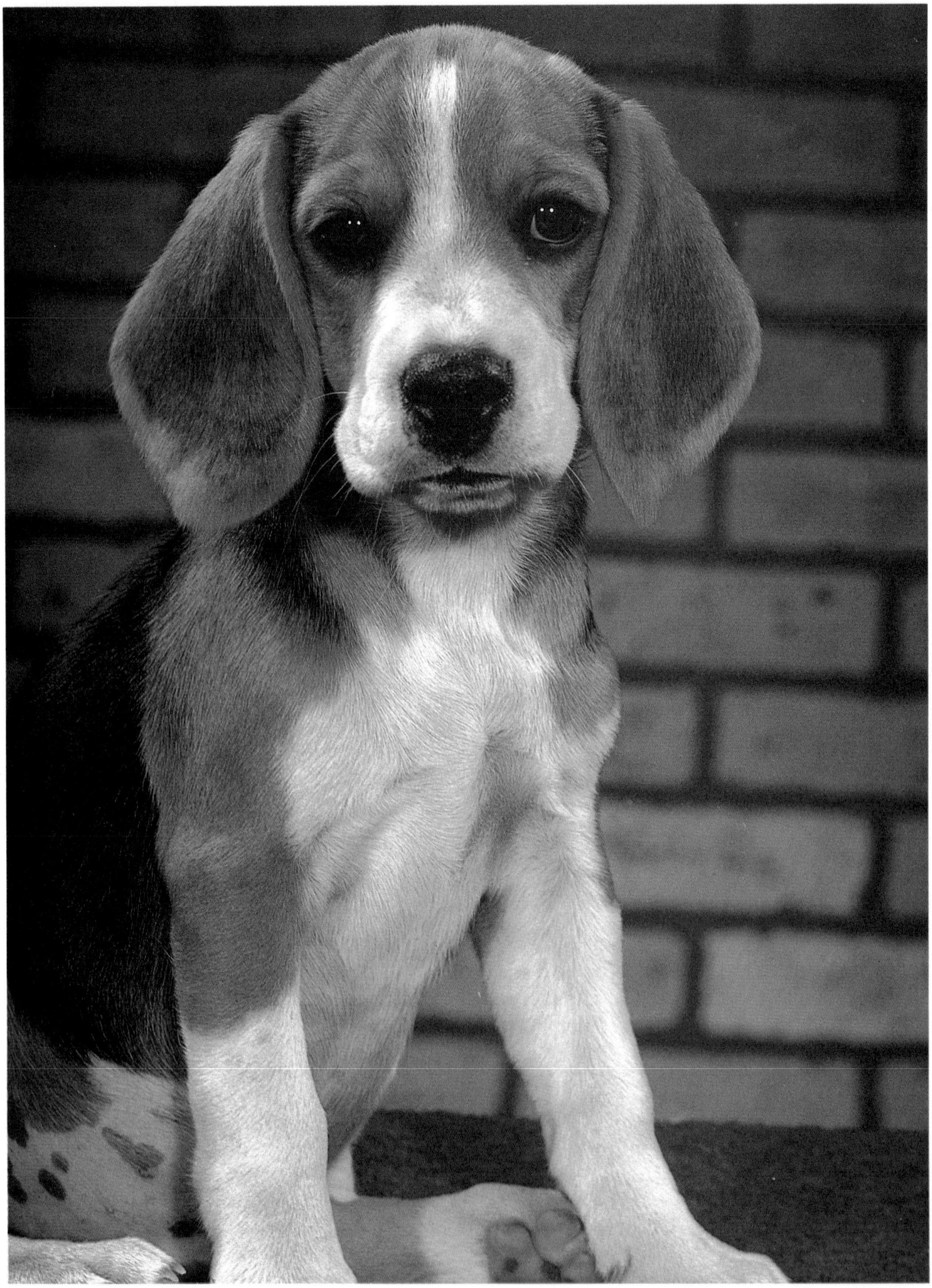

Facing page: Beagle. **Above:** Beagle puppy.

pose, often with certain specific characteristics or proclivities, such as to cancers. This breed is chosen for this heart-rending but medically pertinent task due to its easygoing personality and its adaptability to kennel or pack life, as well as its overall sturdiness.

These same qualities, plus longevity, secure it a permanent place in the heart of dog lovers. In the USA, the Beagle has remained in the top ten registrations for many years, boasting a brief stay in the number one spot during the 1950s. His cocky show strut and merry performances in obedience make him a joy to watch. He is a much-loved pet and companion, although one

may have to deal with his hound's voice and a bit of a stubborn streak. This hound's inquisitive, happy-go-lucky nature and voracious appetite can take him out of his master's good graces, however. To avoid this, training and crating in the owner's absence are advised by breeders.

Beagles are so popular that a verb has been coined, and fanciers are said to be "beagling." The breed is seen frequently in the winner's circle at dog shows, and nearly 3,000 sanctioned Beagle Field Trials are offered each year. Even with all these dogs involved in competitions, the great majority of Beagles enjoy a hunt individually or in pairs with their masters.

BEAGLE HARRIER

COUNTRY: France
WEIGHT: 44 pounds
HEIGHT: 17–19 inches
COAT: Short and smooth
COLOR: Mostly tricolors with a lot of tan; but color is of no importance
REGISTRY: FCI
GROUP: Hound

Baron Gerard of France created this breed by crossing two English hounds, the Beagle and the Harrier. A pack hound used on hare or deer, it looks like the English-type hound from which he came. This dog has the higher set, flat, smaller ears of British dogs. He is stockier and more compact of body than the French hounds and is heavily boned for his size. Small packs of Beagle Harriers are still seen in France with hunters who prize him for his abilities. He is rarely exhibited.

Beagle Harrier.

Beagle Harrier.

Bearded Collie, blue with white markings.

BEARDED COLLIE

COUNTRY: Great Britain
WEIGHT: 40–60 pounds
HEIGHT: 20–22 inches
COAT: Long, harsh, dense
COLOR: Black, brown, fawn, blue, with or without white markings in the Irish pattern. Tan points may occur on all colors.
REGISTRY: FCI, AKC, TKC, CKC
GROUP: Herding

The Bearded Collie evolved from Polski Owczarek Nizinnys, which were left on the shores of Scotland in the 1500s and bred to native herding dogs. One of the earliest notes on the breed described them as: "A big rough tousy-looking tyke with a coat not unlike a doormat, the texture of the hair hard and fibry and the ears hanging close to the head."

In 1898, Alfred Ollivant's book *Owd Bob* carried a description that closely suits the modern Beardie. "Should you, while wandering in the wild sheep land, happen on a moor or in market upon a very perfect gentle knight, clothed in dark grey habit, splashed here and there with rays of moon; free by right divine of the guild of gentlemen, strenuous as a prince, lithe as a rowan, graceful as a girl, with high king carriage, motions and manners of a fairy queen,

Basket of Bearded Collie pups.

should he have a noble breadth of brow, an air of still strength born of right confidence, all unassuming; last and most unfailing test of all, should you look into two snow-clad eyes, calm, wistful, inscrutable, their soft depths clothed on with eternal sadness—yearning, as is said, for the soul that is not theirs—know then, that you look upon one of the line of the most illustrious sheep dogs of the North."

The modern breed as we know it today was introduced to the public sector in the 1940s by its British devotee, G. Olive Willison. An accidental acquisition of a Bearded Collie pup, "Jeannie," so entranced her, she was determined to continue the breed and, after diligent searching, she finally obtained "Bailey" as a mate for Jeannie. Willison's Bothkennar Beardies set the modern lines. Most, if not all, pedigrees lead back to Jeannie and Bailey of Bothkennar.

Beardies met with amazing success in Canada and the USA and were accepted under the ranks of CKC and AKC dogs in nearly record time. They have a steady following, keeping them near the middle of all registrations.

The Bearded Collie breed is one of the few that carries a dominant fading gene. Pups that are born black can begin graying by eight weeks. Blues turn silver, browns lighten to a cinnamon or milky chocolate and fawns become a champagne color. They continue fading until about the age of one year, when the process reverses and they darken again, although they rarely become as dark as they were at birth. The exceptions, of course, are the dogs that do not carry the fading gene. These are called "stay-blacks" (or browns, and so on). Any white markings on these dogs should appear only in the Irish pattern.

Grooming is necessary on a weekly basis, brushing to the skin to remove tangles and prevent mats. Many, seeing the breed for the first time, ask if they are miniature undocked Old English Sheepdogs.

They are becoming one of the most recognizable shaggy sheep dogs, along with their cousin, the OES. The breed's winsome appearance causes them to be in frequent demand for commercials. Beardies are handsome show dogs and loving family pets. Some are therapy dogs and are greeted enthusiastically by residents of nursing homes and hospitals. The breed's parent club is active in encouraging natural instincts and has instituted herding trials.

Beardies are bouncy, bubbly and sometimes boisterous. They are also strong-willed, sturdy and sensitive. Many owners find them both a challenge and a pleasure to train in obedience.

Bearded Collie.

Bedlington Terrier.

BEDLINGTON TERRIER

COUNTRY: Great Britain
WEIGHT: 17–23 pounds
HEIGHT: 15–17½ inches
COAT: Mixture of hard and soft hair that has a tendency to curl, crisp but not wiry
COLOR: Blue, blue/tan, sandy, sandy/tan, liver, liver/tan
REGISTRY: FCI, AKC, TKC, CKC
GROUP: Terrier

Boasting a longer traceable pedigree than any other terrier, the curly-coated Bedlington gives a lamblike illusion. The breed hails from the mining area in the north of England and was first called the Rothbury Terrier in the 1830s. He was originally bred from the wire-coated terriers used locally, probably crossed with hound (i.e., Otterhound) and perhaps Whippet as well. One of the breed's forefathers, "Peachem," is mentioned as both a Bedlington and a Dandie Dinmont. The Bedlington carries a long drop ear and an arch over the loin, both hinting of sighthound. He is also unusual in that he carries the blue or liver colors, probably an inheritance from his sighthound ancestors as well.

He was a favorite with miners and nailmakers for ratting and badgering. In the hunt, he swam after otters and ran down rabbits. A game fellow, he slowly drew a following outside Northumberland, with an English national association for him starting in 1877. At that time, the breed was known to be a tough game dog who would fight to the death if necessary. Gypsies and tinkers kept them as pit fighters, as well as poaching assistants. His skills in poaching caused him still to be known in some remote parts of England as the Gypsy Dog. One of the breed, Ainsley's Young Piper, saved his mistress's toddler from an angry sow. At the age of 14, toothless and almost blind, the same dog drew a badger when other terriers had failed.

Although type has vastly improved over the years, his popularity as a lady's companion tempered his tough working qualities. It was his great heart and lovable nature that endeared him as a pet, and he was no longer selected for his hunting attributes. The American Kennel Club's *The Complete Dog Book* even admits that "when his jealous nature is aroused, he will fight for his place in one's affection"—hardly the same thing as a cornered fox or badger!!

The coat requires periodic trimming to maintain the Bedlington guise. For the show ring, he is hand-scissored to his modern shape, not stripped like other terriers. His terrier heart still makes him a fine alarm dog.

Bedlington Terriers.

Bedlington Terrier.

BELGIAN GRIFFONS

Belgian Griffon

COUNTRY: Belgium
WEIGHT: 2 varieties—up to 6½ pounds and up to 11 pounds
HEIGHT: 7–8 inches
COAT: Hard, long and disheveled
COLOR: Black, black/tan or red/black grizzle
OTHER NAMES: Griffon Belge
REGISTRY: FCI
GROUP: Terrier

Brussels Griffon

COUNTRY: Belgium
WEIGHT: 6–12 pounds
HEIGHT: 7–8 inches
COAT: Long, hard and disheveled
COLOR: Clear red
OTHER NAMES: Griffon Bruxellois
REGISTRY: FCI, AKC, TKC, CKC
GROUP: Terrier

Petit Brabancon

COUNTRY: Belgium
WEIGHT: 6–12 pounds
HEIGHT: 7–8 inches
COAT: Short and dense
COLOR: Red, red/black, red/black grizzle, black or black/tan
OTHER NAMES: Piccolo Brabantino
REGISTRY: FCI
GROUP: Terrier

The descriptions of these little terriers from Belgium are analogous. In fact, AKC recognizes only the breed known as the Brussels Griffon. Its American standard allows all of the color varieties, black through red, as well as the smooth variety (Brabancon). FCI, conversely, divided them into three breeds: smooths (Petit Brabancon), rough reds (Brussels Griffon) and roughs of other colors (Belgian Griffon). Therefore, in Europe they are shown separately, with no interbreeding between the varieties. In America, al-

Petit Brabancon, red.

Belgian Griffon, black.

though the same parameters exist, they are combined into one breed with different color and coat varieties. The history of all three is indistinguishable.

The Affenpinscher was probably the main ingredient in the creation of this "Belgian street urchin." Jan Van Eyck depicted the little Belgian dog in a painting in 1434. A peasant's dog, he was fairly standard in type by the 1600s. Later the breed drew the affection and patronage of French King Henry III, Belgian Queen Henrietta Maria and Queen Astrid. At that time, he was universally rough-coated and longer muzzled, and quite a bit larger than modern specimens, more the size of a Fox Terrier. The Belgian terrier is stouter of build than the Affenpinscher.

In early times, he was called *Griffon D'Ecurie* (Stable Griffon), for he earned his keep by killing the rats and mice in the stable, particularly in those for urban hansom cabs. Their engaging personalities soon created the fashion of riding about town on the driver's seat, next to the cabbie. This gained him wider exposure and, as his popularity as a companion dog increased, he was reduced in size. Many breed historians feel that

crosses to English Toy Spaniels shortened the face and decreased size, as well as removing many of the Griffon's working abilities. Pug blood was also used in the breed's modernization, with the smooth coat and sturdy build coming from that source. Barbets, Smoushond, Yorkshire Terriers and Pekingese are also mentioned as possible members of the family tree. These happy mix-ups that created so many breeds before formal pedigrees were kept may be conjecture or fact.

Their affectionate temperament makes them welcome throughout the world. They reached England in the late 1800s and the United States around the turn of the 20th century.

The Belgian terriers are likeable fellows, intelligent, sensitive, alert with a jaunty good nature, making them precise obedience workers. Their gamin faces invite attention, and they need and enjoy association with people. The breed is not aggressive or quarrelsome. The coat on the wire varieties requires periodic stripping. In America, all three varieties customarily have tails docked short and ears cropped to a very short point, in the fashion of many European terriers.

Brussels Griffon, red.

Above: Body study of the Brussels Griffon. **Below Left:** Body study of the Belgian Griffon. **Below Right:** Head study of the Petit Brabancon.

Belgian Mastiff, fawn with white markings.

BELGIAN MASTIFF

COUNTRY: Belgium
WEIGHT: 99–110 pounds
HEIGHT: 26½–31½ inches
COAT: Short, smooth
COLOR: Fawn, brindle; may have dark mask and occasional white markings
OTHER NAMES: Mâtin Belge, Chien de Trait
REGISTRY: FCI
GROUP: Mastiff

The Belgian contribution to draft dogs was a bobtail mastiff of the butcher's dog type. The breed was used for carting in Belgium and was a calm and obedient dog. The FCI lists this breed in suspension, and the Belgian Kennel Club states that it may be extinct.

BELGIAN SHEEPDOGS

Belgian Sheepdog, Groenendael

COUNTRY: Belgium
WEIGHT: 62 pounds
HEIGHT: 22–26 inches (ideal)
COAT: Medium-long
COLOR: Black
OTHER NAMES: Belgian Sheepdog
REGISTRY: FCI, AKC, UKC, TKC, CKC
GROUP: Herding

Belgian Sheepdog, Laekenois

COUNTRY: Belgium
WEIGHT: 62 pounds
HEIGHT: 22–26 inches (ideal)
COAT: Rough, harsh, shaggy, 2¼ inches long, shorter on muzzle and around eyes
COLOR: Fawn to mahogany, with black overlay
OTHER NAMES: Laekense, Laeken
REGISTRY: FCI, TKC, CKC
GROUP: Herding

Belgian Sheepdog, Malinois

COUNTRY: Belgium
WEIGHT: 62 pounds
HEIGHT: 22–26 inches (ideal)
COAT: Moderately short, dense
COLOR: Fawn to mahogany, with black overlay
OTHER NAMES: Belgian Malinois
REGISTRY: FCI, AKC, UKC, TKC, CKC
GROUP: Herding

Belgian Sheepdog, Tervuren

COUNTRY: Belgium
WEIGHT: 62 pounds
HEIGHT: 22–26 inches (ideal)
COAT: Medium-long
COLOR: Fawn to mahogany, with black overlay
OTHER NAMES: Belgian Tervuren
REGISTRY: FCI, AKC, UKC, TKC, CKC
GROUP: Herding

Belgian Sheepdog Malinois .

Above Left: Belgian Sheepdog Tervuren. **Above Right:** Belgian Sheepdog Groenendael. **Below:** Belgian Sheepdog Laekenois.

The hard-working shepherds' dogs from Belgium have rated raves since the Middle Ages. In those days type varied widely and breeding was based on herding ability. An owner who desired a litter from his good working bitch simply sought out another superb sheep dog, preferably that of a close neighbor. It made little difference if the bitch was fawn and medium-coated, with a refined muzzle and prick ears, and the male was black and shaggy-haired, with a heavy muzzle and half-drop ears. The pups, no matter who they resembled physically, would inherit the working abilities and be in demand. Because of the localized matings, inbreeding was common and dogs began to take on certain standard characteristics. Similar varieties of herding dogs evolved during the same period in Holland, France and Germany.

In 1891, Professor Adolphe Reul of the Belgian School of Veterinary Science cataloged and established standards for the various types of

Belgian Sheepdog Malinois.

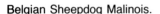

Belgian Sheepdog Groenendael.

Belgian Sheepdogs. He found them remarkably similar in type with the main differences being color, length and texture of the haircoat. The professor divided them into varieties and advised breeding them as separate breeds. At one time as many as eight were documented. Today, however, only four remain: the Malinois (shorthaired fawn), the Groenendael (longhaired black, known in the USA simply as the Belgian Sheepdog), the Tervuren (longhaired fawn) and the Laekenois (wirehaired fawn), all named after the regions in which they were most populous. The standards are identical except for the haircoat.

According to Pagel, the Malinois were the first to establish type, and became so well known that other varieties at one time were called "other-than-Malinois."

The shorthaired *Chien de Berger Belge Malinoix a poil court fauve charbonne* has been given a shorter handle: Belgian Malinois (pronounced *mal-i-nwa*). The Malinois, with its "charcoaled" fawn coat, is a sheepherder par excellence from the area of Malines, giving the variety its tongue-twisting official name. Although still rare in the USA, Malinois are gaining some prominence in police work. Only recognized by AKC in 1965, the breed is slowly gaining a following.

A restaurant owner, Nicholas Rose, is credited with fostering the Groenendael. Rose bred his black bitch, "Petite," to another black herding dog, Piccard D'Uccle, and produced Duc de Groenendael, the keystone sire of the modern Belgian Sheepdog. Wartime was detrimental to breeding programs, but the Groenendael continued to serve its country in finding wounded soldiers and carrying messages on the front. Tales related by American soldiers of these dog heroes paved the way for their introduction to the North American continent. In fact, it was their prowess in war and police work that caused people to confuse them with the German Shepherd Dog. To this day, the term "Belgian Shepherd" is often a misnomer given to black German Shepherds. Today in America, the Groenendael is seen frequently in dog shows, obedience and schutzhund work. The breed also makes a fine family dog.

Brewer M. Corbeel, located near Tervuren, bred his two longhaired, black-tipped fawns, "Tom" and "Poes," producing "Miss," who was purchased by M. Danhieux, developer of the Tervuren variety. Danhieux bred Miss to Piccard D'Uccle, the black foundation of the Groenendaels, and who carried the fawn factor. During the War years, the Terv came close to being only a fond memory, until a lovely specimen, Willy de la Garde Noir, revived interest in the breed. The Terv has made rapid progress since the 1950s in both show and obedience in the USA.

The Laekenois is the rarest of the varieties. This type hails from the area of Boom near Antwerp, which is noted for its lovely and costly linens. The breed's name came from the Chateau de Laeken, one of Queen Marie Henriette's royal residences. The Laekenois was her favorite breed, which she could see helping the shepherds who grazed their flocks on the castle

Belgian Sheepdog Tervuren.

grounds. This contributed to his popularity at that time. The Laeken was used not only for herding but for guarding the fields of Boom where the valuable linens were put out to bleach. The breed still demonstrates its guard instincts and assists both the Belgian army and police. Today the variety is quite rare, and most of its population is in Holland. In 1987, there were 20 specimens in Switzerland, six in Germany and one in Italy as well as a handful of breeders in France and its native Belgium. Although recognized by the Canadian KC, the breed is still scarce in that country as well.

The Laeken likes to be "top dog." To be the dominant partner in the relationship, a Laeken owner should begin training early.

The different varieties—except the Laekenois—have been recognized for many years outside their native Belgium, with the Groenendael being the most numerous. In Canada and in Eu-

rope, the Belgian herding dogs are still considered varieties of the same breed, thus allowing interbreeding. In the USA, however, they have been defined as separate breeds since 1959 and crossbred litters are not registerable. This has created a pickle for breeders because Groenendaels imported from Europe can and do carry the recessive for fawn. It proves to be an unpleasant surprise to Americans to find a "Tervuren" in a litter of purebred Belgians. On the Continent, this "odd man out" could be registered, shown and bred as Terv variety. In the USA the pup would have to be listed as a fawn Belgian Sheepdog, a disqualifying color, and thus be barred from exhibition.

The Belgian dogs are agile and versatile, demonstrating their abilities today in fields other than herding: police and military work, search-and-rescue, dog guides, schutzhund and obedience. They are sturdy and thrive on outdoor excursions, no matter what the weather.

Above: Head study of the Belgian Sheepdog Laekenois.
Below: Body study of the Belgian Sheepdog Groenendael.

Belgian Shorthaired Pointer.

BELGIAN SHORTHAIRED POINTER

COUNTRY: Belgium
WEIGHT: 55 pounds
HEIGHT: 25½ inches
COAT: Short; dense and fine
COLOR: White, with large brown patches; heavy ticking gives the white a gray appearance
OTHER NAMES: Braque Belge
REGISTRY: FCI
GROUP: Gun Dog

This strong, clean-cut pointer from Belgium was known during the last century and was probably most closely related to the French braques. The 1960 edition of the official booklet of Belgian breeds listed him as very rare.

More recently, the FCI has listed the breed "in suspension," and a letter from the Societe Royale Saint Hubert (Belgian KC), dated 11/9/84, says he has "completely disappeared." This indicates no registrations have occurred for many years, and the breed may be extinct.

Bergamasco.

BERGAMASCO

COUNTRY: Italy
WEIGHT: 57–84 pounds
HEIGHT: 22–24 inches
COAT: Abundant, long, hanging in cords
COLOR: All shades of gray, flecked with black, tan or white
OTHER NAMES: Bergamaschi, Bergamese Shepherd, Cane da Pastore Bergamasco
REGISTRY: FCI
GROUP: Herding

These shaggy dogs were brought into Italy by ancient Phoenician merchants—from where, no one knows. We can speculate that the seamen traded for shaggy, corded sheep dogs from the Caucasus or farther east.

Concentrated in the Bergamo area, an old city situated in the north near Milan, the Bergamasco is an intermediate type: a large robust herding dog with flock-guarding ability. Developed by the shepherds of the Italian Alps, he has served his masters well over the centuries.

In his migrations northward, he may have been one progenitor of the shaggy European stock dogs (Briard, Nizinny, Bouvier, etc.). The breed is affectionate and loyal, with a long memory. Owners warn, however, of a natural stubbornness that must be overcome by training.

A thick, corded coat protects him from the elements and prevents injuries from kicks or from bites of wolves or other dogs. The back portion of the coat has a woolly consistency, with the front wiry and rough like goat hair. This hair cascades over his eyes. Like those of his ancestor, the Owtcharka, his cords are never combed out. The Bergamasco presents a unique picture in motion, similar to that of the Puli or Komondor.

The breed is adaptable to any habitat from the open Alpine pastures to a small yard and is devoted to its family but distrustful of strangers. He still demonstrates strong instincts to protect as well as to herd. During a storm, a shepherd encouraged his Bergamasco to sniff a lamb and then the mother of two lost lambs. The dog searched on its own for many hours, finally returning to lead his owner to the lambs, alive and well in a ravine.

Bergamasco.

Noted as easy keepers, they stay vigorous even on their usual pastoral diet of curds and whey. The Bergamasco possesses a heavier muzzle than other members of the herding group.

Until quite recently, he was rare almost to the point of extinction. Dog lovers in Italy, as in so many countries, have worked to save this piece of canine history. He is now promoted as a working dog and can be seen exhibited at Italian and Continental shows. A few specimens have reached other countries, but most of his numbers are still at home. A specialty club is based in Sondrio, on the Swiss border, and where there are dedicated fanciers, there is always hope.

Above and Below: Bergamascos.

Above: Bergamasco tending a flock on Italian landscape. **Below:** Bergamasco.

Berger de Beauce.

BERGER DE BEAUCE

COUNTRY: France
WEIGHT: 66–85 pounds
HEIGHT: 25–28 inches
COAT: Moderately short, close and dense
COLOR: Black/tan or harlequin; previously known colors now unacceptable
OTHER NAMES: Beauceron, French Shorthaired Shepherd, Bas Rouge
REGISTRY: FCI
GROUP: Herding

The earliest reference to the dog from La Beauce plains near Paris appears to be in a Renaissance manuscript, dated 1578. Like their cousin the Briard, this breed has shown its strength, agility and adaptability in various employment. Originally hunters of wild boar, these dogs turned to herding and livestock guarding and eventually to K-9 dogs for the military and police. The Beauce served its country by carrying messages during the Great Wars. A painting at the British War Museum displays a Beauceron wearing a messenger cylinder attached to his collar and leaping over soldiers in a foxhole. The breed also acted as supply transports and the detection of wounded and of mines. Other capabilities are evident by the choice of Beaucerons as dog guides for the blind and as guard dogs. They have much the same versatility as German Shepherds.

The Beauce is currently the second most popular sheep dog in France, following only his countryman, the Briard. He carries strong herding traits, and will attempt to herd any group of two or more. The Bas Rouge designation on the Beauce signifies the reddish tan leg markings, yielding the nickname "Red Stocking." The harlequin coloring is a distinctive black/tan merle, also requiring the red markings. The Beauceron's ears are preferably cropped. In addition to the four regular toes, two large dewclaws are required on each hind foot.

They are aloof with strangers, and protective of their charges, including children. Parents are warned to remove a Beauce from the room if a disciplinary swat to a child is warranted. The breed is said to look kindly only upon its master.

It is an intelligent and calm dog, accepting new situations with aplomb. These dogs enjoy a run and need an outlet for their energy. A strong (not harsh) master is recommended; the Beauceron is not for the meek and mild.

Left: Head study of the Berger de Beauce. **Below:** Beauceron. Notice the prominent upright cropped ears.

BERGER DE PICARD

COUNTRY: France
WEIGHT: 50–70 pounds
HEIGHT: 21½–26 inches
COAT: Medium-long, hard and rough, heavy undercoat, not curly
COLOR: All shades of gray and fawn, no white, except on toes or chest
OTHER NAMES: Picardy Shepherd
REGISTRY: FCI
GROUP: Herding

One of the oldest French sheep-herding dogs, possibly introduced by the Celts, the Picardy is closely related to the Beauceron and Briard. The breed has been, for many years, and still is a flock worker in the Pas-de-Calais region by the Somme in the north of France. Although the breed became endangered during the two World Wars, its easy care and happy, though mischievous, temperament have started the Picardy back on the road to recovery. Nevertheless its numbers are still limited, even in its native country.

Berger de Picard.

Berger de Picard.

The rough, tousled coat does not mat or require special care, yielding a rustic appearance. The standard demands that the ears remain small, so they naturally stand erect.

Like many herding breeds, they require human companionship . . . lots of it, along with exercise . . . lots of it . . . and an owner who will provide both. They are rowdy in their play. The Picardy is a versatile worker. With intruders, they alert and stand their ground. Picardy Shepherds receive high ratings in the official French protection sport. A few specimens of this old breed can be found in the USA.

Berger du Languedoc.

BERGER DU LANGUEDOC

COUNTRY: France
HEIGHT: 16–20 inches
COAT: Usually short, sometimes medium length with short hair on head
COLOR: Various shades of fawn and black/tan
OTHER NAMES: Farou, Cevennes Shepherd
REGISTRY: None
GROUP: Herding

The Farou may be extinct or nearly so. It is smaller with a more pointed muzzle than the northern French sheep dogs; this southern relation otherwise has many similarities. His ears are cropped, and he may have one or two rear dewclaws. The hair can be fairly short or shaggy and moderately long. The face is short-coated in all varieties, similar to the Berger de Pyrenees. His tail is docked similar to the Bouvier's. FCI has recently dropped the breed from its official lists due to lack of registrations or interested breeders.

183

Berger de Pyrenees, long-haired variety, gray-fawn.

BERGERS DE PYRENEES

Berger de Pyrenees

COUNTRY: France
WEIGHT: 18–30 pounds
HEIGHT: 15½–19½ inches
COAT: Long—shaggy, will cord; Goathaired—medium-long, shaggy
COLOR: Fawn, gray, blue, brindle; black is acceptable; white points permissible but not preferable
OTHER NAMES: Pyrenean Shepherd Dog, Labrit
REGISTRY: FCI
GROUP: Herding

Berger de Pyrenees, Smooth Muzzled

COUNTRY: France
HEIGHT: 16–22 inches
COAT: Medium shaggy hair except on muzzle; there should never be hair covering the eyes
COLOR: Harlequin, brindle, fawn, blue and gray, with or without white markings
OTHER NAMES: Smooth Muzzled Pyrenean Shepherd Dog, Berger de Pyrenees a Face Race
REGISTRY: FCI
GROUP: Herding

As happened in so many European countries, the ancient occupation of raising sheep created a triad of shepherd, flock-guarding dog and sheep-herding dog in the Pyrenees mountains of France.

Thus, the history of the little Berger de Pyrenees traces back many years. It seems he was always there, and his characteristics have been set through necessity and use. He was quick and agile for pursuing sheep, and well covered with hair as protection from the elements. Highly resistant to both weather extremes and illness, the breed could go long periods without food. Although brave and ready to defend master and property, he did not need to be large—should an adversary appear to be too much for him to handle, the omnipresent Great Pyrenees was ready to close the gap.

Due to the isolation created by the rugged mountains which form a natural border between France and Spain, each valley individualized the sheep dogs, with small variations in coat length and texture, color and so on. Despite the variety of types, people referred to all of them with the patois name of Labrit, which is still often referred to as a "breed."

Today the breed is often called simply the *Petit Berger*, little shepherd. The French canine body recognized the Pyrenean Shepherd in 1926, and an eminent judge well known in the Great Pyrenees, B. Senac-Lagrange, drew up a standard which remains nearly intact today. At that time, the aforementioned types and valley names were consolidated into two breed classifications.

The Pyrenees sheep dog is slightly longer than tall, with a deep chest, keeping the center of gravity low to the ground. To facilitate all the steep climbing through the mountains, their hocks are a bit close. The thin-soled feet grip

Berger de Pyrenees, goat-haired variety, fawn.

slippery rocks. Their trot is close to the ground; in fact, the French say "he shaves the prairie."

The Berger de Pyrenees has both a longhaired and a moderately longhaired variety. The longer coat will cord if not combed, and is shaggy and long all over. The medium-length coat is called "goat-haired" and is the classic coat, a bit shorter overall, with "cuffs" and "breeches."

The Smooth Muzzled Berger de Pyrenees (literally, bare-faced) is shorter coated, and the hair is nearly smooth on the face and leg fronts. The smooth-faced variety also tends to be more square-bodied and up on leg than his shaggier brothers. They are exhibited in separate classes. Neither variety should have its eyes covered with hair. Working and show specimens have their ears cropped rather short and blunt, and their tails docked. Some pet owners, however, prefer to leave their dogs *au naturale*. The long tail has the shepherd's crook at the end.

The Pyr Shepherd is quite wary and independent, requiring patience and consistent firmness to fit into modern family life. Dogs not ade-

Left: Smooth Muzzled Berger de Pyrenees, blue with tan markings. **Below:** Berger de Pyrenees, goat-haired

quately socialized and trained can become quite unruly—even terrors—breeders warn, although when handled properly they are loyal guardians and a joy to their families. This guardianship is evidenced by a mountain climber's tale. A hiker became ill and had to stop at a Pyrenean shepherd's hut. When the shepherd and flock arrived with nine Pyr Shepherds, the climber was warned of a bear in the area. The shepherds were going down to the village that night for supplies, but planned to leave three dogs to watch the sheep. Three more were assigned to stay with the climber in the hut. Later, he related the dogs willingly came inside and calmly arranged themselves to watch both him and the outside. Although they did not growl or panic when he approached them, they would not let the stranger touch them. They would move silently away and rearrange themselves to continue their watch.

The Pyr Sheep dogs prefer to be with their people, so can be ideal companions for retired

Berger de Pyrenees, long-haired variety, black with white markings.

Smooth Muzzled Berger de Pyrenees, harlequin.

persons, the house-bound or those who enjoy taking a dog with them. They accept the family's children, but have a low tolerance for abuse, intentional or not. Socialization and training are recommended. Their energetic nature calls for long walks or frequent runs. These dogs thrive on having a job to accomplish, whether it be obedience, herding, avalanche and rescue work, or keeping an eye on the family. One dog gave the owner no peace until she entered an excavation she was passing and found an unconscious child. The same dog rejoices in finding lost items: watches, keys, etc. The Petit Berger is described in *The Pyrenean Shepherd Dog* as "a ball of fire . . . so vivacious and quick-witted that . . . . he can . . . perform any task."

Dogs of this breed still work in the Pyrenees, and a number of loyal fanciers promote the breed throughout Europe, as well as a handful doing so in the United States.

BERNESE MOUNTAIN DOG

COUNTRY: Switzerland
WEIGHT: 88 pounds
HEIGHT: 23–27½ inches
COAT: Moderate length hair, straight or wavy but never curly
COLOR: Classic Swiss coloring, black/tan with white markings
OTHER NAMES: Berner Sennenhund
REGISTRY: FCI, AKC, TKC, CKC
GROUP: Mastiff

The Bernese Mountain Dogs trace back to the Roman invasion of Helvetia (Switzerland) 2,000 years ago. Caesar's legions spread throughout Europe and needed guard dogs for their supplies and stations. Their mastiffs supplied the strength. Probable crosses with native flock-guarding dogs provided the ability to withstand the severe weather of the Alps, as well as softening temperaments.

Later used by the weavers of the Berne canton (district) as a draft dog, the Bernese Dog was also a general farm worker and flock guardian, although its benign temperament did not make it a suitable property protector. On market day, these great, patient dogs would be seen pulling

Bernese Mountain Dog.

carts piled high with dairy products or woven baskets into the villages.

The breed had nearly disappeared in the mid-1800s, due to a lack of concerted breeding efforts. Swiss interests had turned to other breeds, particularly the acclaimed St. Bernard, as well as imports that seemed more intriguing than the common native farm dogs. Around the turn of the century, a Swiss cynologist, Herr Franz Schertenleib, combed the countryside to find the last of these dogs his father had told him about. He had some success around the Durrbach district of Berne, which encouraged him to continue searching his country for good representatives of the breed. Zurich Professor Albert Heim joined his efforts. Thanks to the interest of these two men, the Bernese Mountain Dog made a comeback.

At first these dogs carried a variety of local and descriptive names, such as *Gelbbackler* (yellow cheeks), *Vierauger* (four eyes), cheese factory dogs or, most often, *Durrbachler*. Because they were from the entire canton of Berne, not just Durrbach, the club formed at that time changed the breed's name to Berner Sennenhund in 1908. By a 1910 exhibition of Bernese, 107 dogs were shown to judge Albert Heim. While many were without pedigree, three-quarters of the dogs were given the stamp of approval for breeding based on type. The Bernese was on its way!

In the 1930s, one faction made a push to make them seem fiercer, like a guard dog, with some breeding for very light eyes and the split nose. That soon ran its course like other fads, and common sense reigned again.

The Bernese has a huge body of supporters in its homeland, with a strong following in Continental Europe, in Scandinavia and, recognized by AKC in 1936, is steadily gaining ground in the USA. Canada took the breed into its fold in the 1970s, but it remains rare in Great Britain.

These dogs are not giants, and increased size is frowned upon by serious breeders. While the Bernese must be sturdy and strong, ability and soundness are equal prerequisites. Grooming is moderate, with a good brushing every couple weeks making the Bernese sleek and handsome. Their sweet, happy temperament has made them superb family dogs.

Bernese Mountain Dog.

BICHON FRISE

COUNTRY: France/Belgium
HEIGHT: 9–12 inches
COAT: Long, silky, loosely curled outer coat, with undercoat
COLOR: Pure white, although a bit of cream, apricot or gray on the head is allowed.
OTHER NAMES: Bichon Tenerife, Tenerife Dog, Bichon a Poil Frise
REGISTRY: FCI, AKC, TKC, CKC
GROUP: Gun Dog

Fourteenth-century sailors succumbed to the charms of the Bichon, bringing the little furry dog back to France from the shores of Tenerife, one of the Canary Islands in the Atlantic off the coast of Spain. The Bichon from Tenerife has been recorded for nearly as long as the Maltese. The two breeds are closely related, with the Bichon a bit larger. The island was certainly on the Phoenician trade route, and the dogs may have been brought there as items of barter. In Europe, his happy ways soon gained him friends in high places, and he enjoyed 400 years of living among kings and the aristocracy.

In the 1800s, their ride on the crest waned, and the royal whim turned to other dogs. The Tenerife Dog became a dog of the streets, a pet of the commoner. The little Bichon did not remain unemployed long, however. His winsome ways and agility soon gave him new employment as an organ grinder's dog or as a circus performer.

Again, it was servicemen who were entranced by the dog's soft, fluffy appeal. When they took specimens home from France after WWI, French breeders finally began taking the little dogs seriously and, in 1934, they obtained French Kennel Club recognition. They received the nod by the AKC to enter the Miscellaneous Class in 1971, and Canada followed suit in 1975.

Bichon a Poil Frise literally means bichon of the curly coat. The Bichon Frise is distinctive among the bichons, since it is the only one that is double-coated. His coat tends to puff out all over, rather than hang down like his single-coated cousins.

The Bichon is a comparative newcomer to AKC recognition, but is quickly becoming a source to be reckoned with in the show ring. Their sparkling white, poufy jackets and their gait, with a suggestion of a barely contained bounce, make them an attractive show contender.

Bichon Frise.

Bichon Frise.

Bichon Frise.

BILLY

COUNTRY: France
WEIGHT: 55–66 pounds
HEIGHT: 24–26 inches
COAT: Short and smooth
COLOR: Almost pure white, with orange or lemon spots on head and body
REGISTRY: FCI
GROUP: Hound

Developed in the last century by G. Hublot du Rivault, the Billy received its name from Rivault's Poitou estate. Rivault used three breeds, all of which are now extinct, in the development of his dogs. The Ceris was a small, graceful, bright orange-spotted hound used for hare and wolf. Montaimboeufs were large, strong, handsome, and fast dogs used for wild boar; they were also pale orange/white. The Larrye, noted for its exquisite nose, was the creation of Emile de Mauvisse, Count of Villars, in the early 1800s. This occurred in the region of Poitou. Mauvisse is believed to have used what was left of the Poitevins—and then named the breed after the Marquis de Larrye, who founded the Poitevin. Through careful linebreeding, these breeds became the Billy.

The Billy hound is lean-headed with a small, flat ear. He is resourceful and clever, a hound of acute scent, with a light and harmonious voice. He is a master deer hunter, and his pleasing bay—trumpeted through the valleys—differs in tone by the greatness of the game he has sighted. He is sensitive to cold and, when not working, is reported to be a bit quarrelsome with his fellow pack mates. Unknown outside his homeland, his current status in France is not well documented. Although nearly extinct after the last war, a group has fostered his comeback.

Billy.

Black Forest Hound.

BLACK FOREST HOUND

COUNTRY: Czechoslovakia
WEIGHT: 44–49 pounds
HEIGHT: 18–20 inches
COAT: Hard and wiry; ¾–2 inches in length, lying close to the body
COLOR: Black and tan
OTHER NAMES: Slovensky Kopov, Slovakian Hound
REGISTRY: FCI
GROUP: Hound

This Czech national hound is the only scenthound breed native to its country. Although known and used for centuries, formal recognition by the canine governing bodies did not occur until after WWII. He probably descended from dogs of Hungary or of the Balkans, with likely crosses to gun dogs or other non-hound breeds.

This is a distinctive hound. Tough and protective, he makes a diligent watchdog, as the Black Forest Hound lacks the tranquil, naturally obedient nature of most scenthounds. Although affectionate to his master, he requires rigorous early training to serve his purpose. This hound remains widespread throughout Czechoslovakia. The wild boar continues to be his natural prey and he is still hunted extensively in the mountainous regions of Czechoslovakia.

BLACK MOUTH CUR

COUNTRY: USA
WEIGHT: 40–95 pounds
HEIGHT: 16–25 inches
COAT: Short hair, either coarse or fine
COLOR: Reddish golden yellow to fawn or sandy yellow; with or without black muzzle or mask; small amount of white on toes, tip of tail or chest; no white on neck; no brindle or black allowed
OTHER NAMES: Southern Cur, Yellow Black Mouth Cur
GROUP: Hound

The Black Mouth Cur has a burning desire to please his master. A courageous, swift hunter of squirrel, coon, boar or bear, he never retreats. He runs to catch the game and catches to kill. On the track, trailing is semi-open or silent, with a chop or yodel acceptable on tree or at bay. Curs rarely trot, even while hunting, going from a walk to a ground-covering lope.

These dogs are avid hunters, yet work stock well too. Breeders say a pup will train himself—treeing, protecting and/or bunching and penning cattle by six months of age. They are used throughout the southern area of the USA.

The Black Mouth Cur owners claim "Old Yeller" as their property, and that is possible, although the dog in the book was bob-tailed. It is certain, whatever the breed, the family of the canine hero was cur.

Predictable, with even temperaments, the Southern Curs are loyal to their families, giving their lives, if necessary, to protect them. They are especially affectionate to women and children, and aloof with strange men. Some object to parents disciplining children which, of course, endears them to youngsters!

Black Mouth Cur.

BLACK RUSSIAN TERRIER

COUNTRY: USSR
HEIGHT: 25–28 inches
COAT: 2–4 inches, coarse, dense and bristly but close lying
COLOR: Black or salt/pepper
OTHER NAMES: Chornyi, Terrier Noir Russe
REGISTRY: FCI
GROUP: Terrier

In the 1960s, Soviet dog fanciers wished to create their own breed of large working terrier. Using mainly Giant Schnauzers crossed with Airedales, Rottweilers and other breeds, they fashioned a big, agile, tough and weather-resistant dog. It is interesting to note that in times past, the Giant Schnauzer was often called the Russian Bear Schnauzer, indicating the breed's widespread use in the USSR.

Type was fixed in a relatively short time and the Black Russian became widely known in its homeland. FCI has recently granted recognition to this newcomer. This international sanctioning denotes an established written standard and a stability and consistency of breed characteristics.

Many Black Russians are trained and used for professional guard work. They are large enough to be "manstoppers," with adequate coat to protect them from the Russian winters. But the majority of the breed are family pets. They are commonly seen in the larger urban areas, like Moscow and Leningrad, where they serve as companions and watchdogs. Although reliable with their masters, they are suspicious and have an active defense reaction. They are capable of being quite ferocious.

In appearance, they somewhat resemble an uncropped Giant, with a bit more bone and thickness of body as well as a wave to the coat, both gifts of their Airedale inheritance. Very few of the breed are found outside of its native land due to the fact the the Soviets have banned its export.

Black Russian Terrier.

Black Russian Terrier.

BLEUS DE GASCOGNE

Grand Bleu de Gascogne

COUNTRY: France
WEIGHT: 71–77 pounds
HEIGHT: 25–28 inches
COAT: Short and smooth, but not too fine
COLOR: Tricolor; body predominantly white, tan only above eyes, on cheeks and underside of ears, black on head with a few body spots; heavy roaning throughout the white creates the "blue" color
OTHER NAMES: Large Blue Gascony Hound
REGISTRY: FCI
GROUP: Hound

Petit Bleu de Gascogne

COUNTRY: France
WEIGHT: 44 pounds
HEIGHT: 19½–23½ inches
COAT: Short and smooth, but not too fine
COLOR: Tricolor; body predominantly white, tan only above eyes, on cheeks and underside of ears, black on head with a few body spots; heavy roaning throughout the white creates the "blue" color
OTHER NAMES: Small Blue Gascony Hound
REGISTRY: FCI
GROUP: Hound

Petit Griffon Bleu de Gascogne

COUNTRY: France
HEIGHT: 17–21 inches
COAT: Rough, wiry coat
COLOR: Tricolor; body predominantly white, tan only above eyes, on cheeks and underside of ears, black on head with a few body spots; heavy roaning throughout the white creates the "blue" color
OTHER NAMES: Small Blue Gascony Griffon
REGISTRY: FCI
GROUP: Hound

Basset Bleu de Gascogne

COUNTRY: France
WEIGHT: 35–40 pounds
HEIGHT: 12–14 inches
COAT: Short and smooth, but not too fine
COLOR: Tricolor; body predominantly white, tan only above eyes, on cheeks and underside of ears, black on head with a few body spots; heavy roaning throughout the white creates the "blue" color
OTHER NAMES: Blue Gascony Basset
REGISTRY: FCI
GROUP: Hound

Basset Bleu de Gascogne.

Gascony Province lies on the southwestern coast of France, near the Pyrenees Mountains and the Spanish border. Their hounds are of the classic French type, descending directly from the original scenting dogs of Gaul and the Phoenician hound trade. The Gascony stands beside the ancient French griffons as the two types from which most of the modern breeds developed. The Grand is one of the few modern breeds left from the Grand Chiens Courants of the past.

The Grand Bleu originally was used to hunt wolf and, like so many breeds for that purpose, nearly worked himself out of existence with his efficiency in making the European wolf extinct. France's King Henry IV, who reigned in the late 1500s and early 1600s, owned a renowned pack of this breed.

The Grand Bleu is one of the world's largest scenthounds. Only of moderate speed, he is known for his great ability to raise game by his tremendous endurance, his marvelous nose, and a strong and sonorous voice heard at great distance. A reputation as the "coldest nosed" dog is well earned, giving voice long after the "hot" scent has faded. He is built leggy and square, and is aristocratic looking, with no ponderance or heaviness. Many packs remain in France today, and are used on hare, deer and boar.

Many of this breed were brought to America and used in the development of American coonhound breeds. The Gascony probably first arrived in the late 17th century with French explorers. In 1785, General Lafayette gave seven purebred Grand Bleu Gasconies to General George Washington. Washington was known as a hound fancier and breeder, and he noted in his diary that, in October of that first year, one of the French Gascony bitches gave birth to 15 purebred puppies! He also remarked that their melodious voices were like the bells of Moscow. Gasconies were imported to America in the late 1800s and again during the mid-1900s. Because they lacked the trailing speed and the ability to locate quickly that was so desired for American coon hunting, they never gained a foothold as a pure breed in the Western World. But crossed with native hounds, they increased coldtrailing ability and endurance.

The Petit Bleu was bred down from the Grand to handle smaller quarry. Except for size,

Grand Bleu de Gascogne.

he is basically judged on the same standard as the Grand. He tends to be a bit more refined in head and compact of body. As a smaller dog, he is not only speedier but eats less, and is easier to keep and to transport. The breed is especially adept at finding and coursing rabbit, and it is said in France that "going hunting with a Petit Bleu means never coming home with an empty game bag."

The Basset version is a short-legged Grand, and is still a highly prized hunting companion. His handsome appearance, joyous and enthusiastic attitude to the hunt, as well as his pleasant and affectionate personality make him a pleasure to own. Some have found places as companion dogs.

Rarest of the Gascony hounds is the Petit Griffon Bleu, a product of the Petit crossed with wire-coated hounds. Except for his short, wiry jacket and slightly smaller size, he should be similar to the Petit in conformation and color. He is a rustic dog, and is a methodical and untiring worker with a keen nose.

Above Left: Petit Bleu de Gascogne. **Above Right:** Basset Bleu de Gascogne. **Below:** Grand Bleu de Gascogne.

BLOODHOUND

COUNTRY: Belgium
WEIGHT: 70–110 pounds
HEIGHT: 23–27 inches
COAT: Short, thick and hard
COLOR: Black/tan, red/tan, tawny; small amount of white on chest, feet and tip of tail allowed
OTHER NAMES: St. Hubert Hound, Chien de St. Hubert
REGISTRY: FCI, AKC, UKC, TKC, CKC
GROUP: Hound

The ancestry of the modern Bloodhound can be traced straight back to the monastery of St. Hu-
bert and before. These were the ancient dogs called Segusius. The black hounds of the Ardennes were schweisshunds: slow, deliberate, heavy-skinned tracking dogs with persistence, exquisite noses and melodious voices. They originally coldtrailed game such as wolf, big cats or deer, or followed the trail of wounded game. The breed contributed to the development of many European hound breeds, especially the coldtrailing dogs.

When the Normans from France (Gaul) conquered England in 1066 AD, they undoubtedly introduced many of their dogs. The St. Hubert Hound was one of those brought to England, and figured in the formation of the Foxhound. But the original specimen refined with Talbot or

Bloodhound, black/tan.

Southern Hound and called Bloodhound in English also found favor in the British Isles and America.

His ability to discern a cold trail and persistently follow it for many hours gave rise to another profession. Law enforcement officials soon put him to work finding lost persons or trailing criminals. A documented story of a Kentucky Bloodhound named "Nick Carter" tells of the dog following a trail 104 hours old, leading to the discovery and arrest of a fugitive. This same dog's skill resulted in the capture and conviction of more than 600 criminals! Many other records of equally amazing feats are recounted among Bloodhound owners. Trails ranged from a short ten feet to 138 miles; one dog caught 23 escaped convicts in only a day-and-a-half of work.

This reputation as a tracker, especially of fugitives, is the one most people have in mind when they think of the Bloodhound. Movies and fictional stories encouraged the image of a fearsome, baying hound with fangs bared, pursuing escapees through the swamps.

Actually, the Bloodhound is a silent trailer, not announcing his presence. Although he certainly could track down a runaway, he might be more likely to greet the pursued with a licking tongue when he reaches his goal. The track is the only thing in his mind; he is not a pugnacious dog at all! In fact, the Bloodhound is much more frequently put to the trail of lost children or strayed hikers.

The modern Bloodhound is familiar around the world. Although not the identical dog of the monastery, he is officially named the Chien de St. Hubert in Belgium, after his ancient, extinct ancestors. This breed still may be referred to by this title in non-English-speaking countries. But whether Bloodhound or St. Hubert Hound, it is the same large, stolid dog with the long scrolled ears, sad countenance, facial wrinkles and hanging flews and dewlap.

Since he was bred to do his own thing rather than slavishly follow his master's every command, he may seem to be slow on the uptake. Training takes patience, and the instinct to track demands an enclosed yard. His single-mindedness means that, for his own safety, the "sniffer" should not be allowed off leash. Obedience is not his forte, but if you lay a track, you will be able to stand back in admiration. His sense of smell is so much more acute than a human's, it is difficult to fathom; it has been said to be two million times greater. Just think what a garbage can—or a frightened, sweating human—smells like to this breed—a veritable potpourri of scents!

Roger Caras, well-known animal lover and author of *A Celebration of Dogs*, considers "Yankee," the Bloodhound who shared his home, "vain, even arrogant . . . splendid, magnanimous, noble . . . superb . . . a blessing and a miracle."

Bloodhound puppies.

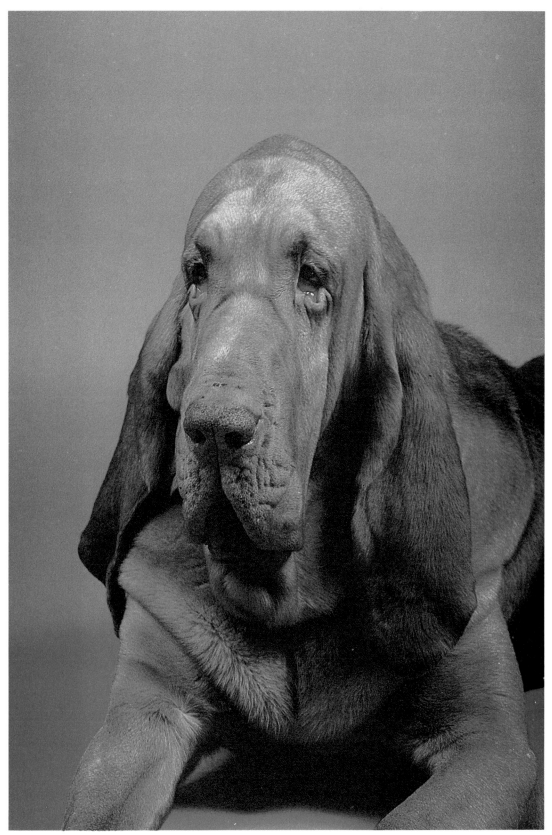

Bloodhound, red/tan.

BLUE LACY

COUNTRY: USA
WEIGHT: 40–50 pounds
COAT: Short, smooth
COLOR: Gunmetal gray, tan, yellow, cream, black; usually solid, but may have minimal white markings
REGISTRY: None
GROUP: Herding

The boast is that a Blue Lacy can do the work of five cowboys, and deluxe workers they are. They arrived "out West" by covered wagon from Kentucky in 1858, brought by the Lacy brothers.

These dogs are in the category of curs, with the emphasis on the herding/droving characteristics. They—like their relatives the Catahoulas—were created for specific needs of colonial Americans. Lacys are said to be the result of Greyhound/scenthound/ coyote cross. Droving dogs could have contributed to the breed as well. The origin of the unusual slate blue color (and blue nose) is a genetic rarity. Few dogs have this coloration—the Bearded Collie, the Neapolitan Mastiff, the Greyhound—so the Greyhound contribution to the Lacy's genetic make-up is a likely one. The so-called coyote in the cross could easily have been feral pariah dogs common in the southeastern United States.

Blue Lacy, black and tan.

Blue Lacy, gray.

Lacys were seen regularly on southwestern ranches for nearly a hundred years. Diane Gentry points out that they came close to disappearing when "modern cowboys on three-wheeled motorbikes" hit the trails.

H.C. Wilkes was determined to save the breed and has worked since 1975 to do just that. They are finding favor with ranchers due to their burning desire to work. A Lacy can handle the meanest longhorn cattle and take to the job instinctively, requiring no training. They can also tackle wild hogs, but can herd chickens in the barnyard as well. Their owners claim they're a good all-around dog, knowing just where to be at the appropriate time and diving into chores without being told to do so. Some will also tree game. They have a gentle nature and take direction with ease.

Bluetick Coonhound.

BLUETICK COONHOUND

COUNTRY: USA
WEIGHT: 45–80 pounds
HEIGHT: 21–27 inches
COAT: Short, dense; a bit coarse to the touch
COLOR: Tricolor, with heavy black ticking in white areas
REGISTRY: UKC
GROUP: Hound

The fine French hounds of the Gascogne, Porcelaine, Saintongeois and others had been brought to America even before colonial times. These patient, persistent, beautifully voiced hounds continued to be bred in fairly pure form in remote areas of the South.

During the early decades of this century, dog dealers made trips into the Louisiana bayou, the Ozark Mountains and other isolated areas,

205

Bluetick Coonhound.

bringing out hounds of remarkably pure type. These dogs, mainly of the heavily ticked blue color, were often referred to as Blue Gascons or French Staghounds. Crossed with various foxhounds and curs, they formed the basis of the UKC Bluetick Coonhound.

Because they were registered as English Coonhounds along with dogs of a very different type, distinct strains of these blue dogs became famous. The Ozark Mountain strain was said to be the closest to pure French and came to prominence in the 1930s. Famous dogs of this strain included "Missouri Valley Echo," "Bailey's Blue Dollar" and "Grant's King Bo."

In the 1920s, the Sugar Creek strain began, with dogs of this bloodline remaining today. They have some old-type Black and Tan in their makeup and are very like the French hounds in their style of hunting. Famous Sugar Creek hounds included the peerless "Blue Bones," who won the first field trial for coonhounds in 1924, and later "Top Notch Drum," "Huey Long," and the prepotent "Cornerstone." Bloodhound, Bluetick, and Porcelaine, as well as Gascogne blood, flowed through the veins of the Old Line strain, another very famous line which included the studs: "Lee's Troop," "Florida Blue" and "Green's Panther." These dogs were much sought after during the late 1930s and the War years, but Old Line is simply gone. The Smokey River and Bugle strains were also prominent in the development of the breed.

Breeders of these blueticked dogs wanted to keep their old style of hunting. They feared a trend to make the majority of hounds registered as English faster and more hot-nosed. To maintain the old-fashioned type, they officially broke away in 1945 and established the breed known as the Bluetick Coonhound.

For a time, blueticked pups from a litter could be registered as Blueticks, and the redticked whelps became English Coonhounds. But soon the stud books were closed, and this practice was no more.

Blueticks still have devout followers and are fine coonhounds. But some owners feel these dogs recently have given way to the current trend of foxhound type and speed in order to participate in the competitive events, as the English hound did before them. Those who want the original big, cold-nosed, old-fashioned type have thus converted to the Blue Gascon and the Majestic.

BOLOGNESE

COUNTRY: Italy
WEIGHT: 5½–9 pounds
HEIGHT: 10–12 inches
COAT: Long, soft, tufty hair without undercoat
COLOR: White, some blond markings are allowed but not preferred
OTHER NAMES: Bichon Bolognese
REGISTRY: FCI
GROUP: Gun Dog

Bologna is a city of northern Italy, well known for centuries as a center of art and learning. The existence of the Bolognese has been recorded since the year 1200, most probably descended from bichon types brought in from southern Italy and Malta. By the Renaissance, the Bolognese had become a favorite of the nobility. Both the Gonzagas and the Medicis bred them and the Duke d'Este gave a pair to King Phillip II of Spain. Supposedly, he indicated that he had

Bolognese, white.

Bolognese, white.

never received a better gift. This breed was also a favorite with La Pompadour, Catherine of Russia, and the ladies-in-waiting of many European courts. Today it is less known, in fact, almost rare in its homeland. Nevertheless, dedicated breeders promote this ancient and admired dog, and there have been recent imports into the United States.

The Bolognese is a typical small bichon dog, intelligent, happy, faithful and companionable. While not hyperactive or high-strung, they are vivacious and full of fun. Breeders report that even ten-year-olds still play like puppies. They are quite fearless and love people.

Bred as companions, they need the attention and presence of their family. In fact, they become so attached to their owners they are like a shadow, following their idols from room to room. "To have a Bolognese in the house is to have someone to love and adore."

The cottony white coat requires daily brushing to keep it free of tangles. But apart from coat care, they are healthy, quiet dogs that make superb companions. They have acute hearing and eyesight, taking notice of anything new or unusual and notify their owners. So, while not barkers, they can be true watchdogs.

207

Above: Bolognese. **Below:** Bologneses, with blonde coloration.

Above: Border Collie, blue merle with tan points and white markings. **Below:** Border Collie, black with white markings, giving ample warning to the sheep in its herd.

BORDER COLLIE

COUNTRY: Great Britain
WEIGHT: 30–45 pounds
HEIGHT: 18–20 inches
COAT: Medium-long (up to 3 inches), thick, straight
COLOR: Black, blue, chocolate, red, with or without tan points and/or white markings—merle can occur in all colors
REGISTRY: FCI, AKC, UKC, TKC, CKC
GROUP: Herding

Border Collie, black with white markings.

The Border Collie probably remains closest in type to the generic "collie" of *auld* Scotland, originating in the border country between Scotland and England. One of the distinct features of the breed is its ability to "eye," a hypnotic stare which wills the sheep to move and turn. The Border was selected for its finesse at strong-eye, coming to prominence with the advent of sheep-herding trials, in which the breed excels. A Border of the early years, "Old Hemp," remains undefeated in English sheep dog trials to this day. Demonstrating his loyalty, another Border stood guard over his dead master for days after the shepherd died while in the hills with the flock.

Although type is distinct, size and coat variations always have been and are still less important than workability. Along with that vital quality, trainability is a prime consideration for the breed.

These dogs are often referred to as "farm collies" or "working collies" and remain excellent working dogs, aiding farmers and stock owners in sheep-herding. They are superb in obedience competition. Two types of temperament are apparent: the workaholic, driven to herd anything and everyone continuously, or the more laid-back family pet. Border Collies are happiest when given a chore and need to have an outlet for their energy. If thwarted in their herding opportunities, Borders will herd the neighbor's stock, other animals, the children—one, in Hawaii, even herds coconuts! A long-time breeder states, "To live with a Border collie is like having a shadow with you."

The Border is recognized throughout the world. The breed is highly exhibited in Australia and as part of the AKC and CKC Miscellaneous Classes. In North America many are registered within their own working-stock dog organizations, bypassing the official registries. Many Border owners fear emphasis on looks and beauty could lead to the breed's ruin. Instead these people encourage a stronger emphasis on working qualities.

BORDER TERRIER

COUNTRY: Great Britain
WEIGHT: 11–12 pounds
HEIGHT: 10 inches
COAT: Rough, wiry
COLOR: Red to wheaten, grizzle/tan or blue/tan allowed; any white other than small spot on chest undesirable
REGISTRY: FCI, AKC, TKC, CKC
GROUP: Terrier

The border area between England and Scotland is rocky with poor soil. Sheep raising is common, and the Border is one of many kinds of dogs developed for going after sheep-stealing foxes and other vermin. He is a small dog with an amazing amount of pluck for his size. The requirements for the Border called for a dog with legs long enough to enable him to cover territory swiftly and to follow a horse, but small enough to go to ground.

His ancestry is without written history, but stems from many of the same origins as the other terriers of northern England. He was previously known as the Reedwater Terrier or the Coquetdale Terrier for valleys or localities of his early existence. He acquired his present name in 1880, perhaps because he was so commonly worked with the Border Foxhounds.

The allowable color of blue and tan suggests a similar background to the Bedlington (whose original members were smaller than the present breed). He probably shares an ancestry with the Dandie Dinmont and the Lakeland as well. Even today an occasional whelp has the soft topknot.

The Border Terrier has not earned the recognition of some of his British relatives, but he is slowly gaining a foothold in the doggy community. In fact, when he was granted English Kennel Club acceptance in 1920, many terrier men were incensed, fearing he would be "prettified" into a show dandy. That fear has not been realized, and he retains his rough-and-tumble looks and qualities. Even though he is recognized by canine governing bodies, his lack of wide exposure in the show ring or as an over-popular pet has maintained his working attributes.

One advantage of the breed is the close, broken coat that affords him protection in the fields. It does not need to be stripped like that of the Wire Fox Terrier, Lakeland Terrier and many others. The standard states that a dog with correct coat should need but a slight "tidying-up of the head, neck, and feet" to go into the show ring. His small size and alert but obedient demeanor make him a marvelous watchdog and companion, as well as a competition-quality obedience dog. Although game, he is not quarrelsome with other dogs. His tail is undocked and carried gaily.

The Border's head should look "like that of an otter," with a broad flat skull, a gradual stop, and a semi-blunt muzzle. He should be built rather narrowly through the shoulder and rear to allow him access to the burrows of foxes and martens.

Border Terrier.

Borzoi, pup.

Borzois.

BORZOI

COUNTRY: USSR
WEIGHT: 75–105 pounds
HEIGHT: 28–31 inches
COAT: Moderately long, silky, flat, wavy or curly; short on head
COLOR: Any color—white usually predominates
OTHER NAMES: Russian Wolfhound, Psowaya Barsaya
REGISTRY: FCI, AKC, TKC, UKC
GROUP: Southern

The best-known Russian dog has been used in its motherland for coursing wolves since the early 17th century. A Russian duke imported several swift sighthounds from Arabia for hunting, but they succumbed almost immediately to the harsh winters. Trying a second time, he crossed the gazehounds with native coated breeds, probably Tartar coursing hounds or long-legged shepherd dogs, taking a step toward the modern Borzoi.

Ceremonial wolf hunts were a display of wealth beyond measure. Everything revolved around the killing of the wolf—from the pairs of aristocratic Russian Wolfhounds chosen from the vast kennels (identical in color and markings to please the noble's eye and equal in speed and strength to reach the wolf at the same time), to the quality horse flesh from the immense stables, the elegant dress of the noble hunters and their servants, and the accompanying opulent celebrations.

As soon as the wolf was sighted, a pair of dogs was unleashed—and the chase was on! It was imperative that the dogs reach the quarry at the same time, to attack from both sides. As the dogs held the wolf down, the nobleman finished off the kill with a flourish of his dagger.

The large, tough hunting dogs were, nevertheless, gentle in temperament and exotic in appearance, making impressive gifts from the czars to the crowned heads of Europe.

In 1903 an admirer of the breed, Joseph Thomas, undertook a pilgrimage to Russia to find the ideal Borzoi. He had little luck, even at the imperial kennels of the czar, until he found the original type in the kennels of Artem Balderoff at Woronzova and of His Royal Highness, the Grand Duke Nicholas at Tula. The dogs Thomas imported were the basis for breeding programs on both sides of the Atlantic.

After the Russian Revolution, many of the kennels were abandoned and breeding of the royal dog ceased. Dogs, through innocent association with the aristocracy, were slaughtered during the chaos. The breed survived through the previous gifts to the Western World and the few dogs that were smuggled out of the country.

Today, there is renewed Soviet pride for their magnificent hound, and they are used by practical hunters throughout southwestern Russia.

Although the Borzoi no longer hunts wolves, it is a competitive courser. Observers thrill to the magnificence of a Borzoi in full stride. Its large size, demand for exercise and great appetite still require more than a pauper's wages. The regal elegance of the breed stands them well in the world of advertising.

Indoors they are graceful and dignified, leaving no havoc behind them, despite their great size. A current breeder's ceramic business would be put to dust by most breeds, yet the Borzoi tiptoe through the shop filled with greenware with nary a mishap. Their calm demeanor and nobility make them an attractive pet for those with enough room.

Borzoi.

Borzoi.

BOSTON TERRIER

COUNTRY: USA
WEIGHT: 25 pounds maximum (classified as under 15, 15–20, or 20–25)
HEIGHT: 15–17 inches
COAT: Short, smooth
COLOR: Brindle with white markings preferred, black with white markings permissible
REGISTRY: FCI, AKC, UKC, TKC, CKC
GROUP: Mastiff

Bred down from pit-fighting dogs of the bull-and-terrier types, the Boston is one of the few breeds "made in the USA." Around 1893, a mixture of Pit Bull, Boxer, English Bull Terrier, French Bulldog and small English Bulldogs produced a pair—Hooper's Judge and Burnett's Gyp—who were the foundation of the Boston Terrier.

It is difficult to believe that these dapper little dogs were once tough pit-fighters. In fact, their weight classifications were once divided as light, middle and heavyweight. Their determination was remarkable, and they are still scrappy enough to defend themselves even with dogs many times their size.

In yesteryear, they were shown under the category of "Round-headed Bull and Terriers, any color." During the infancy of the breed, these little dogs were also called American Bull Terriers and Bullet Heads.

The Irish pattern is well established as the Boston's markings—i.e., white muzzle, blaze on skull, collar, and forechest; white paws and (if they had one) a white tip on tail. Markings are highly important in the show ring, with exact symmetry sought. The Boston's body proportions resemble those of the Staffordshire Terrier, while his short face and screw tail come from his Bulldog ancestors.

During the middle of the 20th century, the Boston Terrier reigned as the American king of purebreds, and his number one position lasted for many years. Because of the breed's large skull and small pelvis, however, many whelpings require Caesarean sections. Although he has stepped down from his throne to join the common dog, he retains his popularity as a pet by devoted enthusiasts of the breed.

Boston fanciers describe them as delightful dogs—keen and intelligent, not yappy. Their biddable nature produces good obedience workers and friends, making them an excellent choice for the elderly. The easily cared for coat and a need to be with their owners accentuate their selection as companions.

Boston Terrier, black with white markings.

Boston Terrier, brindle with white markings.

BOUVIER DE ARDENNES

COUNTRY: Belgium
WEIGHT: 55 pounds
HEIGHT: Medium—up to 24 inches; large—24 inches or more
COAT: 2 inches long, rough and wiry
COLOR: Any color
OTHER NAMES: Ardennes Cattle Dog
REGISTRY: FCI
GROUP: Herding

BOUVIER DES FLANDRES

COUNTRY: France/Belgium
WEIGHT: 88 pounds
HEIGHT: 22½–27½ inches
COAT: Medium length, rough, tousled, "steel wool" hair
COLOR: Fawn to black, pepper and salt, gray and brindle
OTHER NAMES: Belgian Cattle Dog
REGISTRY: FCI, AKC, UKC, TKC, CKC
GROUP: Herding

In times past, all dogs working with cattle were called *bouvier* (bovine herder), and each region throughout the area had its own type. From ancient rough-coated working stock, these dogs were prized as drovers and guardians. As the motorized age arrived, the need for driving cattle to market was gone and so was the call for the dogs that helped in the drives.

The Bouviers were almost eliminated during the long bloody fighting of WWI, and many of the rarer types were lost altogether. Sadly, breeds that are now but a memory include the Bouvier de Roulers, Bouvier de Moerman, and Bouvier de Paret. Still remaining are the Bouvier de Ardennes and Bouvier des Flandres. Both France and Belgium have claimed the dog of Flanders, and the FCI has actually dubbed it "Franco-Belgian." FCI recognizes the Ardennes, although the Belgian KC feels the breed may be nearing extinction—or already gone. A Belgian Army veterinarian, Captain Darby, can be credited with saving the Flandres through the War years. His outstanding Champion Nic de Sittengem won many exhibitions and proved

Bouvier des Flandres, black.

valuable as a sire, with most modern pedigrees tracing back to him.

The Bouvier is a tough, natural working dog, hardy enough to be kept outside all year. He has a forbidding countenance which tends to keep strangers at bay; he makes a good watch dog, but is obedient and affectionate with his master. The Flandres gained a respected reputation serving as an ambulance dog and messenger during World War I. In more recent years, the working Bouvier has served as a defense and military dog. In Belgium, a Bouvier cannot hold the title of show champion until it has passed a working test. He competes in schutzhund and obedience in North America and makes an excellent family guardian.

Ears are not cropped on the Ardennes, with an erect ear preferred. The Flandres' standard specifies cropped ears. Both breeds have short docked tails. The Bouviers' blocky strong head, rough jacket, beard and mustaches give them the appearance of a stern old grandfather. At one time, their harsh coat caused them to be called *pikhaar*, Flemish for hair which pricks, while another nickname *vuilbaard* (dirty beard) is self-evident.

Bouvier des Flandres.

Bouviers des Flandres, salt/pepper, black, and fawn.

Above: Bouvier de Ardennes. **Below:** In its native land, the Bouvier des Flandres is praised for its working abilities—usually.

BOXER

COUNTRY: Germany
WEIGHT: 53–71 pounds
HEIGHT: 22½–25 inches
COAT: Short, smooth
COLOR: Fawn or brindle, with or without white points
REGISTRY: FCI, AKC, UKC, TKC, CKC
GROUP: Mastiff

The Boxer is a refined version of the old *bullenbeisser* (literal translation bull-biter) which has been streamlined in body and sweetened in temperament. His ancestors are thought to have been early Great Danes and English Bulldogs. A similarity to the Boston Terrier, the French Bulldog and the old butcher's dog indicate a definite relationship.

He may have acquired his name through a variety commonly called the *boxl* or through a bastardization of *beisser*. Identifiable and in demand all over the world, the breed has been in its present form since the late 1800s. The promotion of the breed in 1894 by three Germans, Friedrich Robert, Elard Konig and R. Hopner, brought the Boxer to world prominence.

The breed has always been highly favored in its native land and, upon reaching America after the First World War, received steady admiration in the Western World.

White markings are considered "flashy," and should not cover more than one-third of the dog. Occasionally, however, an all-white puppy crops up in a litter of colored dogs. Boxer ears are cropped and the tail docked, but once these puppy cosmetics are performed, he demands little time for grooming. These dogs can be sensitive to extremely high or low temperatures; thus care must be taken during very hot or cold days.

The breed's clean-limbed sturdiness makes it a versatile worker. Boxers have served as police assistants, dog guides or simply defenders of their masters' property.

The stub of the tail wags the rest of the dog. Warm, sleek and loving, they are marvelous children's playmates. Boxers can be rowdy or well-behaved, depending on demeanor and owner demands, but they are always affectionate pets.

Boxer, fawn with white markings.

Boxer, brindle with white markings.

Boxer, fawn with white markings.

Boykin Spaniel.

BOYKIN SPANIEL

COUNTRY: USA
WEIGHT: 30–38 pounds
HEIGHT: 15–18 inches
COAT: Rather wavy or curly and waterproof
COLOR: Solid liver
REGISTRY: UKC
GROUP: Gun Dog

Just after the turn of the 20th century, Alexander White of Spartanburg, South Carolina, was attending Sunday services at church. As he was leaving, he saw a small brown spaniel wandering about and decided to take the tyke home as a pet for his family. The dog, a male, turned out to have some hunting aptitude and was later sent to White's hunting partner, L. Whitaker Boykin, of the Boykin community just outside Camden (South Carolina). With Boykin's schooling, the former stray became a first-rate turkey dog and waterfowl retriever. "Dumpy" was bred to various spaniel bitches who had similar aptitudes, and the little stray became the keystone sire of the Boykin Spaniel family history. Other spaniels, a Springer and an American Water Spaniel, Pointers and Chessies contributed to the breed make-up.

First a turkey dog, he was required to stay down and quiet in the blind while the hunter called the fowl; after the shot, the dog had to be ready to retrieve. The little spaniel fit "just right" into the small boats used on the Wateree River Swamp. As the century progressed, the little southern spaniel adapted well to small water and land birds, in dove hunting and duck shooting. The brown coloring camouflaged him in the woods, and his shortened tail, even if wagged in anticipation, made no sound in the underbrush to give the hunters away.

His area of origin for many years was a winter resort for northerners escaping the cold. Many of these vacationers saw the potential of these local dogs and took one or more home. Today he is used by hunters all along the Atlantic seaboard, with the majority of his admirers still in South Carolina. His history is entwined with that of his state of origin, and South Carolina has designated the Boykin Spaniel its official state dog.

In 1977, several lovers of this rare breed, concerned about indiscriminate breeding, formed the Boykin Spaniel Society to promote and foster him. Among the society's founding members were three descendants of Whit Boykin! They sponsor a field trial and festivities each year in South Carolina for the breed and its fanciers. His prowess is such that the retired head of AKC's Field Trials Department, Ham Rowen, owns a Boykin.

The Boykin is larger than the Cocker, with a smaller, higher set ear. He has considerably less hair and a straighter muzzle. Some coats may be a bit more curly than others, but the practical hunter knows these variations are inevitable and matter little as long as the dog has the abilities. He is a great swimmer and, because of his size, "easy to get in and out of a boat." Most owners report that each of these dogs has a unique personality and an enthusiastic field ability seldom matched by other dogs. His temperament is typically spaniel: docile, pleasant and obedient. Like all gun dogs, he does need abundant exercise, taken care of by long walks on leash or by romping with children in a large yard.

BRACCO ITALIANO

COUNTRY: Italy
WEIGHT: 55–88 pounds
HEIGHT: 22–26½ inches
COAT: Short, dense and fine
COLOR: All white, orange and white, orange roan, chestnut and white, or chestnut roan
OTHER NAMES: Italian Pointer
REGISTRY: FCI
GROUP: Gun Dog

The Italian Pointer is very old and houndlike, and, in fact, may be one of the earliest gun dog types. He has long, folded ears and a slight stop, with a nearly convex muzzle similar to that of the Segugio, and is most likely a descendent or from the same common progenitor. His body, however, is similar to other pointers. His tail is docked to about half its length. Although not known outside of Italy, he is admired at home as an all-purpose gun dog. He is tranquil, docile, obedient and loyal, making a fine family and house dog that doubles as a hunting companion.

Bracco Italiano.

225

BRAQUE D'ARIÉGE

COUNTRY: France
WEIGHT: 55–66 pounds
HEIGHT: 23½–26½ inches
COAT: Fine and short
COLOR: White, with orange or chestnut spots; may have some ticking
OTHER NAMES: Ariége Pointer, Braque de Toulouse
REGISTRY: FCI
GROUP: Gun Dog

The Ariége Pointer probably did not originate from the hound of the area (the Ariégois), since the hound is a breed of the 20th century. The Pointer is considerably older and came from stem hounds of the general area. Being near Italy and the Pyrenees Mountains, he traces back to the Spanish Pointer or Bracco Italiano, both of which he resembles as seen in 17th- and 18th-century paintings. About 60 years ago, the Ariége was modified by crossing with the racier Braque Saint-Germain and even the Braque Francais. These modifications were carried out by Monsieur de Morteau of the Chateau de Molestral in the Ariége during the time of Napoleon IV.

The dog is big and robust, the largest and most powerful of the French pointers. The hare feet, allowable dewlap, long "scrolled" ears and a square muzzle, which tends to the convex ram's shape, are all marks of the hound. For all its power, the breed is elegant and graceful, a tireless worker of slow pace for hunting in rough terrain. The tail is docked a bit in the fashion of many of the Continental pointers and is set on rather low.

The Braque d'Ariége is lively and independent, and needs a master who knows how to dominate him. Although a skilled retriever and hunting dog with a good nose, the breed is known only locally in France. Even at home, it is becoming a rarity.

The Braque d'Ariége was blended with certain pointer-type braques, like the Braque St. Germain, to help save the breed from extinction.

Braque d'Auvergne, black and white.

BRAQUE D'AUVERGNE

COUNTRY: France
WEIGHT: 49–62 pounds
HEIGHT: 22–24 inches
COAT: Short, fine, and shiny
COLOR: Black and white; roaning in the white is desirable to create a blue effect; black must appear on head, covering eyes and ears
OTHER NAMES: Bleu d'Auvergne, Auvergne Pointer
REGISTRY: FCI
GROUP: Gun Dog

Auvergne is in the central southwest of France, near enough to the Gascony region to assume that the Gascony was the hound ancestor of the Auvergne. During Napoleon's occupation of Malta, he decreed the dissolution of the Knights of Malta (*Chevaliers de Malte*). One story tells how the forbears of the Auvergne dogs were brought back to France when the knights returned to their country in 1798. His appearance, however, belies the story. Perhaps the knights brought back dogs who were crossed with local types. The Auvergne is a big, tough hunting dog, built for the Auvergne mountainous areas.

He is lively, sensitive, obedient and affectionate. Like his French hound progenitors, he is light and elegant in the chase. He wags a docked tail, and can be clear white with black spots, but the roaning is much preferred. The heavy roaning is called *charbonnee*, charcoaled. Ears and head should be a solid black and be clean, with no exaggeration and no flew. Among the disqualifications are the tan points, which are the stamp of the hound.

Braque du Bourbonnais.

BRAQUE DU BOURBONNAIS

COUNTRY: France
WEIGHT: 40–57 pounds
HEIGHT: 22 inches
COAT: Short, but hard
COLOR: White, with roaning all over; as few solid patches as possible is preferred; the color may be either liver, brown or orange
OTHER NAMES: Bourbonnais Pointer
REGISTRY: FCI
GROUP: Gun Dog

This provincial hunting dog descended from indigenous breeds of hounds and/or pointing dogs in its native area in central France. A woodcut done by Aldovrandi in 1580 shows a small-eared, short-coupled dog chasing a game bird. The dog is bob-tailed and smooth, with the ticking marks all over his body. Occasionally in times past, a tailless whelp appeared in Braque Francais litters, so some association between the two breeds is possible. Despite first-rate abilities and a good character, the Bourbonnais had never gained much recognition outside its homeland. Recently, however, through the efforts of M. Comte, of the French breed club, breeder M. Francoise Sarret, and the authors of this book, the breed has been introduced to the US. The first litter has been whelped and greeted with much anticipation. He is still a fine hunter of partridge, grouse and pheasant and can also be used on rabbit if trained for small game. French hunters find him a notable gun dog in shooting preserves, and say he is "born trained." A strong breed club now promotes him in France, and he is gaining in popularity, not only with practical hunters, but in field trials and exhibitions as well.

Often referred to as the tailless pointer, pups are usually born with a rudimentary tail. The tail should never be more than three inches in the adult dog. The Bourbonnais is of moderate size with a cobby body and cat feet. Some flew and dewlap are allowed. The standard calls the roan pattern *lie de vin*, a French color that describes wine dregs, while other writers describe the breed's pattern as "dressed like a trout."

Owners describe the breed as serene, sweet and affectionate. The long-time existence of a short-coupled pointing dog with the absence of a tail takes away some of the mystery of the Brittany. Even if one did not come from the other, the genes for cobby dogs with stubby tails were present in France for a very long time.

Braque du Bourbonnais.

BRAQUE DUPUY

COUNTRY: France
WEIGHT: 49–62 pounds
HEIGHT: 25½–27 inches
COAT: Short and fine
COLOR: White with chestnut markings, sometimes in a saddle or mantle
OTHER NAMES: Dupuy Pointer
REGISTRY: FCI
GROUP: Gun Dog

Since the early 17th century, Braques have dwelled in France. They were, at first, of an ancient gun dog prototype, very near the scenthound. Many forms were apparent, some of which, like the Braque Poitou, have disappeared. Others, such as the Braque Francais and perhaps the Dupuy, have survived to the present day.

Several stories concern the Dupuy's origin—and the truth may never be known. Since he is quite houndlike, however, he may go back to the earliest prototype from the hounds of Haut-Poitou. It is known that the breed existed in Poitou before 1808. Legend has it that the breed obtained its name from gamekeepers named Dupuy, who supposedly created it. The story goes that the Dupuy brothers (Homere and Narcisse) kept Braque Francais. A liver/white ticked bitch of theirs named "Miss" was crossed with a dog named "Zidar." Zidar was a *sloughi levrier,* a Sloughi type of Greyhound, brought from Africa by Monsieur Roy, a Lieutenant with the 33rd artillery regiment, garrisoned at Poitiers.

The Dupuy is big (the tallest of the French Braques), racy and elegant, with tight skin, very little stop, the ram's muzzle and a narrow head. His chest is deep and narrow, and there is an arch to the loin. All of these traits are reminders of the classic scenthounds of France, with a hint of the sighthound. Nevertheless, his modern use is for the gun, and he has an excellent nose and good speed over flat open terrain. He is still referred to as *le braque levrier* or Greyhound Braque.

His temperament is described as lively and intelligent, yet dignified. The tail is left intact. He can have patches, ticking or even a mantle of chestnut on his white coat, and the standard warns against the fault of the tan "tri" markings which are a stamp of the hound.

A written standard was published in 1963, but few specimens remain of this unique French breed.

Braque Dupuy.

Braque Saint-Germain.

BRAQUE SAINT-GERMAIN

COUNTRY: France
WEIGHT: 40–57 pounds
HEIGHT: 20–24 inches
COAT: Short, thick, but very fine
COLOR: White, with orange spots and ticking
OTHER NAMES: Saint-Germain Pointer,
Compiègne Pointer
REGISTRY: FCI
GROUP: Gun Dog

In the early 1800s, two English Pointers were purchased from England as gifts for King Charles X of France. They were big running, yellow and white dogs with "grace . . . and elegance of form." They were entrusted to Baron de Larminat, who was the inspector of the forest of Compiègne, northeast of Paris. Although the dog, "Stop," soon died, the bitch was mated to a superior working French Braque. The seven offspring of this mating became the Braque Saint-Germain, an Anglo-French composition. Most of the puppies were given to the Compiègne forest wardens and, when some of these men were transferred to Saint-Germain, their choice working dogs went with them. Since Saint-Germain was close to Paris, these dogs became the rage with Parisian hunters of the time. In fact, for a time, anything orange/white was called "Saint-Germain." Like the Braque Francais, this breed was also called the Braque Charles X, but confusion with the Small French Braque led the committee to drop this name in 1909. Because of his background, he was generally referred to as the *demi-sang*, half-blood braque. The name of his second home has been retained.

This pointer is an elegant, refined, fleet dog with strong searching instincts. The breed has the high headed, high-tailed style of its English heritage. He has a long tail and defined stop; his bright orange and white color also tends to hint at his British ancestors. The Saint-Germain is gentle and affectionate, intelligent and obedient. He is less useful in water due to his fine coat, but he is a first-rate pointer and retriever and competes in French field trials.

While the breed is not the most popular braque in France, it maintains a steady following. Modern owners say, "You only have to observe him to appreciate his elegance and balanced proportions."

Braque Francais, de Grande Taille.

Braque Saint-Germain.

BRAQUES FRANCAISES
Braque Francais, de Grande Taille
COUNTRY: France
WEIGHT: 45–71 pounds
HEIGHT: 22½–27 inches
COAT: Short, thick and dense
COLOR: White, with chestnut patches, with or without ticking
OTHER NAMES: Large French Pointer; French Pointer, Pyrenees type
REGISTRY: FCI
GROUP: Gun Dog

Braque Francais, de Petite Taille
COUNTRY: France
WEIGHT: 37–55 pounds
HEIGHT: 19½–23½ inches
COAT: Short, thick and dense
COLOR: White, with chestnut patches, with or without ticking; or the chestnut is a large mantle which may cover most of the body, but for white on the head and lower extremities
OTHER NAMES: Small French Pointer; French Pointer, Gascony type
REGISTRY: FCI
GROUP: Gun Dog

A very old gun dog from the Pyrenees area of France, the Large French Pointer is probably closely related to the Spanish and Italian Pointers and isn't too far from those early hound/gun dog prototypes. He has always been a prime working dog. It is likely that both sizes were used widely in the creation of other gun dog breeds. The smaller dog was merely bred down from his larger sibling. The large size was originally called *Braque du Pays*, meaning local or native, and the smaller version was known as *Braque de la Railliere* and later the Braque Charles X, after the monarch who was partial to him.

The old-style French Braque was losing favor to foreign breeds at the end of the 19th century, and he was scarce by 1900. Fortunately, two dog authorities, Dr. Castets and Monsieur Senac-Lagrange (later also involved with Great Pyrenees), and Dr. Jean Servier, a dynamic president of the current association, helped save the breed. The push by the Club du Braque Francais in the 1970s brought a modern renaissance to the breed which was rare just a scant 15 years before.

Braque Francais. de Petite Taille.

Braque Francais, de Petite Taille.

More than 500 were registered in 1980, and many have attained success at field trials and dog shows. The modern Braque Francais has recaptured the regard of hobby hunters. In the home, he is obedient, loyal and tranquil, and is good with family members.

The appearance includes a very strong head, with the convex muzzle and a bit of flew and dewlap. A muscular, strong body ends in a docked tail. Known at home as a good hunter, the breed has a stylish point and shows admirable instincts for retrieving and tracking. He works with the stylish "high nose" for air scent, especially in open fields, but can also pick up ground scent in heavy cover and marshes.

The Gascony variation is generally a proportionately smaller version of the Pyrenees type. It has a slightly more refined and tapering head, appearing to have a slightly convex face, and the ears are a bit shorter and higher set. The Gascony tends to be dryer of leg and throat. Its coloring is nearly a solid liver with small white points. Their hunting style is the same as the Pyrenees'.

Braque Francais, de Grande Taille.

Brazilian Terrier.

BRAZILIAN TERRIER

COUNTRY: Brazil
WEIGHT: 15–20 pounds
COAT: Short, smooth
COLOR: Tricolor
OTHER NAMES: Fox Paulistinha, Terrier Brasileiro
REGISTRY: None
GROUP: Terrier

The terrier from Brazil is one of only two native breeds, with the Fila Brasileiro being the other. Jack Russell Terriers, brought to Brazil from Europe in the 19th century, served as the nearest probable ancestor of the Fox Paulistinha. These dogs were crossed with the Pinscher and Chihuahua. Although the Terrier Brasileiro has been in existence for 100 years, the breed has just been registered since 1973.

Despite their size, they are tough, eager hunters and superb ratters. These terriers hunt in packs, surrounding and worrying the prey from all directions until the animal is exhausted.

The native terrier is most common on the outlying ranches and estates. With his alert bearing and bark, he warns of strangers. Lest intruders

Brazilian Terrier.

think they have only to deal with a noisy 20–pound terrier, the barking serves to wake up the tough 100–pound Filas which answer the alarm and handle any threat. The Fox Paulistinha can live in city or country, big or small homes; he "is happy to live with the person he likes."

The Brazilian Terriers are small, game and quick. They are excellent companions, with one fancier professing that "they spring and play all the time they are with the owner." Very intelligent, they "win the owner's heart" and are easily taught. Grooming is a simple chore, taken care of with a few flicks of the brush. Serving as great company for children and the elderly, the little terriers make good family pets. They quickly learn tricks and love to perform.

These smart little terriers of Brazil are unknown in other parts of the world. In their native land, however, they are second only to the Filas in registrations.

BRIARD

COUNTRY: France
WEIGHT: 75 pounds
HEIGHT: 23–27 inches
COAT: Long; slightly wavy, stiff
COLOR: All uniform colors except white—black, fawn, gray or tawny
OTHER NAMES: Berger de Brie
REGISTRY: FCI, AKC, UKC, TKC, CKC
GROUP: Herding

In many areas of the world, the large flock-guarding dog was partnered with a small herding dog. In England, after extermination of the wolves, the giant flock guard was not needed, and smaller herding dogs became the norm (an exception being the Old English Sheepdog). But in continental Europe, the demand was for a large herding dog that offered protection for the sheep, as well as controlling the flock. This type has been established since the Middle Ages, probably stemming from Oriental sheep-herding dogs with crosses to local guarding breeds for size and aggression.

In France this combination created the Briard, an old breed told about in legends. Among the many versions of an ancient tale, Aubry of Montdidier was murdered, with the only witness being his dog. The dog followed the killer, haunting his footsteps continually, making the man's life a misery. The king, being made aware of the situation, ordered a duel between the dog and the accused. (Trials by combat, even with animals, were known to occur in the Middle Ages.) The dog avenged his master's death.

Aubry's dog (in French, *chien d'Aubry*) was a dog of Briard type, and this is a probable source of the breed's name, although it could also be a derivative of the French region of Brie.

Charlemagne gave braces of Briards to friends, and Napoleon so relied on the breed that he took them with him on his military campaigns. Thomas Jefferson added his name to the list of their admirers and imported several dogs to aid the American farmer. Lafayette requested that Briards be sent to him at his American estate.

Briard, fawn.

The Briard is fearless and never timid, hardy and alert and possesses acute hearing. These attributes led the breed to gain a reputation as a noteworthy dog in combat, and to be named the official dog of the French army. The Briard Club of America recounts how these dogs carried supplies to the front lines, served as sentries and found the wounded. Their thick weather-protective coat and sturdiness enabled them to carry machine gun ammunition belts, wrapped around their bodies, to the gunning emplacements. They knew instinctively which soldiers required care and which would not survive. "It was said that any man the Briard passed by was beyond assistance." American soldiers were impressed with the breed, and it wasn't long before the dogs followed the "dog-faces" home.

The Berger de Brie, commonly known as the Briard, and the Berger de Beauce are closely related, with the coat being the major dissimilarity. Both these breeds sport an unusual ear crop, giving them a distinct appearance even today. The ear is shortened and rounded at the tip. The hair on the Briard cascades down off the upright ear, blending into the heavy beard and brows. Both breeds have a "crochet" hook at the end of the tail, which is carried low at rest. The Briard standard, as opposed to those of most breeds, requires the retention of the unusual double rear dewclaws. The best workers were reputed to be those with the extra rear toes, called "bastard fingers" in France.

Personalities are varied: clowns, teases, show-offs, gentlemen, or the "reserved philosophers." Their coarse double coat requires a thorough brushing weekly to remove dead, matting hair and tangles. Their movement is powerful and agile, likened to "quicksilver." They love being outdoors, and some prefer to lie in a snow drift. Briards are protective of their homes, stock and people. Socialization for the young pup is suggested.

Above Left: Briard. **Above Right and Below:** Briard, tawny.

Briard.

Brittany, orange/white.

BRITTANY

COUNTRY: France
WEIGHT: 35–40 pounds
HEIGHT: 19–20 inches
COAT: Flat, fine, only of moderate length, with a bit of a wave; some minimal fringe of ears, underside and back of legs
COLOR: Orange/white, liver/white in USA; International and French standards also allow black/white or tricolor; can have ticking, but clear colors preferred
OTHER NAMES: Epagneul Breton, Brittany Spaniel
REGISTRY: FCI, AKC, UKC, TKC, CKC
GROUP: Gun Dog

The "spaniels" of France are really all small setters. The Brittany may be close to the original couching dogs of medieval Europe. Except for his short tail, his similarity to the all-purpose setters of Germany and the Netherlands, and even the British setters, can be seen. The Brittany has a higher, smaller ear, lighter head and tighter skin than what is expected in flushing spaniels. Similar hunting dogs have been known for a long time in Brittany, and the presence of the Celts in Brittany, Wales and Ireland makes the origin of the red color an interesting topic. Hunting dogs born tailless have a French precedent in the Braque du Bourbonnais.

The modern history of the Brittany dates from the beginning of this century, when Arthur Enaud created a planned breeding program to restore this old, but waning, French breed. The Brit has become a popular hunting dog once again in France and, since its entry into the USA in the 1930s, has enjoyed remarkable success in the States as well.

American fanciers have recently dropped the word "Spaniel," changing the breed name to Brittany. The Brit works much the same as the pointers, the setters, and the *vorstehhunds*. He is an aggressive searching dog and can be pushed out to distance if the conditions warrant. A keen nose and classic point gives him style and dash and, after the point, he retrieves from land or water. His small size is ideal to minimize both the cost of feeding and the space needed to keep and transport him. The Brittany is immensely popular as a personal gun dog in the USA and consistently ranks well in AKC registrations. American Brittany field trials are well attended, and breeders are justifiably proud of a long list of dual champions. The breed also has shown an aptness for obedience competition.

Harsh training is not necessary as they are usually mild and obedient, often quite submissive and wanting to please. The Brit is a good choice for new hunters as the breed is a natural worker that handles easily. He has a tail either naturally short or docked, so that the adult length is never more than four inches. The American and Canadian standards allow only for the orange/white or the rarer liver/white; yet in his country of origin the black/white and tricolors also are recognized. Even the show specimens have not fallen into the trap of exaggerated coat, and grooming is minimal.

Above: Brittany, orange/white. **Below:** Brittany pups.

Above: Brittany, tricolor. **Below:** Brittany, liver/white.

Above: Brittany, tricolor. **Below:** Brittany, black/white.

Brittany.

Above Left: Brittany, black/white. **Above Right:** Brittany, tricolor. **Below Left:** Brittany, liver/white. **Below Right:** Brittany, tricolor.

Bulldog, brindle.

BULLDOG

COUNTRY: Great Britain
WEIGHT: 40–55 pounds
HEIGHT: 12–14 inches
COAT: Short, smooth
COLOR: Red brindle, other brindles, solid white, red-fawn or yellow, piebald (in descending order of preference); black undesirable
OTHER NAMES: English Bulldog
REGISTRY: FCI, AKC, TKC, CKC
GROUP: Mastiff

These dogs were first classified by cynologists as "bulldogs" in the 1630s, although mentioned earlier under "bandogge" or "butchers dogge." They probably shared a common ancestor with the Mastiff, through the Alaunt, which was described in *Master of Game* by Edward, second Duke of York, circa 1406: ". . . Alauntes are treacherous and evil . . . it is the best hound to hold and to nyme [seize] all manner of beasts and hold them fast."

During the heinous days of bull-baiting, dogs caught the bulls by the ear. The early Bulldog, more agile than other fighters, went for the nose and was not as likely to be hooked by a horn. Certainly, the higher legged "bulldogge" of yesteryear could harass the bull into lowering its head for the dog to grab a piece of anatomy, whether the ear or the tender nose. Rules stated that the dog then had to pull the bull backward around the ring—or to throw and pin the beast. Bears, lions, monkeys and badgers were also found worthy to meet the Bulldog in combat. As Pierce Egan recites, the sight brought forth patriotic utterances, as:

> ". . . What creature that, so fierce and
>   bold,
> That springs and scorns to leave his hold?
> . . . It is the Bulldog, matchless, brave,
> Like Britons on the swelling Wave."

Following the demise of this grisly sport, the old-fashioned Bulldog then waded through the bloodbath of the dog-fight pits. This encouraged crosses to various terriers to increase speed, which resulted in the creation of other well-known modern breeds.

The Bulldog of today is not the same as that of the 1600s. After bull-baiting was outlawed in 1835, the original dog evolved into the shorter faced, squattier version we know today, while retaining its powerful undershot jaw.

Bulldogs attained legitimacy in 1860 by entering a different arena—though not quite so bloody—that of the show ring. The bloodthirsty personality of its early years has mellowed into its even demeanor of modern times, while maintaining its threatening appearance. This has earned it the description of "beautiful in its ugliness." Bulldogs are popular mascots, demonstrating the toughness of a team, and have become a symbol of tenacity throughout the world.

The breed has widespread shoulders and a distinctive, rolling gait, making it recognizable anywhere. The exaggerated characteristics have made the Bulldog difficult to mate and whelp, often requiring human assistance through artificial inseminations and Caesarean sections. Care must be taken during hot weather, since the brachycephalic characteristics of the nose and throat tend to restrict air flow.

Bulldog temperament is loving, quiet and gentle. Docile and phlegmatic, their favorite activities are following their masters around the house and taking long naps at their feet.

Bulldog, fawn/white.

Bulldog, brindle/white.

Bulldog, brindle/white.

Bullmastiff.

BULLMASTIFF

COUNTRY: Great Britain
WEIGHT: 110–130 pounds
HEIGHT: 25–27 inches
COAT: Smooth, short
COLOR: Red, fawn or brindle, often with black mask
REGISTRY: FCI, AKC, TKC, CKC
GROUP: Mastiff

In an attempt to decrease the massive size of the English Mastiff, the Bullmastiff was created through crosses with the Bulldog during the late 1800s. This resulted in a more agile, quiet tracker, which retained much of his larger progenitor's power and enabled the Bullmastiff to cover short distances quickly. The Bullmastiff's similarity to the Dogue de Bordeaux, which is centuries older, brings to mind the various Mastiff crosses made throughout history.

These dogs were originally called Gamekeeper's Night Dogs and were set against poachers. Since poaching in England carried the death penalty, those choosing the profession were pre-pared to murder the gamekeepers pursuing them. This called for a tough, fearless, absolutely silent canine assistant.

As the 20th century approached, the need for gamekeepers and their dogs waned. Staged contests were still held, however, to see if a man could outwit the animal. The volunteer was given a head start in woods or moors and, after a few minutes, the muzzled pursuer was slipped off lead. Upon catching his quarry, the dog knocked down the poacher and kept his captive on the ground until the handler arrived. As far as the records show, it was always the dog that won.

Recognition in its homeland came in 1925, and AKC followed suit in 1933. The dark brindles so desirable for night work in its original profession gave way to fawns. British fanciers prefer a dog that appears to have half-Mastiff and half-Bulldog influence from the 19th-century crosses, while Americans seem to desire a 60/40 ratio, with the Mastiff dominating. Hollywood welcomed the Bullmastiff, with both Douglas Fairbanks and producer Harry M. Warner as admirers of the breed.

Nowadays, the Bullmastiff is a calm, though alert, pet. A young dog is often clumsy and demonstrates normal puppy naughtiness. These activities must be "nipped in the bud" before the dog's full size and strength are reached. He is protective of children, other pets and property. These tendencies require a firm, loving owner.

Bullmastiff.

248

Bullmastiff.

Bullmastiff.

BULL TERRIER

COUNTRY: Great Britain
WEIGHT: 52–62 pounds
HEIGHT: 21–22 inches
COAT: Smooth, short
COLOR: White, or any color other than white with or without white markings
REGISTRY: FCI, AKC, UKC, TKC, CKC
GROUP: Mastiff

Bred from crosses of the bull-baiters and the now extinct English White Terrier, with a bit of Dalmatian, the Bull Terrier remains the closest to the original bull-and-terrier breeds. Size, color and head shape were in great variance during its development, and some authorities believe Pointers, Greyhounds and Whippets added their influence. The fighting dogs showed their prowess in the pits, with survivors continuing the fray—this time for ribbons—in the show ring, proudly bearing their battle scars.

Englishman James Hinks first standardized the breed, in the early 1850s, selecting for white color, gameness and the unique egg-shaped head. After type was fixed, the colored variety was added. Ears were originally cropped. Bull Terrier admirers formed a club in England in 1887, with Americans following in 1907.

Bull Terriers were rated by Colonel James Y. Baldwin, Commandant of the War Dogs Training Establishment, as the third most suitable breed in wartime achievements. General George Patton had a Bull Terrier, "Willie," as a companion and a mascot for his troops. One also followed President Theodore Roosevelt around the White House.

The Bull Terrier of today, although still strong and agile, is peaceful and tractable. Stories abound of famed pit-fighting dogs avoiding a confrontation when not "at work." One title-holder actually turned tail and headed for home when challenged by a street-tough cur, which was obviously beneath the champ's ability. Another, losing patience with a defiant Pekingese, picked up the annoyance and dropped it in a waste basket. Bred to defend himself and his human family but not to instigate hostility, he became known as the "white cavalier."

In 1895, when cropping was outlawed, the

Bull Terrier.

Bull Terrier suffered a setback while breeders attempted to obtain the required upright ears without losing other qualities. Naturally erect ears have now been fixed, along with his tiny triangular eyes, giving him a determined but jaunty air. His one-of-a-kind designer head adds to his distinctive appearance, which people seem to find variously exquisite or homely.

BTs are superb athletes, always eager for a game of ball or frisbee. As puppies, this bounding energy combined with amazing strength often makes them rowdy and in need of a firm hand. Their clowning antics have made them a subject of cartoonists and commercials. Like the AmStaff, the Bull Terriers are wonderful people dogs and long-suffering with children. (This, of course, does not mean abuse, but normal, active, clumsy behavior.) Today's Bull Terriers have been out of the pits for many years and most will tolerate family cats and dogs.

Bull Terrier, colored.

Above: Bull Terrier, colored. **Below:** Bull Terrier, white.

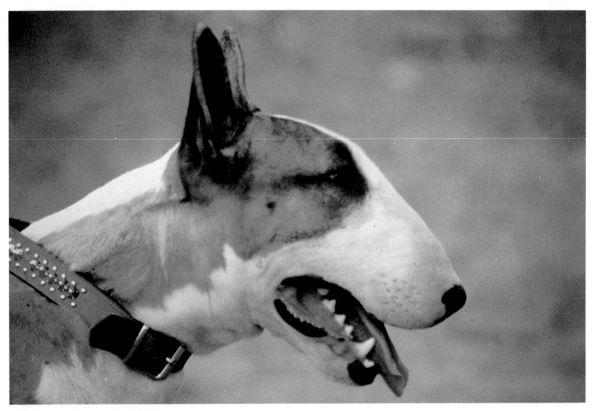

Above and Below: Bull Terrier, colored.

Above and Below: Bull Terrier, white.

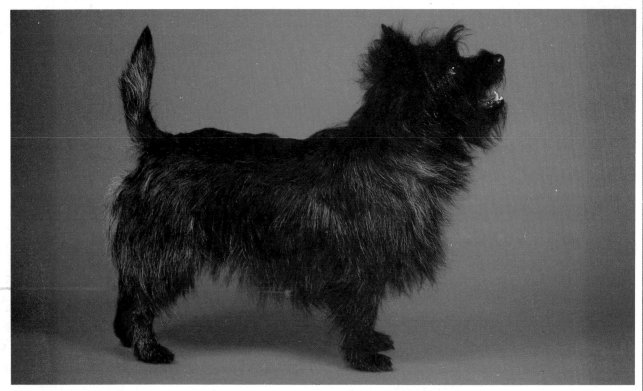

Cairn Terrier.

CAIRN TERRIER

COUNTRY: Great Britain
WEIGHT: 13–14 pounds
HEIGHT: 9½–10 inches
COAT: Rough, wire
COLOR: Any color except white
REGISTRY: FCI, AKC, UKC, TKC, CKC
GROUP: Terrier

The Cairn is a native of the western highlands of Scotland as well as the Isle of Skye, part of the Hebrides Islands, north of Scotland. The breed owes its name and its existence to the pile of rocks erected to identify a boundary or mark a grave. These cairns became favorite hiding places for foxes and other pests. A small but game terrier was needed to go into the cairns and rout out the vermin. The lairds of Scotland kept packs of the tousy terriers for hunting and extermination purposes.

This breed's history is parallel to that of the Skye, the West Highland White and the Scottish Terriers and goes back about 500 years. From a large variety of types in various locales, four distinct breeds slowly emerged: the Cairn, Skye, Westie and Scottie. When the Cairns were first exhibited in 1909, they were called Short-haired Skyes. This produced a howl from the Skye fanciers, resulting in the name Cairn.

Bursting with energy and a joy of life, the Cairn is independent in nature and intently curious, requiring firm instructions. Their terrier nature implores them to dig—whether in a burrow or a flower bed makes no difference to them.

The Cairn has been a neat, compact, cheerful and alert companion since the 1500s. These attributes have made them the favorite terrier in Great Britain, bringing them the honor of being called "the best little pal in the world" by the British Cairn Terrier Club. They reached American shores in 1913, where they have enjoyed a sensible middle-of-the-road status. The breed's sturdiness serves them in good stead as a child's dog.

The short muzzle and erect ears give the breed a keen expression. Its moderately short tail is carried gaily. Ring presentation calls for some "tidying up," since the Cairn's shaggy coat gives the dog a tousled appearance, much like "Toto" in *The Wizard of Oz*.

Cairn Terrier.

Cairn Terrier.

Canaan Dog, liver/white.

CANAAN DOG

COUNTRY: Israel
WEIGHT: 35–55 pounds
HEIGHT: 19–24 inches
COAT: Medium-short, harsh, straight; tail plumed
COLOR: White with large markings in either black, brown or red; browns and black, with or without white markings
OTHER NAMES: Kelef K'naani
REGISTRY: FCI, AKC,CKC
GROUP: Southern

The Canaan Dog has witnessed the birth of the world's greatest religions—Judaism, Islam and Christianity—and has followed the footsteps of Jesus of Nazareth and other Biblical prophets. Queen Jezebel is reputed to have had one of these dogs tied to her throne with a golden chain. They survived long years in the desert, longer even than the travail of Moses and his people. Some hunted with the Bedouins and herded their flocks; others were guards for the Druze on Mount Carmel. Cave drawings as far back as 2200 BC depict dogs resembling the modern Canaan.

When the Jewish people returned to the Promised Land in the 1930s, they discovered pariahs, living fossils, existing like the Dingoes of Australia in a feral state. These dogs were scavengers, surviving despite the hardships of intense heat and a scarcity of water and food. A definite "wild dog" pack order existed. Females left the pack to have their young either in a cave or a "dugout," returning to communal living when the pups were about seven months of age.

In the late 1930s, Dr. Rudolphina Menzel, an Israeli canine authority originally from Germany, was asked to develop a dog for guarding the kibbutz. She and her husband, also a doctor, had observed the pariahs and noted several varieties: *TYPE 1* is a heavier bodied dog, somewhat resembling the flock guards, with a double-coat. *TYPE 2* still has the double-coat and often a tail that tends to curl over the back, but he is lighter in body. This type has a vague resemblance to the northern dogs as well as the Dingo.

Still lighter in build and with a short smooth coat is the *TYPE 3* (the so-called collie-type) pariah, which, when redomesticated, became the Canaan Dog. The *TYPE 4* dog has the appearance of the sighthound, with more raciness and narrowing of the head and body. The wild Type 4 is nearly identical to the Portuguese Podengo and very similar to the Ibizan Hound.

Dr. Menzel cultivated the collie type, starting with "*Dugma*," meaning model or sample, and established the Canaan breed. Although capturing Dugma was a six-month challenge, once enticed to civilization, he was redomesticated with amazing ease.

The Canaan Dogs rose to high favor, due partly to their intelligence and high trainability. They served as sentry dogs and messengers and aided the Red Cross. During World War II, Dr. Menzel trained over 400 for mine detection. Her post-War efforts achieved recognition for the breed as a guide for the blind. They are popular dogs in their native country as companions and guards.

Today their versatility lends them to many tasks: herding, alerting and tracking, making them in demand for sheep dog trials, search-and-rescue, and obedience competition. Their sturdiness enables them to work into their teens.

Owners agree—they do bark, one of their guard attributes. In close proximity, barking can be a problem, and this natural tendency must be curtailed.

Canaan Dog, black with white markings.

Typical of the group, they tend to be aloof. Although they are devoted to their families, they maintain a strong flight reflex, "the highly developed caution toward humans that had allowed her [the breed] to survive in its native land for thousands of years." When confronted with a new or bewildering situation, such as a change in homes, dogs may bolt. Pursuit by well-meaning people seems to puzzle rather than frighten them. They are innately capable of caring for themselves in such a situation. In today's world of multi-lane, fast-moving traffic and dog-control laws, strong measures should be taken to prevent such an occurrence.

Canaans at play are a joy to watch, "boxing" and stalking one another and "talking" back to each other and their families. These dogs first entered the States in 1965. In just a few years, the Canaan has established type and a strong national club. The breed's Israeli standard includes a section on character, indicating that mistrust (of outsiders), endurance, reactability and tractability are all very high. The Canaan Dog is a member of both the AKC and CKC Miscellaneous Classes.

Canaan Dog, white with brown markings.

Above and Below: Canaan Dog, red.

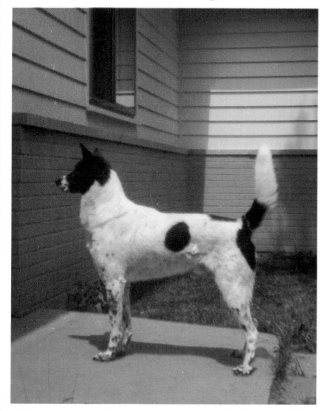

CÃO DA SERRA DE AIRES

COUNTRY: Portugal
WEIGHT: 26½–40 pounds
HEIGHT: 16–21½ inches (most 18 inches or over)
COAT: Long and slightly wavy, coarse goat hair; shaggy on head
COLOR: Shades of yellow, brown, fawn, gray, wolf or black
OTHER NAMES: Portuguese Sheepdog
REGISTRY: FCI
GROUP: Herding

An all-purpose herding and droving dog, the Cão is seen only in Portugal, mainly on the southern plains. It is very similar to the herding dogs of Catalan and to the Pyrenean Sheepdog, possibly crossed with the Briard. The Conde de Castro Guimaraes imported two Briards about 1900, furthering that theory. As with many working breeds, workability was more important than purity, and type was not fixed until 1930. The coat resembles that of the Briard, but carries no undercoat. Although their standard calls for a drop ear, the ears are sometimes cropped. They have long tails and rear dewclaws.

Cão da Serra de Aires.

Cão da Serra de Aires.

The Cão is called the "monkey dog" in his native land, due to his quaint expression. It is widely accepted in Alentejo as a sheep dog. But the breed guards as well as herds—not only sheep, but horses and pigs. These dogs are known for their quick, clever attitude and are particularly adept at bringing back strays. They love their master "above everything on earth," and tend to be a bit reserved with strangers. Adult males may challenge each other for supremacy; the breed requires a firm hand. As a working dog with a need for exercise, they prefer living outdoors, but enjoy an occasional visit in the house.

CÃO DE CASTRO LABOREIRO

COUNTRY: Portugal
WEIGHT: 44–88 pounds
HEIGHT: 20–24 inches
COAT: Medium, short
COLOR: Brindle, also gray and masked fawn
OTHER NAMES: Portuguese Cattle Dog
REGISTRY: FCI
GROUP Flock Guard

In their meanderings out of the Estrela range, many flocks moved to the flat lowlands of the north for winter grazing. The smaller, dark, smooth-coated Estrela dogs are believed to have been the stem of this breed, possibly crossing with native breeds long ago. His place of origin is in the very northern tip of Portugal where he took his name from the small village of Castro Laboreiro, meaning "village of the laborers." Not being part of the great migrations fending

Cão de Castro Laboreiro.

off wolves and bears, the Castro did not grow as large.

Today he is not limited to one village, but is found throughout the country, as one of the most favored of the Portugese guarding breeds. A few have reached other countries and some are used in American flock-guard programs. An owner states his opinion on the Laboreiro's ability: "I believe . . . the Castro could become for the livestock industry what the German Shepherd is to the military."

Due to his naturally suspicious and courageous character, he has adapted easily to police or guard work as well as protecting flocks, herds and isolated homesteads. The Laboreiro's threatening bark is frightening and singular, beginning with a rumbling baritone, quickly climbing the scales to a fortissimo finish.

The breed is bright and learns quickly, but uses its own judgment in decisions. Like many of the flock guards, he is constantly alert, protecting his flock or his family against threats. Totally dedicated to those he keeps safe, the dog is a good companion. Due to his thundering bark, a country home (or understanding neighbors) may be best. His sleek coat and tipped ears need little care other than a quick brush.

Cão de Castro Laboreiro.

CAROLINA DOG

COUNTRY: USA
WEIGHT: 30–40 pounds
HEIGHT: 22 inches
COAT: Short, dense
COLOR: Yellow-gold
REGISTRY: None
GROUP: Southern

Sometime, perhaps 8,000 years ago, dogs of the southern/pariah type migrated across the Bering Strait to the Western World with Asian travelers. These dogs spread the length and breadth of the Hemisphere, laying the foundation for a variety of types and breeds. In western Canada, the Tahltan Bear Dog was of pure pariah type. In the Maritime Provinces to the east, "Indian curs" contributed to the formation of the St. John's retrieving dogs. They also probably formed the basis for the miniaturized and hairless dogs of South America.

To show their widespread existence, a form of feral dog, very similar to the Dingo, lives on the black lava rocks and eats iguana lizards in the Galapagos Islands. His only adaptation is to the 130-degree heat. His ears have grown to im-

mense lengths, standing up like a jack rabbit's ears, to help dissipate body heat.

In what is now the USA, several types once lived. The so-called Basketmaker Dog, now extinct, was nearly a clone of the Dingo and was used by primitive Indians in the southeast. Another type, also lost, named for where his fossils were found, is the Kentucky Shell Heap Dog.

In the Deep South, yet another form of this ancient pariah lives on. Now called the Carolina Dog, because the last remaining specimens were found there, the breed is closely related, or perhaps identical to the other, now extinct, North American pariah breeds. The Carolina Dog was recognized by the Indians, the first explorers and early settlers in the South. Like the Dingo and pariahs before them, they have strong herding instincts. It is probable that the Carolina Dog, crossed with European hounds and other stock, was an ancestor for the American "cur" breeds. In fact, at home the Carolina Dog is of-

Carolina Dog.

Carolina Dog.

ten referred to as "Old Yaller" because of his yellow color.

The Carolina Dog could almost pass for the larger size Dingo with his wedged head, broad, pointed ears, light-boned unexaggerated body, and scimitar-shaped tail. They can be domesticated but, like so many pariah dogs, they have very strong flight reflexes. They tend to be shy and don't like much touching and handling, unless socialized at a very early age. When reared with proper handling, they make fine and well-adjusted family dogs.

Ecologists in the South, including Dr. I. Lehr Brisbin Jr., are searching for pure specimens still in the wild swamps and piney woods of the Savannah River basin. Pups are occasionally placed with selected families to be raised and trained as companions and hunters of small game. Brisbin defines his group's aim as promoting ". . . [the breed's] unique role in the development of today's modern breeds of purebred domestic dogs can be better understood."

Catahoula Leopard Dog, merle.

CATAHOULA LEOPARD DOG

COUNTRY: USA
WEIGHT: 40–50 pounds
HEIGHT: 20–26 inches
COAT: Short and dense
COLOR: Merle and black/tan
OTHER NAMES: Catahoula Hog Dog, Catahoula Cur
GROUP: Herding

Catahoula origin is lost in legends, but similar dogs have long been known in the southeastern United States. The breed is definitely a stock worker, although tougher and more aggressive than many of his shepherd relatives, but his ancestors remain a mystery. It is speculated that he is, in part, descended from the mastiff-type war dogs brought into the area with Spanish explorers. Cathy J. Flamholtz relates how Hernando de Soto cruelly set these dogs to attack the Indians of the area and then abandoned them to be cared for by their victims!

These, if crossed with shepherd dogs of either European or even Indian origin, could have been the breed's roots. There may also have been a drop of hound's blood. The breed will tree and trail although it does take after the shepherd side of the family in more traits. Many old timers still classify the breed as the Catahoula Cur (curs form a group of distinctly American dogs). Henri De Tonti, in 1686, told of seeing dogs with white eyes and mottled spots during his explorations. Jim Bowie owned a pair of Catahoulas, or "Cats" as they were frequently called, in the mid-1800s.

The breed's name comes from the Parish of Catahoula (meaning beautiful clear water), a swampy county in northeast Louisiana, where children went to school by boat rather than bus and where the Catahoula Hog Dog was best known. People from the bayous eked out a living from fishing, trapping, and running a few wild hogs and cattle back in the woods. This stock was wild and unruly, living off acorns and berries, not seeing humans except during the annual round-up.

The hogs, particularly, were nearly impossible to drive. They would turn on most herding dogs and fight rather than run. The Cats were essential to gathering and penning the pigs, and their herding techniques are described by H. Ellen Whiteley, DVM in her article "Catahoula Hog Dog Brings Back Memories of Home." Stragglers were picked out by the dogs and forced into a "fight." Distressed screams from the enraged boar brought the other hogs, especially the lead boar, to the rescue with champing jaws and raised back-bristles. The dogs then turned and ran, escaping the slashing tusks, just fast enough to tantalize the hogs into continuing the chase, which soon led directly into the waiting hog pens. The Cats deftly jumped the back fence, and the hogs were trapped!

Good dogs were worth their weight in gold. A natural selection of breeding stock occurred, since inept or slow specimens rarely made it through the first year of work.

When a person needed a working dog, one was received through a neighbor who had puppies. In the past, Catahoulas were generally not sold, due to the Bible verse in Deuteronomy, which states, "Thou shalt not bring . . . the price of a dog into the house of the Lord thy God . . . "

The modern Catahoula has been adapted for cattle as well as hogs, but he is still better for bringing semi-wild cattle out of the bush than for walking the tame dairy herd into the barn for milking. He is aggressive and heels hard, traits that are necessary for working wild stock, but can spook or injure placid barnyard animals. One breeder, as told to Dennis McClintic, refers to them as "walking sledgehammers." He is also valued for his ability to *wind* cattle (find them by scent) when they are scattered in heavy cover.

NALC (National Association of Louisiana Catahoulas) is the national organization working to standardize type and educate prospective buyers. In 1979, the Catahoula Dog was named the state dog of Louisiana.

Catahoulas use their deep bay to good advantage as watchdogs and hunting companions, even treeing coon. NALC ceased pitting Cats against coons in "Coon on a Log" trials, since it "wasn't fair for the coon to lose all the time." An owner describes her Cat as "strong, made of whipcord and leather," yet gentle with her other dog, though perpetually the "pack leader." The breed is strong-willed, yet sensitive to its owner's needs. They are affectionate and protective of their own family, but often do not welcome visitors.

Catahoula Leopard Dog, merle.

CATALAN SHEEPDOG

COUNTRY: Spain
WEIGHT: 40 pounds
HEIGHT: 18–20 inches
COAT: Long and wavy
COLOR: Fawn with black tips, black, black/tan, grizzle, brindle
OTHER NAMES: Perro de Pastor Catalan, Gos d'Atura Catala, Catalonian Shepherd
REGISTRY: FCI
GROUP: Herding

Catalan Sheepdog.

Catalan Sheepdog.

Catalonia is in the northeastern corner of Spain on the Mediterranean, just across the Pyrenees from France. The people who settled here are of French extraction—not Spanish—coming to Spain from the Pyrenees region. Physically the Catalan Sheepdog is similar to the Pyrenees Sheepdog. Ears may be cropped to stand. The beard, mustache and shaggy coat give them an appearance like the Portuguese Sheepdog or old-type Beardie. A rare, short-coated variety (similiar to that of the Shepherd), the Gos d'Atura Cerda, is noted as needing less care.

They herd horses as well as the sheep that are so abundant in Spain. Although some sources mention a nervous temperament, they are intelligent, vigorous and strong, and adapt well to police, army or guard work.

Caucasian Owtcharka, gray brindle.

CAUCASIAN OWTCHARKA

COUNTRY: USSR
HEIGHT: 24–26 inches minimum; usually much larger
COAT: Moderately short to medium; very thick fringing; some may have abundant ruff and fringe
COLOR: Usually gray, tan, fawn, white, brindle, piebald; any color except brown allowable
OTHER NAMES: Caucasian Sheepdog, Kawkasky Owtscharka, Kaukasische Schaferhund
REGISTRY: FCI
GROUP: Flock Guard

In both the Caucasus and Ural Mountains of the Soviet Union, flock-guarding dogs have long been utilized. Although fine-tuned within the USSR to suit local land and climatic conditions, they trace back to the same Asian/Middle Eastern sources of all flock guardians.

The Caucasus Mountains fill the long finger of land in southwestern Russia that reaches down between the Black Sea and the Caspian Sea to touch Turkey and Iran. In these high elevations (up to 18,000 feet), great flocks of sheep are kept and, for over 600 years, the Owtcharkas have protected them from wild animals and thieves.

Without kennel clubs and written history, there tends to be some variation in type throughout the mountain range.

Russians describe the massive, stocky Grusinian type; the taller, rangier Azerbeidjan from the south near Iran; the smaller, square-built Dagestanian from the southeast between the

269

Greater Caucasus and the Caspian Sea; and the big, strong Kangalian of the Turkish border. The best and most uniform modern examples are in the Georgian Republic. Despite regional differences, the desired Caucasian dog is large-boned, massive and strong, with the mental traits to do livestock guarding work. The proper Owtcharka is confident, strong-willed and fearless, with a large dose of independence. Russians describe him as ferocious and recommend approaching him with caution. He makes an extremely reliable guard dog, being able to naturally discriminate between true threat and benign interference. When real danger threatens, the Caucasian Sheepdog becomes "an incorruptible dare-devil," attacking without warning in utter silence.

Hair length varies with the elevations of lo-cale, and colors can be from the usual flock-guard white or gray/dun to reds, brindles and even piebalds. Ears are cropped short, not to a point, but horizontally and bluntly cut nearly off. Even modern exhibition specimens are still cropped. The tail is usually carried low with a hook at the end, but in excitement may be raised in a loose ring. In some areas of the USSR, tails are still docked.

The first Caucasian Owtcharkas outside their homeland were introduced to East Germany in 1969. By 1979, they had spread to West Germany, winning "the hearts of many dog fanciers by storm." There is now a specialty club in Germany, and these dogs are seen at international shows in Europe. At the present time, the exportation of this breed from the Soviet Union is forbidden.

Caucasian Owtcharka.

Cavalier King Charles Spaniels, Blenheim.

CAVALIER KING CHARLES SPANIEL

COUNTRY: Great Britain
WEIGHT: 10–18 pounds
HEIGHT: 12–13 inches
COAT: Long, silky, free from curl, ample feathering
COLOR: Black/tan, solid red (Ruby), red/white (Blenheim), and tricolor (Prince Charles)
REGISTRY: FCI, AKC, UKC, TKC, CKC
GROUP: Gun Dog

In the 1920s, Roswell Eldridge, an American, wondered if any of the original longer headed toy spaniels seen in early paintings still existed. For five years running, he offered first prizes of 25 pounds at Crufts, England's most prestigious dog show, to be awarded to "Blenheim Spaniels of the Old Type." Whether these types were still found in litters or skilled British breeders did some quick crossing, the prizes began to be claimed.

This revived breed became the Cavalier King Charles, achieving Kennel Club status in England in 1944. This spaniel has accomplished a most remarkable "comeback." Princess Margaret, of the British royal family, acquired one in the 1960s, and this boosted the breed's recognition even more. By the 1970s, this toy spaniel was nearing the top 20 in British registrations. He has been among Canada's recognized breeds since 1957. The American Kennel Club includes the breed in its Miscellaneous Class division. Dog lovers Nancy Reagan, wife of the US President, and Mordecai Siegal, award-winning author, are current fanciers.

The clamor for the breed in England was such that it reached a point of diminishing returns. Breed entries soared and breeders were concerned about the problems that occur at the public's whim. This demand has now sensibly leveled off. With the English passion for the Cavalier in mind and the fact that the breed is charming, one wonders why they haven't caught on more in America. Their coat is long enough for beauty, but isn't so abundant as to require excess care. A variety of colors allows for various tastes. The tail may be docked a bit, or not, allowing the length to balance with the body. In the particolor dogs, there should always be some white at the tip, thus the capriciousness of the color spots dictates whether one pup has his tail cut and another not.

Cavalier King Charles Spaniel.

271

Cavalier King Charles Spaniel, Prince Charles.

United States President Ronald Reagan with Cavalier King Charles Spaniel.

Česky Fousek.

ČESKY FOUSEK

COUNTRY: Czechoslovakia
WEIGHT: 62–75 pounds
HEIGHT: 24–26 inches
COAT: 1 to 3 inches of bristly, rough outer hair, with thick, soft undercoat
COLOR: Liver or liver/white, with or without ticking
OTHER NAMES: Rough-coated Bohemian Pointer, Czech Coarsehaired Pointer, Slovakian Wirehaired Pointer
REGISTRY: FCI
GROUP: Gun Dog

The Česky Fousek is closely related to both the Drahthaar and the Stichelhaar, whom he resembles. The breed was very popular in the area of Bohemia between the mid-1800s and World War I but was almost lost during that war. He was revived in the 1930s, by using some German Shorthaired Pointer blood.

The tail is shortened to two-fifths of its full length. This pointer's rough coat is fairly long on underside and chest, beard and brows. He is described as an aristocratic and noble dog with good abilities. Today, Czechs say he is widespread and frequently hunted in their country.

CHESAPEAKE BAY RETRIEVER

COUNTRY: USA
WEIGHT: 64–75 pounds
HEIGHT: 23–26 inches
COAT: Moderately short, thick, and very coarse, with no beard or brow
COLOR: Dead grass most desirable, liver to hay color allowed
REGISTRY: FCI, AKC, UKC, TKC, CKC
GROUP: Gun Dog

The Chesapeake Bay area has been famous for its first-rate duck hunting ever since the first settlers set foot on shore. Retrievers have always been in demand by the Bay and, for many years, each hunter simply used the best dog he could find bred from other dogs who worked well. The Chesapeake dog was not an overnight creation, taking much of the 19th century to develop.

The oft-repeated story of the breed springing from two dogs saved from a shipwrecked brig is probably another doggy "tale." These two dogs, "Canton," a black female, and "Sailor," a dingy red male with yellow eyes, were probably of the early smaller Newfoundland type and certainly did contribute to the breed. But the fact that they were never bred to each other assures that there were other wellsprings. References point to imported Red Winchesters from Ireland, perhaps bearing some relationship to the breeds which spawned the Irish Water Spaniel. By the last third of the 1800s, owners had formed an organization to promote and standardize the "Chesapeake Bay Ducking Dog." Type was still a variant, with the modern breed taking shape over the next 20 years.

The Chesapeake Bay dog was a favorite of the commercial duck hunter who shot for the restaurant and market trade in the late 1800s and early 1900s. Well-documented records chronicle dogs who averaged a thousand ducks each fall. The icy water and rough waves of the saltwater bay necessitated a dog tough in mind and body who lived to retrieve. And the tougher the conditions, the more the Chessie seemed to enjoy the hunt.

The "dead grass" color was preferred, to provide a camouflage that blended with the fall landscape. His coat is very dense and harsh with an almost oily texture that sheds water and insulates from the wet and cold. The head has a tendency to be smoother than the rest of the body; just a hint of the possible stem to the European water dogs like the Curly-Coated Retriever, Wetterhoun and Irish Water Spaniel. Described as "utilitarian rather than beautiful" and "about as sensitive as a Sherman tank," the breed attracts serious duck hunters.

Bearing the reputation as a hard head, he retains the mental toughness and independent single-mindedness so necessary for his early work. Once the Chessie knows who is giving the orders, he is a hard and willing worker. There are excellent breed members in obedience and field trials, as well as weekend gunners' companions. This is a devoted family dog who loves children. Although most modern families could hardly provide the kind of work performed by one early dog, who "all his life worked an average of five days of every seven," it is necessary to provide a Chesapeake with adequate exercise and some kind of job to make him—and consequently his owner—content.

Chesapeake Bay Retriever.

Chesapeake Bay Retrievers.

Chesapeake Bay Retriever.

277

CHIEN D'ARTOIS

COUNTRY: France
WEIGHT: 40–53 pounds
HEIGHT: 20½–23 inches
COAT: Short and smooth
COLOR: Tricolor in a broken pattern
OTHER NAMES: Briquet
REGISTRY: FCI
GROUP: Hound

Northern France, bordering the English Channel, consists of the historical regions of Normandy and Artois. Normandy, Brittany's eastern neighbor, has the same rolling plains and poor soils. As one moves east into Artois right up on the Belgian border, however, fertile soils and forests abound. The Ardennes area of Belgium, where the St. Hubert was developed, is a near neighbor. Hounds from these regions stem from some of the earliest types.

The d'Artois dog was a favorite by the 17th century. The Prince Alexandre de Gray wrote to the Prince de Galle, in 1609, of his intention to "send a pack of little d'Artois dogs to the king . . ." In fact, this small French hound may have contributed to the formation of the Beagle in England.

By the 19th century, the curse of fashion was laid upon the breed. It became chic among French hunters to avail themselves of the dogs from the British Isles. With the importation of many British types, the inevitable crossbreeding resulted in the deterioration of the pure d'Artois. Crossing also took place with the taller, more elegant, longer, scroll-eared hounds called Normands (now extinct). During the 1800s, only the packs kept at Chantilly and those of the Prince de Conde retained the ancient type.

In the 1880s, Ernest Levair and his cousin, M. Therouanne, began a 20-year effort to breed the original d'Artois, removing the last of the Normand blood. Although their efforts resulted in great success, the war years again nearly destroyed the breed. Once thought to be extinct, there are now about 500 dogs registered in their stud books, making a strong comeback since 1975. They have the small size, shorter head, sturdy body with wide chest, and long, but very flat ears of the original type.

This breed is a supple, rustic hunting dog that is becoming increasingly available to French hunters. Used in small packs for rabbit, other small quarry, or even wild boar, he has a melodious, high bark.

Chien d'Artois.

Chien d'Artois.

CHIEN DE L'ATLAS

COUNTRY: Morocco
WEIGHT: 55 pounds
HEIGHT: 21–24 inches
COAT: Medium-short, dense
COLOR: White preferred; also appears in black; tawny; "washed out" red, black and white
OTHER NAMES: Atlas Sheepdog, Kabyle Dog, Aidi
REGISTRY: FCI
GROUP: Flock Guard

Whether the Aidi crossed into Africa from Spain or was carried from Italy (or beyond) by the globe-trotting Phoenicians matters little. He is a classic flock guard, although a bit smaller and with less coat due to his semi-arid environment.

This breed guards flocks, tents, camels and other belongings of the nomadic tribes in the northern African hills. Several are selected for their attentiveness and aggression, being staked out at night around the campsite. With each other and their masters, they are tractable.

They have exceptional noses, able to track even in the sands of the Sahara and join in the caravan's hunts. They are paired with a Sloughi, the Atlas dog finding the game by scent, then the Sloughi slipped for the chase. In the past he may have been used as a dog of war. The Atlas Sheepdog is versatile, performing as a shepherd, drover, gun, guard, war and police dog.

He is lively and high-strung, but with a job to do, he can be kept in the country or city, even though correspondents say the breed is a dog "of the rural zones." Confident and alert, the Aidi makes an outstanding watchdog.

Moroccans say that a club was organized to promote this national breed only recently. This group is proud of the breed's heritage and wants to preserve the purity of the Atlas Dog. The current standard supplied by the Moroccan Kennel Association describes the thick fur and heavy plume of tail as a sign of purity. Its thick "mane" and "fleece" shelter it from the arid heat and the mountain cold, also protecting the Aidi in fights with jackals and other predators. His ears are tipped to the front; sometimes dogs with cropped ears or a short tail are seen, although the natural condition is the only one recommended.

First-day cover issued by the Moroccan Post Service commemorating the Chien de l'Atlas.

LA FAUNE MAROCAINE

№ 03401

Chien Francais Blanc et Noir.

CHIENS FRANCAISES

Chien Francais Blanc et Noir

COUNTRY: France
WEIGHT: 62–66 pounds
HEIGHT: 26–29 inches
COAT: Short and smooth
COLOR: Actually a tricolor, but the tan is reduced to marks on the head and ears
OTHER NAMES: French Black and White Hound
REGISTRY: FCI
GROUP: Hound

Chien Francais Blanc et Orange

COUNTRY: France
WEIGHT: 62–66 pounds
HEIGHT: 26–29 inches
COAT: Short and smooth
COLOR: Orange and white
OTHER NAMES: French Orange and White Hound
REGISTRY: FCI
GROUP: Hound

Chien Francais Tricolore

COUNTRY: France
WEIGHT: 60 pounds
HEIGHT: 25–28 inches
COAT: Short and smooth
COLOR: Tricolor in a broken pattern all over the body
OTHER NAMES: French Tricolor Hound
REGISTRY: FCI
GROUP: Hound

Besides the previously described French breeds, there are hundreds and hundreds of hound packs throughout France used strictly for hunting. Members of these packs are bred and selected for their abilities without great concern for appearance or type. With so many of the old classic "breeds" disappearing and the existence of all these other crossbred hounds, a committee of French cynologists conducted a survey in 1957 and inventoried all the extant packs. Many of the pack hounds were various crosses of

Chien Francais.

the French hounds) the tan is reduced to spots above the eyes, on the cheeks, and under the ears, so that the body appears to be black/white.

The Orange and White variety was described by the 1957 committee, which decided the breed was not sufficiently set in type to draw up a standard. If exhibited, these dogs are judged, except for color, by the same standard as the Black/White. They are, however, recognized by FCI.

A standard was set for the Tricolor variety after the survey. He is slightly smaller and has much more tan on the body. Otherwise, he is nearly a clone of the Black/White. The Tri is rarely exhibited, but the identification and description of a written standard aids in prevention of crossbreeding and loss of all these ancient types.

Chien Francais Blanc et Orange.

purely French breeds and were fairly similar in type. These were reclassified as the Chien Francais, or French Hound. Those dogs whose French ancestors had been crossed with English hounds for a more British build, were renamed Anglo-Francais (French-English Hound).

The Black and White French Hound is pure Gallic in type, and is mainly derived from crosses of the Gascon-Saintongeois and Levesque as well as others. He has a statuesque, elegant build with the French head and ears.

These dogs are "professional" hunters bred only for their work—yet they are affectionate, tranquil and obedient. Useful for any game, they are specialists on deer. They were the most prevalent of the three French varieties in the pack survey. They are not really black and white, but a tricolor in which (like so many of

Chihuahua, longcoated, black/tan.

CHIHUAHUA

COUNTRY: Mexico
WEIGHT: 1–6 pounds
COAT: Short and smooth; or long and soft with fringing
COLOR: Any color
REGISTRY: FCI, AKC, UKC, TKC, CKC
GROUP: Southern

The Chinese have long practiced the art of dwarfing animals, plants and fish. It is believed that Spanish traders traveled through Mexico on their returns from China and left behind some of their canine acquisitions. These, crossed with the native hairless breeds, made up the modern Chihuahua, which is the smallest dog in the world. Other cynologists have stated he is just a miniaturized version of native pariah dogs. His similarity to the small Podengo of Portugal (another dwarf pariah) is singular.

The tiny dogs may have been named for the State of Chihuahua in Mexico, and many tales lend belief of their existence there. No concrete evidence has been found to prove this theory; in fact, more recent research has provided evidence to the contrary. Explorers reporting the exis-

tence of dogs called the Techichi are now believed to have described a "prairie dog" type of rodent, which the natives "raised, castrated and ate." These little "dogs" lived in holes in the ground.

Whatever their beginnings, Chihuahuas first came to prominence in Mexico City around 1895, reaching El Paso, Texas, shortly thereafter. Dog lovers in the USA refined and perfected the little dog of Mexico—and soon the breed was listed as the top toy in the States. He has maintained his appeal as a companion dog.

The long-coated version was probably produced in the USA, crossing smooth Chihuahuas with other toys like the Papillon, Pomeranian and so on.

Their tiny bodies hide large hearts, making them a favorite for the elderly and those in apartments. They are playful and graceful, with large ears emphasizing their alert appearance. Due to their tiny size (some as small as one pound!), they are not the choice for rowdy families or outdoor living. Breeding and health problems are accentuated in the tiniest specimens. The *mollera*, or open soft spot on the top of the skull, is usually found in the majority of Chihuahuas and is allowed by the standard.

Chihuahuas, longcoated, various colors.

Above: Chihuahua, longcoated, white. **Below:** Chihuahua, longcoated, particolor.

Above: Chihuahua pup, smooth, red.

Chihuahua.

Chihuahuas, particolors.

Chihuahua, orange with white markings.

Chihuahua, blue.

CHINESE CRESTED

COUNTRY: China/Africa
WEIGHT: 5–10 pounds
HEIGHT: Males 13 in. max, females 12 in. max
COAT: Hairless, except for tufts appearing on the head (crest), feet (socks), and tail (plume); Powderpuff—longish, double, soft, silky coat
COLOR: Skin from pink to black, mahogany, blue, lavender or copper, solid or spotted; Powderpuff—any color or combination
REGISTRY: FCI, AKC, TKC
GROUP: Southern

Hairless mutations have occurred in pariah-type litters, and from these the modern hairless breeds have evolved, likely first developing in Africa. Hairless dogs captivated the attention and fancy of ancient dog lovers in Africa, Mexico, Spain and China. During the Han dynasty, the Chinese Crested dogs were cultivated into two types: "treasure house guardians," or deer-type, and the larger, heavier cobby "hunting dog," which, when he didn't bring home meat, was the main ingredient in the cooking pot.

Other hairless varieties, like the African Elephant Dog, or the Abyssinian Sand Dog, developed in similar warm climates.

Fortunately for the breed, Chinese dogs accompanied their masters on trade vessels throughout the world, leaving mementos of their visits behind. True to the dominant genetics, hairlessness would show up in that first litter!

Chinese Cresteds, along with other lovely Chinese breeds, are now rarer than Cadillacs in their native land. Along with the belief of a "Chinese Crested in every pot," the Communist ideology against pets has nearly eliminated dogs on mainland China.

The breed enjoyed a brief stay in the AKC Miscellaneous Class and was exhibited at Westminster in 1885 and at the Sesquicentennial Exposition in Philadelphia in 1926. After a respite of several decades, fanciers organized the Chinese Crested Club of America in 1975, and the breed resumed competition in Miscellaneous Classes again in 1986.

A gay, loving personality, similar to the other hairless varieties, has endeared them to many. Their hair tufts are denser than the sparse wisps on other hairless dogs. They possess a hare foot and can grasp and hold their toys, food or people. Owners describe how they "hug" when held. Perhaps it was that quality or perhaps their "unclad" appearance that enamored Gypsy Rose Lee to their charms.

The powderpuff's veil coat has a soft undercoat with coarser guard hair, and may be short or long. Ears are erect on the hairless variety; the weight of the hair on the powderpuff may cause ears to drop.

Chinese Crested, blue spotted.

Above Left: Chinese Crested. **Above Right:** Chinese Crested powderpuff adult, white, and hairless pup, lavender. **Below:** Chinese Cresteds, pink spotted.

Above: Chinese Crested powderpuff. **Below:** Chinese Crested powderpuff pup, tricolor.

Chinook.

CHINOOK

COUNTRY: USA
WEIGHT: 65–90 pounds
COAT: Short, smooth, dense
COLOR: Tawny
GROUP: Northern

This sledding dog is an American creation, dating from 1915. Arthur Walden wanted to create a sled dog that had both the speed of Huskies and the strength of the larger sled dogs. He used his lead dog, "Chinook," meaning warm winds, as the keystone sire. Chinook, according to Walden, was "half-bred Eskimo" through his dam, whose pedigree led back to Admiral Robert E. Peary's lead dog on his North Pole expedition. Chinook's sire was ". . . mongrel . . . a trace of Saint Bernard."

In 1922 Walden's Chinook team beat three others to win the first Eastern International dogsled race. Walden was asked to be in charge of the teams on Admiral Richard E. Byrd's 1929 Antarctic expedition, and Chinook went with his master. The Admiral wrote in *Little America* that the dogs he prized most highly were the Chinooks. He said, ". . . Walden's team was the backbone of our transport." Loads averaged a remarkable 150 pounds per dog.

Chinook reached a sorrowful end on that trip, according to Admiral Byrd.

. . . the saddest . . . was the loss of Walden's famous lead dog, Chinook. Chinook was Walden's pride, and there was no doubting the fact that he was a great dog. He was old when brought to the Antarctic, too old for hard, continuous labor, and Walden used him as a kind of shock troop, throwing him into a team when the going turned very hard. Then the gallant heart of the old dog would rise above the years and pull with the glorious strength of a three-year-old. The affection between him and Walden was a beautiful thing to see: one sensed that each knew and understood the other perfectly, and it was Walden's rare boast that he never needed to give Chinook an order: the dog knew exactly what had to be done. A few days after his twelfth birthday, Chinook disappeared. We searched the camp for him, without success; in the trampled snow about the ship, it was impossible to find his tracks. . . . Whether he walked out alone to die, because his days of service were done, is something I cannot vouch for: this was the romantic theory advanced by several of the men. At any rate, his body was never found. . . . All this was a deep disappointment to Walden, who wanted to bury Chinook in his harness.

Chinook.

In 1940, ownership of the Chinook dogs was in the hands of Perry Greene, and he was challenged to prove his breed's superiority over the American Eskimo Dog, the Husky and the Malamute. Greene planned the longest race ever undertaken in the USA, 502 miles from northern to southern Maine. The sled was packed with 800 pounds of equipment and supplies topped by Greene's 13-year-old stepson. The journey was mostly by ice and snow-covered roads, allowing good sledding. Some roads, however, were bare. The seven-dog team arrived at their goal, Kittery, 90 hours later, with not a single dog limping. All were in excellent shape; some had gained weight! They achieved a measure of fame from several magazine features, including one in *The National Geographic* about the breed between the 1940s and 1960s, and the fact that one served as mascot of the Operational Chinook Helicopter Unit in Vietnam.

Greene refused to allow anyone else to breed the dogs, and only sold spayed females, fearing that others would ruin the breed. He, as Wal-den, kept the breeding combination to himself. Unfortunately, his misguided altruism caused a decline in the breed.

Chinooks remain in danger of extinction. *The Guinness Book of World Records* listed the Chinook as the world's rarest dog in 1966 when only 125 existed; now there are 150 dogs. Fanciers are working, through the Southern California Rare Breed Club, to gain more recognition, and are actively seeking sledders to work with breeders in programs that emphasize the working qualities. In addition, a breeding program has been charted by biogeneticists, and the Chinook Owner's Association maintains strict guidelines.

Chinooks offer several positive qualities other than the speed, endurance and strength demonstrated by their prowess as a sled dog. They are good, protective family dogs, though headstrong, needing a firm hand. For a large dog, the Chinook boasts a surprising record for good hips and a longevity of 10–15 years. The old-line Chinook's ears were drop, but many are carried erect today.

Chinook.

CHOW CHOW

COUNTRY: China
WEIGHT: 45–70 pounds
HEIGHT: 19–20 inches
COAT: Long coat—long, straight, spitzlike stand-off; smooth coat—shorter spitzlike, more plush, similar to the Siberian or Shiba
COLOR: Any solid color, as tan, red, cream, blue, black, silver gray, or white (rare)
REGISTRY: FCI, AKC, UKC, TKC, CKC
GROUP: Northern

Both the Chow Chow and the Shar-Pei are from mainland China. The Chow is certainly closely related to the other Nordic/spitz dogs, but may not be pure northern, having some sprinkling of mastiff types. This family introduced the heavier heads and thick, wrinkled skin, which some feel the Chow owes to crosses with the Tibetan Mastiff. It is possible some of the Nordic breeds owe their roots to the Chow, rather than the other way around.

Historians trace Chows to the 11th century BC when Tartar hordes invaded China. Art and literature of these eras were often destroyed by the succeeding emperors, and information is sketchy. During the Han dynasty, however, about 150 years BC, bas relief sculpture and pot-tery do depict Chowlike dogs hunting. Later, a T'ang emperor, circa 700 AD, boasted a kennel of 2,500 couples of Chows with a staff of 10,000 huntsmen!

The Chow Chow was relished throughout China as a delicacy, in addition to serving in other less fatal capacities, such as a draft, guard or flock dog. The eating of dog flesh was, and still is, common in Asia. The dogs were fed an all-grain diet and butchered while young. The fur of the longhaired Chow was made into clothing. *The Book of Marco Polo* tells of these dogs being utilized in a Nordic manner, drawing sledges through mire and mud.

Because China had a closed-door policy for centuries, these dogs did not make an appearance in other parts of the world until about 1780. Several types of Chinese dogs, including Pekingese and Chows, were smuggled out by sailors in the 1800s. It was a difficult task to convince these canine grain-eaters to eat the meat that was fed dogs in the Western World. These dogs were displayed in the London Zoo as the "Wild Dog of China" until dog lover and breed savior Queen Victoria took one into her fold.

In the early 1900s, the Chow was still a highly visible dog in China, being sold in market places, with puppies "sitting placidly" in large

Chow Chow, smooth coat, black.

Chow Chow, long coat, red.

blue and white jars on the doorsteps. Nevertheless, it was fortunate that the Chow left China when he did, as the Cultural Revolution declared dogs a useless commodity, and most have been destroyed. A recent visitor to China recorded seeing only three mongrels on her entire trip.

The breed's name is thought to be derived from the pidgin English term *chow chow*, which was a blanket description for the novelties, curios and dogs brought on ships from the Orient. Another theory is that *chou* is Chinese for edible. His Chinese name around Canton, where the breed was numerous, was *Hei She-t'ou* (black-tongued), *Lang Kou* (wolf dog), *Hsiung Kou* (bear dog) or *Kwantung Kou* (dog of Canton).

The breed quickly gained a following and the long, plush coat is admired throughout the world. With popularity ever growing, it is easily recognized and owned in many countries. The smooth coat is not as common, but a few of that variety are being shown in the USA.

As puppies, they have the appearance of live teddy bears. In fact, a belief that Chows descended from bears has been passed through generations. This legend persists not only due to their coat and sure-footedness, but because of the blue-black tongue peculiar to the polar bear and a few Asiatic bears located in the same vicinity. Like bear cubs, Chows do mature, and buyers should be aware that these cuddly pups will one day have their own minds in powerful bodies. Chows have an independent and rather suspicious nature and will guard their property—their family and all their possessions—to the death.

The Chow's black-pigmented tongue, lips, and gums are a stamp of the breed. The massive head and wrinkles make the dog appear to be scowling. Regular grooming is a necessity for the plush coat. Care must be taken in hot weather, especially during periods of high humidity, as the breed suffers greatly and may even be endangered by the combination of heat and humidity.

The breed personifies the one-man dog, and is extremely aloof with strangers. Attention forced on him by outsiders often results in aggressive behavior. But with his own family, he is predictable and loyal. Dangerfield and Howell attest to these characteristics in *The International Encyclopedia of Dogs* with the following statement: "It has been said that the Chow will die for his master but not readily obey him; walk with him but not trot meekly to heel; honour him, but not fawn on his friends and relations."

Chow Chows, long coat, black and red.

Chow Chows, adult and pup.

Cirneco dell'Etna.

CIRNECO DELL'ETNA

COUNTRY: Italy
WEIGHT: 18–26 pounds
HEIGHT: 16½–19½ inches
COAT: Short and smooth
COLOR: Fawn in all shades, white markings allowed
OTHER NAME: Sicilian Greyhound
REGISTRY: FCI
GROUP: Southern

This Pharaoh Hound look-alike was brought to Sicily in the Phoenician heyday, when dogs of this type were a hot item. He has been kept and bred in the shadow of Mount Etna for 3,000 years.

The large island of Sicily, located at the toe of Italy, is the major home of the Cirneco. In more ancient times the breed also was known further north on Corsica, and the Greek name for that latter island, *Cyrnecos*, may have contributed to his name. Mount Etna, the 10,000–foot active volcano on Sicily's eastern side, provides the other portion of his name. The roots and history of this breed are the same as the Pharaoh's and the Ibizan's, repeated on a different island. In fact, in times past the Cirneco was also called the Pharaoh Dog, due to its identical taproots in Egypt.

Even before recorded history, a temple dedicated to the local divinity has existed at Ardano on Sicily. This holy place was supposedly guarded by the Cirneco dogs who had "a supernatural instinct to attack the sacreligious and thief but to welcome enthusiastically the devout."

The breed is prevalent around Ardano, and it is now the only breed which hunts on the slopes of Mount Etna. They were officially recognized by the ENCI (the Italian Kennel Club) about 1940, due mainly to the efforts of Professor Giuseppe Solaro. The FCI has also recognized the breed as distinct from the Pharaoh Hound.

As hunters, they are smaller versions of their relatives from Malta and Ibiza. Although basically sighthounds of an ancient sort, they can also hunt by scent. The Cirneco is a specialist on rabbit and hare, but is so silent that it can also sneak up on any kind of feathered game. He is a lively and friendly companion not known outside of his localized area in Italy. Unfortunately, he is becoming extremely rare at home as well.

Cirneco dell'Etna.

Clumber Spaniel.

CLUMBER SPANIEL

COUNTRY: Great Britain
WEIGHT: 35–65 pounds
COAT: Thick, silky and straight, abundant feathering
COLOR: Lemon/white or orange/white, the more white the better
REGISTRY: FCI, AKC, TKC, CKC
GROUP: Gun Dog

This most distinctive flushing spaniel retained more hound genes than any of the others, except the Sussex, giving him the massive bone and heavy head that is his alone. His type was admired especially by the Duke of Newcastle in Nottingham more than a century ago. The Duke's estate, Clumber Park, was undoubtedly the source of the breed's name, but the breed's background is unknown. There are stories of hounds given to the Duke from French nobles. And yet, the traits may have been selected within the spaniels already extant. The characterization of the Field Spaniel, for example, was accomplished without crossbreeding!

These dogs have enjoyed quite some approval among British royalty. Prince Albert, consort of Queen Victoria, was the first to tout them, and his son, King Edward VII, was extremely proud of those he bred in his Sandringham kennels. As favorites of royalty, these spaniels quickly became fashionable. King George V, son of Edward VII, was a dedicated sportsman and hunter, and continued the tradition of using Clumbers. An interesting note is that this king never allowed his Clumbers to retrieve; his Labradors were brought in for that chore. King George continued to enjoy hunting into advanced old age and this may have contributed to the myth that the Clumber is a slow, plodding worker good only for "old men on shooting sticks " (i.e., hunting seats which are planted in the ground, and on which they waited for the game to come to them!).

The modern Clumber is a big fellow yet is anything but slow. He is birdy, active and can still put in a good day's hunt. Of course, he will not work at the pace of some of his lighter boned cousins, but he is especially useful in heavy cover, for the slower walking hunter, or where game is plentiful. Despite King George's desire to show off his Labradors, the Clumber is a fine retriever as well.

In both England and the USA, the dog is still rare despite his long and noble history. Dedicated fanciers keep his quality high, however, and he has never been in danger of disappearing. Tails, docked to the spaniel one-third, are carried low, never to be pegged in the show ring like a Boxer.

COLLIES

Collie, Rough

COUNTRY: Great Britain
WEIGHT: 50–75 pounds
HEIGHT: 22–26 inches
COAT: Long, dense
COLOR: Sable and white, tricolor, blue merle, white
OTHER NAMES: Scotch Collie
REGISTRY: AKC, UKC, TKC, FCI
GROUP: Herding

Collie, Smooth

COUNTRY: Great Britain
WEIGHT: 50–75 pounds
HEIGHT: 22–26 inches
COAT: Short, smooth, double
COLOR: Sable and white, tricolor, blue merle, white
OTHER NAMES: Scotch Collie
REGISTRY: FCI, AKC, TKC, CKC
GROUP: Herding

Rough Collie, sable and white.

The dog most widely recognized as and usually called simply Collie evolved from the same root stock as the other Scottish herding dogs. The breed often is referred to as the Scotch Collie. It is believed they are the descendants of dogs accompanying Roman invaders of 50 BC interbred with native Scottish dogs. When Queen Victoria visited Scotland in 1860, she first glimpsed the working Collie and brought several back with her to England. The royal stamp of approval skyrocketed the breed to instant fame. Over the next few years the points so admired— the elongated, narrow, chiseled head and the rough coat—were emphasized by breeders, creating the look we know today.

The Collie soon became "the dog of the moment," which accelerated with the Lad stories by Albert Payson Terhune and the Lassie films and television series. During their peak, Collies were a common sight on many farms. The breed rode the crest of popularity, but eventually stabilized to the moderate universal appeal it knows today.

Its sweet expression and tipped ears are considered the stamp of the breed and a highly important consideration in show dogs. The Smooth variety is judged by the same standard as the Rough, with the exception of coat. Their colors are rich and striking, often set off by the Irish pattern of white markings. The rough coat needs regular brushing to maintain its striking good looks; the smooth offers easy grooming.

The Collie is a superb children's loyal companion, always willing to give and accept adoration and to play when human playmates are more fickle. Universally gentle and docile with his family, he is an equally good choice for adults. The first recipient (in 1954) of the Dog Hero award, honored by the Quaker Oats Company Ken-L Ration division, was a Collie, and the breed has continued to garner its share of Dog Heroes since that first year.

Collies are so adoring of their families that they will endure incredible hardships to be with them. One, named "Bobbie," journeyed 2,000 miles to find his people again after being lost on the family's vacation trip!

Smooth Collie, tricolor (*left*); Rough Collie, blue merle (*right*).

Above: Rough Collie, blue merle. **Below:** Rough Collie, tricolor.

Above: Smooth Collie, sable and white. **Below:** Rough Collie, sable and white.

Rough Collie, blue merle.

Rough Collie, tricolor.

CONTINENTAL TOY SPANIELS

Continental Toy Spaniel, Papillon

COUNTRY: France/Belgium
WEIGHT: In proportion to height
HEIGHT: 8–11 inches
COAT: Long, fine and silky, with plenty of fringe on chest, ears, tail and legs
COLOR: Basically white, with patches of any color except liver; color should cover both eyes and ears, leaving a symmetrical white blaze down the face
OTHER NAMES: Papillon, Épagneul Nain Continental Papillon
REGISTRY: FCI, AKC, UKC, TKC, CKC
GROUP: Gun Dog

Continental Toy Spaniel, Phalene

COUNTRY: France/Belgium
WEIGHT: In proportion to height
HEIGHT: 8–11 inches
COAT: Long, fine and silky, with plenty of fringe on chest, ears, tail and legs
COLOR: Basically white, with patches of any color except liver; color should cover both eyes and ears, leaving a symmetrical white blaze down the face
OTHER NAMES: Épagneul Nain Continental, Phalene
REGISTRY: FCI
GROUP: Gun Dog

Continental Toy Spaniel, Papillon

Continental Toy Spaniel, Phalene.

While the King Charles breed was developing in England, a slightly different toy spaniel was being created in continental Europe. He was more refined in bone, with a pointed head and tail curled over the back. Where he came from is conjecture, but miniature bichon dogs were highly esteemed in Europe at the time. Crossings of the more spaniellike miniatures with dogs of bichon type is a possibility. These little charmers created such a clamor that traders brought the dogs from one country to another on mule back and demanded high prices! One of these well-known dog merchants was a Bolognese, so the connection to the bichons cannot be ignored. Originally, all of the Continental "dwarf" spaniels had drooping ears, but later the erect-eared variety emerged.

The wealthy and noble of both Europe and England owned these Continental Toy Spaniels, and many a grand lady refused to have her portrait done unless her tiny dog was included. The breed was seen in paintings by many old masters, including Rubens, Van Dyke, Rembrandt, Fragonard, and others. Madame Pompadour had two Papillons, by name "Inez" and "Mimi." The English admired these little spaniels as well, and in the early days, crosses probably occurred between the English and Continental varieties.

By the time of organized kennel clubs in the late 1800s, the now well-known, prick-eared toy spaniel was universally known as the Papillon. This French word for butterfly aptly describes his large, upright ears which are set at the corners of his head. In fact, the dominant, erect ear became so widespread that many forgot the existence of the drop-eared variety. In the United States, the Papillon is a fairly well-known pet, and the standard describes the "correct" upright ear, but also allows for the drop-eared variety, called Phalene, or moth type. Thus, Americans have only the Papillon, allowing for two styles of ear carriages. In Europe, they also have one breed, but they call it Continental Toy Spaniel. This breed is divided into two varieties called Papillon (erect eared) and Phalene (drop eared). They are also affectionately called *Le Chien Ecureuil*, Squirrel Dog, in France, due to their lovely plumed tails.

Papillons are hardy dogs despite their small size. Their coat is beautiful and easy to care for. They know no enemy and are confident, outgoing, and friendly. Never wildly popular, there are numerous devoted adherents in Canada, America, England, throughout Europe and other countries around the world.

Continental Toy Spaniels, Phalene (*left*), Papillon (*right*).

Continental Toy Spaniel, Papillon.

Continental Toy Spaniel, Papillon.

Continental Toy Spaniel, Papillon.

COTON DE TULEAR

COUNTRY: Madagascar
WEIGHT: 12–15 pounds
HEIGHT: 10–12 inches
COAT: Long, cottony, no undercoat
COLOR: White, white with champagne head or body markings, black and white
REGISTRY: FCI
GROUP: Gun Dog

Bichon dogs from Tenerife were brought to Madagascar and nearby islands on trade ships, probably before the 17th century. From these original imports came the Coton de Reunion, an extinct breed once known on Reunion Island. The descendants of the Coton de Reunion became established near the city of Tulear, Madagascar, and developed into the breed known as the Coton de Tulear.

The Coton (French for cotton) became a favorite of the *merina*, the French nobility on the island during the colonial days. In fact, prior to the 20th century, it was considered criminal for a commoner to own a Coton. This canine social climber soon took on the title of the "Dog of Royalty" and, even today, only socially prominent Malagasy own a Tulear.

This breed is devoted to its masters, wanting always to be in their presence and trying its best to please. Because of these traits, the Coton requires little in the way of discipline to create a fine companion. He is a dog only for a house pet, as he is so happy and friendly that he will not defend himself. Like the other bichon dogs, however, he is alert and intelligent and will inform his master of unusual events. As long as he is primarily a house dog, he adapts well to almost any environment or climate. The breed is healthy and vigorous despite its small size, and requires only a bit of regular brushing to keep it handsome. One of their most endearing traits is a tendency to jump and walk on their hind legs.

Like the other bichons, the hair needs regular grooming to keep the dogs looking their cuddly best. Shedding on all the bichons is minimal and an advantage to allergic owners. The Coton's expression is "enquiring and adoring."

They achieved FCI recognition in 1970 and are being fostered by the Coton de Tulear Club of America. They are still rare throughout the world.

Coton de Tulear, white/champagne.

Croatian Sheepdog.

CROATIAN SHEEPDOG

COUNTRY: Yugoslavia
WEIGHT: 31–44 pounds
HEIGHT: 16–20 inches
COAT: 3–6 inches, soft, dense and wavy, except on the head and front of legs
COLOR: All black, small areas of white markings acceptable
OTHER NAMES: Hrvaški Ŏvcar
REGISTRY: FCI
GROUP: Herding

The Croatian is watchful and pugnacious, although amenable to training. It is only seen as a dog working with flocks and only in Yugoslavia. This is part of the common triumvirate of herding dog, flock guard and shepherd seen in so many European countries. In Yugoslavia, if he needs help protecting the sheep, the Karst Shepherd or Sarplaninac is there to lend a paw. He is still commonly seen among the flocks today.

His prick ears are set on at the corners of his head. If he is born with a tail, it is curled over his back in the style of the Puli, who is probably a close relative. Often the tail is docked. The coat is moderate in length, harsh and wavy, but smooth on the face and fronts of the legs. The body proportions are high on leg and square.

313

Curly-Coated Retriever, black.

breed historians state there were later introductions of Poodle to tighten the coat curl. The Curly-Coated Retriever became a popular hunting dog in Britain in the latter part of the 19th century. He was exported to Australia and New Zealand, where he has remained in demand as a working dog for quail hunting, as well as water birds. These two countries now claim more registrations of the breed than its native land does.

He is in his element in the water, but can retrieve handily on land as well. Owners say he is a natural retriever and easy to train, with a robust constitution and a sweet temperament. But he tends to be sober, independent and wary of strangers, and can be quarrelsome with his fellows in the field. The wonderfully short, waterproof and self-drying coat is a big plus for the sports enthusiast. The Curly-Coated Retriever is fearless, and often doubles as an excellent guardian for his family.

He is a big fellow, built square and up on leg. His tail is left at natural length, and tends to be rather short like a pointer's. There is no trimming required of his curly coat. The coat has no topknot or fringe on the ears, nor is there excess hair on the legs. The proper haircoat outlines the entire body with ringlets all over, like a flapper with a new perm and a tight cap of curls.

Curly-Coated Retriever.

CURLY-COATED RETRIEVER

COUNTRY: Great Britain
WEIGHT: 70–80 pounds
HEIGHT: 25–27 inches
COAT: Small, close, crisp curls all over, face smooth
COLOR: Solid black or solid liver
REGISTRY: FCI, AKC, UKC, TKC, CKC
GROUP: Gun Dog

The Curly is a fairly old breed, if not well-known. He began in the early 1800s from crosses of early British water spaniels with various retrievers or possibly even pointers. Some

CZESKY TERRIER

Country: Czechoslovakia
Weight: 13–20 pounds
Height: 10½–14 inches
Coat: Long, fine and silky, with a tendency to wave
Color: Blue-gray (born black) or light coffee brown (born chocolate)
Other names: Bohemian Terrier
Registry: FCI
Group: Terrier

This handsome terrier is a modern development created by a Czechoslovakian breeder, Dr. Frantisek Horak. The Czesky is a superb ratter and alarm dog that will go to ground.

Dr. Horak was a knowledgeable geneticist and breeder of Scottish and Sealyham Terriers. He was also a sportsman and expected his terriers not only to win shows but to win trophies in the field. Horak crossbred his terriers, starting in 1949, and attained several positive qualities: the gameness and size to go to ground, and all the physical and mental attributes to participate in the hunt. He also attained a dog of style and beauty, accomplishing his purpose within just four breedings and in less than a decade! The first representative of the breed was Javor Lovu Zdar, who drew great attention in the dog world with his silvery blue jacket.

The breed has very slowly gained some

Czesky Terrier, light coffee.

Czesky Terrier, blue-gray.

ground, first in its homeland and now in a few other European countries. FCI recognized the Czesky in 1963, but the breed has been off and on in danger of disappearing.

Although Horak supposedly used only Scotties and Sealyhams, this combination creates many question marks. The Czesky has several traits that are quite uncommon in the majority of terriers. These distinctions include the low carried tail, extreme ratio of length to height, long silky coat, chocolate color, and the fading gene that lightens black to gray and brown to coffee. Both Scottish Terriers and Sealyhams have high-set, gaily carried tails, harsh and wiry broken coats, shortish legs without long bodies, and no hint of the chocolate color or fading factor. The Dandie Dinmont, however, carries most of these traits: the chocolate gene, silky coat, low tail and long, low body. Whether Dr. Horak was able to find these recessives in purely Scottie/Sealyham breeding stock or actually used some other crosses is an unknown.

An easygoing, obedient nature is typical, and he is a fine house dog and children's companion, residing in peace with other domestic animals. The long tail is carried rather low, and the ears fall forward in a semi-drop.

The Czesky has a lovely sheen to its coat, which is clipped on the upper body. A full underline and front is left, along with a profuse beard and eyebrows.

DACHSHUNDS

Dachshund, Miniature

COUNTRY: Germany
WEIGHT: Less than 9 pounds
COAT: Smooth, wire (like a German Wirehair), or long hair (like a setter)
COLOR: One color (includes reds or yellows, can have black tips or overlay); two-color (includes black/tan, chocolate/tan, gray/tan, or white/yellow); or dappled or striped, (includes merle, harlequin and brindle)
OTHER NAMES: Zwergteckel
REGISTRY: FCI, AKC, UKC, TKC, CKC
GROUP: Hound

Dachshund, Standard

COUNTRY: Germany
WEIGHT: 15–25 pounds
COAT: Smooth, wire (like a German Wirehair), or long hair (like a setter)
COLOR: One color (includes reds or yellows, can have black tips or overlay); two-color (includes black/tan, chocolate/tan, gray/tan, or white/yellow); or dappled or striped, (includes merle harlequin and brindle)
OTHER NAMES: Normalgrosse Teckel
REGISTRY: FCI, AKC, UKC, TKC, CKC
GROUP: Hound

While the French were developing their basset varieties for slower, closer hunting, the Germans created the Dachshunds. Short-statured hunting dogs have assisted Germans since the Middle Ages.

Their origin, like those of the bassets, is thought to be from dwarf mutations of the tall hounds. The Dachshund is basically a short-legged version of the schweisshund, although crosses may have been made to various terriers and/or spaniels to obtain the wire and long coats. The Dachsie is a true hound of German type, without exaggerated skin. He carries the ram's muzzle with very slight stop and the large high-set flat ear. *Dachs* means badger, another animal with a sturdy body on short, crooked legs. Therefore, the Dachsbracke is a bracke with short legs "like the badger," and the Dachshund is a tracking hound with similar appendages. Germans usually call the Dachshund a *Teckel*.

Dachshunds have been employed for many hunting chores: chasing rabbits, searching for various game and tracking. They are also small (and brave) enough to go into the lair to bolt hidden prey. To enable them to fill every hunting need, the breed was molded into a number of sizes and coat varieties as well as in a panorama of colors. The Standard, or largest size, was primarily a tracker, although he had ability

Dachshunds, smooth, wire, and long.

Smooth Dachshund.

Longhaired Dachshund puppy.

for searching as well. Smaller varieties were useful in searching, rabbit hunting and going to ground to chase out the quarry. The smallest ones were developed specifically to go into the rabbit warrens and put the inhabitants to flight.

During WWI, the breed was disparaged as was everything German, but he survived the prejudice. He is admired in Australia, the USA and many other countries around the world. The Smooth is a favorite hound in Great Britain, and in the States, Dachshunds cling firmly to their popularity.

In Germany, Dachshund sizes are separated not by weight, as in America, but by chest circumference—the division of classes based on what size hole they could enter! AKC recognizes two sizes, with the Miniature required to be nine pounds or under. FCI and Germany have the same Standard dog (called *Normalgrosse*), but describe two smaller versions. Their *Zwergteckel* (dwarf Dachshund) must not be more than 13.8 inches around the chest, and the little *Kaninchenteckel* (rabbit Dachshund) should not exceed 11.8 inches. All sizes appear in either a short, smooth; short, wiry; or a long, fringed coat. Colors commonly are according to the usual hound tones of black/tan, red or brindle, but more infrequent patterns of merle, blue/tan or gray with yellow markings are also allowed.

White markings are undesirable.

While most of the German hounds are not known outside their native land, the Dachshund has become widely popular throughout the world, fundamentally as a pet dog. In fact, in Gergweis, Germany, the "Dachshund Capital of the World," these little dogs outnumber people two to one. Here Dachsies are rented "by the hour" to tourists for walks. Affectionate and chipper, he is a fine companion and soul mate. Wary enough to be a watchdog, his devotion to his own family, especially to the children, is undying.

His novel shape lends itself to various nicknames: Weiner Dog, Sausage Dog or the Americanized "Hot Dog"! The length of body tends toward back problems, and owners should be careful about their dog's weight, which may intensify or contribute to this ailment.

His desire to hunt is still strong, and he well may excavate your petunia bed to reach a garter snake or gopher. He may even proudly present you with the rat he has killed in the backyard. But his energy and ability to have fun make up for any minor annoyances. All of this talent is bundled into a package with a selection of colors, coats and sizes, giving a prospective owner nearly unlimited choices!

Longhaired Dachshund.

Wire Dachshund.

Longhaired Dachshund.

Above: Longhaired Dachshunds, red. **Below:** Longhaired Dachshunds, dappled.

Above: Wire Dachshunds. **Below:** Dachshund with fallen deer, a large and unusual quarry for these dogs.

DALMATIAN

COUNTRY: Yugoslavia
WEIGHT: 50–55 pounds
HEIGHT: 19–23 inches, over 24 inches disqualifies
COAT: Short, hard, dense and glossy
COLOR: Pure white base, with round, distinct and well-defined spots of either black or liver evenly distributed all over the body
REGISTRY: FCI, AKC, UKC, TKC, CKC
GROUP: Gun Dog

This breed is so unique that it is hard to categorize. Dalmatian history is long and full of legends. His body type mimics both the pointers and the tight-skinned, small-eared hounds of eastern Europe. Since these types developed from one another, it may be a moot point. Since the breed is not used for either scent work or hunting with a gun, it is doubly hard to know his familial tree. Some histories show him used as a gun dog, a trail hound, a shepherd and guardian, a draft dog and even a ratter! Legend has him coming from northern India long ago, being brought to eastern Europe with bands of gypsies. Since some very early records of the breed are found in Dalmatia, from whence comes his name, the FCI lists him as a product of Yugoslavia.

Whatever his origin, the spotted dog that works with horses has been known in Europe since the Middle Ages. With his introduction into Britain, the aristocracy there found the perfect accent for their ornate carriages, liveried drivers and matched high-stepping horses. At first the Dal trotted alongside carriages on long treks to protect the travelers from highwaymen, but eventually the breed became more of an ornament for the wealthy. The Dalmatian dogs went ahead to "clear the way" in the streets or trotted decoratively under the front or rear axles. Popular also in the stables and liveries of the average man, they became known especially for their presence in the fire stations with horse-drawn water wagons. The sight of Dals running through the streets of London clearing the way for the firemen galloping to the scene of a fire gave the breed its nickname of "Firehouse Dog."

From his days in the carriage houses and fire stations of old England, he has made the transition to the modern mascot. A picture of an American firetruck and firefighter without the faithful spotted Dalmatian on the front seat just isn't complete. The breed remains friendly with horses, and he still carries out his task of accompanying horse-drawn equipage. Field events for modern fanciers test the abilities of the Dal to perform these duties. Although he enjoyed a steady, if moderate, popularity, the 1956 book *101 Dalmatians*, published in Britain and later made into a Walt Disney movie, thrust fame upon him!

The Dalmatian is a clean, quiet, discerning pet. He makes a fine watchdog, almost never barking unless there is evidence of something amiss. "Gentlemanly reserve" describes his character, for he has a highly tuned sense of who his master is. Despite good manners, he has a tough inner core and is not afraid to defend his own if pushed.

The breed's simple lines and lack of any need for clipping, grooming or docking appeals to many people. His repute has spread worldwide and he is found in homes, show rings and "on the job" in many countries.

Dalmatian puppies are born pure white, with the spots beginning to fill in during the first few weeks. This is one of the proofs that scientists have used to decide that the Dals' spots are genetically a form of large ticking. Just as the ticking on an Australian Cattle Dog or a German Shorthair doesn't show up until a few weeks or more after birth, such is the nature of the Dalmatian's adornment. Because of the white factor, a certain small percentage of Dalmatian puppies are born permanently deaf.

The Dal is a breed of almost incredible endurance, able to travel at a moderate pace almost indefinitely. Thus their need for exercise is more than casual, and prospective owners should keep that in mind.

Dalmatians.

Dalmatian.

Dalmatian.

DANDIE DINMONT TERRIER

COUNTRY: Great Britain
WEIGHT: 18–24 pounds
HEIGHT: 8–11 inches
COAT: Crisp mixture of hard and soft hair about 2" long
COLOR: Pepper (shades of blue black to light silvery gray) and mustard (reddish brown to pale fawn)
REGISTRY: FCI, AKC, TKC, CKC
GROUP: Terrier

Stemming from the same stock as the Border, Lakeland, Bedlington and Welsh, and from the north where England becomes Scotland, trotted the short-legged Dandie Dinmont. His coat's crisp mixture of hard and soft hair in the blue and liver shades, as well as the long drop ear, puts him very close to the Bedlington in ancestry. Yet crosses involving various hounds and running dogs are suggested because of his distinctive physical traits: the short, crooked legs, the arched loin, and the rounded head and large eye. The standard asks for a body that is one or two inches less in length than twice the height, making him long and not very tall.

This variety was developed as far back as the 1600s as a specialist for otter and badger in the Cheviot Hills and near Coquetdale. Most of these dogs were kept by a few families in the area, like the Allans. Willie "Piper" Allan, who died in 1704, kept an outstanding pack and refused to sell any despite handsome offers. His sons and grandsons continued the tradition, occasionally giving a pair to a friend or for favors. A tenant farmer, John Davidson, obtained a pair and bred them.

With these and similar breedings, the otter terriers were sprinkled sparingly throughout the area, without specific title or pedigree, when Sir Walter Scott chanced upon them in his travels. He immortalized them in his novel *Guy Mannering* (1814), in which one of the characters, a farmer named Dandie Dinmont (modeled after Davidson), kept this breed. Scott describes the attitude of Dinmont's famous six, "Auld Pepper," "Auld Mustard," "Young Pepper," "Young Mustard," "Little Pepper," and "Little Mustard," thus: "they fear naething that ever cam' wi' a hairy skin on't." From then on, the breed came to be known as Dandie Dinmont's Terrier. King Louis Phillipe of France owned a pair of Dandies in the 1840s.

The Dandie has the same intelligent character and guarding ability that make most terriers good companions. The Dandie does tend to be willful, however. His coat doesn't require a great amount of care, but does need combing out and an occasional plucking, especially to accentuate his distinctive soft, silky topknot.

A happy, loving family dog, the Dandie is indifferent to strangers. His serene disposition belies the dormant ratting instinct.

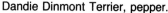
Dandie Dinmont Terrier, pepper.

DANISH BROHOLMER

COUNTRY: Denmark
HEIGHT: 27½–29½ inches
COAT: Short, harsh
COLOR: Light or brownish yellow, black; white marking on chest, feet and tail tip allowed
REGISTRY: FCI
GROUP: Mastiff

In the past, Broholmers attracted attention from royalty and from artists, and are portrayed in paintings of the Danish Renaissance kings, Frederik II and Christian IV. Mastiffs sent by the English to Danish courts were bred with local canines, probably of the early Great Dane type, producing the Broholmer. These dogs assisted in driving cattle to market and were often called *slagterhunden*, the butchers' dogs.

King Frederik VII and his consort, Countess Danner, owned several Broholmers. A painting of the couple completed around 1859 shows a favorite, "Tyrk," lying at their feet; Tyrk was immortalized at his death by being "stuffed" and donated to the Copenhagen Zoological Museum. About the same time, an archeologist, Count Niels Frederik Sehested of Broholm-Funen, began collecting and organizing the breed. This major source gave the breed its modern name. The Count presented numerous puppies to others who promised to support the breed and spent decades standardizing the Broholmer. For a time, the breed enjoyed the friendship of no-

Danish Broholmers, adult and pup.

bility, famed authors and commoners alike. Between the two World Wars, large dogs and their expensive feeding habits went out of fashion. Many thought this Danish dog just an antique.

Cynologist Jytte Weiss, however, stirred interest in restoring the native breed to its former status. In 1974, revival of the breed began with the Committee for National and Forgotten Breeds. The committee, appointed by the Danish Kennel Club, unearthed two quality Broholmers which matched the 1886 standard. Encouraged, committee members Weiss and Ole Staunskjar scoured the country for more, supported in their search by the press, veterinarians and dog lovers. Black variants were found in northern Seeland in the hands of peasants, farmers, lumberjacks and rangers. One of these blacks, named "Manne," became the cornerstone of the modern Broholmer.

The numbers are still not legion, but the Broholmer is gaining strength despite a narrow breed base. Breedings are still approved only through the committee. In 1982, FCI approved the standard and the breed can be exhibited in international shows.

In build, they are more elegant and not as massive as the English Mastiff, although they remain large and impressive. They have a massive, broad head, carried rather low when not alert. The chest is wide and rippling with muscles. The committee encourages the breeding of only steadfast, good-tempered dogs. These powerful dogs are naturally alert and make good watchdogs.

Danish Broholmer, red.

DEUTSCHE BRACKE

COUNTRY: Germany
HEIGHT: 16–21 inches
COAT: Short, smooth, hard and dense
COLOR: Tricolor; tan with black saddle; white limited to blaze, neck ring, chest and belly, feet, and tail tip
OTHER NAMES: German Hound, Deutsche Sauerlandbracke
REGISTRY: FCI
GROUP: Hound

Most German hounds are sturdily boned and a bit low-stationed, with the large but stiff-cartilaged ear that lies flat and wide instead of folding. They tend also to have the "ram's nose" profile with little stop.

The Deutsche Bracke evolved from generic all-purpose, hot-trailing Celtic hounds of varying type used for German forest work. Some earlier types were the Westphalian Bracke and the Sauerlander Holzbracke. These brackes were mainly promoted in the Sauerland and all of Westphalia, which are located in western Germany. For a while, there was some attempt to support the Steinbracke (or in Holland *Steenbrack*), a slightly smaller version of the bracke.

Stein, meaning stone, was an old German weight designation, one stone being about 22 pounds.

All of these fragmented varieties were finally gathered under one breed title, and the Deutsche Bracke is the only official Bracke now recognized in Germany. A club has fostered the type since 1896, although a written standard was not drawn up by the Deutsche Bracken Club until 1955.

In Germany, the Bracke is a dog promoted in the hills and low mountains for hare, fox, rabbit and boar. He is best on the hot scent, giving tongue with his melodious, bell-like voice. His long legs allow him to work quickly and cover a lot of territory.

A superb nose makes him capable of schweisshund work as well, working cold trails of wounded animals. This ability is required more and more, and at this he works silently. Old-time bracken hunters often feared that the use of a dog to trail the wounded deer would make him want to chase healthy ones. This has been proven to be untrue. With quality training methods, the Bracke quickly understands the difference between the hot track and the cold bloodtrail. Modern breeders say that it takes a good deal of patience to teach him to retrieve, but once he is trained, he is reliable.

Deutsche Bracke.

DEUTSCHER WACHTELHUND

COUNTRY: Germany
WEIGHT: 44–66 pounds
HEIGHT: 16–20 inches
COAT: Thick, longish; wavy enough that there is no fringe, smooth on head
OTHER NAMES: German Spaniel
REGISTRY: FCI
GROUP: Gun Dog

This spaniel was created from various breeds in the early 1900s. The "recipe" has been kept a secret, although the Wachtelhund undoubtedly owes much of his ancestry to the ancient European water dogs, as well as to other hunting breeds.

Not only is the Wachtelhund a fine retriever in wet or marshy areas, but he is also used for hare and fox, exhibiting the hound trait of giving tongue on the trail. Aggressive enough to face a fox or even a wolf, the German Spaniel naturally goes for the throat of his furred prey. As a flushing dog, he is useful in finding feath-

Deutscher Wachtelhund.

Deutscher Wachtelhund, brown.

ered game. His sensitive nose enables him to bloodtrail wounded game, such as deer or boar, in the forest.

He is particularly skilled in dense underbrush and areas with standing water. While obedient and affectionate with his master, he has *jagdpassion*, an intense desire to hunt. He is a choice dog for the professional hunter, such as the German forester. A sturdy fellow, a bit low on leg, his tail is docked by a small amount and is always carried low. Germans say he "should only be in sportsmen's hands."

Dingo, light fawn.

DINGO

COUNTRY: Australia
HEIGHT: 19–22 inches
COAT: Short, harsh, double
COLOR: Red to light fawn generally; other colors, such as white spotted or black/tan, exist
OTHER NAMES: Warrigal, Australian Native Dog
REGISTRY: None
GROUP: Southern

First skeletal evidence of the Dingo in Australia was dated about 3,000 years ago, indicating its progenitor probably trudged across the land bridge about the same time as the aborigine. The dogs and people made their trek before Australia was cut off from the mainland to be surrounded by water. The Dingo was first officially noted by Captain William Damphier, who wrote of the wild dog in 1699.

A direct descendant of the original pariahs from the Middle East and southeastern Asia, the

Dingo became feral and returned to the wild. There these canines have remained to the present as one of the only mammals native to Australia. Aborigines adopted pups into their tribes from time to time and raised them as pets and assistants in the hunt. Dogs occasionally interbred with the Dingoes, and the wild dog actually contributed to at least one modern breed: the Australian Cattle Dog.

Today interbreeding domestic dogs with the Dingo is frowned upon. The Australian Native Dog never stood in good favor, since so much of Australian economy is dependent on cattle and sheep production. The Dingo has received much bad press as a livestock killer and is classified as vermin in his homeland, to be killed (eliminated).

But a few people are now concerned with the native dog as a "living fossil" and are working toward studying and preserving him. The Australian Native Dog Training Society, based in New South Wales, has raised and trained many Dingoes. Their members put them on display and hold obedience and trick demonstrations, and the society's motto is: "A Fair Go for our Dingo." These dogs redomesticate quite easily if raised from a young age by a family, but retain the pariah traits of flight and wariness. Early and continued socialization is a must to overcome their shy and sensitive nature. Obedience training is best accomplished by kindness, patience, and a firm but gentle hand. The Dingo chooses a mate for life, sometimes mourning itself to death after the loss of its partner. Females whelp one litter a year in the spring, similar to many of the pariahs. Often a litter is found in the hollow of a tree, totally protected from all sides, with the dams guarding the front. Even so, whelps frequently fall prey to snakes.

Dingoes have strong cooperative instincts and live in small packs. These groups habitually hunt by night. They work silently and only learn to bark from association with other canines, but they do have a wide range of vocalizations, from high yodels to low crows and howls. To survive in the wilderness, they have learned to play possum, shamming death. These dogs' hardiness and resistance to heat have helped them exist in a land that does little to succor their survival. The Dingo has managed to exist without human intervention—and in spite of human dislike.

Dingo, red.

333

Doberman Pinscher, red.

DOBERMAN PINSCHER

COUNTRY: Germany
WEIGHT: 66–88 pounds
HEIGHT: 24–28 inches
COAT: Smooth, short
COLOR: Solid ground color (black, red, blue, or fawn), all with tan markings.
OTHER NAMES: Thuringer Pinscher, Plizeilich Soldatenhund, Dobermann
REGISTRY: FCI, AKC, UKC, TKC, CKC
GROUP: Mastiff

Herr Louis Dobermann was a tax collector cum dog-pound keeper who had to travel through dangerous areas. He needed assistants tough enough to protect him from bandits and to con-vince reluctant tax payers to cough up. He performed his duties with "a grave digger and a bellringer"—and a few basic established breeds. In the late 1860s, he determined to create his own personal guardian, a dog that would look much like a large Miniature Pinscher.

Breed type was fixed in an amazingly short period of time. Dobermann utilized the old German Shepherd type for hardiness, intelligence and soundness, with German Pinscher blood for quick reaction and terrier fire. The Weimar Pointer donated hunting abilities and fine nose, as well as the dilute colors. Added to the strength, guarding instinct and courage of the Rottweiler, the breed needed only the English Greyhound for speed and the Manchester Terrier to give it a short, sleek coat. Dilution factors which produce the reds, blues, and fawns, despite their uncommon appearance, have been present in the general mastiff gene pool since the beginning.

In the early years of the breed, they were extremely sharp, willing to attack "even the devil himself." An early owner, Gottfried Liechti, recorded ". . . it required a good deal of courage to own one." In fact the breed's reputation preceded it to America. One early import won three Best in Shows before any judge had the courage to examine his mouth—only to find several missing teeth, a serious fault in the breed!

Some longhaired and natural bobtail pups were born in the early years. The bobtails were much admired, resulting in the current docking fashion. Earcropping in the long, stylish Ameri-

Doberman Pinscher, cropped ears.

Doberman Pinschers, black.

can show cut or the wider, shorter pet cut aided the ears to stand. Dewclaws were removed, completing the racy appearance.

After Dobermann's death, Otto Goeller continued promotion of the breed and is credited with improvement. Goeller's kennels produced the first notable stud dog, Hellegraf von Thueringen.

The breed began infiltrating American coastlines around the time of WWI. Many Dobermans left in Germany were drafted; others were euthanized, due to the scarcity of food. After the war, the breed's population once again began to rise in its homeland.

The Bulldog may be the official mascot of the US Marine Corps, but the Doberman has the distinction of being named the Marine War Dog. The breed is loyal to its master and will do almost anything requested of it, from exciting drill team performances to schutzhund training. Dobermans have representatives in search-and-rescue, patrol or police dogs and as dog guides for the blind.

One of the breeds that strikes fear in the heart of many, the Dobe's reputation is generally un-earned. It is a natural, loyal guard, but the breed has been mellowed to allow the approach of strangers. Socialization and authoritative discipline are recommended, along with a heritage of sound temperament. The Doberman of today is a handsome, light-footed aristocrat which prefers being with its owners to all other things. Owners suspect they must be part goat in their eating habits, swallowing anything in their path.

Above Right: Doberman Pinscher, red. **Below Right:** Doberman Pinscher, uncropped ears. **Below:** Doberman Pinscher, black.

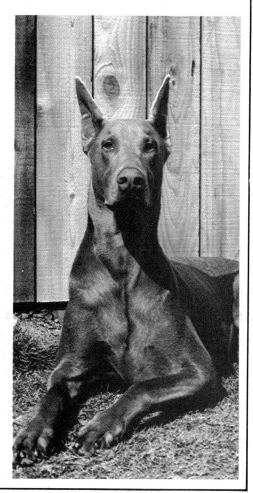

Above: Doberman Pinscher. **Below:** Doberman Pinscher, red.

Above: Doberman Pinscher puppies, four colors. **Below:** Doberman Pinscher, white (*unacceptable color mutation*).

Doberman Pinscher

Doberman Pinscher

Dogo Argentino.

DOGO ARGENTINO

COUNTRY: Argentina
WEIGHT: 80–100 pounds
HEIGHT: 24-27 inches
COAT: Short, thick and smooth
COLOR: White
OTHER NAMES: Argentinian Mastiff
REGISTRY: FCI
GROUP: Mastiff

Distinguished as the only dog developed in Argentina, the Dogo Argentino was created in the 1920s, through the strategem of Dr. Antonio Nores Martinez. A dog lover and avid hunter, Martinez sought a tough guardian: a hunter who was a worthy opponent for wild boar, puma and jaguar. Nevertheless, he also desired a trustworthy family dog. Dr. Martinez believed, "A dog which attacks an intruder and then, at the first threat of injury, abandons its prisoner is worth nothing as a guardian."

The Old Fighting Dog of Cordoba, Spain, was the root stock of the recipe for the Dogo. The general type of the Cordoba was large, white and ferocious, with tremendous variation in appearance. These dogs were only interested in one thing—fighting; they were said to be so vicious, a male would attack bitches during the mating ritual! The Cordoba stemmed from Spanish Mastiff, Bull Terrier, old Bulldog of England and early Boxer.

The Cordoba's original mixture started the recipe for Martinez's "Super Dog" with plenty of spice and hot pepper. The Spanish Mastiff donated power, with the Bulldog contributing chest capacity, stoicism and tenacity. The Boxer's influence gave quiet confidence and trainability. Martinez blended the Cordoba

Dogs with the harlequin Great Dane for height and the Great Pyrenees to maintain the bulk and color. The Pyrenees also introduced hardiness in extreme weather. To heighten the hunting instinct, the English Pointer brought his fine nose and air-scenting ability, and the Irish Wolfhound added a dash of speed. Later crosses to the Dogue de Bordeaux intensified courage, along with body and jaw strength.

Over the next three decades, Martinez demonstrated the Dogo's versatility through its use as a sled dog and dog guide for the blind, as well as a great hunter and guardian. When Antonio Martinez died in 1956, his brother, Agustin, continued promoting and preserving the breed. His post as Ambassador enabled him to introduce the Dogo to other countries and to present these dogs as gifts to those in high positions.

Despite setbacks during political upheavals, the Dogo has achieved the recognition of the Argentina Kennel Club. The breed still hunts big game and guards homes. Argentinian hunts are held in strict silence—by both dogs and hunters. Dogos hunt in packs, ready to attack the tough big game. They are true dogs of heart, showing no hesitancy. The hunters value these dogs, caring for them first after a hunt, as a rider does for a horse.

The breed is well known throughout Europe, especially Germany, and was granted recognition by FCI in 1960. There is an active club in the United States where Dogo owners are encouraging their use as home protector, family dog, and in police or guide work.

The Dogo is loving to children and is a tireless playmate. The breed's stamina and longevity are remarkable, with some dogs still hunting at 16 years of age. In a home situation, if Dogos can't hunt pumas, they'll settle for mice. Their scenting ability was demonstrated by the bitch who picked her own pups out of the wet nurse's litter following her hospitalization. Extremely loyal, they are excellent guard dogs, requiring dominant masters.

Dogo Argentino.

DOGUE DE BORDEAUX

COUNTRY: France
WEIGHT: 80–100 pounds, minimum
HEIGHT: 23–27 inches
COAT: Short, smooth
COLOR: One color—dark auburn or fawn, white on chest allowed
OTHER NAMES: French Mastiff
REGISTRY: FCI
GROUP: Mastiff

The Dogue de Bordeaux is similar to the Bullmastiff in size and type, yet is centuries older, being more closely related to the mastiff from Asia and the molossus that made the trek to Gaul from the Roman arenas. At one time, there were two varieties, the Doguin being the smaller version, which has since vanished into nothing but a sentence in reference books. Dogues have had wide and varied employment since their entrance into France after the fall of Rome. Originally, they served a dual purpose as war dogs and by guarding flocks from wolves and bears.

This was followed by the "glory" of combat with bears and bulls. After humane statutes outlawed the torture of the larger beasts, battles of Dogue against Dogue took the place of dog against bull. Spectators felt the French dog fights rivaled the bullfights in Spain for entertainment purposes. Occasionally, a dull match was sparked by tossing a jaguar in the pit.

This lack of concern for dogs and, in particular, for the Dogue de Bordeaux was written in the 1300s by Gaston Phoebus: ". . . with their thick heads, thick lips, and large ears, they are well suited to hunting bear and pigs because they are stubborn. But they are heavy and ugly and, if a wild boar were to kill them, it would be no great loss."

Following this era, near the end of the Middle Ages, the gladiator turned to cattle droving—not as "glorious" perhaps, but much safer. The breed served as personal protection when fighting was outlawed and the need for cattle drovers declined. His majestic presence decorated many estates. The French Revolution ended that occu-

Dogue de Bordeaux, auburn.

pation, with many of the noble guards giving their lives to protect their masters and property. Fortunately, enough survived to attract the attention of current French cynologists, and the Dogue is now found throughout France, with specimens also in Belgium, Germany, Switzerland, Japan, Africa and the States.

Professor Raymond Triquet headed the rebuilding of the breed during the mid-1960s and stressed that the dogs should be "superb athletes." The massive head is their trademark, with the jaw undershot and the muzzle masked in either black or red.

"Beauty is only skin deep" and despite the dogs' menacing appearance, they are sweet with their masters and children. They will, however, be aggressive with other dogs. The French expression *humeur de dogue* still refers to a person showing a bad temper.

Right: Head study of the Dogue de Bordeaux shows the tremendous size of the breed's skull compared to this youngster. **Below:** Body study of the Dogue de Bordeaux.

DRENTSE PATRIJSHOND

COUNTRY: Netherlands
WEIGHT: 50 pounds
HEIGHT: 22–25 inches
COAT: Thick and straight, with abundant feathering on legs, feet, tail and ears
COLOR: White with brown, orange, or, occasionally, brown/tan patches; with or without ticking or roaning
REGISTRY: FCI
GROUP: Gun Dog

Originating in the province of Drente, the source of his name, the Patrijshond appears in paintings done several centuries ago. He probably was created soon after the first use of firearms. His history is of the same pool of hawking or setting dogs, from which all of the setters and spaniels descended. Always a favorite dog for the weekend hunter in the Netherlands, there are about 6,000 of the breed, almost all in its native country.

He is a pointing dog and a fine retriever, as well as a quiet and well-mannered companion. Hunters also find him good for water work. His most admired quality is that he naturally hunts "under the gun."

Although searching thoroughly, he stays close to the hunter, never straying beyond gun range, and frequently looks to his master for direction. Partridge and quail are not so numerous as they once were in the Netherlands, but the dogs do not have to worry about unemployment—they have adapted well to hunting the still plentiful rabbit and pheasant. Due to his fine nature, he has gained some demand as a companion dog and house pet.

The name is often shortened to Drent (plural Drenten), which is also what people from this province are called. In body type, he is a heavier built dog than the Small Münsterländer, and perhaps most resembles the German Longhair, with a smaller and more refined head. His tail is left long in the style of the setter and, when on scent, is swung around circularly. Due to his gentle, obedient and meek nature, harsh training is unnecessary and, in fact, is counterproductive. The breed base is small, and there is nowhere to go for new blood, so the breed association is actively advising breeders and testing dogs in form and function to ensure all breeding stock is sound.

Drentse Patrijshond, white with brown.

Drever.

DREVER

COUNTRY: Sweden
WEIGHT: 33 pounds
HEIGHT: 11½–15 Sweden; 12–16 inches Canada
COAT: Short, dense and hard
COLOR: Fawn, black, or black/tan; always with the white markings on face, feet, neck, chest and tail tip. Canada allows all colors
OTHER NAMES: Swedish Dachsbracke
REGISTRY: FCI, CKC
GROUP: Hound

Early in the 20th century, Westphalian Dachsbrackes were imported from Germany into Denmark and Sweden. They were appreciated for their hunting abilities. In Denmark, they were mated with Swiss hounds to create a Danish dachsbracke. When these Danish dogs were brought to Sweden, they were backcrossed again to Westphalian Dachsbrackes. This last cross created the breed known as the Drever.

Drev means to hunt in Swedish, and hunting was what the Drever did best. Officially named in 1947, the Swedish KC gave him the nod in 1949. Since then, the Drever has become one of the most popular breeds in his homeland.

He was also introduced to Canada, where he was officially recognized in 1956. But this breed is never seen in a show ring in either country. A slow, steady worker, he hunts hare, fox, and occasionally deer; but this dog has the courage to pit himself against even a wild boar. In such cases, he circles and dodges the prey, warning the hunter by barking furiously. The Drever has an excellent nose and his musical voice is "much larger than his size would seem to warrant."

White markings may appear on his face, neck, chest, feet and tail tip. His legs are straight, never bent like the Dachshund. The ever-wagging tail with its slight brush shows his affable, even temperament.

Dunker, black/tan saddled.

DUNKER

COUNTRY: Norway
WEIGHT: 35–49 pounds
HEIGHT: 18½–21½ inches; some well-built males may go to 22½ inches
COAT: Short, thick and straight
COLOR: Tan with large black saddle and small, symmetrical white markings; or the same color with the black being a splotched, marbled color by action of the harlequin (merle) gene
OTHER NAMES: Norwegian Hound
REGISTRY: FCI
GROUP: Hound

The Dunker was created in the 1820s, supposedly from indigenous dogs and Russian hounds. Although not heavy, he is a powerfully built hound designed for endurance. His name came from the man who originally created him. Today, the Dunker is probably the most numerous scenthound used in Norway and many good specimens can be found there, although he has found no following elsewhere.

The term harlequin refers to the marbled blue color pattern created by the merle gene. This is one of the few hounds carrying this color, along with the dappled Dachshund of Germany, the Irish Kerry Beagle and America's Mountain Cur. Glass (blue) eyes are allowed in the harlequin specimens. Breeding two harlequins is not recommended, as it produces dogs with a preponderance of white and sometimes defects of vision and hearing.

This hound is a robust, noble dog with clean lines and flat, smooth-lying ears. Depth of chest should equal one-half the height at the shoulders, giving plenty of lung power for endurance. Although the coat is described as short, it gives plenty of protection for northern winters. Thus a bit of brush on the tail and the back of the thighs is evidenced.

DUTCH SHEPHERDS

Longhaired Dutch Shepherd

COUNTRY: Netherlands
WEIGHT: 66 pounds
HEIGHT: 23–25 inches
COAT: Long, straight, flat and harsh; short on face and on leg fronts
COLOR: Various shades of brindle, including gray, yellow, silver, red or gold brindles; blue; color tends to lighten with age
OTHER NAMES: Langhaar Hollandse Herdershond
REGISTRY: FCI
GROUP: Herding

Roughhaired Dutch Shepherd

COUNTRY: Netherlands
WEIGHT: 66 pounds
HEIGHT: 23–25 inches
COAT: Medium long, wiry
COLOR: Various shades of brindle, including gray, yellow, silver, red or gold brindles; blue; color tends to lighten with age
OTHER NAMES: Ruwhaar Hollandse Herdershond
REGISTRY: FCI
GROUP: Herding

Shorthaired Dutch Shepherd

COUNTRY: Netherlands
WEIGHT: 66 pounds
HEIGHT: 23–25 inches
COAT: Short, dense
COLOR: Various shades of brindle, including gray, yellow, silver, red or gold brindles; blue; color tends to lighten with age
OTHER NAMES: Korthaar Hollandse Herdershond
REGISTRY: FCI
GROUP: Herding

Longhaired Dutch Shepherd, blue brindle.

The three varieties of the Dutch Shepherds are very similar (except for color) to the shepherds of nearby Belgium and early German shepherd varieties. They, like their Belgian cousins, are judged on the same physical standard. They have been known in their present form since the early 1700s, when examples of the breeds were exported to Australia. The entire inland area of Holland, bordering on Germany, was mainly sheep-herding and flock-tending country. The Dutch Shepherd first came to the fore in Holland around 1870 from the north Brabant area. The dogs demonstrated superb herding abilities and were widespread at that time but, as the flocks dwindled, so did the dogs. Like other herding breeds, they lost more ground when the German Shepherd craze swept the world.

The Dutch Shepherds have been rediscovered in the last few decades and are quickly regaining popularity. Modern owners, proud of this breed's national heritage, are dedicated to retaining working qualities. These dogs have become competent in guard work, and occasionally schutzhund and obedience. But the inborn herding drive is still very acute, and that is what they do best. A few have been brought into the USA.

Above: Roughhaired Dutch Shepherd, brindle. **Below:** Shorthaired Dutch Shepherd, brindle.

The rough coat was prevalent back in the 1940s, but today the smooth coat is seen almost universally, with the wire coat glimpsed but occasionally. The long coat, with shades of gold or silver brindle and liberal featherings on legs and tail, is disappearing. Only about 30 per year are registered in Holland. The simple reason for its rarity is that most of these dogs work out of doors, and the luxurious long coat requires too much care for practical owners who prefer the ease of grooming a short coat.

The Dutch Shepherd pup has indefatigable curiosity and is in perpetual motion, challenging its master to provide activity, new experiences and training. This dog possesses a keen and cunning intelligence. The adult is extremely possessive and territorial, and generally does not tolerate other dogs or thrive in close confinement. If raised with kids or in apartments, they accept the situation, but this is a working animal who is a workaholic and naturally wants to herd and defend. He is happiest in an environment where he has adequate exercise, a territory to defend and plenty of chores to keep both mind and body busy.

Above: Roughhaired Dutch Shepherd. **Below:** Longhaired Dutch Shepherd.

Dutch Smoushond.

DUTCH SMOUSHOND

COUNTRY: Netherlands
WEIGHT: 20–22 pounds
HEIGHT: 14–16½ inches
COAT: Coarse, wiry, harsh, straight, medium length; leg furnishings, eyebrows, mustaches and beard are evident but never exaggerated. No topknot; no tendency to mat
COLOR: Solid yellow, with preference to dark straw color; ears, mustache, beard and eyebrows may be darker
OTHER NAMES: Hollandse Smoushond
REGISTRY: FCI
GROUP: Terrier

In the late 1800s the German Coarsehaired Pinscher, grandfather of the modern Schnauzer, was common throughout Germany. The Germans preferred the black or salt/pepper dogs and usually destroyed the red or yellow whelps which were common in litters at that time. An enterprising Dutch merchant named Abraas

cleverly—and cheaply—bought these German "rejects" and brought them to Holland. They were sold on the streets of Amsterdam as *heerenstalhonden*, or gentlemen's stable dogs.

The yellow, roughhaired little charmers caught on and developed into the Smoushond. The breed enjoyed recognition from the FCI as well as the Dutch Kennel Club and was a popular family dog in the early part of the 20th century. In the years between the Wars, his numbers were greatly reduced, and he all but vanished during WWII. The last two litters were bred in 1949, with none following, and soon he was dropped from official roll calls and declared to be extinct.

In the early 1970s a Dutch woman, who had poignant memories of the Smoushonden owned by herself and friends in the 1940s, decided to recreate the breed. She advertised, asking for anyone owning a mongrel which bore resemblance to the accompanying photo to contact her. In a small country like the Netherlands, it was actually possible to go and check out each of these leads personally. If the "approved" dog was a female, this woman asked the owners to breed the dog once to a stud of her choice, and, of course, chose an appropriate male. She was dedicated to her task and went to look at *each* puppy born and still does even now, assisted by other breed wardens. In fact, this Dutch dog lover sees each Smoushond born in the Netherlands four or five times before breeding age, keeping photo records and recommending possible breeding partners.

By 1977, a specialty club had been refounded and recognition was forthcoming from the Raad van Beheer (Dutch KC) and the FCI. The breed is once again on fairly firm footing, and the modern proponents want to keep it that way. They are very cautious about breeding practices to forestall genetic problems and as yet have no interest in selling any outside the Netherlands.

The Smous is an affectionate and friendly fellow, totally devoid of nervousness, yappiness or wanderlust. His rough but short jacket is quite easy to care for and provides adequate protection. Although the standard allows for an uncut tail, most are docked, leaving one-third to be carried gaily. As the standard states, the Smous should be "a pleasant and easy family dog."

EAST EUROPEAN SHEPHERD

COUNTRY: USSR
WEIGHT: 75–105 pounds
HEIGHT: 24–28 inches
COAT: Moderately short, smooth
COLOR: Black, black/tan saddled, sable, rarely brindle or white
OTHER NAMES: Byelorussian Owtcharka
GROUP: Herding

These dogs are very similar in appearance to a German Shepherd Dog and developed directly from the GSDs brought to the Soviet Union in the 1920s. After over a quarter century of selection, especially for animals to withstand the Russian climate, the breed is distinctly different from the Shepherd known in the West. Although at first centered in Byelorussia and the far western provinces of the USSR, the EESKC has thousands of members all over Russia today. It is presently the leading breed in the USSR. Often dogs of this breed have longer soft hair on the ears, neck, limbs and tail. It is said that their Russian owners spin the cashmerelike wooly undercoat for use in garments.

They are a tough, aggressive guard dog, a favorite of the KGB. For Kremlin duty, the KGB insists on solid blacks. If only one pup of another color is whelped, the entire litter is destroyed, and the breeding is not repeated. Private breeders, however, allow more latitude in color.

Eyes may be brown, amber, blue or odd-eyed. Ears are long and upright, and the paws are large with long toes, giving a snowshoe appearance. Owners equate their temperament to that of a Doberman Pinscher.

The handful that are found in other areas of the world have been smuggled out of East Germany. A photo accompanying an article by Enid Bergstrom in the February 1983 issue of *Dog World* showed them to be a bit squarer in body and longer in muzzle than most modern German Shepherds.

East European Shepherd, black/tan.

East European Shepherd.

Tasy.

EAST RUSSIAN COURSING HOUNDS

Tasy

COUNTRY: USSR
HEIGHT: 22–28 inches
COAT: Short and silky, with fringing on tail and ears
COLOR: Tan, gray or black/tan; usually as spots with white
OTHER NAMES: Mid-Asiatic Borzoi
REGISTRY: None
GROUP: Southern

Taigan

COUNTRY: USSR
HEIGHT: 22–28 inches
COAT: Long, thick and double, sometimes wavy; heavy feathering on tail, ears, thighs, shoulder and front legs
COLOR: Solids in black, gray, fawn or white; can have white markings
OTHER NAMES: Kirghiz Borzoi, Tajgan
REGISTRY: None
GROUP: Southern

Among the lesser known and oldest of the Russian sighthounds are the Tasy and Taigan. The Tasy hails from the endless desert plains east of the Caspian Sea, where he is also an endurance dog. The ringed tail, tapering head and coat with heavy ear fringes—as well as his home area bordering on northern Iran and Afghanistan—may hint at his historical bonds. The fact that the Afghan Hound (who in his native working state had less hair) is sometimes called Tazi is even more intriguing.

Rural hunters have used the Tasy for coursing hare, marmot, fox, hooved game and even wolf. This dog is nimble and can even go into thicket and forest in pursuit. It has a capable nose as well and can search for game by scent before it sees the quarry and begins the chase. Asian hunters sometimes still use trained eagles in combination with the Tasy. These hunts were valuable sources of fur pelts as well as meat and, at one time, one purebred Tasy from the Kara-Tala River area was equated with 47 horses in a dowry. So high was the regard for the Tasy that he was allowed to sleep in the house.

Modern land reclamation and industrializa-

353

Above and Below: Taigan.

tion in these desert regions have forced the breed into remote areas, and today the purebred Tasy is quite rare. They are seldom exhibited, although a few breeders have taken up the banner of this breed and are determined not to see it disappear.

Even further east, in the high altitude Tien Shan region right on the Chinese border, the Taigan came to the fore. This unique breed is not found outside the borders of Kirghizia. It has been adapted for endurance work at six to ten thousand foot elevations and can do scent work as well as retrieve. Both commercial and amateur Kirghiz hunters used this dog for hunting fox, marmot, badger, hare, wildcat, wolf, and hooved game. Trained falcons were often used for the kill. This beautifully coated dog was full of hunting zeal and showed charm and grace with its handler.

Unfortunately, today the purebred Taigan is dwindling rapidly. In a 1986 count, most specimens had been mongrelized and, in the Talass Valley—forever a bastion of the breed—only a few dogs were left. Soviet authorities state that they hope this trend will be reversed.

Norwegian Elkhound.

ELKHOUNDS

Norwegian Elkhound

COUNTRY: Norway
WEIGHT: 44 pounds
HEIGHT: 20 inches
COAT: Short, thick, coarse, stand-off, double
COLOR: Any color of gray, shadings are usual
OTHER NAMES: Norsk Elghund (Gra),
Grahund, Gray Norwegian Elkhound
REGISTRY: FCI, AKC, UKC, TKC, UKC
GROUP: Northern

Norwegian Elkhound, Black

COUNTRY: Norway
WEIGHT: 40 pounds
HEIGHT: 18–20 inches
COAT: Short, thick, coarse, stand-off, double
COLOR: Solid jet black
OTHER NAMES: Norsk Elghund (Sort)
REGISTRY: FCI
GROUP: Northern

Jämthund

COUNTRY: Sweden
WEIGHT: 66 pounds
HEIGHT: 23–25 inches
COAT: Short, thick, coarse, stand-off, double
COLOR: Any color of gray, shadings are usual
OTHER NAMES: Swedish Elkhound
REGISTRY: FCI
GROUP: Northern

The classic elkhound is probably very similar to the northern dog that first appeared at the side of humans during the Stone Age. Skeletons dating back to that era were found in Norway and are nearly identical to today's canine. These types have been selected for their hunting abilities, although at one time they probably were both herding and sledding dogs. In fact, the Norwegian Defense Minister was given the power to mobilize all privately owned elkhounds

Above: Jämthund. **Below:** Norwegian Elkhound.

for sledding hitches to carry military supplies over the snow in case of war. These breeds have remained remarkably the same through the millenia to the present time.

Throughout Scandinavia, dogs of the elkhound type were used and bred without pedigree or formal organizations. These dogs were good workers and bred fairly true, with some minor regional differences. When the FCI attempted to categorize the breeds, they separated them into the above three. The Black Elkhound of Norway is the smallest, with the gray Norwegian dog a bit bigger and the Jämthund the largest, raised and commonly used by the hunters of Jämtland district in Sweden. Although all are very popular dogs in their homelands, only the gray Norwegian Elkhound has achieved any popularity abroad.

Actually, *elghund* translates literally as moose dog, not elkhound, although they were used to hunt elk, lynx, bear and wolf as well as moose. In modern times, these breeds often hunt in pairs and assist sports enthusiasts by finding game and trying to drive it back toward the hunter or keep it within range of the gun. They are not chasers, following game over a great distance like the scenthounds, but work close to the hunter in the northern forests. Small game, such as marten, ermine or grouse, is approached by silently creeping up to it. The elkhounds attempt to block the animal's path or to turn it back toward the hunter. With larger prey, the elkhound feints attack, using this ploy to force the quarry to face the dog. A dog goes in, then dances away to protect himself, barking to keep the victim's attention until his master is within firing range.

Because of the spitz's long association with people, these dogs make fine companions and house dogs, and are especially good with children. They have the classic Nordic/spitz-type head and body, with the tail rolled up tightly on the back. Although lighter shades of gray are the norm of Elkhounds in America, at home they are often very dark gray, having a nearly black face with a mask. The smaller, solid black variety is still the rarest and, except for color, is judged by the same standard as the gray varieties.

Norwegian Elkhound, pup.

Norwegian Elkhound.

Norwegian Elkhound.

ENGLISH COCKER SPANIEL

COUNTRY: Great Britain
WEIGHT: 26–34 pounds
HEIGHT: 15–17 inches
COAT: Flat and silky on body; well, but not excessively, feathered
COLOR: Various solids, or those colors in a broken pattern with white; often have roan patterns
OTHER NAMES: Cocker Spaniel
REGISTRY: FCI, AKC, UKC, TKC, CKC
GROUP: Gun Dog

As the use of flushing spaniels became widespread in England, the smaller ones were called "cocking" spaniels. The name may have come from their use to spring or "cock" the game for the net and, later, the gun. Yet others feel it came from their usefulness on small game such as woodcock. At any rate, the merry little spaniels of England have been popular since the 19th century.

When the Kennel Club of England was cre-ated, just before the turn of the century, it soon recognized the Field, Springer and Cocker Spaniels as separate breeds. Each breed's individual development started from that time. The Cocker of England continued a rise to popularity that took him to the number one spot in his homeland during the 1930s and kept him there for 20 years. He also gained tremendous popularity in other Commonwealth nations.

While the Cocker Spaniel in England was rising to perfection, on the other side of the Atlantic, Americans using basically the same original breeding stock were developing a slightly different Cocker Spaniel. When imports from England were brought here during the 1930s, although there were separate classes for the English variety, there was still interbreeding between the English Cocker and the now native American Cocker. Because the two had become so divergent, most breeders felt that interbreeding was detrimental to both varieties. In 1940, the Kennel Club of England separated the breeds into the Cocker Spaniel and the Ameri-

English Cocker Spaniel, black.

can Cocker Spaniel. Soon after, the AKC followed suit but called the resulting breeds the English Cocker Spaniel (called Cocker in England) and the Cocker Spaniel (called American Cocker in England). FCI used great sense in defining both breeds by country, and the rest of the world calls one the English Cocker Spaniel and the other the American Cocker Spaniel.

The English Cocker in America holds a steady interest, mostly among exhibitors. He is a moderate dog, a bit larger, longer headed, and less coated than the American version. He sports the classic land spaniel tail which is level with the back and constantly wagging in extroverted joy of life. Neither the tail tucked in anxiety or pushed straight up, as seen with some misinformed handlers in the show ring, is typical of the breed. The breed's hunting instincts abound—if any would care to use them. He works close to the gun and uses his good nose to flush out a variety of game. Happy, willing and obedient, he is easy and fun to be with.

Tails are docked on pups. Coat care is a necessity but, if kept up, is not a problem.

Right and Below: English Cocker Spaniel.

English Cocker Spaniels. **Above Left:** Blue roan. **Above Right:** Particolor. **Below Left:** Red. **Below Right:** Buff roan.

English Cocker Spaniel.

English Cocker Spaniel.

English Cocker Spaniel puppy and feline friend.

English Coonhound, red tick.

ENGLISH COONHOUND

COUNTRY: USA
HEIGHT: 21–27 inches
COAT: Short, hard
COLOR: Mainly redtick, also bluetick, tricolor with ticks, white-red, white-black or white-lemon; brindle or too much red or black not acceptable
REGISTRY: UKC
GROUP: Hound

Tracing back to the Virginia hounds, the English Coonhound was bred to adapt to the rougher American climate and terrain. When the English was first recognized by the UKC, it was descriptively called the English Fox and Coonhound, alluding to its capabilities. In fact, at that time, the dogs were used more on fox than on raccoon. They were also capable of going after opossum, cougar and bear.

While the Redbone and Black and Tan were given separate breed status, all other treeing coonhounds were called English after the turn of the century. These included the blueticked dogs, the white tricolors and others, as well as those with redtick markings. There was also great variation in the history and in the style of hunting, from big, cold-nosed, patient trailing hounds to the refined, speedy hot-trailing dogs.

In 1945, the heavily ticked dogs split off from the English, registering themselves as the Bluetick Hound. Later, the tricolored hounds separated into the breed called Treeing Walker Coonhounds. Most modern English Coonhounds are of the redtick color, although they can be bluetick and other hound colors as well.

The breed is the extreme of the fast, hot-trailing competition-type coonhound. An English named "Bones," owned by Colonel Leon Robinson, won one of the first National Coonhound Championships. The breed is still used by practical hunters and competitive hound owners throughout the USA.

ENGLISH FOXHOUND

COUNTRY: Great Britain
WEIGHT: 55–75 pounds
HEIGHT: 23–27 inches
COAT: Very short and hard
COLOR: Bicolor or tricolor, usually with white predominating; blue not allowed
REGISTRY: FCI, AKC, CKC
GROUP: Hound

When fox hunting became the rage in England in the 13th century, a hound was needed specifically for trailing the fast and wily red fox. The trailing hounds of the St. Hubert/Bloodhound type were just too slow for this sport, although their blood formed the basis for the English Foxhound. Crosses were made to faster, lighter hounds and, some say, even to Greyhounds to increase speed.

In England, the foxhound is followed by mounted horsemen, and the dog must be fast with tremendous endurance. Fox scent is a "hot" trail and the hounds do not require the super-sensitive nose of the slow trailing hounds. But they do need good voice, drive and enthusiasm, as well as speed.

For many years each hunt developed its own style of hound, and type was not even. But by 1800, many large standardized packs existed, and the meticulous records kept by each individual Master of Hounds were incorporated in the Masters of Foxhounds Association formed around that time. Thus most Foxhounds in England can trace their pedigrees back, unbroken in written record, for over 150 years.

The first recorded importation of Foxhounds to the USA was in 1738; others soon came to American huntsmen with regularity. George Washington was an ardent hound fancier with many Foxhounds in his kennels. Some of these English dogs remain pure to the present time. Dozens of formal hunts, each with packs of pure English Foxhounds, are held in the eastern United States. Others of these early English imports formed the basis for the American Foxhound and other native coonhounds or scenthounds.

There is no doubt the breed can be prolific. A Foxhound, "Lena," holds the dubious honor of being tops in motherhood, whelping an astounding 23 puppies, with all surviving. Although it is assumed to be the drive to hunt that requires

English Foxhound, tricolor.

367

English Foxhound.

the dam to be restrained from leaving the pups to join the pack, perhaps it is the size of her demanding family!

Physically, the English Foxhound is a square, strongly boned hound with tightly knuckled feet, medium flat ear and lack of any loose or hanging skin. His endurance is evidenced by the fact that many hunt packs are taken to the meet under their own power, which may mean a 10– to 15–mile walk from (and back to) the kennel, with as much as 50 miles of hard running in the interim.

They are described as symmetrical. It was said of "Belvoir Gambler," a great example of the breed in 1885 by Cuthbert Bradley, quoting poet Cannon Kingsley: "Next to an old Greek statue there are few such combinations of grace and strength as in a fine Foxhound."

The practice among formal hunters is not to register hounds until they are a year of age. By that time the qualities of the dog can be assessed and, if he proves to be a good worker, he is formally registered and his ears are "rounded." This process of trimming off the bottom inch or two of the ear length serves to prevent the common nicks and tears to the edge that can repeatedly open and bleed and are so hard to heal.

Owners of individually bred hounds do not practice this trimming. Therefore, in the show ring where both working hounds and home-raised dogs may be competing, a difference in ear lengths may be observed.

Most English Foxhounds who will be used in formal hunts are raised in large packs in kennels, and under those circumstances they tend to be "dog oriented," obstinately interested only in hunting. However, they are calm and affectionate hounds and, if raised within the family from the beginning, make fine companions. They are extremely strong and powerful for their size, and they need to learn discipline early. Supplying adequate exercise and proper training, many owners enjoy them as house pets. They are particularly gentle with children. Neither nervous nor yappy, their pack instincts cause them to enjoy being with their owners and to adapt easily to a human as "pack leader." Like with many of the smooth-coated scenthounds, grooming is almost non-existent. A fair number in the USA have found their way to the conformation and obedience show rings. Pack judging, even for non-hunters, is another outlet for competitive urges. These competitions and formal hunts provide a picturesque setting: scarlet coats (or "pinks") and packs of dogs bounding through grassy terrain.

Foxhounds preparing for a hunt in Great Britain.

English Setter.

ENGLISH SETTER

COUNTRY: Great Britain
WEIGHT: 40–70 pounds
HEIGHT: 24–25 inches
COAT: Flat, of good length without curl, with feathering
COLOR: Tricolor, black/white, blue belton, lemon/white, lemon belton, liver/white, liver belton, orange/white, orange belton, all white
REGISTRY: FCI, AKC, UKC, TKC, CKC
GROUP: Gun Dog

The English Setter stemmed directly from those early couching and hawking dogs that were the basis for so many of the spaniels, as well as of the setters. In fact, the name "setter" derives from his old style of hunting. The breed still bears a strong tendency to creep catlike toward the bird, and may even sink slowly—just a bit—between the shoulder blades as they point. The modern development of the English Setter can be credited to Edward Laverack and Purcell Llewellin, who were contemporaries in mid-19th-century England.

Laverack obtained his foundation stock, "Ponto" and "Old Moll," from the Reverend A. Harrison, who had bred pure for 35 years. Laverack devoted his life and fortunes to developing the English Setter to his ideal. His strain was famous worldwide, and many were exported to the USA. An admirer of attractive appearance, his handsome "Laveracks" are behind many of today's best show strains. But, as with most gun dog breeders of the 19th century, Laverack's primary interest was field trialing and his dogs had these abilities. By the 1870s, long years of inbreeding had set some problems of temperament and infertility in his famous strain and, when outbreaks of distemper followed, the Laverack Kennels reached their nadir. But characteristics of the strain continued through other breeders, including Americans.

Llewellin started his famous field trial strain with high-strung Laverack bitches that, with their fire and high energy, could run to the edges of the course. He owned both Gordons and Irish Setters, and used them in various crosses. When he obtained his Duke-Rhoebes strain, consisting of coarse but sturdily practical English Setters, this proved the perfect nick with the Laverack blood—and made his strain and his name. The Llewellin strain became synonymous with field trial winners, and those imported to America dominated the circuit for many years in the early part of this century. So well known was the strain that there are still people who think the "Llewellin Setter" is a breed unto itself. The last of the straight-bred Llewellins was La Besita, who was the American National Champion of 1915. After that, Llewellins also degenerated by inbreeding, and the pointer soon supplanted the setter as the star of the All-Age Field Trials. Many of the Llewellins were lightly ticked tricolors, and some ill-conceived prejudice against this color remains in the show rings.

Besides these two pillars, whose individual ultimate good for the breed is occasionally—and heatedly—debated, there was a bevy of lesser known fanciers that kept these dogs. When the breed traveled across the seas, he gained the distinction of being America's first gun dog and attained quite a following. As *The New Dog Encyclopedia* attests: "The man who owns one English Setter shouts the praises of the breed to the housetops. The one who owns two English Setters does the same thing—only louder!"

Several of the breed set the tradition for top working field dogs. The modern English Setter is a handsome gun dog that often seconds as a pet. He is quite soft in nature and wilts under harsh treatment. His long coat does require a bit of care, and modern show style dictates some clipping of throat, head and ears. A host of attractive colors are allowed, with the solid white body covered with heavy ticking (called belton) preferred. The show type and field type are still quite far apart, although the breed has recently achieved its first dual championship. With the modern return of interest in the working qualities of many breeds, breeders may yet marry the two.

English Setters, liver belton, blue belton.

English Setter.

ENGLISH SHEPHERD

COUNTRY: USA
WEIGHT: 40–60 pounds
HEIGHT: 18–23 inches
COAT: Long, moderately coarse, dense; short on face, skull and legs
COLOR: Black/tan, tricolor, sable and white, black and white
REGISTRY: UKC
GROUP: Herding

Current owners believe the modern English Shepherd is still very similar to the Roman sheep and cattle dog which accompanied Caesar and his army to the British Isles in 55 BC. The forebears of this breed trotted off an English gangway to American soil, brought by early settlers to the shores of the United States. The English Shepherd was much admired and evolved to its modern type. American farmers found them agile, good workers and an answer to a farmer's prayers. They crossbred the varieties of old Scotch Collie, Border Collie and other

English Shepherd, pup.

English Shepherd, tricolor.

working types to produce today's dog. At first known as the "good ol' farm collie" or farm shepherd, the current name differentiates the breed from other collies. He is not exhibited, or even promoted, but is a simple working dog whose reputation has spread by word of mouth.

Like their cohort, the Australian Shepherd, they are active and good watchdogs. Weather-resistant and hardy, they may greet their owners in the morning from beneath a mound of snow, shaking off the flakes, ready to help with the chores.

They are natural drivers and heelers, good with cattle, sheep, hogs or even poultry. Bred to drive by nipping at heels, they are versatile, but should be started on the poultry or sheep, so they do not become too tough from learning on cattle or hogs. They differentiate between the young stock and adults and act accordingly. English Shepherds are "loose-eyed," in herding, as opposed to the "strong-eyed" Border Collie. The breed works well independently or under direction of a master.

The English Shepherd is a calm and steady all-purpose dog with keen senses. According to owner Diana L. Karr, they are particularly attuned to their family and some swear "by the time he is five or six, you can carry on a decent conversation with him." Owners find them able and eager hunters. They are good with children, pulling carts, helping them learn to walk and acting as referees in their squabbles. Although their tails are usually long, an occasional bobtail is whelped.

English Springer Spaniel, liver/white.

ENGLISH SPRINGER SPANIEL

COUNTRY: Great Britain
WEIGHT: 49–55 pounds
HEIGHT: 19–20 inches
COAT: Close and straight, with good feathering
COLOR: Black/white, liver/white, black tri, liver tri
REGISTRY: FCI, AKC, UKC, TKC, CKC
GROUP: Gun Dog

British flushing spaniels were often called "springing" spaniels, since they were used to spring the game from the cover. In the variety of spaniel sizes, sometimes in the same litter, the smallest were the Cockers, the medium-sized were the Fields and the larger ones became the Springers. Bede Maxwell illustrates the perfectly legal flexibility in those early days: the red/white dog, Corrin of Gerwin, was first registered as a Welsh Cocker, then re-registered as a Welsh Springer and his son became a registered English Springer! The first champion English Springer sired a daughter who was registered as a Field Spaniel.

Cockers and Springers from the same litter were classified by size. The confusion as to "when is a Cocker not a Cocker . . . when it's a Springer" finally led to complete separation of the breeds and a ban on interbreeding. The English gave the Springer official breed status in 1902, and under the direction of the English Springer Spaniel Field Trial Association, the breed became established in the USA.

Known under the pseudonym of Norfolk Spaniel for a time, English Springer Spaniel became the official name by 1900. Sir Thomas Boughey is credited with establishing the modern credentials; his family's stud books on the breed dated from 1812. The Springer is still a fine gunning dog, ideally suited for flushing birds, such as pheasants. The flashy dog show winner and the competitor at the AKC spaniel trials are at extremes of type for the breed. Many Springers show their skill in competition obedience.

The English Springer is not an exaggerated dog and is the leggiest of the flushing spaniels. His pleasant personality and good looks make him a fine house dog as well. The Springer tends to live a long life, staying active into his golden years.

Black/white English Springer Spaniel demonstrating the breed's excellence in obedience trial work.

English Springer Spaniel, liver tri.

English Springer Spaniel.

English Springer Spaniels, adult and pup.

ENGLISH TOY SPANIEL

COUNTRY: Great Britain
WEIGHT: 9–12 pounds
HEIGHT: 10–10½ inches
COAT: Long, wavy, silky and profuse
COLOR: Tricolor (Prince Charles), solid red (Ruby), red/white (Blenheim), or black/tan (King Charles)
OTHER NAMES: King Charles Spaniel
REGISTRY: FCI, AKC, TKC, CKC
GROUP: Gun Dog

Ever since there were spaniels, toy versions have curled in laps and warmed hearts. In England and on the Continent, the charming spaniel personality in a tiny package was valued as a pet. These dogs were selected for smaller and smaller size among the existing couching and setting dogs that established the type for the spaniels. Crosses to other tiny dogs may have occurred as well, but these were basically little gun dogs. Indulged and pampered by the wealthy, they were known as "comforters." Of course, they were mostly admired just for their companionship, but they were also useful as foot warmers in cold and drafty English castles!

Those in England took on the general appearance of a small Cocker Spaniel, and were illustrated frequently in literature and paintings. A medieval scoffer described the "Spaniell gentle . . . These dogs—pretty, proper and fine to satisfie the delicatenes of dainty dames and wanton women's wills . . ." A favorite legend tells that when Mary Queen of Scots was sent to her death in the 16th century, her executioner found one of her devoted little spaniels hidden in the folds of her skirt. To a happier end, in the late 1600s, they were favorites of King Charles II. He had many of them and they enjoyed full run of the palaces. Samuel Pepys, writing at the time, was critical of the king's devotion to them, noting that: "All I observed there was the silliness of the King playing with his dog all the while and not minding his business." Soon the little dogs were universally known as King Charles Spaniels, often referred to as Charlies.

Others who doted on the breed were noted: an advertisement appeared in the *Daily Courant* in 1720, promising a reward for the return of a King Charles Spaniel bitch. With a twisted sense of prideful ownership, one Duke of Norfolk would not sell or give his Toy Spaniels

English Toy Spaniel, Prince Charles.

English Toy Spaniel, King Charles.

away, but instead fed unwanted pups to his eagles!

Over the next century or so, the "King Charles Spaniel" began to change. Crosses to toy dogs from the Orient were likely. Soon the "comforters" became even smaller, with the extreme brachycephalic face, domed head, prominent eyes, and muzzle shortened so the nose was nearly flush to the face. They still had the charming spaniel personalities within a new contour. It is this short-faced version that has arrived at the present time as the English Toy Spaniel.

During the reign of King Charles, most of the specimens were black/tan and, thus, this color has taken on the king's name. The Blenheim color was named after the family estate of the Dukes of Marlborough, whose family owned many of the red/whites over the years. All colors are otherwise judged by the same standard of perfection. When The Kennel Club tried to classify all four colors under the title "Toy Spaniel," Edward VII, also a fancier, did not approve. Therefore, the breed is still also called the King Charles Spaniel—in deference to a king.

The breed is quiet and happy, content to be with its owners, and forgiving in nature. They are physically fastidious. Protruding eyes and hanging ears must be kept scrupulously clean, but otherwise care is minimal. Tails are docked like the other spaniels, and carried level with the back. Ears and their accompanying feathering are so long as to nearly brush the ground.

Above: English Toy Spaniel, Prince Charles. **Below:** English Toy Spaniel, Blenheim.

379

ENTELBUCHER

COUNTRY: Switzerland
WEIGHT: 55–66 pounds
HEIGHT: Under 20 inches
COAT: Short, smooth and dense
COLOR: Black and tan, with white at toes, tail tip, chest, and blaze. The tan always lies between the black and the white
OTHER NAMES: Entelbuch Mountain Dog, Entelbucher Sennenhund
REGISTRY: FCI
GROUP: Mastiff

The smallest of the four Swiss Mountain dogs, the Entelbucher is smooth-coated and bobtailed. *Sennenhund* means dog of the Alpine herdsman. This breed was used by these herdsmen to drive cattle to market.

One owner states the breed is quiet and easy-going. "Barrie does not bark just to hear his echo." He loves height and climbs on top the woodpile, doghouse and grooming table, "perhaps looking for the Alps." This owner sings praises of her dog, uttering only one complaint. Barrie likes to jump up and hit them with his body, even in play, which probably goes back to the dogs' hurling themselves at the cattle.

The breed is conscious of boundaries and is

Entelbucher.

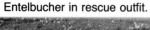
Entelbucher in rescue outfit.

territorial, protective but not aggressive. The dogs make good obedience workers since they love having a job to do. Entelbuchers are independent and self-confident, yet tuned in to their owners, as a Swiss owner demonstrates through the following statement: While her husband was in the hospital, her well-mannered four-year-old Entelbucher suddenly began crying, continuing for a half hour. Shortly thereafter, the family was notified of the master's death. The dog deteriorated and died four weeks later, seemingly of a broken heart.

Although the breed is exceptionally clean and requires little grooming, they enjoy it and demand their turn when others are groomed. All of the sennenhunds delight in the company of people and are friendly with other dogs. Entelbuchers are easy keepers and, in fact, tend to get a mite pudgy if given the opportunity.

Entelbucher.

ÉPAGNEUL FRANCAIS

COUNTRY: France
WEIGHT: 44–55 pounds
HEIGHT: 21–24 inches
COAT: Flat and straight, with feathering on legs, ears, belly and tail
COLOR: Clear white with liver markings
OTHER NAMES: French Spaniel
REGISTRY: FCI
GROUP: Gun Dog

The French Spaniel is a cousin to the Small Münsterländer and the Drentse Patrijshond setter type. The breed is quite old and, while boasting a long history in France, is unknown elsewhere. Fine pointing and retrieving dogs, they show a passion for their work.

They have a strong head that, in recent years, has shown some exaggerated flew and dewlap. As little ticking as possible is desired, with any tan marks disqualifying. The tail is left long, as with the setters. Personalities are—like so many of these breeds—docile, intelligent and trainable.

Épagneul Francais.

Épagneul Francais.

Épagneul Pont-Audemer, solid liver.

ÉPAGNEUL PONT-AUDEMER

COUNTRY: France
WEIGHT: 40–53 pounds
HEIGHT: 20–23 inches
COAT: Long all over and quite wavy, topknot on head, smooth face
COLOR: Solid liver, liver and white with or without ticking in the white
OTHER NAMES: Pont-Audemer Spaniel
REGISTRY: FCI
GROUP: Gun Dog

"He goes where the hunter can't go"—this old saying probably best describes the Pont-Audemer Spaniel, a specialist for water work. His origins most likely go back to the Poodle/Barbet, since they have both been in France for a long time. There may have been crosses to some of the French land spaniels, as well as to British and Irish spaniels, during his formation. He is a water dog of excellence and works the marshes for ducks; the breed has a dual purpose, as it is a fine pointing dog and can be used for other game.

Although a skilled hunter, he has not gained much prominence outside his native districts of Normandy and Picardy in northwestern France. With the invasion of English dogs on French shores and the apathy of French hunters, this breed is in danger of disappearing, perhaps due to its specialization. European hunters prefer a general-purpose dog. Due to the small numbers available for breeding following the War, it became necessary to cross to Irish Water Spaniels in the 1950s. Fewer than 100 registrations per year were recorded in the 1980s, with the numbers decreasing each year, and the breed is plagued with the problems that surface with the unavoidable inbreeding. Fortunately, the Society Havraise is dedicated to the renovation of the breed. The Pont-Audemer has joined forces with the Picardy and the Blue Picardy in a club for all three breeds.

His body is covered with gently curling locks which help him resist the cold, and his narrow, smooth face is topped with a jaunty toupee of curls. Ears are set rather high, and are long and hairy. The tail is docked to a third its original length. Midway between the smaller Brittany and the larger French Spaniel, the Audemer Spaniel is thick-set and robust.

Épagneul Pont-Audemer, liver and white with ticking.

ÉPAGNEULS PICARDIES

Épagneul Picard

COUNTRY: France
WEIGHT: 44 pounds
HEIGHT: 22–24 inches
COAT: Flat and straight with feathering on ears, legs, tail and belly
COLOR: Liver/tan/white tricolor, with heavy ticking
OTHER NAMES: Picardy Spaniel
REGISTRY: FCI
GROUP: Gun Dog

Épagneul Bleu de Picardie

COUNTRY: France
WEIGHT: 44 pounds
HEIGHT: 22–24 inches
COAT: Flat and straight with feathering on ears, legs, tail and belly
COLOR: Black/white, with heavy ticking; tan marks undesirable
OTHER NAMES: Blue Picardy Spaniel
REGISTRY: FCI
GROUP: Gun Dog

The time-honored spaniels of Picardy are closely related to the French Spaniel and others of his genre. At one time the Picard was under the threat of disappearing, but has recently gained a renewed interest among the hunters of France. He is a dog of natural abilities that can find and retrieve game under the most demanding and difficult conditions. If he has a specialty, it is probably marsh work for ducks, but owners say he is equally good for fur and feather in field or woods.

A dog of courage, the Picardy has an even temperament and is always in good spirits, making him a docile, amiable companion. French owners say he "loves to live in the house." He is devoted to his master and looks to his owner for direction. In appearance, he is a square-bodied setter, with the typically long tail and medium head without exaggeration. His colors, with the heavy ticking, are distinctive. With his chocolate/tan/white coat, the ticking throughout gives the Picard a two-tone brown roan jacket.

The soft-natured Blue was created by crossing Picards with British setters, probably blue belton English Setters in the late 1800s. Tan points called "fire marks" are not allowed; his black ticking creates the "blue" pattern. Modern owners say when the Blue accompanies a hunter, "he goes to work." His specialty is hunting the snipe in marshes. Considered a separate breed, the Blue Picardy is judged by nearly the same standard except for color.

Épagneul Bleu de Picardie.

Above Left: Épagneul Picard. **Above Right:** Épagneul Bleu de Picardie. **Below:** Épagneul Picard.

ESKIMO DOG

COUNTRY: Canada
WEIGHT: 60–105 pounds
HEIGHT: 20–27 inches
COAT: 3–6 inches, longer than some of the other sled dogs, thick with lots of undercoat
COLOR: Any color or combination of colors
OTHER NAMES: Husky, Esquimaux, Canadian Eskimo Dog
REGISTRY: FCI, TKC, CKC
GROUP: Northern

The Eskimo Dog has served as the only means of transportation for his people since 1000 BC. This far northern hauling dog—bred to haul sleds in winter, backpack in summer and hunt seals, oxen and bears all year—is closely related to the Greenland Dog. In fact, the Eskimo Dog Club of England considers them the same breed and registers canines imported from Scandinavia (where they are registered as Grønlandshund) as Eskimo Dogs. The FCI still recognizes two breeds, but they are very similar dogs, and there has been much crossing in the last 200 years. The Canadian version is native to the vast areas north of Hudson Bay and east of Alaska and the Mackenzie River—the Northwest Territories, stretching into the Arctic Circle, including Victoria Island, Baffin Island and even Greenland. Because the breed was fostered and saved by the interest of the Canadian KC, the FCI has dubbed it a Canadian breed.

The Eskimo Dog is a hardy, working breed, and has been known to withstand temperatures of -75 to -94 degrees Fahrenheit. The famed Arctic explorer MacMillan once drove a team of Eskimos 100 miles in a continuous run, taking less than 18 hours. The commander of the second Grinnell Expedition, Dr. Elisha Kent Kane, used a six-dog team, which hauled a fully-loaded sledge about 750 miles in two weeks. The packed sled weighed about 700 pounds, more than the usual average load of 100 pounds per dog.

Eskimo Dog, gray.

Eskimo Dog, black/white.

Because of their long history of survival in the harshest of environments, they have an extremely independent nature and go at everything "gung ho!"—fighting, eating, playing and working. They require firm, consistent handling from an owner who will earn their respect as the "lead dog." Owners report that the dogs have very strong pack instincts and that fights and challenges among their peers are common. By the same token, they need sufficient exercise and the company of other dogs. Most are kept outdoors because of their abundant energy, as well as to acclimate the working dogs during the cold months. They must be fenced constantly or walked on lead, since their wild instincts to run and chase are all but impossible to eradicate. In fact, there is some tendency to regard all other animals as food, and they are also inveterate food thieves, characteristics which assured survival in the bitter environs of their homeland.

Despite their strong working background, they are good tempered, affectionate and dignified with people. The mature dog has a certain aloofness similar to a cat and does not relish unsolicited attention. The breed doesn't bark but has a wide range of vocalizations that, owners say, can be quite explicit. The Canadian standard states: "The natural voice is a howl, not a bark. When in a group, the dogs often give voice in a chorus of strangely woven tones, and this is one of the thrilling sounds of the Arctic. A number of dogs will produce a mass crescendo persisting for varying periods until, as if cued by a special note, all will abruptly stop."

The Eskimo Dog is a primitive and natural working dog, representing an era long past. He is a dog only for those who understand his nature and who have the time and facilities to channel his energy. According to Sverdup,"they have the persistence and tenacity of the wild animal, the domestic dog's admirable devotion to their master; they are the wildest breath of nature, the warmest breath of civilisation."

Eskimo Dog, red.

387

ESTONIAN HOUND

COUNTRY: USSR
HEIGHT: 18–21 inches
COAT: Short, dense
COLOR: Black/tan usually; also tan saddled
OTHER NAMES: Gontchaja Estonskaja
GROUP: Hound

The Estonian Republic of the Soviet Union is in European Russia, straight north of Moscow on the Baltic Sea. In the early part of the 20th century, big fast hounds had begun decimating the population of wild goats that were abundant in the area where hare and fox were hunted. Hunters began working to develop a smaller, lower stationed hound that could stalk the small game but were outleagued by the pace of the wild goats.

First they crossed the smallest of the local hounds with English Beagles to reduce size and obtain strong feet, so necessary where snow falls heavily in February. Next into the mixing pot was the Swiss Neiderlaufhund, contributing his musical voice, persistence on the trail and, especially, his very early maturation (as young as five to six months!). A dash of Foxhound was added for endurance.

By 1954, the breed was introduced to the second Soviet Cynological Congress, where he was approved and a standard adopted. He was enthusiastically received by many hunters in other areas of Russia as well. So well had the Estonian breeders done their work that at the 1957 Moscow Exhibition, the Estonian Hound received a special award, and the founders were awarded gold medals.

The Estonian is a strong, rather low-stationed hound that is often ready to hunt effectively before his first birthday. Because of his smaller size and suspicion of strangers, he is often kept in a house or apartment, where he seconds as a watchdog.

Estonian Hound.

Estonian Hound.

ESTRELA MOUNTAIN DOG

COUNTRY: Portugal
WEIGHT: 66–110 pounds
HEIGHT: 24½–28½ inches
COAT: Medium-short or long; coarse and abundant, with dense feathering on tail; in long coats, dense feathering on chest and backs of legs and thighs
COLOR: Brindle, wolf gray and all shades of fawn; usually with black shadings and mask
OTHER NAMES: Portuguese Sheepdog, Cão da Serra da Estrela
REGISTRY: FCI, TKC
GROUP Flock Guard

The Estrela range in the central part of Portugal was the home of this ancient breed. One of the flock guards that spread from Asia to Iberia, the Estrela represents one of the Portuguese branches of the family. Flocks annually moved from the high Estrela plains where they grazed in summer to lower elevations where they stayed from October to March. These Portuguese *Transumancias*, like those in Spain, followed the same routes for centuries, and the migrations were always accompanied by large flock-guarding dogs. As they traveled in search of fresh pastures, the aristocracy confiscated a few of the dogs, finding them excellent guards for their large country estates.

The dogs that cast their lot with the wealthy naturally received better food and care—and more of it. Less agility was needed than that demanded in traipsing over mountains. The estate dogs grew larger, with bigger bone. Eventually, the herds diminished and the flock guards with them, so that the larger dog became more common. With the revival of interest in Portuguese native breeds in the 1930s, the Estrela found many friends, first at home, and later abroad.

The Estrela needs large doses of loving contact and should not be chained or isolated. Yet, they are not demanding of attention and accept what is given them with contentment. As these dogs watched over their flocks, they slept in whatever shelter they could find, often in the open, and they lived on shepherd's leftovers. Little wonder they are easily satisfied now.

As guard dogs, their bark is loud and threatening, and they are sometimes aggressive with

Estrela Mountain Dog, wolf gray.

other dogs of the same sex. Affectionate with their masters and good with children, Estrelas are suspicious of strangers. They can be obstinate and need to be handled with a firm hand, convinced that your way is better than theirs.

Outdoor activity is a necessity. Barking and a passion for wandering, even to jumping fences, can be annoying, both to owners and neighbors. For pet owners, some of this energy can be channeled into obedience work or other chores. Early socialization is recommended.

Planned breedings face "lousy" odds. As breeder/author Roger F. Pye said, "If you start trying when she is just . . . two, you may get her mated by the time she is three and a half."

A breed club fosters their preservation in Portugal, where they still guard flocks and estates. The first Portuguese show recording Estrela entries was Lisbon's in 1908 and a standard was published in 1933. Each year in the Serra da Estrela region, proud owners still gather to compare dogs and talk about their chosen breed at the *concursos* (rather like informal specialty shows). A good number of these dogs have been brought into England where they are exhibited at the larger shows.

Above: Estrela Mountain Dog, fawn. **Below:** Estrela Mountain Dog, reddish fawn.

EURASIAN

COUNTRY: Germany
WEIGHT: 40–70 pounds
HEIGHT: 19½–24 inches
COAT: Long, straight, abundant spitz type
COLOR: Red, fawn, wolfgray, black, or black with limited marks; white and pinto are not yet allowed for breeding
OTHER NAMES: Eurasier
REGISTRY: FCI
GROUP: Northern

The Eurasian is a modern breed developed in the 1960s. Julius Wipfel of Weinheim, Germany, wished to develop a large and distinctive spitz type of dog with all the beautiful colors plus a mellower character for modern times. He crossed Chow Chow males with large German Wolfspitz bitches. From the resulting puppies, he eliminated the Chowlike and more wild wolflike types, keeping the intermediate, imposing spitz-type whelps. He called the new breed the "Wolf-chow." Later he crossed the Wolf-chow bitches with one Samoyed male, and that was the end of the crossbreeding. Good selection since that time has come to establish the breed, known since 1973 as the Eurasian, combining the best of the European and Asian spitz dogs to create a new one.

The Eurasian tends to bond very strongly with his owner and/or family. These dogs need to be with their people, and pine if chained or secluded away from family life or left in a boarding kennel. European owners advise that training should be done by the owner, not a hired trainer, as they respect only their own master. Even changing homes as an adult may be traumatic, if the binding ties are too strong.

Because of the bonding or pack instinct, the Eurasian is very reserved and even distrustful of strangers, making a natural watchdog. When he barks he has a reason to do so. Although friendly and quiet with his family and other dogs in his pack, he can become quite fierce if

Eurasian, wolfgray.

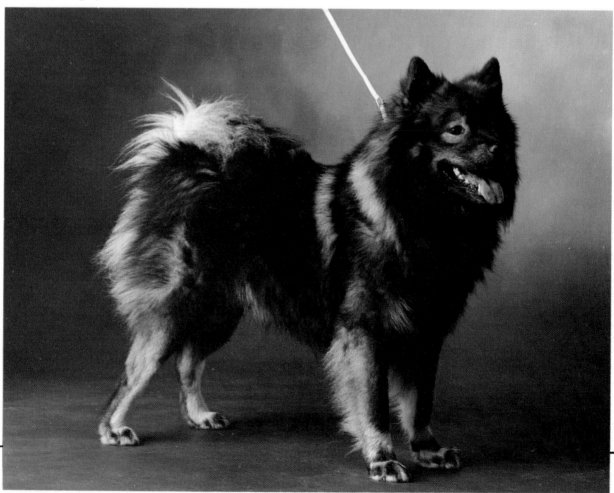

necessary. He will not hesitate to attack someone threatening his people with harm, and is also quite capable of handling himself in a fight, even with larger dogs. Owners warn he must make up to new friends at his own pace, and thus strangers should not pet or handle him until he indicates he has accepted them.

Nevertheless, he is a sensitive dog that wants to please. He is an excellent lady's dog as he responds well to a light hand. Once he has his "pack," he is not a dog that requires constant reminders of who is the alpha animal. Any discord or arguing among his family members makes him truly uneasy, and he may run from one to another, whining and indicating that everyone should calm down and stop their bickering! Upon his family members' returning from even a short time away, the Eurasian will greet them with enthusiasm, dancing on his hind feet in great joy.

The Eurasian is a handsome and imposing spitz dog, gaining in favor all over Europe. They are recognized and shown throughout the Continent, and there are a few specimens in the United States.

Above and Below: Eurasian, red.

FAUVES DE BRETAGNE

Griffon Fauve de Bretagne

COUNTRY: France
WEIGHT: 44 pounds
HEIGHT: 20–22 inches
COAT: Rough, hard hair of medium to short length
COLOR: Solid, in various shades of wheaten to red; small white spot on chest allowed; black hairs highly objectionable
OTHER NAMES: Tawny Brittany Griffon
REGISTRY: FCI
GROUP: Hound

Basset Fauve de Bretagne

COUNTRY: France
WEIGHT: 20–35 pounds
HEIGHT: 13–15 inches
COAT: Rough, hard hair of medium to short length
COLOR: Solid, in various shades of wheaten to red; small white spot on chest allowed; black hairs highly objectionable
OTHER NAMES: Tawny Brittany Basset
REGISTRY: FCI, TKC
GROUP: Hound

The soil in Brittany is poor, and much of the agriculture is devoted to grazing, especially sheep. Brittany is a peninsula in the northwestern corner of France, reaching out into the Atlantic toward Britain. In times past, wolves posed a constant threat to the flocks. Dogs that could track down this predator were an economic necessity. An extra bonus was the diversion from the everyday farm routine provided by the wolf hunts.

The fawn-colored Griffons of Brittany were well chronicled as far back as the Middle Ages. Whether or not these dogs predate the Griffons of Vendee, which is the neighboring province to the south, is debatable. They go back to the same era, and facts of whether one contributed to the other or they came from some of the same stem breeds have been lost in the mists of time.

By 1885, the wolves were gone from Brittany and this breed fell into oblivion or was crossed carelessly with other hounds. Breeders of the present century have worked hard to save the tawny hound. This griffon was easily adapted to other game such as fox and wild boar and, although rarely seen outside of its native area, is still used by modern hunters. Because the breed was becoming bastardized, fanciers have applied a strict standard to eliminate animals that are not of correct type. They are about the same size

Basset Fauve de Bretagne.

as the Briquet Vendeen and are always of the solid fawn, tawny or wheaten color.

The Basset version was probably created from crosses of the large Griffon with bassets from Vendee or elsewhere. The smaller version is quite swift for his size and has a lively and enterprising personality. Brittany Bassets are generally hunted in packs of four, going after smaller prey such as rabbit, hare and wild boar. Along with many other bassets, this variety has achieved some standing in modern society as a companion. He makes a fine pet as long as his need for exercise and his passion for hunting are fulfilled. BFB s are bred and shown in England as well as in their homeland.

Right and Below: Griffon Fauve de Bretagne.

Field Spaniel.

FIELD SPANIEL

COUNTRY: Great Britain
WEIGHT: 35–50 pounds
HEIGHT: 18 inches
COAT: Fair length and density, flat or slightly wavy, silky in texture; with moderately abundant thick feathering on legs, ears, and belly
COLOR: Black, liver, golden liver or mahogany red, or any of these with tan markings; white markings are to be discouraged, and any present should contain roaning and not be clear white
REGISTRY: FCI, AKC, UKC, TKC, CKC
GROUP: Gun Dog

Spaniels were developed in the early 1800s from couching dogs and possibly hounds. Sussex types were the oldest. As the development of the spaniel continued, the Field Spaniel type emerged, with even less of the hound influence. They were first noted in the early 19th century and, in fact, early litters contained both Fields (the larger whelps used for grouse and quail) and Cockers (smaller dogs used for hunting

woodcock). Sometime during the mid-1800s, show interests began to exaggerate and change the Field variety. Led by fancier Phineas Bullock, the whims of fashion nearly ruined the breed. The dog became a caricature, with cumbersome head, very short crooked legs, and elongated weak "hammock-slung" body. According to the *International Encyclopedia of Dogs*, descriptions of the breed at the time noted: ". . . sluggish and crocodile-like," "German sausage," "Caterpillars," with one wag suggesting they needed an extra pair of legs in the middle to keep their sagging bellies off the ground. One dog of the time purportedly was 12 inches at the shoulder and weighed 40 pounds!

As the Field Spaniel craze waned, dedicated owners brought the Field back to a sensible state by the turn of the century. English Springers and perhaps a dash of Cocker Spaniel had a hand in the refinement of the modern breed. The bad taste was not rinsed out of the public's mouth, however, and the Field slipped to the point of extinction. Even though the breed survived the two Wars, by the 1950s its numbers were so small in England that championship status was withdrawn. The breed was literally reduced to a handful of breeders. At a 1967 show in Birmingham, England, every Field in the country (with the exception of a few retirees) was on the bench that day. But numbers slowly increased, and the awarding of challenge certificates was restored in 1969.

Over the years, a few were brought to America. Those arriving in the late 1800s were still classed as Fields or Cockers, depending on weight. Thus, their history in America is tied closely to that of the Cocker Spaniel. After many years without any registrations, a few began to trickle in during the revival in the 1960s. Today, occasional specimens are seen on the show bench, both natives and imports. A handful of litters are registered by AKC each year, so the breed has a pawhold on both sides of the Atlantic.

A Field is the epitome of the basic spaniel, without any exaggeration. Moderate coat and feather, normal stop and flew, slightly more length than height; he stands out for his lack of overdone characteristics. A happy and level-headed fellow, he has both perseverance and endurance in the field.

Fila Brasileiro, brindle.

Field Spaniel.

FILA BRASILEIRO

COUNTRY: Brazil
WEIGHT: Minimum 90 pounds female, 100 pounds male
HEIGHT: 24–29½ inches
COAT: Short, smooth
COLOR: Brindles and all solid colors, except white or mouse gray
OTHER NAMES: Brasilian Mastiff, Brasilian Molosser
REGISTRY: FCI
GROUP: Mastiff

The Fila Brasileiro's ancestors were brought into Brazil by the Portuguese conquistadores. The breed was created in the 19th century through existing mastiff and bullenbeisser stock, crossbred with Bloodhound. The introduction of scenthound into this molosoid blend gave the Fila its longer muzzle (equal in length to back skull), shallow stop and long, folded ear.

Brazilian ranchers of the 19th century were isolated, needing tough dogs for protection, to hunt jaguars and to track runaway slaves. The

397

Fila Brasileiro.

Filas were also intended to give assistance with the semi-wild cattle. When attempting to turn or stop a cow, they might bite and grasp the cheek or nose, but they generally grabbed the ear, just like their Alaunt ancestors. Although the breed has been utilized on ranches since its beginning, formal breeding—according to a standard—was augmented in the 1950s.

An abundance of loose skin hangs on the head and neck, denoting the hound ancestry. Although massive, they should be 40–50 pounds less than an English Mastiff of comparable height. The Fila's hind legs are lighter in bone, longer and less angulated than his front legs, giving him a downhill appearance. The dog sways in a "camel pace," causing a correct rocking and rolling motion to the gait. The pace is unique to the breed, unlike all others which are expected to trot. They are good jumpers, very agile and fast.

The Brazilian standard warns judges not to touch Filas if they wish to keep all their fingers, since aggression is often encouraged. Dogs raised with firm corrections and socialization are shown without incident, however. These dogs are used successfully in schutzhund work in Germany, where they demonstrate their intelligence and ability to be controlled. Passing a shooting test, in which a blank pistol is fired five meters from the dog, is a requirement for all Brazilian champions. They must also pass a temperament test, where dogs (over 12 months) are approached aggressively with a stick. In both cases, the dog should express attention, showing self-confidence and assurance. The judge watches for the dislike the animal shows toward strangers and the self-assurance, courage, determination and bravery of each individual.

The Fila is the most popular breed in its native country. It has not been in the USA long, but has steadily gained ground. *Filar* in Portuguese means to hold or secure. "Faithful as a Fila dog" is an old Brazilian proverb; the Fila's temperament makes it totally loyal to owner and family and naturally distrustful of strangers. A breeder says, "This breed needs a home that understands and needs a dog that will not be friendly with strangers, even those allowed into the home. They should not attack viciously for no reason, but members outside the family should not expect to pet, play or be friendly with an adult." It is totally fearless in the face of danger. The Fila standard states the dog should have a calm, noble, self-assured expression when in repose and a determined, alert, firm one when at attention.

Filas do well in any climate, and their short coat is easily kept up. These dogs adore all members of their human families, including children, and love being close to them, even sitting on their feet. Caution must be taken with visitors, and early socialization is recommended for the pet or show dog. A breeder states the Fila is for "owners with responsible attitudes, not a macho personality."

Above: Fila Brasileiro, pup. **Below:** Fila Brasileiro, fawn.

FINNISH HOUND

COUNTRY: Finland
WEIGHT: 55 pounds
HEIGHT: 22–24½ inches
COAT: Short, but dense and coarse to the touch
COLOR: Tan with black saddle; small white markings on head, chest, feet and tail tip
OTHER NAMES: Suomenajokoira
REGISTRY: FCI
GROUP: Hound

Known since the 18th century, the Finnish Hound was developed by using a variety of English, German, Swiss and native Scandinavian hounds. Although the breed is popular and widespread in Finland, he is uncommon elsewhere. After hunting hare and fox with his master in the summer, he spends the long winters warm and cozy indoors with the family. He is rarely exhibited.

He is a rangy yet strongly boned hound much like a large foxhound. Probably a gift from his German ancestors, his singular ears are large with stiff cartilage, making them stand out somewhat from the head. He is friendly and calm in temperament, yet energetic in the hunt.

Above and Below: Finnish Hound.

Finnish Spitz, red.

FINNISH SPITZ

COUNTRY: Finland
WEIGHT: 25–30 pounds
HEIGHT: 15½–20 inches
COAT: Dense, moderately short, stand-off coat
COLOR: Chestnut red to pale red-gold, lighter shades on the undersides are allowed; puppies born brown
OTHER NAMES: Suomenpystykorva, Finsk Spets, Loulou Finnois
REGISTRY: FCI, AKC, TKC, UKC
GROUP: Northern

The Finnish Spitz is an old, northern breed native to Finland, and has had a written standard since 1812! This handsome red-gold-coated Norseman is the national dog of Finland and is mentioned in several national heroic songs. Improvement of the breed was expedited in the 1890s when forester Hugo Richard Sandberg successfully campaigned to have the barking dog recognized by the Finnish Kennel Club. Writing in *Sporten* that year, he characterized the Finnish Spitz:

"When living in close contact with a family, sharing its bright as well as cloudy days, the Finnish dog has features that resemble its owner, the Finn. The dog shows devotion and self-sacrificing faithfulness towards its master. It has also much more courage than one would expect of such a little dog. Under normal conditions it is a modest animal, but if fettered or shut into a kennel it easily becomes depressed and its fitness for use goes down. It seems to be like a pine: satisfied in poor soil with only a little food, but like a pine it demands air and freedom."

About the same time, Sandberg's cohort, Hugo Roos (another forester and hunter), was dedicated to finding and breeding typical specimens to maintain this handsome hunting dog. Titled English fanciers added support in the 1930s, particularly Lady Kitty Ritson.

In days of old, the Finnish Spitz was used by the Lapps for tracking bear and elk, but is now mainly used for bird hunting, especially capercaillie (similar to wild turkey) and black grouse, the game birds of Finland. His nickname, the

Finnish Spitz.

When a dog has three conformation certificates and either one first or two second prizes from a bird-hunting trial, he becomes a show champion. With a win in the open class at a bird-hunting trial and at least a second prize in a show, he becomes a trial champion. When he has won both titles, he is given the esteemed title of dual champion.

Hunting is considered so important in Finland that the status of the game bird population affects the breeding and registration of these dogs. The late 1970s were bad years for birds, and registrations of Finnish Spitz fell to their lowest level in many years. But when the bird population began recovering, interest in the red dog resumed. In 1980, registration of 1,087 Finnish Spitz was accomplished in Finland, and 116 hunting trials were held in which 579 dogs took part.

Finnish Spitz, pup.

barking bird dog, comes from his unique method of hunting. His lively manner of searching and acute scenting ability lead him to birds. Then by yodeling (barking continuously), he "enchants the bird to sit in the tree and watch the dog."

The dog is said to show "keen disappointment if the hunter misses. When the bird is shot the feet must be given to the dog as a prize, or legend has it, he will refuse to work for such an inconsiderate master."

Bird-hunting trials for the breed are common in Finland, and no Finnish Spitz can become a breed champion without winning a trial prize as well. The trials are set up with the judges following a dog and hunter into the forest. The dog is credited for finding and following birds, holding the bird in the tree, and the number of barks per minute (the more the better). It is claimed he must bark 160 times per minute. He is faulted for disobedience, "false barks" at a tree where there is no bird, ceasing to bark and/or leaving the bird, barking at squirrels or chasing elk or hare.

Finnish Spitz and owner on mountainside in Finland.

The best trial winners can compete in district championships, in the National Haukku contest, and the international contest between Finland and Sweden. Winner of the Haukku Trial is awarded the title "King of Barking" and victor of the international contest wins the crown of "Champion of The North." Breeders support these trials because of their strong desire to maintain working qualities. Because both hunting and the Finnish Spitz are essential parts of the history and culture of the Finnish wilderness, preservation and care of the breed are matters of honor for Finnish kennel clubs and Finnish hunters.

Watchful and alert, the Finnish Spitz makes a fine alarm dog, and is often kept in the home. He is built square and up on leg, with the lightness of build necessary for precise hunting. The tail comes up over the back and down the leg; it must end pressed against the thigh. The small, high-set, mobile ears are a trademark, the translation for his Finnish name, *Suomenpystykorva*, being Finnish cock-eared dog. In England, he is known affectionately as the "Finkie."

Since vocalization is part of their genetic make-up and barking is emphasized in trials, owners must not expect a silent companion. The dogs' beauty, size and happy temperament, as well as their cleanliness, sturdiness and easy care are pluses for family dogs.

The Finnish Spitz was added to AKC's Non-Sporting Group in 1988. He is also registered in Canada (since the '70s), England ('30s), Chile, Australia and several countries in continental Europe.

FLAT-COATED RETRIEVER

COUNTRY: Great Britain
WEIGHT: 60–70 pounds
HEIGHT: 22–23 inches
COAT: Dense, fine textured, as flat as possible, and of medium length, with feathering
COLOR: Solid black or liver
REGISTRY: FCI, AKC, UKC, TKC, CKC
GROUP: Gun Dog

Flat-Coated Retriever, black.

The Flat-Coat is one of the earliest "specialist" land retrievers created in Britain. In the latter half of the 19th century, the breed "appeared" and attracted immediate interest, and attained the reputation as the "game-keeper's dog" for its widespread use on British estates. Two of these dogs, "Old Bounce" and "Young Bounce," owned by game-keeper J. Hull, are credited with being the grande-dames of the modern breed. Very little else is known of his background, but he most likely stems from crossbreeding of trans-Atlantic imports with British setters. The imports were, undoubtedly, of the smaller Newfoundland-dog type, which was also the progenitor of the Labrador and Chesapeake Bay Retriever.

S.E. Shirley, MP, helped stabilize type in the 1880s. The Flat-Coat was a highly esteemed hunting and show dog until WWI. H.R. Cooke, a follower of Shirley, was a great patron of the breed. His Riverside Kennels dominated the breed for 60 years. This may have been the breed's downfall, as many less successful fanciers turned their attention to Labs and Goldens.

Perhaps to his benefit, however, this retriever has never been subject to the great popularity of some of his closely related kin, thus has not suffered the problems associated with "fad" breeds. Registrations are few in both England and the USA, and most dogs are associated with owners who utilize their abilities. The Flat-Coat is a fine land and water retriever with natural talent in marking, retrieving and delivering. He also doubles as a good flushing, upland game hunter. The Flat-Coat is a close-working, calm, biddable dog. Obedience enthusiasts are just beginning to discover his superior qualities of animation, trainability, and willingness to please that make him a top competitor.

The coat is without exaggeration, neither profuse nor over-long, and easy to care for. It has a tendency to wave—in fact, the original name was the "Wavy-Coated Retriever"—and the standard allows for the appearance of those long-ago genes, stating only that the coat should be "as flat as possible." An easygoing personality makes the Flat-Coat a pleasant companion dog, and he needs only adequate exercise to keep him fit.

Flat-Coated Retriever.

FOX TERRIER, SMOOTH

Country: Great Britain
Weight: 16–18 pounds
Height: 15½ inches
Coat: Smooth, but hard and dense
Color: White predominates; liver, brindle or red objectionable
Registry: FCI, AKC, UKC, TKC, CKC
Group: Terrier

FOX TERRIER, WIRE

Country: Great Britain
Weight: 16–18 pounds
Height: 15½ inches
Coat: Hard, wiry
Color: White predominates; liver, brindle or red objectionable
Registry: FCI, AKC, UKC, TKC, CKC
Group: Terrier

Familiar throughout the world, the Fox Terrier most likely came from the same types that produced the Bull Terrier and smooth Black/Tan (Manchester) Terrier. Many other additions, including scenthounds and sighthounds, are probable. Colonel Thornton's "Pitch," recorded in print and on canvas in the 1790s, was of remarkably modern type. Packs with a bit more influence from one breed or another were used by various hunt clubs.

The breed was first exhibited as a sporting dog, due to its remarkable eyesight, keen nose and staying power. Hunters on horseback carried feisty working terriers in a sack or box until the larger foxhounds had driven the quarry to hide. Once the fox was driven into its tunnel, the terriers were loosed and went to ground, routing out the fox.

Francis Redmond is credited for establishing uniform type in the last quarter of the 19th century. The original standard drawn in England in

Smooth Fox Terrier.

Wire Fox Terrier.

1876 has not been changed since, except for a two-pound drop in top weight for males. The dog remains unchanged as well, with his half-dropped ears and long docked tail.

The Wire variety is the same as the Smooth, except for his hard, wiry jacket. Although the rough coat was probably developed before the Smooth, the Wire made its debut into the show ring about 20 years after the Smooth. The rough variety was produced from crossing the Smooth Fox with broken-coated terriers. Reverend Jack Russell, who gave his name to another breed, was a devoted hunter and terrier man. Early Wires needed the elegance, narrow heads and predominance of white which the Smooth already possessed. The Reverend kept the rough-coat strain pure from 1815 to 1870, with one cross to the Smooth for improvement. Today both varieties are judged by the same standard except for coat.

Coat care on the Smooth variety is minimal, but the Wire needs to be "stripped" four times a year. Pet owners often have their Wires trimmed with electric clippers, rather than the time-consuming hand-stripping to remove dead coat.

Their personable and dapper appearance attracts attention whether the dog is in the show ring or playing in the park. Even non-terrier show enthusiasts recall the paragon of Fox Terriers, the remarkable Champion Nornay Saddler. The Fox Terriers are favorites in several countries, with the Smooth being the top terrier in Sweden and the Wire taking that honor in Belgium, Canada, Holland and Italy.

The terrier instinct of "going to ground" may erupt, leading to holes dug in a manicured yard. Given an outlet for their energy, they make sturdy companions for children and are good alarm and watchdogs.

Smooth Fox Terrier.

Above: Wire Fox Terrier puppies. **Below Left:** Smooth Fox Terrier puppy. **Below Right:** Wire Fox Terrier.

Smooth Fox Terrier.

FRENCH BULLDOG

COUNTRY: France
WEIGHT: Under 22 pounds or 22–28 pounds
HEIGHT: 12 inches
COAT: Short, smooth
COLOR: Brindle, fawn (with or without white markings); piebald or white
OTHER NAMES: Bouledogue Francais
REGISTRY: FCI, AKC, TKC, CKC
GROUP: Mastiff

During the 1860s, Bulldogs reached the height of popularity. Toy varieties appeared, which were highly favored, particularly around the English midlands where lace-making flourished. These diminutive Bullys may have been taken to France when some of the lacemakers moved there.

To say the Frenchie was developed totally from English stock is to ignore the fact that many other countries had, at this time, short-faced, bull-baiting and fighting dogs. Spain, especially, had erect-eared bull-baiting dogs. This new breed became highly visible in France, and visiting Americans brought it back to the USA.

Originally, many had the rose ear of their larger counterpart, but the erect, round-tipped "bat" ear has become their hallmark. Americans have been credited with fixing the bat ear. When this breed first "returned" to England to be shown, around 1900, a brouhaha arose. The English were highly insulted that the French had the nerve to use the name "Bulldog" since it was a symbol of Great Britain. Much controversy ensued: letters and editorials in the doggy press and opposition from the existing Miniature Bulldog faction. But despite all this, a specialty club was formed in England in 1903, and soon the Frenchie was recognized and is now known around the world.

Reliable sources on the sinking of the Titantic report a French Bulldog to be the only animal or pet to have perished in this historical disaster. The dog's owner sued for $1,500, a substantial sum for 1912.

The French Bulldog has less body bulk, exaggeration of wrinkle and bowing of legs than its English counterpart. He is born with a bobtail, eliminating the need for surgery. The breed standard is uniform throughout the world with the exception of color. The fawns and creams so favored in North America and Britain are disallowed in continental Europe.

The Frenchie has a bright, alert expression, conveying his fun-loving outlook. He enjoys a large or small family, adults or children. A delight in obedience, he is happy, bright and willing to please. The Frenchie character, alarm bark without yappiness and easy upkeep make these dogs a good choice as companions.

French Bulldog, brindle.

French Bulldog, piebald.

French Bulldog, white.

GALGO ESPAÑOL

COUNTRY: Spain
WEIGHT: 60–66 pounds
HEIGHT: 26–28 inches
COAT: Short, smooth
COLOR: Cinnamon, chestnut, red, black, brindle; solid or in combinations with white
OTHER NAMES: Spanish Greyhound
REGISTRY: FCI
GROUP: Southern

The Galgo has an ancient history. He is named for the Gauls, a Celtic tribe that inhabited the Iberian Peninsula six centuries BC. Celts always appreciated good dogs, and they acquired gazehounds from the Phoenician merchants who plied the Spanish shores. Caesar conquered the area just before the Christian era, and Roman writers of the first and second centuries AD describe the sleek Galgo. Spain was overtaken by the Moors in the eighth century, and additional sighthounds could have been introduced from Africa at that time.

After the Middle Ages, the Galgo maintained type for centuries, especially in Andalusia and Castile. Farmers used him for guard work or for hunting rabbits. Spanish nobility also favored these fleet hounds for formal coursing of live game. Those used for coursing remained the purest in type.

In the 20th century, the Spanish began using the Galgo on the racetrack. Although these coursing canines could "turn on a dime" and maneuver well following live hare through rough country, they were not as fast on the straightaway as their English racing cousins. Imported Greyhounds were crossed with the Galgo to obtain more speed, and large numbers of the ancient Spanish breed were altered by this dilution. Fortunately, fanciers maintained the cause of the old Galgo type.

Today the professional racing dog in Spain is called Galgo Inglés-Español (English-Spanish Galgo) and is *not* the same breed recognized by the FCI and breed purists in Spain. Spanish and European breed clubs formed for the Galgo Español are fostering the breed as a quiet aristocratic companion and a fine coursing dog. Specialty shows are offered for the breed. The Galgo is smaller than the English Greyhound, with a bit more stop and ears that hang straight down. He is a sturdier fellow, built for the demands of coursing and practical hunting.

Galgo Español, brindle.

Grand Gascon-Saintongeois.

GASCONS-SAINTONGEOIS

Grand Gascon-Saintongeois

COUNTRY: France
WEIGHT: 66–71 pounds
HEIGHT: 25–28 inches
COLOR: Tricolor; with tan only in spots on head, black restricted to head and a few body spots, and the white body having some black ticking throughout
OTHER NAMES: Virelade
REGISTRY: FCI
GROUP: Hound

Petit Gascon-Saintongeois

COUNTRY: France
HEIGHT: 22½–25 inches
COAT: Short, dense, and smooth
COLOR: Tricolor; with tan only in spots on head, black restricted to head and a few body spots, and the white body having some black ticking throughout
REGISTRY: FCI
GROUP: Hound

The Saintongeois region of France is on the western coast, just north of Gascony and below Poitou. Prior to the French Revolution, the famous hounds of Saintongeois were acclaimed for hunting the wolf. But following the fall of the nobility, the breed fell into disuse and only scattered specimens of the Saintongeois remained, along with tales of the breed's greatness. In the 1840s, Baron de Virelade crossed what few remaining specimens he could find with the robust Grand Gasconies to create the Gascon-Saintongeois breed. Although formally named for the breeds from which they came, this breed (especially the large size) is often called the Virelade after their creator.

These dogs are nearly as large as the Grand Bleu but are more powerful with a breathtaking, elastic gallop. Originally used for roe deer, they are strong enough for larger game, and today hunt deer, fox and boar. Their ultra-sensitive sense of smell makes them adaptable to and competent in all forms of hunting. A gentle and affectionate hound off the field, the breed is, unfortunately, quite rare today. In 1986, only ten packs were left in France.

Grand Gascon-Saintongeois.

The Petit Gascon-Saintongeois is a smaller version, developed specifically for rabbit or hare. Except for ten centimeters less in height, he has all the same qualities of his larger brother. Both varieties are of the classic French type. The colors are also the same: tricolor with the black restricted to head and a few body patches, topped off with bright ticking. The tan markings are restricted, as described: "On the hindfeet above the hock is a small gray-brown spot called *marque de chevreuil*," or the mark of the deer.

GERMAN HUNT TERRIER

COUNTRY: Germany
WEIGHT: 20–22 pounds
HEIGHT: 16 inches
COAT: Short and coarse, or harsh wire, broken
COLOR: Black/tan, chocolate/tan or red
OTHER NAMES: Deutscher Jagdterrier
REGISTRY: FCI
GROUP: Terrier

During the 1940s, four German sportsmen aspired to establish their own breed of all-purpose game terrier for hunting and going to ground. C.E. Gruenwald, Chief Forester R. Fiess, Dr. Herbert Lackner and Walter Zangenbert, who was also a writer on hunting, used dogs of the old Broken-haired Black and Tan type from England, probably similar to what is now called Patterdale. This type was crossed with German-bred Wire Fox Terriers. The progeny had both smooth and wire coats. With careful selection, type was quickly cemented. FCI recognized the Jagdterrier in a remarkably short period of time.

This breed is a pure hunting machine, not recommended for use as a house dog. He is so aggressive that some label him as cruel to prey. Any animal is fair game: badgers, fox, even the

German Hunt Terrier.

German Hunt Terrier.

dangerous wild boar. This belligerence can make him cantankerous with cats or other dogs. The German Hunt Terrier is also utilized for tracking and retrieving, as well as working underground. Guarding of his master's home and property comes naturally. Those who know him well warn that he may not tolerate friendly advances from anyone other than his master. He is a one-person dog, and even that person has to earn his respect, but once earned, he is devoted. This is a dog that can only fully be appreciated by serious hunters or professional foresters, who have great admiration for his courage and ability.

In Germany, specimens of this breed must pass working tests prior to being granted club approval to reproduce. With the breed club refusing to register offspring of non-working parents, casual fanciers are discouraged to insure maintenance of working qualities. The Jagdterrier is only rarely exhibited.

Some specimens were brought to the USA in the 1950s. For a time, a breed club was in existence, but interest does not seem to have been maintained.

The tail is usually docked to about half the original length, but the ears are left intact to tip forward. At this time, only the rough coat is acceptable.

German Hunt Terrier.

Above: German Hunt Terrier, coarse, black/tan. **Below:** German Longhaired Pointer, solid liver.

GERMAN LONGHAIRED POINTER

COUNTRY: Germany
WEIGHT: 55–77 pounds
HEIGHT: Minimum 21 inches, 25–27½ inches
COAT: Moderate length, wavy but tough in texture, never woolly or curly; not more than 2 inches in length, with some fringe on legs, ears, and underside
COLOR: Usually solid liver—can have white on chest and head; also liver/white spotted
OTHER NAMES: Deutscher Langhaariger Vorstehhund, Langhaar
REGISTRY: FCI, CKC
GROUP: Gun Dog

The Langhaar has been known for nearly as long as the other German *vorstehhunden*, as some of this variety were shown at an exhibition in Hanover in 1879. Longhaired gun dogs populated Europe, and the Longhaired Pointer was originally developed from among these. Later, as field work became emphasized over woods work, the breed was refined by crosses to setters from England. Despite the softer appearance of the flowing coat and liquid brown eyes, the breed is expected to perform all of the exacting hunting chores expected of German dogs—and does them well.

The Canadian Kennel Club recognizes the breed, but the numbers are small there, as they are in Germany today. Some breed interest is awakening in the Netherlands. As long as he has creative outlets for expending his energy (running, long walks, hunting), he is a sweet-natured dog that is "a big friend of the whole family." He enjoys feeling useful, and is easily trainable. An example of the enthusiasm is demonstrated by a female, "Niner," taught to bring the paper from the paperbox to the family in return for a dog biscuit. One morning, after receiving her treat, she returned with a second paper, and then another and another, until quite a heap was gathered. A little detective work showed the dog had "retrieved" all the papers from the neighborhood. The owners quietly returned the papers to their proper places, and ceased the exercise for a time. Niner, however, wasn't content, and ran beside the delivery car until the driver handed her a paper and Niner was again able to perform her task.

Their "long" coat is not so abundant as to require extensive grooming. The beautiful, flagged tail is left intact. They follow the other German utility dogs in conformation, with the high flat ear and the clean head, sans hanging lips.

German Longhaired Pointer, solid liver.

419

German Longhaired Pointer.

German Pinscher, black/tan.

GERMAN PINSCHER

COUNTRY: Germany
WEIGHT: 25–35 pounds
HEIGHT: 16–19 inches
COAT: Short, but coarse
COLOR: Black/tan or red
OTHER NAMES: Standard Pinscher
REGISTRY: FCI, TKC
GROUP: Terrier

As old as the British terriers, the German Pinscher does not possess the same immediate ancestors, although its prototypes probably converged in Europe prior to the Celtic invasion of the British Islands in the centuries before Christ. *Pinscher* means biter in German, referring not to the dog's temperament but to its abilities against adversaries. The German farmer's terrier was slightly larger than its English counterpart. It was a clean, alert guardian, used for home protection and vermin control. The German Pinscher was too large and long legged to go to ground but, nonetheless, could hold his own against anything above ground, even being a manstopper, if necessary.

The breed was officially recognized in Germany in 1879 and has been protected and promoted since 1894 by the German Pinscher-Schnauzer Club. During the years around the turn of the century, both smooth (pinscher) and coarsehaired (schnauzer) pups appeared in the same litters. The club initiated the policy of requiring proof of three generations of pure smooth coats for registration. This quickly helped set type and made them a distinct breed from the Schnauzer.

Over the years, new breeds were created in Germany and others introduced from foreign countries. The Doberman Pinscher and Miniature Pinscher gained acceptance worldwide, and the Standard Schnauzer found favor at home and abroad. The Standard Pinscher, however, fell into obscurity in its homeland and is now nearly unknown elsewhere. There were only ten litters registered in Germany in 1985. Despite the small numbers, interest has been growing lately to preserve this fine breed. There are a handful in the USA, where there is an organization to promote them, and their numbers are once again increasing.

German Pinscher, red.

German Pinscher.

German Pinschers are rough-and-tumble dogs who like a scrap and need a fair amount of exercise. They also need to know who is boss. But within these parameters, they are clean, alert and adaptable to new situations and are eager to please their "pack leader."

Great companions for children, the Pinschers are energetic and large enough for hours of play. Yet they are small enough for easy care, and grooming requires a minimum of fuss. American breeders state the dogs naturally maintain direct eye contact when playing, and are incredibly quick and fast, which means they have retained their capabilities as ratters as well.

Ears are traditionally cropped to a moderate length, much like a pet cut on a Doberman Pinscher, and the tail is docked short when the whelp is just a day or two old. The Pinscher's sleek coat usually is seen in the traditional black and tan, although various shades of red are also allowed.

GERMAN SHEEPPOODLE

COUNTRY: Germany
HEIGHT: 20–24 inches
COAT: Long, hard, shaggy
COLOR: White, also roan and pied
OTHER NAME: Schäfpudel
GROUP: Herding

This breed is unknown outside Germany and is rare, if not extinct, even at home. He had a wavy, poodlelike coat that tended to form in cords like the Poodle, Puli and Komondor. In fact, he was probably related to the Puli, as the importation and exportation of sheep between Germany and Hungary was common. And where the sheep went, the sheep dogs followed.

The Schäfpudel was a good herding dog with drop ears, long tail, and a gentle, tolerant and affectionate nature. Unfortunately, there has been no record of this breed for some time.

GERMAN SHEPHERD DOG

COUNTRY: Germany
WEIGHT: 75–95 pounds
HEIGHT: 22–26 inches
COAT: Moderately short, with dense undercoat
COLOR: Black/tan, sable, all black
OTHER NAMES: Deutsche Schaferhund, Alsatian
REGISTRY: FCI, AKC, UKC, TKC, CKC
GROUP: Herding

The German Shepherd Dog is one of the most widely recognized breeds in the world. The breed is known and favored in many countries for its intelligence, trainability, adaptability and fortitude.

The foundation of this breed is comparatively recent (1899), making the climb to its current numbers and status of renown even more amazing. Rittmeister Max von Stephanitz, proclaimed "the father of the breed," and his friend, Herr Artur Meyer, bought a working dog seen at a show in order to foster a strong, capable German herder. Von Stephanitz led the group that promoted German Shepherds from 1899 to 1935. During that time, he brought the breed to its current status of respect.

With less demand for herding over the years, von Stephanitz was determined not to let the Shepherd decline and encouraged its use by the police and the military. During World War I, there were 48,000 Shepherds "enlisted" in the German Army. Today, the GSD serves perhaps in more ways than any other breed: search-and-rescue (S&R), police, army and sentry, scent

German Shepherd Dog, black/tan.

discrimination and, of course, companion. They are superb dog guides for the blind and helpers for the handicapped.

Perhaps the best testimony to its S&R ability comes from the Hospice at St. Bernard, which still offers refuge to travelers. Today the Hospice raises Saint Bernards as a tourist attraction, but German Shepherds do the rescue work.

Despite fads, poor breeding practices, malignment of character as "attack" dogs, and discrimination against anything German during the years of and following World War I, the breed has thrived. During the German phobia, English owners refused to give up the breed they had come to admire. They did compromise and change the name to Alsatian, which prevailed for nearly 40 years after all hostilities ended. Their American counterparts, in a similar attempt to disguise the breed's origins, temporarily dropped the word "German" from the name. Two German Shepherds helped to soothe the post-War wounds. The film stars Rin Tin Tin and Strongheart reawakened interest in the breed, with their breath-taking adventures and thrilling rescues. During the Second World War, the Shepherd served the Allied forces in the fight against its homeland. These dogs have amazed even their trainers in feats of power and

agility. A shepherd named "Max of Pangoula" scaled a high jump of 11 feet 5⅛ inches, and "Young Sabre" topped a ribbed wall of 11 feet 8 inches.

As late as 1915, there were three coat types— the smoothhaired, the longhaired and the wirehaired. The wirehaired has since disappeared; "long coats" are still born, but do not meet with approval in the conformation ring. They do, however, make fine companions, and there are admirers that prefer them.

Shepherds can tolerate extremes in weather conditions: barking with delight at a romp in below-zero temperatures, rolling in a snowbank; or withstanding the heat of a steamy jungle in a combat zone.

Their ears are required to stand erect naturally, although aid through taping may be given to youngsters with "lazy" ears. A correct, noble Shepherd head can best be described as possessing "the look of eagles." Their tails should reach long and be carried low, with the gentle curve of a saber at the end. All-white coloration is a disqualifying fault, and the Shepherd is one of the very few breeds that is disqualified for viciousness. This commendable practice has accomplished a great deal of good for the breed. It is a GSD, Champion Covy-Tucker Hill's Manhattan, who holds the honor of the most best in shows, over 200, carrying off prestigious wins at Westminster and the AKC Centennial.

The dog is sensible and has a devout loyalty to its family. Perhaps this is why the breed is so popular. Shepherd lovers seem to wear blinders when it comes to their favorite breed, thinking no other can compare. It is claimed the German Shepherd Dog has the intelligence of a seven-year-old child. Shepherds are often top contenders in the obedience ring.

As occurs with any breed that is so numerous, some poor breeding practices exist which perpetuate temperament and health problems. Buyers should study the dam and, if possible, the sire to see if they are physically sound and good-natured. A Shepherd is willing to do anything for the person he loves, to the point of giving his own life. The breed adores its own family and is naturally protective of it and of property. The standard stresses that it must stand its ground and be approachable in public situations.

German Shepherd Dog, solid black.

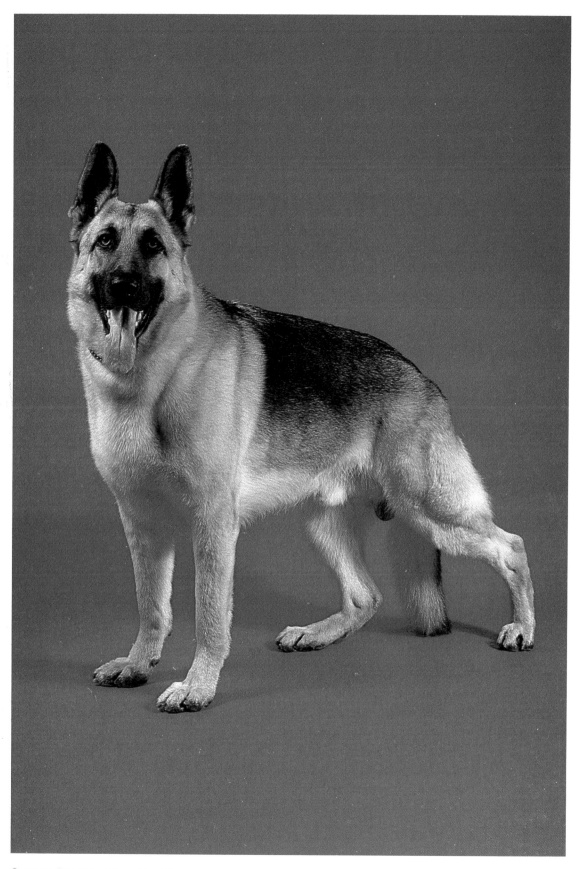

German Shepherd Dog, black/tan.

German Shepherd Dog, pups.

German Shepherd Dog.

Above, Below, and Facing Page: German Shepherd Dog.

GERMAN SHORTHAIRED POINTER

COUNTRY: Germany
WEIGHT: 55–70 pounds
HEIGHT: 23–25 inches
COAT: Short, dense and hard
COLOR: Solid liver, or liver and white, with or without ticking or roaning
OTHER NAMES: Deutscher Kurzhaariger Vorstehhund, Kurzhaar
REGISTRY: FCI, AKC, UKC, TKC, CKC
GROUP: Gun Dog

The slow-working schweisshunds with their superb noses have been found in Germany for centuries. As early as the 1700s, dogs referred to collectively as *huehnerhunden*, bird dogs, were used. No specific types had yet evolved, but they stemmed directly from the existing brackes and schweisshunds present in Germany, refined with pointing dogs. By the 1800s, individual breeds of versatile gun dogs began to be fixed by German breeders.

Prince Albrecht zu Solms-Brauenfels, in the middle of that century, spearheaded a tireless effort to create the ultimate *vorstehhund*—the all-purpose hunting dog. Records show that the Prince owned good schweisshunds and fine Pointers imported from England, and these were probably the basis for the German Shorthaired Pointer.

Early Shorthairs were short and heavy bodied, long-eared and extremely slow-working, showing the strongest influence from the hounds. The oft-repeated story of the Shorthair springing from "Bloodhounds" is merely a lapse in translation. *Schweisshund* translates to "bloodhound," meaning a dog used to follow a bloodtrail, not the breed "Bloodhound." These dogs were long since separated from the Bloodhound (St. Hubert) that we know today. English Pointer blood was later added to existing Shorthairs to increase speed and style, but great care was taken to keep the desired talents in water work, retrieving and tracking, and in toughness.

German Shorthaired Pointer, liver and white with ticking.

German Shorthaired Pointer, solid liver with ticking.

German Shorthaired Pointer, solid liver with ticking.

When the breed was imported into the USA in the early 1900s, it was enthusiastically received by American hunters. In fact, since his official recognition by the AKC in the 1940s, the breed has fared well in AKC registrations. He is one of the favorites of the average weekend hunter because of his natural abilities, ease of training and adaptability to family life. The Shorthair is described as "all business, no frills." In addition, the breed has been successful in the AKC field trials, as well as in American show and obedience rings. The German Shorthaired Pointer Club of America, to its credit, has strongly supported all aspects of breed ability; hence, the Shorthair shows no sign of splitting into two distinct types as have some of the other gun dogs. The breed boasts the most dual champions of any breed in the USA.

His short coat requires little care, even after a day in the field. He is affectionate and good with children, fitting into the venue of pet as long as his basic nature is understood. A dog of immense energy and a desire to hunt, he does not recognize natural boundaries and may become destructive if bored by confinement and a lack of exercise. Behaviorists recommend an outdoor kennel when the owner is not at home.

Tail and dewclaws are clipped when the German Shorthaired Pointer pup is just a few days old. His expressive tail stub wiggles with excitement at his master's attention or becomes rigid on a point. His body, like most shorthaired dogs', is warm and comforting, as are his eyes. The Shorthair is very long-lived, often surviving past his 16th year.

German Shorthaired Pointers, adult and puppies.

German Shorthaired Pointer.

Above: German Shorthaired Pointer diving into water. **Below:** German Shorthaired Pointers holding retrieves.

GERMAN SPITZ

German Wolfspitz

COUNTRY: Germany
HEIGHT: 18 inches minimum
COAT: Long, dense, double, stand-off
COLOR: Wolf gray only
REGISTRY: FCI
GROUP: Northern

Giant German Spitz

COUNTRY: Germany
WEIGHT: 40 pounds
HEIGHT: 16 inches minimum
COAT: Long, dense, double, stand-off
COLOR: Solids only—black, white or brown
OTHER NAMES: Deutscher Grossspitz, Great Spitz
REGISTRY: FCI
GROUP: Northern

Standard German Spitz

COUNTRY: Germany
WEIGHT: 25 pounds
HEIGHT: 11½–14 inches
COAT: Long, dense, double, stand-off
COLOR: Solid colors—white, black, brown, orange, wolf gray
OTHER NAMES: Deutscher Mittelspitz
REGISTRY: FCI, TKC
GROUP: Northern

Small German Spitz

COUNTRY: Germany
WEIGHT: 7 pounds minimum
HEIGHT: 8½–11 inches
COAT: Long, dense, double, stand-off
COLOR: Solids in black, white, brown, wolf gray, or orange (in England particolors are also allowed)
OTHER NAMES: Deutscher Kleinspitz, Miniature German Spitz, Victorian Pom
REGISTRY: FCI, TKC
GROUP: Northern

Toy German Spitz

COUNTRY: Germany
WEIGHT: Under 7 pounds
HEIGHT: Under 8½ inches
COAT: Long, dense, double, stand-off
COLOR: All solid colors
OTHER NAMES: Zwergspitz
REGISTRY: FCI
GROUP: Northern

Besides the three traditional uses for the Nordic breeds, herding, hunting and hauling, spitz have become popular throughout the world as utility and companion dogs. Countries from all over the world have developed their own form, all of which are still similar to one another.

Giant German Spitz, brown.

Small German Spitz, black with white markings.

The German Spitz breeds descend directly from the profusely coated Nordic herding dogs, like the Samoyed or the Lapphund, that are so common in the North. They were probably brought to northern Germany and Holland by Viking plunderers and looters who plagued those areas during the Middle Ages. These dogs spread throughout Europe and even the British Isles, contributing to the development of the true herding and shepherd breeds, as well as being the progenitors of the Spitz.

The Spitz was mentioned in German literature and history as early as 1450. Count Eberhand Zu Sayre Buffon wrote in his 1750 *National History of Quadrupeds* that he believed the Spitz to be the ancestor of all domestic breeds. At the end of the 17th century, citizens of Pomerania were raising a large white Spitz, and those in Wurttemberg had black and brown varieties to watch over their farms and possessions.

These original Spitz dogs have evolved into several sizes and a bouquet of solid colors. Today, the FCI recognizes five varieties based on size. The Wolfspitz, the largest and in gray only, is a similar type to what became the Keeshond in Holland. The Giant is not really a giant, compared to some of the flock guards or mastiffs, and is reminiscent of a small Samoyed or a Lapphund in white, chocolate or black. Standard and Small Spitz, in a wider variety of colors, became much-loved companions with the more recent development of the tiny toy to satisfy the demand for an apartment or lap-sized Spitz. These breeds are popular in Germany and well known throughout Europe, but have not reached North American shores.

The Small Spitz was imported to England from Germany (Pomerania) over 100 years ago and adopted the pseudonym Pomeranian. It was a favorite of Queen Victoria and was occasionally called the Victorian Pom. Gainsborough admired the German Spitz and captured its beauty

437

on canvas.

The Pomeranian has developed separately and divergently with its own standard. These dogs are more refined and have an exaggerated coat. They closely resemble their cousin the Spitz, but are a breed of their own.

With the Pomeranians of the show ring becoming smaller and smaller, many English fanciers lamented the demise of the larger specimens. In fact, Pomeranian show classes for "over 7–pound" dogs had been discontinued in the 1940s. British breeders Janet Edmonds and Averil Cawthera brought in several Klein and Mittel German Spitz from the Continent in the mid-1970s, although they were registered as Poms in England and used in Pomeranian breeding programs.

With the desire to re-establish the larger type Spitz, a special arrangement was created with the Kennel Club of Great Britain. For a six-month period in 1985, any Pom with one or more of four imported Spitz dogs in their pedigrees could have their registries switched to that of German Spitz. After this initial six-month period, the stud books were closed to any further double registration. From this beginning, the German Spitz has been re-established in Great Britain and is now an official breed there.

Breeders say that these dogs are most adaptable, happily accompanying owners on a 30–mile walk or cuddling in front of the fire. They are described as being much like a young child, anxious to please—yet also wanting their own way and knowing how to obtain it. A structured family order exists among these breeds, with the youngest adult delegated to play with the puppies. Like so many of the other northern breeds, the German Spitzes are happy and buoyant, displaying charming smiles and seeming to laugh with you—or at you. They are excellent jumpers and like to stand on their hind legs to beg or to show off. They should never show any nervousness or aggression, being always equable and confident. The alert, watchful personality, needed long ago with the herds, is retained and now suits the watchdog and companion.

German Wolfspitz.

Above: Giant German Spitz. **Below:** Small German Spitz, white with black markings.

Above: Toy German Spitz, chocolate. **Above Right:** Small German Spitz. **Below Left:** Small German Spitz. **Below Right:** Toy German Spitz.

Above: Toy German Spitzes, five colors. **Below:** Small German Spitz.

German Wirehaired Pointer.

GERMAN WIREHAIRED POINTER

COUNTRY: Germany
WEIGHT: 60–70 pounds
HEIGHT: 24–26 inches
COAT: Harsh, wiry and flat lying outer coat, with good beard and brows, never so long as to hide the outline of the dog; plenty of underwool
COLOR: Solid liver, or any combination of liver and white
OTHER NAMES: Deutscher Drahthaariger Vorstehhund, Drahthaar
REGISTRY: FCI, AKC, UKC, TKC, CKC
GROUP: Gun Dog

German Wirehaired Pointer.

The history of the Wirehair in Germany is quite recent. An interest in gun dogs with bristly coats always existed, and several types were in evidence by the late 1800s. At first, the Wirehair Club in Germany fostered all hunting dogs with a wire coat, but the wide variation in types soon saw separate organizations for the Pudelpointer, the Griffon, the Stichelhaar, and the German Wirehaired Pointer. They may all have come from the same stock, as these breeds developed concurrently. From this time on, each breed became individualized.

Like the Shorthair, the Drahthaar was developed to be used as a utility hunting dog and still fills that capacity. Because of the diverse tasks the breed is expected to accomplish, the dog is ideally big and robust, with a coat that affords protection. Wirehairs lead all hunting dogs in German registrations.

The Wirehair came to America about the same time as the first Shorthairs, in the 1920s. But the Wirehair was later in achieving AKC recognition and has never become as widespread as his shorthaired cousins in the States. Wirehairs tend to be a bit more aloof, and sometimes are one-person dogs. Those who support the breed possess a fine, obedient companion and hunting dog.

His tail is docked, like the GSP, leaving about two-fifths. If the coat is proper, it requires very little care. The underwool sheds in the spring and requires bathing and brushing, as is true of most breeds. A good harsh coat will do well with occasional combing out of dead hair. Some slight stripping may be required to neaten him for exhibition, but the coat should never have to be clipped or scissored. Only when the coat is improperly long and woolly does excessive grooming become necessary to give him the proper outline. This improper coat also attracts burrs and sticks in the field, which is why it is discouraged.

Often a clown, the Wirehair provides entertainment for his family. His whiskery face can switch from an imp to a noble show dog or a stern uncle. Sufficient exercise is essential. If bored, his excess energy can turn to destructive entertainment. The more they are taught, the happier they are. The breed needs a mixture of firm training with all-out rough-housing.

German Wirehaired Pointer.

German Wirehaired Pointers.

445

GIANT SCHNAUZER

COUNTRY: Germany
WEIGHT: 70–77 pounds
HEIGHT: 23–27½ inches
COAT: Moderate length, hard, bristly, with woolly undercoat
COLOR: Black or salt and pepper
OTHER NAMES: Riesenschnauzer
REGISTRY: FCI, AKC, UKC, TKC, CKC
GROUP: Herding

Giant Schnauzer, black.

The Giant Schnauzer was developed in southern Germany as a cattle herder from smoothhaired droving dogs, a variety of rough-coated indigenous shepherd dogs and, perhaps, the black Great Dane. He was known as the Munchener Dog at one time, due to the area of origin near Munich. He was used from the 15th century until the arrival of the railroads, when the large cattle drives waned. Farmers then lost interest in feeding these big eaters, and the Giants moved into the towns to become the guardians and mascots of beer halls and butcher shops during the 19th century.

Theory has it that, during this era, breeders noted his similarity to the existing smaller Schnauzers and aimed their breeding programs toward increasing that likeness. This is when most breed historians feel a cross was made to the Standard Schnauzer. The results were called Munich Schnauzers for a time, until the imposing term "Giant" was adapted around the turn of this century.

Introduced to dog shows in Munich in 1909, they attracted immediate attention and a national club was formed. Although they landed on the American shores at about the same time as the German Shepherd, the Giants were simply overshadowed by demand for their native relative. The breed has never gained a large following in North America but, at home, it is still one of the principal breeds used for security work. During both World Wars, the Giant gave valiant service as a police and war dog, suffering so many casualties that many thought the breed was lost. Thankfully, dedicated breeders have maintained the Giant in many countries around the world.

Their coat is similar to that of the other Schnauzers, and requires stripping twice a year. A strong tendency exists to regress to a soft, woolly coat, and care must be taken by breeders to maintain the true Schnauzer "hard" terrier coat. This hair not only is easier to care for than the woolly coat but keeps the breed distinct from its distant relative, the Bouvier. Ears are cropped and the tail is docked. The Giants still retain their guardian instincts and do well in schutzhund trials.

Above: Giant Schnauzer, salt and pepper. **Below:** Giant Schnauzer, black.

Glen of Imaal Terrier, blue brindle.

GLEN OF IMAAL TERRIER

COUNTRY: Ireland
WEIGHT: 35 pounds
HEIGHT: 14 inches
COAT: Medium length, harsh-textured
COLOR: Wheaten or brindle blue
REGISTRY: FCI, TKC
GROUP: Terrier

Although the Glen Terrier is a new furry face to many dog fanciers, it is actually an old breed that was simply ignored for a long time by the dog fancy. The Glen area, in County Wicklow, Ireland, is a scenic but rather bleak area offering poor soil. Many of the local farmers descended from Lowland and Hessian soldiers who had been given the land in the 16th and 17th centuries for services to the crown. These determined, hard-working people had to eke out a living from the rocks and could ill afford a dog who couldn't earn its keep. The fact that the Glen Terrier flourished under such demanding conditions manifests the breed's attributes equal to that of its masters.

With shorter legs than the other Irish terriers, the Glen Terrier could go to ground for badger and fox—not just to put them to flight, for he is game enough to fight to the death. The rat population around homes and barns was kept to a minimum. Saturday nights found owners gathering at a remote spot to match the feisty Glen dogs one-on-one, accentuated by heated wagering.

Besides being good ratters, varmint dogs and Saturday-night entertainment, Glens served as "turn- spits" on the dog wheel. This device was a treadmill, propelled for hours by an energetic little dog, which turned the meat on the spit as it cooked. Their small size, low fronts and strong rears suited them for this task as cook's helpers, and the Glens trotted for miles going nowhere.

Their size is documented in an old story passed down to a current Irish owner from his father, who owned Glens for over 50 years.

Years ago, there were cannons at the Coolmoney Army Camp in County Wicklow, which was held by the British Army. Glen Terriers found their way into camp and were adopted by the men. The claim was that a Glen of Imaal Terrier could always fit into the barrel of those 14–inch cannons.

Folklore says that the Glen Terrier was the result of a cross between the great Celtic hounds and a mongoose, and that the offspring was saved from culling by St. Patrick. The yarn continues that the *Firbolgs*, half snake and half human, ate all the Irish babies and puppies in the land. Upon Patrick's return to Ireland, Glens assisted St. Patrick in ridding Ireland of the snake-people and the snakes. Although touched with the blarney, the tale typifies their prowess and their proud Irish owners.

The breed was recognized formally as recently as the 1930s. In the 1950s, Paddy Brennan and Willie Kane, both admirers of the breed, made a concerted effort to build its reputation and numbers.

To win a championship, the Glen not only had to be judged for conformation, but also had to earn his *teastas misneach* or dead game certificate, accomplished at a badger trial. The terrier was put into a winding tunnel, with his foe, a badger, furiously defending the other end. The dog had to draw or drag the badger out within a certain length of time. Any dog that barked was disqualified.

Modern English owners tell of the grit necessary to face a badger underground. The badger's method of biting can easily ". . . take the face off a terrier. Missing noses and lips, or broken and missing jaws are not unusual in terriers worked to badger." An Irish breeder states that when a Glen Terrier gets a grip on another animal, nothing will induce him to let go until he is "choked out of it" (pressing of the fingers on the dog's throat to loosen the grip). Glens don't shake the rat to break its neck like most terriers do but, with a mighty crunch, bite the rat in half. The Glen has even used its considerable talents to draw the badger from under concrete floors!

Trials with live badgers were outlawed in 1966 and, officially, the test was no longer necessary to make up a champion. But the dog is still a working dog and, no doubt, informal badger trials are still held undercover to determine the gamest of possible breeding stock.

The Glen dog is low-stationed with slightly bowed front legs to give a mechanical advantage while digging. The harsh coat is weather-resistant. Because the "no barking" rule was absolute in trials, this terrier makes a quiet companion. Although the standard calls for a 35–pound dog, Irish breeders state that many Glens are heavier built—more in the 40–50-pound range. The reason for this probably stems back to the years that he was used for dog-fighting, when there were crosses to Bull Terrier, Staffordshire and other larger fighting dogs. Genes are carried forever; hence, the size problem still appears. Compared to some of his relatives, however, the Glen is still a rather moderately sized fellow. There are a handful of Glen enthusiasts in the United States.

Glen of Imaal Terrier, wheaten.

Golden Retriever.

GOLDEN RETRIEVER

COUNTRY: Great Britain
WEIGHT: 60–75 pounds
HEIGHT: 21½–24 inches
COAT: Dense and water repellent, lying flat to the body, flat or wavy, with some fringes—but not silky; good undercoat
COLOR: Various shades of lustrous golden
REGISTRY: FCI, AKC, UKC, TKC, CKC
GROUP: Gun Dog

The Golden is another product from the latter half of the 19th century, when so many of the gun dog breeds were formed. The breed owes much of its development to Sir Dudley Majoribanks (Lord Tweedmouth) whose records from his own meticulous stud books give a good basis of origins. Yellow recessives had always been present in the retrievers from Newfoundland and Labrador, even though in the 1850s the fashion in England was for black "Wavy-Coats" and Labradors. Lighter hues came to prominence later in the yellow Labs, as well in as the Chessie, and then the Golden.

Majoribanks took a liking to the yellow color and acquired a dog of that color, "Nous," from Flat-Coat breeding. To create good water retrievers, Nous was bred to Tweed Water Spaniel bitches, a now-extinct English retrieving dog that was close and curly-coated and a light liver color. Other crossings, of structured linebreeding, were recorded over a period of 20 years, including a Labrador or two, a red setter, possibly a Bloodhound, and other Wavy-Coats.

This, then, is the basic Golden's inheritance. Goldens were registered and shown as golden Flat-Coats until 1913, when they were listed as Golden or Yellow Retrievers and, finally, in 1920, took the name they bear today.

A legend still persists about Russian Sheep-

Golden Retriever.

dogs, acquired from a traveling circus, that contributed to the creation of the breed. No such information has been found among the Tweedmouth archives. Of course, others were breeding these golden-colored retrievers besides Majoribanks, so this strange mixture could have been introduced in other kennels. But most cynologists feel this was a contrived story, which the general public loved to believe. With the possible exception of trainability, the genetics of sheep dogs are diametrically opposed to the necessary abilities of the gun dog, and it is doubtful any knowledgeable dog breeder would have entertained the idea. Supporting this legend, however, the Golden was first exhibited under the name of Russian Retriever or Russian Retriever and Tracker. Thus, the story lives on.

Whatever its foundation, the modern Golden Retriever is a wonderfully versatile dog. He is a good retriever and upland game hunter, is used with increasing frequency as a guide for the blind and makes a loving, easygoing, pleasant companion. In the United States, the Golden dominates obedience competition with his flashy animation, quick reflexes, precision, trainability and intense desire to please. The same attributes

Golden Retriever performing in obedience trial.

Golden Retriever with retrieved pheasant.

stand him in good stead in the show ring.

A Golden requires sufficient exercise to overcome a tendency toward excess poundage. His beautiful coat requires only routine brushing, with a few grooming sessions during the spring when the undercoat is shed. The color can range from a soft, pale moon yellow to a lustrous burnished gold. It is as though the Golden has captured the warmth and beauty of sparkling sunshine in both his coat and temperament. He is a wonderful family pet, as he is loving and long-suffering with children, mannerly in the home, yet always ready to accompany any member in activities. A dog nearly void of guard instincts, his fringed tail always seems to be wagging. His expression is one of straightforward affection and trust.

Golden Retriever.

Golden Retriever on the retrieve.

Golden Retrievers, adults and pups.

Gordon Setter.

GORDON SETTER

COUNTRY: Great Britain
WEIGHT: 45–80 pounds
HEIGHT: 23–27 inches
COAT: Moderately long, flat and straight, long fine feathering
COLOR: Black/tan
REGISTRY: FCI, AKC, TKC, CKC
GROUP: Gun Dog

"Black and fallow" setting dogs have been known in Scotland for at least 350 years. They sprang from setting spaniels. These were crossed with local dogs to create a type for Scottish hunting conditions. In the 18th century, the present name was adapted because of the famed dogs kept by the Duke of Gordon.

An unknown writer in the late 1700s might well have been talking about a modern dog: "The Gordon Castle Setters are as a rule easy to break and naturally back well. They are not fast dogs but they have good staying powers and can keep on steadily from morning until night. Their noses are first class and they seldom make a false point or what is called at field trials a sen-

sational stand . . . . [but] When they stand you may be sure there are birds."

Early kennels had black/whites, tricolors, and reds as well as the black/tan, but this last color soon became the most desired—and thus the mark of purity. Red whelps still may crop up occasionally in a litter, as the standard warns.

Because of their handsome looks as well as their field abilities, they were imported and welcomed into America in the mid-1800s. Their lack of breakneck speed and breathtaking style to compete with the English Setter and Pointer at the big Circuit Trials may have been their rescue from the breed split seen in other gun dogs. They remained a favorite with hunters who wanted a full game bag. The Gordon is a handsome competitor in the show ring. They make a good showing in the AKC field trials, and there are a few duals.

Gordons are the heaviest headed of the setters, showing some flew, and long, low-set ears. His typical setter nature allows the weekend hunter to have a house pet as well. He does tend to be a bit more suspicious of strangers than the other setters and serves well as a home guardian.

Gordon Setter.

GREAT DANE

COUNTRY: Germany
WEIGHT: 100 pounds or more
HEIGHT: Minimum 28–32 inches; 30–32 inches or over preferred
COAT: Short, smooth
COLOR: Black, blue, fawn, brindle, harlequin
OTHER NAMES: Deutsche Dogge, German Mastiff
REGISTRY: FCI, AKC, UKC, TKC, CKC
GROUP: Mastiff

Except for lacking the undershot jaw, the Great Dane represents the closest modern example of the Alaunt. In Italy, the breed is called *Alano*, the Italian word for mastiff. Although not the heaviest, they are the tallest of the mastiffs, and their racier build may indicate a cross to hounds in past centuries. Merle hounds or shepherd dogs could have introduced the merle (harlequin) gene.

That the type is ancient is without question. Dogs of Dane or Alaunt type are depicted in drawings in the tombs of Beni-Hassan, dating

Great Dane, harlequin.

about 2200 BC. Some of these dogs are shown as harlequins. Other pre-Christian replicas appear on coins, on bas reliefs and in paintings.

His name is the only thing about him that is Danish. He is all German, used long ago by Germanic and Celtic tribes as a war dog, and is called Deutsche Dogge by the FCI. Only in English-speaking countries is he still a "Dane."

At first a giant bull-baiter, he was also used as a boarhound since the Middle Ages. In 1592, the Duke of Braunschweig showed up for a boar hunt with his pack of 600 male Danes! The breed was declared the national dog of Germany in 1876. A great favorite of the Iron Chancellor, Bismarck, they were his body guards and constant companions. In modern times, the Dane serves as a guardian and friend. His noble, statuesque appearance gives him the designation of "Apollo of dogdom."

An early admirer and owner was William "Buffalo Bill" Cody, when specimens were brought to American shores in the mid-1800s. Some of these early imports came directly from German estates where they had been trained in attack work. Thus the breed gained an early false reputation for ferocity. Temperament was soon "tempered." They were first shown under the name of Siberian or Ulm Dog. The Dane was introduced to British exhibitors in 1877, where his great, majestic height amazed spectators.

As a giant, it is essential for buyers to research their purchase, finding pups of strong, sound, good-natured parents. Large males may often reach as much as 180 pounds, though the tallest dog on record, a Great Dane named Shamgret Danzas, weighed 238 pounds at 41½ inches!

Although Danes are as content living in an apartment as on an estate, it is necessary to allow them to stretch those long legs frequently. Grooming, as with most of the mastiffs, is minimal—and feeding costs are maximum! They require involvement with family activities. If bored, these giants can become destructive—and a large dog can turn a table into toothpicks in minutes.

Danes' ears have been cropped for many years on the Continent and in the States; however, it is becoming more common to see natural drop ears even in the show ring.

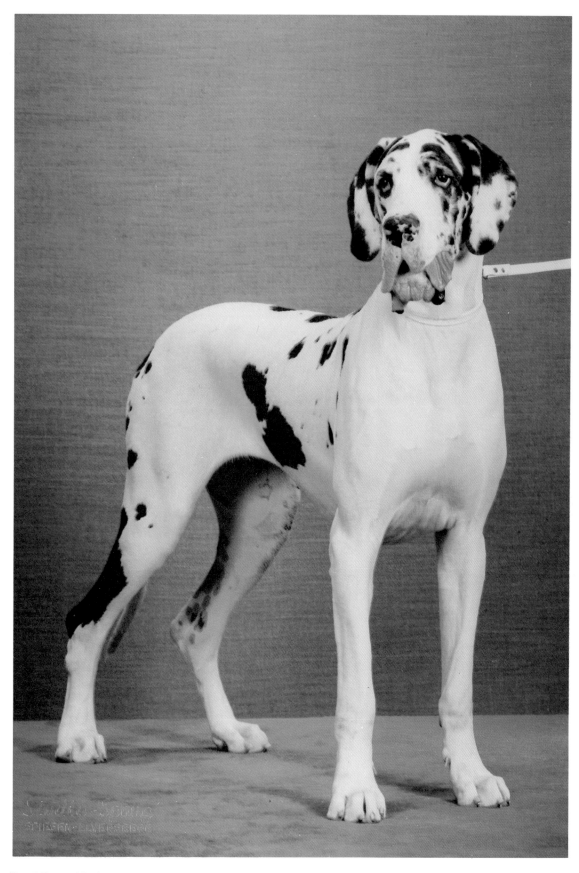

Great Dane, black.

Great Dane, brindle, ears cropped.

Great Dane.

Great Dane.

Great Dane.

GREATER SWISS MOUNTAIN DOG

COUNTRY: Switzerland
WEIGHT: Around 130 pounds
HEIGHT: 23½–28½ inches
COAT: Short, dense
COLOR: Black and tan, with white at toes, tail tip, chest, and blaze. The tan always lies between the black and the white. Red tricolors do occur but are not acceptable.
OTHER NAMES: Grosser Schweizer Sennenhund
REGISTRY: FCI, AKC
GROUP: Mastiff

The "Swissy" is the largest—and probably the oldest —of the four Swiss varieties, bred from the mastiff types left behind by the Roman armies. It was used for centuries in rural cantons, with no formal breeding program, as a butcher's dog and as a draft dog pulling produce to market. Farmers loved them. The dogs worked as hard as horses but didn't eat as much, and litters were large—up to 18 pups!

At that time, he was referred to as "Old Blaze." He started to disappear as the popularity of the red/white St. Bernard soared in the mid-1800s. There were many crossbreedings, and anything with the dominant red and white was called St. Bernard. Likely, many Swissies became Saints in one generation!

Right after the turn of the century, only a few remained on isolated farms. Franz Schertenleib found one and bought it as a "white elephant." Eager to hear what the knowledgeable judge, Dr. Albert Heim, had to say about this find, he exhibited the dog at a 1908 show, entered in the Bernese class. Heim knew the history of the Swissy and—having thought the breed extinct—praised the dog and admonished Swiss dog lovers to scout the farms and find enough animals to revitalize the breed.

The Swiss took a renewed interest and worked to keep these dogs from dying out. In 1910, these breeders accomplished another goal when the GSMD was accepted by the Swiss registry. Today's Greater Swiss Mountain Dogs

Greater Swiss Mountain Dog.

Greater Swiss Mountain Dog.

trace back to seven or eight animals, a very narrow breed base. Up until the 1930s, "foundlings,"dogs which exemplified the breed but did not possess a pedigree, were still used in breeding programs. A problem with lack of size was conquered, possibly by crossbreeding with smooth Bernards.

Their natural protective instinct is demonstrated by the tale of "Nero." After an evening in the pubs, Nero's owner and his friends headed home. Instead of following his owner as usual, Nero chose to accompany a man who was in his cups. When the man fell in a creek, Nero fished him out, escorted him home and stayed overnight. When the gentleman came to his senses and opened the door the next morning, Nero immediately headed for home. This instinct is today channeled into schutzhund training and as watchdogs for the homes.

As peace loving as the Swiss people, the breed is calm, even-tempered and sturdy. Not a roamer, the Swissy hates to be tied or confined and is happiest with his family. He still loves to pull carts or sleds, especially if the passenger is a child.

The Swissy is an attractive, easily groomed show dog with an aptitude for obedience. The breed was introduced to the States in 1968, and in 1985 was accepted into the AKC Miscellaneous Group.

GREAT PYRENEES

COUNTRY: France
WEIGHT: 90–140 pounds
HEIGHT: 25–32 inches
COAT: Medium to medium-long
COLOR: White
OTHER NAMES: Pyrenean Mountain Dog, Chien de Montagne des Pyrenees
REGISTRY: FCI, AKC, UKC, TKC, CKC
GROUP: Flock Guard

Certainly the most recognizable and populous example of the flock-guarding breeds, the Pyr originated in the Pyrenees Mountains that separate France from Spain. The exact history of the dogs' arrival is not known, but they have been guarding the flocks in France for millenia. Fossils of the breed type have been found predating the Bronze Age (1800–1000 BC). "Discovered" by the French nobility before the Revolution, like the Maremma in Italy, they could be found guarding the large chateaux in southern France. Dauphin Louis XIV named the breed the Royal Dog of France.

Great Pyrenees.

465

This didn't secure the Pyr in the hands of royalty, however. The peasants continued to make use of his abilities as flock guard. Although physical characteristics such as strength, keen hearing, and big paws for sure-footedness were deemed highly preferable, the psychological aspects of the dog were considered of prime importance. If a dog didn't bond to the sheep and protect them despite his own discomforts, the dog was killed, abandoned or sold (at a steep price) to a tourist who didn't care about these attributes.

Pyrs also bore the ignominy of being dupes for smugglers. These majestic dogs wore a backpack stuffed with contraband, taking it across the border between France and Spain. Their sure-footedness enabled them to take roads impassable to humans, allowing the dogs to avoid detection by customs officials.

Early Pyrenees were brought to the Canadian Maritime Provinces by Basque fishermen and stayed long enough to mix their genes with local retrievers, creating a genetic base for the Newfoundland and Landseer. General Lafayette sent two of these dogs to a writer friend in America, touting the Pyrs' expertise in flock guarding.

The early 20th century found these dogs nearly extinct. Bernard Senac-Lagrange, a French aristocrat and well-known dog authority, can be credited with saving the breed. He consolidated various factions, went into the mountains to obtain good specimens and created the first written standard.

Imported into America soon after Lagrange's time, the Pyr achieved AKC recognition in 1933. During World War II, the breed carried messages and packs for the French troops. In America, deemed too large for military service, they were trained for pack work designed for an Alaskan campaign, if such a service was needed. When this idea was discarded, the Pyrs were "honorably discharged."

This lovely show dog has been sweetened considerably in temperament from the strong guarding dogs of the mountains, and has become one of the gentle giants. Specimens hailing directly from the Pyrenees may still have more of the typical independence and wariness.

Great Pyrenees.

Above: The Great Pyrenees, illustrated here with a young lamb, is a reliable and talented flock guard. **Below:** Great Pyrenees.

There is no need to feel that the breed has been ruined by exhibition, however. Because of his greater availability and higher profile, he is one of the breeds most commonly (and successfully) called upon for predator control. Farmers or ranchers introduce the puppy to the flock very early. By the time the pups are six months old, they are usually fully bonded to the sheep and are beginning to protect them. This breed does well with all livestock and with other dogs.

Pyrs have double dewclaws on the hind feet. A consistent regime of grooming is necessary to keep the dog shiny, unmatted and healthy. They are loving and protective of their home and family and need to be a part of activities. Lagrange said, "Only the true breed possesses this bewitching, almost indefinable expression in the eyes, both distant and caressing, contemplative and just a little sad. As you look in these eyes the immense moral value of the breed pierces your soul."

Above: Great Pyrenees puppies posing over mountainous terrain. **Below:** Body study of the Great Pyrenees—more commonly in Europe do beige patches appear on the breed's head and body.

GREEK HAREHOUND

COUNTRY: Greece
WEIGHT: 38–44 pounds
HEIGHT: 18½–21½ inches
COAT: Very short; thick, a little coarse
COLOR: Black and tan saddled, with a white spot on chest allowed
OTHER NAMES: Hellinikos Ichnilatis, Hellenic Hound
REGISTRY: FCI
GROUP: Hound

Greek Harehound.

The native hound of Greece is very similar to the Yugoslavian Balkan Hound. Southern Yugoslavia borders on the north of Greece and forms the western edge of the Balkan Peninsula. The two breeds probably had similar origins or are actually two strains that have developed from the same ancient breed.

Although renowned locally for his skilled nose and resonant voice, the Greek dog is known only in his native land. Formal dog breeding and exhibiting is limited in Greece, but this type of hound has remained pure because of his abilities. Used especially over the rocky terrain so prevalent in his homeland, he is hunted singly, in pairs or in small packs.

JRQuinn

Greek Sheepdog.

GREEK SHEEPDOG

COUNTRY: Greece
WEIGHT: 80–90 pounds
HEIGHT: 26 inches
COAT: Thick, dense
COLOR: White
GROUP: Flock Guard

Greece, just across the isthmus from Turkey, probably acquired its flock guards with early migrations of people to the West. These dogs have been used throughout Greece, particularly around the northern provinces in the Balkan foothills.

Said to look much like the Maremma or the Kuvasz, the breed is renowned for its ferocity. The dogs occasionally took it upon themselves to protect the whole countryside. A heavy log or other object attached to the collar curbed this zealotry. People walking in rural areas—sometimes even the shepherds—armed themselves with stout sticks or a pocketful of rocks.

According to Hughes, "Travels in Greece" (1800s), a traveler tells how he "was attacked by one of those fierce . . . dogs which shepherds use to protect their flocks. He flew at my horse's heels. I had to wheel the horse and discharge my fowling piece over his head."

Shepherds of the old school felt cropping the right ear improved the dog's hearing. This practice caused a peculiar lopsided look with a short stub on the right and a drop ear on the left.

Since there are no kennel clubs in Greece and few dogs are raised for pleasure, it is difficult to know the modern status of this ancient breed. They have never been introduced to any other country, but the great white dogs are still used by Greek shepherds. They breed them in the practical sense; best worker to best worker, with little regard for "fine points." But the type has remained pure. Modern Greek cynologists lament the fact that many Greeks feel imported breeds such as Dobermans and Rottweilers create more snob appeal and status that the native breeds.

GREENLAND DOG

COUNTRY: Scandinavian countries
WEIGHT: 66 pounds and up
HEIGHT: 24 inches
COAT: Medium, dense, stand-off
COLOR: Any color allowed, except albino
OTHER NAMES: Grønlandshund
REGISTRY: FCI
GROUP: Northern

The Greenland Dog is closely related to other northern hauling huskies. At one time, there were dozens of breeds and varieties, but many have disappeared due to modern use of snowmobiles and other machinery, which has supplanted the use of these dogs. Much crossing of types occurred as the modern settling of northern areas provided contact between previously remote areas. The Grønlandshund is one of the breeds saved and fostered by fanciers, especially in the Scandinavian countries. Sadly, the breed is no longer numerous even in its native environment.

Before use of the more recent method of chaining sled dogs when not working, the practice among the natives was to keep them tethered with thongs of seal hide. Of course, dogs chewed through their ties, so most working sled dogs had their incisors broken (the small cutting teeth in the front of the canines), which necessitated cutting their meat. Since most of the dogs were fed frozen meat or fish, the rations were chopped into small pieces which could be swallowed whole. In *The Voyage of the Fox*, McClintock recalls how he once cut 65 pounds of seal meat into small pieces, and his 29 hungry Eskimo dogs devoured every morsel in 42 seconds!

Greenland Dogs were also used by the natives as hunting dogs, utilizing their keen sense of smell to find seals' breathing holes in the ice. Once the hole was found, the dog and master sat back to wait, as sooner or later the seal came up for air and it would be speared. In the summer months, the dogs carried backpacks of supplies up to 33 pounds.

The breed remains principally a working dog. They have the typical, Nordic, good, loyal, affectionate temperament, but when the dogs work in teams, they don't have the opportunity to develop a relationship with one master. They are independent and self-willed, and rowdy and boisterous in their play. The thick, stand-off outer coat and dense underwool allow them to withstand constant outdoor living in temperatures that can reach -50 or even -75 degrees Fahrenheit.

Greenland Dog, fawn.

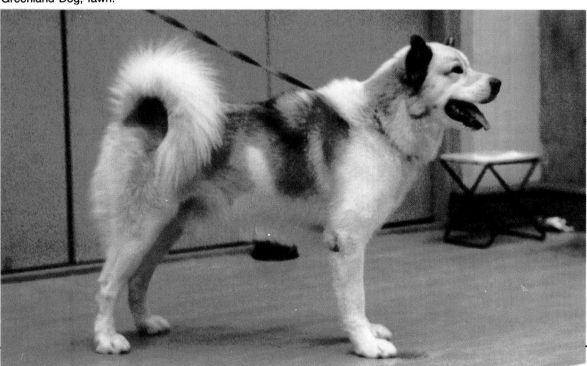

471

Above: Greenland Dogs pictured working on a snow-covered landscape in their homeland. **Below:** Greenland Dog.

Greenland Dog.

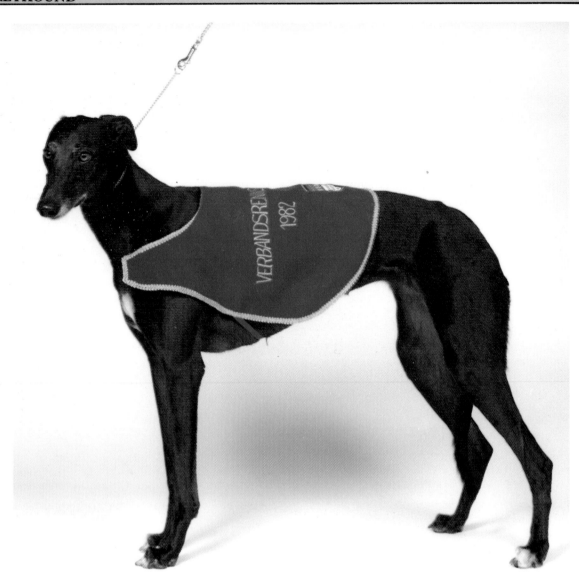

Greyhound.

GREYHOUND

COUNTRY: Great Britain
WEIGHT: 60–70 pounds
HEIGHT: 27–30 inches
COAT: Short, smooth
COLOR: Any color
REGISTRY: FCI, AKC, TKC, CKC
GROUP: Southern

> Heded like a Snake and necked like a
>   Drake.
> Foted like a Kat. Tayled like a Rat.
> Syded lyke a Teme. Chyned like a Beme.
>   *Boke of St. Albans,* Dame Berners, 1486

Edward, Duke of York, described the Greyhound in *The Master of Game* as "shuldres as a roe buck; the for legges stregth and grete ynow, and nought to hind legges; the feet straight and round as a catte, and great cleas, the boones and joyntes of the cheyne grete and hard as the cheyne of an hert; the thighs great and squarred as an hare, the houghs streight, and not crompying as an oxe."

This "duke's" mixture portrayed the sleek, muscled and racy Greyhound, admired for its speed for thousands of years. Tombs of Egypt from the Fourth dynasty, between 4000 and 3500 BC, show drawings of dogs similar to Greyhounds and Salukis, making it obvious that dogs of this type were much esteemed during this era. During the ensuing centuries, Greyhounds proved to be in great demand as an item of barter, and spread through the Near East and Europe. They were developed to standard in England, where they became a status symbol. A Welsh proverb states, "You may know a gentlemen by his horse, his hawk and his greyhound."

The source of the Greyhound name is accredited to various plausibilities: from as simple an explanation as the breed's early colors or the Latin word *gradus*, i.e., swiftness; to the Old English *grech* or *greg* meaning dog; or a corruption of "gazehound" or "great hound."

The dog was a favorite of English nobility, who limited ownership by the common folk under the *Laws of Canute* formulated in 1016: "No mean person may keepe any greyhounds, but freemen may keepe greyhounds so that their knees be cut before the verderors of the forest, and without cutting of their knees also, if he does abide 10 miles from the bounds of the forest." In wide flat expanses, a hunter was handicapped—no brushy forest to conceal the human presence or to hamper the animal as it attempted to bolt. With its powerful eyesight and great speed enabling him to overtake the quarry, the Greyhound proved an invaluable

Greyhound, brindle.

Greyhounds, fawn.

aid. One of them, "Bang" by name, jumped an astounding 30 feet while coursing a hare.

When dogs became more than a means to a full cooking pot, the Greyhound excelled in coursing, and later track racing, hitting a speed of nearly 45½ mph, maintaining its reputation as the fastest dog on earth. Only the cheetah tops him for speed in the animal world. His track abilities have given him an advantage over all other breeds. The racing Greyhound is the only recognized breed in America not afflicted with the curse of hip dysplasia. Several Greyhounds made their fame and their masters' fortune on the track, some winning as much as $50,000 during their racing peak. The sale of one dog, "Indian Joe," copped the biggest price in dogdom: $72,000.

"In 1867 a shiftless tenant of an Irish nobleman was sleeping off the effects of a drunken spree on the banks of a stream running through the estate when he heard muffled cries coming from a sack caught on the root of a rotting stump. Staggering to the stream's edge the tenant drew from the water a half-drowned Greyhound puppy. When grown this puppy . . . became the most famous of all racing greyhounds—Master McGrath . . . defeated but once in his entire racing career, and then only because he fell through the ice of a frozen stream during a course."

Modern Greyhounds make gentle, well-behaved, graceful pets, elegant show dogs or thrilling competitors. They are affectionate with their families and, like many sighthounds, aloof with strangers. An interesting piece of trivia is that a Greyhound named "Low Pressure" has the distinction of being the most prolific dog. During his eight-year breeding span, he sired 2,414 registered pups, with another 600 unregistered!

Greyhound, brindle with white.

Griffon Nivernais, blue-gray.

GRIFFON NIVERNAIS

COUNTRY: France
WEIGHT: 50–55 pounds
HEIGHT: 21-24½ inches
COAT: Long, hard, rough and bushy
COLOR: Preferably blue-gray, dark gray or wolf gray; roan, black/tan, tawny rarely seen
REGISTRY: FCI
GROUP: Hound

One of the oldest of the French hounds, the Griffon Nivernais originated in the Nivernais district of central France, just south of Paris. The genesis of the wire-coated hounds is un-known, although crosses to the Phoenician sighthound types could have introduced the wire gene. Shaggy coats were also exhibited by the Eastern-type herding or water dogs so these, too, could have been the source of the rough jacket. Whatever the origin, the wire coats furnished protection from the brush and rocky terrain. The bristly beard, mustache and body coat give the wire coats an unkempt, "devil-may-care" appearance.

The Nivernais can be traced back as far as the 1200s, when they were called the *Chien Gris de St. Louis* (St. Louis's Gray Dogs) as the favorites of Louis IX. These gray dogs probably came from the Balkans after the fourth Crusade. At home they were refined with crosses to other hounds. They remained in good standing, as they were also favored by the Sun King, Louis XIV, nearly 400 years later.

The breed was originally bred for hunting boar and wolves in packs and was the forerunner of many other scenthounds. Hunts, embellished with trumpeters and liveried beaters, involved hundreds of these hounds. These celebrated Nivernais packs were scattered following the Revolution. More than 100 years later, many dog lovers feared the noble Nivernais was gone forever, but a club founded in 1900 managed to gather remaining specimens and worked to restore the breed. Called *Chien de Pays*, meaning a local breed or native dog at home, he has made a comeback.

The breed is now used for smaller game and is particularly prized by "Sunday hunters" because of its ease of care, willingness to work and adaptability to any terrain including water. His expression should be "a little sad," but he should never be timid. The standard also demands a dog that is "simple and hardy," built for long hours of hard work rather than speed. Therefore the weekend hunter, who must follow the dog on foot, has a hunting companion that meets those needs. Four or five *barbouillards*, (nickname for the breed, meaning dirty and besmirched), are claimed to be better than a dozen hounds of other breeds. He is now utilized throughout France and has been exported to several countries, including Greece, as well as the United States and Canada, where he is used to hunt bear.

Above: A pack of Griffon Nivernais pictured with their masters in front of a castle in their native France. **Below:** Body study of the Griffon Nivernais.

GRIFFONS VENDEENS

Grand Griffon Vendeen

COUNTRY: France
WEIGHT: 66–77 pounds
HEIGHT: Minimum 23½ inches, larger preferred
COAT: 1¼–2½ inches, hard and rough; never soft
COLOR: Various shades of orange, gray, tawny, or black/tan, usually as spots on white background
OTHER NAMES: Large Vendeen Griffon
REGISTRY: FCI
GROUP: Hound

Briquet Griffon Vendeen

COUNTRY: France
WEIGHT: 35–53 pounds
HEIGHT: 20–22 inches
COAT: 1¼–2½ inches, hard and rough; never soft
COLOR: Various shades of orange, gray, tawny, or black/tan, usually as spots on white background
OTHER NAMES: Medium Vendeen Griffon
REGISTRY: FCI
GROUP: Hound

Grand Basset Griffon Vendeen

COUNTRY: France
WEIGHT: 40–44 pounds
HEIGHT: 15–16½ inches
COAT: 1¼–2½ inches, hard and rough; never soft
COLOR: Various shades of orange, gray, tawny, or black/tan, usually as spots on white background
OTHER NAMES: Large Vendeen Basset
REGISTRY: FCI
GROUP: Hound

Petit Basset Griffon Vendeen

COUNTRY: France
WEIGHT: 25–35 pounds
HEIGHT: 13–15 inches
COAT: 1¼–2½ inches, hard and rough; never soft
COLOR: Various shades of orange, gray, tawny, or black/tan, usually as spots on white background
OTHER NAMES: Small Vendeen Basset
REGISTRY: FCI, TKC, CKC
GROUP: Hound

Grand Basset Griffon Vendeen, black/tan.

La Vendee is a district on the western coast of France, south of Brittany. The hounds of Vendee are some of the oldest varieties, bred directly from the white Southern Hound with crosses to rough-coated dogs reportedly from Italy. Crosses also occurred to the Griffon Nivernais. One of the first breeders was a king's recorder (clerk) in the 15th century. Clerk in French is *greffier*, and the reference to the "greffier's dogs" gradually became "griffon." The name was first used to describe these breeds and later to indicate many of the wire-coated hunting dogs. Several griffons were given to King Louis XII, bringing him much pleasure. In fact, the breed was once called *Chiens Blancs du Roi* or the King's White Hounds.

The French Revolution nearly sounded the death knell for these breeds, but they were fostered and revitalized by devoted breeders in the 20th century with the first club forming in 1907. The large (Grand) size was originally used in packs for big game such as boar and wolf. They were noted for their stamina and courage. The Grand is still a passionate and persistent hunter.

But hunting land in France, as in much of the world, is becoming restricted and is decreasing. This leaves a limited environment for the Grand, whose style is to follow the quarry for many hours. This variety is the rarest of the hunting Vendeens, and owners voice concern about "a dark future for this breed." Enthusiasts hope that more serious breeders will take up the banner of this old hound. One breeder in America has imported stock and is working to establish these dogs.

Briquet is the French term for a smaller hound used for hare coursing, and the Briquet version of the Vendeen Hound is just a slightly smaller variety. He is used today in small packs or singly as a personal hunting dog, literally beating the bushes for all types of game. Not a commonplace dog either, he has a wider appeal as a single hunter's dog, so is less likely to face extinction than the Grand.

There are two *Basset*, or short-legged, varieties of the Vendeen Griffons. The two sizes originally occurred even in the same litters, and interbreeding was allowed. It was 1950 before the Petit was given separate status, and 25 years later that crossing of the two sizes was forbid-

Petit Basset Griffon Vendeen, tawny.

den. These short-legged Bassets were ideal for the Vendee landscape, which is heavily interspaced with hedges and roads, making winter passage impossible on horseback. Hare-coursing is done on foot, and hounds that stayed close to the hunters were in demand. In both the large and small Basset varieties, the body retains its full size with only the legs being shortened by the dwarf mutation. In France and elsewhere the Vendeen Bassets are still used individually or in packs for hunting all sorts of quarry, including deer and wild boar, as well as smaller furred and feathered game.

Because of its extroverted, lively nature and jaunty expression, the Petit Basset has won some degree of popularity as a companion dog. Petit Basset Griffon Vendeens (often called *PeeBee-GeeVees* or just Petits in America to put a handle on their tongue-twister name) have been granted recognition in Canada, and there are a good number in the USA, including some hunt

A hunting pack of Grand Griffons Vendeens on lead with master.

packs. A PBGV baby, "Alexander," created a minor sensation by winning Best Puppy at the acclaimed 1983 Professional Handler's Super Match before most of America knew what the breed was. An American organization is fostering this breed, and their proponents hope for AKC recognition in the near future. Affectionately called Roughies in England and Griffons in Denmark, in French speaking countries they are still called PetitBassetGriffonVendeen, fluently rolled out as if it were all one word!

All these varieties are classic French hounds clad in a rough jacket, with lean heads and long folded ears. A lack of excessive loose skin, and the high-set, proudly carried saber tail completes the picture. The coat is medium length, rough and wiry, with plenty of undercoat for protection. It is not as long and shaggy as the Griffon Nivernais and is never trimmed, even for exhibition.

Although black/tan tricolors are allowed by the standard, the more commonly seen brighter shades of red, orange or tawny with the predominance of white sets these dogs apart from many hounds. The Grand Basset always has straight (albeit short) legs, while the Petit's legs may be either straight or a bit bowed.

Vendeens, like most scenthounds, are vocal when hot on a scent. Hunting is instinctive. So is digging. Non-hunters should be aware of these inclinations, never leaving these hounds loose—or they will be gone, over hill and dale!

All of the sizes are energetic, independent and—breeders warn—not naturally obedient. They must be taught control and be made to understand who is "top dog" from the beginning. Once that obstacle is overcome, they are nonstop tail waggers who win hearts wherever they go.

Above Left: Grand Griffon Vendeen, orange. **Above Right:** Briquet Griffon Vendeen, orange. **Below:** Petit Basset Griffon Vendeen, dark tawny.

Above: Petit Basset Griffon Vendeen, pups. **Below:** Grand Griffon Vendeen, orange.

Above: Petit Basset Griffon Vendeen. **Below:** Briquet Griffon Vendeen, orange.

Haldenstövare.

HALDENSTÖVARE

COUNTRY: Norway
WEIGHT: 44–55 pounds
HEIGHT: 19½–23½ inches
COAT: Short, shiny and dense
COLOR: Tricolor, with white predominating
OTHER NAMES: Halden Hound
REGISTRY: FCI
GROUP: Hound

Norwegian scenthounds have been popular hunting dogs in their native land since the 1800s, but have never gained a following elsewhere. The Haldenstövare was named after the town of Halden, where the breed was developed from indigenous hounds and foxhounds. A graceful and rather lightweight hunter, he is used especially for fast chases over wide open spaces—even in snow.

He has a clean, dry head and neck without excess skin, and moderately long ears that reach the middle of the muzzle when pulled forward. The body should give the impression of supple power, with a deep chest and ribs carried well back, wide muscular loin and straight, strongly boned legs. Feet are particularly important because of the terrain he must hunt. Toes are high and tight but long enough to grip the snow, and there must be dense hair between the toes for protection. In color, the white must predominate. Black patches occur on the head and body, and the tan is limited to the spots above the eyes, on the cheeks, legs and breast, and under the ears and vent. Color is quite important in this breed, since the predominantly white hound is distinctly different from most of the darker hued Scandinavian stövare.

Although a fine hunter, numbers of this native Norwegian hound are limited. Because of their relative scarcity, promoters warn that great care must be used in breeding programs to prevent various inheritable defects.

486

HAMILTONSTÖVARE

COUNTRY: Sweden
WEIGHT: 50–60 pounds
HEIGHT: 18–23½ inches
COAT: Short; very thick with lots of undercoat in the winter
COLOR: Tricolor: golden tan with black mantle, white on breast, muzzle, on feet and tip of tail; a partial collar is now permitted. No color should predominate.
OTHER NAMES: Hamilton Hound
REGISTRY: FCI, TKC
GROUP: Hound

About 100 years ago, Count A.P. Hamilton created the breed that carries his name. The Count was the founder of the Swedish Kennel Club and a connoisseur of hounds. His dog and bitch, "Pang" and "Stella," were basically of English Foxhound and/or Harrier breeding. Hamilton imported German hounds, like those of Hanover, Holstein and Curlandia, to cross with his British-bred dogs. From these hybrids came the Hamiltonstövare. Today it is a favored hunting dog in Sweden. Since 1968, a few have been imported into Britain, where they are slowly gaining a pawhold.

The Hamilton is always hunted singly, like the brackes of Germany. He accompanies the hunting parties into the vast Swedish pine forests, where he finds and flushes game back towards the guns, baying to indicate his whereabouts. Also adapted to snow cover, he is robust enough to trail large game.

His temperament is sweet and gentle, and he fits well into family life. However, the hunting instincts are strong and the need for activity is great. Those two factors must be kept in mind by prospective owners. Large space is necessary for long walks. Owners warn that, even when well trained, these dogs should be kept on leash in areas with game, as hunting instincts may override training. Once off on a scent, they will hunt for hours before returning to their original starting point, working up a hearty appetite. Owners describe them as real "chow hounds." But if enough physical activity is provided, these hounds are happy, bouncy and extroverted pals which relate well to people and other animals.

The Hamiltonstövare is popular enough in Sweden to be a part of the nation's folklore. A small elf, Tomten, is said to help Swedish homemakers in the house. He is accompanied by a Hamilton called "Karo."

Hamiltonstövare.

HANOVERIAN HOUND

COUNTRY: Germany
WEIGHT: 84–99 pounds
HEIGHT: 20–24 inches
COAT: Short, thick and shiny
COLOR: Light to dark red, more or less dark-streaked; face with or without dark mask
OTHER NAMES: Hannoverscher Schweisshund
REGISTRY: FCI
GROUP: Hound

Schweisshund literally means bloodhound, which is a generic term for a dog, such as the Hanoverian or Bavarian, that follows a bloodtrail. When large game is wounded during a hunt, it may travel many miles in heavy cover only to hide and die a long, slow death. The development of dogs for trailing the wounded animal are common on the Continent. The honor code of the German hunter demands an obligation to find all shot game—dead or wounded. A deer injured with an arrow or bullet may leave only occasional drops of blood many yards apart. The dogs, although brought in even hours later, can follow the cold trail for many miles and lead the hunter to the wounded animal. Sometimes the search goes on for days, but it is never aban-

doned until the wounded animal is found, dead or alive. This sort of hunting, actually trailing, is not often employed in the USA. It requires a dog with an excellent cold nose and great cold-trailing ability.

The Hanoverian was developed in the 19th century by gamekeepers around the city of Hanover in Upper Saxony, including the central plains of Germany. The breed fathers started with heavy tracking hounds known since the fifth century, like the Solling-Leitbracke, which was a close kin to the St. Hubert and other hounds of the Segusian type. These were crossed with lighter type Celtic Bracken, such as the Haidbracke and hounds from the Harz to create the modern form.

The Hanoverian is specifically a big-game tracking and trailing dog of superb nose, although quite slow on the move. His body is low on leg and heavy for his height. He carries some flew, but his hallmark is the huge stiff ear set rather high on the head. The Hanoverian has the marvelous nose necessary for bloodtrailing, and he is also an able assistant on live game. Although hunted in packs long ago, he is now usually worked singly. His blood flows in the veins of many of the European utility gun dogs, which is where these latter dogs inherited their nose, tracking ability and perseverance.

The Hanoverian is valued beyond rubies by gamekeepers and forest wardens. Even though gun dogs like the German Shorthair are trained to bloodtrail, if these non-specialists fail to find a wounded animal, the Hanoverian may be brought in—sometimes days later—and put on the trail. No wounded animal is left to waste in the forest.

One current German forester proudly tells of starting his Hanoverian on a track more than a week old. Over several days, they followed the trail 30 miles, finally successfully finding the quarry.

These dogs are calm, quiet, poised and very attached to their master and family. But when hunting, they are "hard, single-minded and persistent." They are highly specialized and must be worked steadily to bring out the best of their talents. Thus, they are not dogs for the casual hunter. Most are owned and utilized by foresters and game wardens.

Hanoverian Hound, brindle.

Above: Hanoverian Hound, red. **Below:** Hanoverian Hound.

489

HARLEQUIN PINSCHER

COUNTRY: Germany
WEIGHT: 22–26 pounds
HEIGHT: 12–14 inches
COAT: Short and smooth
COLOR: Variations of harlequin (merle blotching on either white or black)
OTHER NAMES: Harlekinpinscher
REGISTRY: FCI
GROUP: Terrier

The Harlequin Pinscher was selected from smaller specimens of the German Pinscher, specifically for the merle color. Since the merle gene is dominant and it is a color unknown in other terriers, a cross to another group is likely to have introduced this hue. Merle dogs show a preponderance of white, and many German breeders felt lack of pigment tended to introduce a multitude of problems. Thus the Pinscher-Schnauzer Club denigrated this variety and refused to recognize them.

Fanciers claimed the breed had outstanding temperament and made an ideal companion that thrived on indoor life. These factors suggest that small herding dogs, like the Sheltie or Berger de Pyrenees, may have contributed to the breed, introducing both the merle color and a more gentle personality. Hounds offer other possibilities, such as dappled Dachshunds. The Harlequin Pinscher is most likely now extinct. No formal registrations have been made since the 1930s, but there is some talk of a revival in the offing.

Harlequin Pinscher.

HARRIER

COUNTRY: Great Britain
WEIGHT: 48–60 pounds
HEIGHT: 19–22 inches
COAT: Short, coarse and hard
COLOR: Any hound color including blues
REGISTRY: FCI, AKC, CKC
GROUP: Hound

Harrier, brown and white, saddled.

The Harrier is, in actuality, a perfect small version of an English Foxhound: crosses of various old-style, heavy scenthounds with lighter, smaller hounds, such as the Beagle, with a dash of this 'n that. These dogs are the same in form and ability, and developed directly from the same stock that created the larger hound. Records show an established pack of Harriers was owned by Sir Elias de Midhope as early as 1260. The Cotley Pack of Somerset was organized by Thomas Deane in 1796, with many Harriers brought to the "colonies" during that time. Their original capacity was for following the large, slower European hare in front of their masters who hunted on foot. Later hunters on horseback followed the packs.

Like the English Foxhound, most Harriers were raised by specialized hunt clubs for use by their members. Many of these packs were renowned, their fame continuing for several generations. The Quarme Harriers, which have a distinctive pale color, were disbanded following the last World War, after a long and illustrious history. The Minehead Harriers still hunt in the County of Somerset. Other packs have been bred and hunted continuously for more than a hundred years. Pack Harriers in England are registered and regulated by the Association of Masters of Harriers and Beagles. This group's stud books have two sections—one for the English Harrier and one for the West Country Harrier, recognizing differences in type.

The sport of hound trailing is very popular in the Lake district and the area bordering England and Scotland. The hounds, following a drag track, are run for speed only; the first one arriving at the finish line is declared the winner. Since the sport attracts as much betting as the racing dog tracks, formal rules and regulations have been passed. For this activity, they use crossbred hounds that are basically Harrier, but with various surreptitious additions to create the necessary speed.

Harriers as a pure breed have subsisted in the United States although never in large numbers. If pack raised they are more dog-oriented, like the Foxhound. When reared in individual homes, they are like any other hound. The dogs are gentle, never biting nor snapping. Grooming is minimal, and they are healthy and hardy souls.

The hound stubbornness and single-mindedness do require firm, early discipline. A basic obedience course is recommended for any Harrier, even if the owner does not plan to pursue exhibiting in that arena. Training helps establish the proper relationship of who gives the orders.

This breed is a rough-and-tumble, independent lot, perfect for the family that works hard and plays hard. The Harrier thrives without pampering, and does well if the family is gone all day. Exercise is a must, however, making this dog an excellent companion for long hikes, bike rides or horseback jaunts.

HAVANESE

COUNTRY: Cuba
WEIGHT: 7–12 pounds
HEIGHT: 8–10½ inches
COAT: Profuse, wavy to curly, double-coated
COLOR: Wide variety of colors or color combinations
OTHER NAMES: Bichon Havanais, Havana Silk Dog
REGISTRY: FCI
GROUP: Gun Dog

These charmers descended from bichon types of the Old World, but there is some argument about which specific type was the origin. Most researchers say they came with the Spanish as they colonized the West Indies, which would probably point to Tenerife and the Bichon Frise as the progenitors. But Cubans seem to feel the dog originally came to their island with Italian sea captains, thus pointing to Malta or Bologna as the source. Captains often carried illegal contraband to be sold to wealthy Cuban families. "Hence, the entree gift of one of these precious little dogs to the wealthy Señoras [sic] opened the doors of her home to them."

The Havanese was soon a favorite of the very wealthy, and a frequent sight in the palaces and country estates. Catalina Laza, the wife of a wealthy Cuban sugar mill baron, raised the dogs for her own pleasure and to present to society friends. When the Cuban Revolution threatened the existence of these dogs and their owners, they were smuggled out by families fleeing their homeland. Quite rare today, they are now being revived and promoted by fanciers in the USA who have formed the Havanese Club of America.

Temperament for this breed is similar to all its bichon cousins—charming, intelligent and alert. Adults can be aloof with strangers. The Havanese has been known to guard children heroically and is a loving and devoted companion. Natural clowns, they are superb circus and trick dogs. Like the Bolognese, they make good watchdogs because of their alert demeanor and close relationship with their owners. One owner says they are "fantastic little friends." Their sturdiness and longevity make extra pluses as companions and their brilliance of colors, including cream, gold, silver, blue, black, chocolate (appropriately called "tobacco brown"), the rare white, or combinations of these adds to their appeal. Modern show dogs are kept free of tangles, but any trimming, fussing or coiffing is prohibited.

Havanese, white.

Above Left: Havanese, pup. **Above Right and Below:** Havaneses.

HAWAIIAN POI DOG

COUNTRY: USA
COAT: Short
COLOR: Variety
OTHER NAMES: Ilio
REGISTRY: None
GROUP: Southern

Hawaiian Poi Dog, white.

Pariah dogs came to Hawaii with the Polynesians during the first settlement more than 1,000 years ago. The dogs came under the care of the women and children, with a pup sometimes given as a present to an infant at birth. Nursing from the baby's mother supposedly gave the dog a protective instinct. If the child died, the dog was killed and buried with his tiny master. If,

as was often the case, the canine predeceased his young owner, his teeth were pulled and given to the child to wear as a necklace, continuing the "protection."

Unfortunately for the Poi Dog, writer Elinor Dewire observes, the island's people "made no distinction between the enjoyment of an animal's consumption and its companionship." Dogs played with during the day were fed as a delicacy to visiting chieftains and royalty that same night. The dogs were fed *poi* (a paste made from ground, baked and fermented taro root) to fatten them for eating.

Their vegetarian diet over a long period of time resulted in a change in the bones of their heads. The heads became large and flat, due to the disuse of the bones from a lack of chewing.

Not used for any purpose but to be eaten, the Poi Dogs gradually evolved into small, lazy animals, waddling around with distended bellies and shortened legs. These pariah types never reverted to the feral state, since the Hawaiian habitat was not suited to that lifestyle. Besides they probably were too lazy to bother scrounging for food when they could become fat on human handouts! They grew to be slow, lazy and dull witted, much like a slug in mind and body.

On one of his explorations in 1779, Captain James Cook described them, when he said the Poi Dogs seldom barked, came in many colors and ran with the hogs (which also held the dual role of pet/pork chop).

Early in the 19th century, other dogs had so intermingled with the Poi Dog that it was no longer pure. Years later two men conducted a breeding program at the Honolulu Zoo, attempting to reconstruct the breed. After 12 years, it was deemed to be a failure and the experiment was discontinued, and another breed was lost to the world of dogs.

HERTHA POINTER

COUNTRY: Denmark
WEIGHT: 45–60 pounds
HEIGHT: 23–25½ inches
COAT: Short and fine
COLOR: Yellow-orange; with small white markings on feet, tail tip, chest and muzzle
GROUP: Gun Dog

When the war between Germany and Denmark ended, the defeated Danish soldiers made their way home. Accompanying one group of veterans in 1864 was an orange-red pointer-type bitch. No one knew her origin or how she came to join the men, but they named her "Hertha" and she proved to be a fine gun dog. A sportsman bought her and presented her as a gift to his friend, a well-known hunter and supervisor in one of the great state forests of Jutland.

The island of Als has long been a political football for Denmark because of its position in the south of Jutland near the border of Germany. During the monarchy, the Dukes of Augustenborg made their home on this island. At the time of the Danish-German War, the Duke of Augustenborg was Frederik Christian, pretender to the Danish throne. He was a famous and daring breeder of quality hunting dogs and fine horses, and his kennel of (English) Pointers was renowned. Because of selective inbreeding, his dogs all had a solid orange-red color with distinctive small white markings. Although Hertha was of general gun dog type, she did not particularly possess the English Pointer look. But because of her color, many who saw her thought that she probably came from the Duke's kennels.

Hertha was bred to "Sport," who *was* a Pointer from the Duke's breeding, and the results of this pairing were the wellspring of the Hertha Pointer breed. For many years, hunters fostered the "Hertha dog" or "Hertha hound." Soon a breed club was formed, predating the Danish Kennel Club by 54 years (they changed the name to Hertha Pointer, which may have been an unforeseen mistake), and these dogs became common throughout Denmark. A standard has been in effect since 1897, and photos and description were included in the 1902 edition of Henri de Bylandt's book *Les Races de Chien.*

495

Hertha Pointer.

From this long history of breeding true to type, with pedigrees going back 123 years, the breed is as yet having a difficult time being accepted and recognized by the central canine authorities. The Pointer Club of Denmark and the Danish Kennel Club's official position is that the Hertha Pointer is merely a color variant of the English Pointer. In 1982 the Hertha Club was bitterly disappointed that, despite providing proof of what they felt were the criteria for what constitutes a breed, their petition for recognition was again denied.

There are perhaps some political stumbling blocks to the official acceptance of the breed. The tag of "Pointer" may have set in many people's minds that the dog *was* a Pointer. Over the years, most kennels that have Pointers have crossed their dogs to Herthas to gain the fine field abilities (Herthas, on the other hand, now are never bred to Pointers!). Therefore, while virtually all Pointers in Denmark today can find a trace of Hertha and Sport in their pedigrees, a multitude of purebred Herthas exist without Pointer blood! If the breed were declared a separate entity, this source of crossing would be closed to the Pointer fanciers, and some feel this is a motive for them to block the separation. The fact that the Duke of Augustenborg turned out to be an enemy of Denmark and lost his

dukedom to the Germans could also be a psychological factor against the breed. These and other problems, not of their own making, led to the creation of a group called the Committee for National and Forgotten Breeds, which fosters native breeds and works for their preservation and recognition. Cynologists everywhere would applaud this idea, which could be copied profitably elsewhere!

At any rate, the number of Herthas continues to climb slowly and their proponents are not daunted in the desire to have their breed recognized. These dogs have bred true for over one hundred years, with their sinewy aloofness and their distinctive color pattern. They are moderately sized, extremely athletic gun dogs with fine natural field abilities. The limited white markings remind one somewhat of those seen on the Perdigueiro Portugueso and, occasionally, the Small French Braque. The Hertha people find the presence of a small white spot on the forehead desirable. Although the standard warns against the purely self-colored individual (with no white), the presence of too much white is equally undesirable and untypical. The authors hope that the descendants of "Old Hertha" will soon find their place among the recognized breeds of the world.

HOVAWART

COUNTRY: Germany
WEIGHT: 65–90 pounds
HEIGHT: 24–28 inches
COAT: Long, thick with only slight wave
COLOR: Black, black/tan, red fawn
REGISTRY: FCI, TKC
GROUP: Herding

Dogs named *Hofewart*, meaning estate dog or farmyard warden, were mentioned and reproduced in documents and pictures since the 13th century. This dog was used to guard the courtyard, and a writer of that era told of his rescue as a baby by a wounded Hovawart. When the family castle was besieged, he was carried by the dog to a neighboring estate.

In those early times, stealing the Hovawart was penalized with a fine and a demand to replace the dog. The fine was higher for a nighttime theft than a day-time one because their worth as guards was so highly valued. The original Hofewart seemed to disappear with the German aristocracy. No mention of the breed was seen in formal dog circles for centuries. The breed reappeared around the turn of this century under the impetus of enthusiast Kurt Konig.

Much controversy exists over whether the 20th-century Hovawart was a "reinvented" breed or a resurrected one. Believers of the reinvention theory state that breeders used Leonbergers, German Shepherds, Newfoundlands, Kuvasz and the semi-wild African veldt dogs to create a tough working breed which looked like the Hofewart of old. It is hard to imagine type being established and dogs breeding true in a short period of time, after this extreme cross-breeding procedure—especially since neither the German Shepherd nor the Leonberger were themselves fixed in type at that time.

The resurrection proponents believe dogs of the old-type Hovawart survived on isolated farms and in remote rural areas of the Harz and Black Forest. These people contend that Konig and his cohorts scoured these areas, acquiring dogs that had the desired looks and temperament. It was these farm dogs that formed the base for the "new" breed.

Whatever the true story, type was well set in the early decades of this century and the German Kennel Club (VDH) recognized the Hovawart in 1937. The War years were hard on the breed. The new beginning of the breed had a tenuous hold, not only because of the cessation of breeding and scarcity of food during those years, but because many of the kennels were

Hovawart, black/tan.

Above: Hovawart, black/tan. **Below:** Tug o' war underway, Hovawart holding his own against worthy opponent.

designated as part of the eastern zone when Germany was divided in 1945. Interested owners reaffirmed their dedication, and the Hovawart—although not in large numbers—now is firmly established in Germany. In the 1960s, breed enthusiasts saw sponsoring organizations formed in Switzerland, the Netherlands, Austria, Denmark, Finland, Sweden and Scotland. Hovawarts were introduced to America in the 1980s.

Characterized as "weatherproof," intelligent, trustworthy and responsive to training, the Hovawart, however, tends to stay puppyish for a long time, and needs patience in training. Bred to protect their home and family, they are void of any hunting or roving tendencies. They work well with livestock in their role as farm dogs. Natural guardians even in puppyhood, the Hovawarts require a dominant hand. Care must be taken to assert the "pack leader" position of the human in this relationship. An aptitude for obedience and schutzhund work is apparent. A "job" and extensive exercise keeps them happy and fit. Hovawarts are good house dogs, being quiet in nature and requiring minimal coat care.

The breed is classified in Europe as a working dog, in the same group as German Shepherds, Boxers, Dobermans, Rottweilers and Giant Schnauzers. The breed organizations are very strict in selecting for good conformation, proper color, sound hips and health, and proper guardian temperament, which includes a gun shyness test. Puppies are guaranteed and German stock is 95-percent free of hip dysplasia.

Hygenhund, red/brown with white.

HYGENHUND

COUNTRY: Norway
WEIGHT: 44–53 pounds
HEIGHT: 18½–23 inches
COAT: Not too short; very dense
COLOR: red/brown or red/yellow, often with
black tipping, with or without slight white
markings; black/tan, usually with white
symmetrical markings; or white with red/brown,
red/yellow or black and brown spots and/or
ticking
REGISTRY: FCI
GROUP: Hound

Norwegian breeder Hygen created his hound in
the late 1800s from German Holsteiner hounds
and various other hound breeds. The Hygenhund was bred as an endurance hunter which
can go over the arctic snows for long periods
without fatigue.

Structurally, they are quite short-coupled
with a solid, tight build and no excess skin.
Reminiscent of the Swedish Smålandsstövare,
the head is a bit shorter and more wedge-shaped
than most of the other Scandinavian hounds. In
addition, the ears are smaller and higher set, allowing them to stand out slightly from the head
instead of hanging straight down. The high-
arched toes have plenty of protective hair between them. Tails are rather short, barely reaching to the hock, and carried in a slightly upward
curve.

A happy dog, he is a serious hunter with great
staying power. Like the Halden Hound, his
population is small and strict breeding rules
govern his sponsors. The standard warns that
the wonderful characteristics of this native Norwegian cannot be retrieved from other breeds if
lost, and thus a close eye must be kept on breeding programs to maintain his fine qualities.

IBIZAN HOUND

COUNTRY: Spain
WEIGHT: 42–55 pounds
HEIGHT: 22½–27½ inches
COAT: Shorthaired or wirehaired; short is close and hard, with perhaps a little brush on back of thighs and under tail; wire is hard, coarse, and 1–3 inches long, with a possible generous moustache and longer on back, thighs and tail. Neither coat is preferable to the other.
COLOR: Solid red or lion tawny, solid white or—more usually—a combination of the color with the white, either in a pied or an Irish pattern
OTHER NAMES: Podenco Ibicenco, Ca Eivissencs
REGISTRY: FCI, AKC, TKC, CKC
GROUP: Southern

Ibizan Hound, shorthaired.

In early times, the same ancient Middle Eastern, prick-eared dogs that created the Pharaoh Hound were brought by trading ships to the Balaeric Islands off the coast of Spain. One of these islands, Ibiza, gave this breed its name. Despite their isolated development, far from Malta, the dominance of their ancient characteristics allowed these two independently developed breeds to look very much alike even after many centuries. Ibizan Hounds were said to have ridden atop Hannibal's elephants when he invaded Italy; the fact that this Carthaginian general was actually born on Ibiza gives weight to the story. Ibizan Hounds have been known in their present form on the islands of Ibiza and its neighbor, Formentera, eight miles to the south, for more than 5,000 years.

The Ibizan was welcomed as an admirable hunter of rabbit and other small game on this poor island, where these prizes supplemented the diet of inhabitants whose food was scarce. Owners couldn't afford to feed many puppies, and often the weaker pups and most of the males were drowned in the sea. The survivors were easy keepers who could stay healthy and spirited on a diet of a few fish heads, an occasional bit of goat meat, and whatever game they could scrounge for themselves.

They were also known and worked in the nearby mainland provinces of Catalonia in Spain (where the breed is called in the Catalonian language, *Ca Eivissencs*) and the Provence and Roussillon area of France. Due to a silent style of hunting, the Ibizan or his crosses were often the choice of French poachers, who called him *Charnique* or *Charnegue*. These clandestine activities led to a declaration of this dog being banned in France.

Continuing in this vein as a simple hunting dog brought the Ibizan halfway through the 20th century. At that time, the breed came to the attention of a dog authority and judge from Spain, Doña Maria Dolores Olives de Cotonera, the *Marquesa de Belgida* of Barcelona. She wanted to save this now indigenous Spanish breed. Her kennel, located on the larger Balaeric island of Majorca (Mallorca), soon was producing high quality dogs which she promoted throughout Spain and the Continent. When interest generated in America, she per-in the air from a standstill. In straight-away racing, they have been clocked at 40 mph. The often-seen white mark on the head between the ears is called the "ax mark" and, probably due to an old superstition, is a highly prized characteristic.

Ibizan Hound, wirehaired, white with red.

Ibiizan Hound, shorthaired, white with red.

sonally saw that good quality representatives were sent to begin breeding programs in the USA.

Soon the Ibizan Hound was seen in many countries of the world, as a pet, as an exhibition dog, on race tracks, and in hunting or coursing competitions. In 1958, a special commission from the Egyptian government was sent to Ibiza and Formentera to see examples of the breed and bring specimens to their country. After 5,000 years, the Ibizan Hound returned home!

Their style of hunting utilizes scent and sound (with their huge antennae ears), as well as sight. They can follow their quarry in and out of brush, over walls and through any type of obstacle course. If they lose sight of their prey in heavy cover, they stand on their hind legs to relocate the game. Guns are unnecessary. When hunting to provide food for their masters' table, the Ibizans locate the prey by scent, flush and chase until they catch it and break its neck, then gently retrieve the prize to hand.

The American Kennel Club gave its official sanction to the Ibizan Hound in 1979. Ibizans are extremely hardy and agile. They are capable of jumping great distances both in height and width and can leap six to eight feet straight up

Iceland Dog.

ICELAND DOG

COUNTRY: Iceland
WEIGHT: 20–30 pounds
HEIGHT: 12–16 inches
COAT: Thick, coarse, quite short, stand-off
COLOR: Wheaten, black, wolf sable, "dirty" all-white; often with small symmetrical white markings, sometimes a black mask
OTHER NAMES: Icelandic Sheepdog, Iceland Spitz
REGISTRY: FCI
GROUP: Northern

There is probably no other country that has chronicled its history better than Iceland. The revered *Sagas* tell of Vikings bringing small herding dogs when they colonized Iceland in 880 AD. Actually just a smaller version of the Buhund, the Iceland Dog is directly descended from these dogs.

Pistol, a character in Shakespeare's *Henry IV* (ca. 1600), says, "Pish for thee, Iceland Dog. Thou prick-eared cur of Iceland." Sir Richard Burton wrote *A Summer in Iceland* in 1875, and made note that a good dog equaled the value of one horse. It was said that a dog can find a sheep buried under 11 yards of snow.

Denmark established a written standard for the Iceland Dog in 1898. The breed became rare in its native land after nearly all dogs in Iceland were destroyed by distemper near the end of the last century. In 1928, dog breeding was further curtailed by the ban on all importation of mammals into Iceland. The breed was reconstructed by British and Icelandic breeders by using what stock was left and carefully introducing other Nordic herding dogs. Mrs. Sigridur Petursdottir was instrumental in the revival of the breed, and in 1969, a club was formed to support the Iceland Dog.

The breed is void of hunting instincts, as it was developed exclusively as a herder like the Buhund. Lively, active, and affectionate, he is still developing mentally at 18 months. He needs to have close contact with his humans as well as calm, firm discipline to develop the desirable character. Naturally friendly, · they are alert enough to be watchdogs. They have the same cleanliness and easy-care coat of the Buhund and bear the same lack of interest in hunting or wandering.

Iceland Dog.

INCA HAIRLESS DOG

COUNTRY: Peru
WEIGHT: Small 9–18 pounds; medium 18–26 pounds; large 26–55 pounds
HEIGHT: Small 10–16 inches; medium 16–20 inches; large 20–28 inches
COAT: Hairless; short fuzzy hair on top of head, edge of ears, feet and tail
COLOR: Solid dark skin
OTHER NAMES: Peruvian Hairless Dog
REGISTRY: FCI
GROUP: Southern

Hairless dogs have been bred in Peru since the time of the Incan civilizations. But today very few professional breeders of Inca Hairless Dogs live in Peru; only a handful breed dogs according to genetic studies and with careful planning.

Inca Hairless Dog.

A few of the Hairless dogs were sent to Germany, where rare breed club members helped the Peruvians draft a standard and obtain FCI recognition in 1985. A few are found in the United States.

Like the Inca Orchids, the Inca Hairless have missing premolars, often causing their tongues to hang out the side of their mouths. They also have the two coat varieties, with the same dominant hairless gene. In fact, owners say that the Peruvian dogs choose their canine friends on the basis of the length of their hair. Unlike their relatives of the night (Orchids), however, they have small eyes "from squinting in the sun."

Appreciation of their warmth was expressed by a peasant owner who said they are "nice to have in bed . . . warm as an oven on a chilly night. They are very clean, and they have no fleas."

They are agile dogs, with a light gait which comes "from centuries of walking the endless coastal sand." Two gaits are seen: the free trot and the restricted front rhythmic movement. Dogs with very straight fronts walk in tiny little steps, giving an impression of the Paso Fino horse.

Inca Hairless Dog, powderpuff variety.

IRISH RED AND WHITE SETTER

COUNTRY: Ireland
WEIGHT: 40–70 pounds
HEIGHT: 23½–27 inches
COAT: Flat, straight, and slightly coarse, longer for the feathering
COLOR: White ground color with clear red patches, roaning or ticking objectionable—but, if present, a minimum amount on face and below hock and elbow only
REGISTRY: TKC
GROUP: Gun Dog

The red/whites may actually predate the solid reds. The coat of arms of the Irish Nash family bears three red and white setters, and Sir Thomas Staples of County Tyrone and Evans of Gortmerron kept red/whites in the 18th century. Lord Rossmore of Monaghan can boast the same tradition and, indeed, the Red and White is, to this day, occasionally referred to locally as the Rossmore Setter.

Nevertheless, by the turn of the 19th century, while the solid red continued his rise to fame on

Irish Red and White Setter, pup.

both sides of the Atlantic, his spotted brothers retreated to remote areas of Ireland. They never completely disappeared, however. Being a recessive, the spotted dogs can, and still do, occasionally crop up in red litters. A few Irishmen, over the years, preferred to hunt over the more easily seen red/whites. A rare breeder or two also stubbornly continued to foster the type. The Reverend Noble Huston of County Down, Ireland, bred the variety in the early part of this century to keep the red-and-white flame alive.

In the 1940s, a breed club was formed, especially to foster the hunting qualities of the red-white. Shortly after, the Cuddys of County Cork, Ireland, began their interest in the breed; nearly all modern specimens trace their pedigree back to Cuddy dogs. In the early 1970s, the Irish Kennel Club awarded the task of monitoring the present-day revival to the Irish Red Setter Club. They created a committee to monitor all pups prior to registration, because the breed base was so small and crossings to the Red are close up in most pedigrees. From a low of seven registered animals at that time, the "Red-n-White" has begun a slow climb to full recognition. Owners of a red/white litter in Ireland, until recently, had to take them to the breed committee for the approval signature! To the credit of the Red Club and its wholehearted cooperation, the Red and White is now regarded as self-sufficient.

Irish Red and White Setter.

A dog belonging to the Gormleys of County Dublin was entered at Crufts in 1980, in the "Any Variety Not Separately Classified" class. So unknown was the breed that the show committee tried to switch the entry into the Irish Red Setter class! Full championship status was given to the breed at Crufts in 1987, much to the pride of those who worked so hard for him. A few of the Red-n-Whites have been brought into the United States, where owners formed a breed club and interest is growing.

Character and appearance of the two breeds are very similar, with a few minor exceptions. The Red/Whites have a higher set ear, are a bit shorter, wider and sturdier of body, and have less of the long, heavy feathering. The practical hunter, unlike the show dog enthusiast, finds excessive feathering a bother. The Red/White probably looks very similar to the Irish (Red)

Setter of 100 years ago! In temperament, the spotted dogs have "the same joyous exuberance as their Red cousins but are less forthcoming with strangers." Ann Millington interjects that "they are 'thinking' dogs and consider you well before deciding you are worthy of their friendship."

They still make good practical gun dogs and are particularly known for their stamina. Stories such as that of the field trial dog from bygone days, who ran ten miles behind his master's carriage to the trial grounds and then home again at night, are common. Color has to be carefully monitored, and dogs with an excess of ticking (roan, or belton, patterns like the English Setter) are faulted. A note of interest: 150 years ago there was described a third color of Irish Setter, called a "Shower of Hail" Setter, which was an all-over, heavily ticked pattern.

Irish Red and White Setter.

IRISH SETTER

COUNTRY: Ireland
WEIGHT: 60–70 pounds
HEIGHT: 25–27 inches
COAT: Moderately long, flat and straight, with abundant feathering
COLOR: Mahogany or rich chestnut red
OTHER NAMES: Irish Red Setter
REGISTRY: FCI, AKC, UKC, TKC, CKC
GROUP: Gun Dog

Irish Setter.

Setting dogs of both the solid red and the red-white spotted coats have existed in Ireland since the 1700s, when hawking was the fad. Development of a dog for wing shooting was accomplished from existing hawking dogs and other hunting types. The fact that the Celts, who settled Ireland, also populated Brittany is interesting with the existence of red or orange spaniels from the latter area. The Irish state their Setter is pure spaniel, the only setter with no crossing to pointer. Bede Maxwell, author of *The Truth About Sporting Dogs* says, "Irishophiles may prefer to believe their Setter sprung full-formed from among the shamrocks, but history yields no proof of it."

Yet the Irish Setter is physically the most pointerlike (i.e., houndlike) of all the setters. The Celts were famous for their scenthounds as well as their spaniels, so perhaps the crossing was among pure Celtic hounds, instead of the pointer breeds that sprang from them. Throughout the 18th—and for most of the 19th—century, the Setters bred in Ireland were still of both color types. In the late 1800s, several top winners, such as Ch. Palmerston, flaunted the solid red coat, and their popularity increased. When a club was formed for the breed in 1882, it took on the name of The Irish Red Setter Club and, from that time on, the red variety prospered while the red/white declined.

Irish Setters were brought to America in the late 1800s, mainly as gun dogs. They proved most useful, and many early ones were hunted as well as shown. Head types varied greatly, from the "dish" face, mimicking the English Pointer, to the stopless downface, like those found on the best German hounds. But the flashy red-jacketed bodies had great consistency and, as the show fraternity embraced the dashing redhead, they quickly succeeded in fixing head type.

The Red Setter became and has remained popular among both the show fancy and the pet-owning general public, due to his personality as well as his looks. Big, elegant and athletic, with his flowing red coat, and the happy, head-up, tail-wagging attitude, the Irish catches the eye of any judge. And that rollicking devil-may-care personality has captured the hearts of many owners. Like most all sporting dogs, however, he needs plenty of exercise, discipline, and a purpose to prevent his brain from finding other unwelcome activities to relieve his energy and boredom. More and more modern Irish owners and show fanciers are reemphasizing the hunting qualities that sometimes were forgotten in the race to fill the demand for puppies. There are dual champions, with more to come, and other owners are testing their dogs' abilities in noncompetitive events like the new AKC hunting tests. The Irish Setter people have likewise used his trainability and verve to advantage in the competitive obedience ring. The breed is a sensitive one, and does not react well to harsh training methods.

Irish Setters.

Irish Setter.

Irish Terrier.

IRISH TERRIER

COUNTRY: Ireland
WEIGHT: 25–27 pounds
HEIGHT: 18 inches
COAT: Harsh, wire, broken coat
COLOR: Red to red wheaten
OTHER NAMES: Irish Red Terrier
REGISTRY: FCI, AKC, TKC, CKC
GROUP: Terrier

Called the Irish Red Terrier in the past to distinguish him from the other native terriers of Erin, this breed may be the oldest on the Isle. Dogs like these were known for centuries and were valuable only to poor Irish farmers with small holdings. Not much was written about them as they were not a dog of the aristocracy, who weren't in as dire need of ratting expertise. The type was descriptively mentioned in the Brehon laws (the earliest Irish legal code, first passed by word-of-mouth and then recorded in early medieval times) as the "dog of the dungheap." The dungheaps were the piles of manure that were inevitable in the farmyards and were breeding grounds for rats.

Dog expert, Stonehenge (J. H. Walsh), writing in 1887, shows his contempt for all things not inherently British with his refusal to believe that the Irish Terrier was a distinct breed from the "old Scotch terrier." But the differences were distinct. The truth might be that the raiding Irish could have introduced the prototype to Scotland many centuries ago. Or perhaps the Celts, who conquered both Scotland and Ireland four centuries before Christ, brought the archetypical terrier with them, and differences developed after that.

Whatever the early history, by the middle of the 1800s, the Irish Terrier, jacketed in black/tan and brindle as well as the more desirable red, was a common sight. During these years, many of this breed were seen with cropped ears, a sure sign they were used for dog-fighting. The Irish Terrier's punishing jaws bode the end of many an Irish rat. But despite the instincts to destroy vermin, he could be a soft-mouthed retriever and often wore two hats: ratter and hunter. There was still variation in size and type at the breed's debut at an Irish show in 1875. Out of the 50 dogs that strutted the ring, entries included some in the under nine-pound division and one that was over 30 pounds; a pure white entry competed against many that would have passed for Cairns. These differences existed despite the rule that the dogs must have a pedigree to enter. Many had notes attached reading, "Breeding information available at such-and-such an address." The winner, "Boxer" by name, was brazenly labeled as "Bred by owner, pedigree unknown!" This mass confusion prompted the formation of a strong breed club still in existence today.

By the turn of the century, only the red dogs were accepted, type had become fairly well standardized and ear cropping (along with fighting) had been prohibited. The reputation of the breed was made during the First World War when the Irish Terriers were used as messenger dogs. The noise and confusion of trench warfare was no deterrent to the fearless Irisher, and many a soldier owed his life to these dogs.

A taller and racier dog than the Fox Terrier, the Irish still carries plenty of bone and substance. Always good-tempered, affectionate and loyal with his people, the breed should still show the characteristic fire, animation, and "heedless, reckless pluck" that has earned him the nickname daredevil. These dogs exude charm, and their cocksure strut belies the warmth within. They are particularly good with children and are said to be dogs "o'the little people." Writers Dangerfield and Howell, in their *Encyclopedia of Dogs*, noted, "A growing lad could wish no finer friend to grow up with; mischief overlooked by the one will certainly be exploited by the other!"

The Irish was the first native terrier from Ireland given Kennel Club recognition (19th century) and has gained worldwide acceptance since that time.

Irish Terrier.

Irish Water Spaniel.

IRISH WATER SPANIEL

COUNTRY: Ireland
WEIGHT: 45–65 pounds
HEIGHT: 21–24 inches
COAT: Tight, crisp ringlets on body, neck and 2 inches down tail, longer hair with loose curls on legs and topknot; smooth on face, remainder of tail, and back legs below hock
COLOR: Solid liver
REGISTRY: FCI, AKC, UKC, TKC, CKC
GROUP: Gun Dog

The exact origins of this most distinct breed are argued to this day. Several types of water retrievers coexisted in Ireland, but this specific breed appeared in the 1830s, mainly from the kennels of Justin McCarthy. His dog "Boatswain," whelped in 1834, is the acknowledged "sire" of the modern breed. McCarthy never revealed the sources of his breeding, and the Irishman kept his secret to the grave.

An ancestor of McCarthy fought with the Irish Brigade against England in France for Louis XII. Since several stem types have graced France since early times, specimens of the early Barbet/Poodle types could have been brought back to Ireland and later crossed with local Irish or British dogs. But those of the Portuguese Water Dog genus may have also been brought to British and Irish shores with Portuguese sailors. It is known that two types of water spaniels populated the Emerald Isle, the northern variety being small and particolored with a wavy coat. His southern counterpart was larger and sported a curly coat. This latter dog likely contributed to the modern IWS. Controversy notwithstanding, it is known he is from water dog stock and that his distinctive type, with high-held head and tail, long thighs and low hocks, and smooth tail, was fixed early.

Remarkably similar to the dogs of 150 years ago, he remains a popular working and show dog in his native Ireland. Although recognized in the USA since 1878 and supported by an active breed club, he is few in number. The breed was appreciated by hunters of waterfowl, who supplied American tables with various delicacies and who admired the breed's qualities of diligently working long hours day after day. The terrain and cover in Ireland were similar to those housing waterfowl in America, enabling the dog to do well in marshy bogs and making him a logical choice for the serious gunner.

He is a quality retriever in any cover and for a variety of game, but his real skills are seen in water, even in currents, where he is a strong swimmer and often dives to go after wounded ducks. His expertise lies in retrieving wounded fowl, which might otherwise escape the hunter. Large and strong enough to handle even geese with ease, his heavy coat affords him protection from long exposure in icy water. His coat needs to be groomed, but not clipped like a Poodle; it sheds water and doesn't become wet to the skin.

There are several well-known obedience workers in the breed, and the first sporting dog to win an obedience title in the USA was an Irish Water Spaniel. His nature is one of initiative and courage, yet he is innately trainable. Owners insist he is a dog with a sense of humor, and his enjoyment of games makes him a good family dog. He is, however, discerning with strangers. His head is capped with a characteristic topknot, and his expression is quizzical, adding to his appealing appearance.

Irish Water Spaniel.

IRISH WOLFHOUND

COUNTRY: Ireland
WEIGHT: Minimum 105 pounds for females and 120 pounds for males
HEIGHT: Minimum 30 inches for females and 32 inches for males, 32–34 inches more ideal
COAT: Rough and hard, especially wiry and long over eyes and on underjaw
COLOR: Gray, brindle, red, black, pure white, fawn, or any other color that occurs in the Deerhound
REGISTRY: FCI, AKC, TKC, CKC
GROUP: Southern

The Irish Wolfhound is the tallest of the running hounds, combining speed and power to the "nth" degree. Their history, equally sketchy, probably parallels that of the Scottish Deerhound. Imposing sighthounds have been recorded in Ireland since histories were kept. The Celts invaded Greece and sacked Delphi in 275 BC. There they could have acquired dogs of the Greyhound/Afghan type who accompanied them on their conquest of Europe. Celtic tastes in dogs ran to great speed and size, and these running hounds may have been crossed with rangy mastiffs even before they reached Ireland, the furthest reach of the Celtic migrations. The Romans found the dogs there when they invaded British shores in the first centuries AD.

A letter written in 393 AD by Roman consul Symmachus to his brother Flavianus, then stationed in Britain, thanked him for the seven Irish hounds sent previously. He states "All Rome viewed them with wonder"—this a jaded citizenship who regularly saw huge mastiffs and men fighting bears and lions in the arena! The Irish dogs must have been imposing figures even then.

In early times the great Irish hound came in smooth and rough coats as well as in a variety of dark and light colors. While type might have been quite variable, their qualities of heart, loyalty to master, strength and speed were universal and became legendary. From Ireland's heroic age of 200 BC to 200 AD, magnificent tales of these dogs abound.

One saga involves the hound "Ailbhe," who supposedly defended the entire province of the king of Leinster. The story says the dog was so fast that he could run around Leinster in a single day, and he possessed keen wisdom and supernatural intelligence. In one episode, Ailbhe is asked to decide whether the men of King Conor or those of Queen Maeve are more heroic. Unfortunately, the dog is killed while pursuing the frightened men of King Conor!

The bitch "Bran" was another famous legendary hound, the best of a famous pack of the 4th-century king of Ireland, Cormac. Cared for by Fionn MacCumhaill, the dogs in the pack supposedly were said to have magical powers. "Bran was especially prized for her incredible speed, her bravery in facing wild boars and her ability to warn Fionn and his men against enemy attacks." Fionn's men rescued Bran and other hounds when they were stolen by a servingman who intended to sell them in Britain.

From other written records of the fifth century, we know that dog breeding in Ireland was so organized and the dogs so valued that merchants sold them abroad by the shipload! At least the majority of the dogs to be sold were of the wolfhound type, and these Irish cargos may

have contributed to the development of breeds in Europe.

In the 1100s, it was purported that the King of Ulster offered 4,000 cows for a coveted Wolfhound. When the offer for "Aibe" was refused, it started a war. A long Icelandic saga of the 13th century sets a dog in a prominent role. One of the principals, Gunnar, received an Irish hound as a gift from a friend, who said "he is a big animal and will make as good a comrade-in-arms as a powerful man. He has human intelligence and will bark at every man he recognizes as your enemy, but never at your friends; he can tell from a man's face whether he means you well or not. He would lay down his life rather than fail you. His name is Samr." In this tragedy of feuding and revenge, the dog serves Gunnar well. When enemies come to assassinate Gunnar, they pay a farmer to kill the dog first. Samr fights mightily and is killed only because they manage to drive an ax into his head. With his dying gasp, he emits an eerie howl which serves to warn Gunnar of the approaching enemies.

From this grim tale of the past, we know that

Irish Wolfhound, gray.

Irish Wolfhounds, fawn.

Irish dogs were already so exalted as to be featured in the literature of another country. It also shows they were regarded as princely gifts and the world knew of their strength and speed. The tale of the theft of Bran and her pack indicates how a poor man might make a few dollars selling these valuable dogs abroad.

Certainly a section on Wolfhounds would not be complete without the most famous—and true—story. In the 13th century, Llewelyn, prince of North Wales, had a place at Beddgelert, where he enjoyed hunting in the company of "Gelert, the Faithful Hound." One day, Gelert was unaccountably absent as the prince left on his hunt. On Llewelyn's return, the truant, stained and smeared with blood, joyfully sprang to meet his master. The prince, alarmed, hastened to find his son, and saw the infant's cot empty, the bed clothes and floor covered with blood. The frantic father drew his sword and plunged it into the bloody hound. The dog's dying yelp was answered by a child's cry. Llewelyn searched to discover his son unharmed, but lying near the body of a mighty wolf, which Gelert had slain. The prince, filled with remorse, is said never to have smiled again. Gelert's grave in northern Wales is marked by a monument that says: "He buried Gelert here. The spot is called Beddgelert."

From the medieval chores of battle, guarding, and hunting boar, stag and the long extinct Irish elk (which stood six feet high at the shoulder), the Wolfhound gradually turned to the specialized hunting of wolves by the 15th and 16th century. It was during this time that they became more consistent in type and more like the Wolfhound of today.

By the mid-1600s, Cromwell decreed the exporting of Wolfhounds to be illegal because wolves were still a major problem on the British Isles and the great hounds were not plentiful. The last wolf was killed in Ireland before 1800 and, within 50 years, the great hounds—having lost their purpose—were reduced to low numbers. The Great Irish Famine of the 1840s also took its toll on the large dogs. Because of the 150–year ban on exportation, there was nowhere else to go for new breeding stock.

Almost no one in the early 1800s had ever seen a live Wolfhound and, with their exagger-

515

Irish Wolfhounds, fawn.

ated tales in literature, there was much argument among period authorities over what a true Wolfhound had looked like. (Most assumed they were extinct.)

R.D. Richardson stirred some interest in the breed by writing articles in the 1840s. He also acquired a dog named "Bran" who was of the old type, and bred him to several wolfhounds and deerhounds, and their descendants became the ancestors of all modern Wolfhounds through the Kilfane and Ballytobin Kennels.

Finally in the latter half of the 1800s, Captain G.A. Graham made the restoration of this ancient Irish breed his life's work. He acquired descendants of Richardson's Bran and bred them to deerhounds of the Glengarry strain. With careful selection and occasional outcrosses to Borzoi or even Great Dane to increase size, he recreated the old type. It bred true. Shown successfully in the 1870s, the Irish Wolfhound was on the road to recovery and a breed club was formed in 1885.

The breed is admired and owned in many countries around the world, still prized for its gentleness and unswerving loyalty. His stature as the tallest dog in the world precludes him ever becoming a common pet, but he is a quiet house dog who can be successfully kept content if his regular need to run is met. The rough coat requires occasional combing only. Modern owners can take advantage of lure coursing and other running events.

Irish Wolfhound, gray.

Italian Greyhound.

ITALIAN GREYHOUND

COUNTRY: Italy
WEIGHT: Two varieties—8 pounds maximum; over 8 pounds
HEIGHT: 13–15 inches
COAT: Short, smooth
COLOR: All shades of fawn, red, mouse, blue, cream and white; black/tan not allowed
OTHER NAMES: Piccoli Levrieri Italiani
REGISTRY: FCI, AKC, TKC, CKC
GROUP: Southern

Evidence of miniature Greyhounds was found in the tombs of Egypt, but this exquisite version of its larger counterpart was bred to perfection during Roman times in Italy. Like many of the toy varieties, the little Italian was not bred to serve his masters in any way but as a lap dog. In fact, the miniature Greyhound may well be the first breed bred exclusively as a pet. Some believe that the Latin motto, *cave canem* (beware the dog), did not warn guests of the tough mastiff kept as a guard, but instead asked them to be careful not to harm the tiny Italian Greyhound.

The Italian Greyhound was fancied by the ladies of the court, quickly winning the hearts of Mary Queen of Scots and Anne of Denmark. King Lobengula, chief of a 19th-century Matabele tribe, was so entranced by their prancing movement he gave a breeder 200 head of cattle for one Italian Greyhound! Frederick the Great succumbed to their charms, as did countless others. The king carried his favorite pet with him, even into battle. It is said during the Seven Years' War that Frederick found it necessary to hide from the enemy under a bridge. If the dog had barked a warning or whined in fear, Frederick and Prussia would have met an early and tragic fate. But the dog hugged his master in silence.

During the 19th century, miniaturization of the breed was carried to grotesque extremes in Europe and Britain. The pathetic results were often sterile. Fortunately, by 1900, good sense again reigned. Although the two World Wars dealt harshly with the breed in Europe, good stock abounded in Canada and the USA to export, replenish and rejuvenate the Italian Greyhound.

Their current devotees sing praises of their easy care, their cleanliness, their quiet behavior. Owners are warned, however, to take care that they are not chilled. They definitely are house dogs, not candidates for kennels or cold outdoor living. Unlike most of the sighthounds, their size lets them receive plenty of exercise by following their people around the house. Their quiet demeanor invites gentle care.

Italian Greyhounds, mouse and white.

Italian Greyhound, fawn with white markings.

JACK RUSSELL TERRIER

COUNTRY: Great Britain
WEIGHT: 12–18 pounds
HEIGHT: Two sizes: 9–12 inches and 12–15 inches
COAT: Rough, broken (very short wire), or smooth
COLOR: At least 51 percent white (preferably more) with markings of tricolor, brown or black; brindle not allowed
REGISTRY: None
GROUP: Terrier

Jack Russell Terrier, broken, white with red.

Although a man of the cloth, the "Hunting Parson," Rev. Jack Russell, was a passionate fox hunter of the mid-1800s and pursued the sport until his death at age 88. Fox hunters needed small dogs to roust the foxes who had escaped to ground. Many hunters employed smaller or shorter legged terriers, which had to be carried on horseback to the fox's lair. But the Reverend Jack liked a longer legged type that could follow the hounds on foot. He developed his own strain, based on a crossbred terrier bitch, "Trump," which he bought from a milkman.

How Russell continued with the breeding program was never recorded, but even modern proponents of the breed admit a certain amount of crossbreeding occurred. First, fighting bull-and-terrier dogs were used to add the white color (easily differentiated by the hounds from the fox) and increase the aggression and tenacity. Unfortunately, this often resulted in a dog that silently killed the fox underground, thus spoiling the sport of the hunt for the others! Small "pocket" Beagles were used to temper this hard edge, as well as adding the tendency to give tongue. The result was a dog that was often one thought ahead of the fox.

Game to this day, a good Russell Terrier is still capable of going to ground. One owner described how her three JRTs chased a bull raccoon down a drain pipe near her home. When they hadn't emerged by the next morning, she had a backhoe brought in and started digging. The crew cut a ditch, reaching 300 feet, over the next 12 hours, and finally discovered the raccoon backed up against the cellar wall. Not only were the terriers none the worse for the ordeal, they were still jockeying for position with one another to get closest to the prey. It is not unusual for this breed to forego food, water and other creature comforts once it has the whiff of the quarry.

Although the Parson never used his dogs for the purpose, the JRT is also a plucky ratter. In 1977, an Englishman and his team of four Jack Russells took three tons of rats out of chicken farms in just one day! Another modern JRT owner gave this practical advice to a writer from *Sports Illustrated* to pass on to anyone planning to take part in this sport with their dogs: "If you take your terrier ratting, always wear slacks or breeches tucked either into your Wellingtons or into your socks so that the rats cannot run up your trouser legs or skirt. This happens far more often than one might imagine, and, although it may be excruciatingly funny to the rest of the party, it is no joke for you."

Despite all this emphasis on its ability and desire to fight and kill pests, JRTs are excellent house dogs and children's pets. They have a unique sense of humor, are clean in their habits

521

and are sweet and affectionate to people. They do require plenty of exercise. When there is more than one, they have a tendency to go off hunting on their own if not fenced. The old instincts to get down in the ground may cause some to be passionate diggers. But they are happy companions and their fans are delighted with them.

The Jack Russell Terrier has its own registering body in both Britain and the USA, but in neither country is there much desire for formal recognition of the breed. Owners prefer the unrefined nature of their dog. They worry about novice owners caring more about show points and good looks, allowing a loss of the working characteristics that have been so painstakingly kept over the years. A typical opinion is stated: "If these terriers ever become soft-bred show dogs, John Russell will turn over in his grave."

In fact, there is a reverse snob appeal about this breed, due to the fact that they do not want to be AKC recognized. This, in addition to the fact that they possess an affinity for horses, has made them a popular addition to many horse

A Jack Russell Terrier seated with master on horse while the hounds execute the initial task of scenting.

Jack Russell Terrier, rough.

farms and estates of the wealthy, especially on the East Coast.

In all physical characteristics, form follows function. The size of a good Jack Russell should be about the same as that of a fox; if the fox can go down the hole, then the terrier should be able to follow without difficulty. The standard demands that the chest be narrow enough to be spanned by two hands behind the shoulder blades. Chests that are chunkier create a dog that can be stuck in the hole! The docked tail of an adult specimen should end up about four inches, just enough length to be able to grab in order to extract the dog from the burrow. The predominance of white differentiates him from the fox.

Most of the larger sized dogs sport the rough or broken coat (similar to a smooth, with fuller hair on the legs and a bit of wiry hair on the chin creating a beard), while the shorter legged variety, carrying more of the cross to the pocket beagle, are more often smooths. Although they often live to 16 years as a house pet, their fearless nature tends to shorten their lifespan in the country. One breeder estimates the average lifespan on a farm to be only six years.

Above: Jack Russell Terrier, rough, white with brown. **Below:** Jack Russell Terrier, smooth, tricolor.

523

Japanese Chin, black and white.

JAPANESE CHIN

COUNTRY: Japan
WEIGHT: Two divisions—over 7 pounds; or under 7 pounds, the smaller the better
COAT: Profuse, long, straight, and rather silky; the abundant thick feathering tends to stand out, creating a mane
COLOR: Black and white or red (includes all shades of sable, brindle, lemon or orange) and white in a broken pattern
OTHER NAMES: Japanese Spaniel
REGISTRY: FCI, AKC, TKC, CKC
GROUP: Herding

Although he has similarities to both of the other two types of toy spaniels, the Japanese Chin probably has an entirely different origin. He has been known in Japan for many centuries, most likely stemming from dogs of the Asian continent. Argument continues over whether they arrived as gifts to the Emperor with a Korean emissary of 732 AD or emigrated with Buddhist monks and teachers from China, who taught Zen Buddhism, as early as 520 AD. Perhaps both are true. The Japanese Chin may share a common ancestor with the Pekingese and Pug.

In Japan, they were owned only by nobility. They were fed only rice and saki to stunt their growth; some were so tiny that they were kept in hanging cages like canaries! Dogs were protected from intentional injury by strict laws, and special care and housing were given to sickly or aged dogs. Dogs held a place of honor, perhaps because the Emperor was born during the Year of the Dog, and were considered gifts of high value. When Perry opened Japan to the West in 1853, he brought some of these little dogs back with him. Their appearance in Europe created a great demand, and hundreds of Far Eastern spaniels made the long journey by ship from the Orient to the West. Ten of these little dogs appeared in an 1882 New York dog show. The present Japanese Chin Club in America dates from 1912, and the breed's entry into Canada was about the same time. His ownership now encompasses more than Japanese nobility. The breed is a beloved pet in its homeland and other countries.

The Chin is a charming and sensitive companion, adapting well to almost any indoor lifestyle. He is clean and intelligent. The thickly feathered tail plumes up over the back.

Japanese Chin.

Japanese Chin.

Japanese Spitz.

JAPANESE SPITZ

COUNTRY: Japan
WEIGHT: 13 pounds
HEIGHT: 10–16 inches (English standard); often about 15 inches
COAT: Thick, long, and stand-off
COLOR: White only
REGISTRY: FCI, TKC
GROUP: Northern

The Japanese Spitz is a miniature lap spitz, descended from longer haired Nordic dogs brought to Japan in the early part of this century. The most likely type is the Siberian native Samoyed, which was bred smaller and smaller in size after arrival in Japan. This breed does not enjoy the wide acceptance of the Shiba, but has been exported into the Scandinavian countries. There these spitz were happily adopted and are shown.

In the 1970s, Dorothy Kenyon brought some from Sweden into England. They immediately became popular, and are allowed to compete for championships in British dog shows. They are very similar in size and appearance to the Miniature variety of the American Eskimo, which probably will preclude their ever developing any following in the USA.

Intelligent, bold, and lively, they have all of the character of the other spitz breeds. Their coat is self-cleaning, and they enjoy pleasing their owners. They are less suspicious in nature than some of their Nordic cousins, making them a true companion dog.

Their natural hunting instincts surface when they sight a squirrel or rabbit. Small enough to be a lap dog and large enough to enjoy a romp, the Japanese Spitz is an ideal choice for children or adults.

Above: Japanese Spitz, puppies. **Below:** Japanese Spitz.

JAPANESE TERRIER

COUNTRY: Japan
HEIGHT: 12–13 inches
COAT: Short, smooth
COLOR: Tricolor, with white predominating
OTHER NAMES: Nippon Terrier
REGISTRY: None
GROUP: Terrier

The Smooth Fox Terrier traveled all the way from Holland to Japan in 1702 to produce the first Japanese Terrier, bred from crossings with native breeds of that era. Type was refined in Yokohama and Kobe, harbor towns. They were designed exclusively as pets, to be carried about when their owners went out. Nicknames include *Oyuki* (snowy) Terrier and Mikado Terrier.

Very much like its progenitor (the Smooth Fox), the terrier from the Land of the Rising Sun has a certain elegance almost hinting of the Whippet. Its slick, smooth coat makes grooming an easy chore, and its lively terrier temperament makes it a spirited pet. Tails are docked and ears are set high and fold forward. It is unknown outside of Japan.

Japanese Terrier.

KANGAL DOG

COUNTRY: Turkey
WEIGHT: 75–150 pounds
HEIGHT: 28–34 inches
COAT: Short, smooth
COLOR: Chamois, dun or grayish dun; with a black mask; white chest blaze and feet characteristic; never white
OTHER NAMES: Karabash
GROUP: Flock Guard

Kangal Dog, grayish dun.

These ancient guardians have served the shepherds of the mountains and plains in the Kangal district of eastern Turkey for thousands of years. In the Sivas area, the family headed by the Aga of Kangal has produced illustrious leaders in central Turkey since their ancestors, the Turkoman Beys, invaded Asia Minor around 1000 AD. They were a great land-owning family of the 16th through 19th centuries. These people were—and still remain—renowned breeders of beautiful animals: the Arabian horse, sheep and the Kangal Dog. The dogs were also owned by others in the area, but both the dogs and the region are named for the family.

Turkish natives all know and identify the Kangal Dog. When a traveler mentions Kangal, Turks answer, "big, thick head, black-masked dog." Their pride is such that the Kangal Dog is depicted on a national stamp. Yet, they are not found as pets in their homeland. As Moslems, most Turks do not allow dogs in their homes, and the majority of pets are owned by Europeans or Americans living in Turkey. Work is the only reason for the Kangal's existence, and to find a specimen, the shepherds and the flocks must be sought. Like other flock guards, the dogs are easy keepers and fierce, awesome guards. Nevertheless, children of the shepherd families can play with the dogs, with the little ones sometimes riding on the huge animals' backs.

The old term *karabash* means black head, and was sometimes used to describe this type. But the name Kangal is more accurate, both historically and geographically.

The nobility of the old Ottoman Empire strongly fostered the maintenance of purebred types. The sultanates and landed aristocracy fell in the 20th century, however, and this last vestige of support for pure dogs was lost. Despite the lack of regulatory groups, the dogs remain pure to type in the Kangal area. A recent non-doggy tourist to Turkey reported seeing the great dun-colored dogs among the flocks in the mountains north and east of Sivas.

Because there is no Turkish registry body nor dog shows, the dog remains a working animal in its native country. Ears are cropped or, more accurately, "chopped" by shepherds in Turkey. Kangals are now trickling into the United States and other countries, where they are used for guardians and livestock protection, in addition to being exhibited at rare breed shows.

Kangaroo Dog.

KANGAROO DOG

COUNTRY: Australia
WEIGHT: 65–70 pounds
HEIGHT: 27½–29½ inches
COAT: Smooth and fine, sometimes coarser on the body
COLOR: All colors, black not desirable
OTHER NAMES: Kangaroo Hound, Australian Greyhound
REGISTRY: None
GROUP: Southern

Early Australian settlers used large sighthounds, such as Greyhounds, to hunt kangaroos, wallabies and Dingoes. Deerhound blood was added for increased size and power, and the resulting progeny were known as Kangaroo Dogs. In appearance, the Kangaroo Dogs resembled the English Greyhound, but were heavier.

These dogs did not have the fortune to attract the support and attention of breeders and have never reached registry status. With national protection of kangaroos and wallabies, the Kangaroo Dog became increasingly rare and is found only on remote sheep and cattle stations in Australia, and is possibly even extinct.

KARELIAN BEAR LAIKAS

Karelian Bear Dog

COUNTRY: Finland
WEIGHT: 44–49 pounds
HEIGHT: 19–23½ inches
COAT: Short, harsh, stand-off
COLOR: Black (preferably dull or with a brownish cast); white blaze, throat, chest, feet and tail tip
OTHER NAMES: Karelsk Bjornhund, Karjalankarhukoira, Karelischer Barenhund
REGISTRY: FCI, CKC
GROUP: Northern

Russo-European Laika

COUNTRY: USSR
WEIGHT: 45–50 pounds
HEIGHT: 21–24 inches
COAT: Short, harsh, stand-off
COLOR: Black, with symmetrical white markings
OTHER NAMES: Lajka Ruissisch Europaisch, Karelian Bear Laika
REGISTRY: FCI
GROUP: Northern

Large hunting laikas from Karelia and neighboring areas on the Russian/Finland border have become popular throughout European Russia as well as in Finland. The breed that the Finns fostered took on the name Karelian Bear Dog. In Russia (Karelia is now a territory of the Soviet Union), the breed is called Russo-European Laika, but they are much the same dog in background, appearance, and hunting style. The Russian strain called the Karelian Bear Laika is larger and more aggressive, creating a more specialized elk and bear dog. But all of them are big dogs, slightly longer than tall, and they boast a robust, athletic stature. Although the tail preferably plumes over the back, natural bobtails do exist and, while frowned upon, are still conceded by both the current Finnish and Soviet standards.

The dog always was employed for a variety of game, but interest was aroused in the breed by his reputation as a big game hunter. This was especially true of the Russian aristocracy in the last century. Bear Dog was accepted as its name, which gives the breed a certain dignity and stature. Although the breed remained fairly pure in backwoods villages for centuries, in the 1930s the Finnish Kennel Club took this breed into its

Karelian Bear Dog.

Russo-European Laika.

planned breeding programs, furnishing the boost needed to guarantee the breed's preservation.

The Winter War (between Russia and Finland in 1939–40) nearly decimated the breed and only a few fanciers remained. By the 1960s, the Karelian Bear Dog was seriously declining in Finland. Poor breeding practices—using parents without good abilities—were creating puppies which disappointed hunters. Conscientious breeders brought this laika back to today's strength in both numbers and abilities.

The Karelian Bear Dog in Finland has been used mainly as a hunter of elk. Now trials to choose breeding stock are held and are said to be very demanding on both dog and hunter. Erkki Tuominen, a Finnish breeder, says of the breed, ". . . its future depends on how we can retain and further develop its ability as an elkdog."

He described the dog eloquently in a letter: "A definite kind of abruptness, which could also be named self-respect, belongs to the tempera-

ment of the Carelian Bear Dog [Finnish spelling]. In a pinch it is unfailingly brave, never yielding, even merciless. This is the dog for a big-game hunter both in essence and character . . . . If one would have to describe the Carelian Bear Dog with a word, it would be *grand* . . . . Its black-white colour, the fiery look of . . . dark eyes and the stateliness and strength of its essence capture the eyes of a hunter . . . like a piece of wild and untamed wilderness . . . firm barking in [the] autumn landscape, the angrily puffing elk; that is Finnish big-game hunting at its best."

These big-game hunters are used for other types of quarry as well, depending on their owner. In Russia the laikas hunt squirrel, fowl and mink as well as bears, moose, boars and even wolves. American owners agree that the Karelians are excellent squirrel dogs. Contrary to the name, *laika* meaning barker, these dogs are always silent trailers, beginning their barking only when the game is treed or otherwise cornered. At that point, they begin their continuous barking to keep the quarry occupied until the hunter is within shooting range. They generally hunt singly, due to their aggressive tendencies.

Karelian Bear Dogs are owned and bred in Canada, America and other European countries as well as Russia and Finland. Owners emphasize they are a working breed and must have plenty of exercise, and that the dogs are most happy when owned by an outdoor enthusiast. Most are housed outside to keep them acclimated to the colder temperatures. They are tough and independent, but form a strong bond with their owner. These characteristics make them sharp guard dogs. The breed is aggressive with other dogs and will fight an intruder—human or canine—to the death, if need be. The Karelian does not make a good pet for those unable to control him. Training, socialization and leash control in public are advised.

Above: Russo-European Laika. **Below:** Karelian Bear Dog sounding a warning.

Karelo-Finnish Laika, fawn.

KARELO-FINNISH LAIKA

COUNTRY: USSR
WEIGHT: 25–30 pounds
HEIGHT: 15–19 inches
COAT: Dense, moderately short, stand-off
COLOR: Fawn in various shades, lighter tones on the undersides are allowed
GROUP: Northern Dog

The Karelo-Finnish Laika is very similar to the Finnish Spitz. Nordic hunting breeds developed long before current national boundaries. The red hunting dog fostered in Finland took on the name Finnish Spitz, and the same general type promoted in European Russia was named Karelo-Finnish for the area from which it came. The area called Karelia is actually a part of northwestern Russia, just east of Finland and south of the Barents seaport of Murmansk. The Russian term *laika* means barker or barking dog, similar to the term applied to his Finnish counterpart. All of the Nordic-type dogs from Russia are called laika, describing their distinctive hunting style. The actual Karelo-Finnish Laika is unknown outside of Russia, but at home he is very popular with hunters; in fact he is the most numerous of all the Russian laikas, due to his fine abilities and small size.

Maturing very early, he finds employment for various types of bird hunting—grouse, pheasant and duck—as well as squirrels. Many Soviet fur hunters also find this breed useful for trailing and entering fox, marten or raccoon burrows, and he is even brave enough to dance face to face with a bear. This energetic, small, quick dog is the least likely of the laikas to bog down and suffocate in the deep snow drifts.

In temperament, the Karelo-Finnish is high-strung and excitable. He is willing to please and cannot stand rudeness, punishment or unfair treatment. Russians say "everything about this dog, its eyes, ears, and tail, express joy and cheerfulness." But if ill-treated, the bond between Laika and hunter is broken, and the hunt will lose its joy.

Karelo-Finnish Laika.

Keeshond.

Keeshond.

KEESHOND

COUNTRY: Netherlands
WEIGHT: 55–66 pounds
HEIGHT: 17–19 inches
COAT: Long, dense, double, stand-off
COLOR: Wolf gray; lighter shadings on head and undersides, creating the typical spectacles around the eyes
OTHER NAMES: Wolfspitz, Chien Loup
REGISTRY: AKC, UKC, TKC, CKC
GROUP: Northern

Dogs of the spitz type have long been common in Friesland (northern Holland), left over from the Viking invasions. Legend tells of a Viking ship that went down at sea. The only survivor, a chieftain's son, was rescued during the storm by a Christian fisherman of Friesland and his dog. Wolfert (the fisherman) and the Viking finally landed in unknown territory and built a chapel to St. Olaf for their deliverance. This chapel became a village at the mouth of the Amstel River, where a dam was built in later years. The town was known as Amstelredam, later Amsterdam. The dog, a participant in the entire legend, was never forgotten. The seal of the city of Amsterdam shows an ancient vessel with a dog of definite spitz type watching over the side. Carrying a dog on board a vessel thus became a good omen, and later a custom. A ship's canines came under the sea laws, as the pets represented ownership. In the owner's absence, no one dared ransack a ship if there was a dog on board! So throughout Dutch history, boats and

537

Keeshond.

cially like and adopt the large, wolf gray type. The Dutch dearly loved their dogs and passed laws for their protection. One such law shows the value placed on companionship: "He who kills a hunting dog shall be fined eight pieces, but if he kills someone's pet dog the fine shall be twelve pieces."

Although known for centuries, he acquired his modern name from Cornelius de Gyselaer, a Dutch patriot at the time of the French Revolution. De Gyselaer's nickname was Kees (pronounced *kays*), and Kees's dog became a symbol of the common and middle-class Dutch Patriot Party that followed de Gyselaer. With the eventual defeat of de Gyselaer's cause, the dog fell into disrepute. Prominent people proved not to have the loyalties of their dogs—they did not want to be seen with a Kees dog. The breed dropped from sight among the urban and upper classes.

In 1920, nearly 150 years later, Baroness van Hardenbroek took an interest in the breed and began her search for good specimens. She was startled to find that among the bargemen, farmers and truckers of rural areas, there were still many enthusiasts of the breed. The dogs they had maintained were of remarkably good type, with many of these owners keeping their own rudimentary stud books. With the renewed interest that the Baroness stirred when she began breeding, the Keeshond again was seen throughout Holland. It was introduced in the 1930s into the USA and England simply as the Dutch Barge Dog. Never a dog of fads or crazes, the Keeshond has continued to have a steady and loyal following throughout the world. Although the FCI does not register the Keeshond, considering it the same breed as the German Wolfspitz, the USA, Canada and Great Britain consider him an entity.

Kees require only moderate grooming and are happy, family-oriented dogs, so much so they are sometimes called "the laughing Dutchman." They can be a bit self-willed, however, and may balk at being forced into doing things that they don't want to do. But with firm, consistent guidance, they prove compliant. The Kees is clean, personable and alert and has made the move from the boats of Holland to 20th-century apartments with ease.

barges traditionally carried dogs on board, for vermin control, as watchdogs and simply for companionship and good luck.

Keeshonden are of the same stem stock as the German Spitz, but the Dutch seemed to espe-

Keeshonden.

Kerry Beagle, black/tan.

KERRY BEAGLE

COUNTRY: Ireland
HEIGHT: 22–24 inches
COAT: Hard, close and smooth
COLOR: Black and tan, blue mottled and tan, black/tan/white, or tan and white
OTHER NAMES: Pocadan
GROUP: Hound

From very early times, a large distinctive scent-hound has trod the Emerald Isle. He most likely arrived with the Celts and has been refined over the years with crosses to the Southern Hound and French hounds.

By the 18th and 19th centuries, their numbers had dwindled until they were primarily in only one kennel owned by the Ryan family of Scarteen, County Limerick. With interest in native breeds growing, however, there are now a good number of fine packs with Kerry Beagles hunted throughout rural Ireland. Many specimens came with Irish immigrants to the USA, where they contributed to the famous Trigg strain of American Foxhounds as well as being one of the major stems of the American Black and Tan Coonhound. The breed is unsponsored by any formal dog organization, even in its homeland.

The origin of his description as "beagle" is unknown, as he was never a small dog like the familiar Beagle. In fact, in earlier times, he was even larger, but has carried the label of Beagle for centuries. The present-day word for the breed in the Irish language is *pocadan*, which describes him as a hunting dog. In the beginning, he was mainly used for stag hunting, a sport requiring speed and stamina. He is now generally utilized for hare hunts as well as drag trials.

The exhilarating sport of foot hunting for hare is pursued in Ireland mainly for the enjoyment of following a fine pack of hounds. Watching these dogs from a high vantage point as they work the rocky mountainsides is a never-ending thrill, and listening to their beautiful voices echo across the valleys culminates the hunt. *The Native Dogs of Ireland* says that, "it is extremely rare if a hare is caught. The Hunt Master invariably calls off the hounds should the hare be in any danger or distress."

Drag trials are held in Ireland for the Kerry Beagle. The Kerry hounds fan out in a large circle when casting, and automatically turn to the first dog that finds the scent and indicates it by "opening" with a loud bay. They have astonishing speed and independence.

The Kerry Beagle sports long ears, full chops and a robust, athletic build. The black-and-tan jacketing is the classic coat, although a great variety of other "hound" colors as tan or red bicolors, tricolors, or even the very rare blue-mottled (merle) color, are seen and allowed. One 19th-century writer's description of him as "an indifferent bloodhound" was not meant to be unflattering, but merely indicated that they looked much like a Bloodhound without the exaggeration of bone and skin. One hopes that sufficient interest is maintained in this ancient Irish hound to ultimately find it included among the recognized and exhibited dogs of the world.

KERRY BLUE TERRIER

COUNTRY: Ireland
WEIGHT: 33–40 pounds
HEIGHT: 17½–19½ inches
COAT: Soft, profuse, dense and wavy
COLOR: Born black and clear to any shade of blue by the age of 18 months
REGISTRY: FCI, AKC, TKC, CKC
GROUP: Terrier

Like his cousin the Irish Terrier, the Blue Terrier of Eire has little literary reference before the 1800s. Oft repeated legends tell us that the Blue's ancestor swam ashore from a ship wrecked off Tralee Bay in the late 1700s, or even that it was from Spanish ships of the Armada in 1588. "This dark survivor was supposed to have mated with local terriers to produce a dog with a dark blue coat and the type and temperament of a terrier." There are also references to "blackish blue" terriers indigenous to County Kerry and other areas going back further that could have been the rootstock and to what the "dark survivor" was bred.

His rather soft wavy coat is distinct among the terriers. With all of the above evidence, even if the story of the shipwreck survivor is true, it is hard to know what type of dog he was. Would he have been a shaggy sheep dog type who instilled the herding ability and longer coat with fading pigment into the local terrier population? Or was it a water dog, of the type that produced the Poodles, Porties and Water Spaniels, who introduced the graying factor, soft wavy coat and water ability? All interesting speculation—the answer to which is lost in the mists of Irish lore.

Although used for all jobs required of terriers, the Kerry was said to be the only dog that "will tackle an otter, single-handed, in deep water." He also was used in his native land to tend stock.

This "true blue" native of the Emerald Isle enjoyed a peak in the 1920s, when no less than four clubs sponsored him in Ireland. The Kerry represented more than 25 percent of total Irish Kennel Club registrations in 1924. It was during this time that the struggle for national independence from Britain was going on, and the Kerry became a mascot for Irish patriots. His favor was such that, even during those bitter times, the Dublin Blue Terrier Club of 1920 was made up of members on both sides of the political fence. Politics were tolerated—or ignored—when it came to dogs, however. According to breed history, the first show held by the group was set up without permission of the ruling British KC. It was judged by Dan Nolan (at the time on the British authority "wanted" list for being a member of the Irish Republican Army). Among the spectators and competitors at this event were members of the English KC as well as an Inspector from the Constabulary. Yet all turned a blind eye while they competed for the Wyndham Quinn Challenge Cup for best Kerry!

American fanciers first exhibited the breed at Westminster in 1922. Among more contemporary owners, Mrs. William Randolph Hearst and heavy-weight champion Gene Tunney both owned Kerrys.

The Kerry in Ireland is required to be shown in an untrimmed, natural state. Elsewhere, the dog is exhibited with a sculptured, scissored coat. He is reported to be a long-lived dog. Like his close cousins, the Irish Terrier and the Soft-Coated Wheaten Terrier, he is a leggy, rangy dog.

Kerry Blues are born black and, if correct, have the dominant gene for coat fading. The color begins to fade to gray and acquires its adult solid slate gray color by 18 months. This is the same graying or fading gene seen in some Bearded Collies and Poodles.

While he sometimes suffers from an undeserved reputation for surliness, he can be described today as he was in 1922 by fancier E.M. Webb: "His temperament is well nigh faultless, if a slight tendency to diminish the cat population be excepted. He is . . . . unrivalled as a ratter, charming as a companion, trustworthy as a watchdog."

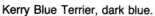

Kerry Blue Terrier, dark blue.

Kerry Blue Terrier, grayish blue.

Kerry Blue Terrier

Above: Kerry Blue Terrier, dark blue. **Below:** Kerry Blue Terrier, pups.

KOMONDOR

COUNTRY: Hungary
WEIGHT: 80–150 pounds
HEIGHT: 25½ inches minimum ("the bigger, the better")
COAT: Long, corded
COLOR: White
REGISTRY: FCI, AKC, UKC, TKC, CKC
GROUP: Flock Guard

A working flock guard in Hungary and a unique show dog of the United States and Great Britain, the Komondor serves as a link between yesterday and today.

Hungarian legend tells us that tenth-century Serb shepherds found a litter of wolf cubs and selected those that behaved most like dogs. These were trained to work with sheep, and crossed with native dogs, supposedly produced the Komondor.

Despite fanciful legends, the Komondor is directly descended from the Owtcharki brought to Hungary by the nomadic Magyars around 1,000 years ago. The source of his name cannot be pinpointed, but it may have been derived from the term *komondor kedvu* (meaning somber,

surly or angry), apt adjectives for the ancient flock guard.

A fixture in Hungary for centuries, the Kom has only been in North America since the 1930s. They are routinely seen in shows, besides participating in flock-guarding programs. Heavyweight boxer Gene Tunney owned an illustrious Komondor bitch. The breed, however, has never become well known in Great Britain.

The Kom protects and dominates whatever animals are under his care and includes children in that responsibility. He is an alert, tough guard and serves as a police dog in some areas.

Breeder and owner Joy C. Levy says, "The dog's protective instincts, and his instincts to make decisions for himself, have been selected for centuries. If we breed two imported dogs, their offspring carry on this temperament, which gets them into trouble in Modern American Society [*sic*]. This happens especially in modern suburbia, where fences do not exist and people regularly trespass in the eyes of the dog. Hordes of children rushing into houses without ringing or being let in often look as bad to a Komondor as that villain who steals his family's

Komondor.

Komondorok.

Komondor.

trash, or the one who comes into his house with a weapon, in the form of a plumber's wrench. In the USA some of the best dogs are put down as vicious, when all they did was try to defend their owner and his property.''

True to the flock guards, they are not easy breeders. The bitches only cycle once a year, and the studs are not avid performers. As an additional hindrance, the long, corded coats make matings difficult.

The corded coat is not seen on more than a handful of breeds. Now a unique conversation piece, the cords served a purpose for the flock guard. These twisted ringlets were never combed and, in adulthood, served as armor, impervious to climate and predators' teeth. The cords also serve to make them look like one of the semi-wild sheep. In his native land, the working Kom is shaggy, heavily matted, and untidy. Show conditioning necessitates a neater appearance.

Cording takes special care, requiring meticulous training during puppyhood and from four to eight hours blow-drying the coat after bathing. In addition, owners spend up to two hours per week hand-separating the cords. Maintaining the white color complicates the care.

Outside the show ring, Koms serve as guardians for animals, property and families. They are part of several flock-guard programs in the USA. Breeders recommend obedience training, as the Kom likes to be the boss.

Kooikerhondje.

KOOIKERHONDJE

COUNTRY: Netherlands
WEIGHT: 20–24 pounds
HEIGHT: 14–16 inches
COAT: Moderately long, with slight wave;
fringed, as a spaniel
COLOR: Red and white
OTHER NAMES: Kooiker Dog
GROUP: Gun Dog

Kooiker Dogs have been extant in the Netherlands for many years, helping the hunters draw the *kooikers,* a type of duck. It was a Kooiker that was credited with saving the life of Prince William of Orange (1533–1584). The dog barked at intruders, alerting the Prince to escape. Dutch artists Jan Steen and Jan Vermeer captured the breed in paintings during the 1600s.

History then skips any mention of the Kooiker Dog until the early 1940s when Baroness v. Hardenbroek van Ammerstol began her search for one of this native breed. The Baron-

ess gave a likeness of the Kooiker Dog to a peddler and showed him the coat color, asking him to search for such a dog in his travels. The peddler was fortunate to find a Kooiker bitch, "Tommy," in the northern Netherlands. Two males, "Bobby" and "Bennie," were also found in the same area.

Tommy's first litter was born in 1943, and these three dogs set the foundation of the modern breed. Originally, tricolored dogs were allowed, but are now not permitted.

The Kooikerhondje is called the "decoy" in the Netherlands for its method of aiding the hunter. Pipes set with wire netting are placed around ponds and lakes. Feed is sprinkled near the end, with tame ducks eating the fodder and drawing the attention of the wild ducks. The Kooiker Dog leads the ducks in, attracting them with his bushy white tail. When they are under the netting, the hunter appears, frightening the birds into the netting. Young and rare birds are ringed and set free. The nature reserves in the

Netherlands employ about a hundred decoys.

Baroness v. Hardenbroek van Ammerstol received a gold pin of honor from the Council of Cynological Management for her work to solidify the futures of the national breeds including the Drent Partridge and the Dutch Kooiker Dog.

This old Dutch breed has only enjoyed an organized breed club since 1967; acknowledgement of the breed came in 1971. Fanciers feel FCI will accept the breed in the near future. Matings are still a problem, with strict breeding requirements and a narrow breed base. (All specimens are in the Netherlands.) However, those same regulations are improving soundness of the breed.

The Kooiker Dog is medium sized, very much like a small setter or spaniel in appearance. The tail must be long and bushy; hair on the ears is long, preferably with black tips called earrings. He is cheerful, easy to manage and affectionate with his owners. These qualities make him not only a good hunter's companion, but a delightful family and obedience dog.

Above: The Kooikerhondje demonstrating its obedience trial abilities. **Below:** A family of Kooikerhondjes from the Netherlands.

Krasky Ovcar.

KRASKY OVCAR

COUNTRY: Yugoslavia
WEIGHT: 55–88 pounds
HEIGHT: 20½–24 inches
COAT: Medium, dense and harsh
COLOR: Iron gray with shadings
OTHER NAMES: Karst Sheepdog, Istrian Sheepdog
REGISTRY: FCI
GROUP: Flock Guard

Nestled up against the Alps of Italy and Austria is the northern border of Yugoslavia. The area called Karst (or Kras) encompasses much of northern Yugoslavia, including the Istrian Peninsula jutting out into the Adriatic Sea. The local livestock-guarding dog is closely related to the Sarplaninac of the south. Both the Karst and the Sar are obviously related to the flock guards of Greece, Rumania and the eastern Balkans.

Americans, looking for examples of this breed in the late 1970s, were told that if any existed, "all the[se] dogs were now only in the south" of Yugoslavia. But their obituary was premature. A few lovers of this breed worked to see it saved in its homeland, Europe and even in America.

Most of these breeders were people of Yugoslavian descent who saw the Karst as a living piece of their country's history. The FCI has now granted international recognition to the breed.

The Krasky Ovcar is only seen in the iron gray color, preferably with darker shadings on the back and "spectacles" around the eyes. The ears are small and set fairly high, hanging down in a flat *v*. The long tail is heavy with hair, forming a flag. Muscles must be strong and well developed, giving an impression of mammoth strength. Its leathery footpads enable it to go over nearly impassable terrain and rocks.

A good domestic dog, the Karst has been described as a cheerful, delightful companion. He is wary of strangers and not easily won over, and these characteristics combined with abundant courage make him an excellent guardian. He is smaller and less aggressive than some of the other flock guards. Sporadically, a specimen of the breed is exhibited at rare breed shows in America and FCI events in Europe. The breed has not been promoted like the Sar for livestock guarding in America, but it has served in that capacity in its homeland for centuries.

551

Above: Kromfohrländer, wire. **Below:** Kromfohrländer, long straight.

552

KROMFOHRLÄNDER

COUNTRY: Germany
WEIGHT: 26 pounds
HEIGHT: 15–18 inches
COAT: Two types: rough wire; medium-long straight hair
COLOR: Mainly white with tan (light to very dark) markings in a broken pattern, including saddle and head
REGISTRY: FCI
GROUP: Terrier

The Kromfohrländer is a breed of the 20th century. In 1945, American soldiers marched into Germany from France. One group, arriving in the town of Siegen, Westphalia, was accompanied by a shaggy, tawny dog. Although his family tree was unknown, his appearance and French origin indicated a Breton Griffon (Griffon Fauve de Bretagne). The dog was taken in by a townswoman, Ilse Schleifenbaum. "Peter" became a beloved house pet and later "fell in love" with the next-door neighbor, "Fiffi," a fe-

Kromfohrländer, medium straight.

Kromfohrländer, wire.

male of uncertain pedigree, but possibly Fox Terrier extraction. The resulting puppies were uniform and so handsome that Mrs. Schleifenbaum decided to develop them into a new breed. Ten years later, in 1955, she succeeded in having the German Kennel Club officially recognize them, with the FCI giving them the stamp of approval shortly after.

Lively, loyal and obedient, the breed was developed specifically as a companion dog. The muzzle tapers slightly, ears are high and fall in a complete drop, and the happy tail is carried gaily, forming a loose ring over the back. This German terrier carries robust sporting dog proportions.

He is alert, watchful, devoted to his family and does not roam. Since the breed was a happy accident, these dogs do not hunt but are strictly companions and watchdogs. A current German owner relates how Kromfohrländers are a part of his family and says, "We did not know that dogs could be so intelligent."

KUVASZ

COUNTRY: Hungary
WEIGHT: 110 pounds maximum
HEIGHT: 26 inches maximum
COAT: Wavy, medium length
COLOR: White to ivory
REGISTRY: FCI, AKC, CKC
GROUP: Flock Guard

Kuvasz, white.

Many cynologists believe the Kuvasz was brought to Hungary by the Kumans, nomadic shepherds of Turkish origin in the 13th century. These dogs may have moved north with much earlier migrations, however. They are obviously part of the flock-guarding family, both as ancestors and descendants. Their similarity to the Akbash Dog is striking.

Kuvasz may have been derived from the Sumerians, ancient Eastern people who originally fostered dogs of this type. *Ku-assa*, in Sumerian, is dog horse, indicating a dog that guarded and ran along beside horses and riders. The term *ku-assa* is found on a clay board at the site of Akkad in northern Mesopotamia, circa 3000 BC. Most of the migrating peoples who came from Asia to populate eastern Europe were horse-riding tribes whose wealth was in large herds of range cattle. Those who settled what is now Hungary brought their white guard dogs with them.

The breed savored a moment of splendor in the 15th century in the court of King Matyas (Mathias) I, who claimed to trust his Kuvasz dogs more than his fawning courtiers. This king used his Kuvaszok for hunting wild boar and as personal guardians. The breed was never an exclusivity with royalty, however, and aided herdsmen and peasants in protection. He is still seen frequently in Hungary today.

The Kuvasz has been bred and exhibited in the United States since the 1920s. He successfully patrols American ranches for predator control. The breed has never become recognized in Great Britain.

A typical flock guard in temperament, he is wary and suspicious of that which is not familiar. This is correct temperament for the breed—and the group—as a whole.

Owners should be responsible, with enough experience and knowledge to control the macho temperament. The Kuvasz will continue to test his owner's dominance. Once he has given his devotion, he will be a one-family dog and will protect that family from all intruders, including a new neighbor or the toll-taker. The Kuvasz has an intense loyalty to that which is his own and needs proper socialization and control to become a dependable companion dog as well. The thick, white coat is also demanding of attention.

Kuvasz, ivory.

Kyi Leo, black/white particolor.

KYI LEO

COUNTRY: USA
HEIGHT: 8–12 inches, outside limits; 9–11 inches preferred
COAT: Long, thick and straight or slightly wavy, tends to part along the spine
COLOR: Usually black/white particolor, but also gold/white, or self colors, some dogs may fade from black to slate
REGISTRY: None
GROUP: Herding

In the 1950s, around the San Francisco Bay area of California, a few people experimented with crosses of Maltese dogs and Lhasa Apsos. Why this was begun is not recorded, but the result was small adorable dogs with sparkling personalties, causing people to succumb to their charms. One lady from San José linebred these shaggy dogs for many years, developing a type to her liking. When Harriet Linn acquired one of these Maltese/Lhasa Shaggies in 1965, little did she know that she was beginning a lifetime commitment. After breeding a litter from that first dog, she knew she was hooked. Mrs. Linn was the driving force behind the coalescing of this new breed. She acquired other specimens, including several from the San José kennel when it closed its doors in 1969. Three years later, sufficient interest in the breed brought owners and breeders together for a formal meeting.

They decided on the name Kyi Leo for their new breed. *Kyi* is Tibetan for dog, giving credit to the Lhasa, and *Leo* is Latin for lion, acknowledging the Maltese's contribution. A club was formed and an interim standard adopted. The breed club keeps detailed registration information on all Kyi Leos since the breed is not yet recognized by any formal kennel authority. A quarterly newsletter is sent out to all owners and interested parties, and the group sponsors an annual picnic (the Kyi Leo Get Together) for Kyi Leo lovers to meet one another and talk about their favorite subject!

Above: Kyi Leos, particolor. **Below:** Kyi Leo.

The Kyi Leo has many of the good points of both of his ancestors. Although a small dog, he is not as tiny and fragile as the Maltese. His muzzle is longer and lacks the underbite seen in most Lhasas. While his hair is long, it never reaches the excessive floor length of the show specimens of his forebears. Although other colors are seen and allowed, the black and white pied dogs are the trademark of the breed.

Known for their agility and catlike quickness, they are playful and people-oriented. These dogs are outgoing, happy and intelligent with an abundance of willingness to please. Yet they have a tendency to be a bit reserved with strangers, making them ideal small alarm dogs. Although, occasionally, they show a hint of stubbornness, most owners tolerantly see this as merely asserting their own characters. They charm their way into hearts. The breed is known in a dozen states, as well as Canada, and is growing in numbers each year.

Labrador Retrievers, yellow, chocolate, and black.

LABRADOR RETRIEVER

COUNTRY: Great Britain
WEIGHT: 55–75 pounds
HEIGHT: 21½–24½ inches
COAT: Moderately short, dense, hard and without wave; thick undercoat
COLOR: Solid black, chocolate, or yellow (from fox-red to light cream)
REGISTRY: FCI, AKC, UKC, TKC, CKC
GROUP: Gun Dog

As far back as the 17th century, water dogs were used by fishermen and hunters in Canada. These were called Newfoundland, Labrador (Greenland was once called Labrador) or St. John's Dogs, depending on their geographic location. These early dogs were moderate in size, had curled coats, carried the genetic factor to produce spotting, and tended to a high tail. Not much formal breeding was attempted, but from these eventually stemmed the modern Newfoundland and Landseer, as well as the Labrador, Flat-Coat and Chesapeake Bay Retrievers.

Throughout the world, fishing vessels, trading ships and exploratory expeditions provided continuous traffic. Most ships had dogs on board, and the crossing of various imported types with the native population of dogs was well documented. By 1800, these retrieving dogs were being sold into England by ships plying from the Canadian coast. But, later that century, a heavy dog tax caused a great reduction in the breed in Canada and, more importantly, the creation of the English quarantine laws essentially stopped further importation. Thus, although the root stock came from Canada, the modern development of the breed occurred in England.

Early Labs sported a large variety of types and colors, including spotted and brindle. The Flat-Coat was enjoying great favor during the 19th century, and the Labrador was not granted Kennel Club recognition until after the turn of the century. But, once he came to prominence, he stayed on top. Labs are now in the first five breeds in both England and America and maintain their popularity as duck dogs par excellence. In American retriever field trials, the Labrador dominates to the point of exclusion. He enjoys a sterling reputation as an upland bird flusher, companion, drug detector, obedience competitor and guide dog for the blind. In fact,

"Polly" lovingly served her blind master for a record 13 years! The Lab is well known and utilized also in Australia, Canada, and many other countries.

Willing-to-please perhaps best describes the Lab. The breed, overall, is sensible, even-tempered, intelligent, and possesses strong natural abilities in marking and retrieving. The short, easy-care coat and docile temperament make the Lab a favorite pet, who can—year round—run with the kids, catch a flying disc in the park, join the family by the fire, and still double as a hunting companion. Because of his fairly large size and his designated lifestyle as an active, athletic dog, soundness is of prime importance.

The ideal Lab is described as slightly longer than tall, with a robust, muscular build. His distinctive "otter" tail is covered by short, thick hair; he should *never* show any fringe on the underside of the tail! The double coat is quite waterproof, requiring frequent brushing only during the spring shedding season.

Labrador Retriever, yellow.

Labrador Retriever, chocolate.

Labrador Retriever, black, with a retrieved mallard.

Labrador Retriever, black.

Labrador Retriever, yellow.

LAKELAND TERRIER

COUNTRY: Great Britain
WEIGHT: 17 pounds
HEIGHT: 13–15 inches
COAT: Hard and wiry
COLOR: Blue, black, liver, black/tan, blue/tan, red, red grizzle, grizzle/tan, wheaten
REGISTRY: FCI, AKC, TKC, CKC
GROUP: Terrier

From solid-colored, broken-coated terriers of the lake districts of northern England, this fine working terrier emerged. The entire area—the northern counties of Cumberland, Northumberland and Westmoreland—was the fount of many terrier varieties. The dog that eventually developed into the Bedlington and Dandie Dinmont was probably the origin of the Lakeland and the Border Terrier as well. A century or more before organized dog shows, the Lakeland assisted in informal hunts. These were organized by farmers—with a couple of hounds and terriers—when foxes were raiding the sheepfolds.

These dogs were not like the "fox" terriers developed further south which were expected to bolt the quarry. The Lakelands were practical working terriers, required to face and kill the fox underground. When exhibited, they were still shown under the all-embracing term: Colored Working Terrier.

The breed was then called the Patterdale or Fell Terrier and came in a variety of colors as well as white. When they were first exhibited in the 1880s–90s, they were divided into white and colored dogs. Masters of Foxhounds judged the terriers not on their looks, but for their ability as working "fox" terriers. Soon the white terriers were used exclusively for otter work. (Young hounds, in their excitement, often mistook a dark dog for an otter and mauled the dog instead as both bolted from the hole.) The dark dogs were kept to hunt for foxes in the mountain rock piles.

Stories of Lakeland courage are plentiful. In 1871, Lord Lonsdale had a Lakeland that crawled 23 feet under rock after an otter. In order to extricate the dog, it was necessary to undertake extensive blasting operations. The dog was taken out, still in fine fettle, three days later. Still other dogs were recorded to have

Lakeland Terrier.

Lakeland Terrier.

LANCASHIRE HEELER

COUNTRY: Great Britain
WEIGHT: 6–12 pounds
HEIGHT: 10–12 inches
COAT: Short, smooth
COLOR: Black/tan
OTHER NAMES: Ormskirk Terrier, Ormskirk Heeler
REGISTRY: TKC
GROUP: Herding

Developed as a cattle dog during the 1960s–70s, the Lancashire still herds cattle, horses and goats in its namesake territory. The breed's roots trace back to Corgis and Manchester Terriers. Both ancestries are apparent in his skills and make the breed a perfect farm and family dog. Terrier attributes are evident in hunting rabbits, exterminating rats and alerting to intruders. Yet the little dog is a courageous heeler, built low to escape kicks. The Lancashire has such strong heeling instincts, one family says their dog even will try to round up cattle seen on television!

Lancashire Heeler.

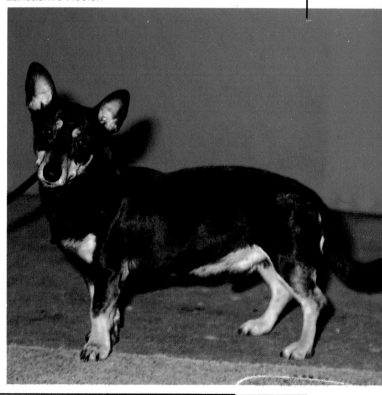

been taken out alive after 10–12 days. Of course, many paid the ultimate penalty.

In 1921, a group of fanciers met to resume pre-War activities and dubbed the breed after its lake district. Seven years later, the name Lakeland became official. The first president of the breed club was Lord Lonsdale, whose family had raised Lakelands for 50 years.

The Lakeland coat must be groomed in a manner similar to that of the Wire Fox and other rough-coated terriers. Although not as well known as some other terriers, they are consistently successful in the show rings. One famous champion, Stingray of Derryabah, was Best in Show at Crufts in 1967, followed by a BIS at Westminster, in New York, the following year. He became the only dog to win these prestigious shows on both sides of the Atlantic. Actor Bill Cosby is an ardent terrier fan, co-owning several top-winning dogs, among them a Lakeland, a Wire Fox and a Welsh Terrier.

They capture more than shows, however, winning hearts as well. Lakelands are down-to-earth, level-headed dogs who make fine companions. The breed adores children and matches their energy step for step.

Small physiques encase a large dog personality, and these dogs are protective of their turf. Yet, Lancashires are playful, intelligent companions and excellent obedience dogs. Their small size belies their strength, agility and hardiness. Although rare in numbers and known only in England as yet, they are increasing in favor because of their versatility, happy temperament and ease of care. They are sturdy and long-lived and particularly good playmates for children.

The Lancashire is adaptable to new circumstances. Only recently entering the show ring, the breed has a good attitude and is athletic, showing high promise in that realm as well as the farm and home.

Lancashire Heeler.

Landseer.

LANDSEER

COUNTRY: Scandinavian countries
HEIGHT: 26–31½ inches
COAT: Moderate length, soft, fairly dense, fine to the touch; short on head and fronts of legs
COLOR: Clear white, with large distinct black spots on back and rump; head should be black with a symmetrical white blaze
REGISTRY: FCI
GROUP: Mastiff

The original "Newfoundland" imports from Canada were much different from our present breed. Sir Edwin Landseer created several famous paintings of "Newfoundland dogs" in the early part of the 19th century, and these gave the type its name. The painting *Off to the Rescue*, (1827) of "Bashaw," a black-and-white variety belonging to the Right Honorable Earl of Dudley, and *A Distinguished Member of the Humane Society*, (1838) of "Paul Pry" owned by Mrs. Newman Smith, were notable. The dogs were portrayed as spotted, having a tapering head, longer legs and a more "open" coat, with a tendency to curl.

As the century progressed, two quite different types of Newfies developed in Europe, not just in color but in other characteristics. In the 1881 edition of the official German stud books, two varieties of Newfoundland dogs were clearly described. The "wavy-haired" was solid black (white not desired), with a shorter nose, overhanging lips and more massive build. The "curly-haired" Newfoundland (i.e., Landseer) had the described spotted pattern and the longer, dryer and more tapering head. The latter type also stood higher on leg with a slightly lighter frame.

Fanciers on the Continent continued to breed this variety of the black and white Landseer Newfoundland. Although the First World War took its toll on giant breeds, efforts were made in the 1930s to re-establish the Landseer as a separate breed. Brothers Otto and Alfred Walterspiel spearheaded efforts in 1933 to bring the Landseer back to prominence. The breed base was so small that some crossing to the black Newfoundland occurred in the early days. At this time, the Landseer has been bred pure for many years.

FCI recognizes the two breeds and, in 1976, the German Landseer Club was born as the first organization promoting the Landseer separately from the Newfoundland. Holland and Belgium have joined in that premise.

Above and Below: Landseers.

LAPINPOROKOIRA

COUNTRY: Finland
WEIGHT: 66 pounds or less
HEIGHT: 19–22 inches
COAT: Medium short, stiff and coarse, dense undercoat
COLOR: Black, black/tan
OTHER NAMES: Lapland Reindeer Dog, Lapponian Herder, Lapponian Vallhund
REGISTRY: FCI
GROUP: Herding

For centuries the Laplanders of northern Finland hunted reindeer, using pure northern spitz dogs to assist them. As the wild herds disappeared, the Lapps changed to herding domesticated reindeer. With this modification of lifestyle, they needed a different kind of dog to assist them and crossed their native dogs with herding breeds brought in from Europe. The result was a strong, natural herding dog with a good nature.

The Lapinporokoira is a true intermediate between the Nordic and herding breeds—closer to the Nordic type—but with a bit more leg, less curl to the tail and a longer, less tapering head.

Originally the dogs worked outside in the elements throughout the year, keeping the herds together and bringing back strays. The Porokoira sometimes ran over 60 miles a day, usually through deep snow. Years later, in the 1960s, the snowmobile became very popular with the herdsmen, and nearly spelled the doom of the Lapponian Herder. It wasn't long before the high cost of the machine and its fuel made the Lapps take a second look at the old herding breed. The natural energy of the Lapp dog and its accompanying lower "fuel" bills acquired a greater appeal.

Olli Korhonen, chair of the Finnish KC in the 60s, spearheaded the creation of a standard (1966) and the organization of breeding the Lapponian Herder. Through these efforts, an efficient system has evolved. The Lapps want good working dogs, mostly males, and have little interest in raising litters. Many Porokoira fanciers in the south of Finland are attracted to the breed by its good nature, easy care and obedience. They cooperate with the herdsmen in the north, bringing the best working males south to breed with their females and sending the male pups north to work. This system also insures the retention of natural working qualities in the breed.

Lapinporokoira, black/tan.

Finnish Lapphund, sable.

LAPPHUNDS

Swedish Lapphund

COUNTRY: Sweden
WEIGHT: 44 pounds
HEIGHT: 17½–19½ inches
COAT: Long, thick stand-off, with heavy underwool, and fringing on leg backs, belly and tail
COLOR: Black or liver, usually solid but sometimes with symmetrical white marks
OTHER NAMES: Lapplandska Spetz, Swedish Lapp Spitz
REGISTRY: FCI
GROUP: Northern

Finnish Lapphund

COUNTRY: Finland
HEIGHT: 18–20½ inches
COAT: Long, thick, stand-off; heavy underwool, and fringing on leg backs, belly and tail
COLOR: Any color, as long as the color dominates, and any white markings are small and symmetrical
OTHER NAMES: Lapinkoira
REGISTRY: FCI
GROUP: Northern

These two breeds are almost identical, although the FCI recognizes both, and the Swedish and Finnish Kennel Clubs each recognize their own breed as distinct. The standard for the Finnish variety allows for a slightly larger size, although recent correspondence from Finland states that most dogs are in the smaller range and there is thought of changing the standard.

Part of the confusion lies with the Lapp people. They are an old group native to the Arctic Circle, and the area they populated has always been known as Lapland, although never comprising a separate country. The area called Lapland actually includes parts of northern Norway, Sweden, Finland and even northwest Russia. Thus, any dogs developed by the Lapps were named for them; those brought south into Sweden were called Swedish Lapphunds, and the ones coming into Finland became the Finnish

Lapphund. Lapland is not far from the area of the Samoyede people in central Siberia, and the Lapland herding breeds bear much resemblance to the Samoyed dog.

The Lapphunds are natural herders of the ancient Nordic spitz type. Although much of reindeer herding has disappeared over the centuries, the dogs have adapted to work with sheep and cattle. Lapphunds were first brought to Finland from Pello in Lapland in the 1930s. These dogs were later bred with the longhaired Karelian Bear Dog, creating a breed called the Cockhill's Finnish Lapphound. When the Finnish Kennel Club decided to separate the Lapphound and the Lapponian Herder, the Cockhill variety was abolished, and breeders looked to Lapland to restore the original type.

Because of their moderate size and their courageous, affectionate nature, they make fine

Swedish Lapphund.

Above: Finnish Lapphund, black/tan. **Below:** Finnish Lapphund.

house pets that are natural alarm dogs. They have the longer coat and look very much like the German Spitz (i.e., Keeshond) as well as the Samoyed. Although the standards allow Irish white markings, self-colored dogs seem to predominate. The heavily plumed tail is carried up on the back.

The Finnish Kennel Club is concerned about preserving this breed, and notes particularly that breeding programs must emphasize the differences between the Lapinkoira and the Lapinporokoira. The Lapinporokoira (or Lapponian Herder) is larger, shorter coated, and has a body that is longer than tall. To keep the modern breeds distinct, the emphasis is on breeding Lapphunds that are moderate in size, nearly square-bodied, and long-coated.

LATVIAN HOUND

COUNTRY: USSR
HEIGHT: 16–19 inches
COAT: Short, dense
COLOR: Black and tan
GROUP: Hound

Latvia is another of the Russian Baltic states, where hunting is a passion in the heavy forests. The hunting of deer and boar in Latvia has followed an unusual format. The forest is blocked out into 1600-foot squares separated by wide clear-cut paths. Hunters may only shoot deer in the cut areas. During a hunt, each hunter is assigned a spot in the clearings, and beaters with dogs line up at the far side of the block. The hunting horn sounds, the hounds are slipped, and the chase is on. The dogs must be ultra-obedient to keep within the prescribed area, finding and flushing any game out to the waiting hunters in the clearings. These dogs needn't have the endurance or persistence, as they have to cover only the 1600 x 1600-foot block and are never expected to chase beyond that, even if the quarry is wounded.

Throughout the 19th century, Latvian gentry hunted deer with long-legged dogs called Curland Hounds, which had been created from a blend of Lucernese, English and Polish hounds. By WWI, good selection of these hounds had ceased, and they were often crossed with mongrels and Dachshunds. In 1920, the Latvian Department of Forestry banned the use of dogs larger than 20 inches, and hunters selected many of the Curland/Dachshund crosses, often blending them with English Beagles. It wasn't until 1947 that the Council of Hunters and Fishermen of the Latvian SSR resolved to fix the Latvian Hound as a specific breed. Despite great difficulty, they found and purchased 40 dogs of the desired type from private owners and began a breeding program. By 1971, type was fixed and a standard adopted.

The modern Latvian Hound is a dog of general basset type with cat feet, short straight legs, a strong arched back and a wedge-shaped, tight-lipped head. They are selected for their ability to raise game quickly and to be obedient to any of the handlers during the hunt.

Leonberger.

LEONBERGER

COUNTRY: Germany
WEIGHT: 80–150 pounds
HEIGHT: 25½–31½ inches
COAT: Medium-to-long thick hair on body, short on face and front of legs
COLOR: Lion-colored, golden yellow to red, with black mask
REGISTRY: FCI
GROUP: Mastiff

Mayor Heinrich Essig created the Leonberger in the 1840s to honor his German town. He wanted to produce a noble dog close in appearance to the lion in the Leonberg town crest. The monks at St. Bernard cooperated and encouraged him by sending some dogs for use in his breeding experiments. This proved to have a twofold benefit as the breeding program at the monastery had suffered severe setbacks from distemper outbreaks, as well as decreased vigor due to prolonged inbreeding. Some of Herr Essig's crosses were returned later to the monastery and incorporated into the monks' breeding program.

In the 1840s, Essig began by crossing a Landseer Newfoundland with a St. Bernard, then backcrossed to a Great Pyrenees. The results were large, strong dogs that quickly gained popularity as working animals and a leonine status symbol for the city of Leonberg and surrounding estates.

It is probable another solid-colored dog was incorporated into the base stock, as the Landseer and Saint are both particolored, and major white markings on the Leonberger are now undesirable. Conjecture has pointed to German or Austrian scenthounds, Greater Swiss Mountain Dogs or Kuvaszok contributing to the formation of the modern Leonberger.

The Leonberger displayed attributes from his progenitors: affection for people, great size, working aptitude, majestic appearance and, from the Newfoundland, his love for water. These qualities attracted attention from German breeders and from Austria's Empress Elizabeth, who quickly acquired one. There followed a parade of illustrious owners: the Prince of Wales, the King of Belgium, a Russian czar, Chancellor Otto Furst von Bismarck, Emperor Napoleon III, German composer Richard Wagner and Italian patriot Giuseppe Garibaldi.

The World Wars were devastating to the Leonberger. With owners barely able to obtain food for themselves and their families, feeding giant animals was out of the question. Breeders fled or were killed, leaving the dogs to fend for themselves and, in some instances, the animals

themselves were slain. At the end of WWI, only five dogs remained, and these were carefully nurtured and bred from until WWII, when the devastation struck again, leaving but eight Leonbergers to be found. Five litters were bred in 1945, resulting in 22 puppies. The following year, only 17 puppies survived. According to a present owner, it has taken 25 years to re-establish the breed.

While still considered a rare breed, the Leonberger is gaining ground and serves as a rescue dog and family watchdog, as well as companion. These dogs enjoy water—playing with it, being in it, or just lying in a child's wading pool, if there is no alternative. They even blow bubbles in their water bowls! The "Gentle Lion" is fascinated by and genial with small creatures—dogs, other animals and especially children. Most, given a choice, would prefer to be with children over anything else. Give them kids and a pool and they are in dog heaven! They will stand and watch for hours beside a playpen in utter contentment.

Due to the dogs' size and strength, owners stress the importance of human companionship and the need for early training, or you'll find yourself telling a new version of the old joke: Where does a 150-pound Leonberger sleep? . . . *Anywhere he wants!*

Leonberger.

LEOPARD CUR

COUNTRY: USA
WEIGHT: 45–70 pounds
COAT: Dense and smooth
COLOR: Leopard spotted (merle) or black/tan most common; occasional yellow, brindle, and blue (mouse color); all can have white points or neck rings
OTHER NAMES: Leopard Tree Dog
GROUP: Hound

The name "cur" to most of our minds, and according to *Webster's Dictionary*, is a mixed breed dog or a mongrel. Actually, Curs are a specific type of American dog with a long, proud history. Old-time coon hunters liked to say the word cur came from a dog that had been "cur-tailed" or docked since, at the birth of the breed, the Leopard Cur was born bob-tailed or was cur-tailed.

The early settler in the American South wanted a single dog of medium size that could hunt and tree the native game but also be aggressive and tough enough to guard against Indian attacks, work the semi-wild livestock and even fight if necessary. Probably originally created by crosses of various hounds, stock dogs, and possibly native American pariah dogs, these Cur types followed the pioneer into the American West. Curs had the natural inclination to tree their game, and thus figured prominently in the development of the coonhounds.

The Leopard Cur was probably the fountainhead of these types, beginning in eastern North Carolina in the early part of the 18th century. Spanish conquistadors had brought war dogs, often of the blue-splotched color, with them to America as early as 1542. The French, also, came to the southern region accompanied by their dogs, including not only their famous hounds but perhaps the big, bold Beauceron of the harlequin variety. The area was later settled by people of English, Scotch and Irish descent, who brought a variety of both hounds (including the mottled Kerry Beagle) and herding dogs (like the merle Collie). So, attempting to pinpoint the origin of the "leopard" color (blue merle) is impossible. It could have come from either the hound or the stock dog side.

In early pioneer times, the farmstead and

Leopard Cur, black/tan.

Leopard Cur, merle.

fields were fenced to keep the livestock *out*. The cattle and the semi-wild hogs ran free in the woods, fending for themselves and being rounded up once a year. For this task, the farmer needed a stock dog that was tough and aggressive and would go for the nose like the "bulldogs" of old. But he also wanted a hunting companion who would accompany him into the vast forests to shoot squirrel, raccoon, and other game as well as be tough enough for hunting big game like the panther (the eastern mountain lion). This type, called variously Leopard Dog, Leopard Cur, or just Cur, was well known before the American Revolution.

The Leopard Dogs moved west into Tennessee, Kentucky and beyond with the pioneers. Later, particularly after the Civil War, the dogs continued into the developing southwest of Texas and Oklahoma.

This creation was unique from the past hounds in two ways. First, their disposition was to want to please their master, while in general the pure hound is a more independent creature. This factor definitely came from those willing to please—the herding dogs. The second trait was the natural tendency and ability to tree game. Where this came from is pure conjecture. Perhaps it was from the war dog/bulldog mentality; perhaps it was just a happy accident. At any rate, the treeing instinct combined with the presence of the raccoon in America created a demand for this skill. Other hounds were just trailing dogs, but it was the addition of the Cur blood to those foxhounds and others that eventually created the treeing American Coonhounds.

By the early 20th century, the lifestyle of even the most remote mountain areas had changed enough that there was little need for the old style Leopard Dog. Few dogs of reasonable purity remained in the early 1950s.

About the same time, three men, working independently, began searches through remote areas. These men, J. Richard McDuffie, Leroy E. Smith and A.W. Carter, each established breeding programs to renew this old American breed. When they met in 1959, they created the American Cur Breeders Association to foster and promote the breed. They tried to register only dogs that traced back to the origins in North Carolina. In 1974, McDuffie, the registrar, transferred the registration office to Billie Williams of Missouri. His organization, the ACBA, continues to promote the breed today. McDuffie and others became alarmed, however, that a few unscrupulous breeders were crossing the old-style Leopards with other hounds and, because the merle gene is dominant and mottled pups result, registering them as Leopard Curs. Thus these men began the Leopard Tree Dog Registration Office in 1977 to register only those dogs tracing back to original North Carolina pedigrees on both sides. Many modern breeders have their dogs double registered with both the ACBA and the LTD.

The true Leopard Cur has a look, a psychology and a hunting style that is distinctly "cur." They have fine noses and are open trailers capable of excellent speed on a cold track. But they are "chop-mouthed"; that is, they have more of a bark than the drawn-out bay of a hound. These dogs also "run for blood," which is defined as the fight at the end of the track as the primary interest. To the pure hound, following the trail is the prime motivation.

The Leopard Dog has small, shorter ears set fairly high on the head, and tight cat feet. Today, most Leopard pups are born with long tails, which are not docked. This Cur is very affectionate to his master and has an intense desire to please. He tends to be a one-man dog, wary of strangers and, although always preferring to run from someone not known to him, if cornered will turn and stand his ground. Highly muscled and alert, the Leopard gives the impression of a coiled spring, ready to bound into action. The breed is courageous, with great stamina, able to work in temperature extremes.

Breeding for color alone is highly discouraged, as the ability of the hound is far more important than his jacketing. The American Cur Breeders Association history states, "Regardless of color, if he did a superior job, he was used as breeding stock. If he didn't, he stopped a bullet." Plain and simple! The breeding of leopard to leopard color is never allowed, because of the possibility of white pups which may be deaf or blind.

Leopard Cur, merle.

Levesque.

LEVESQUE

COUNTRY: France
WEIGHT: 55–66 pounds
HEIGHT: 26–28 inches
COAT: Short and smooth
COLOR: Tricolor; with the tan limited mainly to the head; the black occurs as a large mantle or blanket; white clear with no ticking
REGISTRY: FCI
GROUP: Hound

The hound bearing this name was created in 1873 by Rogatien Levesque. Levesque used Bleu Gascony, Virelade (Grand Gascon-Saintongeois) and English Foxhound to create a breed somewhat similar to the Grand Gascon in size, color and conformation. Originally bred to hunt in packs, the Levesque has a fine nose and is fast and sturdy. He is used for all types of game. The Levesque is a lighter built dog than some of the other large French hounds, even though still good sized. Today the Levesque is quite rare, having been crossed with other breeds, or may even be extinct. Many French cynologists feel that the remaining specimens were incorporated into the creation of the Chien Francais Blanc et Noir in 1957.

Lhasa Apso.

LHASA APSO

COUNTRY: Tibet (China)
HEIGHT: 10–11 inches for males, less for bitches
COAT: Heavy, straight, hard and dense
COLOR: Golden, sandy or honey (these preferably with black tips on ear, tail and beard hair); also grizzle, slate, smoke, particolor, black, white, or brown
OTHER NAMES: Tibetan Apso
REGISTRY: FCI, AKC, UKC, TKC, CKC
GROUP: Herding

Much of Oriental history has not become known to the Western Hemisphere, and the origins of Far Eastern dogs are sketchy. It is known, however, that the Tibetan Terrier, the shaggy herding dog of Tibet, was the basis for many other breeds and types.

Selection for giantism had long ago created the Tibetan Mastiff from large wolf dogs. A selection for dwarfism (brachycephalicism) among the Tibetan Terriers created a dog with slightly shortened muzzle and lower stationed, slightly bent legs. Maintaining the heavy coat and the tail up over the back, the result was a dog of the Lhasa Apso type. Small shaggy dogs were known in Tibet as far back as eight centuries before Christ.

These little "holy dogs" were presented to guests as tokens of luck or as "thank you" presents. They were welcomed not only for their alarm-dog tendencies, but because they were believed to bring peace and prosperity to their households. As the nomadic "guests" traveled through the Eastern Hemisphere into Europe, the appeal of their dogs spread also.

The impetus for fixing the Apso type, however, was the conversion of Tibet to Buddhism in the seventh century AD. Lions had been, even before Buddhism, a traditional symbol of Tibetan royalty, with their famous lion throne of the Dalai Lama and the flag displaying the king of beasts. This symbol of the mighty lion was used, in slightly modified form, to emphasize the power of Buddha. The god was said to have shown his complete domination over the animals by making the lion guard his temples and follow him around "like a pet dog." A leonine colored and shaped dog was a good example to show primitive people proof of this story.

Lhasas, "lion dogs," became fixtures inside the homes of Tibetan nobility and in lamas' monasteries. Of course, the little dogs were purported to be guardians which, with their wariness to strangers and sharp bark, they probably were. But, with a Tibetan Mastiff tied outside the dwelling to provide the heavy artillery, the Apsos were mainly the beloved companions and friends of people in an inhospitable part of the world. Legend says that lamas (priests) that failed to reach Nirvana came back reincarnated as Lhasa Apsos. With this prestigious background, it is obvious why they were treated so well by the Tibetans.

The origin of the breed's name is a matter of controversy. In Tibet, the Lhasa is called *abso seng kye*, which indicates a barking, sentinel lion

dog. Most numerous around the religious capital of Lhasa, the resulting combination might have contributed to his Western name. There are those that feel the name came from the Tibetan word *rapso*, which means goatlike, a description of the coat. In Britain, he is sometimes called, more generically, the Tibetan Apso.

Documented evidence exists that, for centuries, the Dalai Lamas—the spiritual heads of Tibet—sent gifts of small lion dogs to the imperial courts of China as tokens of esteem and good fortune. These dogs were incorporated into the strains of Chinese dogs and helped in the formation of breeds such as the Shih Tzu and Pekingese. The last of the Manchu empresses was known to have bred the Lhasas into her Chinese dogs "to improve coat."

Lhasa dogs began to appear in the West around the turn of the century, brought back by British explorers, emissaries and other travelers to Tibet. There was much confusion at first, with shaggy Oriental dogs of a variety of sizes being called "Lhasa Terriers." It was only later

Lhasa Apso.

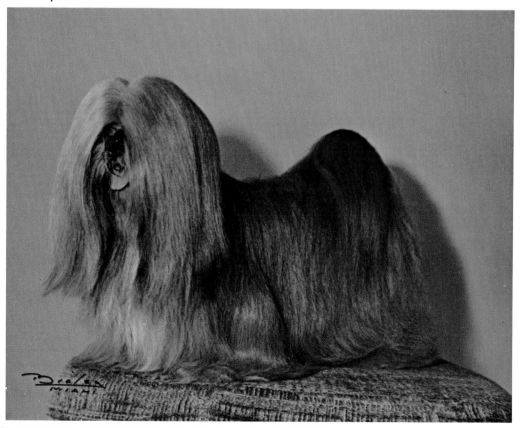

Lhasa Apso.

that authorities distinguished between the leggier and longer headed Tibetan Terrier and the smaller Lhasa Apso. Many early Shih Tzus also may have been a part of this confusion. But by the 1930s, the Lhasa Apso had his own identity and a supportive breed club in Britain. The breed was introduced into the United States about this same time, from an initial pair given as gifts by the 13th Dalai Lama to visiting Americans, the C. Suydam Cuttings, forming the famed Hamilton line. In fact, the dogs in Tibet were never sold, but given away to esteemed friends as good luck talismans that kept evil spirits away.

Later, when the Shih Tzu first arrived in the States, they were mistakingly registered as Lhasas. Some of these dogs were naturally bred to Lhasas, causing a great deal of trouble between breeders. Even today one will find stress placed on the "pure Hamilton line," indicating no Shih Tzu blood flows in their veins.

The Lhasa has become a favored companion dog in many modern nations. His small—but not toy—size combined with his surprising hardiness and ability to distinguish friend from foe have endeared him to many. Owners are amazed by his ability to adapt to a variety of climatic conditions and lifestyles, but he does need human contact to fulfill his destiny. Despite their natural companionability with man, some can be a bit strong-minded, and early introduction to rules and firm, loving discipline are recommended.

They are well known for their longevity; dogs of 18 are not uncommon and one champion of this breed lived to be 29! In the show ring, the Lhasa is the ultimate in coiffed glamour, with hair completely covering his eyes and head and reaching the floor. Even those specimens intended as pets require regular grooming to prevent a disaster of tangles and mats. Due to the brachycephalic nature of their genetic background, undershot jaws are the norm.

Lhasa Apso.

Lhasa Apso.

Lhasa Apso.

LITHUANIAN HOUND

COUNTRY: USSR
HEIGHT: 21–24 inches
COAT: Short and glossy
COLOR: Black with dapples
GROUP: Hound

This newest of the Russian scenthounds is a product of the present century. Lithuanian hunters crossed local big game hounds with Beagles, Bloodhounds (St. Hubert), Polish Hounds and later Russian Hounds, in an attempt to recreate the old-type Curland Hound (associated at one time with the Latvian Hound). Although progress was made at first, the breed was gasping for life in the 1970s and very low in numbers. During the 1976–77 hunting season, many fine dogs were killed by boars, and the breed was threatened with extinction. That year the Lithuanian Cynological Council appointed a specialist to be responsible for perpetuation of the breed, created a special kennel facility for raising them and adopted a standard. The breed seems to be on its feet now, although it is still found only in the Lithuanian Republic.

This hound is a good-sized, robust dog of clean, sleek, yet muscular proportions. He has the fervor, speed and persistence to track hare, fox and even boar, and is known for his glorious voice.

Lithuanian Hound.

Löwchen.

LÖWCHEN

COUNTRY: France
WEIGHT: 8–18 pounds
HEIGHT: 10–13 inches
COAT: Long, silky, wavy but not curly
COLOR: Any color or combination of colors
OTHER NAMES: Little Lion Dog, Petit Chien Lion
REGISTRY: FCI, TKC
GROUP: Gun Dog

Favorites of the Florentine nobles of the 15th century, the Löwchen catered to the whims of the elite. Ladies at court clipped the hair from the dogs' backs and used them as hot water bottles. Developed in Europe, the breed has been traditionally clipped similar to the Portuguese Water Dog in the "lion" trim. In fact, with his clip, his waving hair, his tail held high over his back and his color varieties, one can almost imagine him a miniature of that breed. This is probably not his immediate origin, but the simi-

larity of the bichon family and the water dogs is emphasized by these comparisons. The Little Lion Dog undoubtedly evolved from the family of bichons, as they traveled from the Mediterranean into Europe. Many feel that the breed was developed in Germany, but FCI lists France as the official country of development.

The Löwchen has been established in Spain, France and Germany since the 1500s. One of this type was painted by Goya in the late 18th century in a portrait of the beautiful Duchess of Alba. These dogs with the lion cut are often depicted at the feet of armored knights on tombs in old churches. The story goes that if a knight was killed in battle, he had a figure of a lion at his feet, demonstrating his courage. Otherwise he had the "little lion dogs," the Löwchens, as did the ladies—perhaps to provide them courage or comfort in their battles of the afterlife.

In more modern times, the Löwchen fell out of favor and nearly disappeared. The few that were left were turned out into the streets to fend

for themselves during the stress and uncertainty of the War years. Thanks to the post-war efforts of Madame M. Bennert of Brussels, a dedicated fancier, the Little Lion Dog was slowly brought back from obscurity. She combed the streets, collecting typical specimens. These contributed to the resurgence of the breed. Her work was carried on by a German, Dr. Richert, after her death. In 1960, the Löwchen was named the rarest breed by the *Guinness Book of World Records*.

They are now recognized in many countries of the world, including Great Britain, but are still fairly rare. No longer, however, do they win the dubitable claim to fame as the "rarest breed." Despite its diminutive size, the Löwchen is robust and full of energy, yet sensible and not hyperactive. A dog of intelligence and affection, he is exclusively a house pet and companion, and is winning admiration in the US.

Above: Löwchen, dark gray. **Below:** Löwchen, fawn.

Lundehund.

LUNDEHUND

COUNTRY: Norway
WEIGHT: 13–14 pounds
HEIGHT: 12½–14½ inches
COAT: Short, rough, stand-off
COLOR: Brown with black tipping and some white markings; rare blacks or white with black tipping allowed
OTHER NAMES: Norwegian Puffin Dog
REGISTRY: FCI
GROUP: Northern

This quaint dog is believed by some to have survived the Ice Age by feeding on sea birds. Its purity was assured by the isolation of Maastad and other Arctic islands. As early as 1591, Schonnebol told of these dogs in his travels.

The puffin (*lunde*) is a brightly colored bird which waddles on land, but fights fiercely to protect its young. Puffins breed in large colonies, with nests built deep in the rocky crevices on coastal islands in the Arctic seas. Nest rob-

bing is only for the very brave or foolhardy person, as the birds fight desperately to protect themselves with their vicious beaks and claws. Nevertheless, the young birds were sought to be salted, preserved and eaten during Lent. It is said they tasted enough like fish to satisfy even pious consciences. The puffin down and feathers were also valued.

When the fledglings were about 40 days old, the danger of the hunt was eased as the adults abandoned their young to the ways of the world. All that was left to battle was the folding, pleating and mutilating of oneself into the crevices. No human was up to that. Enter the Lundehund—physically a breed nonpareil—ideally suited to fit the job requirements.

The Puffin Dog is a typical Nordic dog, but with several modifications to fit his specialized job. His upright ears are placed so high and forward that, upon pricking them, they afford the added protection of almost closing to the front. This creates a shield from the constantly dripping water and dust in the caves. He is able to mold his body to fit in narrow passages because of the extraordinary range of motion in his joints. The head can be bent backwards, almost touching its back, and the forelegs can turn to the side at 90-degree angles.

The Lundehund certainly has the most interesting feet in dogdom. Small-bodied for agility among the rocks, the breed has been selected for polydactylism (supernumerary toes), so that it has at least two large functional dewclaws and up to eight plantar cushions per foot. The extra toes aid in the clamber up the rocks after the puffin. The standard states that there must be at least six toes on each foot and, of those, at least five toes on the forefoot and four on the hind foot should support the dog. On the front paw, five of those toes are triple-jointed, similar to our fingers, and one toe is double-jointed. Four toes on the rear foot have three joints, and one is split into two digits, each with two joints, all

giving the dog incredible grasping abilities, even on the rocky climbs. These characteristics must be on the judging table during competition.

Parson Petter Dass (1647–1708) wrote of the puffin hunt in a poem, *Nordlandstrompet*:

"A puffin hatches an only egg,
it is hidden in the scree as inside a wall
in the innermost caves of the rocks.
A nest is built so near the other,
that one bites the other's wing and feather
in the crevices, where they hide.
But the farmers who have a plan
know well to intrude upon those puffins
   with loot,
and that by trained dogs,
which by formation are supple and small,
so they can creep into the narrowest nook
and pull out live puffins.
When the dog snatches that puffin by the
   neck,

Lundehund modestly demonstrating his extraordinary flexibility.

which lies in front, whose life is for sale,
it begins straightway to set out.
At once the puffin, which sat behind
grasps the foremost by the tail and goes
   together,
whereas one is left behind.
By this it happens that a single dog
drags out at once from the darkest ground
twelve, thirteen—even fourteen and more,
and supplies its awaiting master
with so much booty, as he can handle,
whereby his profit may flourish."

The little dog was considered as valuable as a cow, and neighbors squabbled over having more Lundehunds than each other. Around 1850, however, nets took the place of the Puffin Dogs. Dog enthusiast Sigurd Skaun read about the Lundehunds and tracked them down to the island of Veroy. He published an article on the breed in the Norwegian hunting and fishing union's 1925 periodical. Twelve years later Eleanor Christie read that article and began her search for the native dog. About 50 samples of the breed were finally found in Haastad on the southwestern part of Veroy.

Mrs. Christie obtained four pups from Monrad Mostad in 1939. In 1942, a severe distemper

Lundehund.

The Lundehund's double-jointed neck and closeable ears are mutations unique to the breed.

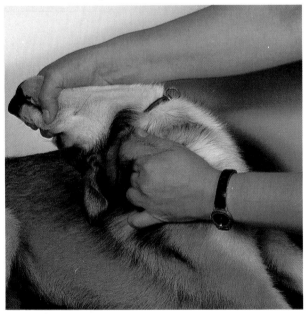

outbreak left only one survivor on Veroy. Christie came to the rescue with some of her breeding. One of these, although never hunted previously, took 14 puffins on his first outing.

It was impossible to obtain vaccine during the War years and, in 1944, distemper came to the Christies' kennel, leaving her with only an aged bitch. This time Mostad returned her generosity and supplied her with breeding stock. The breed was virtually down to the essentials, with only one bitch and one male in a breeder's hands. Eleanor Christie was determined not to let one of her country's national treasures become extinct, and has built the breed up to a respectable number today. Norwegian law now protects the colorful puffin and has exempted the Lundehund from taxation, allowing both species to flourish and multiply.

Despite the breed's odd proclivities, the Lundehund is perfectly normal when it comes to being friendly and enjoying his family. Though perhaps a bit obstinate, they make entertaining companions, joining in a variety of activities.

MAGYAR AGĂR

COUNTRY: Hungary
WEIGHT: 49–68 pounds
HEIGHT: 25–27½ inches
COAT: Short and a bit coarse
COLOR: All sighthound colors
OTHER NAMES: Hungarian Greyhound
REGISTRY: FCI
GROUP: Southern

When ninth-century Magyars invaded Hungary, they were accompanied by cattle/sheep herding dogs and running hounds from the steppes of Russia. During the early centuries, these dogs crossed with native sighthounds, present since Celtic times, and created the Agăr. These speedy and keen hounds were utilized for centuries by the nobility for formal hunts and coursing and by the peasants for poaching. In the 20th century, Greyhounds were introduced for greater speed and elegance. Many Hungarians felt this was destroying the old-type Agăr, diluting it until it is nothing more than a Greyhound's "poor cousin." In fact, the Agăr is often referred to today as a half-breed. But recognition by the FCI in 1966 revived interest in the true breed, both in its homeland and elsewhere in Europe.

The Agăr is used on hare and foxes in Hungary and chases the mechanical lure on the track. Although larger than the Galgo, he is still smaller than the Greyhound. Also distinguishing him from his English counterpart are a wide head and muzzle and the coarser haircoat for protection. He is a calm and affectionate dog.

Magyar Agăr, brindle/white.

Majestic Tree Hound, white with brown markings.

MAJESTIC TREE HOUND

COUNTRY: USA
WEIGHT: 75–110 pounds
HEIGHT: 24½–30 inches
COAT: Short, thick and dense
COLOR: Any color or combination of colors
GROUP: Hound

The creation of this breed is very recent, but the stem stock goes clear back to medieval northern France and the hounds of St. Hubert. The motives of this breed's creators were much the same as those who sponsor the American Blue Gascon Hound. These hunters wanted to save the large, cold-nosed, methodical working hound as a type in America, but the Majestic Tree Hound's forebear was the working Bloodhound.

Big game hounds of the old Bloodhound/Talbot/St. Hubert type inhabited American soil for

591

and jaguar, and are able to drive the big cats from their hiding places. Newhart offers a hunter's account of the scene: "It was a wild sight. The maddened hounds bayed at the foot of the pine. Above them in the lower branches stood the big horse-killing cat, the destroyer of the deer, the lord of stealthy murder, facing his doom with a heart both craven and cruel."

They also make superior coon hunters where the speed and numbers treed are not as important as the skill, voice and persistence of a fine hound. (This is true also of American Blue Gascon and Plott Hounds, both big game hunters.) An exquisite nose finds a track where other hounds would fail, and the coldtrailing ability keeps him on it long after others would have given up and gone home.

This is an extemely good-natured and affectionate hound, accepting equally both praise and correction. He is not quarrelsome with his fellows and has a noble and dignified expression.

Majestic Tree Hound, pup, tricolor.

Majestic Tree Hound, pup, brown/white.

many years, and these were crossed with a variety of other hounds for coldtrailing work. The Majestic people say they crossed these Bloodhounds with "western big-game hounds." These dogs may have been of the Gascon type like the Old Line dogs or even strains from those long ago Porcelaines that went west with the Rousseau family.

Lee Newhart, Jr., and several others created the National Majestic Tree Hound Association in 1980, and registered the first hounds in that year. These are *big* hounds with males averaging over 100 pounds. They have the long, low-set earage (with a minimum length specified), heavy flew and dewlap of their ancestors from the Ardennes. They carry more excess skin in general than the American Blue Gascon, and are noteworthy for their abundant flew and dewlap, as well as facial wrinkles.

Intended for rugged terrain and long endurance, they are most suited for lion, bear, bobcat

Maltese.

MALTESE

COUNTRY: Italy
WEIGHT: Less than 7 pounds, 4–6 pounds preferred
COAT: Long, flat silky hair hanging nearly to ground, no undercoat
COLOR: White; light tan or lemon on the ears only is allowed although not preferred
OTHER NAMES: Bichon Maltiase
REGISTRY: FCI, AKC, UKC, TKC, CKC
GROUP: Gun Dog

Small dogs referred to as "bichons" have been present and popular around the Mediterranean for thousands of years. The question of which breed is the oldest and which came first follows the puzzle of the chicken and the egg. They are all, essentially, miniaturized water retrievers,

coming from the same stock that produced the Portuguese Water Dogs, the Barbet, the Poodles and others. Those that lived on Tenerife were called Bichon Tenerife, those from Bologna called Bolognese and dogs on Malta were known as Maltese. Some may have developed independently, but all have similar type and character. All bichon varieties are cute, cuddly and coaty, giving them a winsome appeal.

Pets that fit the description of the Maltese have been known since very early times. The island of Malta, off the southern coast of Italy, was colonized by the Phoenicians about 1000 BC. These small, white dogs could have been brought to the area by the Phoenicians and/or spread elsewhere by them, since they sailed and traded around the known world. The Maltese dogs were entirely bred as companions and

Maltese.

Maltese.

"comforters," being especially favored by the ladies who often carried them in their sleeves or held them in their laps when in their carriages "taking air." But they won the hearts of more than the women; the Roman governor of Malta in the first century AD so adored his Maltese that he requested a portrait painted and poems written about her.

The Maltese maintained its demand as a companion through the centuries. Dr. Caius describes these small white dogs in the 1500s, and, in 1607, a writer described one that sold for $2,000! At that time, they were described as the size of a squirrel or a common ferret, as small as today's tiniest specimens.

The Maltese remains a much-loved pet and glamorous show dog. They are fastidious, refined and loyal. Devoted to their owners, they are friendly with everyone. Their snowy white, soft coat is without undercoat so they don't create yearly shedding problems, although they definitely require frequent combing to keep out tangles. Their tails are natural length and curve gracefully up over the back. The Maltese is playful and sturdy, despite its petiteness.

Maltese.

Malteses, adult and pups.

MANCHESTER TERRIERS

Manchester Terrier

COUNTRY: Great Britain
WEIGHT: 12–16 pounds; 16–22 pounds
COAT: Short, smooth
COLOR: Black/tan
OTHER NAMES: Black and Tan Terrier
REGISTRY: FCI, AKC, TKC, CKC
GROUP: Terrier

Toy Manchester Terrier

COUNTRY: Great Britain
WEIGHT: 7–12 pounds
COAT: Short, smooth
COLOR: Black/tan
OTHER NAMES: Black and Tan Toy Terrier,
English Toy Terrier
REGISTRY: FCI, AKC, TKC, CKC
GROUP: Terrier

Described by Dr. Johannes Caius's chronicle of English dogs (1570s), the Black and Tan Terrier was probably the original ratting terrier, highly skilled in his duty. The Black and Tan was coarser in head and body, and shorter on leg than many of our modern terriers and may have looked much like the modern smooth-coated Patterdale. The wellspring for many of the terrier breeds, these black/tan dogs also contributed to the formation of some fighting breeds.

The poor man's sports of rat killing and rabbit coursing reached a zenith in the Manchester district of England during the mid-1800s. John Hulme, as well as other sporting men, determined to produce a dog with "true grit" that could be used in both arenas, crossed the Black and Tan Terrier with the coursing Whippet. This combination created the breed now known as the Manchester Terrier. Backcrossing to fix type was mainly to more terriers, but the Whippet (sighthound) influence is evidenced still by

Manchester Terrier.

Toy Manchester Terrier.

the arched loin and slightly Roman nose with very little stop to the head. But grit they did have! The famed "Billy" was pitted against 100 rats, with a time limit of eight-and-a-half minutes. Billy killed them all in six minutes, 35 seconds, later lowering his time by another 22 seconds—only three-and-a-half seconds per rat!

Although the breed became celebrated, the name did not, many feeling it was too restrictive for a dog known throughout the British Isles. During his heyday in the Victorian era, he was often referred to as the "Gentleman's Terrier." For a time, around the turn of the present century, the original name (Black and Tan Terrier) was reintroduced.

With a great deal of size variation in the early Manchester stock, the Toy variety was created by selecting and breeding the smallest among them. Although called the Toy Manchester in the USA, the English version has retained the interim name of Black and Tan Toy Terrier. This smaller version also peaked in popularity during Queen Victoria's reign, with breeders fascinated with producing tinier and tinier specimens until health and normalcy were threatened. Two-and-a-half-pound adult dogs were not unusual.

Since ears always had been cropped, selection for ear size and carriage was unimportant. When ear cropping was outlawed in 1889, breeders of both varieties had difficulty in obtaining dogs of correct type that also had the good button ear. Also, the newly adopted standard required precise markings. This discouraged many breeders. By this time, ratting trials had been outlawed as well. The breeds lost favor and became quite rare. Due to the persistence of a few devotees, the Manchesters were maintained, without the size extreme favored in earlier times and with much-improved ears.

Manchester Terrier.

By 1923, American and English fanciers elected to stay with Manchester Terrier as a name for the breed. In the same year, the Manchester Terrier Club of America was formed.

Except for size and ears, the standard and Toy varieties are judged by the same standard. The larger is allowed folded ears, similar to those of the Fox and Lakeland Terriers, or erect ears, often cropped in a long cut (except in England). Ideally, the tan markings on the legs and toes should contain "pencil marks" of black. Any white in the coat is highly objectionable.

Their sleek beauty, graceful movement and intelligence make them a choice for the show ring. In the home, they are great friends with a long lifespan. All of these qualities, plus their easy-care coats and an alert bark, make them a good choice for the elderly.

Today, the Toy is a nearly identical smaller replica of the standard Manchester Terrier. The "little brother" has high-set erect ears that do not fold or drop, and cropping is a disqualification.

MAREMMA SHEEPDOG

COUNTRY: Italy
WEIGHT: 65–100 pounds
HEIGHT: 23½–29 inches
COAT: Profuse, long, never curly
COLOR: White, some yellow or pale orange tolerated on ears only
OTHER NAMES: Pastore Abruzzese, Cane da Pastore Maremmano-Abruzzese
REGISTRY: FCI, TKC
GROUP: Flock Guard

The Maremma is directly descended from the first flock guarders that migrated from the Middle East, probably across the Adriatic from Greece. A first-century writer, Lucius Columella, refers to the Maremma in his book on Roman rural affairs, and Marcus Terentius Varro, "most learned of the Romans," describes such a dog in 100 BC.

The breed was used all along the Apennine mountain range, the spine that runs the length of Italy. The pattern of the Tuscan farmers persisted for centuries. During the winter months, pasture was adequate in the dry, low areas (like Maremma) along the sea coast to support the flocks. White dogs protecting these animals were naturally called Maremmani. The summer heat dried up nearly every blade of grass in the lowlands so the shepherd, sheep and grand white dogs climbed the mountains to stay for many months in greener pastures.

Although many guarded flocks in the Abruzzi Mountains (and thus were called Abruzzese), they were also known further north and south along the Adriatic coast. When the shepherd went home at night, the sheep were left in a net enclosure to prevent wandering. The dogs never followed the master home, but stayed to protect the sheep. These dogs were also a traditional feature of the fine country houses of Tuscany. A story about British troops capturing some Italian soldiers with a Maremma tells of the dog placed in a pen with six trained Royal Air Force Alsatians (German Shepherds). In the morning, the white dog was calmly lying in the pen next to six dead Alsatians!

The Maremma is similar in type to the Great Pyrenees and Kuvasz, though without as great a

600

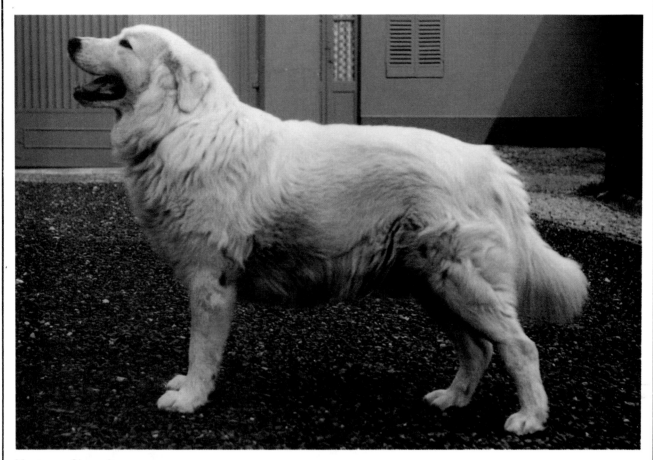

Maremma Sheepdog.

bulk. The dogs are often fed only curds and whey or a mealy pap, and yet they seem well nourished.

Fear of ruination by "improvement" kept the Maremma away from the public eye for many years. In the 1950s, a meeting finally took place in Florence, where a discussion of the types ensued. Although the Abruzzese was often considered a separate breed, sturdier with a more profuse coat, a decision was made that these were only normal variations based on climate. A standard was approved for a single breed, allowing for some variation of coat length. The official breed name in Italy includes both geographical labels to keep everyone happy.

These dogs have the typical flock-guard independence and must be handled with respect. While it is necessary to establish dominance, a Maremma that is beaten or ill-used will not hesitate to bite his master. They have a strong natural concept of their owners' belongings and feel the need to protect them. In a modern world, this encompasses home, grounds, cars and be-

longings, as well as family members. The Maremma will not allow anyone, even his master, to interfere with his guarding duties. He feels, often rightly so, that he knows best! As explained in the Maremma Sheepdog Club of Great Britain booklet, "It may be inconvenient if they [the children] deserve a spanking which he will not permit, or when he will not allow strangers to pick up their toys."

He has had an active following in Great Britain for more than 50 years, where the breed may compete for championships and is used to guard country estates. The Maremma has found favor in Sweden as well. Introduced into the United States in the 1970s, it serves only in the flock-guarding programs and is occasionally seen at rare breed shows. In just a short time, however, the breed has won the enthusiastic praise of stock owners. Some dogs, in fact, take their work too seriously. The Hampshire College program placed a six-month-old Maremma with a flock in Arkansas that had suffered losses from predators. The pup immediately took charge,

Maremma Sheepdog.

ending the kills. "Lady" became so attached to "her" sheep and their territory that when the sheep were sold and soybeans filled the pasture, she transferred her protection to the soybeans!

As with many of the flock-guarding breeds, the Maremma seems plagued with infertility and disinterest in breeding. Irregular heat cycles are reported, along with female aggression toward suitors. Researchers at Hampshire College have two bitches that have never had a litter, even though precautions were not taken to prevent matings. This modern breeder dilemma may actually have been a desirable trait in working dogs to prevent distractions from their duties. Once they conceive, they are likely to have good-sized litters. In their native land, working dams give birth under a tree or in some protective cavity.

They have a great instinct concerning "their" sheep. One working dog picked up an ill lamb in his mouth, and brought it to his master. An Italian breeder states, "In Italy sheep raising on the mountains would be practically impossible without these dogs."

The Maremma is not as large as some of the other flock guards and has the ability to appear larger or smaller than it is in reality. When unhappy, the dog will curl up and appear much smaller than normal. But when he is threatened or alerted, he draws himself to full size, flares his ruff, and holds his tail high over his back, seemingly increasing his bulk. The spiked collar, also used in Italy, increases the dog's aura even more.

Although the adult Maremma does not fawn on its master and is hesitant to show devotion, it will lay down its life to protect its family. It will remember its master "though many years may pass in his absence." It will also remember an unkindness.

MASTIFF

COUNTRY: Great Britain
WEIGHT: 175–190 pounds
HEIGHT: Minimum 27½–30 inches
COAT: Short, smooth
COLOR: Apricot, fawn or fawn-brindle, all with black mask
OTHER NAMES: Old English Mastiff
REGISTRY: FCI, AKC, TKC, CKC
GROUP: Mastiff

Early cynologists disagree just where the Mastiff originated, but they concur it is an ancient type. These dogs were depicted in bas reliefs as early as the Babylonian era, about 2200 BC, with their roots most likely leading back to the ancient Tibetan Mastiff. When the Romans arrived in England, the Mastiff had already preceded them, likely brought by ancient dog-traders. The English dogs' courage and power so impressed the Romans that they took examples of the breed back to Rome to fight in the arenas. These English powerhouses often defeated the homebred variety of molossus.

It was the Mastiffs' use as bandogs that brought them to prominence. Mastiffs, a derivative of the Latin *mastinus* meaning house-dog, roamed the grounds of estates and guarded castles, as well as lowly huts. Peasants were compelled to keep at least one Mastiff for every two serfs to ward off savage beasts and villains. The Legh family of Lyme Hall, Cheshire, is recorded to have kept Mastiffs since 1415. English kings showed their pride in the dogs and displayed generosity by gifting Spanish royalty with the breed. Henry VIII sent Charles V a battalion of 400 Mastiffs as war dogs. The mastiff type was so common in England at the time of the Norman invasion that the French word *dogue*, meaning mastiff, was incorporated into the English language to describe all of the canine species!

Mastiffs served time in the pits facing large, tough opponents during the Elizabethan era. Following the decline of the forbidden matches, these dogs entered a downward trend. During the mid-19th century, the breed was revitalized and believed to have been crossed with the Al-

Mastiff, fawn.

Mastiff, brindle.

pine Mastiff (St. Bernard). It was during this period that Mastiff fanciers "laid down the law" against the original longer head, now unfashionable. The wide use of one stud, with short, blocky head—but otherwise very faulty—created almost insurmountable problems.

Interest waned. From 63 Mastiffs at an 1871 English show, the entry dropped to zero just a few years later. The war years of the next century took further tolls on the breed. In 1945, only eight Mastiffs of breeding age were left in all of Britain! But a pair of fine pups, donated by a top Canadian kennel, helped restore the breed in its homeland, where it now is firmly entrenched.

In 1941, it was recognized in America and, currently, the Mastiff holds steady mid-way in AKC registrations. Throughout the years, Mastiffs have traveled the usual hills and valleys of popularity: large dog vs. small dog; hairy vs. smooth; tough vs. mellow.

Despite his giant size and forbidding appearance, the Mastiff is a good family pet, with those same qualities making him a worthy watchdog. He is a creature of habit and does not transplant easily, meaning that buyers who choose the Mastiff should plan to keep him for life. Tragically, like so many of the giants, he is not long-lived.

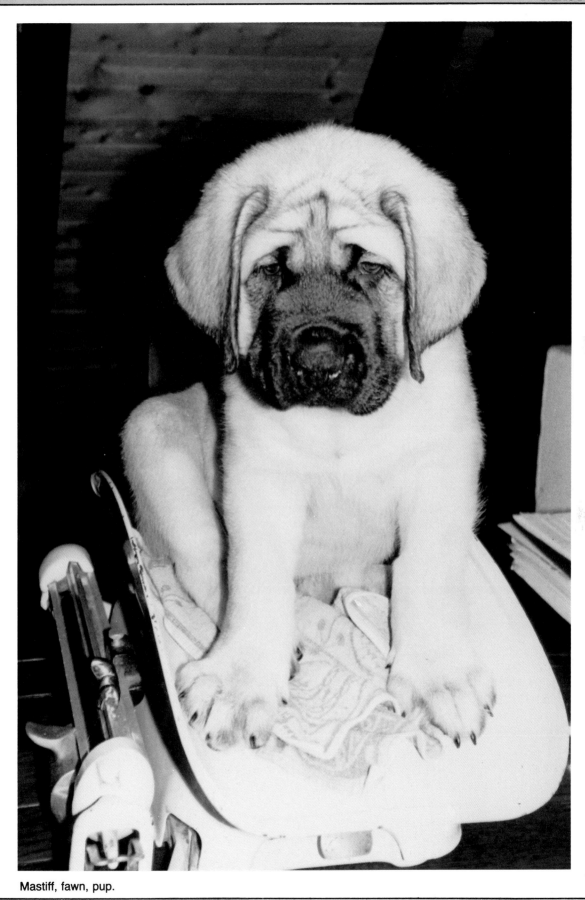

Mastiff, fawn, pup.

MIDDLE ASIAN OWTCHARKA

COUNTRY: USSR
HEIGHT 23½–25½ inches minimum; usually larger
COAT: Short and thick
COLOR: Black, white, gray or brindle; with or without white markings
OTHER NAMES: Mid-Asian Shepherd
GROUP: Flock Guard

The ancient home of the Middle Asian Owtcharka is east of the Urals into Siberia and even Mongolia. There he has aided and protected the nomadic tribes and their flocks for centuries. But modern changes in lifestyles have reduced the numbers of this breed. The best modern examples are in the Turkmen Republic, although he can be found in the Republics of Uzbek, Tadzhik, Kazakhstan and Kirgiz. He has never been exhibited nor been established outside mid-Russia.

Most are similar to the largest and thickest set of the Caucasian dogs, and they not only have their ears lopped off short, but have their tails bobbed as well. Many feel he resembles his ancestor, the Tibetan Mastiff, because of his thick skin with neck folds and facial wrinkles. He also comes in a variety of colors, but especially black. He is well adapted to the heat and scarce water conditions of Central Asia. Because of his strength and bravery he is sometimes used in hunting boar or snow leopards. In some areas he has been crossed with local Borzois to create a shepherd that seconds as a hunter. These crosses tend to be more refined in bone.

Middle Asian Owtcharka, black with white and tan markings.

Middle Asian Owtcharka.

Miniature Bull Terrier, colored.

MINIATURE BULL TERRIER

COUNTRY: Great Britain
WEIGHT: 10–40 pounds
HEIGHT: 10–14 inches
COAT: Short, harsh
COLOR: Solid white; white with head markings; brindle, red, fawn, black/tan, black brindle, with or without white markings in the Irish pattern
REGISTRY: FCI, AKC, TKC, CKC
GROUP: Mastiff

Good things come in small packages, and the Miniature Bull Terrier is all the fire and clowning of its larger version seen through the reverse side of a magnifying glass. Bred to aid their larger brothers in ratting duties, they were a great favorite of those who preferred a smaller, more manageable house pet. At one time, Bull Terriers ranged from as tiny as three pounds to a macho 30-plus. The Toy variety, under ten pounds, suffered the problems often seen in extreme miniaturization and has disappeared, but the Mini is picking up fans daily.

In 1938, Englishman Colonel Glyn founded the Miniature Bull Terrier Club, and the Minis were eligible for challenge certificates shortly after. Although they were shown in the United States early in the 1900s, they reached a lull and have only recently (1963) begun showing in the Miscellaneous Class again. The CKC also includes them in that class, while they merit full FCI recognition.

They adore their owners and are excellent playmates for children, as well as being good alarm dogs. Breeders warn owners to be careful not to leave precious or dangerous objects lying around, since the Mini thinks any object within his reach is fair game for lunch. Puppies are "energized" and can be destructive if left alone.

Strong and solid, the Minis can pull owners on skateboards or cross-country skis! They're adaptable to any lifestyle, from active to sedate, from large families with children to a single person or an elderly couple. These dogs enjoy being the center of attention, and will put up with a great amount of "foolishness" from children, including being dressed in doll clothes. All of this is often accompanied by a "Bully" smile.

This "pocket edition" of the Bull Terrier is even-tempered, but requires a controlling hand. Owners note that physical care is a breeze.

Miniature Bull Terrier, colored.

Miniature Pinscher

MINIATURE PINSCHER

COUNTRY: Germany
WEIGHT: 10 pounds
HEIGHT: 10–12½ inches
COAT: Short and smooth
COLOR: Black/tan, chocolate/tan or stag red
OTHER NAMES: Zwergpinscher
REGISTRY: FCI, AKC, UKC, TKC, CKC
GROUP: Terrier

The well-known "Min-Pin" has been bred for several hundred years, stemming directly from his larger cousin, the German Pinscher. Some feel that small Dachshunds and Italian Greyhounds were introduced to the smallest pinschers to obtain the diminutive size. These dogs are often called "Reh Pinscher," due to their resemblance to the small roe deer found in Rhineland forests.

When the German Pinscher-Schnauzer Club was formed in the 1890s, it embraced all pinscher sizes. For a time, the Miniature Pinscher's quest was for "the tinier, the better." These Lilliputian specimens were bedecked and bejeweled and were judged while lying on exquisite pillows or being held protectively in their owner's arms.

The club's influence helped establish type and spread interest. By WWI the breed had regained its soundness and was back on the ground, showing off its trademark: the high-prancing gait. Even with some reduction of breeding activities during the First World War, the breed continued to gain ground. It was first shown in American dog shows in small numbers during the 1920s, and has slowly increased its numbers in the United States since that time. Progress has been slower in Great Britain, due to strict quarantine laws as well as the ban on cropping. British breeders now are making good progress in breeding strains with small, naturally erect ears.

The Min-Pin was taken under the auspices of AKC in 1929 and first shown as a terrier. Now listed as a Toy, like the Yorkshire, he is all terrier! His natural presence makes him a born showman in the ring, giving him the title of "King of Toys." The Min-Pin is the top toy breed in Denmark, Holland and Italy.

Ears are usually cropped, and the tail is docked like the Standard Pinscher's. The similarity to their larger versions goes beyond mere looks, since guarding instincts and a robust and confident nature are evident, making them capable of biting an intruder—in the ankle. They can be suspicious and protective. Overall, they are fun-loving dogs who need little care to keep them in good condition.

Miniature Pinschers, red.

Miniature Pinschers, black/tan.

MOSCOW LONGHAIRED TOY TERRIER

COUNTRY: USSR
WEIGHT: 4½–6½ pounds
HEIGHT: 8–11 inches
COAT: Long and straight, with abundant fringe on ears, legs and neck ruff
COLOR: Black, brown, sable, fawn or tan, usually with tan points, but may be solid; merle also occurs
OTHER NAMES: Moscovian Miniature Terrier
REGISTRY: None
GROUP: Terrier

This newest of the Russian breeds is a definite charmer. Approved only in 1981, he is becoming the rage in the cities. The Longhaired Toy Terrier was developed especially as an urban pet, notably for senior citizens, which could withstand Russian winters. Limited information exists on which breeds were used, although it is thought that long-coated Chihuahuas and small English toys like the Yorkshire were used. The existence of the merle color, as well as good guarding ability, makes one think of small European terriers like the Harlequin Pinscher. The result is a gracious, aristocratic, lively and handsome dog that is easily trained and cared for.

His petite face tapers sharply, and the large ears cascade with flowing hair. His docked tail is held upright, and his every movement is light and quick. A wide range of colors adds to his appeal. He is unknown outside the Soviet Union. But at home, demand far outweighs supply due to their small litters.

Moscow Longhaired Toy Terrier, black with tan points.

MOSCOW WATCHDOG

COUNTRY: USSR
WEIGHT: 100–150 pounds
HEIGHT: 25–27 inches
COAT: Moderate length, thick with fringing
COLOR: Red/white
GROUP: Mastiff

This recent innovation was created by Moscow dog fanciers who wanted a large, strong watchdog that would be more receptive to taking and following orders. After World War II, breeders began with Caucasian Owtcharkas for wariness and ferocity. The St. Bernard was then chosen for its size and strength, but more benign temperament. A blend of the two has created the Moscow Watchdog, with the beautiful physical qualities of thick coat and strong muscles, as well as the mental characteristics these people wanted.

Moscow Watchdog.

Moscow Watchdog.

MOUNTAIN CUR

COUNTRY: USA
WEIGHT: 35–65 pounds
COAT: Short or slightly longer and heavy
COLOR: Brindle, yellow, black/tan or mouse blue; with or without white neck ring and points
GROUP: Hound

The Mountain Cur is of the same general gene pool as the Leopard Cur. They originated at the time the United States was new and were particularly common in the Ohio River Valley. As frontiersmen, followed by entire families, moved to open the West, their Cur dogs accompanied them. Those that foster this breed say that besides the herding dog and hound, there is a dash of "Indian cur" (a pariah-type dog) in their makeup. Although called "mountain" because of their particular advantage to settlers in wooded, wild areas, they were just as welcome in swampy or arid areas, or other places with harsh living conditions.

This breed tends less to the hound than some of the other Cur breeds, perhaps because of that elusive Indian background. He is very stocky, wide and muscular with a strong wide head and the short, higher set ear. Although the full length tail is allowed, many are born tailless.

Trailing ability varies with strains, but they have enough nose to follow game and are particularly strong in treeing ability. Usually they are silent trailers. And they are very tough, willing to face a squealing razorback or an angry wild cat when it is cornered. This breed does not have any of the blue-mottled color.

Mountain Cur, yellow.

Mountain Cur.

The book *Old Yeller*, about a boy growing up in frontier Texas and a dog for which the book is named, is a typical Mountain Cur (unlike the movie which starred a dog of Lab type). In the book, Old Yeller is a short-haired, yellow bobtailed dog that hunts and trees, naturally goes for the nose when he faces a mad bull, and isn't afraid to fight a full-grown bear when it threatens his own. The author is precise in describing this old-fashioned breed and its use to the pioneer, without ever naming the breed. Of course, in those days, the breed really didn't have a name or an individual identity.

The blanket name "cur" is slowly being sorted into individual types. The name Mountain Cur used to encompass what is now the Treeing Tennessee Brindle and the Stephens Stock as well, but these two have attained enough individual identity to justify their own registering groups.

By the end of the last war, there were very few of these old-time Mountain Curs left. A few die-hard owners still maintained some stock in isolated swamps and remote mountain regions of the southeast. Recently, they began to enjoy a modest revival, similar to the other Cur breeds. The Original Mountain Cur Breeders Association fosters and registers the breed today.

MUDI

COUNTRY: Hungary
WEIGHT: 18–29 pounds
HEIGHT: 14–20 inches
COAT: Short on head and fronts of legs, 2 inches on rest of body, coarse and bristly, with a tendency to curl.
COLOR: Black, white, pied
REGISTRY: FCI
GROUP: Herding

A truly rare breed, the Mudi has total accumulative registrations numbering only in the 300s. Despite the Mudi's small stature, he shows abundant courage in his duties as an all-around farm dog. The Mudi works the cattle, exterminates rodents—and hunts boar on his day off. The tail is usually docked. Almost all Mudis are in Hungary, although an occasional specimen is seen at European dog shows.

Mudi, black.

MÜNSTERLÄNDERS

Large Münsterländer

COUNTRY: Germany
WEIGHT: 50–70 pounds
HEIGHT: 23–25½ inches
COAT: Sleek, moderate length, with feathering
COLOR: Black and white, heavy ticking or roaning is preferred over the clear white patterns
OTHER NAMES: Grosser Münsterländer Vorstehhund
REGISTRY: FCI, TKC
GROUP: Gun Dog

Small Münsterländer

COUNTRY: Germany
WEIGHT: 33 pounds
HEIGHT: 19–22 inches
COAT: Sleek, moderate length, with feathering
COLOR: Liver and white, with ticking
OTHER NAMES: Kleiner Münsterländer Vorstehhund, Heidewachtel
REGISTRY: FCI
GROUP: Gun Dog

Back in the days of the generic *huenerhunden*, bird dogs in Germany came in all sizes and coat colors and textures. These were interbred, based on function only. In the latter part of the 19th century, the interest in individual breeds grew, and the types were separated.

When the club for the German Longhaired Pointer drew up its written standard, for some reason, it accepted only the liver/white dogs. Litters were often of mixed colors in those days, and the black/white pups denied registration were usually given away. Farmers and hunters, many from the Münster area, were the recipients of these well-bred gun dogs and cared little about their color or registration status. They continued breeding the black/white longhaired pointers, perhaps crossing to other dogs of the setter or spaniel type, and in 1919 formed a club for the Münsterländer.

The Münster has found friends throughout Germany and has been brought to England as well. He is an all-purpose pointing/retrieving gun dog and is expected to perform in the utility trials in Germany. In England, he competes with the other Continental gun dogs in the HPR (Hunt Point Retriever) Field Trials.

Large Münsterländer.

Although bred for training and ability to withstand the pressures involved, the breed wants to please and can be soft in nature. His beautiful, fringed coat is never exaggerated. The tail may be left intact or have just a tiny bit of the end removed. They love to retrieve, and naturally like to carry things about in their mouth.

As with all of their hunting relatives, they require sufficient exercise. But if walked or run enough, a Münster can adapt easily to indoor life, even in the city. He tends to be vocal and owner-oriented. Owners say if they are gone for even a moment, a Münster enthusiastically greets their return by "talking" in his low rumble and bringing them "their treasured possessions." The Münster does well in obedience, and is good with other animals and with children.

The smaller variety is of more recent origin, from the early 1900s; they are pointing dogs—as setters are—rather than flushers. The Small Münsterländer was the result of crosses of the German Longhair to Continental spaniels. This Münster appears only in the liver/white ticked color, and his tail is left long.

He is a good hunter, with a happy tail-wagging nature. Both the Large and Small Münsterländers are known in Canada, England, and in various European countries, although not in large numbers.

Above: Head study of the Large Münsterländer. **Below:** Small Münsterländer.

Neapolitan Mastiff, gray.

NEAPOLITAN MASTIFF

Country: Italy
Weight: 110–150 pounds
Height: 23½–30 inches
Coat: Short, smooth
Color: Solid gray (in all shades), black, mahogany, blond
Other names: Mastino Napoletano
Registry: FCI, TKC
Group: Mastiff

Neapolitans are direct descendants of the molossus of the Roman arenas, probably very similar to the old type known 2,000 years ago. Over the centuries the dog has been used in war and for police, guard and draft work, as well as being a collaborator in crime. The Italian standard calls for a dog of "rustic but majestic appearance."

Although the breed has existed in southern Italy since Roman times, the Neapolitan was first presented to the general public at a Naples dog show in 1946. They so impressed a painter, Piero Scanziani, that he collected superior animals and started his own kennel. He is now considered the modern father of the breed. Scanziani set up the written standard, and obtained recognition for the breed from the Italian KC (ENCI).

Their appearance belies their affectionate temperament. Neos are gentle to friends, yet are natural guards and territorial, never wandering off their property. An owner of Neos says, "My husband would exercise our dogs by bicycle. All manner of dogs would come rushing off properties and out of driveways, challenging them as they passed. Surprisingly, the mastiffs would just stop and look, neither growling nor raising their hackles. It was almost as if the mastiffs were perplexed at the audacity and impudence of these up-starts!"

Although bred for combat, they are not pugnacious to other dogs and are good mothers. A

Neapolitan Mastiff.

breeder says that it is quite humorous to watch such a large dog tiptoeing with exaggerated daintiness amongst her pups in the whelping box.

As a fighting breed originally, the dogs were selected for their stoicism and still exhibit that trait today. Neapolitans are adaptable to various environments and climates, transferring smoothly from kennels in Italy to life as house dogs in North America. A Canadian breeder states, "It is always a little nerve-wracking arriving at the airport to collect a very large dog that you know nothing about temperament-wise, not to say . . . the apprehensiveness experienced driving home with a strange dog's head resting on your shoulder." This is especially true when it is a 130-pound dog, but there was no need for worry—as both she and the dog always arrived intact.

Neapolitan Mastiff.

Neapolitan Mastiff, mahogany.

The proper gait is typical of the larger mastiffs: slow, free and bearlike. Neos have distinctive physical traits, however. Skin hangs in exaggerated folds around the head, making it seem double or even triple-chinned. If the ears are cropped (as is the custom), they are "almost amputated, and docked to the point where it forms a nearly equilateral triangle." One-third of the tail is removed. Exhibiting an elegant and majestic aloofness, they give the appearance of someone you wouldn't want to meet alone at night in a dark alley. Neos enjoy a very active fancy in Italy, with growing numbers of good breeders in other countries. Enthusiastic programs can be found in Germany, France, Spain, England as well as other European nations, Canada, the USA, and Israel.

NEWFOUNDLAND

COUNTRY: Canada
WEIGHT: 110–150 pounds
HEIGHT: 26–28 inches
COAT: Medium length, very dense
COLOR: Solid black, bronze, particolor
(Landseer)
REGISTRY: FCI, AKC, UKC, TKC, CKC
GROUP: Mastiff

As canines were molded to fill whatever job was needed, residents of the banks of Labrador, St. John's and Newfoundland developed dogs for aiding the fishermen. The early history of these animals consists mainly of unsubstantiated stories and fanciful tales.

Newfoundland folklore tells of an early Tibetan Mastiff-type dog which accompanied Indians migrating across the polar region to the Maritime Provinces. Four thousand years later, in 1001 AD, when the Vikings arrived, they supposedly had "bear dogs" of similar origin. The fusion of these two "long-lost cousins" supposedly created the base for the Newfoundland breed.

By the 1600s, records show European fishing vessels were frequent visitors to the Maritimes and, since nearly all these fleets brought dogs with them, crosses probably occurred with various European breeds who "jumped ship" for a night on the town. Portuguese and Basque fishermen were the earliest, and both Portuguese Water Dogs and Great Pyrenees in turn probably contributed water-proofing, coat variations and water-working qualities, along with size and nobility.

Soon two distinct types developed: the so-called Lesser St. John's Dog (which developed into the Labrador Retriever) and the Greater St. John's Dog (which became the Newfoundland and Landseer).

Early Newfoundlands aided crews and became invaluable aboard ship, rescuing sailors and barking the danger of reefs. Newfies were strong swimmers, and retrieved both people and boats in distress. With the highest tides in the world (reaching 70 feet) in the Bay of Fundy near Newfoundland, it seems likely they were called upon frequently. Not all work was so romantic, however; daily duties found these dogs

Newfoundland, black.

swimming from ship to ship, carrying lines, or retrieving objects and drunken sailors who had fallen overboard.

By the 18th century, examples of these Newfoundland dogs were brought back to England on British trade ships. Early Newfs were a mixed lot, generally smaller and lighter boned than today's specimens, with a wide variance in colors (often spotted). Coat textures were rough, curly or long, and the high tail often curved in a circle.

Crossing may have occurred again in Europe, but type was eventually stabilized. The Newf evolved into a large, sturdily boned, low-tailed dog still in several colors and usually spotted. About the time a written standard was introduced in the late 1800s, the solid black variety became the rage in England, so much so that the black almost became known as the "only Newfoundland in Britain and North America." Today the spotted Newfoundland is considered a color variety, called Landseer, recognized by FCI as a separate breed. They also come in solid chocolate (bronze).

Nobility, peaceful personality, sleek good looks and superior strength attracted more than seafarers and Indians to the breed. None can forget Lord Byron's epitaph to "Boatswain," his Newfoundland:

Newfoundland backpacking in mountains.

Newfoundland, bronze.

When some proud son of man returns to
    earth,
Unknown to glory, but upheld by birth,
The sculptor's art exhausts the pomp of
    woe,
And storied urns record who rests below.
When all is done, upon the tomb is seen
Not what he was, but what he should have
    been.
But the poor dog, in life the firmest friend,
The first to welcome, foremost to defend.
Whose honest heart is still his master's
    own,
Who labors, fights, lives, breathes for him
    alone,
Unhonored falls, unnoticed all his worth,
Denied in heaven the soul he had on earth.
Ye who perchance behold this simple urn,
Pass on,—it honors none you wish to
    mourn;
To mark a friend's remains these stones
    arise;
I never knew but one—and here he lies.

Newfoundland, black and white particolor (Landseer).

Patriots, presidents and politicians have joined celebrities and royalty in their admiration for these dogs: Benjamin Franklin, Samuel Adams, George Washington, Robert Kennedy, Bing Crosby, King Edward VII, the Rumanian Queen Marie and her son King Michael, and, of course, Queen Victoria. A black Newfoundland named "Seaman" accompanied Meriwether Lewis on his boat, *Discovery*, up the Missouri River in 1804.

In 1886 Newfoundland owners formed a specialty club and drew up a standard. The gentle giant debuted in the show ring and enjoyed a small but respectable status. About 1935, the Newf began an upward climb, drawing a steady group of fanciers. The Newfoundland Club of America encourages the retention of natural ability by hosting water rescue tests. Basic tests include retrieves, find and retrieves, carrying lines, towing a boat, following instructions in the water, and lifesaving. Advanced dogs participate in more complex retrieves and lifesaving.

Their owners' only complaint is that the dogs don't know when the testing is over and "fun in the sun" time begins. Newfs tend to be overzealous in their rescues, occasionally dampening the fun of a swimming party by "rescuing" the swimmers.

For landlubber owners, the club also hosts draft-dog tests. The dogs are harnessed to carts and must back, follow commands, haul a load and maneuver an obstacle course. Breeders recommend Newfs be included in family activities and, if possible, water play. If ignored, they become bored and even depressed.

Like cuddly, sweet bear cubs, the Newfoundland pups grow to be large, impressive animals. Unlike the cubs, however, they retain the gentle demeanor and "benevolent expression." Surprisingly, the giant, economy-sized Newf eats only as much as most retrievers. Breeders credit this to his tranquil behavior and disposition. The breed is known to be easygoing and extremely patient with children and with animals.

Newfoundland.

NEW GUINEA SINGING DOG

COUNTRY: New Guinea
WEIGHT: 20 pounds
HEIGHT: 14–15 inches
COAT: Medium-short, dense
COLOR: Red; with or without symmetrical white markings
REGISTRY: None
GROUP: Southern

The island of New Guinea, second largest in the world, is home to many strange creatures. Its variation from the tropical clime in the lowlands to Alpinelike cold in the higher elevations is uncommon. Early domesticated southern dogs spread from the Middle East to southeastern Asia with various human migrations many thousands of years ago. Some drifted to Australia to become the Dingo and others to Malaysia (the Telomian).

Not far from Australia, a dingo-type dog took up residence in New Guinea. The torrid forests and chilled mountain peaks spawned a hardy animal called the New Guinea Singing Dog.

Many lived as pariah dogs with the village natives in the lower elevations. Other dogs climbed to the mountains, where they turned feral. In

New Guinea Singing Dog.

New Guinea Singing Dogs.

the cold climes, they developed a thicker, double, slightly longer coat than most pariahs. But curled tails, the foxy, wedge-shaped heads and high prick ears follow the usual pariah characteristics.

Although smaller than its near relative, the Singing Dog is similar to the Dingo but with unique propensities. It possesses the erect ears and is a swift hunter with social instincts. Unlike the Dingo, the New Guinea female cycles twice a year in captivity.

Its howl has an eerie yet synchronized quality which gives the breed its name. The howl can be spurred by agitation or excitement. One tone blends with the next, sending goosebumps up a listener's back.

In 1948, a pair of the dogs was brought to the Taronga Zoo in Sydney, Australia. Several other zoos clamored for the progeny, and pairs were brought to Europe and Russia in the 1950s–60s. For a time, the Singing Dogs fascinated the public. The interest in keeping and viewing a dog—albeit a feral dog—waned, although two pairs still live in zoos in the States.

"Singer" and "Dancer" sing for their supper at the Minnesota Zoo, with another pair at the Sedgwick County Zoo in Wichita, Kansas. The Minnesota duo once "accompanied" Metropolitan Opera star Benita Valente on television. The Singing Dogs are tame enough to be handled and petted, but don't tolerate these attentions for long. These dogs are believed to be scarce or even extinct in New Guinea.

Norbottenspets.

NORBOTTENSPETS

COUNTRY: Sweden and Finland
WEIGHT: 26–33 pounds
HEIGHT: 17 inches
COAT: Short and stand-off
COLOR: Basically white, with a few color spots preferably in yellow or brown; black spots permissible
OTHER NAMES: Nordic Spitz, Pohjanpystykorva
REGISTRY: FCI
GROUP: Northern

The little spitz of Sweden and Finland began long ago as a hunter of small game. Called the *Pohjanpystykorva* in Finland, it was taken by immigrant farmers to northern Sweden where it was given an even longer name, the *Norrbottens-skollandehund*. Although widespread for many years as a common hunting and farm dog, the average owner "didn't know that they had a breed," and breeding programs were not planned. As hunting with this dog waned and the popularity of foreign breeds increased, people lost interest.

The Norbottenspets was thought to be extinct and was dropped from the rolls of the Swedish KC in 1948. Lovers of the breed continued to scour both countries, discovering good specimens in remote villages and reestablishing breeding programs. It was reinstated by the kennel clubs in Sweden (1967) and in Finland (1970s) and is now quite popular again in both countries. His demand today is as a house companion and for hunting game birds such as grouse and hazel hens. A few have won high prizes in bird-hunting trials. The Norbottenspets has a plus as a house pet—he is not the great barker that most of the other Nordic hunters are.

His coat is quite short for a Nordic dog and his tail curves loosely over the back, turning down to lie against the thigh. He is square and firm bodied. His character is alert, lively, calm and friendly—also described as brisk—but never shy, nervous, or aggressive. The breed is particularly good with children. He is most happy when owned by a hunter, even if a hobby hunter.

NORFOLK TERRIER

COUNTRY: Great Britain
WEIGHT: 11–12 pounds
HEIGHT: 10 inches
COAT: Hard, wiry, broken, lies flat to the body
COLOR: Red to wheaten
REGISTRY: FCI, AKC, UKC, CKC, TKC
GROUP: Terrier

The Norfolk has many similarities to the Border in size, color and coat, but his head is more fox-like and he has the erect ear. His ancestors may have included some of the same brave fellows that produced the Border and his relative, the Cairn, in the north, and many cynologists feel that red terriers from Ireland figured in his history. The town of Norwich is in the county of Norfolk just north of London in the eastcentral area of England called East Anglia.

In the 1800s, there was no official recognition of the Norwich/Norfolk, which was just another general type farm dog and hunting terrier used in the area. In the 1880s, he became the rage with the undergraduates at Cambridge University and his popularity soared. Some even felt he should be called the Cantab Terrier in honor of the collegiate atmosphere which promoted him. In the early 1900s, the keystone sire was named "Rags." One of the prominent breeders after World War I was named Frank "Roughrider" Jones, a horseman, who had Glen of Imaal Terriers and a dark red brindle Cairn-type bitch. Some of these were bred to Rags, as was a terrier bitch named "Ninety," of Dandie Dinmont and hunting terrier stock. The harsh-coated red progeny were retained by Jones and these formed the foundation for the Norwich/Norfolk. Early specimens imported into the USA were often called Jones Terriers.

In America they were utilized by several Masters of Foxhounds for their original purpose of assisting the foxhound with the prey that had gone to ground. In fact, the Cheshire Hunt Club of Philadelphia and a few others of the 1920s maintained purebred kennels of Norwich to assist in their hunts. Bred to hunt in packs, they are sociable dogs. The breed obtained official recognition from English and American governing bodies in the 1930s.

Norfolk Terrier.

Like the Border, the Norwich is shown in a nearly natural coat. He is an alert, handsome, and charming fellow who makes a fine companion as well as a working terrier. Up until 1979, the breed was allowed to be shown in the USA with either a prick (erect) ear or a small forward-folding drop ear. At that time, AKC followed the example of The Kennel Club of England and called the prick-eared variety the Norwich Terrier and established a new breed name, the Norfolk Terrier, for the drop-eared variety. The town of Norwich is in the county of Norfolk; thus one was named for the town and the other for the whole county.

They are very similar except for the ears. "Wich" is the Norwich, and "wich" is the Norfolk? The Norwich has pointed ears like a *witch*'s hat, and the Norfolk's ears *fold*.

Both terriers do fine in the house, with sufficient opportunity to "stretch their legs" outdoors. Responsive, but still scalawags, these little dogs bring to mind the warning of terrier man Jerome K. Jerome, "Terriers are born with about four times as much original sin in them as other dogs."

Norfolk Terrier.

NORTHEASTERLY HAULING LAIKA

COUNTRY: USSR
HEIGHT: 23–24 inches minimum
COAT: Medium, thick, double coat
COLOR: Any color
OTHER NAMES: Northeastern Sleigh Dog
GROUP: Northern

During the 1940s, Russian cynologists attempted to consolidate the multitude of existing Northern draft/hunting/herding type dogs from Siberia and the Soviet Union into six distinct breeds. This amounted to an exercise in "lumping." They established four hunting or hunting/sledding breeds, one sledding/ herding breed and one pure sledding breed, although they recognized there were other types that did not fit into these parameters.

The pure sledding breed is the Hauling Laika, which is probably an amalgamation of various native draft types. The standard established is one for a large hauling dog, very similar to the Eskimo Dog or the Malamute.

Soviet cynologists recognize the necessity for sled dogs in the most remote areas of Siberia and the Arctic. They say dogs and vehicular transportation, even in the 1980s, complement each other.

Should a visitor arrive in the lower Kolyman and Anadyr River areas of far east Siberia during their short summer, says a modern Soviet dog writer, he would immediately notice many idle, dirty dogs. They wander about, covered with clumps of shedding hair and mud, seeming quite useless to the visitor. But the locals know that the long, bitter winter is not far off. Then the dogs grow a beautiful winter coat and work constantly. They pull skiers (doing "skjoring") and haul sleds to all parts of the tundra. They deliver the physician and veterinarian and supplies as well as mail and news from afar.

This dog furnishes warmth to his master when, during a sudden blizzard, every living creature digs into a snow drift. And he can unerringly find his way home even in blinding snow. Hauling dogs often second as hunting dogs as well. A team of six to ten Hauling Laikas, pulling a load of 88–110 pounds per dog, may average three to four miles per hour. This figures to 40–48 miles a day for a four to six day trip in -40 to -50 degree weather, all on only about three pounds of fish a day per dog! Thus to this day, the northern peoples of the Soviet Union love and respect their amazing helpmates.

Northeastern Russian laikas slumbering on a snow covered peninsula.

NORWEGIAN BUHUND

COUNTRY: Norway
WEIGHT: 26–40 pounds
HEIGHT: 17–18 inches
COAT: Thick, harsh, short, and smooth-lying with a soft wool undercoat.
COLOR: Wheaten, black, wolf sable, small symmetrical white markings, and/or a black mask
OTHER NAMES: Norsk Buhund, Norwegian Sheepdog
REGISTRY: FCI, TKC
GROUP: Northern

The Buhund is one of the earliest known Nordic herding types, although it was not officially recognized until the 20th century. As humans from the North began to live in permanent settlements in the Scandinavian countries, they brought with them the hauling and reindeer-herding dogs used for centuries. This stock was used to create a herding dog for cattle, sheep and horses that doubles as an all-purpose farm dog. *Bu* in Norwegian means homestead or mountain hut and Buhund is the name given to their sheepdog. The Buhund was already widespread in the Middle Ages and has maintained a similar appearance ever since that time. John Saeland fostered the breed to recognition and formed a club in 1936.

Modern breeders state that the breed can be adapted not only for sheep and goat herding, but also for turkeys, ducks and domestic pheasant. The Buhund is now seen in several countries outside of Norway, and is a lively, courageous and energetic companion. He has become fairly numerous in Great Britain and is gaining a following in Australia as well. Quite adaptable to a variety of tasks, including child's companion, obedience dog, or hearing dog, he is a security guard that is never off-duty.

These dogs are in tune with owners, communicating with various noises and body language. They are highly trainable, great farm dogs and stay within call. The Buhund is a creature of habit and, as one owner said, knows the household routine and is usually one jump ahead.

An English owner tells of walking home from town after dark with her Buhund and another

Norwegian Buhund, wheaten.

dog. She was attacked from behind and, while the other dog ran off, the Buhund sank its teeth into the aggressor's leg and doggedly held on, allowing her master to escape. In fact, even after the woman was safe, it took several calls for the dog to back off the attack and join her!

Another report tells of a bitch left alone in a home with her newborn pups. When fire broke out in the house, the bitch could have escaped, but chose to stay and protect her pups. Fortunately, she was discovered and saved by her 14-year-old owner.

Their herding and protective instincts come to the fore even when untrained and, occasionally, when unwanted. A town bitch was seen correctly and proudly herding sheep when she was a guest at a farm. Another "aided" her owner in a climb in Wales by tugging at her coat.

Like most of the Nordic dogs, Buhunds are clean, intelligent and fun. They also have the northern traits of great energy, the desire for human companionship, and the need for a firm, consistent master to overcome their strong will.

NORWICH TERRIER

COUNTRY: Great Britain
WEIGHT: 11–12 pounds
HEIGHT: 10 inches
COAT: Hard, wiry, broken, lies flat to the body
COLOR: Red to wheaten most common
REGISTRY: FCI, AKC, UKC, TKC, CKC
GROUP: Terrier

The Norwich was separated from the Norfolk only recently and has an identical history. It has many similarities to the Border in size, color and coat, but his head is more foxlike and he has the erect ear. His ancestors may have included some of the same brave fellows that produced the Border and his relative, the Cairn, in the north, and many cynologists feel that red terriers from Ireland figured in his history. The town of Norwich is in the county of Norfolk just north of London in the eastcentral area of England called East Anglia.

In the 1800s, there was no official recognition of the Norwich/Norfolk, which was just another general type farm dog and hunting terrier used in the area. In the 1880s, he became the rage with the undergraduates at Cambridge University and his popularity soared. Some even felt he should be called the Cantab Terrier in honor of the collegiate atmosphere which promoted him. In the early 1900s, the keystone sire was named "Rags." One of the prominent breeders after World War I was named Frank "Roughrider" Jones, a horseman, who had Glen of Imaal Terriers and a dark red brindle Cairn-type bitch. Some of these were bred to Rags, as was a terrier bitch named "Ninety," of Dandie Dinmont and hunting terrier stock. The harsh-coated red progeny were retained by Jones and these formed the foundation for the Norwich/Norfolk. Early specimens imported into the USA were often called Jones Terriers.

In America they were utilized by several Masters of Foxhounds for their original purpose of assisting the foxhound with the prey that had gone to ground. In fact, the Cheshire Hunt Club of Philadelphia and a few others of the 1920s maintained purebred kennels of Norwich to assist in their hunts. Bred to hunt in packs, they are sociable dogs. The breed obtained official recognition from English and American govern-

Norwich Terrier.

The Norwich Terrier and the Norfolk Terrier, once both called the Norfolk Terrier, are recognized today as two individual breeds. The Norwich Terrier is prick-eared (*left*) while the Norfolk is drop-eared (*below*). White is undesirable in both breeds but marks or patches are permissible in some standards.

BEST OF BREED

ASHBEY PHOTO

ing bodies in the 1930s.

Like the Border, the Norwich is shown in a nearly natural coat. He is an alert, handsome, and charming fellow who makes a fine companion as well as a working terrier. Up until 1979, the breed was allowed to be shown in the USA with either a prick (erect) ear or a small forward-folding drop ear. At that time, AKC followed the example of The Kennel Club of England and called the prick-eared variety the Norwich Terrier and established a new breed name, the Norfolk Terrier, for the drop-eared variety. One was named for the town and the other for the whole county.

They are very similar except for the ears. "Wich" is the Norwich, and "wich" is the Norfolk? The Norwich has pointed ears like a *witch*'s hat, and the Norfolk's ears *fol*d.

Both terriers do fine in the house, with sufficient opportunity to "stretch their legs" outdoors. Responsive, but still scalawags, these little dogs bring to mind the warning of terrier man Jerome K. Jerome, "Terriers are born with about four times as much original sin in them as other dogs."

Above and below: Norwich Terriers.

Nova Scotia Duck Tolling Retriever.

NOVA SCOTIA DUCK TOLLING RETRIEVER

COUNTRY: Canada
WEIGHT: 37–51 pounds
HEIGHT: 17–21 inches
COAT: Moderate length, lying close; thick, straight to slightly wavy, plenteous undercoat, fringing fairly abundant
COLOR: Red (from deep golden red to dark coppery red), usually with small white markings on feet, chest, tail tip and sometimes face
REGISTRY: FCI, CKC
GROUP: Gun Dog

The clever manner in which foxes work together to obtain a duck dinner has been observed over the centuries. While one of a pair conceals itself near the waterline, the other fox leaps and cavorts about on the shore, swishing his magnificent tail. The rafts of ducks out on the water soon become curious and move in closer and closer to see what all the commotion is. Soon, some are close enough to be caught by the undercover partner. Indians utilized this mesmerizing practice by stringing a fox skin across a length of shore and yanking it quickly back and forth, simulating the movement of the fox.

Dogs have been taught to draw ducks towards the hunter in the style of the fox. This process is called tolling, from the Old English *tollen*, to entice. Long ago, Europeans used tolling dogs to draw ducks into the net. For more than a hundred years, in the Little River district of Yarmouth County in southwestern Nova Scotia, hunters used tolling dogs, fashioned after the MicMac Indian Dog, which lured waterfowl in the manner of the fox.

These dogs were the result of various retriever crosses, estimated as Golden, Chesapeake, Labrador and Flat-Coat, with speculation of a dash of Cocker, Irish Setter (for its beautiful red coat) and various small farm collies and/or playful spitzlike dogs. Their unique hunting style has been set for more than a hundred years, but a formal registration and written standard is of recent date (1945). The breed used to be called the Little River Duck Dog or the Yarmouth Toller, but when the Canadian Kennel Club began registering them in the late 1950s, the present name was decreed. FCI gave them full international recognition in 1982. There are a fair number of Tollers and a breed specialty club in the United States.

The Duck Toller's unconventional style of hunting begins with the hunter concealed in a blind near the shore. A small stick or other retrieving item is tossed toward the water. The dog rushes out with tremendous animation, twirling and prancing as he retrieves the object and returns to the blind, tail wagging at all times. Some Tollers vocalize as they fetch. The object is thrown again and again. Sometimes the ducks are immediately curious. Other times they may watch the dog make 50 retrieves. The dogs must maintain the animation and enthusiasm for as long as it takes to draw the fowl. Sooner or later, ducks and geese become curious and move nearer, often hissing and beating the water with their wings as they approach the shore.

The properly trained tolling dog never breaks concentration to peer at the ducks as they inch closer, but continues his "game." When the ducks are within range, the hunter calls the dog back into the blind, stands up to put the ducks to flight and then shoots. After the shot, the Toller dons his other hat—that of a fine natural retriever.

Hunting with a Toller means being able to come home with a full game bag, even on those sunny, "blue bird" days that are notoriously poor for waterfowl hunting. A small 30–pound bitch is credited with retrieving a Canada goose (no small trophy) from the Atlantic Ocean during a storm. Another retrieved several of these geese, despite a face full of porcupine quills.

One breeder laughingly laments an over-enthusiastic dog, who thoroughly ruined his day's shooting, though providing her master a story for all time. This bitch persisted in catching quail on the wing, and brought the birds to him unharmed.

Tollers are like other retrievers in that they are companionable and easy to train, but as dogs of high energy they need a great deal of exercise. As long as an outlet is found to satisfy that need, they make fine house dogs. More and more owners are finding that obedience is another talent. The Toller's strong retrieving desire and playfulness are natural traits, both necessary for his tolling ability. Tolling is also a natural trait (like pointing) and cannot be taught. These dogs have an intense, natural excitement about their duty. Young dogs need to practice, but training sessions involve establishing a close relationship and having children throw sticks for them to retrieve. Nova Scotians still refer to working a tolling dog as "playing" the dog. Another owner says, "Tollers are retrieving fools. If anyone ever makes the mistake of throwing a ball for them, they will keep the unfortunate soul throwing until his arm gives out."

Nova Scotia Duck Tolling Retrievers.

The breed is sensible and devoted to its family. An owner in Michigan credits her well-being to her dog, after he twice saved her, once legitimately and more than once "illegitimately." The first instance occurred on a hiking expedition, when she ended on a precarious ledge. This medium-sized dog braced himself so that his owner could grasp his collar and pull herself to safety. The other instance involves her swimming attempts—he won't allow her deeper than ankle-high water!

The Toller may be a bit more reserved to non-family than the Golden Retriever. The coat requires the same care as other retrievers. Some Tollers have very little white, while others evidence the Irish pattern, even to a large facial blaze. The white tip of the tail is highly prized since it can be seen from a distance by the fowl, much like the white tip on Reynard's tail!

Above and Below: Nova Scotia Duck Tolling Retrievers.

Above: Nova Scotia Duck Tolling Retrievers burrowing in the snow. **Below:** Nova Scotia Duck Tolling Retriever.

Old Danish Bird Dog.

OLD DANISH BIRD DOG

COUNTRY: Denmark
WEIGHT: 40–53 pounds
HEIGHT: 20–23 inches
COAT: Short, dense, and tight
COLOR: Liver and white, a small amount of ticking allowed
OTHER NAMES: Gamle (or Gammel) Dansk Honsehund, Old Danish Pointer
REGISTRY: FCI
GROUP: Gun Dog

One of only two hunting dogs native to Denmark, this breed was developed in the early 1700s from various farm *blodhundes*, (probably a form of the St. Hubert Hound), and early pointing dogs brought from Spain by gypsies. The man most responsible for the breed's early development was Morten Bak, and the breed is sometimes still called the Bakhund locally.

The Old Danish Bird Dog was initially used as a retriever, but its skills as a close working gun dog increased over the years. Unfortunately, the breed began to wane and, in 1939, during the War, it nearly disappeared. Due to the persistence of a few enthusiasts, the Honsehund has gained steadily in popularity since that time. Today, in Denmark, its owners boast it is listed as third hunting dog in the number of registrations.

Modern Danish field trial standards for the breed demand a dog that works fairly close and takes direction from his handler while thoroughly hunting the terrain. He must have great stamina, clean retrieves and, although the high point is most desirable, the old style of creeping and/or dropping to a lying position is still seen and allowed. His tail moves eagerly and, upon scent, circles in full rotation. Because of the breed's superlative nose, many are trained for schweisshund work (seeking wounded deer) as well as for bomb detection.

Danish owners say that the breed's abilities are quite universal, with almost all dogs being used for hunting or some other form of work. But they also are a quiet, friendly family dog who can get by with a minimum of exercise. One fan says to live with a Honsehund is like having a "clever and good friend."

The heavy neck skin of the breed is a mark of its ancient hound lineage, but the standard warns against allowing too much exaggeration to creep in. His body proportions are that of a rectangle, being only slightly longer than tall, and his tapering tail is never docked. The Honsehund has had very little exposure outside Denmark, although recently, one was invited to compete in the European World Cup competition for all Continental pointing dogs.

Old Danish Bird Dog.

OLD ENGLISH SHEEPDOG

COUNTRY: Great Britain
WEIGHT: 66 pounds or more
HEIGHT: 22 inches or more
COAT: Long, profuse, hard texture, shaggy
COLOR: Any shade of gray, grizzle, blue or blue merle; with or without white markings
OTHER NAMES: Bobtail
REGISTRY: FCI, AKC, TKC, CKC
GROUP: Herding

Despite the name "Old English," evidence suggests the breed is neither old nor all English. An 1835 painting by Sidney Cooper gives us the first illustration of the Bobtail. Its ancestry is through the European shepherd dogs, such as the Bergamasco or Russian owtcharkas, bred to the sheep dogs of the British Islands. The body structure of the OES is more like that of the heavier shepherd dogs seen on the Continent.

Contrary to its nickname, the "Bobtail" was created (by docking), not born. In the 18th century, drovers' dogs, which helped drive the herds to market, were exempt from taxation. To mark these dogs, their tails were docked. The lack of a tail was not a hindrance to the drover's dog, which didn't require the quick turns and stops of the herder. The Bobtail made a good drover's dog: eager, protective of his charges and weather-resistant with his heavy, dense

Old English Sheepdog.

Old English Sheepdogs, adult and pups.

coat. No one spent time on grooming these dogs, however, and they were sheared down annually in the spring along with the sheep. Farmers' wives spun the dog shearings, as well as the sheep's wool, into warm clothing.

Everywhere the breed debuted in shows, it was received with delight. The OES won dedicated fanciers not only in England, but in Canada, the States and other countries around the world, due to its distinctive coat and its singular, rolling gait. That same coat with its time-consuming care, however, has kept its numbers sensible and has not allowed him to become a "dog of the moment." While the pet owner may still resort to the "shear down," the exhibition specimen requires hours of care.

The modern OES retains the appearance of a fluffy clown with the heart of a faithful guardian. The breed is a popular competitor with spectators in the obedience ring and scent hurdle races, and they perform well despite their veil of hair. They tend to be very protective of their possessions. Fanciers recognize the need for a firm hand in training to overcome their strong will.

Old English Sheepdog.

Otter Hound, grizzle.

OTTER HOUND

COUNTRY: Great Britain
WEIGHT: 65–120 pounds
HEIGHT: 23–27 inches
COAT: Medium length; hard and crisp in texture, with an oily waterproof nature and abundant underwool
COLOR: Generally grizzle or wheaten; black/tan, liver/tan, tricolor
REGISTRY: FCI, AKC, TKC, CKC
GROUP: Hound

To the American eye, the Otter Hound seems a bit of an oddity, with most hounds being of the smooth type like Beagles and Coonhounds—a shaggy dog seems out of sync. But in France, a wide variety of rough-coated hounds have hunted for centuries. The great Griffons of Nivernais, Brittany and, especially, Vendee are most surely the direct ancestors of the Otter Hound. He was perfected in England, with additions of various hounds (including Bloodhound) and water spaniels.

The greffier-type hound in France is a cold-trailer of great endurance, and these characteristics were useful in developing a dog to hunt otter. Otters, once in abundance, are predators that decimated the fish in English rivers. This furnished an excuse for avid hunters, since otters were the only game in season from April to September. Otter hunting thus became a minor sport during the 18th century.

European otters, weighing up to 24 pounds, live in holes dug in river banks with the entrance under the water surface. These otters can swim for great distances underwater, coming up only occasionally for air. The scent trail they leave on land is called a "drag" and on water is termed a "wash." The Otter Hound has an exquisite scenting ability like that of the Bloodhound, and he easily can pick up and follow a drag ten to twelve hours old. When pursuing a wash, the hounds sometimes swim as long as five hours, an activity requiring the ultimate in both nose and endurance. His oily, thick undercoat and webbed feet make him an Olympic-ability swimmer.

Several British monarchs carried the title of Master of Otterhounds: John; Richard III; Charles II; Edward II and IV; Henry II, VI, VII and VIII; and even Elizabeth I. During the height of otter hunting in the latter half of the 1800s, there were 18 to 20 packs in use throughout Britain each season. Famous hounds, such as the Hawkstone Pack of the Honorable Geoffrey Hill, killed more than 700 otters during a 20-year span. Squire Lomax of Clitheroe was a stickler for the formality of the hunt, and the manner in which his hounds worked was more important than the end result. During the late 1860s, his famous pack was so well trained that it was said they took their cues from him with only a minimal wave of his hand. Many of the major packs of those times would send a "couple" of hounds to the larger bench exhibitions, and the Carlisle and Kendal working packs were also noted for their show winners.

The Otter Hound, like previous hounds that hunted the wolf, was efficient enough to almost annihilate his own existence. The otter numbers were reduced so that fewer and fewer packs

Otter Hound, wheaten.

643

Otter Hound.

could be justifiably supported. In addition, many hunt clubs began crossing the shaggy Otter Hound with Foxhound to gain added speed. By 1900, there were very few purebred Otter Hounds left in England, although a number of good specimens had been exported to the United States. Today the breed is rare on both sides of the Atlantic, save a few fanciers who sponsor it at shows.

Otters are now a protected species in England, and otter hunting with dogs has never been practiced in the USA. This canine's background of persistence on a cold trail could perhaps make him useful on other game if anyone cares to try.

His rough, shaggy coat and large size make him the most distinctive of the hounds in America. He requires brushing about once a week. Sometimes the Otter Hound drinks by submerging his entire head in water. It is always at that moment that he decides to show his love for his master and lays his soggy beard in a lap!

These dogs have the independence of hounds yet possess great devotion to their masters. They are affectionate and boisterous, much like the children they enjoy playing with. Their hound attributes of a loud bugle and self-willed nature, combined with substantial size, need the skills of a knowledgeable trainer.

OWCZAREK PODHALANSKI

COUNTRY: Poland
WEIGHT: 100–150 pounds
HEIGHT: 24–34 inches
COAT: Long, thick, hard, straight or wavy
COLOR: White
OTHER NAMES: Tatra Mountain Sheepdog, Owczarek Tatrzanski, Polish Mountain Dog
REGISTRY: FCI
GROUP: Flock Guard

The Podhale, where this breed originated, is a small region in southern Poland, against the Tatra range, which are the highest peaks in the Carpathians. The Podhalanski's history follows that of similar dogs from Czechoslovakia, Hungary and Rumania, all of which trace back to the white guardian dogs of the Eastern World. The Polish *owca* (pronounced "ofsta") means sheep, and *owczarek* (pronounced "ofcharek") is the generic term for sheepdog. This is the same meaning as the Russian word *owtcharka* or the Yugoslavian *ovcar*.

This native Polish breed is an outstanding mountain worker. The tail is used as a handhold while following the dog through rough and steep terrain!

Beside the traditional use as a livestock guardian, the Polish people often use these dogs for personal protection and as guard dogs in factories. Much like the people who breed them, the Podhalanskis are independent, self-sufficient and courageous. They are coveted for their attributes: heartiness, adaptability and bravery. Their personalities are more easygoing than most of the flock guardians, with irritability or cowardice being a fault. This may be due to the dogs' use for hauling carts among the dairy, horticultural and bakery trades. The same dogs may be used in the mountains during the grazing season and in winter brought to town to help with other chores.

Young dogs that show high intelligence are selected for police, military or guide dog work. Every dog serves the people in some way, and is treated well in return. Even the dogs lacking in

Owczarek Podhalanski.

Owczarek Podhalanski.

ment, proper dominance must be exerted by the master early in the relationship to overcome the dog's natural independence. Otherwise he might quietly put his head on the owner's shoulder!

The Podhalanski is placid and cheerful, but American owners warn about his tendency to bark if left outside alone at night. This breed is constantly on the alert.

The breed is popular in Poland and was introduced in the United States and Canada by a few imports in the 1980s. An American Foreign Service Officer stationed in Poland came to admire the breed. Once back in the States, he arranged to acquire three of these magnificent Polish dogs. They left Poland "by a whisker," leaving the very day martial law was declared in 1981. From this modest beginning, the Polish Tatra Sheepdog Club of America has been formed to help promote the breed and to bring owners together for a common cause.

Owczarek Podhalanski, pups.

talent are kept for their wool, with the combings used for upholstery and fine woolens!

Their owners claim the breed is easy to care for in both grooming and feeding. The coat is self-cleansing and "never requires bathing." Like many of the flock guards, Podhalanskis are surprisingly economical to feed.

The Podhalanski doesn't need people to be content. These dogs develop their own routines, and quickly attach themselves to environment, buildings, people or animals. As with the other flock-guarding breeds, dominance is exerted over another dog. The dominant one quietly puts his head on the other's shoulders as a reminder. Despite the more tractable tempera-

PATTERDALE TERRIER

COUNTRY: Great Britain
WEIGHT: 12–13 pounds
HEIGHT: Less than 12½ inches
COAT: Short and coarse
COLOR: Black, red, chocolate or black/tan
OTHER NAMES: Black Fell Terrier
REGISTRY: FCI
GROUP: Terrier

Avid terrier people in Yorkshire and the lake districts to this day breed strictly working stock, often generally referred to as fell terriers. As is common with working dogs, they show physical variation, since mating is based only on working qualities and gameness. But one distinct type that emerged is the Patterdale Terrier, named for a village in Cumbria.

These dogs are particularly hard and tenacious. "Many [Foxhound] masters would not thank you for attempting to bolt his [sic] fox with a hard bitten Patterdale, for the dog is more likely to get hold and have a go, possibly kill the fox rather than allow him to bolt. . ."

thus spoiling the hunt with the hounds. The fells of the north country, with the protection afforded foxes in *borrans*, rock tips, mines and scree, created the need for a hard terrier able to scramble over the terrain and fearless enough to go to ground. The Patterdale filled—and still fills—that need.

Dan Russell of *Shooting Times and Country Magazine* relates the following story of having run a fox to ground in a rough place: "Turning to his terrier, Fury, Joe said 'Thee and me's bin good pals, but t'times come when we mun part, for if tha gaas in here ah'll nivver see thee agen.' In went Fury and soon there were sounds of a terrific battle underground. The fox refused to bolt and after a while Fury came out, badly bitten from ear to ear. The dog was sent to the nearest farm for treatment and tools were sent for. At the end of three hours digging an entrance was made into the borran and there, inside, were all the signs of an Homeric struggle and in the corner, piled on top of each other, were three big foxes."

Further testament to the high esteem in which Patterdales are held is evidenced in the

Patterdale Terriers, red and black.

following exchange reported by Nigel Hinch-cliffe: "A Welshman once rang me and asked to buy a black terrier, preferably one fully working. When asked what kind of work, I was told 'a bit of ratting on the allotments and the occasional rabbiting in Pembrokeshire.' I declined him, advising him to buy locally, for buying a 'black-un' for such work was like buying a Rolls Royce in which to deliver milk."

The first Patterdales were brought to the USA in 1978. This dog is a laid-back terrier, not as yappy as some, who enjoys "curling up by the heat duct" in the house. Modern owners say he can be kenneled with two or three other terriers, as long as he has enough work and hunting to keep him exercised and content. If stale or bored, he may pick fights with a kennel mate.

They are game and tough when hunting, and hunters often take three or four dogs with them on a jaunt. In the States, these dogs hunt "anything with fur"—woodchuck (groundhog), fox, coon or even badger. An American Patterdale, aptly named "Rocky," a flyweight at 13 pounds, recently drew a 34–pound badger!

An owner says his Patterdales are sensible dogs. When they first enter a burrow, they'll bark and fuss, trying to incite the quarry to bolt. If the prey refuses to budge, only then will the terrier go in for a hold.

The Patterdale has a bit thicker and cheekier head than many of our modern show terriers, suggesting a hint of the Bull Terrier. This may have been what they looked like originally, or this look might have come from a later cross.

Patterdale Terrier, red.

PEKINGESE

COUNTRY: China
WEIGHT: 6 pounds, 6–8 pounds, and 8–14 pounds
COAT: Long, straight, harsh and profuse; heavy feathering and abundant undercoat
COLOR: All colors allowed: red, fawn, black, black/tan, sable, brindle, white and particolor (two colors evenly broken all over body); black masks and spectacles around the eyes and lines to the ears are desirable
OTHER NAMES: Peking Palasthund
REGISTRY: FCI, AKC, UKC, TKC, CKC
GROUP: Herding

The Pekingese may be the ultimately dwarfed version of the hairy dogs from Tibet. Or, like the Pug, it may contain some miniature versions of the brachycephalic mastiff dogs. A combination of these two sources could have resulted in this unique canine creation. Whatever the origin, similar miniature dogs have been known in China since the T'ang dynasty of the eighth century. In ancient superstitious times, the "terrifying" lionlike appearance of these dogs, and the "Fo Dog" idols that represented them, were supposed to frighten away evil spirits. The Peke was known by a variety of names: Lion Dog, like his close relatives the Lhasa and Shih Tzu; Sun Dog, for the prized golden color; or Sleeve Dog, when he was small enough to be carried around in a voluminous Chinese sleeve.

The Chinese emperor Ming Ti converted to Buddhism in the first century AD, and the leonine connection to Buddha was bestowed on the Pekingese, as well as others, to be protectors of the faith. As the centuries passed, the popularity of these and other types of small pet dogs among the wealthy ebbed and flowed. By the beginning of the 19th century, dogs of the Pekingese type had become the darlings of the Chinese imperial court and the next several decades saw them reach their zenith. There were thousands of them around the various imperial palaces, and 4,000 eunuchs were housed and employed in Peking solely for the purpose of breeding, raising and caring for the Pekingese dogs. Slave girls wet-nursed the imperial puppies after their own expendable daughters were slain. No one out-

Pekingese, sable.

side of the nobility was allowed to own one, and the dogs knew nothing but pampering and gentle care. Two little Pekes announced the appearance of the emperor with short, sharp barks; two more followed daintily carrying the hem of his imperial robe. Stealing one was punishable by death.

When Peking was sacked by the British in 1860, the imperial family gave instructions to destroy all the dogs so that none would fall into the hands of the "foreign devils." Nevertheless, soldiers found four guarding the body of the emperor's aunt, who had taken her own life. These small dogs (all "sleeves" under 6 pounds) were transported back to England where one was given to Queen Victoria who, with grim humor, called her "Looty." Others were soon obtained from Peking through more normal channels, and before long the breed became

fashionable and quickly rose to the esteemed position where it has remained. At the end of the 1800s, the regent dowager Empress T'zu Hsi presented a Pekingese to an American artist, Miss Carl, in return for a painting of her favorite dog. She also presented a dog to Alice Roosevelt upon her visit to Peking. J.P. Morgan was another admirer of these dogs and brought a pair home to America. The Peke was accepted by the AKC in 1909 and in England the following year.

The Dowager Empress is also credited with the following instructions concerning the little royal dog: it was to be fed sharks' fins and curlews' livers, breasts of quails, tea or milk of antelopes, broth made from the nests of sea swallows; if ill it was to be ". . . anointed with the clarified fat of the leg of a sacred leopard and give it to drink a throstle's egg shell—full of the juice of the custard apple in which has been dissolved three pinches of shredded rhinoceros horn. . . '' Her full description of the Pekingese included an ideal that "its forelegs be bent so that it shall not desire to wander far or leave the Imperial precincts.''

In rural northern China today, a very small version of the Pekingese is still bred. This miniscule canine, under one pound, is considered good luck. Always in the piebald pattern, their spotted coats are "read" like tea leaves.

The Pekingese does have rather distinctive physical characteristics that, while pleasing to some, may not be appealing to others. The extremely shortened muzzle puts the nose directly between the eyes, creating a wide "smiling" mouth and a very flat face. This same characteristic causes them to suffer on hot, humid days. Pekingese eyes are prominent and prone to injury. The head is wide and flat, the neck short with relatively massive shoulders and chest, and front legs are short and crooked. Combined with a long body, short stature and rather narrow hips, the breed characteristically moves with a bit of a roll.

Pekingese do have marvelous personalities, exhibiting confidence, charm and a bit of stubborn independence. They are fearless but never aggressive, and their sole purpose in life is to give comfort and companionship to their owners.

Above: Pekingeses, particolor. **Below:** Pekingese, fawn.

Pekingese, red.

PERDIGUEIRO PORTUGUESO

Country: Portugal
Weight: 35–60 pounds
Height: 20½–22 inches
Coat: Short and smooth; longhaired (old type)
Color: Yellow or chestnut, solid color or with some white in the Irish pattern (not pied)
Other names: Portuguese Pointer
Registry: FCI
Group: Gun Dog

Perdigueiro means partridge in Portuguese, and this breed is the native partridge dog. The dog, known by Portuguese hunters as "the National," enjoys a proud history which remains today. The pointer of Portugal stems directly from ancient hawking dogs of the fifth and sixth centuries. Where the hawking dogs came from is unknown, as Portugal was on the ancient sea trade routes from all directions.

Afonso III, living in the 13th century, painted dogs of the type known today. Hawking dogs, then called Podengo de Mastra (pointing hound) were described in a Portuguese book of hunting by João I in the late 1300s. During the same era, Gaston Phoebus described the big, beautiful body, the grand head and the white and cinnamon color of the Portuguese falconer's dog.

Well established for so long and with the extensive travel and trade of the Portuguese, this breed may have contributed much to the development of European hunting dogs. The Portuguese Pointer was introduced to England by a Portuguese businessman in the early 1700s. H. Symonds describes the Iberian connection in *A Treatise on Field Diversions* in 1776 and says the "pointer" was first seen in England "about 40 years ago." Although refined for English tastes, the origin of the "dish" face on the Pointer of England is certainly explained by this history.

The Portuguese Pointer is a big, classical, athletic dog still commonly used by hunters throughout his native country. The head has the short muzzle and a slight convexity which is unique to him and his English cousin.

Perdigueiro Portugueso, longhaired, old type.

Hunting instincts of the Portuguese are strong and natural. Owners say these dogs begin sight pointing and retrieving sticks and other objects by two or three months of age, without any training. As soon as they are taken to the fields for instructions, they naturally begin an intense searching pattern. They can withstand extremes of climate and do well in any terrain.

This dog is exceptionally sweet and affectionate to his master. In fact, the official standard says he can "go to extremes of affection, occasionally embarrassing, which can be easily corrected by . . . training." One current owner describes a female that would sit for hours in front of him, staring in adoration. His wife would jokingly say that the dog was the reincarnation of an old lover—the only way to describe the sweet, tender expression in the dog's eyes.

Obedience and sociability in large doses are built into this breed as well. Despite his abundance of attributes and his prestige at home, he has not gained a following outside Portugal.

Right: Perdigueiro Portugueso, longhaired, old type. **Below:** Perdigueiro Portugueso, smoothhaired.

653

Above: Perdigueiro Portugueso. **Below:** Perdiguero Navarro.

Perdiguero de Burgos.

PERDIGUERO DE BURGOS

COUNTRY: Spain
WEIGHT: 55–66 pounds
HEIGHT: 20–24 inches
COAT: Short and fine
COLOR: Liver and white, with ticking
OTHER NAMES: Perdiguero Burgales, Spanish Pointer
REGISTRY: FCI
GROUP: Gun Dog

PERDIGUERO NAVARRO

COUNTRY: Spain
WEIGHT: 55–66 pounds
HEIGHT: 20–24 inches
COAT: Short or long as a setter's
COLOR: Orange/white, liver/white
OTHER NAMES: Old Spanish Pointer, Navarra Pointer, Bracco Navarone, Pachon de Vitoria
GROUP: Gun Dog

The basis of the Spanish Pointer is unknown, but the breed has been known since the 1600s. A current breeder speculates that long ago hunters crossed Spanish breeds, such as the Pachon Iberico and the Sabueso Hound, to create a pointer. The breed maintains physical similarities to both of these.

Don Alonso Martinez, writing during the time of King Phillip VI (1700s), described dogs with characteristics of the Perdiguero de Burgos. Velasquez painted Prince Baltasar Carlos in hunting dress accompanied by Spanish Pointers of Burgos type. The Perdiguero hails from the provinces of Leon, Vitoria and Burgos in northern Spain.

During the Spanish Civil War (1936–39) and WWII (1939–45), the breed waned and came within a breath of extinction. Señor Ayza, a modern breeder, says it became a "forgotten breed." But thanks to a few people, such as Don Manuel Izquierdo, Don Gerardo Sadornil and others who with much self-denial and perse-

Perdiguero de Burgos.

verance, . . . won the revival of the breed."
There are now fine examples of the Burgos
throughout Spain once again.

He was used in times past by monarchs and
the nobility for large game such as deer. Nowadays, he is a specialist for smaller game, but still
demonstrates the bravery necessary for facing
larger prey. The Spanish Pointer is especially esteemed in the mountainous regions, where he is
tireless, although type varies according to the
terrain that is hunted.

He can do equally well finding and retrieving
rabbits, pointing quail, or bringing back ducks
no matter how deep and cold the water. His
crowning achievement is in assisting in hunts for
the famed Spanish red-legged partridge, the
Perdiz.

Sports enthusiasts come from all over the
world to hunt this bird that flies like a phantom
jet and is hard to shoot. The hunts, which are
organized with shooters in blinds in a line and
beaters to drive the birds toward them, still do
not guarantee birds. But if you hit them, the
Perdigueros are there to retrieve them. The authors take this opportunity to note that the
Spanish government supports the maintenance
of Perdiz flocks by having their game wardens
keep track of the bird population. If the numbers on one farm are low, the government pays
the farmer market price for his crops so they
won't be harvested, leaving ground cover and
food for the Perdiz to prosper. This is decided
farm by farm, year by year. In a world where
game is disappearing, Spain has kept a large ex-
panding population of these famed game birds.
Shooting is only done where permitted.

In hunting, the breed is only fast enough to
cover the terrain meticulously and methodically,
hunting with an elegant, high head. Keen on
scent, he points a fair distance from the game.
He is also noted for his soft mouth.

He has no following away from home; nevertheless, the breed is still very popular in Spain
because of its natural abilities, its resistance to
extremes of weather and terrain, and its docile,
affectionate and likable nature. He is good with
children, and most dogs are kept in the home as
pets.

This is a big dog, but not heavily boned. The
body is lean, muscular and tough, with a strong
head, noticeable dewlap, and prominent lips.
His tail is docked.

The Perdiguero de Burgos was already spread
throughout Spain when the Spanish Kennel
Club first recognized the Navarro in 1911. Yet
the Navarro is an ancient type of pointing dog,
and actually may have been the prototype for
other breeds. He was known in Spain for centuries, but was thought to be lost. A group of people in Navarra and Alava (Basque country) are
trying to revive and restore the breed.

Where he came from cannot be pinpointed,
but the breed always had both smooth and longhaired varieties. He may have figured in the
early development of the feathered setting dogs
of Europe, as well as of the vorstehhunds and
braques, because of the scope of Spanish influence in Europe during those times.

His distinctive feature is his split or double
nose, something mentioned in the histories of
other European hunting dogs, such as the German Shorthair. The Navarro is similar to the
Burgos in hunting style and is also used in the
Perdiz hunts.

Perdiguero Navarro.

PERRO DE PASTOR MALLORQUIN

COUNTRY: Spain
WEIGHT: 45–60 pounds
HEIGHT: 19–22 inches
COAT: Short (pelo corto) or medium (pelo largo)
COLOR: Usually dark brindle or black
OTHER NAMES: Ca de Bestiar
REGISTRY FCI
GROUP Flock Guard

This is a livestock guardian and farm dog originating on the Balearic Islands of Spain. He is a bit smaller than the Portuguese Cão de Castro Laboreiro, but otherwise closely resembles that breed and may, therefore, have a similar history. Their true background is unknown. They have the temperament and mental characteristics of the flock-guarding dogs, but are dark, small and smooth-coated.

The breed was brought to the Balearics on early trade routes through the Mediterranean. Since these dogs were isolated on islands, either crossing with other types occurred or a mutation appeared, giving the Perro de Pastor the ability to withstand extreme heat. Whether they were shipped around the Iberian Peninsula to Portugal or the other way around is unknown.

Unknown outside Spain, the Perro de Pastor is quite common there and is seen everywhere on farms and in rural villages. Farmers produce a litter when they need a replacement and give or barter the remainder to their neighbors. Although type is set, there are few breeders or exhibition dogs. In fact, the farmer who owns one might be quite surprised to find out he owns a pure breed. To him, it's just a "farm dog."

The Perro de Pastor is effective and extremely territorial, combining aggression and courage to make any rural family feel safe. He is good and loyal with his owners, but is rarely a house dog.

A limited number have been exported to Brazil and a few breeders support the Pastor dog there. No more than a handful of breeders who live on the Iberian Peninsula produce pedigreed specimens.

His dark coat requires little care, and the ears and tail remain natural. His rose ears fold back into his neck ruff. The FCI recognizes the breed, listing both the short-coated and long-coated varieties. Today, the long coat is rarely seen and may already be gone. The dogs are universally shorthaired and dark for ease of care.

Perro de Pastor Mallorquin.

Above Left, Above Right and Below: Perro de Pastor Mallorquin.

Perro de Presa Canario, brindle.

PERRO DE PRESA CANARIO

COUNTRY: Spain
WEIGHT: 84–110 pounds maximum
HEIGHT: 21½–25½ inches
COAT: Short, smooth, but coarse
COLOR: Brindles, fawn; some white permissible
OTHER NAMES: Canary Dog
GROUP: Mastiff

The Canario has recently been reborn, although once near extinction. The Canary Islands belonging to Spain were actually named for the fierce dogs found there, not for its little yellow singing birds. From the Latin *cane* came the "Island of the Dogs." These tough, smooth-coated, livestock and farm dogs, called Bardino Majero, were probably similar to the Perro de Pastor Mallorquin and the Cão de Castro Laboreiro and were present before Hispanic times.

When English settlers came to the archipelago in the 19th century, they brought mastiffs and old-style bulldogs which were crossed with these native dogs. The result was the Canary Dog.

This breed was selected and bred specifically for organized fights and became an extremely game, powerful and able fighting machine. Outlawed in 1940, dog-fighting continued as a clan-destine activity, with the quality and purity of the breeding stock deteriorating.

By the 1960s, when the Canary Dog was at an all-time low, the German Shepherd Dog was introduced to the islands. The Shepherd became the breed in vogue, almost causing the demise of the native canine. In the early 1970s, however, interest was renewed in the native breeds, and Spaniards began to search for examples of the Canary Dog. Fortunately, pure specimens had been retained by farmers in rural and isolated areas where the Canario was found to be a good farm hand. Ten years later, breeders produced good examples of the breed, which can be seen today at dog shows. An active breed club is promoting him at home and elsewhere in Europe. Dr. Carl Semencic conducted research and introduced the breed to North America in recent years. Fanciers feel confident the breed is close to FCI recognition.

These dogs have a wide, solid head, often with an undershot jaw. A bit of loose, hanging skin appears on the chin and throat, and the ears are cropped to a point. The Canary Dog, despite his size, is quiet and subdued in the home. Devoted to his family, he makes an excellent home guardian.

Perro de Presa Canario.

Perro de Presa Canario pictured with child. The breed's tremendous size is evident.

PERRO DE PRESA MALLORQUIN

COUNTRY: Spain
WEIGHT: 150 pounds maximum
HEIGHT: 23 inches minimum
COAT: Short, smooth
COLOR: Yellow with black mask
OTHER NAMES: Ca de Bou, Mallorquin Bulldog
REGISTRY: FCI
GROUP: Mastiff

Ever since the days of the great Alaunts, the sports of bull-baiting, and later dog-fighting, have been notorious spectator sports in Spain. Large, agile fighting dogs were renowned in Spain, where they are generally called *Perro de*

Presa, meaning a gripping or holding dog and loosely translated as bulldog. Although bull-baiting is no longer practiced, dogfighting still has avid followers in Spanish rural areas and places settled by Spaniards (South America, Puerto Rico, etc.).

For many centuries the local fighting breeds were the white Cordoba Dog (see Dogo Argentino) and the dark-colored Perro de Presa España, the Spanish Bulldog, very like the original bulldogs of 16th-century England. The Presa had long, straight legs, even or slightly undershot mouth and great power with agility. He was around 100 pounds, with a long neck and a long tail held high; he was said to look much like the old smaller Doguin form of the Dogue de Bordeaux. He has long been extinct. The Cordoba Dog's influence is still seen in the Dogo Argentino and those brought to the Americas, forming various white dogs used to hunt wild boar.

As organized dog-fighting waned on the rest of the continent, it continued on the islands off the Spanish coast. On the Balearic island of Mallorca, one breed has been recognized by FCI. Officially called the Perra de Presa Mallorquin, much controversy exists over whether he is now extinct or not. Although he is still listed on the FCI roster, Spanish judges and dog breeders say the Mallorquin has completely disappeared. Americans at a recent rural Spanish show for Pit Bulls and other fighting dogs said, however, six times as many Mallorquin Bulldogs were entered as Pit Bulls. Whether these dogs represent a reconstruction of the breed or a revival is a matter to be settled in time.

The Mallorquin Bulldog was often called *Ca de Bou* in the native Catalan language. Up to a hefty and impressive 150 pounds, he had his ears cropped in a short, rounded cut to make him look like a panther. The Mallorquin Dog was brought in great numbers to Puerto Rico and other Spanish islands of the Caribbean where, in the early part of this century, dog-fighting was common. Although laws have not been passed against it, the "sport" is no longer organized. This breed was the fighting dog of the islands. Puerto Ricans say many Mallorquin crosses exist, but are not sure whether any pure specimens remain.

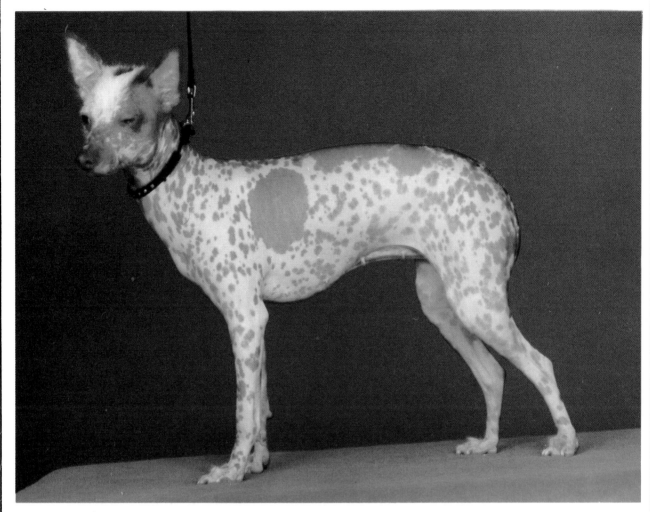

Peruvian Inca Orchid.

PERUVIAN INCA ORCHID

COUNTRY: Peru
WEIGHT: 20–38 pounds
HEIGHT: 15½–20 inches
COAT: Hairless—with crew-cut length hair on top of head permissible; Coated—with moderate length silky hair all over
COLOR: Heavy skin mottling of any color combination on pink or white background; or solid color
OTHER NAMES: Perro Flora, Moonflower Dog
REGISTRY: UKC
GROUP: Southern

Like their gentle Inca Indian masters, the Inca Orchid dogs are tranquil and intelligent. In the original Peruvian tongue, Oeuchua, the breed is called *caa-allepo*, which translates to dog without vestments.

When Spanish explorers landed in Peru, they found these hairless dogs in the homes of the Incan nobility, surrounded by orchids decorating the darkened rooms. The Inca Orchid dogs were kept inside during the day because of their sensitivity to the sun's rays. At night they ran free under the light of the moon—hence the origin of both names.

The Incans exercised selective breeding among their own people—even brother/sister marriages to assure purity and a predictable consistency—and carried over the practice to their animals. Incan nobility prized the light-colored dogs and rivaled among themselves for creating the palest hues. The common people strove to

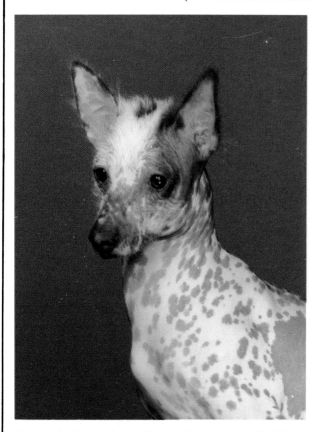

Above, Below Left and Right: Peruvian Inca Orchid.

breed the best quality dogs possible as a means of barter for favors from the nobility. Peruvian Indians still raise the dogs as beloved house pets but, reportedly, also as an occasional main dish.

The hairless head may be completely bald or be topped with a crew cut. The rarer powder-puff variety is not shown, but is kept for breeding purposes to correct teeth and skin problems that plague the hairless breeds. The ears of the hairless variety stand pricked at attention; the powderpuff's hair tips the ears forward, similar to a Sheltie's.

Oil is added to the dogs' food to keep the skin soft and healthy. The Inca Orchid must be protected from the sun, not only to ward off blisters and burns, but to prevent possible skin cancers. The Inca Hairless is dark-skinned, furnishing protection, and is considered the "daytime dog."

Deerlike in structure and movement, the breed is light boned but supple, lithe and swift. They are extremely sensitive in temperament and wilt under any roughness, even so much as a raised voice. They are laid back and unaggressive, and bloom with adult companionship. Kindness is repaid with utter devotion. The warmth received from their affectionate natures and heat-radiating bodies make them appealing to many as house pets. They can be found in America and Europe as well as in South America.

Above: Peruvian Inca Orchid, coated. **Below:** Fellow Peruvian, Inca Hairless Dog.

Pharaoh Hound

PHARAOH HOUND

COUNTRY: Malta
HEIGHT: 21–25 inches
COAT: Short and glossy; ranging from fine and close to slightly harsh with no feathering
COLOR: Self-colored tan, rich tan, or chestnut; white markings allowed only as follows— strongly desired white tip on tail and acceptable white on chest (called the star), toes, and slim snip on face
OTHER NAMES: Kelb-tal Fenek
REGISTRY: FCI, AKC, TKC, CKC
GROUP: Southern

Artifacts created in the Nile Valley during the Stone Age, perhaps as long ago as 4000 BC, display the image of a general type hound, such as the Pharaoh, Ibizan and Sicilian breeds. These dogs had the typical large, upright ears and descended from pariah-type southern dogs selected for their speed. Depicted widely during the Egyptian dynasties, these dogs bear a striking resemblance to the dog-god Anubis, who guided souls to their place in the afterworld.

But long before Egyptian times, the Phoenicians busily traded sighthounds of this kind around the known world. In most cases, these

Pharaoh Hound, chestnut.

dogs were molded and shaped into new breeds by crossing with native dogs. But, in certain cases, the canine cargo was left on isolated islands where they bred true for millenia. Such is the case with the Pharaoh Hound.

Phoenicians colonized the island of Malta about 1000 BC, probably bringing fleet hounds with them at that time. Over the years, the people of this poor-soiled rocky island learned to value the dogs for hunting rabbits. This is where they acquired the name Kelb-tal Fenek, or rabbit dog. After the decline of the Middle Eastern civilizations, Malta was left on its own for many centuries (although legend says that the Apostle Paul was shipwrecked near Malta in 60 AD when the inhabitants of these islands were converted to Christianity). For almost 2,000 years, the original dogs bred true on the island, without the introduction of any other type. Today the Pharaoh is the national dog of Malta and a piece of living history, showing us what dogs looked like thousands of years ago.

Although some Pharaoh Hounds were brought to Britain in the 1930s, they attracted little attention and soon disappeared. It wasn't until the breed was reintroduced in the 1960s that these dogs began to stir interest. A specialty club was organized in England as recently as 1968, with official Kennel Club recognition soon following. Specimens were introduced to North America in the late 1960s and gained much respect for their abilities in lure coursing and in field trials for sighthounds. Canada recognized the breed in 1979, with America following suit in 1983.

The Pharaoh is an unusual sighthound who can also competently hunt by scent. His temperament is friendly and affectionate, even playful. This, combined with his intelligence, often makes him a competitive obedience dog, a trait not common among the independent gazehounds. Despite his great speed and agility, his nature makes him quiet and unobtrusive in the home. The long, whiplike tail is carried high in a gentle curve when he is in action, very much like his ancient pariah ancestors and his cousin the Canaan Dog.

His alarm tendencies and easy care make him a viable choice for those who are willing to provide a workout. It has been noted by modern owners that Pharaohs lick rain water off each other, obviously a desert instinct to take advantage of any water. When excited, they blush a rosy pink, highlighting their faces and the inside of their ears. It is said "his face glows like a god."

Pharaoh Hound, pup.

Plott Hound, brindle.

PLOTT HOUND

COUNTRY: USA
WEIGHT: 50 pounds
HEIGHT: 22 inches
COAT: Short, thick and dense
COLOR: Usually brindle; from light golden brindle to "saddled" brindle with large black mantle and brindle only on the legs; occasional smokey blue dogs; buckskins barred from registration
REGISTRY: UKC
GROUP: Hound

The story of the Plott Hound parallels that of the Plott family and their neighbors in the Great Smoky Mountains that join North Carolina and Tennessee, in what was Cherokee territory. Sixteen-year-old Johannes Plott emigrated to this area from Germany in 1750 with his brother Enoch, who died on the journey. With them came their Hanoverian-type schweisshunds. The descendants of these hounds were fostered, bred and hunted by seven generations of Plotts.

As generations of Plotts married and began families in other parts of the mountains, their hounds spread with them. The Plott's hounds ran the mountainsides for over 200 years. Used on a variety of game, these hounds were bear dogs par excellence. They didn't carry any specific breed name in the early days. Those belonging to Plotts were called Plott's Hounds, those bred by the Cables of Swain County were named Cable Hounds, etc., even though the hounds were all basically the same type and breeding. The original schweisshunds were crossed with other hounds and with cur types especially for their treeing ability. At one time, the breed was even referred to as the Plott Cur. But through the years, each of these clans maintained the original type of a tough, persistent, coldtrailing hound. H.T. Crockett, the Hannahs, the Cruse family, the Reece brothers, the Will Orr family and Blain Blevins all had notable strains.

By the 1920s, the old strains of these brindle mountain-bear dogs needed a boost. The Blevins Hounds were a strain of black-saddled tan hounds also known in the Great Smokies. Gola Ferguson, who had bred hounds of the Plott type for many years, crossed some of his with those of Blevins' type. The result of this cross,

"Tige" and "Boss," was two legendary hounds that became known throughout the vast mountain range. Bred back to Plott types, they provided the boost that was needed to revive this old breed. Almost all modern registered Plotts trace to one or the other of these pillars. Even the Plott families, always able to appreciate a fine hound, bought dogs from Ferguson to improve their own stock. This cross also introduced the black-saddled brindle pattern.

When this breed was suggested for UKC registration in 1946, there were those that wanted them called Ferguson Hounds or Cable Hounds. Although many contributed to the breed, the Plott family received the honor in the final selection.

Plotts are very tough hounds who not only can coldtrail a 500–pound bear or a boar, but can stand up to that type of game when they have it cornered. As Ferguson said of one of his dogs, "Against bear, he was a one man army." One hunter's eager female Plott always tore up a bear's ear, which she'd grab and hang on to stubbornly. The Plotts are hounds of fine nose and beautiful voice, and are easily trained.

Hack Smithdeal, a well-to-do, avid bear hunter of Tennessee, did much to publicize the Plott breed. He claimed this breed to be the best he could find for bear hunting, and much of his famous pack came directly from John Plott and his son, George Plott, in the 1930s. A 1946 demonstration with Smithdeal's hounds for the Conservation Department opened bear hunting with dogs in Michigan. From Smithdeal dogs came the hounds of the Pioneer Kennel of Dale Brandenburg, who has produced many outstanding Plotts.

Although the lighter brindle color was common earlier, after the Blevins cross the most usual pattern was a black-saddled brindle, some almost a solid black with brindling only on the legs. Other colors appear in the breed, including slate blue from the Blue Delch strain and a very few buckskins. The buckskin color has recently been barred from registration due to the fact that some of that color had come from Redbone crosses. The Plott breeders, like the Blue Gascon and Majestic promoters, want to maintain the old hunting type without adulteration from hot-nosed speed hounds.

PODENGOS PORTUGUESOS

Podengo Portugueso Grande

COUNTRY: Portugal
WEIGHT: 66 pounds
HEIGHT: 22–28 inches
COAT: Short, coarse, longer than most of the sighthounds; Wirehaired—medium-long, shaggy and coarse
COLOR: Yellow, tan, dark gray with white markings
OTHER NAMES: Large Portuguese Hound
REGISTRY: FCI
GROUP: Southern

Podengo Portugueso Grande, wirehaired.

Podengo Portugueso Pequeño

COUNTRY: Portugal
WEIGHT: 10–12½ pounds
HEIGHT: 8–12 inches
COAT: Same as Grande
COLOR: Fawn and white combinations
OTHER NAMES: Small Portuguese Hound
REGISTRY: FCI
GROUP: Southern

Podengo Portugueso Pequeño, wirehaired.

Podengo Portugueso Medio, shorthaired.

Podengo Portugueso Medio

COUNTRY: Portugal
WEIGHT: 35–44 pounds
HEIGHT: 15½–22 inches
COAT: Same as Grande
COLOR: Shades of fawn or gray, usually with white markings
OTHER NAMES: Medium Portuguese Hound
REGISTRY: FCI
GROUP: Southern

Portugal's contributions to the sighthound classification can trace their ancestry to the running dogs of northern Africa. They are probably closely related to the Pharaoh Hound and most likely joined their relatives on board trading vessels, disembarking on Portuguese shores. Because they were not as isolated as those on islands, the availability of other breeding stock allowed for some variations over the years.

These dogs were most prevalent in northern Portugal where they were renowned rabbit dogs. Hunting singly or in packs, the Podengo developed into varieties allowing for the type of terrain to be covered. In more open country, the large size used its longer legs to overtake the prey with greater speed. Today the Grande is not seen as much as in times past. He is a natural dog, without docking or cropping. The Grande is an outstanding guard dog and an eager hunter.

Fitting snugly in between and bridging the gap is the Medio. While not as fast on the flat, he has more maneuverability in rougher cover and uneven terrain. It is the most common form seen with hunters in modern Portugal. His comparatively smaller size is easier to house and feed.

The Pequeño, looking much like a sturdy Chihuahua, still demonstrates the hunting instincts despite his diminutive size. He is touted as the world's smallest hunting dog, and is used (like the Kaninchen Dachshund) to enter the rabbit warrens and flush the prey into the open—either for the gun or for the larger Podengos to run down. The Pequeño is also commonly seen as a "crew member" on boats where his job is to dispatch rats. While all of the sizes can second as house pets, the small version fits best and most popularly into this venue.

These are breeds which have never been sponsored outside of their native Portugal. FCI recognizes all three varieties, and one sees them occasionally exhibited at Portuguese shows. Like the Ibizans and Pharaohs, they are quiet, easy keepers and simple to groom. The added value of filling the game bag has kept them in the forefront with Portuguese hunters. All three Podengos appear in both smooth and wire coats and are lively, affectionate companions.

Podengo Portugueso Pequeño, shorthaired.

Above: Podengo Portugueso Medio, wirehaired. **Below:** Podengo Portugueso Grande, wirehaired.

Pointer, black with white.

POINTER

COUNTRY: Great Britain
WEIGHT: About 44–66 pounds
HEIGHT: Around 21–24 inches
COAT: Short, dense, and smooth
COLOR: Liver, lemon, black, or orange, either solid or in combination with white
OTHER NAMES: English Pointer
REGISTRY: FCI, AKC, UKC, TKC, CKC
GROUP: Gun Dog

Pointing dogs popped up all over Europe around 1650, but the English version has remained the modern prototype. What exactly was used in its creation is not known, but development occurred within the British Isles; there was ample trade to Britain in dogs from all over the world. The strongest influence may have been the Portuguese Pointer, with his ancient lineage and his dished face.

The earliest Pointers were actually present before the age of wing shooting, assisting in the "hare-coursing" rage. The Pointer was sent out to find and "point out" the presence of a hare. Then Greyhounds were brought up and slipped as the hare bolted. When wing shooting came into vogue after 1700, the Pointer began to prove his real worth. The earliest Pointers really "set," dropping to the ground on the flush of game, a quality that has been bred out long since. Yet the ardent desire to hunt, speed of search, intense style, and exceptional nose have been retained to the present day. The Pointer has, over the years, been used in crosses in countries all over Europe to add elegance and dash to the native gun dogs.

The Pointer has remained in high esteem throughout the world. The great majority in the USA are registered with the Field Dog Stud Book, and have been bred for great speed and ground coverage, as well as tremendous courage and stamina for the required three-hour heats. This type now dominates the great Open All Age American Field Trial Circuit. Hunting of this sort, in front of mounted handlers covering vast acreages, is not available to most hunters. Therefore, the American Field type of Pointer may be "too much dog" for the average hunter who wants a pleasant day of sport and a full game bag. The AKC-registered Pointer, on the other hand, tends to be a closer working dog, competing in the AKC field trials, which are more the venue of the true gun dog.

The Pointer's distinctive "dished" face that hints of a mastiff background, the undocked tail of moderate length and taper, and his big, graceful elegance make him stand out among hunting dogs. He is especially known for his endurance in hot weather, but his longtime susceptibility to the cold and his reluctance in water remain a part of him. The breed is not always as enthusiastic and adept at retrieving as some of his Continental cousins. The passion to hunt is intense.

The classic good looks of the Pointer, with his proud bearing, demand attention at shows. Show Pointers do not often compete in field trials, making the first dual championship attained in the mid-1980s a piece of history. With adequate exercise, the Pointer makes an affectionate, clean and quiet companion dog.

Above: Pointer, liver with white. **Below:** Pointer, orange with white, in motion.

Above and Below: Pointer in field.

Above and Below: Pointer.

Pointer, liver with white.

Pointers.

POITEVIN

COUNTRY: France
WEIGHT: 66 pounds
HEIGHT: 24–28 inches
COAT: Short and glossy
COLOR: Tricolor or orange/white, with large body patches of both or all three colors; the tri has a black saddle
OTHER NAMES: Haut-Poitou
REGISTRY: FCI
GROUP: Hound

Wolves were plentiful in Poitou in the 1600s. This province on France's western coast is above Saintongeois and below Vendee and Brittany. In the 1690s, the Marquis Francois de Larrye of Poitou created a big, courageous hound specifically for wolf. Hunting in packs, these hounds were remarkable for their nose, voice and speed over rough ground. French hunters stated, "It was the best dog in the world for hunting wolves; capable of following its prey from sunrise to sunrise."

Most of the kennels were lost following the Revolution and an 1842 rabies outbreak decimated the last pack, leaving just one dog and two bitches. Determined fanciers of the 20th century have restored the breed, using some crosses including foxhound. Despite this revival, the Poitevin is still not widespread, perhaps because there is no demand for his "specialty." But he still has proponents in France, and recently there have been a handful of imports to an American hound fancier. An elegant and racy scenthound, he carries less ear than many of the classic French hounds.

Poitevin, tricolor.

Polish Hound, black and tan saddled.

POLISH HOUND

COUNTRY: Poland
WEIGHT: 55–71 pounds
HEIGHT: 22–26 inches
COAT: Short, smooth, and very dense, with a slight fringe on under side of tail
COLOR: Black and tan, or black and tan saddled
OTHER NAMES: Ogar Polski
REGISTRY: FCI
GROUP: Hound

The Polish indigenous hound, like so many of the European hounds, is unfamiliar outside his home borders. He is a big, slow, heavy dog, but without the ponderous head, long ears, and excessive skin of the St. Hubert type. He is proba-

bly related to the deliberate tracking dogs of Germany and Austria. He has the German hound's large, stiff, flat ears with a bit of flew. In past centuries, he was highly prized for his superlative tracking ability. The War years decimated the breed, but it made a post-War comeback, achieving FCI recognition in 1966. At one time, a smaller version called the Gonczy Polski existed as well.

During the hunt he moves at a steady trot or a heavy gallop, and is highly prized for his perseverance and beautiful voice. Adapted to all terrain and weather, he is a dog of kind and gentle spirit. In recent years, he has again become scarce and is reputed to be quite rare.

681

POLSKI OWCZAREK NIZINNY

COUNTRY: Poland
WEIGHT: 30–50 pounds
HEIGHT: Maly—up to 14 inches; Sredni—16–18½ inches; Duzy Ponad—over 19 inches
COAT: Thick, long, with shaggy hair covering the face
COLOR: All acceptable, including piebald
OTHER NAMES: Valee Sheepdog, Polish Lowland Sheepdog
REGISTRY: FCI, TKC
GROUP: Herding

The Nizinny may well be the missing link between several modern, shaggy herding breeds and the ancient, corded herding dogs of the East. Of ancient lineage, bred from the Puli and the long-coated, medium-sized Hun herding dogs, some of these Nizinnys were traded by Polish sailors along their coastal destinations. Before long the sailors had a dog in every port. The Nizinny was instrumental in the ancestry of the Bearded Collie and Schapendoes.

Bred as a working dog since the 16th century by farmers and shepherds, the Nizinny was nearly extinct at the end of the Second World War. Most of the Polish people were concerned mainly with survival, not with the procreation and perfection of dogs, but—thankfully—a few breeders continued their lines from the scant six bitches and two dogs considered acceptable for breeding. A Polish veterinarian, Dr. Danuta Hrzniewicz, has been tireless in her efforts to rebuild the breed's foundation. These breeders' tough culling program produced today's version, which remains trainable, intelligent, and affectionate with children, yet alert to danger. Several of these dogs have been chosen to partici-

Polski Owczarek Nizinny.

pate as therapy dogs, visiting the hospitalized.

The sheepdog of Poland, divided into three sizes in its homeland, is best known in its medium-sized (Sredni) version. As with most breeds developed for working purposes, the Nizinny is wary of strangers. In Poland, a working certificate must be earned before a championship can be awarded, and the dogs are more populous in the country, where they still herd, than in the cities.

They have short tails, docked if necessary. Otherwise, in appearance, they are much like one of their descendants, the Bearded Collie. Their gaze is described as "penetrating," whereas the Beardie's is termed "inquiring," the end result being the same—that of being able to win the admiration of whosoever eyes they captivate. According to breeders, the memory of a Nizinny is long, and years later, they will remember an offense or a caress. They have won friends in some countries outside of Poland, including a fair number in the United States.

Right: Polski Owczarek Nizinny. **Below:** Polish owners in traditional dress accompanied by Polish Lowland Sheepdogs and Owczarek Podhalanski pup.

683

POMERANIAN

COUNTRY: Great Britain
WEIGHT: 3–7 pounds
HEIGHT: 11 inches maximum
COAT: Very abundant spitz-type coat
COLOR: 12 allowed colors: black (and black/tan), brown, chocolate, beaver (dark beige), red, orange, cream, orange sable, wolf sable, blue, white, or particolor
REGISTRY: AKC, UKC, TKC, CKC
GROUP: Northern

The origins of this breed hail from European herding spitz dogs. When the first specimens were brought to England from the German province of Pomerania, they were larger (up to 30 pounds), usually white and less profusely coated than our modern specimens. Litters often included smaller pups, and soon the smallest species was preferred.

Queen Victoria fell in love with the tiny ball of fluff, bringing it home with her in 1888. She exhibited Poms extensively at British shows, and hers were generally in the 12–18 pound range. Large by modern standards, hers made the Poms of that day look monstrous by comparison. This encouraged an upsurge throughout England, where they were exhibited at that time as "spitzdogs." British breeders systematically bred them for smaller and smaller size, and more and more coat. Modern show specimens are usually four to five pounds! So, although they have been named for their homeland, they are considered to be an English breed, developed in Britain to their modern form. The FCI, however, does not separately register the Pomeranian, considering it the same breed as the German Zwergspitz. The Pomeranian came to North America around the turn of the century and quickly gained favor on that continent as well.

The Pom is a beloved companion dog throughout the world. Despite its diminutive size, the breed retains the spitz personality with a brilliance of colors. Pomeranians have the alert, active, and curious character of their larger brethren, and are useful alarm dogs and fine, accurate obedience dogs. The breed is "full of itself," and likes nothing better than to "strut its stuff" in a show ring or on a neighborhood walk.

Weekly grooming keeps Poms neat. They make wonderful playmates for children who are old enough to be considerate of their tiny stature. Their easy care, beauty and diminutive size suit them as companions to the elderly.

Pomeranian, black/tan.

Pomeranians, cream.

Pomeranian.

Pomeranian, red.

POODLES

Poodle, Standard

COUNTRY: France
WEIGHT: 45–70 pounds
HEIGHT: Over 15 inches
COAT: Profuse, dense, harsh, closely curling coat (will cord if not combed)
COLOR: Any solid color
OTHER NAMES: Caniche, Barbone
REGISTRY: FCI, AKC, UKC, TKC, CKC
GROUP: Gun Dog

Poodle, Miniature

COUNTRY: France
HEIGHT: 10–15 inches (USA), 11–15 inches (Great Britain)
COAT: Same as the Standard
COLOR: Same as the Standard
OTHER NAMES: Caniche, Barbone
REGISTRY: FCI, AKC, UKC, TKC, CKC
GROUP: Gun Dog

Poodle, Toy

COUNTRY: France
HEIGHT: Under 10 inches
COAT: Same as the Standard
COLOR: Same as the Standard
OTHER NAMES: Caniche, Chien Canne
REGISTRY: FCI, AKC, UKC, TKC, CKC
GROUP: Gun Dog

Where and when the Poodle breed developed remains a matter of controversy. Shaggy water dogs, often with the clipping which has become a tradition, were known in many countries predating the Christian era. These developed, over time, into the specific breeds we know today. Poodle types were depicted in artwork as early as the 15th century. Germany may have been the actual country of origin, where, known as the *pudel*, he was well established as a water retriever before that century. It is believed the breed entered France with German troops.

Standard Poodle, black.

Standard Poodle, white.

From the marshes of Germany, the Poodle climbed to world-wide popularity. Welcomed by the French, he is still called Caniche, from the French *chien canard* for duck dog. In France, he evolved into his modern form. His quick intelligence and charm soon found him favor as a performer, and since the dawn of European circuses, Poodles have entertained as trick dogs. One Poodle, named "Domini," was credited with telling time and playing a challenging game of dominoes. The exaggerated pompons were clipped to match those of the clowns. Small Poodles or Poodle crosses were also used extensively as truffle dogs, sniffing out the delectable underground fungus for their partners, the Dachshunds, who then unearthed the truffle.

The courts of Europe, especially in France, escalated the fad of the pampered pet, a position the Poodle has not lost to this day. Because he assumed most of his modern characteristics in France, FCI has identified that country as his place of origin.

The Standard Poodle may be the oldest of the varieties, but has always has been the least in numbers. His size and coat care require both space and time. To his credit, the modern Standard Poodle is an athletic yet urbane companion. He is still a hearty swimmer and can jog, hike, or compete in obedience with *joie de vivre*. Yet his long history as a companion enables him to be a gentleman in the home.

The Miniature variety appeared on the scene shortly after its larger siblings became celebrated. In circuses and homes, the smaller size was cheaper to feed and easier to care for. The Miniature has remained the most common of all the Poodle varieties. In fact, in the 1950s and 60s, he soared to a phenomenal popularity all over the world. The numbers were so great that inevitably, some genetic problems occurred. Today, however, the Poodle has returned to a position of security. The Miniature makes a lively, yet mannerly, companion for all lifestyles.

As the Poodle became the rage with the nobility in the 17th and 18th centuries, smaller and smaller specimens were desired, resulting in the birth of the Toy variety. Toy Poodles were portrayed by the German artist, Durer, circa 1500, and by Goya toward the end of the 18th century in Spain. Many in Louis XVI's court fancied the charming dog.

Miniature Poodle.

The Toy Poodle has all the same intelligence and friendliness of the two larger versions in a smaller package. As is true with any extreme miniaturization, a few more problems are inherent in the small size, such as in whelping puppies. The ideal for the breed defines a Toy as any Poodle under 10 inches—most show dogs, however, are around eight inches. Some breeders have attempted to produce even smaller specimens, calling them "Teacup" Poodles. No such variety is defined by the standard, and these very tiny dogs are prone to many more in-born problems.

People occasionally disparage the trim as an exaggerated bid for attention but, originally, the Poodle's clip had a practical purpose. The jacket was kept heavy around the joints and organs, for protection in cold water, and the remaining coat was shorn for efficiency. Following that sensible period, came an era of ridiculous embellishments. As revealed by Shirley Kalstone in "Origins of Trimming the Poodle" (AKC *Gazette*), groomers clipped the dog in any design the owner requested: a family coat of arms, monograms, fleurs-de-lis, with moustachios and imperiales (Van Dyke beards). If desired, they capped it off with a pompadour to match the owner's.

The Poodle coat requires either frequent home-grooming sessions or regular visits to professionals. The modern show ring allows only two coat clips—the English Saddle Clip and the Continental, with the pompons—both with full-length body hair requiring great attention. But most pet owners have their Poodles cut down into a kennel or Dutch clip, with shorter hair making care easier. Early show dogs were occasionally shown with a corded coat and, recently, this style has reappeared.

Poodles have their tails cut to about half-length when the whelps are just a few days old. Except for their size, all three varieties are judged by the same criteria. They move with a light, springy gait, almost as if they were dancing. The Poodle, in all of his varieties, probably remains the most popular companion dog in the world and jockeys with the Cocker Spaniel for AKC's top dog.

Standard Poodle.

691

Standard Poodles, white and apricot.

Above: Poodle, harlequin—particolor not recognized by any major registry. **Below:** Poodle in corded coat. Some fanciers have begun showing the breed in this style coat.

Poodle.

Miniature Poodle, light apricot.

Poodles, Standard and Miniature.

Miniature Poodles, apricot and silver.

PORCELAINE

COUNTRY: France
WEIGHT: 55–62 pounds
HEIGHT: 22–23 inches
COAT: Very short and fine
COLOR: Nearly solid white with a few spots of orange especially on the ears
OTHER NAMES: Chien de Franche-Comte, Franc Comptoise
REGISTRY: FCI
GROUP: Hound

The province of Franche-Comte is in the east in the French Alps up against the border of Switzerland. The hound from this district is very old, having descended from the Montaimboeufs, that ancient breed that stemmed directly from the Talbots. During his heyday in the 1700s, the Porcelaine or Comptoise was considerably larger than the modern breed. He is probably closely related to the Schweizer Laufhund of Switzerland. At first called by his area of origin, he began to be known locally, and finally universally, by his current descriptive name. During the French Revolution, he actually disappeared but was "reconstructed" in 1845 with the help of Swiss breeders and their Laufhunds.

During the Revolution or before, many of the French nobility fled France, often taking their hounds with them. A good number of this breed found its way to America. For example, a family named Rousseau was granted large tracts of land in the Louisiana Territory by King Louis XIV, and kept many hunting hounds there. Reportedly, just before the American Civil War, there were 250 Porcelaine hounds on the Rousseau plantations in the South. A painting owned by the family, and exhibited in Paris in 1906, shows 31 Porcelaines killing a panther in the Louisiana canebreak. After the Civil War, when the southern plantations were broken up, the descendants of the Rousseau family moved west into Texas. The pack of hounds was scattered as gifts to area ranchers. Although purebred Porcelaine breeding did not survive that move, the blood of these French hounds figured prominently in the creation of many of our native American hound breeds, especially in the southwest.

Bred to hunt hare and roe deer, the breed is energetic, impetuous, and fierce in the hunt, but serene when at home. He is a classic French hound in type with very long ears. The name Porcelaine came from his shining white coat which gives him the look of a porcelain statuette.

Porcelaine.

Portuguese Water Dog, white.

PORTUGUESE WATER DOG

COUNTRY: Portugal
WEIGHT: 35–55 pounds
HEIGHT: 16–22 inches
COAT: Shiny, wavy and loosely curled; or thick, with shorter curls
COLOR: White; black, liver, with/without white markings or spots in varying proportions
OTHER NAMES: Cão de Agua
REGISTRY: FCI, AKC, TKC
GROUP: Gun Dog

The Portie is from the same stem as other water dogs of Europe, with the speculation being that he arrived on the Iberian Peninsula with the Moors via northern Africa. They have the same body and coat type as the other water dogs, with a slightly different method of retrieving.

For centuries, the Portuguese fishermen of the Algarve area have found these dogs to be indispensable. Their great swimming ability and webbed feet enabled them to take messages between boats and to aid the villagers in handling the nets in the water, as well as "herding" the fish into the nets. They caught any fish that escaped from the nets, and would dive into deep water to retrieve lost articles and "men overboard." These dogs are credited with good sight and scent, announcing a school of fish from their place in the bow. At the end of the day, they guarded the catch and gear and were rewarded for their chores with a meal of fish.

Sitting in the bow during heavy fog, they served as a predecessor to the foghorn, barking continuously to warn others of the boat's presence. Their easygoing nature and trainability were a necessity in the tight quarters of the fishing boats. Size differences allow them to fit comfortably into all boats, from the smallest skiff to a larger vessel. So vital was their contribution to the fishing villages that one was actually put on a fisherman's payroll, and it was officially noted that anyone who harmed the Cão de Agua would be punished.

In more modern times with radios and other conveniences, this distinct dog has been disappearing from his native working environment. In 1960, only 50 specimens were believed to remain. Fortunately, the breed has found people to foster its perpetuation. In his native Portugal, the United States and other countries, dedicated breeders are demonstrating the great charm of the breed to others. Vasco Bensaud revived the breed when mechanical replacements threatened the robust, affable native dog. Deyanne Miller, a Connecticut breeder, is credited with introducing the breed to the USA, which may very well have served to rescue the Portie from anonymity or worse. A very adaptable dog to any environment, the Portie fits as well into a family situation as into the bow of a boat. His unique sense of humor makes him a valued family member, and he loves other dogs as well. His bark adds to the breed's individuality, by climbing "up and down an octave."

The Portie coat offers several solid colors and combinations, as well as two textures. The coat

Portuguese Water Dog.

Portuguese Water Dog, black.

can be clipped in both the traditional working retriever clip (moderately short all over) or the lion clip (trimmed short on abdomen, legs, tail and face, with the hair left long on the thorax and end of the tail). When excited or on the alert, his tail curls up over the back in a gentle curve.

He is a trainable, pleasant companion, yet athletic enough to be a retriever, obedience worker or walking companion. Recognized in several European countries, he was granted full AKC recognition in 1984. Famous admirers of the breed include a real "water man," Jacques Cousteau, as well as landlubber Raymond Burr. The Portie's coat is comparatively "non-shedding" and is not as aggravating as some other breeds' to people suffering from allergies. Breeders pass a word of warning to today's owners: guard against obesity and give sufficient exercise.

Above: Portuguese Water Dogs and masters outside castle in Portugal.
Below: Portuguese Water Dog, puppies.

Pudelpointer.

PUDELPOINTER

COUNTRY: Germany
WEIGHT: 55–70 pounds
HEIGHT: 24–26 inches
COAT: Hard, coarse and thick, but not very long, slight beard and brow
COLOR: Chestnut to dead leaf, solid with a small amount of white on paws and chest allowed
REGISTRY: FCI, CKC
GROUP: Gun Dog

A combination of pointers and "poodles" in name and genetic make-up, this breed was created in the late 1800s by Baron von Zedlitz. He started with 90 "pointers" (probably of the utility dog type, i.e., Shorthair, Wirehair, and others) and seven "poodles." Some who have studied the breed espouse his use of the modern Poodle; however, others feel the breed's forebears were actually Barbets, ancestors of the Poodle. Nevertheless, the Pudelpointer inherited the intelligence, attachment and obedience to owners, love of water and natural retrieving ability demonstrated by Poodles. The pointers contributed other hunting skills, including the sensitive nose and fiery attitude toward game.

While working on establishing the mental characteristics and hunting attitude, physical type was slowly fixed. Today his short, rough, waterproof jacket with its camouflage coloring and other qualities enable him to figure prominently in German utility trials. The breed cannot achieve stud book status in its native land until the dog has passed these demanding ability tests. The dog must also pass a hip radiograph exam, as well as have a conformation rating.

Field trials in Germany demand formidable performance from the dogs. In the utility search competition, 25 requirements have to be passed. Judgment is made on work in the woods, water, field and in retrieving—and all dogs must have acquired at least a "good" rating in conformation before being allowed to compete.

The retrieving portion of the test necessitates finding and bringing back a hare and a fox; another fox must be retrieved over a high jump. Field work judging is based on nose, searching, pointing, retrieving of feathered game, and manners. The dog must not only track wounded duck but retrieve from deep water.

The difference between hunting styles becomes fully apparent in the woods. While the utility dog is never actually used to hunt deer, its ability to search for wounded game such as boar, hare, fox, and/or deer and stag is utilized throughout Europe. Especially in Germany, the sporting hunter makes every effort to find each piece of game that he wounds but fails to kill. As Dr. Fritz von Dewitz-Colpin relates, "All hunting is done under the motive: The subsequent search defines the value of the huntsman."

The dog must track a wounded hare and a fox, most preferably giving tongue while on the trail, and then retrieve the animal. He must find and put to flight furred game such as rabbits. And last, he is expected to follow the bloodtrail of a wounded deer or boar (in trials, simulated by dripping just one drop of blood every yard or so over a trail of 500 meters with a deer skin left at the end). To start, the dog tracks on lead, but as he becomes closer to the game and sure of his quarry, he is unleashed to go on by himself. When he reaches the dead game, he has to indicate his success. The *verbellen* (verbal) dog bays loudly to announce the find. This is the most desirable way since, in actual hunting situations, he may find the wounded deer alive and, having cornered it, bay until his master reaches him. Some dogs are naturally *verweisen* (mute), and these dogs usually are trained to take in their mouths a short strap, called a *bringsel*, that hangs from their collar, and return to the handler. This symbolic retrieve of the *bringsel*, literally "the bringing thing," indicates that the dog can lead the handler to dead game that is too

Pudelpointer.

large to retrieve.

Until 1933, the dog was also expected to pass a sharpness test in which he killed a "big cat" or a fox. These species preyed on both hare and birds, so it was important to game wardens that the numbers of cats and foxes be kept low. These tests have been outlawed, but owners of the utility breeds may find hints of this sharpness still present.

A limited number of Pudelpointers are in Canada and the USA, almost exclusively in the hands of hunters. Most comparable to the German utility tests are the trials sponsored by the North American Versatile Hunting Dog Association (NAVHDA), and the Pudelpointers perform commendably in these events. NAVHDA judges the dogs against a standard and expects them to perform a variety of hunting chores.

Pudelpointers do as well hunting in the desert as they do in a snowdrift. The breed has tremendous stamina and needs a large amount of exercise. Their tail is docked like that of a Shorthair.

PUG

COUNTRY: China
WEIGHT: 14–18 pounds
HEIGHT: 10–11 inches
COAT: Short, smooth
COLOR: Apricot or silver-fawn (both with black mask), black
OTHER NAMES: Mops, Carlin
REGISTRY: FCI, AKC, TKC, CKC
GROUP: Mastiff

The Pug is a miniature mastiff, with boxy head, large bone and typically thick, wrinkled skin. He hails originally from the Orient, where the Chinese have always favored the snub-nosed dog. This little dog could pass for a flat-faced miniature Tibetan Mastiff or a long-legged, smooth cousin of the Pekingese.

The Dutch East India Company traded around the world, including the Far East, where they found the Pug in China and brought it home to Holland, probably before the 16th century. By the time of William I, Prince of Orange (1533–1584), this breed was admired in the Netherlands. In fact, because the Prince had

Pug, black.

them, Pugs became the symbol of those who supported the royal family (the Orangists), just as the Keeshond was the mascot of the Patriots or commoner's cause. When William rose victorious after the unrest, the Pug soared in popularity.

When Protestant William III took over England's throne after Catholic James II was ousted, the Pug accompanied the Dutchman to the islands and to British favor. Thus, the Pug is not only a symbol of politics, but of religion. Years later, another famous couple, the Duke and Duchess of Windsor enjoyed the company of this miniature mastiff.

It is possible that the original Pug may have been larger, and it may have been he who contributed to the pushed-in faces of several breeds in Europe, i.e., the Affenpinscher and English Bulldog. His name source is controversial. Fanciers can make their own choice: the Latin *pugnus*, meaning fist, describes the dog's shape; the fact that many of the fighting breeds were descended from the Alaunt, which came down from the the Pugnaces; the old English term *pugg*, meaning someone tenderly loved, which was in general usage in England long before the breed's arrival.

Until the late 1800s the breed was only seen in fawn. The English Lady Brassey returned from the Orient in 1877 with a pair of black Pugs, introducing the second color.

Classified by AKC as a toy, the Pug is more solid than many others in the group and is sturdy enough to romp and play with children. His pushed-in nose and bright, button eyes give him a teddy-bear look. Children must be warned, however, that the little dog is not a teddy bear, but a living thing that can be hurt.

The breed motto is *multum in parvo*, a lot in a small package, which aptly describes the Pug. He has been the chosen companion of those who prefer a smaller dog that still evidences the character of a larger counterpart. Fanciers emphasize the Pug's laid-back temperament, cleanliness and affection for his master as attributes of the breed.

Quiet, but alert, affectionate and patient, they are true "gentlemen" and "ladies." If they attend too many tea parties, however, they tend to become grossly overweight.

Pug, apricot.

Pug, silver-fawn.

Pug, silver-fawn.

PULI

COUNTRY: Hungary
WEIGHT: 18–39 pounds
HEIGHT: 14–19 inches
COAT: Long, thick, coarse, wavy, forming cords
COLOR: Any solid colors–rusty black, black, all shades of gray, and white
REGISTRY: FCI, AKC, TKC, CKC
GROUP: Herding

Much of the Hungarian culture came from the Far East with invading Magyars, including its flock-guarding and herding breeds. The Puli is very much like the Tibetan Terrier in structure and instincts. It shows the Asian influence in its short-coupled body, the thick coat covering its body and, particularly, the tail curled over the back.

Its working abilities are of utmost importance. In fact, the dogs which do not measure up are not even given the breed name—they are just plain dogs and are not kept. The breed name is derived from the *Puli Hou*, the "Destroyer Huns" of Asia. One branch of these nomadic huns, the Magyars, migrated into eastern Europe with their sheep, dogs and horses in the ninth century and settled Hungary. In their native land, more than two dogs are called *Pulix*;

Puli.

in America the plural is *Pulik*. The Puli came close to being lost during the many wars that tore its country, but the breed has survived.

Recognizing the native breed's value as a herding dog, due to its intelligence and eagerness in performing its chores, Emil Raitsits brought the breed back from the edge of extinction.

The Puli coat is remarkable and resembles a rag mop. The idea that the coat is unkempt or not touched is a fallacy. Owners spend a great deal of time keeping their dogs' cords clean. The painstaking cording procedure is begun when the dog is a young puppy. Drying after a bath is time-consuming. Coats may be brushed into a woolly Afro, rather than corded in the States, but only corded coats may be shown in Hungary, Canada and Mexico.

A working Puli is a picture of agility and flying cords. The adult corded coat affords protection from the elements and a cushion from the hooves of cattle.

Pulik have been used for police work in some parts of the world. They have been successful in the show ring and obedience work in North America. In Hungary, these dogs are still seen with flocks.

Pulik.

Pulik.

PUMI

COUNTRY: Hungary
WEIGHT: 18–29 pounds
HEIGHT: 13–19 inches
COAT: Medium-long, curling hair, not felty like Puli type, never cording
COLOR: Solids—Black, all shades of gray, and reddish brown, white not favored
REGISTRY: FCI
GROUP: Herding

The Pumi was bred from Pomeranian or Hutespitz dogs brought from Germany and crossed with the Puli brought along with the merino sheep imported in the 17th and 18th centuries. This dog has evolved into a breed of its own over the last 300 years and is gaining popularity in its homeland. Developed to drive cattle, it is daring, energetic, mouthy and high-spirited. Its standard describes the Pumi as "unable to keep quiet." His character makes the breed a fine watchdog in remote areas.

The Pumi's tail is set high and carried gaily. One-third of the tail is removed The ears are upright and tipped forward. The coat is distinct from the Puli's in that, although thick and long, the hair does not form into cords. The Pumi is considered the town dog in Hungary, while the Puli remains on the *puszta*, high plains.

Above and Below: Pumi.

Pyrenean Mastiff.

PYRENEAN MASTIFF

COUNTRY: Spain
WEIGHT: 120–155 pounds
HEIGHT: 28½–32 inches or more
COAT: Moderate length on the back; longer on tail, neck, chest and backs of legs
COLOR: Basically white with body or head markings of grays, brindle, black, orange or fawn obligatory
OTHER NAMES: Perro Mastin del Pireneo, Mastin d'Aragon
REGISTRY: FCI
GROUP: Flock Guard

Massive flock-guarding dogs arrived on the Iberian Peninsula over 30 centuries ago. Cargos of Assyrian and Sumerian-type dogs were traded around the Mediterranean by the Phoenicians. Many of these dogs were left in Spain, where they found ample employment with the great flocks. As they spread throughout the peninsula, the dogs developed several regional variations. Moving north into the ancient kingdom of Aragon, the Pyrenean Mastiff was born.

Until nearly 1500, Spain was divided into several small, ever-changing, often warring, principalities. But a most civilized system of sheep raising developed that transcended political and economical uncertainties.

The *Trashumante*, or the formal mass migration of flocks to and from grazing grounds, paralleled the history of the Pyrenean Mastiff. The Visigoth King Eurico created the first regulations for these migrations in 504 AD, which continued through the 18th century. The routes (always north and south from the mountains to the lowlands) for each grand flock were formally delineated, and the shepherds, sheep and sheepdogs were allowed to cross political barriers and to supersede wars in their search for grass. The

Pyrenean Mastiff.

sheep were divided into herds of 1,000 head, each assigned a shepherd and five mastins—no more—with the canines each receiving the same food allotment as each human. The dogs protected the flocks from wolves and bears and were highly esteemed.

Named for the area of the Trashumante source, dogs coming with flocks from Aragon were called Mastin d'Aragon. Those accompanying the migration from Navarre were dubbed Mastin Navarro, etc., with minimal type variations.

It wasn't until 1946 that any attempt at consolidation occurred. At that time, the smooth-coated, heavier headed, more solid-colored dogs from La Mancha, Extremadura, Castille and Leon were lumped together under the name Spanish Mastiff (Mastin de Español). The longer coated dogs with more white from the north and northeast were grouped as the Pyrenean Mastiff.

The Pyrenean dogs, once in danger of extinction, are now benefiting from a resurgence of pride in Spain for the native dogs of that country. They are magnificent companions and guardians, a living piece of Spanish history.

A proper Mastin del Pireneo should be distinctly different from both the Spanish Mastiff and the Great Pyrenees. The Spanish Mastiff is smooth-coated; has lower set, larger ears and more stop; and has more color—often solid-colored. Differing by his much more refined head, the Great Pyrenees is also rangier for his size and is all white. The Pyrenean Mastiff carries a very deep head frequently accompanied by a considerable wealth of dewlap, as well as "showing the haw." His ears often fold back into his neck ruff, like so many dogs in this group.

His temperament is benign, even with other animals, as long as property and beings under his watchful eye are not threatened—then he can be formidable. Owners say he has a "clear concept of his strength" and doesn't need to show it off. The breed has a good many proponents at home, with a fair amount of interest established in Sweden, Norway and Finland.

RAFEIRO DO ALENTEJO

COUNTRY: Portugal
WEIGHT: 95–110 pounds
HEIGHT: 30 inches maximum
COAT: Medium-short
COLOR: White with spots of black, red, yellow, gray or brindle
REGISTRY: FCI
GROUP Flock Guard

The Rafeiro was spawned from several breed sources in the Alentejo, the flat lowland area in southern Portugal. Some flocks from the Estrela Mountains came south to the Alentejo for the winter and contributed the genetic influence from their dogs. Other stems may have been the Mastin de Español from the other side of the border.

In the lowlands, the smooth-coated specimens gained favor. Used as estate guardians as well as shepherds' assistants, they tended to be large, with the massive head and rolls of dewlaps much like the Spanish mastins. The impassive appearance underscores their aggressive nature. These dogs are fierce as well as being willful and hard-headed.

This dog rarely makes a good house pet, being used to the space available outdoors; nor does he fit in well with necessary home routines. Some who have met the Rafeiro say he is too much dog for most people.

Americans searching for examples of this old breed were told the dogs still existed, but the travelers were unable to find pure specimens available for use in USA flock-guard programs. The Rafeiro is still raised and worked in the Alentejo, however, and a Portuguese specialty club today supports the breed.

Rafeiro do Alentejo, white with brindle.

Rat Terriers, tri.

RAT TERRIER

COUNTRY: USA
WEIGHT: 12–35 pounds; under 8 pounds; 4–6 pounds
HEIGHT: 14–23 inches; under 14 inches; 8 inches
COAT: Short, smooth
COLOR: Tri-spotted, red/white, solid red, solid black/tan, blue/white, red brindle
OTHER NAME: Feist
REGISTRY: None
GROUP: Terrier

The American Rat Terrier developed from crosses of Smooth Fox Terrier and Manchester Terrier. This mixture, started in England about 1820, proved to be one of the best in the rat-baiting pits. Contests fired bets on how many rats the dog could kill in a certain period of time. The record is held by a Rat Terrier that killed 2,501 rats found in an infested barn over a seven-hour span.

When brought to the USA in the 1890s, they were still their original black/tan. They became a favorite of Teddy Roosevelt, who gave them the name Rat Terrier, and who took them on several big game hunts. An old photo in *Outdoor Life* magazine shows this President with three of the black and tans. American breeders crossed them again with the Smooth Fox Terrier (thus introducing the modern predominance of white), as well as Beagle and Whippet. The Beagle increased bulk, trailing and hunting ability, along with the red color. Speed and agility were donated by the Whippet, who was also the probable source of both the blue and brindle colors.

In addition to its ratting chores, the standard or large-sized Rat Terrier is most used by American hunters for squirrel, coon, wild boar, varmints and deer. The medium size can be just as effective on the smaller quarry, but may not be able to tackle boar or deer. These terriers are sometimes put into dens in trees or in ground holes to eliminate their prey. The larger sizes are strictly hunting dogs and are quite fearless. A breeder reports that they are natural, tenacious hunters, with overwhelming instincts, making the dogs hyperactive and constantly eager. He says they should only be owned by those who hunt with them, as "they don't deserve to be ruined by people who might just want 'pets.'" They do make good farm and guard dogs.

Pups may be born tailless or are docked at two days. Ears are either upright or tipped. Breeders concerned with working dogs are not as fussy about the specifics of looks. Both of the larger varieties are extremely rugged and do fine outdoors. Although many of the small sizes are house dogs, they can do well outside too, with adequate protection during the coldest weather. A small or toy version was created by cross-breeding with Chihuahua and Toy Manchester.

The Toy Rat Terriers are commonly seen on farms and in homes as pets. They are excellent companions and are sturdy and robust. Despite their size, they are good guards who can (and often will) deliver a punishing bite if they deem it necessary.

Rat Terrier.

REDBONE COONHOUND

COUNTRY: USA
HEIGHT: 21–26 inches
COAT: Short, smooth and hard
COLOR: Solid red preferred; small amount of white on brisket or feet not objectionable
REGISTRY: UKC
GROUP: Hound

In the 18th and 19th century, breeders began creating faster, hotter nosed coonhounds that were quicker to locate and faster to tree. Using the available foxhound strains as well as other hounds, and perhaps a little dash of cur, the specific treeing coonhound breeds were born. All of these hounds were more American Foxhound type than any other, exhibiting strong, moderately sized bodies and clean heads with smaller ears.

Red hounds have been common in America since very early times, when the pioneers' essential tools were: an axe, a spade, a saw, a gun and a "huntin' dawg." Records show Scottish immigrants bringing red hounds to the States in the late 1700s and the importation of red Irish hounds to an American hunter before the Civil War. Colonel George F.L. Birdsong is known to have acquired red hounds that figured in his strain as well as the subsequent July line of foxhounds. Although the exact origin of the red coonhound is based on speculation, there were certainly plenty of European hounds of that color to choose from.

Early hounds were often given the name of their breeder, strain or color. Some say Peter Redbone, a Tennessee promoter of this type of hound, gave his name to the hound, while others feel the name evolved from its color. At any rate, by the latter part of the last century, a well-known treeing dog called a Redbone Hound was available in solid red, red with white marks, red with a black saddle (called Saddlebacks) or, occasionally, even black and tan. Registration began shortly after 1900, with some attempt to breed only red hounds with white trim.

One of the early greats was a dog named "Midnight Flyer," bought in 1920 from breed promoter Sam Stephenson. In 1927, the first Leafy Oaks Coonhound Field Trial Champion-

Redbone Coonhound.

ship was won by a Redbone named "Little Sheik," who pocketed a $1,000 prize. "Jungle Jim," a great-great-grandson of Midnight Flyer, born in 1938, put the Redbone name on the map. His owner Brooks Magill was a dedicated supporter of the breed and the originator of the "Nite Hunt." Jim's good looks, fine abilities and his prepotency as a sire made him a household word in the breed. He lived until 1950, and most modern Redbone pedigrees contain his name.

UKC began formal registration of the American coonhound breeds in 1940. Stephenson backed the breed saying, "He is always ready for a hunt, no woods is strange to him, no night too dark or water too deep or too cold. He will stop at nothing until the coon is safely up a tree and will stay and bark at the tree for hours or until you go to him." With the adoption of a written standard for the Redbone, breeders made an even greater effort to eliminate the white markings and soon had a nearly solid red dog. The concentration on color set the breed back a bit, but dedicated hunters demanded performance as well as color, and soon both attributes were set in.

Redbones are a widely used hound, blessed with a marvelous nose and voice, trailing ability and a strong desire to tree their game. Owners feel they have a good-looking dog that pleases the eye but, most especially, one that has the talent to make the hunter proud. As breed historian Col. Dorman W. Clouse states, "They have proved their greatness in the swamp lands in the deep south to the mountains in California to have the guts, grit and desire to please their master."

The even-tempered Redbone Coonhound is no longer only a breed of the USA; it has spread into Canada and Mexico, and traveled across the seas to Japan, South Africa and South America. It received some fame in the Walt Disney production, *The Hound That Thought He Was a Coon.*

RHODESIAN RIDGEBACK

COUNTRY: South Africa
WEIGHT: 65–75 pounds
HEIGHT: 24–27 inches
COAT: Short, dense, sleek and glossy
COLOR: Light to red wheaten, a little white on toes and chest allowed
OTHER NAMES: African Lion Hound
REGISTRY: FCI, AKC, TKC, CKC
GROUP: Southern

This breed is one of those conglomerates that makes it hard to classify. Dutch, German and Huguenot immigrants came to South Africa in the 16th and 17th centuries to start new lives.

Rhodesian Ridgeback.

Rhodesian Ridgeback.

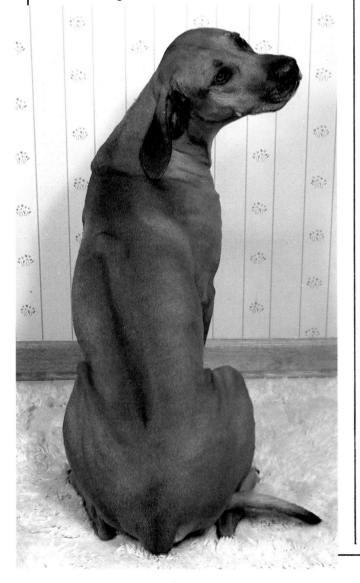

With them came their mastiffs (like the Great Dane), scenthounds and other dogs. The Hottentots (or Khoikoi, the name preferred by anthropologists) were a tribe of this area who had, over the previous thousand years, migrated from northern Africa. With them came dogs of the sighthound type that had a distinctive ridge of hair growing the opposite way down their backs. Anthropologists have placed similar dogs bearing a ridge and of a fiercely loyal type in South Africa prior to 1505.

The Phu Quoc Dog, from its namesake island near Thailand, was said to be pariah/hound type. This dog, now probably extinct, is the only other purebred to bear the distinctive ridge. The Phu Quoc could have been brought to Africa aboard Phoenician ships and passed its trait to African dogs.

The European emigrants came to be known as Boers, who were mostly farmers. They needed large, brave dogs which would protect their families and stock from wild animals and marauders, and could also be used for hunting deer and feather. Of necessity, the breed had to be able to withstand the harsh climate, as well as the deadly tropical diseases and parasites in the African *veldt*, or grassland. For a hundred years after

Rhodesian Ridgeback.

1700, European immigration was closed, so breeding had to be accomplished with what was available. Dogs brought originally with the first emigration from Africa were crossed with the native ridged dogs, and the distinctive Rhodesian Ridgeback was formed. The Ridgeback had the courage, solid body and good nose of the European hound/mastiff but retained the ridge, speed and acclimation to the African environment from the Hottentot dogs.

In the 1870s, the Reverend Helm brought a few of these dogs into Rhodesia (now Zimbabwe), an area where the big game hunters were active. Famous hunters of the day, such as Selons, Upcher and especially, Van Rooyen, found these South African Boer dogs to be outstanding for the sport of hunting lions on horseback. The Ridgeback had the nose and trailing ability to follow the giant cats and the heft and courage to face a quarry of that size. Cornelius Van Rooyen, living in the Bulawayo area, refined and perfected his pack over a period of 35 years, with the breed often being called Van Rooyen Dogs in those early days.

In 1922, after Van Rooyen's death, a group of fanciers created a club to standardize and foster the breed. At first this group asked the South African Kennel Club for the name Rhodesian Lion Dog, but because of the fierce connotation of the moniker, it was soon changed to Rhodesian Ridgeback. The breed first came to England in 1928 and was recognized by the AKC in 1959.

He is a powerful dog without being cumbersome, and is known for his clean, quiet and obedient nature. The ridge is his hallmark: a line of hair growing in the opposite direction from the other hair, up the center of the back with two whorls (called crowns) on either side of it near its beginning between the shoulder blades. For show specimens, the exact length, symmetry and shape of this ridge is of the utmost importance. Inheritance of the ridge is very dominant, and one can see mongrels in Africa today that look very much like shepherds, Boxers, Great Danes or others, all carrying the ridge up their back.

The Ridgeback is known in countries throughout Europe and North America with a small but loyal following. The breed can be headstrong and easily bored. The ideal owner will provide an outlet for his energy and train with a firm but fair hand.

Rhodesian Ridgeback.

Rottweiler.

ROTTWEILER

COUNTRY: Germany
WEIGHT: 90–110 pounds
HEIGHT: 22–27 inches
COAT: Short, smooth
COLOR: Black/tan only
REGISTRY: FCI, AKC, UKC, TKC, CKC
GROUP: Mastiff

As Roman soldiers marched across Europe, they were accompanied by their food "on the hoof." With the armies came specific types of mastiffs used for driving and guarding the cattle; the dogs also changed the minds of would-be thieves and army deserters. As the cattle were eaten, dogs were discarded along the way as excess baggage. Others were left as guardians at the various outposts established by the Romans. Since the main route of travel was over the Alps through St. Gotthard Pass, these dogs figured in the background of many of the Swiss breeds. The northern boundary of the army's ventures traced through southern Germany, including the town of Rottweil, which became a major European center for livestock commerce during the next 18 centuries.

The Roman's canine contribution to Germany produced the "butcher" dogs of Rottweil, driving cattle and pulling wares to market. The trip was dangerous, with highwaymen lying in wait for the unwary, and traders tied their money belts around the Rottweilers' necks. When the railroads eliminated the need for cattle drives and drover dogs, the strong, courageous workers were pushed to find other employment. Large dogs were expensive to feed when they didn't earn their keep, so small dogs were deemed better pets. The breed had almost disappeared in the early 1900s when its capability as a guard and police dog became evident. Backers formed clubs in Germany in 1907, with the Rottweiler achieving AKC and CKC recognition in the 1930s.

The Rottie is a strong-minded and courageous animal which has reached a pinnacle of popularity. Breeders warn the Rottweiler is tough with other dogs and will argue the point of dominance with people—even their own people. Training, firm discipline and maintenance of the alpha position are the breeders' prescriptions. The Rottie excels at schutzhund, happily joining in obedience competition, tracking and other activities that let him feel useful.

The Rottweiler's tail is docked to a small stub. He frequently is born with rear dewclaws, which are removed when the tails are docked. The small drop ears are left natural to hang down close to the cheeks. In Germany, strict Rottweiler breeding policies are dictated to control common conditions such as hip dysplasia. Reputable American breeders advise using the same high standards in order to continue producing sound animals.

Right: Rottweiler. **Below:** Rottweiler. Adult and pup.

Rottweilers.

Rottweiler.

RUMANIAN SHEEPDOG

COUNTRY: Rumania
WEIGHT: 70–90 pounds
HEIGHT: 24–26 inches
COAT: Medium-long
COLOR: White, often with colored spots on head
OTHER NAMES: Carpathian Sheepdog
GROUP: Flock Guard

The flock guard of Rumania was fostered in the Carpathian Mountains of eastern Rumania and is closely related to the mountain dogs of Hungary, Czechoslovakia and Poland.

Like his Greek and Yugoslavian relatives, the Rumanian Sheepdog is noted for his surly temper. The practice of attaching a log to the collar was also common with these dogs, as a protection for passersby—and for the dogs themselves. Not only did this keep him nearby, but it identified him as owned property. Dogs without the log and collar were often shot on sight!

Farther south, near the Balkans, the Rumanian was larger, smoother coated and found in many dark or even piebald colors. This variety was used for hauling and carting as well as flock guarding. Most probably, their differences were due to crosses with mastiff or pariah types found near the coast. In the higher, isolated elevations the white mountain strains remained pure.

The usual practice was to dock the last third of the tail. In excitement, the shortened tail brush was held aloft like a feather duster.

These two types were described by the cynologist, Clifford Hubbard, in the 1940s, but information since that time has been scarce, and none of these dogs have found their way to the Western World. Like so many of these old working breeds, they remained in use in remote areas. Today, the Rumanian Kennel Club recognizes the types as two distinct breeds. They are still used only by shepherds solely as working animals. Cynologists today worry about the dilution that is occurring in these Rumanian dogs as the number of purebred specimens dwindles. Rumanian dog lovers hope others will join them in sufficient numbers to sponsor and promote these native breeds.

Rumanian Sheepdog.

Russian Harlequin Hound.

RUSSIAN HARLEQUIN HOUND

COUNTRY: USSR
HEIGHT: 22–26 inches
COAT: Short, dense
COLOR: Tricolor, white predominant
OTHER NAMES: Russian Piebald Hound,
Gontchaja Russkaja Pegaja
GROUP: Hound

English Foxhounds were brought into Russia during the reign of Empress Anne (1730–1740), and by the latter part of the 19th century, these English dogs had been blended with the Russian Hound to form a breed called the Anglo-Russian. After 1951, it was renamed the Russian Harlequin Hound.

In those early days, hounds were valued just for their voice and fierce speed as they tracked the quarry only until sighted, at which time the Borzoi were slipped. For this, the Foxhound excelled. But as hunting changed over to using only the scenthound, this blend of English and Russian dogs created an outstanding dog for the Red Chase, so called because of the traditional term red game for fox or wolf.

This hound had the beautiful voice, speed, size, persistence and endurance of both its ancestors, plus the Foxhound's smart, visible color. This color was important to be able to distinguish the game from the hound, even in heavy cover.

The Harlequin Hound is squarer in build than the Russian Hound, carrying a strong head, with a well-defined stop and plenty of flews.

Today, the Harlequin Hound is being improved in type and uniformity. The members of the Dynamo Sport Society of Tula have produced a particularly fine, uniform pack of Harls used for wolves. In the 1980s hunters from Moscow and its suburbs began to utilize the best Tula dogs to upgrade their own stock. At current Soviet dog shows, the quality of the Harlequin is now considered equal to the best Russian Hounds.

RUSSIAN HOUND

COUNTRY: USSR
HEIGHT: 22–27 inches
COAT: Moderately short, very dense
COLOR: Yellow/red; may or may not have a black saddle and/or small white markings
OTHER NAMES: Kostroma Hound, Russian Drab Yellow Hound, Gontchaja Russkaja
GROUP: Hound

Scenthounds have been used in Russia as far back as any European country, probably before the Middle Ages. In fact, the Russians feel that their indigenous Russian Hound was crossed with the laikas many years ago to obtain the smaller ears, oblique eyes, thick grayish undercoat and more wedge-shaped head. By the early 16th century, writings confirmed the presence of fine hounds with "loud and melodious baying" that were used for hunting hare.

Although the Russian Hound has changed gradually over its long history through the introduction of European hounds and selective breeding, it maintains many of its earlier qualities. It is the hound most suited to the Russian hunt, as well as the country's climate, and hunting with hounds is the Russian national sport.

In the early 20th century, the Russian Hound had many minor regional differences based on its locale or breeder, and was often named for these places or people. The first Soviet Cynological Congress adopted a standard for the breed in 1925, based on the dogs bred in the Kostroma region. Soon regional distinctions were obliterated, and today the Russian Hound is one of the most populous breeds in the country, with many thousands registered. These dogs are slightly longer than tall and thick set, with a quiet, even temperament.

Although at one time hunted in packs, modern dogs are usually hunted singly. They are hounds with a keen nose and particularly great persistence and endurance in pursuing game (mainly hare, but occasionally fox). Their voices are rich and melodious and must carry across vast distances. Soviet hunters say they can recognize individual dogs from afar by their distinctive sound, either bass, baritone, tenor, alto or a high-pitched treble. As the Russian dog researcher Dmitri Dimov describes, the hound's voice is the symbol of the hunt, "singing to the glory of the joyous hunt in the autumn Russian forest. In these moments, a true hunter forgets about his gun. Tears come to his eyes, and emotions take his soul. . . . For such moments, do the true fanciers keep their hounds."

Russian Hound.

Russian Spaniel, white with black.

RUSSIAN SPANIEL

COUNTRY: USSR
HEIGHT: 15–17 inches
COAT: Silky, with fringing ears, belly and back of legs
COLOR: Variety of colors allowed
GROUP: Gun Dog

Following WWII, urban Russian hunters sought a small hunting companion. To fill this demand, they created the Russian Spaniel, using a variety of European spaniel breeds. Their invention was recognized by Soviet dog authorities in 1951. In the 1970s, a few were exported to East Germany, where a following has ensued.

This dog is not well suited to areas poor in game or very dense or harsh conditions. He is small and can become exhausted. But, in areas with plentiful game, he has plenty of verve and ability to search, flush and retrieve feathered or small furred game. Although regions rich in waterfowl are dwindling in the USSR today, the Russian Spaniel can make a good duck dog as well. Hunters use his abilities in hunting quail, corncrake and sandpiper or in flushing hare and wild goats from the forests. This spaniel is also talented in trailing wounded game, often successfully following a track as old as 36 hours. When the dead game is found, he either bays or brings back the *bringsel* strap, indicating that he can lead the handler to game too large to retrieve.

His handsome appearance and agreeable nature make him a good companion, and most are kept at home. In general appearance, he is reminiscent of a robust and leggy Springer Spaniel. Easy to train, he is devoted to his master, never letting him out of sight. The Russian Spaniel is also amiable with children and serves as an alarm dog when the need arises.

Saarlooswolfhond.

SAARLOOSWOLFHOND

COUNTRY: Netherlands
WEIGHT: 79–90 pounds
HEIGHT: 27½–29½ inches
COAT: Short, dense
COLOR: Agouti, wolf gray, woods brown, may have small areas of white markings
REGISTRY: FCI
GROUP: Herding

As a student of genetics, Leendert Saarloos studied various species, including several breeds of dogs. In the 1930s, Saarloos entered a cooperative effort with a Dutch zoo. He obtained a female wolf which he intended to cross with his German Shepherd, attempting to bring purebred dogs back to their "natural ability and sturdiness." His belief was that the domesticated dog had "degenerated" to an animal full of diseases and softness. He thought that the germs which were so debilitating and even fatal to dogs would not affect the wolf, but his theory was immediately proven wrong when the zoo animal succumbed to a virus. Fortunately for his program, the zoo provided another wolf, and his plan began to unfold.

Over the years, he selected for health and character from the wolf/dog progeny, breeding the get back to German Shepherds. Despite setbacks, he persisted, seeking the advice of a Dutch geneticist, Professor Hagendorn. Saarloos achieved some small successes in using these "European Wolfdogs" as dog guides for the blind. His faith in the breed was such that he also tried to encourage their use as police and rescue dogs, but to no avail. He fought a continual battle against the wild wolf characteristics of caution, reserve and flight in his breeding program. Several thwarted attempts were made to obtain recognition of the breed. Others noted his efforts, but he discouraged their interest, wishing to monopolize control of the program.

Saarloos died in 1969 before his dream of a newly recognized breed was realized. Not much improvement was attained until after his death when the genetic base expanded. Other interested owners created a strong club and finally attained recognition from the Dutch Kennel Club for these dogs in 1975. They honored the father of the breed by changing the name to Saarlooswolfhond. The association is very strict in its requirements against hip dysplasia, spondylosis of the spine and other health and temperament problems. Casual breeding is discouraged.

Saarlooswolfhonds are exceptionally strong-willed and do not take well to obedience or schutzhund work. They are still pack-oriented and need a strong alpha leader and a social atmosphere. Seclusion intensifies anti-social behavior, and the dogs panic if locked in an enclosure. Owners must establish the dominant alpha position, be willing to spend a great deal of time with them and train with patience. The breed is quiet, seldom barking, alerting homeowners in other ways. They do well in packs, with a leader emerging and keeping order. Problems can occur, however, if a dog who does not understand the established order is introduced to the pack. The club's publication notes that most owners of the breed have at least two to provide the necessary "pack." The Saarlooswolfhond is not known outside the Netherlands.

Above and Below: Saarlooswolfhond.

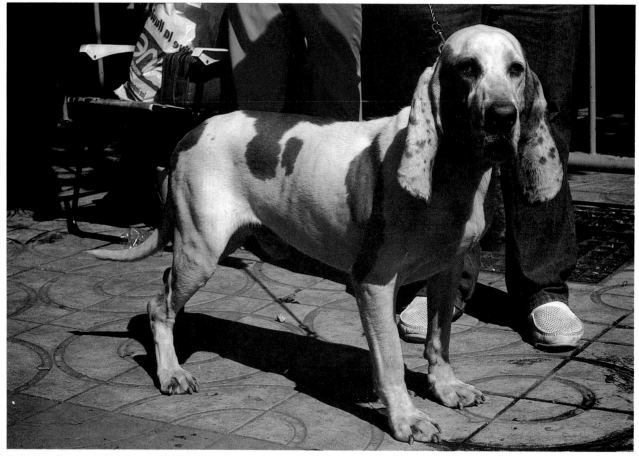

Sabueso Español de Monte, white with red.

SABUESOS ESPAÑOLES

Sabueso Español de Monte

COUNTRY: Spain
WEIGHT: 55 pounds
HEIGHT: 20–22 inches
COAT: Short and glossy
COLOR: Basically white, with red or black patches distributed evenly all over
OTHER NAMES: Large Spanish Hound
REGISTRY: FCI
GROUP: Hound

Sabueso Español Lebrero

COUNTRY: Spain
HEIGHT: Under 20½ inches for males or 19½ inches for females
COAT: Short and glossy
COLOR: Nearly solid red; with white usually reduced to an Irish pattern of blaze, neck ring, socks, belly and chest patch, and tail tip
OTHER NAMES: Small Spanish Hound
GROUP: Hound

Brought to Spain long ago by the Celts and isolated on the Iberian Peninsula, this breed has remained fairly pure. The Sabueso is a classic mastiff or St. Hubert-type hound with heavy bone, large ponderous head, long pendulous ears, lots of flew and dewlap, low-set tail and short on leg.

Hunted in packs at one time, these dogs are now used mostly by law enforcement authorities for tracking. They are particularly adapted for long hours of work in the heat, and have an abundance of energy. The breed needs discipline in training since it can be temperamental and self-willed. But these same qualities have given this dog the perseverance necessary to follow cold trails for many hours. They are loyal and affectionate to their masters. The two types are similar with the exception of size and minor color differences.

SAINT BERNARD

COUNTRY: Switzerland
WEIGHT: 110–200+ pounds
HEIGHT: 25½–27½ inches minimum
COAT: Two varieties—short and smooth or medium-long
COLOR: Red and white
OTHER NAMES: St. Bernhardshund
REGISTRY: FCI, AKC, UKC, TKC, CKC
GROUP: Mastiff

High in the Swiss Alps is the Hospice du Grand St. Bernard. Located at St. Gotthard's pass near the Italian border, this monastery is one of the highest and oldest human settlements in Europe. The Romans erected a temple to Jupiter there as they marched north to conquer Europe.

In the tenth century, Bernard of Menthon (later canonized St. Bernard) built a Hospice over the old ruins and dedicated his life to helping the poor and needy pilgrims who traveled through the pass on their way to Rome, often on foot.

The monks at St. Bernard's worked to aid travelers and to rescue victims of avalanches and bitter winters. By 1707, the overworked monks soon realized that dogs, with their superior noses, strength and weather-resistant coats, were better equipped to guide and rescue travelers. Humans couldn't follow the treacherous narrow trails when deep snow covered them, and often plunged to their death. But the sure-footed dogs showed them the way. The dogs' amazing sense of direction was a godsend in blizzards, when even the native monks became lost and disoriented.

Initial attempts utilized a hodge-podge of mastiff cast-offs from the Roman era. But by 1800, the monks had established a kennel and their own breeding program, generally calling the dogs Alpine Mastiffs.

Edwin Landseer, at the age of 17, immortalized

Saint Bernard.

Saint Bernard.

Tales of their great rescues abound, with 2,500 lives credited to the dogs. One of the most famous dogs, "Barry," reportedly saved 40 lives. On his 41st mission, his rescue attempt ended in tragedy when the person killed Barry in a misbegotten "fit of cowardly terror." Around 1810, the breed was often referred to as Barry hounds.

They were, at first, all moderately sized and shorthaired. In the 1830s the canine population at the Hospice was decimated by losses, disease, inbreeding and bad winters. Over the next few decades, the monks outcrossed to other breeds to regain vigor and establish the St. Bernard as we know it today. As a side effect, crosses to larger breeds, such as the Newfoundland, increased the size and introduced the longhaired variety. Today the St. Bernard dogs are still mascots at the monastery.

The Reverend J.C. Macdona, an English owner, brought the breed before the public around 1870. He and other fanciers of that time standardized the St. Bernard. It never takes long for a breed creating a sensation to reach America, and the first Saints competed at Westminster Kennel Club in 1877. Asking prices were listed for a few of the dogs in the Westminster catalog, with some of the St. Bernard price tags greater than $1,000.

These dogs are gargantuan in size and in accomplishments, with three listed in the *Guinness Book of World Records*. "Benedictine" won the honor of the largest dog on record by tipping the truck scales at 305 pounds. A Saint named Ayette's Brandy Bear shifted the heaviest load, 6,400½ pounds of steel on a wheeled cart, for 15 feet in less than 90 seconds. And a bitch, appropriately named "Careless Ann," tied the record for the largest litter with 23 puppies whelped.

As true giants, they have the physical problems associated with the other large breeds. Their gait is lumbering, they slobber and are expensive to feed. Families that are willing to cope with these aspects have majesty at their feet.

Saints are not always "saints," but they are always large. The combination takes an owner who is willing to discipline that adorable ball of fluff right from the start. Responsible breeders urge buyers to be selective, choosing from sturdy-bodied parentage with gentle temperament.

these dogs on canvas, and established not only their fame but his own as a dog portraiteur. One work, entitled *Alpine Mastiffs Reanimating a Distressed Traveler*, portrays two dogs standing over a fallen traveler. One of the rescuers bayed its alarm, and the other, with the all-important brandy cask around its neck, attempted to revive the man by licking his hand. Landseer's whimsical addition of a non-existent brandy keg has carried through the years as a symbol.

The youngsters accompanied adult dogs on their missions, learning from their experienced elders. It is said if a person were found, one Saint lay down on each side, furnishing body heat. Another licked the face, attempting to revive the victim, and yet a fourth dog returned to the monastery for assistance.

Saint Bernard

SALUKI

COUNTRY: Iran
HEIGHT: Males 23–28 inches; bitches may be considerably smaller
COAT: Smooth and silky, with feathering on legs, back of thighs, under tail and on ears; or a smooth variety which is void of feathering
COLOR: White, cream, fawn, golden, red, grizzle/tan, tricolor, black/tan
OTHER NAMES: Persian Greyhound
REGISTRY: FCI, AKC, UKC, TKC, CKC
GROUP: Southern

The Saluki and the Sloughi have parallel histories and most likely date back to the same stem in the ancient Middle East. Some of the very earliest representations of running gazehounds include those with the attractive fringing of tail, ears and thighs. A painting at Hierakonapolis, dated 3600 BC, shows a Salukilike dog. The breed's ancient name may have come from the long-disappeared southern Arabian city of Saluk, with its reputation for fine armor and dogs, or it may be derived from the town of Seleukia in the old Greek empire of Syria.

A translation from the Diwan of Abu Nuwas, court poet and jester, 800, AD says: "It is as though behind the place where his eyelashes meet there are burning coals constantly kindled . . . Like a hawk swooping on sand-grouse, he peels the skin of the earth with four feet. He runs so swift! They do not touch the earth as he runs . . . "

These graceful dogs were esteemed by sheiks of the desert throughout the centuries and called *El Hor*, the noble one. The Salukis coursed gazelles and other game, either alone or as an adjunct to the falcon. Like their near relative, the Azawakh, they were slipped loose when near the quarry, enabling them to run down game and hold it for the arrival of the master who made the kill. Training for their part in the hunt began when the pups were four months old.

These dogs held places of honor in the tents of the Bedouins. The breeding of fine Arabian horses and gazehounds was an art taught to sons by their fathers. Pedigrees, kept pure for thousands of years, were never written down but were committed to memory and passed to each new generation by word of mouth. A Saluki was

Saluki, grizzle/tan.

Saluki, tricolor.

Saluki, fawn.

never sold, but given as a treasured gift or as a trade for favors. Some were obtained in this fashion by Europeans during the Crusades (11th–13th centuries), but were absorbed into the native dog populations when returned to Europe.

A pair of these desert hounds was presented to Lady Florence Amherst in the late 1800s, and she was so taken with the dogs that she strove to have the breed recognized in England. But it wasn't until after the end of WWI that the breed made any headway in the British Isles, with the Saluki recognized there in 1923. Breeding stock came to the USA from England at this time and the AKC recognized the breed in 1927. In the late 1930s, Esther Bliss Knapp of Ohio took up the breed and imported many lovely specimens from England, Arabia, Egypt and Persia into her Pine Paddock Kennels. This stock, directly from the desert, was the basis for quality breeding programs that have continued in America. Canada followed with recognition in 1938. In fact, such good specimens are produced in America and in England that oil-rich sheiks have been known to come to the Western World today to buy Salukis. Despite the modern trap-

pings of luxury cars and business suits, these desert men can still compare the current pedigrees and the dogs to those legendary ancestors of yesteryear.

One of the common practices in the desert was the cropping of Saluki ears. While the thought of chopping off those lovely graceful appendages seems a crime, it was done to prevent injury and infection in a climate where flies and disease abound. Many of the first specimens brought in from the deserts were cropped, thus precluding their being shown in the States. It was their offspring who first made appearances in American dog shows.

Like all sighthounds, the Saluki is a fine pet and companion but not for everyone. Exercise is a must, but so is control over their excursions. They are generally very hardy dogs, having been selected by nature's cruel "survival of the fittest" for so long. Indoors they are like cats, clean, quiet and enjoying attention when they feel like it. Heavy feathering between the toes protects the feet from the heat of the sand. The smooth version is sometimes called Shami, although it was also called *slughi* at one time.

Saluki.

SAMOYEDS

Samoyed

COUNTRY: Scandinavian countries
WEIGHT: 50–65 pounds
HEIGHT: 19–23½ inches
COAT: Long, stand-off, with dense underwool
COLOR: White, white with biscuit, cream, all biscuit
REGISTRY: FCI, AKC, UKC, TKC, CKC
GROUP: Northern

Nenets Herding Laika

COUNTRY: USSR
WEIGHT: 40–50 pounds
HEIGHT: Over 18 inches for males, over 16 inches for females
COAT: Long, stand-off, with dense underwool
COLOR: White, gray, black or tan, either solid or piebald pattern with white
OTHER NAMES: Russian Samoyed Laika, Reindeer Herding Laika
GROUP: Northern

The herding-type dogs of the North were used by many ancient peoples for their reindeer. These dogs were chosen for demonstrating *no* hunting instincts, since the practice of leaving the dogs untied, especially in the summer, meant that dogs with hunting urges could kill the reindeer. These northern herding dogs were the basis of several breeds later developed in Europe. Some of them have remained pure herders while others were also adapted for sledding.

The Samoyedes and Nentsy, ancient nomadic tribes of northcentral Siberia, have always relied on their dogs. Many of the inland northern nomadic peoples used their dogs for herding reindeer, and the dog of the Samoyedes started out in that role. Never a hunter, he was later adapted for pulling and as a guard and companion. His close association with people, even sharing the *choom*, or portable tent, made him the friendly dog he remains today.

The first European explorers in the area described the longhaired white or black dogs. The adventurer Tooke wrote, in 1779, that the Samoyede people "used their dogs to haul sledges

Samoyed.

738

Samoyeds.

and . . . wore clothes of shaggy dog skins." In his first polar expedition in the 1890s, Fridtjof Nansen used white and black/white Samoyed dogs. Fur traders traveling to Siberia for sable brought the first samples of the breed back to England. Ernest Kilburn-Scott brought one home with him in 1889, and he and his wife became great admirers and breeders of the Samoyed. A Sam named "Etah" led his team on the first trip to the South Pole for Norwegian explorer Roald Amundsen in 1911. The breed was also established early in Australia, being brought there after Scott used them in his second attempt to reach the South Pole.

Only 12 dogs are credited as the foundation of the Samoyed breed today. Most were obtained through explorers and a handful of English breeders who traveled to the region.

The black colors were soon eliminated, and the pure, sparkling white is nearly universal today. The proper outer coat is harsh and straight, never wispy, silky or wavy, and is longer than other Arctic breeds. This hair texture provides the maximum protection from the elements, while demanding minimum care. Even though white, a properly coated Sammy stays very clean looking, with mud simply brushing off as it dries. The correct coat has a glorious silver sheen. His very dense double coat does require regular brushing, especially in the spring and summer. Shedding of the heavy underwool, if not removed from the coat, can cause matting and subsequent skin problems. This hair can be turned to positive purposes and spun into elegant wool.

Because of the centuries of working and living closely with humans, the Samoyed is exceptionally people-oriented. The breed quickly caught on as a beautiful and charming companion dog. He happily tackles any task or game with a carefree air and typically joyous abandon. The Sammy "smile" is a mark of the breed and of his cheerful personality.

During the creation of the six amalgamated laikas of the Soviet Union, the Nenets was the only sledding/herding breed established. The Nenets Herding Laika is probably very similar to the Samoyed the rest of the world knows and loves. It is possible that the Russian breed represents the dog in its native land, where color variation is still allowed. Early imports of the same stem became the Samoyed of today.

The Nenets dog, unlike the hunting laikas who need to be independent thinkers, looks to his master for direction. He is a cheerful, devoted dog willing to work long hours on the tundra, rounding up strays, bringing in weak calves which have fallen behind, or huddling the herd when necessary.

His longer coat, like the Samoyed's, forms a face ruff and thick trousers on the thighs. Not only is this protection in the winter when he works all day and sleeps all night in a snowbank, but it is a barrier to the biting mosquitos and midges of the short Arctic summer.

A variety of colors exists, since this breed has never been selected for color, and pure white dogs often have blue eyes.

Modern Soviet cynologists have encouraged the continued use of these ancient herding dogs and have recently introduced them as herders into reindeer breeding programs in Eastern Siberia and the Kamchatka Peninsula.

Samoyeds.

Samoyed.

SANSHU DOG

COUNTRY: Japan
WEIGHT: 44–55 pounds for large size
HEIGHT: Small size 16–18 inches, large size 20–22 inches
COAT: Short, harsh; stand-off, abundant
COLOR: Red, black/tan, tan, fawn, salt/pepper, or pied
GROUP: Northern

Breeders developed the Sanshu Dog about 1912 on Honshu, Japan's main island where all of the major cities and population centers are located. They started by crossing indigenous middle-sized Japanese dogs with the Chow Chow from China.

The robust Sanshu looks very much like a small Akita (or a large Shiba), but his tail tends to curl more loosely over the back.

He comes in a wide range of attractive colors. Both varieties are popular as companion dogs throughout Japan. Despite this, he has never achieved any official recognition.

Sanshu Dog.

Sarplaninac, tan.

SARPLANINAC

COUNTRY: Yugoslavia
WEIGHT: 55–80 pounds
HEIGHT: 22–24 inches
COAT: Dense, medium length (about 4 inches), rough or smooth
COLOR: Tan, iron gray, white or black
OTHER NAMES: Sar Planina, Illyrian Sheepdog
REGISTRY: FCI
GROUP: Flock Guard

Pronounced "shar-pla-née-natz," the breed name is taken from the mountain range in the south of Yugoslavia which is the dog's home. This geographical area was once known as Illyria, the original name given to the breed. The region is now called Macedonia, but the dogs worked mainly in the mountains and were renamed for the range. One of the oldest breeds in Yugoslavia, the "Sar" is one of only two breeds officially recognized by the Yugoslavian Kennel Club.

These dogs are similar to their probable ancestors, the Greek Sheepdogs and Akbash Dogs

to the east. As various western migrations penetrated southeastern Europe, they were accompanied by their flocks and their guardian dogs. Numerous in its homeland, the Sarplaninac is still part of the great flocks. It is versatile and occasionally works cattle or serves as guard. In fact, a military line of Sars was created in Marshall Josip Tito's kennels.

The Sar holds allegiance to only one master; everyone else is the enemy. They are aggressive in defending their flocks and are dedicated to their charges. A traveler relates: "One of these dogs just jumped off a high embankment on the side of the trail onto my horse's back. I might have been dragged from the saddle, but I beat on his head with my iron handled whip . . . . They are of mastiff size with thicker hair, brown to dun, long fine muzzle and magnificent tail."

The first Sar in America, a pure white bitch, was imported into the USA in 1975. She was brought down from the Yugoslavian mountains by muleback and shipped to California. The Hampshire College Livestock Dog Project brought in several more in 1977. From these beginnings, the Sarplaninac has infiltrated farms

and ranches all over the States and Canada. Sheep and goat raisers are discovering advantages to owning a Sar when the majority of their predator problems disappear.

One six-month-old Sar in a USA flock-guarding program began working with sheep in a barn, and couldn't be coaxed away from "his" barn, even to play. In the spring, however, some sheep were sold, others purchased and the flock was put out to pasture. "Bruno" was the ideal employee, happily adapting to new sheep and new quarters.

The Sarplaninac is one of the few flock guards that comes in solid colors other than white. Although a bit smaller than some of the other related breeds, these dogs have the natural guarding qualities and independent thinking typical of the group. Their temperaments are calm, contrasting sharply to the ferocity that can quickly erupt when the situation warrants. A Missouri sheep rancher and Sar owner summed it up: "Owning a Livestock Guardian Dog can be a rewarding experience if placed in the proper perspective. The use of any of the[se] unique breeds . . . . is not to be taken lightly, it requires work, time and, like anything else on a farm, proper management."

They tolerate family members including children if raised with them, but remain aloof with outsiders. The Sar's protection incorporates all of its territory and living creatures within it.

Above: Sarplaninac.
Left: Sarplaninac puppy with sheep.

Schapendoes.

SCHAPENDOES

COUNTRY: Netherlands
WEIGHT: 33 pounds
HEIGHT: 17½–20 inches
COAT: Long, dense, harsh, with a tendency to wave
COLOR: All colors acceptable, blue gray to black preferred
OTHER NAMES: Dutch Sheepdog
REGISTRY: FCI
GROUP: Herding

The Schapendoes is the shaggy sheep dog of Holland. With the rough, dense, long coat and drop ears, the breed is physically similar to the Beardie, Puli, Nizinny and other European varieties. Root stock is believed to be the same as that of Briard, Bearded Collie and Bergamasco.

Although the Dutch Sheepdogs have been in existence for many centuries, they are not well known. They did not attract the attention of royalty but remained a dog of the common people; therefore they were rarely immortalized in art or literature. More recently, small flocks of sheep in Holland were subsidized by the government as "show" for tourists, presenting a pretty picture of green pastures dotted with white sheep. The native sheep dogs did not reap the same government benefits as their charges. Due to a lack of interest in the native breed and the importation of English Border Collies, the Schapendoes dwindled into small numbers prior to the Second World War.

Dutch inspector and publicist P.M.C. Toepoel discussed the dog's characteristics with others who were interested in the breed and became the driving force behind preserving the Schapendoes. Following his lead, a few enthusiastic Dutch owners became dedicated to resurrecting the breed and, in the 1940s, the first specimens were shown. Their cheerful temperaments, coupled with a rough-and-tumble appeal, stirred in

Schapendoes.

noses and shoulders. They are lively, courageous and intelligent, although a bit high-strung. Daily running expends energy and aids in keeping them fit. Their tireless playfulness makes the Schapendoes an ideal children's companion and, since they are alert without aggression, they also serve as watchdogs. Their herding instincts, like many of their counterparts, are such that they will herd anything—even children, if necessary.

Owners say they are sweet, merry buddies, a "flower for the future." They are meant to look like a shaggy dog, not plush and sleek like a Tibetan Terrier or to be only a decoration. During puppyhood some mats form; a routine brushing schedule removes them.

Schapendoes.

terest in the Schapendoes. Growth in numbers has been tempered with caution by wise breeders. Even large kennels only keep four or five dogs with a few pups, and waiting lists are long. The breed is known in several European countries.

The weather-resistant coats serve them in good stead in inclement weather, although like many modern dogs, they much prefer being indoors with their people to being kept outdoors. Thoroughly brushing the hair to the roots every two weeks is recommended for adults, with puppies requiring a bit more care. The finished product should appear clean, but a bit unkempt. Their feet are lighter in color than the body coat. The tail is all-expressive, carried high (but not curled over the back) when trotting or in his usual gallop; while jumping it serves as a helm. Although slightly elevated at attention, the tail is carried low when at rest.

These sheepdogs are still worked in their native land, firmly nudging the animals with their

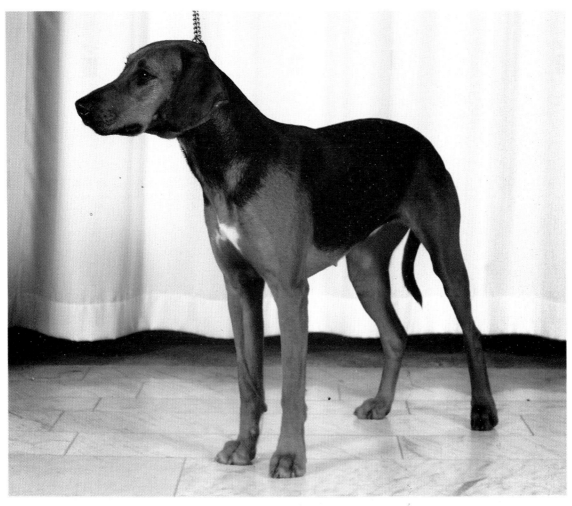

Schillerstövare.

SCHILLERSTÖVARE

COUNTRY: Sweden
WEIGHT: 40–53 pounds
HEIGHT: 19½–24 inches
COAT: Short, but very thick with plenty of undercoat
COLOR: Self-colored tan with a black saddle; no white desired
OTHER NAMES: Schiller Hound
REGISTRY: FCI
GROUP: Hound

The Schillerstövare's ancestors have hunted the Swedish forests since the 1400s. The modern breed evolved through crossing these native dogs with scenting hounds from Germany, Austria and Switzerland.

Per Schiller, the father of the breed, showed two of his dogs at the first Swedish dog show in 1886. These two hounds, "Ralla I" and "Tamburini," became the pillars of the breed. The Swedish registering body did not recognize the breed, however, until 1952.

Of only moderate size, he is strongly boned and sturdily made. He carries no exaggeration in earage, skin or head. His square body contains tremendous power, and he is noted for his speed. The Swedish KC booklet says he is the fastest of all the Scandinavian hounds. He is self-colored tan with the black saddle or mantle and no white.

These dogs are particularly useful in hunting snow hare, as they seem to be immune to the cold suffered during long hunts in deep snows.

Schipperke.

SCHIPPERKE

COUNTRY: Belgium

WEIGHT: 18 pounds maximum

COAT: Abundant, harsh and straight, with ruff, cape, jabot, and culotte, (terms for the stand-off hair on parts of the body, with the ruff describing the neck, the cape for the shoulder, the jabot for the chest, and the culotte for the backs of the rear legs; jabot means a lace frill on the front of a shirt and culottes are trousers that are full in the leg)

COLOR: In USA, solid black only; FCI allows other solid colors such as chocolate, sable or cream, but black preferred

REGISTRY: FCI, AKC, UKC, TKC, CKC

GROUP: Northern

These small watchdogs from the Belgian province of Flanders have been known for many hundreds of years. Although there are those today who say the Schip is a miniature version of the black Belgian Sheepdog, it is more probable that he evolved from northern spitz dogs of early Viking days. Since the shepherd dogs trace their family tree to the same stock, one could still claim an ancient relationship.

The Schipperke's legend tells of a shoemaker who, in 1609, became irritated at the persistent thieving of his neighbor's dog and, after finally catching him at it, cut off his tail. The much improved appearance of the mutilated thief supposedly was copied, starting the trend for docking. In those days, the breed was still called *spits* or *spitske* and was immensely popular among shoemakers and other tradesmen. In the years before 1700, it was the custom of these craftspeople to parade their little black, tailless dogs on alternate Sundays. The dogs wore wide brass collars worked with intricate designs, perhaps done by a metal worker. This may have led to the Sunday dog show custom! At any rate, the Schipperke may be credited with the first specialty (one breed) show, an exhibition put on for them in 1690 by the "Guild Workmen."

It was his common presence on the canal boats of Flanders, however, that earned the breed its modern name of Schipperke, Flemish for little boatman. A barge owner named Reussens promoted the breed in the 19th century, using the dogs as guards on his canal trips between Brussels and Antwerp. The frugal Belgians liked this small guardian who alerted them to trouble, yet ate little and occupied minimum space.

Queen Marie Henriette, wife of Belgian King Leopold II, saw a victorious Schipperke at a show in 1885 and acquired it, thus starting its rise to favor as a fashionable pet.

The Schip remains a welcome house dog today, with a sharp, perky personality and kind nature. The breed displays tendencies of alarm dogs, however, investigating every noise or movement. Schips have even been known to hunt small game with their owners and to be good mousers. Their intelligence and alert, athletic bearing make them potentially good obedience workers.

While the tail is usually entirely removed at birth, a Schipperke who has the tail left intact has a beautiful plume that curves up over its back. Proponents of the natural look feel the tail acts as a barometer of the dog's mood. The breed is a perfect miniature Nordic dog, like a small Buhund or Elkhound. With his standard's requirement for the jabot, culottes, cape and ruff, he's a dandy in full dress on the runway at the dog show. He requires only a minimum of care and generally provides his family with many years of mutual affection.

Schipperke, black.

SCHNAUZER, MINIATURE

COUNTRY: Germany
WEIGHT: 13–15 pounds
HEIGHT: 12–14 inches
COAT: Wiry, rough
COLOR: Salt and pepper, black or black/tan
OTHER NAMES: Zwergschnauzer
REGISTRY: FCI, AKC, UKC, TKC, CKC
GROUP: Terrier

SCHNAUZER, STANDARD

COUNTRY: Germany
WEIGHT: 33 pounds
HEIGHT: 18½–19½ inches
COAT: Wiry and rough
COLOR: Salt/pepper or black
REGISTRY: FCI, AKC, UKC, TKC, CKC
GROUP: Terrier

Schnauze means muzzle in German. Early smooth-coated Standard Pinschers were crossed to obtain a wiry coat. What they were crossed with remains a matter of controversy, with claims being made for black Poodles, gray Wolfspitz, "dog of Bologne," or even shepherd's dogs like the extinct Schafpudel. Possibly they were all used. Whatever the source, the type has been recognized for many centuries. Artist Albrecht Durer owned a Schnauzer-type and painted the dog in several works, including the 1492 watercolor *Madonna with the Many Animals*.

The Standard Schnauzer filled many needs: ratter, drover's dog, stock tender, and guardian in the home and stables. He pulled carts loaded with produce to market and watched the children in his spare time, causing him to be called a *kinderwachter*. In other words, the Schnauzer was an all-around farm dog.

Standard Schnauzer, salt and pepper.

he was first classified as a terrier. He now competes in the Working Group. Today he is a spirited and courageous companion as well as a fine obedience worker.

The Miniature version was created either from the Standard Schnauzer or Min-Pin crossed with Affenpinschers or perhaps both. He debuted in the show ring in 1899 and reached the States around the same time as his larger brother. He is a popular and much-loved companion dog throughout the world. His terrier background makes him alert and spunky, not a mellow lap dog. Today's Miniature Schnauzer temperament has been softened so that he is a delightful and charming companion. He also makes a sparkling obedience competitor.

Schnauzers are lively and demanding of owners' time for game-playing and coat care. Some people elect to have the jacket professionally groomed—leaving *all* their time for games. The broken coat requires periodic stripping or clipping; routine care allows for a smart appearance and a pet that does not smell doggy. The Schnauzer trim leaves an abundant beard, mustache and eyebrows, and furnishings on the legs and feet.

Miniature Schnauzer, salt and pepper.

Originally, wires and smooths sometimes occurred in the same litter and the "pinscher" and "schnauzer" were not considered separate breeds. In 1880 the medium-sized Schnauzer club published its first breed standard. Within ten years, the Pinscher-Schnauzer Club of Germany had separated the two coat varieties. Still called a Wire-haired Pinscher, the winner of the first classes for the breed in 1879 was named "Schnauzer." Possibly this was the source for the breed's name.

The Standard Schnauzer was the earliest of the three varieties. Brought to the USA in 1925,

Miniature Schnauzer.

Miniature Schnauzer, black with white markings.

Miniature Schnauzer.

Standard Schnauzer, puppy.

Standard Schnauzer.

SCOTTISH DEERHOUND

COUNTRY: Great Britain
WEIGHT: 75–110 pounds
HEIGHT: 28–32 inches
COAT: Harsh, wiry, crisp and 3–4 inches long, softer on head, belly and breast; a slightly silky coat is preferable to the highly objectionable woolly coat
COLOR: A variety of dark self colors, as dark blue-gray, dark or lighter grays and brindles, or the yellow, sandy red or red fawn with black mask and ears. A small amount of white on breast and toes allowed, but the less the better.
REGISTRY: FCI, AKC, TKC, CKC
GROUP: Southern

Exactly when the first sighthounds came to the British Islands is lost in the mists of the moors. The Phoenicians sailed as far as Britain ten centuries before Christ and could have brought their famous trade goods. Celts conquered areas of the Middle East and probably acquired dogs of this sort before migrating to the British Isles. Whatever their original source, great running hounds were well known there by the time of the Roman invasions.

In the harsh environment of the Scottish Highlands, the early silken-skinned African Greyhounds (forerunner of the Deerhound) were at a great disadvantage. They were probably crossed with shaggy native breeds to acquire weather protection. Beneath that wiry coat remains an almost classic Greyhound outline. A historical monument, the Hilton of Cadboll stone, eighth century AD, shows two hounds attacking a deer, and early English literature tells of "highland Greyhounds" with long, rough hair.

Under the feudal system of the Middle Ages, the great lords of Scotland had the time and wherewithal to pursue the sport of "deer driving," using packs of these fleet hounds to run down the quarry. The dogs' use and ownership by the highland clan chieftains became so exclusive that, at one time, laws were passed preventing anyone below the rank of earl from owning a Deerhound. This may have been a ploy to insure that there were adequate deer for the noble-bred Scots to hunt! At any rate, it also insured that there were very few of these stately dogs. "A leash of Deerhounds was held the fine whereby a noble lord condemned to death might purchase his reprieve."

By the 18th century, three factors combined to nearly spell the end of this great breed. The invention of firearms made hunting with large packs of running hounds unnecessary, as well as drastically reducing the numbers of the large Scottish stag. The increased use of land for agriculture deprived hunters of the vast unfenced spaces necessary for running down a stag with hounds. Those huge hunts became but a memory. And after 1745, when the Scots lost the Battle of Culloden to the British, the clan system collapsed and disappeared. Thus the dogs lost their purpose as well as their sponsors, and their days in the highlands seemed numbered.

It wasn't until the early 1800s that two brothers, Archibald and Duncan (Lord Colonsay) McNeill, undertook the task of the revival of this great Scottish hound. These gentlemen began a search for good specimens, followed by careful breeding for the lost ideal. Their success is demonstrated by this period being called the "Colonsay revival." As the numbers slowly increased, several prestigious English persons took up the banner of the Deerhound. Queen Victoria, who could—and did—gainsay the popularity of a breed by her interest alone, became a patron. The Deerhound was often painted by the famous dog artist, Landseer, who was so expert at "capturing all the essentials of the breed: gentleness, strength, dignity and courage."

Sir Walter Scott called his Deerhound, "Maida," "the most perfect creature of heaven." After the great hound's death, Scott buried his dog with a monument bearing this inscription:

*Beneath the sculptured form
which late you wore,
Sleep soundly, Maida, at your
Master's door.*

The breed was brought to North America during this Victorian resurrection of the late 1800s. Canada had a total of seven Deerhounds registered during 1888–89. There were nine entered in the first Westminster Kennel Club show of

Scottish Deerhound.

1877, two of which had been bred by Queen Victoria and were offered for sale, carrying the royal price tag of 10,000 pounds sterling each!

Typical of dedicated dog lovers, during the difficult years of the Second World War, Norah Hartley of Peterborough, England, struggled to keep her Deerhounds going. She carefully put aside some food and bred an occasional litter. She told an inspector, "A lot of people are having their dogs destroyed, but I'm not going to have mine destroyed until I must. Put one box of cartridges on the top shelf, and that will be one for each of the Rotherwoods [her kennel name] that remain if the occasion becomes necessary to use them. If I can't feed them, they'll be shot. If I can feed them, then I shall keep them." The box of cartridges remained on the top shelf.

Dedicated promoters of the Deerhound still reside on both sides of the Atlantic, and the breed is in no danger of extinction. Due to the dogs' size, however, the cost of feeding and pro-

viding the necessary space will always keep the breed limited, and they remain near the bottom of AKC registrations—which satisfies their fans just fine. The Deerhound has the gentle, quiet nature of most sighthounds, silently curling up or tiptoeing around the house. Once outside, the urge to run can carry them great distances in a short span of time. Grooming is at a minimum; all that is required is an occasional brushing to remove dead hair. Some modern owners compete in the lure-coursing events to test their hounds' instincts and to give the great beasts a chance to do what their inner natures tell them to do—run full out after an object. At least an hour daily of trotting, alternated with galloping, is necessary to keep the breed in good physical and mental conditioning.

The Deerhound adores his family in a quiet, dignified manner. He is a good pet for those who are willing to fulfill his needs. The breed found fame in the film *Out of Africa* as one of Baroness Karen Blixen's Deerhounds.

Scottish Terrier, black.

SCOTTISH TERRIER

COUNTRY: Great Britain
WEIGHT: 19–23 pounds
HEIGHT: 10–11 inches
COAT: Wiry as bristles
COLOR: Black, brindle, wheaten, grays, or grizzled
REGISTRY: FCI, AKC, TKC, CKC
GROUP: Terrier

The Scottish Terrier seemed to appear from the mists of the moors. Until 1859, no mention of the breed was recorded and, yet, that year Scotties were exhibited as a pure breed. For a time, they were dubbed the Aberdeen, due to the central locus of the breed in that area. It is certain the West Highland White and Scottish Terriers are closely related, the ancestors of both centralizing in the Blackmount region of Perthshire and the Moor of Rannoch. Although the hunters of the era, like the shepherds, were more interested in ability than purity, certain families had a pride in developing and retaining their own pure strain—and this is where the various types blossomed into specific breeds.

Those that favor the "Scottie" prefer to believe that the hairy beast described by Caius was the old version of the Scottish Terrier. Untrimmed, he would, indeed, be covered with hair. Another very old type—perhaps a prototype of the Scottie *and* the Cairn—crossed with a shipwrecked Maltese, created the more glamorous Skye that we now know. Wire-coated terriers could have all come originally from the Far North where their foundation Nordic breeds lived.

In 1881, a standard was drawn and shortly after, a club was organized. One scant year later, the Scottish Terrier landed in Canada, where the breed is now firmly entrenched. The first Scottie registered in the USA was Canadian bred. After the breed's initial introduction, it became a common sight.

True terrier temperament is apparent to the extreme in the Scottie, causing him to be alert, quick and feisty. These qualities make him an ideal watchdog and varmint controller. Unfortunately, this "killer" tendency sometimes extends to the neighbor's cat or an unwary bird. Without proper firmness, he can become a bossy brat and even a biter, but consistent discipline allows his great character and loyalty to shine.

It is startling to some that Scotties are not always black. That image has been perpetuated through Franklin Roosevelt's Scottie, "Fala," as well as the famous Black and White™ Scotch advertising. Early specimens were often red with a black mask, and today a wide variety of colors can and do occur.

The prominent eyebrows and mustaches draw attention to the elongated head and give him a scowling appearance. Stripping takes care of the show dog coat, with pets usually being clipped. Owners should be aware, however, that clipping softens terrier coats and lightens colors, so if they change their minds and decide to show their companion, a lengthy process of coat repair is involved. The Scottish Terrier is a frequent winner in shows throughout the world.

Above: Scottish Terrier, gray. **Below:** Scottish Terrier, wheaten.

Scottish Terrier, black.

Scottish Terrier, wheaten.

Sealyham Terrier.

Sealyham Terrier.

SEALYHAM TERRIER

COUNTRY: Great Britain
WEIGHT: 22–25 pounds
HEIGHT: 10–11 inches
COAT: Wiry outer coat with undercoat
COLOR: White, although lemon, tan or badger markings are allowed on the head and ears
REGISTRY: FCI, AKC, TKC, CKC
GROUP: Terrier

Bred in Wales in the mid-1900s, the Sealyham went after badgers, foxes and other vermin, including polecats. Captain John Owen Tucker Edwardes of Sealyham, Pembrokeshire, determined to produce his idea of a perfect terrier. He wanted a breed that was small enough to go to ground after badgers and be courageous enough to fight otters with the Captain's pack of Otterhounds. He is believed to have begun with the Corgi and incorporated the Dandie for short legs and pluck. The West Highland White Terrier, Bull Terrier, Wire Fox Terrier and the extinct Old English White Terrier are all possible contributors to the type known today. There is also speculation about an infusion of "Flander's Basset," one of the low-stationed hounds of northern France. Edwardes's survival-of-the-fit-test breeding program trained pups on rats, and his tough culling methods selected the "keepers."

Captain Edwardes placed his puppies with his tenant farmers to work rats and other vermin in the barnyards while the pups matured. When he went around later to visit the pups, he was accompanied by a pair of his most belligerent adult terriers and a shotgun. He expected the youngster on the farm to firmly stand his ground when approached by the aggressive older dogs. If they gave an inch (backed up or turned), a shot ended the cowardice.

Those that passed this test faced a second one at a year of age. A live polecat (skunk) was hidden in a burrow after being dragged in a sack for some distance. The prospective yearlings were placed at the start of the drag. Spiritedly, they had to follow the scent trail to the burrow opening, enter without any hesitancy and dispatch the dangerous and furious animal. The Captain waited by the entrance with his trusty shotgun for the faint of heart or those with second thoughts. Others with slow reflexes or a lack of strength were also culled—by the polecat. Obviously, the Edwardes strain became extremely game and aggressive.

Since this was the breed of only one man, it was fortunate that, after Edwardes's death in 1891, other people took up the cause of the Sealyham. One of these was Fred Lewis, whose tireless work in promoting the Sealyham and sponsoring an organization gained him the label of father of the breed, although there is no doubt the actual "father" was Edwardes. The British canine authority recognized the Sealyham in 1911, the same year the USA recognized the breed.

Independent and long-living pets, Sealyhams need frequent brushing and occasional trimming and plucking. Even more grooming is necessary for the show dog. The breed has rather low-set, drop ears and a docked tail. Despite their past history of toughness, the modern breed has mellowed considerably. He is still game and self-assured, but certainly more peaceful. Firm, fair discipline is the best way to approach training.

Sealyham Terrier.

Segugio Italiano a Pelo Raso, fawn.

SEGUGIOS ITALIANOS
Segugio Italiano a Pelo Forte

COUNTRY: Italy
WEIGHT: 40–62 pounds
HEIGHT: 20½–23 inches
COAT: Hard, wiry and dense; lying close to the body, without bushy brows and very little beard; hair never to exceed 2 inches
COLOR: Black/tan or fawn (from deep red to very pale wheaten); any white is to be discouraged
OTHER NAMES: Roughhaired Italian Hound
REGISTRY: FCI
GROUP: Hound

Segugio Italiano a Pelo Raso

COUNTRY: Italy
WEIGHT: 40–62 pounds
HEIGHT: 20½–23 inches
COAT: Very short, thick and shiny
COLOR: Black/tan or fawn (from deep red to very pale wheaten); any white is to be discouraged
OTHER NAMES: Shorthaired Italian Hound
REGISTRY: FCI
GROUP: Hound

The Italian hound is a distinct type, as an intermediate between sighthound and scenthounds. He probably originated from crossing early Celtic hounds in southern Gaul with sighthounds of the Phoenicians. Two ancient statues, *Diana The Huntress* in the Naples Museum and *Diana With Bow and Arrow* at the Vatican Museum, display dogs of the classic Segugio type.

The Segugio's appearance and abilities were improved and fixed during the Renaissance, when the breed was in demand by all classes of society for hunting. At the Segugio's apex, the pomp and circumstance of the Italian nobility's hunts included participants with finely appointed horses, as well as trumpeters and beaters in full livery, with hundreds of these hounds.

As the grand hunts ended, the breed fell into a period of neglect for several hundred years, with much crossbreeding done by those "just wanting a good rabbit dog." Fortunately, the 20th century brought a renewed interest in fostering this unique Italian breed. The Segugio is now one of the most numerous dogs in Italy and, under the guidance of the Societa Italiana Pro Segugio, quality continues to improve.

The Segugio is a large but refined dog of moderately light bone and a racy body with "no fat." The muzzle is long, tapering and slightly convex with very little stop and no excessive skin. The unique and characteristic ear is very long, narrow, low-set and folded toward the tip. No surplus skin appears anywhere on the body. The tail is carried like a saber, high in a sickle curve.

Fanciers in Italy are divided equally among those preferring the wire coat and those with smooth-haired stock. The smooth coat is described as being "like glass."

Temperaments are mild but vivacious. These are sociable dogs, as are most hounds, and they are ardent in the hunt. Today the Segugio hunts rabbit, hare and wild boar, and expertly handles these chores in both flat, open country and in mountainous areas with heavy cover. Especially noted for their endurance and "steel legs," these dogs often hunt a full 12-hour day without a rest, willing and able to repeat the performance the next day—and the day after that! A pleasing harmonious bark rounds out the hunting attributes. Although a streak of stubbornness may surface, this can be eliminated by initiating training as a young pup.

Segugio Italiano a Pelo Forte, fawn.

Above: Segugio Italiano a Pelo Raso, fawn. **Below:** Segugio Italiano a Pelo Forte, black/tan.

Shar-Pei, fawn.

SHAR-PEI

COUNTRY: China
WEIGHT: 45–55 pounds
HEIGHT: 18–20 inches
COAT: Short, bristly, stand-off outer coat; very short, called *horse* coat; slightly longer, called *brush* coat; no undercoat
COLOR: Fawn, cream, red, black or chocolate
OTHER NAMES: Chinese Fighting Dog
REGISTRY: FCI, AKC, UKC, TKC
GROUP: Northern

Although the breed gained recognition as a fighting breed with obvious mastiff characteristics, the Shar-Pei also attributes its background to the Nordic genes and perhaps others. Chow-type dogs may have been crossed with Western mastiffs brought in on the early trade routes. The pariah may have even added a drop or two of its blood.

Whatever his background, the Shar-Pei has existed for centuries in the southern provinces near the South China Sea, with Dah Let, Kwan-tung Province given as its source. The breed aided the peasants through hunting, herding and protection—and provided them entertainment through dog fighting.

The loose skin enabled the dog to turn on its opponent even when grasped firmly in his enemy's teeth. He was said to be capable of turning around in his own skin. The tiny ears and deep-set eyes were other qualities much desired to prevent injury. His short, bristly coat was distasteful in an opponent's mouth.

While the Chow Chow was gaining popularity abroad, the Shar-Pei breed was being decimated at home in China. They finally disappeared in mainland China, and only a few remained in Hong Kong. It was during that time a clever owner, Matgo Law, became concerned that his beloved breed might disappear entirely. He wrote to an all-breed dog magazine, beseeching Americans to become involved with the plight of the Shar-Pei. His impassioned plea and the accompanying photos brought immediate response from the Western Hemisphere.

Shar-Pei, brown.

Shar-Pei, fawn.

When a few specimens were brought to the United States in the 1970s, they were considered the rarest dog in the world. Their unusual features swiftly made them the darling of the talk shows which, in turn, ignited the excitement among those people craving the unique and eclectic. Shar-Pei numbers are increasing rapidly and they have been accepted for registration with the UKC and the AKC's Miscellaneous Class.

Except for even more skin, the very tiny drop ear (like no other breed of dog), and the thicker padding of the muzzle, they are much like a very smooth-haired Chow. They also have the black mouth pigment and tongue, making the relationship obvious. The tail may be carried in a tight curl, loose curl or arched.

Breeders describe the head as being "reminiscent of a hippopotamus," with a broad muzzle padded with flesh and described as a meat-mouth. The horse coat is preferred over the slightly longer brush coat, solid colors chosen over "flowered" (spotted) and solid black tongues chosen over flowered ones.

All pups are cute and tempting, but there is perhaps none more fascinating than a baby Shar-Pei clad in skin many sizes too large for him and definitely not permanent-pressed. Prospective

Shar-Peis.

Shar-Pei, cream.

buyers must be aware of the breed's idiosyncracies and be prepared to deal with them. The skin requires as much attention as a heavy-coated dog, since the wrinkles make them prone to skin disease. Eye problems can also result, and some breeders have the abundant eye skin "tacked" by the veterinarian at three or four weeks until about 8–10 weeks of age. Adults grow into their over-sized coat and wrinkles often appear only on the face and shoulders when mature.

Their mastiff heritage contributed dominant temperaments, and they may pick fights among their housemates. Their strong personalities require firm training and socialization. They want to be with their people, and their early house-breaking habits assure acceptance in the home. A kennel existence is torture for them.

Shetland Sheepdog, sable.

SHETLAND SHEEPDOG

COUNTRY: Great Britain
HEIGHT: 13–16 inches
COAT: Long, dense, harsh with abundant undercoat
COLOR: Black, blue merle or sable, marked with varying amounts of white (in Irish pattern) and/or tan
REGISTRY: FCI, AKC, UKC, TKC, CKC
GROUP: Herding

During the 1700s fishing boats arrived regularly on the Shetland Islands, bringing black and tan King Charles Spaniels, "Yakki" dogs from Greenland and spitz-type herding dogs from the Scandinavian countries. These dogs were allowed to "stretch their legs" during their onshore leave, and often left little remembrances of their visit on the islands. The Shetland Sheepdog is obviously related to the other collies, either directly or through a common ancestor. The progeny of these "sailors" and the native island dogs proved to be alert, eager working stock and came to be known as *Toonie* dogs, for the *toon* or town (or from *tun*, Norwegian for farm). Obviously, they were good workers in town or on the farm.

The Shetland Islands are bare and rugged. The terrain furnishes inhospitable territory for raising stock, but its natives were rugged, too, and developed animals that didn't need lush flora to survive. Their miniature cattle, dwarf sheep and tiny Shetland ponies were herded by correspondingly small sheep dogs. The small farms were known as crofts, and the crofters thought highly of their gentle little herding dogs. The Shelties' gait carried them lightly over rough terrain, and their easygoing manner made them gentle with stock.

Early literature refers to the dogs as "nondescript." Eventually a Shetlander named Loggie standardized type for the show ring, and the breed was entered in Crufts in 1906, where they were shown with the Collies, as miniatures. After the destructive years of WWI, a fancier introduced a Collie into the surviving lines, and created the type known at this time.

Quick workers, Shelties are highly intelligent and willing to please, making them one of the outstanding obedience breeds in the ring today. These "apartment-size" collies make ideal pets—they are amiable, healthy, docile and great with children. As with the other collies, a regular grooming schedule keeps their plush coats looking attractive.

The Sheltie standard is precise in height and marking requirements. Due to the relatively recent cross with the Rough Collie, a tendency exists for some specimens to be larger than desired. Puppies termed as "mismarks" and youngsters that go over-size, however, still make delightful companions.

Above: Shetland Sheepdog, blue merle. **Below:** Shetland Sheepdog, sable.

Above and Below: Shetland Sheepdog, sable.

Shetland Sheepdog, sable.

SHIBA INU

COUNTRY: Japan
WEIGHT: 20–30 pounds
HEIGHT: 13½–15½ inches
COAT: Fairly short, harsh, plush, straight, stand-off, double
COLOR: In order of Japanese preference—deep red, red sesame (red and black hairs with the red predominating), black/tan, black sesame (same as red sesame, except here the black hairs predominate), white, lighter red. American standard has no order of preference and also includes brindles and white markings.
REGISTRY: FCI
GROUP: Northern

In Japan, a small package filled with a keen disposition and talent is generally compared to the Japanese pepper. This term fits the Shiba dog, spicy though small. His name literally means small dog. The Shiba should look like a small version of the Akita.

Wending its way through the southern regions, perhaps over land bridges from Korea and China, Shibas originated in the mountainous landlocked areas of Japan, where the type has been known for nearly 3,000 years. The Shiba is a result of interbreeding ancient types: the Sanin, the Mino and the Shinshu.

Shibas were used as hunters of ground birds and small game. The little dog occasionally assisted the hunter for boar, bear and deer, as well. Originally, more than one type were bred in different areas. Modern breeders have combined the various types, selecting from among them for the desired qualities of small size, curled tail, triangular-set "Oriental" eyes, deep red color, and warmth and affection for the master.

Because of its native ability and environment, the modern Shiba enjoys the out-of-doors and cold weather. In fact, some Japanese owners put their dogs on ice and blow fans on them to grow lush coats!

Agile and quick, they delight in a good run with owners. A warning to use a leash accompa-

Shiba Inu bitch owned by Andrew De Prisco and Rick Tomita.

nies this suggestion, for it is said, "you can never outrun a Shiba." They are catlike in their cleanliness and have the northern dog tendency of aloofness to strangers and an independent nature, being natural guardians. Although affectionate to their family, they are sometimes scrappy with other dogs.

Owners describe their cunning intelligence, saying that they could charm a stone! Breeders warn they are not a dog for everyone, even though many who see one find it appealing. Prospective owners must understand the spitz-type personality and be prepared to deal with it before they will truly enjoy owning one. They are perky and sturdy for their size, making them ideal children's playmates. If there are no children around, nor adults available, a Shiba is perfectly able to entertain himself for long periods. They are loving and ready for fun, but are not always underfoot when their people are busy. An owner says, they "love to live and live to love."

The Shiba has been the most popular dog in Japan for a number of years, where his size is welcome in a small country with a high population. The Shiba is making headway in the USA, with at least two organizations promoting and registering the breed, and the breed has a good number of enthusiasts in other countries.

Above: Shiba Inu. **Below:** Shiba Inu with three Japanese girls in traditional dress.

Shih Tzu.

SHIH TZU

COUNTRY: Tibet (China)
WEIGHT: 9–16 pounds ideal, 19 pounds maximum
HEIGHT: 8–11 inches
COAT: Long and dense; appearing harsher than it feels
COLOR: All colors allowed, but white blaze and tail tip are highly prized
OTHER NAMES: Chrysanthemum Dog
REGISTRY: FCI, AKC, UKC, TKC, CKC
GROUP: Herding

Although the Shih Tzu's roots are in Tibet, his perfection occurred in China. If the Lhasa is a mildly dwarfed Tibetan Terrier, the Shih Tzu is a slightly more exaggerated dwarf form of these breeds. The Chinese prized the smaller individuals from the Lhasas sent to China and pre-

ferred the very shortened face. Although some writers feel crossing to the Pekingese occurred, simple selection for the most dwarfed forms of the Lhasas could easily have created this charmer.

To further link the two breeds, the Chinese call their version *Shih Tzu*, which means lion dog, the same label that the Lhasa dog bears in Tibet. The scenario can easily be imagined: Tibetans sent pairs of charming smallish lion dogs to the imperial court of China. The Chinese also called them lion dogs (in Chinese, of course). Over the centuries the smaller, shorter legged and shorter faced specimens were selected or crossed with native toy breeds, and the result evolved into our modern Shih Tzu.

The dogs lived lives of luxury in the palaces of China, and were bred as loving companions. After China became a republic in 1912, occasional specimens made their way into Britain. Fortunately, enough were brought to England and Norway, and later North America, to begin good breeding programs prior to the Communist takeover when dogs were virtually eliminated in China.

The British awarded championship status to the breed in 1949 but it was not recognized in North America until the 1960s. When allowed to be shown in America in 1969, one of the specimens exhibited went all the way to Best in Show the first time he was shown. The breed is well known for its marvelous movement, with tremendous reach and drive pushing that little body smoothly ahead like a locomotive. Shih Tzus have enjoyed tremendous success in show rings all over the world. In Canada, where their standard allows for a slightly larger specimen, they are a part of the Non-Sporting Group. The

Shih Tzu.

Shih Tzu.

Shih Tzu is shown in the Toy Group in the United States.

The Shih Tzu is also being "discovered" as a fine companion dog. Less suspicious of strangers than his erstwhile cousin, the Lhasa, he is vivacious and athletic for his small size, and very people-oriented. Full of confidence and self-importance, his arrogant carriage is described in the standard. His beautiful, flowing coat does require a fair amount of grooming to look its best. It is the hair that grows upward from the short nose that gives the Shih Tzu the "chrysanthemum" look described by the Orientals. In fact, the original standard issued by the Peking Kennel Club may have been the most descriptive in dogdom. Included in the requirements were a "lion head, bear torso, camel hoof, feather-duster tail, palm-leaf ear, rice teeth, pearly petal tongue and movement like a goldfish." Shih Tzus consider themselves extremely dignified, yet can be charming clowns.

Shih Tzu.

Shih Tzu.

SHIKA INUS

Kishu

COUNTRY: Japan
HEIGHT: 17–22 inches
COAT: Short, coarse and straight, soft, dense undercoat, fringe on cheeks and tail
COLOR: White most common, but can be red, sesame or brindle
REGISTRY: FCI
GROUP: Northern

Kai Dog

COUNTRY: Japan
HEIGHT: 18–22½ inches
COAT: Short, straight and coarse with soft, dense undercoat, hair longer on the tail
COLOR: Black brindle, red brindle or brindle
OTHER NAMES: Tora (Tiger) Dog
REGISTRY: FCI
GROUP: Northern

Kishu, white.

Kai Dog, brindle.

Shikoku

COUNTRY: Japan
HEIGHT: 17½–22 inches
COAT: Short, harsh and straight with soft, dense undercoat
COLOR: Brindle or red
REGISTRY: FCI
GROUP: Northern

The Kishu, Kai Dog and Shikoku fall into the category of Shika Inu, or medium-sized Japanese dogs. They are very similar with overlapping colors and have only small differences in size and other fine points. Originally, these were all dogs that assisted the *matagi*, the professional hunters, with wild boar or deer. Known for their bravery, it is said that the Shika dog "will

Shikoku.

not concede a step before danger."

Although mainly working dogs, they all have been more or less adapted as companions and guardians since the matagi profession has nearly disappeared.

The Kishu is the matagi's dog from the mountainous regions of Wakayama and Mie prefectures and has been known since before the Christian era. Although previously used for deer, it was best known for boar hunting. The hunter's weapon was the firelock, which could be fired only once before reloading. If a wild boar was wounded, it could fatally charge the hunter, and the dog was expected to courageously run interference until the hunter could reload. It is not difficult to discern why the breed was noted for its "scarred glory."

These dogs are clean, silent and docile. Although they are useful in herding, as watchdog, fishermen's helpers, or hunters' aides, many are also kept in the home. The Kishu is distinguished from the Ainu Dog because he is a bit longer in body proportions and, although cautious, is more benign of temperament. The white coat tends to disappear in the snow, but has the advantage of being easily distinguished from his dark-colored prey.

Used more for deer, the Shikoku and the Kai are other varieties of the Shika (mid-sized) dogs. As former hunting dogs of the matagi, they were often referred to as "deerhounds." Coming from the mountains around Fuji and the southern Alps region of Yamanishi prefecture, the Kai was considered too rough to make a good house pet, being close to the wild in temperament. Modern dogs are milder and some are now seen in homes. He is, however, loyal to his master and a fine hunter. The Japanese say he is a one-man dog with people. Hunted in packs, he is companionable with other dogs. Brindling may not be apparent until after six months of age.

The Shikoku is the final variety of Shika dogs, and is similar to the other two. His home is Shikoku Island, across the inland sea from Osaka, where he was also used for hunting. This smallest of the middle-sized dogs comes only in solid reds and brindle color. None of the Shika dogs are known outside Japan.

Siberian Husky, gray.

SIBERIAN HUSKY

COUNTRY: USA
WEIGHT: 45–60 pounds
HEIGHT: 21–23½ inches
COAT: Thick, peltlike, stand-off; dense undercoat
COLOR: Any color acceptable, grays, blacks, reds, and even pied are common, usually with light shading around the head and underside
OTHER NAMES: Arctic Husky
REGISTRY: FCI, AKC, TKC, CKC, UKC
GROUP: Northern

A variety of primitive paleo-Asiatic tribes have been present in Siberia for half-a-million years, during the time when the vast North was a warmer and more hospitable hunting ground. These tribes continued to live much as they had during the Stone Age. Each group relied on dogs as helpers, and each developed a specific

Siberian Husky, black.

type, based upon such factors as hunting requirements and snow cover, terrain and temperature.

The Chukchi tribe, often referred to as the "Dog Breeding" Chukchi, was based along the coasts of the Arctic and Pacific Oceans on the peninsula that reaches out from Siberia toward Alaska. When a harsh cold settled into the area about 3,000 years ago, the Chukchi people adapted by creating a culture based on the long-distance sled dog. The tribe lived in permanent inland settlements and had to go long distances to hunt the sea mammals which fed both people and dogs. A small sledding dog was ideal, one that could exist on very little food. Neither sprinters nor freighters, these dogs were endurance animals and could pull light loads of killed game at moderate speeds over incredible distances. When a Chukchi needed to haul something heavier, he merely borrowed extra dogs from friends and harnessed up 16 or 18 instead of the usual six-to-eight hitch.

All males except the finest lead dogs were castrated after a year in harness, not only to control the breeding urges but to help maintain fat on their bodies. By keeping all but the unneutered lead dogs tied during the winter when the bitches came in heat, a workable system of line-breeding was established. Because the Chukchi women did most of the dog care and selection, these dogs were used to children and were accustomed to being a part of the family.

Siberian Chukchis were brought into Alaska in the early 1900s, and quickly gained a reputation for sledding. The Chukchi dog in pure form, or crossed with other native sledding breeds, became universal, especially in chores where speed with endurance was of utmost importance, such as mail delivery and long-distance sled dog racing. He was, at that time, still called Chukchi or "husky," a generic term for a sled-pulling dog.

Siberian Husky.

As the breed gained a foothold with American dog fanciers, the name Chukchi was replaced by the more general term Siberian Husky, and that became his official name. Thanks to the Chukchi selection for good temperament, he is people-oriented and a popular companion dog—thus not a very good guard dog. Nevertheless, he is a working dog and, if not given adequate attention, exercise, training and discipline, can be stubborn and easily bored. The Siberian Husky is still the most popular breed for modern "mushers" or owners who want to try him with a sled, since the breed happily ignores frigid temperatures and deep snows. He has tiny, high-set erect ears and a plush coat. Because of their long association with people, they still maintain the fastidious cleanliness which was always demanded of them. The United Kennel Club recognizes the breed as the Arctic Husky.

Siberian Husky.

Siberian Husky, copper.

SIBERIAN LAIKAS

West Siberian Laika

COUNTRY: USSR
WEIGHT: 40–50 pounds
HEIGHT: 21–24 inches
COAT: Short, stand-off
COLOR: Solid or piebald in white, gray, tan, red or black
REGISTRY: FCI
GROUP: Northern

East Siberian Laika

COUNTRY: USSR
WEIGHT: 40–50 pounds
HEIGHT: 22–25 inches
COAT: Short, stand-off
COLOR: Usually black or black piebald; tan or white allowed
REGISTRY: FCI
GROUP: Northern

These are the other two breeds (in addition to the Karelo-Finnish and the Russo-European Laikas) established by the Russian council in 1947 as hunting/sledding laikas. They are combinations of types from various native tribes throughout Siberia.

The West Siberian Laika is the most numerous of the two, in fact, outnumbering all hunting dogs registered in the USSR, except the Russian Hound. They are bred by Khantu and Mansi hunters throughout the giant upper Irtysh River basin in the eastern slopes of the Ural Mountains. These vast forest areas are hunted for their valuable fur animals: mink, sable, marten, squirrel, otter and even bear. As the local hunters say, "Without a dog, there is no hunter!" The most valuable of the dogs hunt sable (in winter called ermine), the prize termed the "white gold."

This takes tremendous speed and endurance over snow or in forests littered with fallen trees. The praiseworthy dog must take one stride for

West Siberian Laika, tan.

East Siberian Laika, piebald.

each four or five bounds of the sable, continuing for long hours. Thus, these Laikas are selected for size and power with emphasis on being tall and a bit light to work in deep snow. Even the most accomplished workers "earn retirement after eight years of hunting," so demanding is their chore. Temperaments are calm and even.

The last 25 years have seen tremendous progress in the number of uniform specimens, as well as in the high level of quality work of the West Siberian.

The East Siberian Laika, on the other hand, is still considered more of a conglomerate with only a temporary standard in existence. Many laikas are used in Eastern Siberia, but the vast territory has created a large variety of types and strains, each with slightly different appearance and style of hunting. These dogs are generally larger and tougher than the Western Laikas.

Large scale breeding programs for the Eastern form began in the 1980s, and Soviet breeders hope to consolidate type and improve the skill level of this breed in the future. Although the overwhelming majority are hunting dogs, some of these are seen in the cities as companions.

Above: West Siberian Laika. **Below:** East Siberian Laika.

Silky Terrier.

SILKY TERRIER

COUNTRY: Australia
WEIGHT: 8–10 pounds
HEIGHT: 9 inches
COAT: 5–6 inches, flat, fine, glossy and silky
COLOR: Blue/tan
OTHER NAMES: Australian Silky Terrier, Sydney Silky, Silky Toy Terrier
REGISTRY: FCI, AKC, TKC, CKC
GROUP: Terrier

The histories of the two native Australian terriers are tied inextricably—one to the other. Both the Australian Terrier and the Silky Terrier were developed in the 19th century by Australians using various British terrier breeds. Records show that blue and tan broken-coated terriers of about ten pounds were renowned watchdogs around Tasmania, even in the early 1800s. Other terriers of that era in Australia were sandy colored.

Sometime in the 1820s, one of those early small-sized blue/tan bitches was taken to England and bred to a Dandie Dinmont. The result-

Silky Terrier.

ing progeny eventually returned to Australia and became the foundation for the Silky Terrier. The Dandie imparted the silkier coat and back length, as well as the tendency to an arched back and high rear still seen in modern specimens. Not all of the credit for silky coat belongs to the Dandie, however, since Skyes, used in the make-up of the Aussie, sometimes produce a faulty predisposition to silky coats. Selection for the Skye's faulty trait contributed to the desirable coat of the Silky. Additional backcrosses to Yorkshire Terriers may have fixed the small size and blue color.

MacArthur Little was an early prominent breeder of these "silkys," and when he migrated to Sydney with his kennel, the name of Sydney Silky Terrier was adopted. Because the "Silky" was not accepted as an official name until 1955, the term Sydney Silky is heard still.

The Silky standard was accepted in 1906 in New South Wales, and another—different—standard was drawn in Victoria. It wasn't until 1959 that all discrepancies were smoothed out, and AKC recognized the Silky shortly after the revised standard was approved. Although officially the Silky Terrier in the USA, he is called Australian Silky Terrier in his native Australia and Silky Toy Terrier in Canada.

The Silky was developed as a pet and house dog and needs only regular brushing to keep his coat in good condition. The Silky's coat is long and soft, but is never intended to cascade clear to the floor like that of the Yorkie's. It must stop at about knee level, leaving feet and pasterns exposed.

Modern dogs all have the erect ear, although for many years both prick and drop ears were allowed. This was probably another throwback to the Skye, which has both ear carriages. The Silky, like his cousin the Australian Terrier, has his gaily carried tail docked short. Although the Aussie is still classified by AKC as a Terrier, the Silky is in the Toy Group. Despite his diminutive size, he is still capable of killing rodents and snakes and shrilly announcing the presence of intruders.

Australian judge, Frank Longmore, describes the Silky, as "The little dog that fits into our hearts and homes, no matter how large the former nor how small the latter . . . ."

SKYE TERRIER

COUNTRY: Great Britain
WEIGHT: 25 pounds
HEIGHT: 9½–10 inches
COAT: Hard, but long (5½ inches) and straight
COLOR: Solid black, grays (from platinum to dark blue), fawn or cream
REGISTRY: FCI, AKC, TKC, CKC
GROUP: Terrier

One historian says the Skye hailed from the Isle of Skye more than 400 years ago, and was described by Caius nearly in its present form, ". . . brought out of barbarous borders fro' the uttermost countryes northward . . . which, by reason of the length of heare, makes showe neither of face nor of body." Another theory suggests that shipwrecked Maltese types from the ill-fated Spanish Armada mated with local terriers (probably Cairns or Cairn prototypes) to create the breed in the 1600s. Certainly, other breeds added their influence to create the extreme ratio of length to height. Once called the Terrier of the Western Islands, he evolved to his present form isolated on the rocky Isle of Skye.

Whatever his history, he is a distinctive terrier. His silken beauty has given him the nickname of the "heavenly breed." Queen Victoria added the Skye to her kennel, and its reputation was established. The coat was silky on the original working dog, although not as long.

The Skye has not changed much over the years, and has not followed the whims of fashion. The motto of the Skye Club of Scotland is: *Wha daur meddle wi' me*. This could refer to the fact that the tough terrier dares anyone to challenge him, but it could also be a warning to future owners and breeders not to meddle with a good thing! The only variable has been the ears. Prior to 1890, most Skyes had drop ears, but the prick ear became more prevalent. Although either type is allowed, the pendant ear is rarely seen today.

Around 1858, an Edinburgh shepherd died without family or friend—other than a little Skye Terrier named "Bobby." The little gray dog took up vigil on the shepherd's grave in Greyfriars' churchyard. Although he was coaxed from the graveyard time after time and offered the comforts of a home, he preferred to stay

Skye Terrier, gray.

SLOUGHI

Skye Terrier.

with his master. Finally, Bobby was given a permanent license and allowed to stay in the graveyard. Fed by the townspeople, he continued his vigil until his death, ten years after his owner's. A monument was later erected at the cemetery gate, paying tribute to his loyalty and steadfastness.

Still loyal and predictable in demeanor, Skyes are gentle and tuned into their owners, but reserved with others. They often loathe being touched by strangers, especially without a proper introduction, and their terrier nature may make them answer a casual pat with a bite. Pluses for the breed are its longevity and contentment with only small amounts of exercise.

The Skye has a longer, stronger muzzle than the Cairn and larger ears. He carries his tail low, which is an oddity among terriers. The long coat parts down the back and hangs, spilling over the ears and face, necessitating regular brushing.

SLOUGHI

COUNTRY: Morocco
WEIGHT: 45–60 pounds
HEIGHT: 24–28½ inches
COAT: Short, fine and dense
COLOR: Sand, sable, red sable, charcoal sable, brindle; with or without black mask and/or black manteau (saddle or black tipped hairs on back)
OTHER NAMES: Slougui, Arabian Greyhound
REGISTRY: FCI, TKC
GROUP: Southern

While several of the gazehounds claim the distinction of being the world's oldest breed, the point may be moot. "Breeds" as such did not exist in those ancient times, and types tended to mold and change over the years and with transitions to other environments. The Sloughi, however, is certainly one of the oldest types, and is still being used in the same area in which he began. The breed is found throughout the Sahara in what are now portions of Morocco, Tunisia, Algeria and Libya. Due to its modern presence and promotion there, the breed was declared by the FCI to be of Moroccan origin, although it is still often called the Arabian Greyhound.

There are rock engravings of dogs manifesting the Sloughi/gazehound type found in North Africa that date back to the Neolithic Period (8000–6000 BC). The old Berber culture of the Sahara worked hounds of this type. As civilizations arose, these dogs were in demand by the wealthy for organized hunting. Supposedly the Sloughi was Tutankhamen's favorite dog and many were depicted in paintings and artifacts found in his tomb. Hannibal was accompanied by Berber cavalry when he crossed the Alps and, since these horsemen were never without their hunting dogs, Sloughis (as well as the previously mentioned Ibizans) may well have been introduced to southern Europe at that time. Crossed with native scenthounds, these dogs would account for some of the sighthound characteristics seen in the hounds of Italy.

But their main role was as dogs of the desert tribes. They have lived for literally thousands of years with their nomadic masters, chasing down desert game and guarding the encampments.

Their long webbed toes enabled them to grip the hot desert sands while running.

The Moslem culture generally denigrated the dog as "unclean," especially the detested pariah dog. One of the greatest fears for people of these areas was the fate of non-burial after death, with their bodies being eaten by the scavenging pariahs. But the gazehounds had become an exception to the hatred of dogs. These sighthounds were highly valued and shared their masters' tents.

Such was the bond between Sloughi and nomad that these beloved dogs are, even to the present time, treated like members of the family—at least male members of the family! The birth of a Sloughi litter is cause for celebration among friends, treated with the same joy as the birth of a son. Sugar or a lamb, the traditional funeral offerings, are brought as solace when a Sloughi dies. Photo albums are kept of the dogs and their ancestors and shown to friends. One modern enthusiast describes the usual scene of a Sloughi and his master comfortably relaxing in the living room, while the wife and daughters are stuck working in the kitchen!

In the mountains, the brindle color camouflaged the Sloughi; in the desert, the coloring was like that of sand. Saluki and Sloughi enthusiasts debate whether or not they are the same breed. Saluki owners dismiss the Sloughi as a smooth-coated member of their breed, while Sloughi fanciers insist their dogs have distinct differences. The Sloughi is larger and heavier boned.

Sloughis are quiet, sensitive dogs that bond strongly and early with their masters. This trait makes it very difficult for them to change homes as adults. Their gentle manners and fastidiousness make them welcome in the home, which is where they must be to satisfy their great need for human companionship. They do need adequate outlets for their energy, and a place for regular gallops or long walks is necessary. Digging can be a problem, as they once dug holes to the cooler sand for relief from the heat.

In their homeland, their qualities are not al-

Sloughis with owners at meeting of Club for Native Moroccan Breeds.

ways looked upon by the townspeople with the same fatherly affection as by the nomads. Because of their instinct to chase, they are considered a predator, and hunting with Sloughis is now regulated in most areas. The modern world contains small pet cats and dogs and fenced livestock that the Sloughi may view as rabbits or gazelles. Therefore, care and control must always be used. It stands to reason that chase games are favorites when two or more can join the fun.

The breed is not numerous, but enthusiasts in both Morocco and abroad are keeping the Sloughi from slipping away to extinction. The CRCN (Club for National Dog Breeds) in his homeland has published a standard, holds exhibitions, and in other ways promotes this old, native breed. The Sloughi has found enthusiasts in several European countries and Great Britain, with a few appearing in the USA as well. Sloughis may be seen competing in Continental dog shows.

Slovak Cuvacs.

Sloughi, sand.

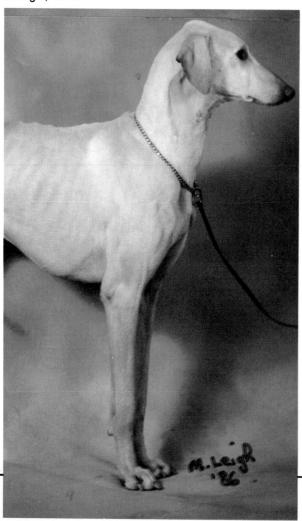

SLOVAK CUVAC

COUNTRY: Czechoslovakia
WEIGHT: 85–105 pounds
HEIGHT: 25–28 inches
COAT: Medium length; thick and wavy
COLOR: White
OTHER NAMES: Slovensky Tchouvatch, Liptok
REGISTRY: FCI
GROUP: Flock Guard

The Carpathian mountain chain originates in Rumania and skirts Hungary, filling much of eastern Czechoslovakia as it pushes north, ending in the Liptok Mountains of the High Tatra range in the southeastern corner of Poland. The great white guardian prototype followed the mountains northward. The Czechoslovakian flock guard could easily pass for a Kuvasz, a Rumanian Sheepdog or a Podhalanski. Their histories are undoubtably similar. The breed name is spelled *Cuvac* in Czechoslovakian, but the English and German spelling, *Tchouvatch*, reflects the pronunciation (chew-votch).

The breed has been well documented as far back as the 17th century. But as the wolves slowly disappeared from the European mountains and modern herding practices were instituted, the Cuvac also began to be a relic from the past. What few specimens were left in the 1950s were bred carelessly. Credit for reviving the breed and fixing characteristics is due Dr. Antonin Hruza, in cooperation with the Veterinary School of Brno. A written standard was established and approved in 1964.

Currently, a few breeders of the Cuvac are scattered throughout Czechoslovakia and other European countries, as well as the USA. The Cuvac is still quite rare, but at least fanciers are working to save the breed. An owner in Germany describes her dogs' marvelous temperaments with children. Yet she warns about the Cuvac's stubborn, independent nature which must be overcome with proper training. Once they have learned something, she says, they never forget it.

Their tremendous speed for their size and bulk is noteworthy. This is probably the origin of the Czech lore that says the Cuvac was the result of crossing a Greyhound and a wolf.

The Cuvac is a dog requiring adequate space, and thus owners should have a good-sized yard for exercise. These dogs thrive best in an environment of a large family, children and livestock to care for. Farms and ranches make the best homes. These dogs are natural animal guardians and children watchers, taking to this busy lifestyle like a junkfood junkie to a bowl of peanuts. They are gentle and loyal to their family and its possessions. This handsome white flock guard has diversified from slaying wolves or hunting big game to border patrol or search-and-rescue.

Regular grooming keeps the white coat clean and attractive—and furniture free from white "mohair." The annual shed of the dense underwool requires vigorous brushing and bathing sessions in the spring.

Slovak Cuvac.

Smålandsstövare.

SMÅLANDSSTÖVARE

COUNTRY: Sweden
WEIGHT: 33–40 pounds
HEIGHT: 17 inches
COAT: Thick and heavy, but short
COLOR: Black with tan markings; any white to be discouraged
OTHER NAMES: Smålands Hound
REGISTRY: FCI
GROUP: Hound

Like the Schillerhound, the Smålandsstövare is a Swedish hound that traces its roots back to ancient periods. They were probably used as far back as the Middle Ages. The hound of Smålands is indigenous to central Sweden and possesses some singular physical traits.

Although the occasional hock-length tail is conceded, it is universally born (never docked) with a short tail; no other scenthound sports the short version. The head is shorter and more wedge-shaped than most hounds, with the ears very small and flat; the body is cobby and small, all of which indicate that a long-ago cross of hounds to native Nordic-type dogs may have occurred to produce this breed. But he has keen scenthound abilities and is used in all terrain and weather for trailing game. They are most commonly employed in the hunting of fox and hare throughout the dense forest of Smålands district in southern Sweden.

SOFT-COATED WHEATEN TERRIER

COUNTRY: Ireland
WEIGHT: 35–45 pounds
HEIGHT: 18–19 inches
COAT: Profuse, soft and silky, not harsh
COLOR: Any shade from light wheaten to golden reddish
REGISTRY: FCI, AKC, TKC, CKC
GROUP: Terrier

In times past, all of the terriers of Ireland were known collectively as Irish Terriers, so it is hard to know whether ancient references to this strain are about the generic type or specifically about the red breed known today. People who foster the Wheaten feel that he is as old or older than the red "daredevil," both coming from the same stem breed. Actually, the Wheaten, Kerry and Irish Terriers share a similar leggy, racy, square terrier appearance that stamps them with generally analogous origins.

The Wheaten Terrier of 200 years ago was also a dog of the poor, and was so common that few considered it worth notice. There are some references to wheaten-colored, open-coated dogs with punishing jaws, mainly in the Kerry and Cork areas. These dogs were used especially for otter and badger. Under the Irish penal laws of the 1700s, tenant farmers were prohibited from owning a dog worth more than five pounds, and thus the soft-coated dog was the bargain basement one commonly owned.

He had no wealthy aristocrats to foster him and was only recognized as a separate breed when the Wheaten was issued its present name in 1937. Around that time, a group of fanciers wanted to save this historic Irish breed. So, although the Wheaten is a very old breed, it is a latecomer to the modern world of purebred dogs. Irish canine authorities recognized the breed in 1937; AKC approval did not come until 1973, with Canada following in 1978.

His temperament can best be described as "defense with aggression"; however, he is not a fellow who picks a fight. Having lived in homes with families for hundreds of years, he is a gentle and loyal pet. He is lively and puppyish all his 10–14 years, and firm—but fair—discipline is necessary.

The breed is noted for its late maturity, with dogs rarely at their best for exhibition until two years of age. Although pets and show dogs should be trimmed for best appearance, this should be accomplished only with scissors, not clippers. Although the original Irish standard admonished a sculptured appearance, modern show specimens are exhibited more and more this way. When the coat is properly cared for, the dead hair is brushed out rather than falling all over the carpeting, a fact pleasing to most homemakers.

Soft-Coated Wheaten Terrier.

Soft-Coated Wheaten Terrier.

Above: Soft-Coated Wheaten Terrier. **Below:** Soft-Coated Wheaten Terriers, bitch and pups.

SOUTH RUSSIAN OWTCHARKA

COUNTRY: USSR
WEIGHT: 110–155 pounds
HEIGHT: 25–26 inches minimum; 30-34 inches usual
COAT: Long, dense, silky with woolen undercoat
COLOR: Pure white; white with head spots in shades of fawn or gray
OTHER NAMES: Ovtcharka de Russie Meridionale, South Russian Sheepdog
REGISTRY: FCI
GROUP: Flock Guard

In the inhospitable elevations of the mountains, a larger and heavier coated dog evolved. This giant pastoral guarding breed has a long history in the steppes of the Ukraine in European Russia. The old-style Owtcharka, originally with a heavy-corded coat, probably stemmed from large dogs of a similar type from Tibet or elsewhere in the East. These dogs were brought west with the migrations centuries before Christ. Some were left in the Ukraine, while others accompanied the nomads further west into Hungary to form the basis of the Komondor.

In 1797, shepherds' dogs were brought to the Ukraine from Spain with imported merino

South Russian Owtcharka, white.

South Russian Owtcharkas.

sheep, but proved too small (at 20 inches) and weak to protect the flocks from the Russian wolves. These Spanish dogs were crossed with the original corded Owtcharkas to begin the breed now known as the South Russian Owtcharka.

In the early part of this century, representatives of the breed were brought to England via Baltic trade ships. Some reached the USA and enjoyed a brief stay in AKC's Miscellaneous Class. Not long after that they disappeared into the Russian interior and were lost to the West. Those at home became scarce as well, although a few are seen at the larger dog shows in Russia. The majority in their homeland are bred by the Red Army, who found the breed useful for guard work. They are often left to guard isolated facilities or industrial plants, or used on duty with troops. The military, naturally, selects the more aggressive tendencies and forbids the exportation of these dogs.

Recently, several of these closely guarded white giants have been secreted out of Russia, reintroducing them to Europe and the West. A Swiss couple, who own three of these Owtcharki and praise their qualities, encountered "James Bond" adventures smuggling their dogs out of Moscow and Leningrad. They emphasize that,

although not as aggressive as the Red Army dogs, this breed is extremely protective and intelligent, requiring a strong-minded "alpha" owner. They have a quicker trigger than many other guardian breeds, giving very little warning before attacking when they perceive danger to their owner. With a firm, but loving hand and proper early socialization, the breed can be a desirable companion and guardian. But a breeder warns this animal is not for a novice or timid dog owner: "You can spoil this breed into a murderer."

He does require sizeable outdoor room, not only for adequate exercise, but because "he needs a kingdom to keep intruders out." Modern Russian owners say he is ever vigilant, "although it may seem that his eyes are closed, he does see everything." The modern SRO, although his coat is long, shaggy and profuse, does not cord like the old-style Owtcharka. It does need extensive grooming to maintain his appearance and good health. His speed is amazing for a dog of giant size, and he has lightning reflexes. The Swiss have found this dog to be a natural as *Katastrophen Hund*, a dog used in emergencies, such as finding avalanche victims or persons trapped in earthquake rubble.

Spanish Mastiff, reddish.

SPANISH MASTIFF

COUNTRY: Spain
WEIGHT: 110–132 pounds
HEIGHT: 26–28 inches
COAT: Short, very thick
COLOR: Reddish, wolf gray, fawn, white and black, white and golden yellow, white and gray, grizzle
OTHER NAMES: Mastin de Español, Mastin de Extremadura, Mastin de Leon, Mastin de La Mancha
REGISTRY: FCI
GROUP Flock Guard

The Spanish Mastiffs, although named mastiff, fill flock-guard positions. They share a similar history to all flock-guarding dogs from Spain and Portugal. Landing with the Phoenicians, they were part of the tradition of the Trashumante (flock migrations) in the southern routes of Spain. Those that spilled over into Portugal became the Estrela and the Rafeiro do Alentejo.

Still found guarding cattle and sheep in the hills of Spain, this dog is a powerful, protective animal with infinite color variance. As is true of many large animals (and humans), he does not feel the need to show his obvious strength. He is alert, but calm and unruffled. The stock guardian sounds the alarm to the shepherd, then becomes quiet and attentive, not attacking.

The breed is still natural in its behavior and instincts. Expectant dams find a secluded place to bear and raise their puppies.

The Spanish Mastiff is gentle with other animals—even cats—and loving to his owners. He enjoys being with his family and doing a job for them. This dog is easily satisfied with minimal exercise and grooming. Owners that do not raise stock find them apt family guardians, search-and-rescue dogs or obedience workers. Currently, there are breeders in Switzerland and Germany, and the dogs are beginning to infiltrate the USA and other countries. They are seen occasionally at international dog shows.

Above: Spanish Mastiff, grizzle. **Below:** Spanish Mastiff, pup.

Spinone Italiano, chestnut roan.

SPINONE ITALIANO

COUNTRY: Italy
WEIGHT: 71–82 pounds
HEIGHT: 24–26 inches
COAT: Hard, dense and shaggy
COLOR: All white, orange and white, orange roan, chestnut and white, or chestnut roan
OTHER NAMES: Italian Coarsehaired Pointer
REGISTRY: FCI, AKC, TKC, CKC
GROUP: Gun Dog

The Spinone is truly an antique. Although he stemmed from native hounds, probably of Segugio type, as did the Bracco, his history is not complete. For instance, what gave him his wiry coat? This may be evidence that the griffons of France and the Spinone are closely related, with the griffons springing from early Spinones—or both coming from common ancestors. The presence of the corded shepherd dogs in Italy could have accounted for the bristling wiry coats on these breeds. He is also credited with being a very old blend of coarsehaired setters from Italy, bred with those left by Greek traders and others from the Adriatic coast, and a cross to white mastiff. The truth in dog histories is entwined with legends.

The breed is noted for its superior nose and ultra-soft mouth. The Spinone is especially good in heavy cover or cold, wet conditions where his protective coat serves him well.

Even dogs that do not hunt are served well by their coat, as evidenced by a 12–week-old pup exposed to the cold and damp after falling into a well shaft and spending ten hours there. This same inquisitive pup enjoyed a tastier experience when he discovered the milkman's delivery and "was soon having his extra pint."

Still hunted throughout Piedmont in Italy, he is beginning to be appreciated and fostered in England, in other European countries and the USA. There seems to be a split in his homeland between show and field interests, with a separate standard for each of the two types.

The Italian working standard specifies: "When the quarry tries to get away, the Spinone steers it downwind, mastering the direct emanation of the scent . . . he moves forward with extreme caution, avoiding as far as possible dry branches or crackling leaves." Despite his size and usual "long, tidy trot," the Spinone can turn into a powerful, swift hunter should the quarry take flight.

He is given credit by various sources as a "thinker," and will use this ability to adapt to various conditions. He is called "Nature's gentleman." His expression toward his master is lowering of the head, with an upward look in "silent communication."

The Spinone is big but docile and affectionate. They love playing with other dogs, but in play they can "crush all opponents by using their considerable weight." They can be stubborn, however, and need training and direction. With careful selection and proper socialization, they are "big cuddly teddy bears." In fact, owners have few complaints, other than his "wet beard in their faces." The bristly head gives the appearance of a wise, old, whiskery grandfather. His tail is docked to about half its natural length.

Above: Spinone Italiano, orange and white. **Below:** Spinone Italiano pointing.

Stabyhoun, black with white markings.

STABYHOUN

COUNTRY: Netherlands
WEIGHT: 33–44 pounds
HEIGHT: 19½–21 inches
COAT: Moderately long and sleek, no curl although a bit of wave over the croup is acceptable; the "feathering" on tail and breeches is thick so it appears bushy; ear feather is long at the base of the ear, decreasing to short hair at the tip
COLOR: Black, chocolate, or orange, with white markings, in which there may be ticking and roaning
REGISTRY: FCI
GROUP: Gun Dog

Like the Dutch Wetterhoun, the Stabyhoun originated in Friesland, where he has been known since the 1600s. The Spanish occupied the Netherlands until the mid-16th century, and there is speculation that they brought setting and couching dogs from other parts of Europe. These imports developed into the native spaniel/ setters: the Drentse Patrijshond, the Kooikerhondje, and the Stabyhoun in Holland, as well as the German Longhaired Pointer, Large Münsterländer and Small Münsterländer of Germany. Frisian writers of the early 1800s describe the Stabyhoun in his present form. Similar dogs are depicted in early Dutch paintings. Exhibition of the breed didn't begin until the 1940s, and soon after, official recognition was granted by both the Dutch and international dog organizations.

The "Bijke," as he is affectionately called at home, is a quality pointing and retrieving dog, doubling as a mole and polecat catcher, guard and children's companion around the home. He is used in duck and pigeon hunting, calmly staying down and unobserved until called upon to make the retrieves. Wounded game is searched out and returned in his soft mouth. In field and woods, he enthusiastically searches for game and is an excellent pointer. As one owner says, "His nose never lies."

The larger specimens have also been used as

draft dogs, undoubtedly because of the breed's calm and even temperament. The mole-catcher needed to be of a size to be carried "in a basket on the back of a small man's bicycle." With children, even those not known to them, they are soft and gentle. Its good temperament is described in brief by the Dutch Stabyhoun Wetterhoun Club as "A spontaneous Frysk . . . (that) wears its heart on its sleeve."

The bushy feathering of the tail and breeches, and the ear that is fringed at the base but smooth haired at the tip, are distinctive breed characteristics. The low-set tail is not docked.

To maintain his good qualities, the Dutch Club has very strict breeding policies. Before dogs can be bred, they must have hips radiographed free of dysplasia, receive an excellent or very good rating at a conformation show, have prior permission granted by the breed committee, and meet other restrictions to insure the production of quality puppies. The Stabyhoun is promoted by Dutch breeders, not only because of his character and abilities but also because of their desire to protect a native breed with a long and proud history.

Stabyhoun.

Staffordshire Bull Terrier, red.

STAFFORDSHIRE BULL TERRIER

COUNTRY: Great Britain
WEIGHT: 24–38 pounds
HEIGHT: 14–16 inches
COAT: Short, smooth
COLOR: Red, beige (fawn), white, black, blue or brindle; with or without white markings
REGISTRY: AKC, FCI, TKC, CKC
GROUP: Mastiff

This was the original "Bull-and-Terrier." Crossing the 19th century bulldog with the old English Terrier produced the modern Staffordshire Bull, which still looks very much like its bull/terrier ancestor. Upon arrival in the United States in the early 1800s, the breed was crossbred to become larger and taller. The results were the American Staffordshire Terrier and the American Pit Bull Terrier. Those which remained in England retained their original form, and came to the United States about 1870, where they were recognized as the Staffordshire Bull Terrier.

Staffordshire Bull Terrier, red with white markings.

During these early years, the Staff was bred and used for dog-fighting but, by the 1930s, the law had begun to make this activity disappear. Rather than see his beloved dogs vanish with their profession, fancier Joseph Dunn organized a club and worked to have this breed recognized by The Kennel Club of England. Another name besides Bull-and-Terrier had to be chosen (since the Bull Terrier had already assumed that one), so the locale of greatest interest, Staffordshire, was chosen as its dog tag.

After official acceptance in 1935, the breed's good qualities elevated these dogs to a position of popularity in their homeland, and they have retained that favor. Most Staffs brought to North America came after World War II. The breed was recognized in Canada in 1952, fol-lowed by American acceptance in 1974.

The basic difference between the Staff, AmStaff and Pit Bull, other than size, is the fact that ear cropping is not allowed on the Staff. A folded-back "rose" or half-drop ear is required.

These dogs need activity to keep their hard-muscled physique and are happy to join their owners in jogging or other sports. Like similar breeds, they are devoted to their families, are gentle with children and accept other pets.

The Staff does require firm, consistent han-dling as a pup. With maturity, he is laid back, loves social contact and is a real "character." He can competently defend his own if necessary, and he knows it. Thus he rarely shows any bra-vura of snapping or snarling. He is quiet and calm—until needed.

Staffordshire Bull Terrier.

STEPHENS STOCK

COUNTRY: USA
WEIGHT: 35–55 pounds, over 55 pounds disqualifies
HEIGHT: 16–23 inches, over 23 inches disqualifies
COAT: Short, smooth
COLOR: Black, a few white markings permissible
OTHER NAMES: Stephens Cur
GROUP: Hound

In the years after World War II, five strains of mountain curs were recognized. Hugh Stephens's family, of southeastern Kentucky, had owned one strain for over 100 years, always preferring their "Little Blacks." Stephens was first Vice President of the Mountain Cur Club but, in 1970, it was felt the Stephens strain and the McConnell lines were distinct enough to form their own registry.

At that time the name Stephens Stock was chosen for the breed, honoring the Stephens family. These curs were more houndlike than many of the others, as they worked a cold track and opened on the trail. Several hunters preferred them, due to the dogs' sound on the trail, good change of voice at the tree and their competitive hunting spirit. Colors other than black do occur but are not registerable.

Stephens dogs are quick, sensible and easy to train. Natural at treeing, they are specialists at squirrel and coon. Although Stephens Stock are too small to go after big game alone, they are very courageous and will work as a team on mountain lions and bears. These dogs are very responsive to kindness and are family-oriented but wary of strangers.

Hugh Stephens, founder of the breed, with "Jack," a black Stephens Stock.

Stichelhaar.

STICHELHAAR

COUNTRY: Germany
WEIGHT: 44 pounds
HEIGHT: 22–26 inches
COAT: 1½ inches, hard and bristly, but lying close to the body; only a moderate amount of mustache, eyebrows, and feathering of belly, chest, legs and tail
COLOR: Brown and white, in a roan or spotted pattern
OTHER NAMES: Deutscher Stichelhaariger Vorstehhund, German Brokencoated Pointer
REGISTRY: FCI
GROUP: Gun Dog

The history of the Wirehair in Germany is quite recent. An interest in gun dogs with bristly coats always existed, and several types were in evidence by the late 1800s. At first, the Wirehair Club in Germany fostered all hunting dogs with a wire coat, but the wide variation in types soon saw separate organizations for the Pudelpointer, the Griffon, the Stichelhaar, and the German Wirehaired Pointer. They may all have come from the same stock, as these breeds developed concurrently. From this time on, each breed became individualized.

The Stichelhaar, meaning broken hair, carries a very harsh, short, but flat-lying coat. Except for his beard and brow, the wire jacket is not noticeable until it is touched. His similarity to the German Wirehaired Pointer in both appearance and hunting style blurred the lines between the two breeds. Most dogs that were once of Stichelhaar breeding are now under the label of Drahthaar. The FCI and the German authorities do still recognize the Stichelhaar. Currently, the breed is quite scarce, with only 10 to 15 registrations per year.

Strellufstöver

STRELLUFSTÖVER

COUNTRY: Denmark
HEIGHT: 12–15 inches
COAT: Short, straight and dense; slight fringe on tail
COLOR: Any color, with white markings
OTHER NAMES: Danish Dachsbracke
REGISTRY: FCI
GROUP: Hound

The Strellufstöver is a 20th-century creation. Frands Christian Frandsen, of Holsted, Jutland, envisioned a hound with the persistence and independence to hunt a variety of game in the Holsted area. About 1912, he acquired Smålandsstöveren from Sweden, Westphalian Dachsbracken from Germany and Berner Laufhunds from Switzerland, and crossbred these hounds, selecting the desired traits from the progeny.

By the mid-1920s, Frandsen had fixed the type he wanted, and hunters from all over Denmark were using the new Danish Dachsbracke.

By 1929, fanciers formed the Dansk Stovarklub, which still supports the breed, soon named Strelluf after Frandsen's kennel. FCI recognized the new hound in 1937, seven years before his benefactor's death.

Later, the Danish Dachsbracke moved on to Sweden, where these dogs contributed to the makeup of the Drever. By 1960, Scandinavian dog authorities agreed that the Drever and Strellufstöver were so close as to be essentially the same breed. They are now listed as one breed with one standard, but in Denmark his advocates still prefer to call him Strelluf. He has a slow, steady following (500) in his homeland, as compared to 11,000 Drevers in Sweden!

The Strellufstöver is used for fox, deer and hare. He works slowly over large estates, baying constantly and driving the game out to the hunter.

This dog is watchful, calm, never nervous or aggressive. His bold white markings must be visible from both sides, as well as from the front and back.

STUMPY-TAIL CATTLE DOG

COUNTRY: Australia
WEIGHT: 35–45 pounds
HEIGHT: 17–20 inches
COAT: Medium-short, harsh, straight, dense
COLOR: Blue speckled with black markings on head; red speckled with darker red markings on head
GROUP: Herding

Sharing much of the same history and appearance as the Australian Cattle Dog, the Stumpy-Tail Cattle Dog is a cross of the Smithfield and Dingo, accomplished by a drover named Timmons. The Smithfield was a longhaired, black and white bobtail, similar to a small Old English Sheepdog. The first samples of Stumpy-Tails were red in color, bob-tailed and were tabbed Timmons Biters. A later influx of Blue-Merle Collies added the blue coloration. The Stumpy-Tail was bred selectively for the three to four inch bobs.

Like the AuCaDo, the Stumpy bites low—at the foot still touching the ground—and immediately crouches to avoid the ensuing kick. A natural selection was easily accomplished by the cattle themselves. A bite to the heel of the hoof in the air, or a tendency to stay erect, served only to lay open the skull of the under-achiever.

The tail must be a natural bob of less than four inches. The Stumpy's close relative, the Australian Cattle Dog, is sometimes born tailless as well. The Stumpy-Cattle Dog is unknown outside Australia and is becoming rare in its native land as well.

Stumpy-Tail Cattle Dog.

STYRIAN ROUGHHAIRED MOUNTAIN HOUND

COUNTRY: Austria
WEIGHT: 33–40 pounds
HEIGHT: 17½–23 inches
COAT: Rough but not wiry; short and straight, without shine
COLOR: Red or reddish yellow
OTHER NAMES: Steirischer Rauhaarige Hochgebirgsbracke, Peintinger Bracke
REGISTRY: FCI
GROUP: Hound

Ancient Middle Eastern hounds aboard Phoenician and Greek vessels were traded to Celtic and Germanic tribes. This stock, coming down through the centuries, is the basis for these and other Austrian hounds.

Much of Austria is mountainous with extreme climatic variations, and the Austrian hounds have been adapted for these conditions. *Hochgebirgs* means high mountains, and the Rauhaarige is especially adapted to that environment. Styria, the land of *lederhosen* and embroidered capes, is in the south of Austria on the Yugoslavian border. The rough-coated hound from that area is a cross of schweisshund-type trackers with the wirehaired hounds of Istria. This blend created a tough utility scenthound for use in the highest elevations.

One of the first crosses was done by Herr Peintinger in 1870, through mating his Hanoverian bitch, "Hela I," to an Istrian dog. Many other crosses and experiments occurred before the breed was stabilized, but soon Peintinger was exhibiting and hunting the third-generation pure type. The breed was recognized by its official name in 1889, but is still often called by the name of its founder.

The Styrian is of robust build, and is muscular and sturdy. The head is straighter with a bit more stop than the Brandl. He has small feet with high, arched toes. The rough hair is never very long and he sports no moustaches. His head and coat give him "a serious . . . nearly a threatening facial expression." Yet, he is not a vicious dog at all, but calm and gentle.

Competent in silent trailing as well as the vocal pursuit on a hot scent, he is both serious and intelligent. He is particularly noted for being an easy keeper and for his ability to overcome cold, damp, heat, thirst and other discomforts while following his prey through the mountains. Modern hunters from Austria and Yugoslavia prize this resistant, tough, but good-natured hound.

A strict breed club that requires proof of ability as well as health and soundness before approving a breeding helps to assure that these dogs retain their attributes.

Styrian Roughhaired Mountain Hound.

Sussex Spaniel.

SUSSEX SPANIEL

COUNTRY: Great Britain
WEIGHT: 40–45 pounds
HEIGHT: 13–15½ inches
COAT: Flat, silky and moderately long, with abundant feathering
COLOR: Solid golden liver, white spot on chest faulty
REGISTRY: FCI, AKC, TKC, CKC
GROUP: Gun Dog

While the rest of Europe was developing the pointing spaniels, the British created their equivalent in the form of the flushing land spaniel. Although the flushing spaniel owes most of his inheritance to the couching dogs of early days, other additions changed his size and style of hunting. What these crossings were is a matter of conjecture, but they may have come from the small, though massive, heavy-skinned influence of the low-stationed hound. The result was a passionate and happy hunting dog that flushed rather than pointed. These dogs became very popular with British gunners, and a variety of sizes and color types developed.

The Sussex is probably a remnant of the oldest type, maintaining a hint of hound in both his heavy-skinned appearance and his urge to give tongue when on scent (especially fur). His earliest proponent, in the 1790s, was A.E. Fuller of Rosehill Park, in the British county of Sussex. By 1803, the British dog press was praising "the golden Spaniel of Sussex, the largest and strongest of the Spaniels." This proves that not only was the Sussex in England at that time, but other types of spaniels also existed with which to compare him.

Since its original introduction, this rare spaniel has constantly verged on extinction. Despite fine abilities and the beautiful golden color, the breed has never attracted a wide circle of fanciers. British breeder Joy Freer may have held the longest interest, acquiring her first Sussex in 1923 and maintaining her sponsorship until her death in 1984. She literally carried the breed through the Second World War, borrowing a little of her hogs' rations here and butcher's scraps there to maintain her eight dogs through the years of food rationing. She continued a limited breeding program through those difficult years, regimentally and carefully placing the one litter a year with others who loved the breed. Nearly all modern dogs trace to these eight survivors of the War.

To say the breed base is narrow does not begin to define the problems. With so few in existence, all closely inbred through necessity, it has been a difficult task to upgrade stock. But much to the credit of fanciers on both sides of the Atlantic, improvement is being accomplished. Great care is taken with the placement of each precious puppy, since every dog may be needed for promotion of the breed or for breeding stock.

In appearance, the Sussex has a tendency to loose skin, heavy and long, low-set ears and prominent flew, reminiscent of the hound—with the setter's heavy fringed coat and merry, docile disposition. The breed is a sturdy hunter with great stamina, though not quick. This probably proved its downfall in later years, against the more agile swift retrievers and setters.

This is a laid-back spaniel who, while friendly, is a bit more territorial than most others of his group. Devoted to his family, he rarely lets them out of his sight. Owning one means having a shadow around the house. Sussex Spaniels take correction well and learn quickly. Many have the endearing habit of "smiling" when excited, or when asking forgiveness after a scolding. Swimming is a passion taken to naturally. If not hunted, the Sussex will find his own quarry: birds, insects and butterflies.

Joy Freer described them like this: "There is no other animal which has his coloring except the lion . . . [the Sussex] also have the same big bone and big feet, and something of the same steady way of regarding you that the lion does."

SWISS LAUFHUNDS

Schweizer Laufhund

COUNTRY: Switzerland
WEIGHT: 34–44 pounds
HEIGHT: 18–23 inches
COAT: Short, thick and hard
COLOR: White with orange, yellow or sometimes red markings
OTHER NAMES: Swiss Hound
REGISTRY: FCI
GROUP: Hound

Schweizer Laufhund, white with orange.

Schweizer Neiderlaufhund

COUNTRY: Switzerland
WEIGHT: 30–40 pounds
HEIGHT: 13–16½ inches
COAT: Short, thick and hard
COLOR: White with orange, yellow or sometimes red markings
OTHER NAMES: Small Swiss Hound
REGISTRY: FCI
GROUP: Hound

Bruno Jura Laufhund

COUNTRY: Switzerland
WEIGHT: 34–44 pounds
HEIGHT: 18–23 inches
COAT: Short, thick and hard
COLOR: Tan with black saddle, or black with tan points
OTHER NAMES: Jura Hound, Bruno de Jura
REGISTRY: FCI
GROUP: Hound

St. Hubert Jura Laufhund

COUNTRY: Switzerland
WEIGHT: 34–44 pounds
HEIGHT: 18–23 inches
COAT: Short, thick and hard
COLOR: Tan with black saddle, or black with tan points
OTHER NAMES: Jura Hound
REGISTRY: FCI
GROUP: Hound

Jura Neiderlaufhund

COUNTRY: Switzerland
WEIGHT: 30–40 pounds
HEIGHT: 13–16½ inches
COAT: Short, thick and hard or short wire
COLOR: Tan with black saddle, or black with tan points
OTHER NAMES: Small Jura Hound
REGISTRY: FCI
GROUP: Hound

Berner Laufhund

COUNTRY: Switzerland
WEIGHT: 34–44 pounds
HEIGHT: 18–23 inches
COAT: Short, thick and hard
COLOR: Tricolor; white ground color with black head and body spots and tan markings above eyes, on cheeks, under ears and on legs; very little ticking in the white
OTHER NAMES: Bernese Hound
REGISTRY: FCI
GROUP: Hound

Berner Neiderlaufhund

COUNTRY: Switzerland
WEIGHT: 30–40 pounds
HEIGHT: 13–16½ inches
COAT: Short, thick and hard
COLOR: Tricolor; white ground color with black head and body spots and tan marking above eyes, on cheeks, under ears and on legs; very little ticking in the white
OTHER NAMES: Small Bernese Hound
REGISTRY: FCI
GROUP: Hound

Luzerner Laufhund

COUNTRY: Switzerland
WEIGHT: 34–44 pounds
HEIGHT: 18–23 inches
COAT: Short, thick and hard
COLOR: Tricolor; with heavy ticking in the white creating a blue effect
OTHER NAMES: Lucernese Hound
REGISTRY: FCI
GROUP: Hound

Luzerner Neiderlaufhund

COUNTRY: Switzerland
WEIGHT: 30–40 pounds
HEIGHT: 13–16½ inches
COAT: Short, thick and hard
COLOR: Tricolor; with heavy ticking in the white creating a blue effect
OTHER NAMES: Small Lucernese Hound
REGISTRY: FCI
GROUP: Hound

Schweizer Laufhund, white with orange.

The scenthounds of Switzerland are called *lauf-hunds* (walking dogs), or dogs to follow on foot. As with the French hounds, the Swiss hounds' history leads back to the Celtic/Phoenician connection, with varieties established during the Middle Ages. Twelfth-century Zurich cathedral art shows hounds of quite good modern type. Correspondence between parties in Milan, Italy, and Switzerland in the 1500s recounts the fine nose and grand tracking ability of the "famous" Swiss hounds. These dogs have come down to the present time with the same appearance and abilities and are still used on hare, fox, stag and roe deer by practical hunters throughout Switzerland.

The Swiss hounds are all very similar, excepting color and size, and strongly resemble the classic French hounds in type. All of them have an intense love of hunting and for this reason are not recommended as just watchdogs or pets. Hunting and chasing instincts are strong, and if these are not satiated, the dogs must be taken out on leash for plenty of supervised exercise.

When a laufhund comes to a fresh trail, he announces it with a "rare hauling bark." In fact, the voice that is so important in the hunt may cause his owners trouble if he is kept in town. Because of this mouthiness, his ownership is forbidden in some populated areas. However, if given a supervised outlet for energy, he is a friendly, gentle and loyal friend for the home as well as the hunt. Besides practical hunting, the Swiss breed organization holds tests for both hunting and coldtrailing to assess abilities.

With its geographic distribution near the French border, the richly colored Schweizer Hound shows a close relationship to the Porcelaine of Franche-Comte and other orange-and-white French hounds from which the breed stemmed. In repayment, the Schweizer was used in the reconstruction of the Porcelaine.

The Jura Mountains run along the western edge of Switzerland bordering on France. The hound that developed there had no white and is a bit more akin to the old-style pure Celtic hound. He probably developed from French and Belgian dogs of the St. Hubert type. There are two distinct varieties of the Jura. The Bruno variety, often called the Bruno de Jura, is very like the French hounds and the other Swiss hounds, while the St. Hubert variety has a big head, exaggerated heavy ears, and an abundance of loose skin on the head, lips and neck.

Lucerne is in the northcentral lake region of Switzerland, the home of the Lucernese Hound. He probably stemmed from the French Petit Bleu de Gascognes and is very similar to them in appearance.

The Bernese variety was probably named, not for the city of Bern, but for the Bernese Alps which are further south. He is closely akin to French hounds like the Ariége and Artois, with their moderate size and clear white without ticking.

The short-legged hound varieties that the French call *basset* and the Germans name *dachshund*, the Swiss term *Neiderlaufhunds*. Each of the Swiss hound varieties comes in "petit" as well as "tall," which are otherwise judged by the same standard as the large sizes. The Neiderlaufhunds are especially noted for their full-bodied voices which resound pleasantly during the hunt. The Neider variety of the Jura is more like the Bruno than the St. Hubert type. The Berner Neiderlaufhund is the only one of the Swiss hounds that can be seen in a rough wiry coat. These dogs are all gentle and patient with children. Given sufficient exercise and an outlet for hunting instincts, they are good, sturdy companions. One, which fell into a hole in rocks, was finally rescued after ten days of working to retrieve him. He was still alive although he had no food or water available!

Bruno Jura Laufhund.

Above: Bruno Jura Laufhund, tan with black saddle. **Below:** Jura Neiderlaufhund, black with tan points.

Above: Berner Laufhund. **Below:** Berner Neiderlaufhund.

Above: Schweizer Neiderlaufhund. **Below:** Bruno Jura Laufhunds.

Above: Luzerner Laufhund. **Below:** Luzerner Neiderlaufhund.

TAHLTAN BEAR DOG

COUNTRY: Canada
WEIGHT: 15 pounds maximum
HEIGHT: 15 inches maximum
COAT: Short, dense, close-coated, with bushy tail
COLOR: Black or blue with small white markings
REGISTRY: CKC
GROUP: Southern

Raised by the Tahltan Indians to hunt bear, the Tahltan Bear Dog was a mighty power in a small package. Before a hunt, the dogs were ceremonially bled by stabbing them in the hindquarters with the fibula bone of a fox or wolf. The morning of the hunt, two dogs were carried in a sack over the Indian's shoulder until fresh bear tracks were sighted. Upon release, these little dogs moved lightly over the crust of snow while the bear was slowed down by the deep drifts. Their foxlike staccato yaps harassed the bear into submission or confused him until the Indians could come close enough for a kill. To prepare for a foray against big cats, a claw from a dead lynx was used to ceremonially mark the dog's face.

The Tahltan Bear Dog had the courage to face a bear, but was friendly and gentle with smaller animals and with humans. They lived in the tent with the family, sharing bed and board. A Jesuit of the 17th century described the Indians' communal houses in winter, saying he "could not decide which was worse—the smoke, the fleas or the dogs."

Descended from pariah-type dogs that had come with prehistoric migrations, the Tahltan Dogs were centralized in the remote mountainous areas of northwestern British Columbia and the southern Yukon. Their usual diet was small bits of birds, meat and fish, and they flourished in the bitter cold. Outside their native environment, they succumbed to distemper, heat prostration and problems due to dietary changes. As white explorers came into the territory, bringing a variety of other dogs, the Tahltan Dog became diluted.

Like others of their group, they had a peculiar yodel. Foxy in appearance, their main distinction among dogs is their novel tail. Short, bushy and carried erect, it has been described variously as a shaving brush or a whisk broom.

The CKC has recognized the breed for many years, but it has been over 20 years since the last Tahltan Bear Dog was registered. In 1984, only two spayed bitches of this type were recorded as living in Canada. Sadly, it appears the breed may be doomed.

Tahltan Bear Dog, blue.

Telomian.

TELOMIAN

COUNTRY: Malaysia
WEIGHT: 18–28 pounds
HEIGHT: 15–19 inches
COAT: Short, smooth
COLOR: Any shade of sable, with white in Irish pattern or piebald, occasional black mask
REGISTRY: None
GROUP: Southern

As pets of the aborigines, the Telomians were an integral part of their lives, protecting the villagers from snakes. The dogs were sight hunters of small game and caught fish in the midst of a stream. These natives ate mostly tapioca, rice and a small amount of fish and fruit, a diet shared with their pets. The masters' huts were built on six-to-eight foot stilts, and the Telomians climbed the ladders to the quarters to sleep. Entering first, a dog chased out and killed any snakes and small animals that had taken up residence during the family's absence. Today, the breed retains that climbing agility and is difficult to confine.

The breed reached the public eye in 1963 when anthropologist Dr. Orville Elliot discovered specimens protected by aborigines in the jungles of Malaysia. The Telomian was named for the Telom River near their source. Due to increased access to the jungles, the little dog's lifestyle was changing and threatened. The natives communicated their concern for their beloved dogs to the doctor and his wife. To prevent dilution or extinction of the breed, the Elliots obtained a pair.

Dr. Elliot sent this pair to Dr. J.P. Scott, at Jackson Laboratory in Maine, for inclusion in his study on animal behavior. They were bred in laboratory situations until their introduction to the public in 1970 by research assistant Audrey Malone Palumbo. That year the Telomian Dog Club was formed and became interested in obtaining another pair of dogs, as the current stock was intensely inbred. Elliot once again traveled to Malaysia to search for a pair, which arrived in 1973.

The Telomians carry many similarities to the Basenji and other pariah dogs: the wrinkled brow, almond eyes, light square body structure and annual estrus cycle. They vocalize in the same manner—a unique howl/growl/crowing effect.

Telomians love to play and run, needing to work off energy, making them excellent pets for children. Similar to their playmates, they are attracted to almost anything—balls, sticks, frisbees, toads, skunks. A characteristic of the breed is the use of their paws, opening doors, holding toys and chewbones, much like a human infant.

They require a maximum amount of human handling at four-to-eight weeks of age, starting earlier than the peak socialization period of other breeds. Without this bonding, they remain aloof to people and unable to adjust to new situations. If socialized, Telomians become marvelous and fascinating friends.

Mostly companion dogs, they are lure-coursed and do well in coursing trials. At 35 mph, they are swift competitors. The Telomian Dog Club, based in the United States, helps place Telomian puppies in appropriate homes. All Telomians existing today in America stem back to only two original pairs.

TIBETAN MASTIFF

COUNTRY: Tibet (China)
WEIGHT: 180 pounds or more
HEIGHT: 22–28 inches
COAT: Thick, medium length, double
COLOR: Gold and black/tan most common; also black, grizzle, sable, brown, blue/tan and others
REGISTRY: FCI, TKC
GROUP: Mastiff

It is highly possible that the Tibetan Mastiff is the missing link between the flock guard and the mastiff breeds. He is from the area which gave us the stem of the original mastiff; yet he has a longer coat than most, and a tail curled over the back. It is possible that the Tibetans crossed the original archetype with other dogs to obtain today's breed. While the answer is lost in

Tibetan Mastiff, black/tan.

Tibetan Mastiff.

the mystery of Tibet, the breed, thankfully, has survived. It has been around since recorded history—or before—and is just now gaining some acceptance in the West, primarily in the US and Europe. The Tibetan Mastiff certainly is the forebear of several modern breeds.

Two types of mastiffs originally aided the lamas and villagers of Tibet: the Bhotia, an agile livestock guardian, and the Tsang Kyi, a larger territorial sentinel. The latter dog has for centuries protected nobility and religious orders. A pup was kept tied from two months of age to make him fierce; in fact, the Tibetans' name for their mastiff is the *Do-kyi*, dog you can tie up. Chaining or tying intensifies aggression, and these dogs bear the reputation of guarding an entire village. Like the bandogs of England, he was secured during the day and set free at night. Because of this habit, the breed tends to be sociable with other dogs and livestock, though he will defend himself if challenged.

The Tibetans say that a white spot on the chest is a good sign, signifying a brave heart. A white tail tip, however, is cut off as it denotes weakness. Tibetan natives make their dogs a protective woolly collar from the finest stiff hairs of a yak's tail. The hair is dyed red, and

when a TM is wearing the collar, he appears even larger and more threatening.

Tibetan dogs traveled with Alexander the Great from "the roof of the world" to European countries, where they planted the seed for so many of today's mastiff and flock-guarding breeds.

The modern Tibetan Mastiff has been known outside Tibet for more than a century. The Prince of Wales owned at least one specimen in the 1880s, and a British standard for the breed was in existence in the 1930s. President Eisenhower received two as gifts from the Dalai Lama. Yet others reached America in the early 1970s through drug smugglers who placed packets of illegal substances under false bottoms in dog crates. These dealers then shipped the largest and toughest Tibetan Mastiffs to the States, where no customs inspector dared to inspect their crates!

A positive aspect of this crime is that many specimens escaped Communist China and reached the hands of concerned breeders. Others were brought in by more conventional routes. The TM is now recognized in many European and Asian countries, and there are national organizations for the breed in both North

Above: Tibetan Mastiff, gold. **Below:** Tibetan Mastiff.

America and Europe. In the US they have been used as guard and sled dogs, as well as family companions.

The American Tibetan Mastiff Association recommends mating only genetically sound animals. Besides physical soundness, breeders are advised to choose stock with proper guardian tendencies and a stable family-oriented temperament. Bitches cycle only once a year.

The breed has incorporated many of the giant attributes of "impressive stature, formidable appearance and great strength." A controlled environment with moderate weight gain and adequate exercise is recommended by breeders to forestall many of the problems that often plague large breeds. The eight-week-old fluffy clown, often described as a teddy bear, will grow into a large, aloof adult with a strong sense of territory and an instinct to defend it. Socialization, discipline and routine grooming should begin early.

Despite their tough, protective instincts, they are gentle with their own families. In their homeland, they are controlled by even the smallest child, who can handle them and call them off intruders with ease. The Tibetan Mastiffs were bred to withstand the extreme temperatures of their native mountain land and are still capable of playing in a snowdrift in below zero temperatures or of performing an obedience routine at 90 degrees.

Tibetan Spaniel.

TIBETAN SPANIEL

COUNTRY: Tibet (China)
WEIGHT: 9–15 pounds
HEIGHT: 10 inches
COAT: Moderately long, silky, double; shorter on face and front of legs, heavy feathering on tail, breeches and ears
COLOR: All colors and combinations of colors permitted
REGISTRY: FCI, AKC, TKC, CKC
GROUP: Herding

As with other Oriental dogs, mystery surrounds this old, but only lately unveiled, little breed. It is known that, just as the Tibetan Terrier isn't a terrier, the Tibetan Spaniel isn't a spaniel. So much for nomenclature! The breed's close relative, the Pekingese, didn't reach its state of "perfection" until about 150 years ago. Prior to that time, based on what is depicted in Chinese art, the Peke was less exaggerated in coat and body form. In fact, many paintings of the period depicting palace dogs show a type very similar to the modern Tibetan Spaniel. Early Pugs, long known in China, had lengthier muzzles and also appeared much like smooth versions of the "spaniel" from Tibet.

The close political ties between ancient Tibet and China resulted in a steady stream of trade between the two nations. Just as the Shih Tzu was created from dogs that came from Tibet to China, the Tibetan Spaniel may have resulted from dogs going in the other direction. Early Chinese Pekingese-type dogs that were given as gifts to Tibetan officials formed the stem from which the Tibetan Spaniel developed. As the dogs that were left in China slowly evolved into our modern Pekingese, those that went to Tibet maintained the older type. An exaggerated brachycephalic dog, with the short face causing restricted nasal capacity, could not survive in the high altitude of Tibet.

The Tibetan Spaniel was fostered and loved in the monasteries of Tibet for many centuries. Monks carried the little dogs under their flowing robes in the winter, with both benefiting from the additional warmth. The spaniels reputedly turned the prayer wheels for the monks, in

Above: Tibetan Spaniels, adults and pups, various colors. **Below:** Tibetan Spaniel.

addition to serving as alarms. Like the Lhasas that the lamas also favored, these dogs were considered to bring good luck. The first examples of this breed were brought back to Great Britain by medical missionaries in the 1920s. The great popularity of the Pekingese seemed to have left no room for these plainer brothers. But they had established a toehold and, after WWII, the Tibetan Spaniel finally became firmly established in England, gaining distinction as both a show dog and family pet. The first specimens were brought to Canada in the mid-60s and the CKC recognized the breed in 1979. Their introduction to the USA came later and was slower; AKC finally recognized this breed in 1983.

While the unknowledgeable might view this relative newcomer to the Western dog scene as a poor quality or crossbred Pekingese, he is his own dog, with distinctive appearance and character. One of the things his adherents like about him is the very lack of exaggeration. He has the exotic charm of so many of the Oriental breeds without any gross distortion of body or a plethora of coat. Full of intelligence, owners find the breed gay and assertive. None of the delicate, fragile toy is displayed in him, and he enjoys an energetic romp. Affectionate with his own family, he tends to be a bit aloof with strangers.

TIBETAN TERRIER

COUNTRY: Tibet (China)
WEIGHT: 18–30 pounds
HEIGHT: 14–16 inches
COAT: Long, shaggy, covering face
COLOR: White, gray, black, golden, with or without white or tan
OTHER NAMES: Dhokhi Apso
REGISTRY: FCI, AKC, TKC, CKC
GROUP: Herding

Despite his name, this ancient Tibetan is not a terrier, but a true herding dog. The spunky lit-tle animal developed through ancient breeds, the North KunLun Mountain Dog and the Inner Mongolian Dog, which resembled a Poodle and stemmed back to the owtcharkas. Others believe this breed to be one of the prototypes of the herding family.

One talent specifically mentioned by Margareta Sundqvist is the Tibetan Terrier's ability to assist the shepherds on their journeys down from the mountains, by leaping to the backs of the sheep and down again in narrow passages.

They also served as alarm dogs in remote Tibetan villages, alerting the Tibetan Mastiffs of

Tibetan Terrier, black with white marking.

835

Tibetan Terrier, gray with white marking.

intruders. Tibetans that were too small for such a rigorous life were given to the lamas and utilized and bred by the Tibetan monks for many centuries, developing into Lhasa Apsos.

Brought into Europe by the Magyars, the TT is a likely contributor to the Puli's makeup, being similar in size, shape, tail carriage and working traits. Other modern breeds acquired some of his qualities as he made his way through Europe.

The triad of shepherd, flock guard and herding dog has worked as a partnership throughout the world and over the centuries. None thrives alone in its sheep tending, so each has learned to rely on the other. Ancient Tibetan natives conceived this workable arrangement, with their Tibetan Mastiff doing the guarding and the Tibetan Terrier taking care of the actual herding. As the barbarians of the East invaded Europe, their families and flocks came with them, along with their two types of dogs. These Mastiffs and herders were left in all countries which absorbed these migrations, where they became individualized for the local region.

Poland developed the mighty Podhalanski and the shaggy Nizinny; in Hungary, the corded Komondor watched the flocks while the Puli did the footwork; northern Italy brought forth the Maremma and the accompanying Bergamasco. Spain boasts the Spanish Mastiff and the Gos d'Atura. Even tiny Portugal, on the coast, has the Estrela Mountain Dog which works with the Cão de Serra de Aires. And the French Great Pyrenees plays guard while the Berger de Pyrenees runs interference.

In each of these regions, the flock-guarding dogs have remained very similar. The sheep-herding dogs have retained many characteristics that lump them together with the sheepdogs of the East, rather than those that came by way of the North. These sheep dogs tend to be shaggy all over their bodies. Many have the tail that tends to curl over the back. Grizzled colors of grays and fawns predominate, rather than the black/tans so common in the northern shepherd dogs.

An English physician, Dr. H.R. Grieg, saved a Tibetan citizen's life and was honored with one of these shaggy Tibetan herding dogs. She later obtained another and brought them back to England; although she was not successful in breeding them, her dogs did serve to introduce the breed to the Western World. The Tibetan Terrier has been recognized in India since 1920, and in England since 1937, where they compete in the Utility Group. A comparative newcomer to the United States, they have been shown in Non-Sporting since 1973.

While the Tibetan Terrier of past centuries was tousled and shaggy-coated, today's show dog is adorned by an elegant coat necessitating hours of skillful grooming. Their long, elegant tails wrap protectively around themselves while sleeping. Another charming characteristic is that of using their paws in a catlike manner, holding, grasping and batting at balls. They can be stubborn if pushed into compliance. The Tibetan makes a merry household pet, small enough for apartments and sturdy enough for children's roughhousing.

Tibetan Terrier.

TOSA INU

COUNTRY: Japan
WEIGHT: 100–200 pounds
HEIGHT: 24½–25½ inches minimum (usually much larger)
COAT: Short, smooth
COLOR: Solid red preferred; brindle, dull black, fawn and white markings permitted
OTHER NAMES: Tosa Ken, Tosa Token
REGISTRY: FCI
GROUP: Mastiff

Tosa Inu, red.

Dog-fighting has been a passion in Japan for many years, and the Tosa was bred particularly to fill that demand, coming from Tosa, Kochi prefecture. After the National Isolation Policy was lifted in 1854, original spitz-type fighters, such as the Akita, habitually were defeated by European breeds. Fighting enthusiasts wouldn't put up with such loss of face and bred the native dogs to St. Bernards, Mastiffs, Great Danes, Bulldogs and Pointers from the West. This increased size and strength, creating the modern Tosa, a dog similar in type and ability to the European "heavyweights."

The dogs were trained with two whips: one had a loud snap but a small sting and the other was used for punishment, inflicting pain. These canine "sumo wrestlers" were chosen for their silent and stoic fighting—they would not scream or utter a whimper though fighting to the death.

Fights were ceremonial occasions, with the dogs paraded to the ring. They were controlled by thick white ropes tied around their necks and held by strong men bracing their legs. Fights were usually stopped if one combatant eased up or gave ground. Contests for top national honors, however, were sometimes allowed to go the bitter and deadly end. Winners received ceremonial aprons, beautiful and valuable, with some priced at $31,000!

The breed suffered setbacks during World War II, as did other large dogs around the world. Favorites were sent to isolated areas in northern Japan, where they continued to be bred. Later fighting enthusiasts standardized appearance and revived the breed to its former glory. They have been exported, in small numbers, to other areas, including the USA and Germany, where they exist as companions and guards only.

The standard notes its aggression toward other dogs. The Tosa gives no ground; it attacks head on. Although massive, the Tosa is agile and athletic, requiring an owner willing to discipline and capable of physically handling and mentally dominating a large, powerful dog. Nevertheless, if properly handled, the Tosa Inu is a quiet, well-behaved breed and is a good family companion.

Tosa Inu in traditional Japanese festival dress.

Toy Fox Terrier.

TOY FOX TERRIER

COUNTRY: USA
WEIGHT: 3½–7 pounds
HEIGHT: 10 inches
COAT: Short, smooth
COLOR: Tri preferred, with white predominating
OTHER NAMES: AmerToy
REGISTRY: UKC
GROUP: Terrier

The Toy was bred directly from the Smooth Fox Terrier, which was brought to the USA from England in the 1870s. At that time, size varied considerably. Although AKC only recognizes the standard size, UKC registered both sizes as Fox Terriers until 1936. The breed then was divided into two varieties: the Fox Terrier and the Toy Fox Terrier.

The AmerToy is widely known in America, with several clubs and organizations fostering him. He has all of the desirable terrier attributes in a small, attractive package. Many people from rural backgrounds recall having these little dogs around the farm "forever." Often appearing in Fox Terrier litters, they were termed runts.

In today's apartment and condo, the Amer-Toy finds himself equally at home, although the instincts remain. One breeder was called by a farmer who had purchased a pup as a pet for his wife some time earlier. The dog had been exclusively a spoiled house dog all of its life. One day the dog accompanied the farmer out to the silo where it spotted a rat. This tiny, pampered pet ran to the rat, grabbed and killed it with a quick shake, as though he had been doing it all of his life. The farmer related that the dog now serves dual duty, and the farm is nearly rat-free!

AmerToys have also proven their worth as Handi-Dogs, which are trained to assist the deaf and handicapped. These dogs can pick up and return a dropped pencil, fetch a shoe or the paper, and bark on command to indicate the need for help. For people with limited abilities of their hands or who are confined to a wheelchair, Handi-Dogs give their masters increased independence.

The AmerToy is a breeze to groom, and provides its own exercise. Ears are erect, and the tail is docked. His frisky clowning endears him to his owners.

TRANSYLVANIAN HOUNDS

Transylvanian Hound, Short

COUNTRY: Hungary
HEIGHT: 18–22 inches
COAT: Short and coarse
COLOR: Red and tan (with a brown nose); small amounts of white acceptable
OTHER NAMES: Erdelyi Kopo, Short Hungarian Hound
GROUP: Hound

Transylvanian Hound, Tall

COUNTRY: Hungary
WEIGHT: 66–77 pounds
HEIGHT: 22–26 inches
COAT: Short and coarse
COLOR: Black and tan
OTHER NAMES: Erdelyi Kopo, Tall Hungarian Hound
REGISTRY: FCI
GROUP: Hound

When the Magyars invaded the Carpathian Mountains of eastern Hungary in the ninth century, they brought hounds with them. Crossbred with native or Polish dogs, the Transylvanian basis was formed. The Carpathians are heavily forested, so thick that by the time a young hunter on foot walked through the woods, he would be an old man. Therefore, the dogs of the area were strong, bred to go after game following mounted riders.

Heavy winter snows and sultry summers required hounds that were particularly adapted to extremes of climate. In the past, they were used extensively by Hungarian kings and princes for hunting wolf and bear in the mountains. In more modern times, the long-legged variety was used on stag, lynx and boar, while the shorter legged version kept pace with the fox and hare.

The Transylvanian is known for its keen sense of direction and orientation to the environment, vital in mountainous and forested cover. This is a dog without exaggeration, moderate in bone and head with tight skin and a medium flat ear. Prized as an obedient, trainable, good-natured hound who is an easy keeper, he was never known outside Hungary. Recent reports indicate that the Transylvanian dogs face extinction, with their numbers dangerously low.

Tall Transylvanian Hound.

TREEING TENNESSEE BRINDLE

COUNTRY: USA
WEIGHT: In proportion to height, around 45 pounds
HEIGHT: 16–24 inches
COAT: Short, dense and smooth
COLOR: Brindle, or black with brindle trim; small amount of white on breast or feet allowed
GROUP: Hound

Treeing Tennessee Brindle, brindle.

The second of the "mountain" curs is the Treeing Tennessee Brindle. As opposed to the Mountain Cur, this breed tends a lot more to the hound. His roots are the same as the other coondogs, and the rather honest statement of the Association sums up this dog's history. "Our original breeding stock came from outstanding brindle tree dogs from every part of the country." The Plott dogs as well as the Curs may have played prominently in the formation of the Tennessee dog.

Hunters used the small brindle hounds for generations. They didn't have a name for them then; they just knew that these unpretentious dogs were fine open trailers and were superb locators, fearless with game such as coon and squirrel but very companionable with men and dogs.

It wasn't until 1967 that a group formed to foster and register the breed and give it an official name. Founded by the Reverend Earl Phillips who is in his late 90s and still working his dogs, the Treeing Tennessee Brindle Breeders Association has grown from modest beginnings to over 500 members in 30 states. In 1978, the TTBBA turned its registry over to the American Coon Hunters Association and the Treeing Brindle was recognized as this group's ninth breed of coonhound. The TTBBA has recently applied to AKC for Miscellaneous Class status for their breed.

Hunting characteristics are much like the other coonhound breeds, with ample nose for trailing game, open trailers with a coarse chop mouth, and fine treeing ability. Small hounds, they have tight cat feet and small ears. They are fast and courageous hunters and, as companions, are intelligent, affectionate and easygoing. Their promoters say these dogs have "heart and try" in abundance.

Puppy buyers are encouraged to look for one that is happy, bold, confident and inquisitive. The breed is particularly sensitive to neglect or abuse, and breeders warn that care must be taken in training not to destroy that heart—"You can take it out, but you can *never* put it back!" Traits such as large size, long low ears, stub tails and colors other than brindle are warned against, since all would put him into another canine category.

TREEING WALKER COONHOUND

COUNTRY: USA
WEIGHT: 45–70 pounds
HEIGHT: 20–27 inches
COAT: Short, smooth and glossy
COLOR: Tricolored preferred; bicolors allowed
REGISTRY: UKC
GROUP: Hound

Like the other coonhounds, the Treeing Walker has the Virginia hounds to thank for its beginnings. From the English Foxhounds, the Virginia hounds begat the Walker Foxhound, which in turn begat the Treeing Walker. Sometime in the 1800s, a dog known as "Tennessee Lead," a stolen dog of unknown origin, was crossed into the Walker Hound. He was a prepotent dog, excelling in game sense, drive and speed, and having a clear, short chop mouth.

This breed has a higher percentage of foxhound and is swift and hot-nosed. The breed broke off from the English Coonhound in 1945. One owner says he believes they are the best breed for coonhound field trials because of their speed, ability to locate quickly and good treeing ability.

Treeing experts like the Redbone, these dogs can be used for other game, but specialize in raccoon and opossum. They learn their trade early and adjust easily to most living conditions. Another owner says his hounds have brought him many hours of enjoyment while hunting and showing in field trials, as well as for "the pure pleasure of going out in the stillness of the night and treeing a coon." Almost all of these dogs are working hounds.

High-strung but loving and eager to please, the Treeing Walker is intelligent and confident. Although there are tan and white dogs in the breed, they must never be called "red," most likely to distinguish them from the Redbone.

Treeing Walker Coonhound, tricolor.

Tyroler Bracke, black/tan.

TYROLER BRACKE

COUNTRY: Austria
WEIGHT: 33–48 pounds
HEIGHT: 16–19 inches
COAT: Short; very tough and dense hair
COLOR: Self-colored in black, black/tan, red or yellow; small white markings allowed
OTHER NAMES: Tyrolean Hound
REGISTRY: FCI
GROUP: Hound

Celtic brackes, known throughout the Alps since the Middle Ages, were the basis for many German and Austrian hounds. These Alpenbracken slowly developed into many modern breeds. By 1860, hunters in the Tyrol began to select their own specific type, and this developed into the modern, capable Tyroler Bracke. The first specimen was exhibited at Innsbruck in 1896, after which the standard was accepted.

The Tyrol is the long western finger of Austria, bordering on the Swiss and Italian Alps. Its high altitude mountains have frigid winters and steamy summers, and the Tyrolean Hound is perfectly adapted to this harsh environment.

These dogs are used for hunting rabbit and fox, but can be utilized as a *Nachsuchenhund* (that is, to search for sick or wounded deer). They are especially adapted for tracking and trailing after the shot has been fired.

Most common in the Tyrol, modern hunters in other parts of Austria and in a few other countries have recognized the Tyroler Bracke's outstanding qualities. He is an ideal companion for the hunter, especially in high elevations.

He works the hot trail *spurlaut,* (i.e., he gives tongue to let the hunter know he is on to a scent), what American hound owners call "opening" on trail. He is a lively and spirited dog, with a superb nose and great endurance during the hunt. Intelligent and easygoing, the Tyrolean is tractable and fits into home life well. He is most happy, however, when he is used for his intended work.

A tracker, the Tyroler is built with much the same lines as the Bavarian dogs with strong bodies, but rather short legs. This Austrian hound is smaller than his German cousins. Owners say too many white marks on the limbs are frowned upon.

VASGOTASPETS

COUNTRY: Sweden
WEIGHT: 20–32 pounds
HEIGHT: 13–16 inches
COAT: Medium length, thick and hard
COLOR: Shaded gray preferred, followed by shaded red, then brindle, blue-gray; white markings, if any, must be less than 40 percent
OTHER NAMES: Swedish Vallhund, Swedish Cattledog
REGISTRY: TKC
GROUP: Herding

An old, indigenous breed from the Vastergotland plains of Sweden, known for its cattle herds, the Vallhund's similarity to the Welsh Corgis—especially the Pembroke—is intriguing. Pembrokeshire is accessible to the coast, and Viking raiders struck along the Irish and Welsh coast. Whether the Vikings introduced the short-legged dog to the Welsh or seized the hard-working little dog as part of their spoils is speculated, but uncertain, and tends to be colored by whether it is a Vallhund or Corgi owner telling the story.

The Vasgotaspets, meaning spitz of the West Goths, was known at one time as the Vikingarnas Dog. It has very small prick ears and a natural bobtail (more than four inches is a standard disqualification, as is docking). This Corgi-type dog is higher on leg and shorter in body than its close relative in Great Britain. Its head is foxy, even more so than the Corgi's. The breed is used on farms, not only for cattle droving, but also as a vermin catcher, watchdog and over-all farm dog.

With the *Vallhund*, forest dog, in danger of extinction in the 1930s, dedicated Swedish breeders, led by Count Bjorn von Rosen, motivated a comeback for this handsome little dog. Officially recognized by the Swedish KC in 1948, the breed is now quite popular in its homeland and has found some following in other countries. A good number live in England where it was granted recognition in 1984, and the Swedish herding dog has recently been introduced to America.

Exhibiting a unique sense of humor, he is a natural showoff. Once he realizes a particular stunt brings laughter or applause, he will repeat it over and over. Affectionate and sensitive to his owner's mood, the Swedish herder reflects joy or quiet contemplation. The Vasgotaspets is intelligent and spirited and does not hesitate to vocalize his joy at being alive. He is a sturdy little dog and is easy to care for.

Vasgotaspets.

VIZSLA

COUNTRY: Hungary
WEIGHT: 49–62 pounds
HEIGHT: 22–24 inches
COAT: Shorthaired—smooth and fine; Wirehaired—bristly but quite short (1–1½ inches) and conforming to the outline of the dog, some beard and brow desirable
COLOR: Various shades of gold to sandy yellow
OTHER NAMES: Magyar Vizsla
REGISTRY: FCI, AKC, UKC, TKC, CKC
GROUP: Gun Dog

The exact origin of this striking Hungarian hunting dog is difficult to pinpoint. Some historians think the Vizsla goes back in pure line to the days of the Magyar hordes that overran Hungary from the East. Others feel it is a creation of the present century! Perhaps the reality is somewhere between.

The home of the Vizsla is the hot central plain of Hungary, the Puszta, an area of rich and diverse agriculture and plentiful game. Etchings of nearly a thousand years ago show Magyar huntsmen with dogs and falcons. It is known that they had good hounds (such as the Transyl-vanian), and they must have used these hounds in selective breeding for dogs to use with the falcon. Legends persist about the "Yellow Turkish Hunting Dog" used in the Vizsla's development. This will continue to be a mystery, as there is no modern equivalent of this type, and it isn't known even what kind of "hunting" dog the extinct breed was. Of course, it is only logical to assume that good hunting dogs were brought with the migrating Magyars as they left Asia Minor for Europe. But the modern fine tuning of this breed as an all-purpose hunting dog probably occurred fairly recently, possibly with crosses to other established European breeds.

The Vizsla suffered greatly between the two Great Wars, and much of the modern breed is based on dogs taken out of Hungary by owners emigrating to other countries. The breed has gained some following in several European countries, as well as in North America. Because of his origin on the hot plains, he has been noted for his stamina in hot weather. Some Vizsla historians note that at some point during the 1930s, after crosses were made to the German Wirehair, the Drotszoru or wirehaired ver-

Vizsla, wirehaired.

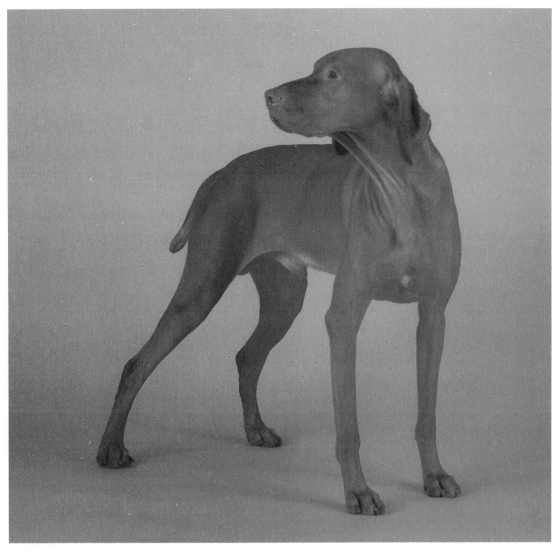

Vizsla, shorthaired.

sion appeared. This variety has not been officially recognized in the USA, but the wire coat is encouraged in Hungary since it can better withstand the winter weather, especially while retrieving ducks from ice-cold water and sitting (wet) for hours in a boat.

The Hungarian pointer is expected to be an all-rounder, searching diligently, not ranging too far, and marking and retrieving from land and water. These are gentle dogs, willing to please but not adapting well to a harsh hand. Their character is defined by their Hungarian name, *Vizsla*, meaning alert and responsive.

The breed is more refined than many of the other European utility dogs, only moderate of bone, standing high on cat feet, with a hint of an arch to the loin. Perhaps that "yellow dog from Turkey" had some of the sighthound in him! But breeders are warned to avoid letting their dog degenerate into one too refined and shelly to stand up to the work expected of him.

The Vizsla is making a good name for himself among American hunters, and his bright gold color stands him well in the show ring. A steady trickle of dual champions is being produced by dedicated breeders who don't want a breed split. Obedience has also found him a capable participant. In 1987, a Vizsla captured the first and only triple American championship, a special award created by AKC for a dog that has won his bench title for the ideal appearance, his field trial championship, and an obedience trial championship won after the UD title is obtained.

Vizsla.

Vizsla.

VOLPINO ITALIANO

COUNTRY: Italy
WEIGHT: Less than 10 pounds
HEIGHT: 11–12 inches
COAT: Long, thick spitz coat
COLOR: Pure white or sable (rare)
OTHER NAMES: Florentine Spitz, Cane de Quirinale
REGISTRY: FCI
GROUP: Northern

Spitz types were found throughout the ancient world. Specimens from this group have been found preserved in European peat bogs which anthropologists trace to 4000 BC. The remains—with curly tails, foxy heads and small erect ears—have been found, dating back over 5,000 years. These little pets wore decorative ivory bracelets and collars. Engravings of similar dogs were found in Greece, and these have been determined to date about 400 BC.

The Volpino has been known and loved by Italian royalty for centuries, being an especial favorite of the ladies. Although bearing a strong resemblance to the Pomeranian, the breed is much older and thus has a different background. The northern dogs found their way south very early in canine history. The Italian word for wolf is *lupo*, and the Keeshond is called both Lupino and Volpino in Italian, so Volpino may be an old term for wolfdog or wolfspitz. Despite his long history, the Volpino is unknown outside of Italy and is now quite rare even in his homeland.

Volpino Italiano, white.

Weimaraner, shorthaired.

WEIMARANER

COUNTRY: Germany
WEIGHT: 70–85 pounds
HEIGHT: 23–28 inches
COAT: Shorthaired—short, fine and hard;
Longhaired—1–2 inches and fringed as a setter
COLOR: Solid light gray
REGISTRY: FCI, AKC, UKC, TKC, CKC
GROUP: Gun Dog

The Weimaraner, favored at the court of Weimar, also looks to the brackes and schweisshunds of Germany for his ancestry. Pointers, a little heavier, a little slower than those used to develop the Shorthair, contributed to his genealogy. Although a dog of Weimaraner type appeared in a Van Dyke painting of the early 1600s, the breed was closer to hound type at that time, and was used for tracking and hunting

851

large game such as bear, wolves and big cats.

As wing shooting began to displace hunting of the diminishing big game, the Weimaraner was crossed with "huenerhunden" to secure more bird dog characteristics. The Weim is a true versatile gun dog, still carrying more of the ancestral hound stamp than many of his German cousins. The large, stiff, flat ear is very similar to the type seen on the German schweisshunds. He is a tough and able hunter, carrying out all of the desirable "after-the-shot" jobs so important to the European hunter.

Breeding of the gray dog was kept close to the vest in Germany for many years by a very strict breed club. Although quality was high, there was never a large number of the breed, even in its homeland.

Only a few were brought to the USA prior to the War but, in the 1940s, interest grew both in America and in other European countries. Unfortunately, the Weim's introduction in the US was accompanied by much hoopla and media hype about his natural all-around abilities. The promoters failed to mention the rigorous training necessary to develop the finished German utility dog. Many gullible new owners were dis-

appointed that the "Gray Ghost" wasn't a wonder dog who came pre-trained! Fortunately, his modern fanciers are following a more prudent path of hunting, showing, field trialing and obedience training their dogs—creating a showcase for the dog-owning public to see. Weims are fine companions and hunting dogs and have accomplished much in the way of obedience and tracking titles as well as a good number of duals. They are resilient enough to be trained in schutzhund protection work.

The longhaired variety is well known and accepted in Europe, although it constitutes a disqualification in the AKC standard. Governed by a recessive gene, the longhairs still, legitimately, pop up now and then in American litters. Although they are prohibited from registration, the longhairs still make fine hunting dogs or obedience prospects. Several Americans have imported registered German Longhaired Weimaraners into the USA in an attempt to have the variety recognized. Although the shorthaired variety has the tail docked to about half the original length, the long coats often are left undocked, more in the venue of the setter.

Weimaraner, longhaired.

Weimaraner.

Weimaraner.

Weimaraner.

Cardigan Welsh Corgi, brindle.

WELSH CORGIS

Welsh Corgi, Cardigan

COUNTRY: Great Britain
WEIGHT: 28–30 pounds maximum
HEIGHT: 12 inches
COAT: Medium-short, harsh and dense
COLOR: Red, sable, brindles, black, tricolor, blue merle, usually with white in Irish pattern; predominant white is a serious fault
REGISTRY: FCI, AKC, UKC, TKC, CKC
GROUP: Herding

Welsh Corgi, Pembroke

COUNTRY: Great Britain
WEIGHT: 24–28 pounds
HEIGHT: 10–12 inches
COAT: Medium-short, dense
COLOR: Red, sable, fawn, black/tan; self-colored or with white markings on legs, chest and neck, and a minimal amount on the head
REGISTRY: FCI, AKC, UKC, TKC, CKC
GROUP: Herding

Although the Cardigan is not as well known as the Pembroke variety, the Cardi is thought to be the older, being brought to Wales with the Celts (about 1200 BC). The Pembroke is a comparative newcomer to the Welsh, entering with Flemish weavers around the tenth century. Another theory contends that both breeds descended from Swedish Vallhunds brought to the Welsh coast by Viking invaders in the ninth century.

The derivation of the name Corgi is attributed to the Celtic word for dog (*corgi*). Other tales passed on through generations say that the little dogs were named for *cor*, dwarf, and *gi*, dog, or for *cur*, watch over.

The crofters of Wales had no land of their own to graze their cattle, as they were allowed to fence only small areas around their dwelling. These poor farmers were granted, however, the liberty of driving their cattle to pasture on the Crown's open range. An intelligent, hard-working droving dog was an asset. Corgis met those requirements and gave an added benefit: they were short-legged, cattle-heeling dogs, developed to run under the legs, avoiding dangerous kicks.

The two breeds are very similar to each other with a few minor differences. In fact, until the 1930s, Pembrokes and Cardigans were interbred. Since that time, each breed's fanciers have emphasized the individualities. The Cardigan is a bit larger, heavier boned and longer bodied, and displays a long, low tail. The Cardi has been called the "yard-long" dog, being the same length from the tip of its nose to the end of its outstretched tail as a Welsh yard. His ears are larger and set wider than the Pembroke's. Color and coats also differ. Legend says that the blue-merle color of the Cardi was brought by fairies one dark night.

The dog from Pembrokeshire has straighter legs and is known for its foxier look, due to its more wedge-shaped head and smaller, higher earset. Occasionally, their pups are born tailless. Those that aren't are docked flush with the body, leaving not even a stump to wag. To remember which is which, word association can help: the Cardigan has a long tail, like the long sleeves in a cardigan sweater, and the Pembroke has a "broke" tail.

Pembroke Welsh Corgi, sable.

Cardigan Welsh Corgi, blue merle.

Although the Cardigan has never become as prevalent, the Pembroke has been in vogue, due to being a favorite of the British royal family. The latter breed has become one of the most prominent dogs in England and Australia.

Both are handsome, loving, learn quickly and are good obedience workers. They are often chosen as small companions by large breed fanciers, because Corgis possess the heart of a larger dog. Full of their own self-importance, they are jaunty little characters. Their working background and sturdy bodies allow them to handle the roughhousing of large, rowdy dogs—or large, rowdy families.

Pembroke Welsh Corgi, red with white.

Cardigan Welsh Corgi.

WELSH SPRINGER SPANIEL

COUNTRY: Great Britain
WEIGHT: 35–45 pounds
COAT: Straight and flat, with moderate feathering
COLOR: Red and white
REGISTRY: FCI, AKC, TKC, CKC
GROUP: Gun Dog

Wales's distinctive red/white spaniel has been portrayed by artists even earlier than the other British spaniels. The Celts originally settled Wales, Ireland and Brittany, and some relationship to the red/white hunting dogs of those areas could easily be established. He was also part of that happy mixture of British spaniels prior to the 20th century. Consequently, a long and pure history is not pretended. His standardization coincided with the time period of the Cocker and the Springer. Breeder A.T. Williams, around 1900, promoted the breed both on the bench and at working trials.

The Welsh differs from the English Springer by reason of his more tapered head, the body, which is lower on leg, the smaller and higher set ear, as well as his clear red and white jacket. A true individual, he should not be dismissed as a "dumpy English Springer" or a "big coarse Cocker." He doesn't show any exaggeration of feathering or coat, which may carry a bit of a wave.

A natural flushing spaniel, he is a keen and tireless worker, and is particularly good in water. In Wales, he is also known as a "Starter." The breed has never become numerous in the United States or in any other country. But his happy spaniel temperament has won loyal friends who continue to foster the breed.

Welsh Springer Spaniels.

Welsh Springer Spaniel.

Welsh Terrier.

Welsh Terrier.

WELSH TERRIER

COUNTRY: Great Britain
WEIGHT: 20 pounds
HEIGHT: 15 inches
COAT: Wire
COLOR: Black/tan
REGISTRY: FCI, AKC, TKC, CKC
GROUP: Terrier

The old black and tan Broken-Coated Terrier (or Old English Terrier) of northern England was used in the foundation of so many of our modern terriers. Today's modern Welshie is probably the closest and the most direct descendant of this ancient strain, with legs stretched and head elongated a bit. They were all shown under the same classification until 1888. One dog, "Dick Turpin," won prizes over a three-year period in both breeds. English owners wanted the type called English Broken-haired, and the Welsh wanted to retain their claim. The Welsh terrier-like persistence won over The Kennel Club.

Used for ratting and for badger and otter hunting like so many other terriers in the last century, the breed is also known for its good nature and ease of handling. To be most efficient in the Welsh hills, he had to be long-legged enough to climb and to run after a horse. He has been compared in general appearance to a small version of the Airedale.

He is broader headed than his cousin, the Wire Fox Terrier, and is always wire-jacketed in black and rich tan. The breed requires stripping four times a year to retain its smart appearance. His tail is docked.

A Welshie has an almost catlike curiosity, which can cause him—and his owners—problems at times. His playfulness and energy call for a firm hand and an outlet such as swimming (which he enjoys immensely), obedience training or romping with older children. He is affectionate and calm in the home.

WEST HIGHLAND WHITE TERRIER

COUNTRY: Great Britain
WEIGHT: 15–22 pounds
HEIGHT: 10–11 inches
COAT: Rough, wiry
COLOR: White
REGISTRY: FCI, AKC, UKC, TKC, CKC
GROUP: Terrier

From the general rough-coated terrier stock of Scotland, white whelps were selected to form this breed. Colored pups were culled, just as the whites were given away or destroyed when creating the purebred Cairn and Scottish Terrier. Like all the other terriers, the Westie was used for vermin control.

These white dogs were easy to distinguish from their surroundings and the wildlife. Thus, white terriers have run the Scottish Highlands for over 300 years. Records show that King James I, a Stuart who ruled England in the 1620s, requested some game "little white earth dogges" out of Argyleshire—possibly Westies.

Colonel Malcolm of Polltalloch, Argyleshire, Scotland, accidentally shot and killed his favorite terrier (a dark-colored one) on an 1860 hunting excursion, and determined to have only white dogs from then on. The Malcolms may have been the originators of the Highland Terrier—as game white terriers were kept by this family since the 18th century or before. At that early time, they were often called Polltalloch Terriers.

Others in this shire also fostered the breed. The Duke of Argyll's estate at Dumbartonshire (Scotland) was called Roseneath. In the 19th

West Highland White Terriers, adult and pup.

West Highland White Terrier.

century, Westies became generally known as Roseneath Terriers, indicating the Duke's patronage and interest. The breed was also known as the White Scottish Terrier in the first organized dog shows in the late 1800s. In 1904, they were first classified under the name of West Highland White Terrier. Westies first charmed Westminster spectators in 1906.

The breed has survived fads exaggerating certain breed points, such as the straight short forelegs, and returned to the sensible structure of today. Its shaggy white coat, small erect ears and black button nose give the Highland Terrier a cute and cuddly image. But it is all terrier with too much energy and spirit for much of that "cuddling nonsense"!

The Westie resembles a Cairn more than the Scottie. Modern show dogs have taken on a clip that accentuates the head. The hard-textured hair causes mud to just fall off when dry. They clean up with a few strokes of the brush, so keeping the coat white is not a major problem.

The breed is hardy, devoted and happy-go-lucky, exhibiting typical terrier tendencies: sturdiness, alarm barks, digging, cock-of-the-walk strutting and one-upmanship with other dogs (especially males). But this dog is not as volatile as some of the others in his group. In fact, the Westie standard warns against excessive pugnacity. Inclement weather is no deterrent to his energetic personality, and he makes a fine family pet.

Westphalian Dachbracke, red with white markings.

WESTPHALIAN DACHSBRACKE

COUNTRY: Germany
HEIGHT: 12–15 inches
COAT: Short, smooth, hard and dense
COLOR: Tricolor, as the Deutsche Bracke, or red with the described white markings
OTHER NAMES: Westfälische Dachsbracke, Sauerlander Dachsbracke
REGISTRY: FCI
GROUP: Hound

Just as the French developed their bassets for closer or slower hound work, the Germans created their dachshunds and dachsbrackes. Short-legged versions of the bracke have been known for a very long time in the western German areas of Westphalia and the Sauerland. Modern authorities feel his development included short-legged mutations of the larger brackes, as well as crosses to the dachshunds of the time. Cynologists Ludwig Beckmann and Otto Grashey first officially described and named the breed in 1886, although portraits from the Middle Ages show the little dog. The Westphalian Dachsbracke was recognized by the German Kennel authorities in 1935, and is fostered and protected today under the umbrella of the Deutsche Bracken Club.

This Dachsbracke has been recruited for hunting hare, fox, wild boar and rabbit in the central high mountains. Hunting in the mountain woods is impossible without dogs. He searches for game, is especially good for the "circle chase" with rabbits and is employed for blood-trailing as well. Often the prey is not as fearful of the smaller Dachsbracke and allows the dog to approach closer before fleeing.

This short hunter performs well unless the snow is very deep. He must be willing to give tongue, but only when sure of his quarry. This vocal attribute is highly desirable, and silent dogs are neutered. The "loud" hunting is utilized only for short distances, often when he chases the quarry around in a circle and back to the waiting hunter. More and more, the Westphalian dog is also used for schweisshund trailing work. This is a pleasant and companionable dog.

Westphalian Dachsbracke, tricolor.

WEST RUSSIAN COURSING HOUNDS

Chortaj

COUNTRY: USSR
HEIGHT: 25–26 inches
COAT: Thick and smooth
COLOR: Many colors allowed, often solids
OTHER NAMES: Eastern Greyhound
REGISTRY: None
GROUP: Southern

South Russian Steppe Hound

COUNTRY: USSR
HEIGHT: 24–28 inches
COLOR: Solid colors
OTHER NAMES: Steppe Borzoi
REGISTRY: None
GROUP: Southern

While the AKC Borzoi has had all the world-wide publicity because of his association with royalty, the lesser known *borzoi* (sighthounds) of the Soviet Union are far older and are still widely bred and hunted. In the northern half of Russia, hunting is done either with scenthounds or laikas. But in the south, across the vast plains and steppes, the villagers still hunt on horseback with one or two sighthounds and sometimes an eagle or falcon instead of a gun. This is a centuries old tradition of the Tartars and Cossacks who settled these regions. The proximity of this area to the Middle East probably answers the question of source, although these dogs came into the area so long ago, they are now considered indigenous breeds.

On the immense steppes from the north Caucasus Mountains, west of the Caspian Sea, up through the Volga and Don River estuaries, abundant game flourished, allowing the continuation of the Cossack tradition of coursing.

In these areas, hunters use both the Chortaj (pronounced *hortai*) and various strains of the South Russian Steppe Hound. They ride out looking for game, depending on the Chortaj, who has eyesight keen enough to spot game up to 280 yards away. Once seen, the pursuit is on. These dogs are endowed with tremendous endurance to withstand the lengthy chases which fi-

Chortaj, gray.

Chortaj.

WETTERHOUN

COUNTRY: Netherlands
WEIGHT: 33–44 pounds
HEIGHT: 21½–23¼ inches
COAT: Thick, tight curls all over, except smooth on the head, bottom third of the ears and the legs
COLOR: Liver, liver/white, black, or black/white; ticking or roaning may appear in the white
OTHER NAMES: Otterhoun, Dutch Spaniel
REGISTRY: FCI
GROUP: Gun Dog

Friesland is a county in the northwestern corner of the Netherlands. The Frisian people have their own culture and language, and have developed two of the native Dutch hunting dogs. The Wetterhoun is one of these distinctive Frisian breeds. The breed's history goes back to the

Wetterhoun, black/white.

nally exhaust the game. A Borzoi, although possessing greater speed, would be worn out himself before the fox, hare or antelope could be run down on the spacious steppes. The Steppe Borzoi can, however, put on short bursts of tremendous speed to turn the quarry before it is able to find safety in a thicket or heavy brush. Young dogs are coupled with experienced ones to train them; those that don't make the grade are shot.

Modern Russian cynologists admit that many dogs of these two breeds have, until very recently, been kept and trained under exceedingly primitive conditions and poor nutrition. Often they roamed at will in the villages. The authorities are diligently working to educate the South Russian hunters in the practical value of proper care and selection. Now more and more of the dogs are being kept penned or leashed. Russians emphasize the importance of dog shows and field trials to compare quality and learn how to improve the breed. A few Chortaj have been exhibited at Moscow shows recently and type is improving. The Chortaj looks very much like a smooth Borzoi, with a stopless down face and rosed ear, while the Steppe Borzois (those that are fixed in type) often are reminiscent of a Sloughi.

Wetterhoun, black/white with roaning.

1600s, or earlier, although their exact origin is unknown. It is surely related to the generic water dogs of Europe, but the tail curled over the back suggests a possible cross to dogs of Nordic type.

Originally, the Wetterhoun (literal translation from the Frisian is water dog) was used to find and kill otters in the lake district of his homeland. For this chore he needed to be tough and fearless. There is little present-day need for an otter dog, but the Wetterhoun is also an excellent close-working flushing dog. He works like many of our modern land spaniels, searching for game and indicating its presence. After the shot, he retrieves well from land or water. Breeders say that while hunting in heavy cover the Wetterhoun "goes like a tank." They love the water and happily swim even in freezing weather. When thwarted in hunting, a pet may turn to stalking moles and mice.

The breed is quite distinctive as a gun dog in both appearance and character. He has a rather wide and powerful body with a strong head and a tightly spiraled tail. The coat must never be woolly, the curls correctly being large bundles of hair with an almost greasy, waterproof texture. An admirer says, "It is a go-getter and goes up to the fish-otter without any fear at all, just like it approaches the polecat and the wildcat as if they didn't bite at all. The Musks even fear the Wetterhoun. . . . "

The Dutch say these dogs are much like the Frisian people, obstinate but, once their hearts are won, loveable and loyal. His standard calls for him to be of stubborn character and reserved with strangers. The Dutch Wetterhoun Club describes the breed: "A cautious Frysk with a heart of gold." While quiet in the home, loving with their people and excellent with children, they do need plenty of daily exercise for their energies. Their reticent nature also makes them natural watchdogs. With their masters, they learn quickly and take well to training, as they love their work.

WHIPPET

Country: Great Britain
Weight: 28 pounds
Height: 18–22 inches
Coat: Short, fine and close
Color: Any color
Registry: FCI, AKC, UKC, TKC, CKC
Group: Southern

English miners loved to gamble, but didn't have the finances for horses or even large dogs, so these sportsmen turned to the "snap" dog trials in the 1800s. Rabbits released in an enclosure were chased down and killed by dogs racing against the clock. The English terriers were outstanding at killing rats, but suffered embarrassment when pitted against the speed of rabbits. They couldn't catch them to kill them!

These terriers were modified with Greyhound blood to increase speed, and some say the Whippet was the result. Later humane laws put a crimp in the gambler's "fun," and the passion turned to racing. Lure or "rag racing" was substituted for the live rabbit. At that time, small greyhound types, such as the Italian Greyhound, added refinement to the terrier blend. Lancashire textile workers, immigrating to New England in the early 1900s, introduced the Whippets and their racing to North America.

Whippet, brown brindle.

As the poor man's race horse, Whippets served the purpose of the working class, who wanted a piece of the racing action. Because these men didn't have fancy oval tracks, and had to arrange their races in back alleys and empty lots, the Whippet became a straight-away sprinter. His acceleration ability gives him jackrabbit starts, covering 200 yards in 12 seconds! Whippets have been clocked at up to 37 mph.

They have a fragile appearance, but that is belied on the track. Slim and powerful as a marathoner, Whippets have the clean lines and dignity of their larger half-brothers the greyhounds. Many breed champions also hold a racing merit award. They make quiet, sturdy and affectionate pets and obedience dogs, delighting in the company of people and other dogs—especially other Whippets!

Recently the appearance of a longhaired version has stirred much controversy. The American parent club has denied them status.

Whippets.

Whippet, brindle.

WIREHAIRED POINTING GRIFFON

COUNTRY: France
WEIGHT: 50–60 pounds
HEIGHT: 22–24 inches
COAT: Hard and coarse, "like a wild boar" with heavy beard and eyebrows
COLOR: Solid chestnut or chestnut with white or steel gray (roan) markings
OTHER NAMES: Korthals Griffon, Griffon d'Arret a Poil Dur
REGISTRY: FCI, AKC, CKC
GROUP: Gun Dog

Edward K. Korthals, a Dutchman who later moved to Germany, created this versatile hunting breed. Its development took place in the 1860s–70s, when so many of the shooting dogs were being developed. Korthals's basic stock started with a bitch named "Mouche," and continued with other griffons of Barbet origin for coat, love of water and intelligence. What he

Above: Wirehaired Pointing Griffon, chestnut with roaning. **Below:** Wirehaired Pointing Griffons.

Wirehaired Pointing Griffon.

crossed the griffons with is not known for sure. Experts speculate that he used various setters or pointers for pointing ability and air scenting; German Shorthairs, Small Münsterländers and others of this type were in abundance in Germany at this time. Many feel he used the Braque Francais. Herr Korthals served as an agent to the Duke of Penthievre in France. Interest soon generated a following for his new breed in that country. Thus, France was the source of much crossbreeding and the area of first interest, which is the reason FCI lists the breed as French.

The Pointing Griffon was brought to the USA in the very early years of this century, and, in fact, was the first of the Continental "all-purpose" breeds to gain official recognition here. But, like so many of the excellent working Continental breeds that followed him, he tended to be denigrated by the American dog press as too slow and unstylish. The United States, at that time, was still a nation of abundant game and vast, unfenced spaces, where the big running pointer/setter was at his glory. Only recently has the modern American hunter had to come to grips with the commonplace situation in Europe

a century ago: urban expansion, increased use of all land for crops and livestock, and shrinking habitat for wild game. Therefore, only lately have American hunters begun to appreciate the Continental breeds, which may be slower but never miss a "single"—dogs who work closer and are more biddable in small farm fields, who trail a wounded running bird so it won't be lost, and retrieve in water as well as on land.

Even though the Korthals breed has been a long-term resident of the USA, it has never reached great heights of popularity, which is acceptable, perhaps preferable, to those who foster it. He has maintained a steady, if small, following among practical hunters. His keen nose and passion for the hunt are still present. Only a few are ever seen in American show rings. The breed club in America is adamant in stressing working qualities and soundness. The Korthals is still bred in Europe as well.

His tail is docked to leave a third, and his wiry, bristly coat requires a minimum of brushing. He is an intelligent, affectionate dog, but is also active and energetic. The Pointing Griffon needs plenty of exercise, especially if he is to be kept in the house.

XOLOITZCUINTLIS

Xoloitzcuintli

COUNTRY: Mexico
HEIGHT: 13–22½ inches (Standard and Miniature)
COAT: Hairless, with a wisp of short, thin hair on head and nape, feet and tail tip; Powderpuff variety
COLOR: Skin can be dark solid charcoal, slate, reddish gray, liver or bronze preferred; pink or coffee colored spots are permissible
OTHER NAMES: Standard Mexican Hairless
REGISTRY: FCI
GROUP: Southern

Xoloitzcuintli, Toy

COUNTRY: Mexico
HEIGHT: 11–12 inches (size of small Fox Terrier)
COAT: Hairless, with a wisp of short, thin hair on head and nape, feet and tail tip; Powderpuff variety
COLOR: Skin can be dark solid charcoal, slate, reddish gray, liver or bronze preferred; pink or coffee colored spots permissible
OTHER NAMES: Mexican Hairless, Tepeizeuintli
REGISTRY: CKC
GROUP: Southern

Ancestors of the Aztec Indians brought hairless dogs called *Biche*, meaning naked, with them when they arrived in Mexico from Asia. The Aztecs enjoyed the hairless dogs as pets, but also found them useful as bedwarmers and sacrificial offerings. The Mexican Hairless and the larger variety, Xoloitzcuintli (pronounced *show-low-eats-QUEEN-tlee*), warmed their stomachs—inside and out. Clay figures and remains of these dogs, dating from 300 to 900 AD, have been found in burial sites, where the dogs guided the souls to a happy afterlife—and furnished nourishment until it was reached.

After the Spanish conquest, the great Aztec society disappeared, and with it the pampered pet/culinary delicacy. Small numbers of Xolos survived in remote villages. They were not forgotten, however. Famed Mexican artist Diego Rivera captured them in his murals. In the 1950s, the Mexican Kennel Club made a concerted effort to re-establish this distinct national breed.

The toasty warm body heat of these hairless dogs made them in demand as ancient hot-water bottles, relieving stomach pains and rheumatic joints, or simply warming chill nights. Extreme cold made for a "Three Dog Night." The breed's palliative qualities magnified until its "healing powers" became a panacea. The

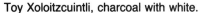

Toy Xoloitzcuintli, charcoal with white.

warmth from these dogs is still enjoyed today, particularly by the elderly.

The Xolo and Mexican Hairless are identical except for size. The Mexican KC feels that the size variation is acceptable and recognizes them as one breed, the Xolo. In the USA, however, the smaller variety has been renamed the Mexican Hairless. The ancient link of both varieties to the pariahs and sighthounds is evident in the racy, elegant body, streamlined head and lighter bone. Ears must be erect. Structurewise the Xolo is similar in appearance to the standard Manchester Terrier.

Their character is one of happy, though calm, temperament without fear. In fact, the Xolo makes a good alarm dog, noisy only when necessary. Considered totally hairless, he sometimes has a bit of fuzz on the top of the head and a hair or two on the tail. They are admired for their elegance, unique appearance, personality—and hairlessness. The very fact that they have no hair makes them a choice for allergic owners,

Toy Xoloitzcuintli.

Toy Xoloitzcuintli, slate.

with the side benefits of cleanliness, no doggy odor and no fleas!

Time saved on coat grooming, however, is spent on skin care. The fragile skin is susceptible to sunburn, drying irritations and tears from other dogs and objects. All hairless breeds must be protected from the cold by providing the knit sweater or coat that Nature left off. Although powderpuff coats occur in about one of three, they are disqualified and may not be shown.

The Mexican Hairless was recognized by AKC until 1959, when a lack of registrations and show entries caused it to be dropped. The CKC still recognizes the breed, and a nucleus of dedicated fanciers in North America still promote the small Mexican.

Above: Toy Xoloitzcuintli, coated variety. **Below:** Xoloitzcuintli, slate.

Above: Toy Xoloitzcuintli, coated variety, charcoal and white. **Below:** Toy Xoloitzcuintli, reddish gray.

YORKSHIRE TERRIER

COUNTRY: Great Britain
WEIGHT: Under 7 pounds
HEIGHT: 9 inches
COAT: Long, straight; glossy, fine and silky
COLOR: Blue/tan
REGISTRY: FCI, AKC, UKC, TKC, CKC
GROUP: Terrier

The Yorkshire came from the same district as the Airedale, appearing for the first time around 1850, with "Huddersfeld Ben" listed as the first Yorkie. His background is not well documented, although speculation says Old English Black/Tan Terriers contributed the general terrier outline and mental qualities. Maltese donated the long, silky coat and petite face. The Skye fixed terrier temperament while retaining the coat. Each breeder, however, may have used a different "recipe."

These small, silky-coated terriers were in great demand by the wealthy families of Yorkshire. Poor farmers and workers occasionally established a lucrative sideline by producing puppies to fill that demand, and the competition to "corner the market" made these breeders closed-mouthed about their formulas.

Yorkshire Terriers, adult and pup.

They were originally called Broken-haired Scotch or Yorkshire Terriers, although their coat is not similar to the other brokenhaired terriers. About 1870, the breed became known as the Yorkshire Terrier. He was promoted in the eastern US by Americans who adored the little sprite, as well as in England. The size of today's toy was set by choosing the smaller specimens of the original 12–14 pound variety. While the selective breeding was occurring, size varied from under three to 13 pounds. Coat, too, was much shorter, though silky even at that time. Terrier advocates of the time degraded the "dresser drawer dog" and predicted little future for him. How wrong they were! By the 20th century, he was prized throughout the world.

Yorkies are spunky, which was aptly evidenced by "Smokey," spoils of WWII. American William Wynne found the Yorkie in a shell hole near Japanese lines in New Guinea. Nobody claimed her, and she seemed not to understand either Japanese or English. Smokey backpacked through the rest of the war, accompanying Wynne on 150 air raids and 12 air-sea rescue missions. She even survived a typhoon at Okinawa. In between these feats, she learned tricks which entertained the troops and enabled her to assist the Signal Corps by carrying a telegraph wire through a 70–foot, eight-inch pipe. No timid toy, Smokey also jumped from a 30–foot tower with her specially made parachute. After the War, Smokey and Wynne were a hit at veterans' hospitals. A few years later, another Yorkie entered politics when "Pasha" trotted the halls of the White House with the Nixon family.

Their handy, pick-me-up size makes them ideal travel companions. As with most tiny toys, the Yorkie is not the best choice for young children. The smallest dog ever recorded, according to the *1985 Guinness Book of World Records*, is "Sylvia," a Yorkie adult, at ten ounces. Despite their size, however, they possess the typical terrier temperament and are spirited and self-assured. Affectionate and devoted to their owners, they won't hesitate to sound the alarm if danger lurks. Born black/tan, the black slowly changes to a dark steel blue by adulthood, enhanced by the rich tan markings. Routine grooming is necessary.

Yorkshire Terrier.

Trio of Yorkshire Terriers.

Yorkshire Terrier.

YUGOSLAVIAN HOUNDS

Balkan Hound

COUNTRY: Yugoslavia
WEIGHT: 44 pounds
HEIGHT: 18–21 inches
COAT: Short, but coarse, thick and flat
COLOR: Black and tan saddled
OTHER NAMES: Balkanski Gonič
REGISTRY: FCI
GROUP: Hound

Bosnian Roughhaired Hound

COUNTRY: Yugoslavia
WEIGHT: 35–53 pounds
HEIGHT: 18–22 inches
COAT: Long (4 inches); hard and bristly, with a thick undercoat
COLOR: Grain yellow, reddish yellow, earth gray, blackish; bicolors and tricolors also acceptable
OTHER NAMES: Bosanski Barak
REGISTRY: FCI
GROUP: Hound

Bosnian Roughhaired Hound, gray.

Yugoslavian Mountain Hound.

Istrian Hound, Smoothhaired

COUNTRY: Yugoslavia
WEIGHT: 35–50 pounds
HEIGHT: 18–21 inches
COAT: Short and fine
COLOR: White; orange or yellow markings mainly on ears, with a few markings allowed on body, especially at base of tail
OTHER NAMES: Kratkodlaki Itrski Gonič
REGISTRY: FCI
GROUP: Hound

Istrian Hound, Wirehaired

COUNTRY: Yugoslavia
WEIGHT: 35–53 pounds
HEIGHT: 18–23 inches
COAT: 2–3-inch wiry outer coat, close to the body; with eyebrows and beard; woolly undercoat
COLOR: White; orange or yellow markings mainly on ears, with a few markings allowed on body, especially at base of tail
OTHER NAMES: Resasti Itrski Gonič
REGISTRY: FCI
GROUP: Hound

Posavac Hound

COUNTRY: Yugoslavia
WEIGHT: 40 pounds
HEIGHT: 18–23 inches
COAT: ¾–1½ inches, thick, hard and wiry
COLOR: Shades of wheaten or red; white on chest, abdomen and paws allowed
OTHER NAMES: Posavski Gonič
REGISTRY: FCI
GROUP: Hound

Yugoslavian Mountain Hound

COUNTRY: Yugoslavia
WEIGHT: 44–55 pounds
HEIGHT: 18-22 inches
COAT: Thick, flat, short but coarse
COLOR: Black and tan
OTHER NAMES: Jugoslavenski Planinski Gonič
REGISTRY: FCI
GROUP: Hound

Posavac Hound.

Yugoslavian Tricolor Hound

COUNTRY: Yugoslavia
WEIGHT: 44–55 pounds
HEIGHT: 18–22 inches
COAT: Thick, flat, short but coarse
COLOR: Tricolor with lots of tan, white only on face, chest, tail tip, feet and legs
OTHER NAMES: Jugoslavenski Tribarvni Gonič
REGISTRY: FCI
GROUP: Hound

Although Yugoslavia was designated a country only in this century, the Slavic people who live there have an ancient history. Because the Yugoslavian ports on the Adriatic were on the major trade routes of the Phoenicians, all Slavic hounds have long roots reaching back to ancient times. They most likely are a mixture of the early sighthounds, which were almost pariah in type, crossed with the scenthounds of Europe.

These Yugoslavian dogs (and their Greek

Yugoslavian Tricolor Hound.

Smoothhaired Istrian Hound.

pitched, full voice.

The dogs of Istria differ from the other hounds of Yugoslavia because of their distinctive white-and-orange color. The lighter the shade of orange-yellow spots, the purer the dog is considered. They have a racier build, cat feet, a head with less stop and a higher set ear. The thinner the tail, the more valued the dog. The Wirehaired version, with his beard and brows, is slightly larger but judged by the same standard as the smooth. In recent years, the Wirehaired Istrian has been gaining proponents among nonhunters in Yugoslavia. His peaceful character makes him a fine house companion, and his striking appearance draws attention at dog shows.

The fertile northcentral plains along the Sava River of Yugoslavia are the home of the Posavac Hound. Little known outside its own locale, this dog is an esteemed hunting companion at home and is used for hare and deer. His bright red wheaten color creates a handsome effect. Much like the other Yugoslavian hounds, he is a bit low on leg. He is obedient and affectionate with the family.

Bosnia marks the beginning of the mountainous inland area in northcentral Yugoslavia. In the last century, the rough-jacketed Bosnian Hound was bred especially for withstanding bad weather and going over rough terrain. He is unknown outside his native country. The standard calls for a body length ten percent greater than height, a strong muzzle with beard and moustaches, heavy ears, and the four-inch rough coat.

The last three smooth-coated hounds of Yugoslavia are all from the south and are quite similar. The Mountain Hound is from the Planina range in southwestern Yugoslavia, the Balkan Hound is from the eastern regions near the Bulgarian border and the Tricolor is also from the south. Used over hostile terrain, they are all strong and untiring hunting "pros" for hare, fox, deer and even boar. The Balkan is known particularly for his high-pitched voice and his ability as a tracking dog. These breeds are not promoted outside their specific areas. Current correspondence from Yugoslavian breeders indicates that the Tricolor and Mountain Hounds are now very rare.

cousins) are the sole scenthounds of southeastern Europe and the Balkans. All are quite similar in type. They are moderate in size, slightly longer than tall and possess fairly good bone. The squarish head has no loose skin and moderate flat ears. While they are passionate hunters, untiring even over the roughest terrain, they all seem to be tranquil, good-natured and affectionate in the home.

Istrian dogs were probably the oldest of these, or at least most like the original type. Istria is a peninsula in the northwestern corner of Yugoslavia jutting out into the Adriatic Sea. Hounds from this area, now called Slovenia, are hunted in small packs or pairs over rough and heavy terrain for fox and hare and are especially sharp against the wild boar. The Istrian Hound is also a talented bloodtrailer and is known for his low-

Above: Smoothhaired Istrian Hound. **Below:** Wirehaired Istrian Hound.

Glossary

AKC. The commonly used abbreviation of American Kennel Club.

American Kennel Club. The official registry for purebred dogs in the United States. Publishes and maintains the Stud Book and handles all litter and individual registrations, transfers of ownership, and so on. Keeps all United States dog show, field trial, and obedience trial records; issues championships and other titles in these areas as they are earned; approves and licenses dog show, obedience trial, and field trial judges; licenses or issues approval to all championship shows, obedience trials, and recognized match shows. Creates and enforces the rules, regulations, and policies by which the breeding, raising, exhibiting, handling, and judging of purebred dogs in the United States are governed. Clubs, not individuals, are members of the American Kennel Club, each of which is represented by a delegate selected from the club's own membership for the purpose of attending the quarterly American Kennel Club meetings as the representative of the member club, to vote on matters discussed at each meeting and to bring back a report to the individual club of any decisions or developments which took place there.

Angulation. The angles formed by the meeting of the bones, generally referring to the shoulder and upper arm in the forequarters and the stifle and hock in the hindquarters.

Autosomal. All genes that are inherited on the regular chromosomes (NOT on the X/Y chromosome). Thus, they follow the regular rules of Mendelian dominance and recessiveness.

Balance. Symmetry and proportion. A wellbalanced dog is one in which all of the parts appear in correct ratio to one another: height to length, head to body, skull to foreface, and neck to head and body.

Beard. Long, thick hair growth on muzzle, especially the lower jaw.

Bench Show. A show where dogs are judged on their appearance. Although most modern shows allow the exhibitor to show his dog and then leave, in the past the dogs were put on display on a "bench" all day for spectators. Thus the term bench showing has remained as a general synonym for conformation showing.

Best in Show. The dog or bitch chosen as the most representative of any dog in any breed from among the group winners at an all-breed dog show. (The dog or bitch that has won Best of Breed next competes in the group of which its breed is a part. Then the first-prize winner of each group meets in an additional competition from which one is selected the Best in Show.)

Bitch. A female dog.

Bite. The manner in which the upper and lower jaws meet.

Black/Silver. A true black and silver has the solid black body with grayish silver markings above the eyes, on the cheeks, under the ears, on the forechest, on the feet and inside of the legs, and under the tail (e.g., Schnauzer).

Black/Tan. Just like the black/silver except the grayish silver points are tan in color (e.g., Rottweiler).

Black/Tan Saddled. The tan marks, as in the black/tan, are much larger including much of the head, upper legs, neck, and belly, and leaving the black only as a "saddle" on the back, as well as on the top of the neck and tail (e.g., German Shepherd Dog).

Blue. There are four distinct colors that are called "blue;" all are inherited differently:
1) *Blue (dilute)*: Dogs born a solid steel or gun metal gray, *always* with a gray nose and paw pads (e.g., blue Great Dane or Chow). 2) *Blue (silvering, graying)*: There is another "blue" that starts black and fades to a blue-gray in adulthood, *always* with a black nose (e.g., Kerry Blue Terrier). 3) *Blue (ticking)*: Another "blue" is created by black roaning on white, *always* with a black nose (e.g., Grand Bleu de Gascogne). 4) *Blue Merle*: This is a marbled gray on black, *always* with a black nose, sometimes with blue eyes. Can also be called harlequin or mottled (e.g., merle Collie).

Bone. Refers to the girth of a dog's leg bones. A dog called "good in bone" has legs that are correct in girth for its breed and for its own general conformation. Well-rounded bone is roundish in appearance, flat bone rather flattish. Light bone is very fine and small in diameter, almost spindle-like in appearance; legs are extremely slender. Heavy bone refers to legs that are thick and sturdy.

Breed. Purebred dogs descended from mutual ancestors refined and developed by man.

Breeder. A person who breeds dogs.

Brisket. The forepart of the body between the forelegs and beneath the chest.

Brood bitch. A female dog used primarily for breeding.

CACIB. A Challenge Certificate offered by the Federation Cynologique Internationale towards a dog's championship.

Canadian Kennel Club. The principle dog registry in Canada. Formed in 1887, the organization devoted itself to the promotion of breeding and exhibiting 'thoroughbred' dogs in Canada, the formulation of rules for the governing of dog exhibition, as well as the recommendation of able judges and the official opening of a registry for purebred dogs.

Canines. Dogs, jackals, wolves, and foxes as a group.

Cat foot. The short-toed, round tight foot similar to that of a cat.

Ch. Commonly used abbreviation of champion.

Challenge Certificate. A card awarded at dog shows in Great Britain by which championship there is gained. Comparable to our Winners Dog and Winners Bitch awards. To become a British champion a dog must win three of these Challenge Certificates at designated championship dog shows.

Champion. A dog or bitch that has won a total of fifteen points, including two majors, the total number under not less than three judges, two of whom must have awarded the majors at AKC point shows.

Character. Appearance, behavior, and temperament considered correct in an individual breed of dog.

Cheeky. Cheeks which bulge out or are rounded in appearance.

Chest. The part of the body enclosed by the ribs.

Chiseled. Clean-cut below the eyes.

Chop Mouth. A hound that does not have a long, drawn out bay, but more of a short, choppy bark as he follows the scent trail.

Chops. Pendulous, loose skin creating jowls. *See* Flews.

CKC. Abbreviation for the Canadian Kennel Club.

Close-coupled. Compact in appearance. Short in the loin.

Closed Trailing. Refers to a dog that follows a scent trail silently.

Coarse. Lacking in refinement or elegance.

Coat. The hair which covers the dog.

Cold Nosed. Refers to a hound that is capable of following a "cold" scent, one that is either very old and/or one that is very difficult to find and follow.

Cold Trailer. Refers to a hound, usually slow working, that has the inherent ability of nose as well as the desire, endurance and tenacity to follow a cold trail.

Condition. General health. A dog said to be in good condition is one carrying exactly the right amount of weight, whose coat looks alive and glossy, and that exhibits a general appearance and demeanor of well-being.

Conformation. The framework of the dog, its form and structure.

Couching. This is a very old term describing hunting dogs that, when they scented game, slowly crept nearer while lowering themselves to the ground. This was a trait desired when birds were captured with nets, or when the dog found birds for the falcon.

Coupling. The section of the body known as the loin. A short-coupled dog is one in which the loin is short.

Crest. The arched portion of the back of the neck.

Crop. Cut the ear leather, usually to cause the ear to stand erect.

Croup. The portion of the back directly above the hind legs.

Cynology. A study of canines.

Dam. Female parent of a dog or bitch.

Dentition. Arrangement of the teeth.

Dewclaws. Extra claws on the inside of the legs. Should generally be removed several days following the puppy's birth. Required in some breeds, unimportant in others, and sometimes a disqualification—all according to the individual breed standard.

Dewlap. Excess loose and pendulous skin at the throat.

Dish-faced. The tip of the nose is placed higher than the stop.

Disqualification. A fault or condition which renders a dog ineligible to compete in organized shows, designated by the breed standard or by a leading dog registry.

Dock. Shorten the tail by cutting it.

Dog. A male of the species. Also used to describe male and female canines collectively.

Dog show. A competition in which dogs have been entered for the purpose of evaluation and to receive the opinion of a judge.

Domed. A top-skull that is rounded rather than flat.

Double coat. A coat consisting of a hard, weather-resistant, protective outer covering over a soft, short, close underlayer which provides warmth.

Down-faced. A downward inclination of the muzzle toward the tip of the nose. Also called a "ranis nose."

Drag. A trail having been prepared by dragging a bag, generally bearing the strong scent of an animal, along the ground.

Drive. The powerful action of the hindquarters which should equal the degree of reach of the forequarters.

Drop ear. Ears carried drooping or folded forward.

Dry head. One exhibiting no excess wrinkle.

Dry neck. A clean, firm neckline free of throatiness or excess skin.

Dual champion. A dog having gained both bench show and field trial championships.

Elbow. The joint of the forearm and upper arm.

Even bite. Exact meeting of the front teeth, tip to tip with no overlap of the uppers or lowers. Generally considered to be less serviceable than the scissors bite, although equally permissible or preferred in some breeds. Also known as level bite.

Expression. The typical expression of the breed as one studies the head. Determined largely by the shape of the eye and its placement.

Fancier. A person actively involved in the sport of purebred dogs.

Fancy. The enthusiasts of a sport or hobby. Dog breeders, exhibitors, judges, and others actively involved with purebred dogs as a group comprise the dog fancy.

Fawn. There are two different colors which can be referred to as "fawn."
1) *Fawn (brown)*: A tan color ranging from light chamois to red wheaten, often with shadings of the red or even black tips on the hairs. *Always* with a black nose. Genetically, this color is the same as sable (e.g., Boxer). 2) *Fawn (gray)*: There is another color sometimes called "fawn" which is a pale grayish brown dilution of brown and blue. These dogs *always* have a pale gray to flesh-colored nose (e.g., Weimaraner).

FCI. Abbreviation of the Federation Cynologique Internationale.

Feathering. The longer fringes of hair that appear on the ears, tail, chest, and legs.

Federation Cynologique Internationale. A canine authority representing numerous countries, principally European, all of which consent to and agree on certain practices and breed identifications. Recognizing each breed of the countries it includes, the FCI registers about 400 breeds—each of the breeds that are federated are thusly eligible for International Championship.

Fetch. Retrieving of game by a dog, or the command for the dog to do so.

Field champion. A dog that has gained the title field champion has defeated a specified number of dogs in specified competition at a series of American Kennel Club licensed or member field trials.

Field trial. A competition for specified Hound or Sporting breeds where dogs are judged according to their ability and style on following a game trail or on finding and retrieving game.

Finishing a dog. Refers to completing a dog's championship, obedience title, or field trial title.

Flank. The side of the body through the loin area.

Flat bone. Bones of the leg which are not round.

Flat-sided. Ribs that are flat down the side rather than slightly rounded.

Fld. Ch. Abbreviation of field champion, used as a prefix before the dog's name.

Flews. A pendulous condition of the skin at the corners of the mouth.

Flush. To drive birds from cover. To spring at them. To force them to take flight.

Flying ears. Ears correctly carried dropped or folded that stand up or tend to "fly" upon occasion.

Foreface. The muzzle of the dog.

Front. The forepart of the body viewed head-on. Includes the head, forelegs, shoulders, chest, and feet.

Gait. The manner in which a dog walks or trots.

Gallop. The fastest gait. Never to be used in the show ring, but often used when hunting, racing, etc.

Game. The animals or wild birds which are hunted.

Gay tail. Tail carried high.

Gazehound. A general name for the swift hounds that run by sight; a synonym for sighthound or windhound.

Get. Puppies.

Groom. To bathe, brush, comb, and trim your dog.

Groups. Refers to the variety groups in which all breeds of dogs are divided.

Gun Dog. One that has been specifically trained to work with man in the field for retrieving game that has been shot and for locating live game.

Guns. The persons who do the shooting during field trials.

Gun-shy. Describes a dog that cringes or shows other signs of fear at the sound or sight of a gun.

Hackney action. High lifting of the forefeet in the manner of a hackney pony.

Hard-mouthed. A dog that grasps the game too firmly in retrieving, causing bites and tooth marks.

Hare foot. An elongated paw, like the foot of a hare.

Haw. This is the red membrane (third eyelid) in the inner corner of a dog's eye. When a dog has a lot of heavy facial skin or loose hanging lids, the haw is more apparent.

Hock. The joint between the second thigh and the metatarsus.

Honorable scars. Those incurred as a result of working injuries.

Hot nosed. Refers to a dog that can follow a fresh trail, one made by an animal that has a scent that is easy to follow (like a fox).

Hot trailing. Refers to a hound that follows a hot scent, usually at much greater speed than the cold nosed dog.

Int. Ch. An abbreviation of International Champion.

International Champion. A dog awarded four CACIB cards at F.C.I. dog shows.

Jowls. Flesh of lips and jaws.

Kennel. The building in which dogs are housed. Also used when referring to a person's collective dogs.

Kennel Club. The Kennel Club of Great Britain is the principle dog registering organization in the country and was founded in 1873. The registry's objective and purpose is set forth in its rule number I as "promoting the improvement of Dogs, Dog Shows, Field Trials, Working Trials and Obedience Tests." Functioning in an advisory capacity to the organization is an elected body of persons with similar objectives to the club, breeding, training and exhibiting purebred dogs.

Layback. 1) Describes correctly angulated shoulders. 2) Describes a short-faced dog whose pushed-in nose placement is accompanied by undershot jaw.

Leather. The ear flap. Also the skin of the actual nose.

Level bite. Another way of describing an even bite, as teeth of both jaws meet exactly.

Lippy. Lips that are pendulous or do not fit tightly.

Liver. A brown color ranging from reddish to chocolate, *always* with a brown nose and paw pads (e.g., Irish Water Spaniel).

Loin. Area of the sides between the lower ribs and hindquarters.

Loose-eyed. Refers to sheep-herding dogs that can direct sheep by eye contact (see strong-eyed) but can also round up by heeling; their eye contact is not as intense as the strong-eyed dog.

Lumbering. A clumsy, awkward gait.

Lure coursing. Sighthounds used to course after live game, but most modern contests use a rag or mechanical lure for the dogs to chase.

Mane. The long hair growing on the top and upper sides of the neck.

Mate. To breed a dog and a bitch to one another. Littermates are dogs which are born in the same litter.

Merle. *See* Blue Merle.

Miscellaneous Class. A class provided at AKC point shows in which specified breeds may compete in the absence of their own breed classification. Dogs of breeds in the process of becoming recognized by AKC may compete in this class prior to the eventual provision of their own individual breed classification.

Mustache. Long, thick hair growth on the upper muzzle.

Muzzle. 1) The part of the head in front of the eyes. 2) To fasten something over the mouth, usually to prevent biting.

Nick. A successful breeding that results in puppies of excellent quality.

Non-slip retriever. A dog not expected to flush or to find game; one that merely walks at heel, marks the fall, then retrieves upon command.

Nose. Describes the dog's organ of smell, but also refers to his talent at scenting. A dog with a "good nose" is one adept at picking up and following a scent trail.

Obedience trial. A licensed obedience trial is one held under AKC rules at which it is possible to gain a "leg" towards a dog's obedience title or titles.

Obedience trial champion. Denotes that a dog has attained obedience trial championship under AKC regulations by having gained a specified number of points and first place awards.

Occiput. Upper back point of skull.

O.F.A. Commonly used abbreviation for Orthopedic Foundation for Animals.

Open trailing: Refers to a hound that begins baying as soon as he has found the scent (opens) and continues as long as he is on the trail.

Orthopedic Foundation for Animals. This organization is ready to read the hip radiographs of dogs and certify the existence of or freedom from hip dysplasia. Board-certified radiologists read vast numbers of these files each year.

O.T. Ch. An abbreviation of the obedience trial champion title.

Pad. Thick protective covering of the bottom of the foot. Serves as a shock absorber.

Parti-colored. A spotted dog, *see* Pied.

Patterned white. White markings restricted to a symmetrical pattern on feet, tail tip, chest mark, facial blaze, and sometimes a collar, also called "Boston" or "Irish" spotting (e.g., Boston Terrier).

Pied. Patches of color on a white background, also called piebald, parti-color, or "broken" pattern. When there are two colors, it is called bi-colored and, if there are three, the dog is referred to as tri-color (e.g., Pointer).

Pile. Soft hair making a dense undercoat.

Plume. A long fringe of hair on the tail.

Poach. To trespass on private property when hunting.

Police dog. Any dog that has been trained to do police work.

Quality. Excellence of type and conformation.

Racy. Lightly built, appearing overly long in leg and lacking substance.

Rangy. Excessive length of body combined with shallowness through the ribs and chest.

Reach. The distance to which the forelegs reach out in gaiting, which should correspond with the strength and drive of the hindquarters.

Register. To record your dog with your dog-registering organization.

Roach back. A convex curvature of the top-line of the dog.

Roan. Individual colored hairs in the white markings. Red hairs create a "red roan" and black hairs give a steel gray appearance called "blue" or "blue roan" (e.g., Australian Cattle Dog).

Rolling gait. An aimless, ambling type of action correct in some breeds but to be faulted in others.

Sable. A rich reddish brown with shadings of color, may or may not have black tipping on each hair. Genetically it is the same as tan fawn (e.g., Rough Collie).

Scissors bite. The outer tips of the lower incisors touch the inner tips of the upper incisors. Generally considered to be the most serviceable type of jaw formation.

Self-colored. When a dog is a solid color, without white markings.

Semi-open trailing. Refers to a dog that will bark some of the time on trail (e.g., chop mouth), but really begins howling when he has the quarry treed.

Shelly. A body lacking in substance.

Shoulder height. The height of the dog from the ground to the highest point of the withers.

Sire. The male parent.

Soundness. Mental and physical stability. Sometimes used as well to denote the manner in which the dog gaits.

Stake. A class in field trial competition.

Standard. The official description of the ideal specimen of a breed. The Standard of Perfection is drawn up by the parent specialty club (usually by a special committee to whom the task is assigned), is approved by the membership and by the American Kennel Club, and then serves as a guide to breeders and to judges in decisions regarding the merit, or lack of it, in evaluating individual dogs.

Stifle. The joint of the hind leg corresponding to a person's knee.

Stop. The step-up from nose to skull; the indentation at the juncture of the skull and foreface.

Straight behind. Lacking angulation in the hindquarters.

Strong-eyed. Refers to sheep-herding dogs who have intense qualities of staring down and almost hypnotically directing sheep by eye contact.

Stud. A male dog that is used for breeding.

Stud book. The official record kept on the breeding particulars of recognized breeds of dogs.

Substance. Degree of bone size.

Tail set. Manner in which the tail is placed on the rump.

Thigh. Hindquarters from the stifle to the hip.

Throatiness. Excessive loose skin at the throat.

Ticking: Small dots of color in the white markings, "freckles" (e.g., English Springer Spaniel).

TKC. Abbreviation for The Kennel Club of Great Britain employed in this atlas. *See* Kennel Club.

Tongue: This term is used as a synonym for bay, howl or "open," all terms meaning the dog is vocal when he is following a scent trail.

Topline. The dog's back from withers to tail set.

Trail. Hunt by following a trail scent.

Tricolor. Indicating black/tan or chocolate/tan in combinations of white. There are several forms of the color.
1) *Pied tricolor*: White and black spots broken over the entire body, plus tan marks over eyes, on cheeks, under ears, on feet and around vent (e.g., English Toy Spaniel, Prince Charles variety). 2) *Saddled tricolor*: White and tan spots evenly distributed, plus the black saddle (e.g., Foxhound). 3) *Patterned tricolor*: A true black/tan color plus white blaze, chest, feet, tail tip (e.g., Bernese Mountain Dog).

Trot. The gait at which the dog moves in a rhythmic two-beat action, right front and left hind foot and left front and right hind foot each striking the ground together.

Tuck-up. The amount of "waist line" behind the rib cage, measured as the depth of body at the loin. The Greyhound has a large amount of tuck-up, while the Mastiff has very little.

Type. The combination of features which makes a breed unique, distinguishing it from all others.

UKC. Abbreviation for the United Kennel Club.

Undershot. The front teeth of the lower jaw reach beyond the front teeth of the upper jaw.

United Kennel Club. United Kennel Club (UKC) was established in 1898 by Mr. Chauncey Z. Bennett and is the second largest all-breed registry in the United States. It is privately owned and controlled, and has developed the only complete computer registry system. Through its outstanding registration system, the UKC offers a six- or seven-generation pedigree to qualifying registrants. The UKC is the first registry to recognize all six breeds of Coonhound.

Upper arm. The foreleg between the forearm and the shoulder blade.

Vent. A synonym for the anus, or the area under the tail.

Walk. The gait in which three feet support the body, each lifting in regular sequence, one at a time, off the ground.

W.C. An abbreviation of Working Certificate.

Withers. The highest point of the shoulders, right behind the neck.

Working Certificate. An award earned by dogs who have proven their hunting ability and who are not gun-shy.

Bibliography

Alzugaray, Domingo and Catia, eds., *Fox Paulistinha*, Editora Tres Ltda, Sao Paulo, SP.

American Chinese Crested Club official brochure.

American Kennel Club official publication, *The Complete Dog Book*, Doubleday & Co., Inc., Garden City, NY, 1968.

American Kennel Gazette, "Dogs from the Roof of the World," 3/37.

Anatolian Shepherd Dog Club of America Newsletter, 2/84.

Anatolian Shepherd Dog Club of America official pamphlet.

Archer, Colleen, "Canada's Native Dog," *Dog World*, 8/85, p. 22.

Arnold, Cecilia, "A Tribute to History," *Pure-Bred Dogs/-American Kennel Gazette*, 12/86, pp. 34-41.

Ash, Edward C., *Dogs: Their History and Development*, Vol. I, 1st published London, 1927, reissued by Benjamin Blom, Inc., New York, 1972.

——. *The New Book of the Dog*, MacMillan Co., New York, 1939.

v. August Grimpe, Druck, Deutsches Hunde-Stamm Buch, Hannover, 1881.

Australian Kennel Control Council official publication, *Dogs of Australia*, Hedges and Bell Printing, Singapore, 1984.

Balmain, Margot, "The True Blue Australian," *Dog Fancy*, 3/87, p. 44.

Barker, A.J. and H.A., *The Complete Book of Dogs*, Bison Books, Ltd., London, 1982.

Barnard, Charles N., "The Descendants of Walden's Dog," *True*, Feb. 19??, pp. 37-38, 62-63.

Beresford, Pat, "A Golden Jubilee," *Pure-Bred Dogs/American Kennel Gazette*, 11/86, pp. 70-73.

——. "Duality of Purpose," *Pure-Bred Dogs/American Kennel Gazette*, 1/87, p. 61.

Bergstrom, Enid S., "Ovcharka—the 'New' Police Dog?" *Dog World*, 2/83, pp. 14-15.

Berners, Dame Juliana, *Boke of St. Albans*, 1486.

Bernues, Juan Fernando, Carlos Contera Alejandre, et al., *El Libro del Mastin del Pirineo*, Guara Editorial, Zaragoza, Spain 1983.

Bixler, Alice, "The Loverly Lowchen," *Dogs in Canada*, 12/81, pp. 14-15.

Bobb, Maggie, "Confessions of a Filaphile," *Dog World*, 1/86, pp. 26, 83-86.

The Borzoi Club of America, Inc., official publications.

Boxhall-James, Betty, "Chinese Crested Powderpuff and Hairless," English Club Newsletter.

Boykin Spaniel Society official brochure, Camden, SC.

Brandenburger, Dale, *Plott Hound History*.

Braund, Kathryn, *The Uncommon Dog Breeds*, Arco, New York, 1975.

Braund, Kathryn and Deyanne F. Miller, *The Complete Portuguese Water Dog*, Howell Book House, NY, NY, 1986.

Brearley, Joan McDonald, *The Book of the Afghan Hound*, T.F.H. Publications, Inc., Neptune City, NJ, 1978.

——.*The Book of the Akita*, T.F.H. Publications, Inc., Neptune City, NJ, 1985.

——. *The Book of the Bulldog*, T.F.H. Publications, Inc., Neptune City, NJ, 1985.

——. *The Book of the Cocker Spaniel*, T.F.H. Publications, Inc., Neptune City, NJ, 1982.

——. *The Book of the Maltese*, T.F.H. Publications, Inc., Neptune City, NJ, 1984.

——. *The Book of the Yorkshire Terrier*, T.F.H. Publications, Inc., Neptune City, NJ, 1984.

The Briard Club of America official brochure.

Brisbin, Dr. I. Lehr, Jr., "Primitive Dogs," *Pure-Bred Dogs/American Kennel Gazette*, 3/87, p. 79.

Brown, E. Jane, "Polish Pup Shows Pizzazz," *Dog World*, 7/83, p. 132.

Browne, A. Gondrexon-Ives, *The Hamlyn Guide to Dogs*, Hamlyn Pub. Group, Ltd., London, 1974.

Bruce, James Jr., "Early History," Redbone Coonhound Club of America Yearbook.

Burger, Carl, *All About Dogs*, Random House, 1962.

Burgoin, Gillian, *Guide to the Weimaraner*, The Boydell Press, Suffolk, England, 1985.

Butrick, Carol, "A Terviffic Event, An Historic Perspective," *Pure-Bred Dogs/American Kennel Gazette*, 11/86, p. 63.

Byrd, Richard Evelyn, *Little America*, G.P. Putnam's Sons, New York, 1930.

Caius, Iohannes (Johannes), *Of English Dogges*, London, 1576; modern reproduction DaCapo Press, NY, 1969.

Calif, Lee, "Keeping the Memories Alive," *Canine Chronicle*, 5/31/86.

Calkins, Diane, "Pit Bulls," *Dog Fancy*, 8/86, pp. 36-37, 41-43.

Canaan Club of America, Inc., brochure, "Canaan Dog."

Canadian Kennel Club official publication, *The Canadian Kennel Club Book of Dogs*, General Publishing Co., Ltd., Toronto, Canada, 1982.

Canine Chronicle, "Chinese Crested to Rejoin Miscellaneous Group Feb. 1," 1/4/86, p. 32.

Canine Chronicle, "Petit Basset Griffon Vendeen Find a

New Home with CKC," 7/31/85, p. 26.

Canine Classified, ed. Anne Page, "Petit Basset Griffon Vendeen," Vol. IV, issue 3, 3/86, pp. 16, 18, 20.

Caras, Roger, *A Celebration of Dogs*, Times Books, 1982.

————. "A Plea for the Chinook," *Long Island Newsday Magazine*, 3/20/84.

Cavill, David, *All About the Spitz Breeds*, Pelham Books Ltd., England, 1978.

Clouse, Col. Dorman W., "History of the Redbone," Redbone Coonhound Club of America Yearbook.

Cooper, Mrs. B.M., "The Origin and Development of the Australian Kelpie."

Coppinger, Lorna and the International Sled Dog Racing Assoc., *The World of Sled Dogs*, Howell Book House, NY, NY, 1977.

Coppinger, Lorna and Raymond, "So Firm a Friendship," *Natural History*, Vol. 89, No. 3, 3/80.

————. "Livestock-Guarding Dogs," *Blair & Ketchum's Country Journal*, Vol. VII, No. 4, 4/80, pp. 68-77.

————. *Livestock Guarding Dogs for U.S. Agriculture*, Livestock Dog Project, Montague, MA, 1978.

Crisp, W.G., "Tahltan Bear Dog," *Dogs in Canada*, 12/56, pp. 13-15.

Dangerfield, Stanley and Elsworth Howell, eds., *The International Encyclopedia of Dogs*, Rainbird Reference Books, Ltd., London, 1971.

Dannen, Kent and Donna, "The Samoyed," *Dog Fancy*, 2/87, pp. 36, 41.

Darwin, Charles, *The Zoology of the Voyage of H.M.S. Beagle*, Nova Pacifica Pub., Wellington, NZ, 1833.

Davis, Henry P., revised and updated, *The New Dog Encyclopedia*, Stackpole Books, Harrisburg, PA, 1970.

De Bernes, Suzanne, "The Italian Spinone," *Our Dogs*, England, 5/20/82, p. 10.

Debo, Ellen Weathers, *The Shar-Pei*, T.F.H. Publications, Inc., Neptune City, NJ, 1986.

Demidoff, Lorna and Michael Jennings, *The Complete Siberian Husky*, 1st Ed., Howell Book House, NY, NY, 1978.

Deutscher Landseer Club (1976-1981), E.V. Zuchtbuch, Netherlands, 1983.

Dickerson, S.M., *Chinese Crested*.

Diwan of Abu Nuwas, Court Poet and Jester, 800 A.D.

Dimov, D., *Dogs of the Soviet Union*, Vadim Yudin, translator, unpublished manuscript.

Dogo Argentino Club of America, Goodland, IN, "The Dogo Argentino," *Canine Chronicle*, 12/17/86, p. 4a.

Dogs USA, Susan Pearce, ed., Elizabeth Dunn, pub., Ontario, Canada, 10/86.

Dog World Magazine, official standards issue, Maclean Hunter Publishing Corp., Chicago, IL, 6/86.

Donahue, Jane B., "Puli Power," *Pure-Bred Dogs/American Kennel Gazette*, 1/84, p. 41.

Donovan, John A.K., *The Irish Wolfhound—the Great Symbol of Ireland*, Alpine Publication, Inc., Loveland, CO, 1986.

Dorl, J., "The 'Imperial' Pekingese," *Pure-Bred Dogs/American Kennel Gazette*, 5/86, p. 37.

Draper, Dr. Samuel and Joan M. Brearley, *The Book of the*

Chow Chow, T.F.H. Publications, Inc., Neptune City, NJ, 1977.

Drury, Mrs. Maynard K., *This is the Newfoundland*, T.F.H. Publications, Inc., Neptune City, NJ, 1978.

Dullinger, Betty R., "The Yorkshire Terrier," *Dog Fancy*, 5/87, pp. 36, 41.

Durant, John, "Prodigious Perry Greene," *The Saturday Evening Post*, 1/11/17, pp. 26-27, 63, 66, 68-69.

The Dutch Sheepdog Club official brochure, Kloosterburen, Netherlands.

Egan, Pierce, "The Bull Bait," *Sporting Anecdotes*, 1820.

English, Dorothy, "Can You Name This Dog?" *Dog Fancy*, 1/87, p. 60.

Eskimo Dog Club of Great Britain, *The Eskimo Dog*.

Fiennes, Richard and Alice, *The Natural History of Dogs*, Bonanza Books, New York, 1968.

The Finnish Spitz Club of America official publication.

Fiorone, Fiorenzo, *The Encyclopedia of Dogs; The Canine Breeds*, Thomas Y. Crowell Company, New York, (first pub. in Italy as *Enciclopedia del Cane* in 1970), translation copyright 1973 by Rizzoli Editore.

Flamholtz, Cathy J., *A Celebration of Rare Breeds*, OTR Publications, 1986.

Foy, Marcia, *The Basset Hound*, T.F.H. Publications, Inc., Neptune City, NJ, 1985.

Foy, Marcia and Anna Katherine Nicholas, *The Beagle*, T.F.H. Publications, Inc., Neptune City, NJ, 1985.

Fraser, Jackie, "Chow Mania, An Ancient History," *Pure-Bred Dogs/American Kennel Gazette*, 8/86, p. 65.

————. "Dignified and Loving," *Pure-Bred Dogs/American Kennel Gazette*, 1/85, p. 37.

————. "The Early Days," *Pure-Bred Dogs/American Kennel Gazette*, 2/86.

————. "Evolution of the Miniature Pinscher," *Pure-Bred Dogs/American Kennel Gazette*, 6/86, p. 55.

Freedman, Alix M., "Rabbits Can Relax When a Basset Pack is Hunting for Them," The *Wall Street Journal*, 11/19/85.

Gentry, Diane K., "Blue Lacys—Instinctive 'Cowboys'," *Dog Fancy*, 3/87, pp. 46-47.

Gordon, J.F., *An Illustrated Guide to Some Rare and Unusual Dog Breeds*, John Bartholomew & Son, London, 1975.

Great Lakes Canaan Club official brochure, Hoffman Estates, IL.

Green, Jeffrey S. & Roger A. Woodruff, *Guarding Dogs Protect Sheep From Predators*, U.S. Sheep Experiment Station, Dubois, Idaho, 1/83.

Guillet, Dr. Emile, *Les Chiens Courants D'Aujour D'Hui*, ed. du Passage, Paris.

Gyes, Nancy, "Introducing the Hovawart," *Animal Times*, Palo Alto, CA, 9/86.

Hancock, David, "Saving the Danish Breeds," *Pure-Bred Dogs/American Kennel Gazette*, 7/86.

Harling, Donn and Deborah, *Australian Cattle Dogs—The First 5 Years 1980–1985*, Sun Graphics, Parsons, KS, 1986.

Hart, Ernest H., *Encyclopedia of Dog Breeds*, T.F.H. Publications, Inc., Neptune City, NJ, 1975.

————. *The German Shepherd Dog*, T.F.H. Publications, Inc., Neptune City, NJ, 1985.

Hartop, Judith J., "Man & Animals," *Pure-Bred Dogs/American Kennel Gazette*, 11/84, pp. 54-57.

Helle, Nancy, "The Portuguese Water Dog Makes Waves in America," *The Greenwich Review Magazine*, 3/77, pp. 18-21.

Hinchliffe, Nigel, "The Patterdale Terrier," *The Working Terrier Yearbook*, Vol. 3, 1985.

Holler, Heinz, *Schnauzer und Pinscher*, Eugen Ulmer GmbH & Co., 1986, pp. 42-43.

Hovawart Club of Germany, *Unser Hovawart*.

Howe, Dorothy, *The Labrador Retriever*, T.F.H. Publications, Inc., Neptune City, NJ, 1985.

Hubbard, Clifford L.B., *Dogs in Britain*, MacMillan & Co., Ltd., London, 1948, pp. 291-293.

————. *Working Dogs of the World*, Sidgwick and Jackson Ltd., London, 1947.

Huddleston, Arthur, *The Boston Terrier*, Denlinger's Publishers, Ltd., Fairfax, VA, 1985.

Irick, Mackey J. Jr., *The New Poodle*, 6th Ed., Howell Book House, NY, NY, 1986.

Jerome, Jerome K. in Wood, Margaretta, "Norfolk/Norwich Terrier column," *Pure-Bred Dogs/American Kennel Gazette*, 2/87, p. 156.

Junko, Fujino, "The Dogs of Japan," *The East*, Vol, VIII, No. 3, 3/72, pp 28-35.

Kaleski, Robert, *Australian Barkers and Biters*, The Endeavor Press, Sydney, Australia, 1933.

Kalstone, Shirlee, "Origins of Trimming the Poodle," *Pure-Bred Dogs/American Kennel Gazette*, 4/87, pp. 14-15.

Kanzler, Kathleen, Sheila Balch, Dolly and Robert Ward, "The Arctic Breeds—The Similarities and the Differences," *Kennel Review*, 10/81, pp. 1-3.

Karr, Diana L., "The English Shepherd as a Watchdog," *Bloodlines*, 7-8/81, pp. 30-31.

Kenyon, Dorothy and Ann, *Japanese Spitz*, E.G. Parrott, Torquay, 1979.

Kline, David Van Gordon, "The Border Terrier," *Dog Fancy*, 5/87, pp. 42-43.

v. Kramer, Eva Maria, "Der Schapendoes aus Holland," *Hendewelt*, 9/86, pp. 270-271.

Lane, Marion S., ed., *Pure-Bred Dogs/American Kennel Gazette*, Anniversary Issue, 2/87.

————."To the Harness Born," *Pure-Bred Dogs/American Kennel Gazette*, 7/86, pp. 42-43.

Lanting, Fred, "An American Dog Watcher in Japan," *Dog World*, 8/85, pp. 12-13, 135, 137, 146-147, 149.

Large Munsterlander Club brochure, Bishop's Stortford Herts., England.

Larsen, Linda and Richard W. Eichhorn, *The Tibetan Mastiff Owner's Manual*, Drakyi Tibetan Mastiffs, Sherman Oaks, CA, 1982.

Laws of Canute, No. 31, 1016 A.D.

Lehman, Patricia F., "The West Highland White Terrier," *Dog Fancy*, 1/87, pp. 36-41.

Levy, Joy C., "Problems in a Rare Breed," *The World of the Working Dog*, 7-8/76, pp. 21-22.

Litell, Richard J., "The Puffin Dog," *SAS Magazine Scanorama*, 4-5/76.

Llewellyn, Zell, "An Introduction to the Shar-Pei," *Bloodlines*, 11-12/82.

————. "The Barbet Dog—National Water Dog of France," *Portuguese Water Dog Cruise Lines*, 1-2/87, pp. 14-15.

Lorenz, Karl, *Man Meets Dog*, Penguin Books, 1973.

MacLeod, Norm and Altoona, *The Australian Kelpie Handbook*, Victoria, Australia, 2nd Ed., 4/85.

McLeroth, Diane, *The Briard: A Collection*, Aubry Assoc. and The Briard Club of America, Baraboo, WI, 1982.

McLoughlin, John, *The Canine Clan: A New Look at Man's Best Friend*, The Viking Press, NY, 1983.

McWhirter, Norris and Ross, David A. Boehm, Maris Cakars, *Guinness Book of World Records*, Special Edition, Sterling Publishing Co., Inc., New York, 1985.

Malo Alcrudo, Rafael, et al., eds., *El Libro del Mastin del Pireneo*, Guara Editorial, Zaragoza, Spain, 1983.

Mansencal, Guy, "Pyrenean Sheepdog," Tarbes, France.

The Maremma Sheepdog Club of Great Britain, official booklet.

Martin, Bobi, "Chinooks: Fighting to Survive," *Dog World*, 10/85, pp. 14, 118.

Martin, Inge, "The Inca Hairless Dog," *Americas*, 7/-8/83, pp. 26-29.

Maxwell, C. Bede, *The Truth About Sporting Dogs*, Howell Book House, Inc., New York, NY.

Menzel, Drs. R. & R., *Pariah Dogs: A History of the Canaan Dog Breed*, translated by Bryna Comsky, 1982.

Messerschmidt, Donald A., PhD, "The Tibetan Mastiff Color, Coat and Collar," *Dog World*, 9/83.

Middle Atlantic States Komondor Club, Inc., booklet, 1980.

Miller, Felicity, "Letters," *The Sled Dog*, Glemsford, Suffolk, England, 8/86, pp. 15-17.

Millington, Ann, "A Very Rare Breed, Indeed!" *Canine Chronicle*, 4/84.

Miniature Bull Terrier Club of America pamphlet.

Mondador, Arnoldo, ed., *Le Enciclopedic di Arianna*.

Mureen, Sigrid, "Island Working Dogs," *Pure-Bred Dogs American Kennel Club*, 9/86, p. 71.

Nederlandse Vereniging Voor Stabij-En Wetterhounen, *De Fryske Hounen*, n.d.

Nelson, David D., "The Kangal Dog of Turkey," *Dog World*, 3/85.

Nelson, David D. and Judith N., "Akbash Dog, A Turkish Breed for Home and Agriculture," The Akbash Dog Assn. Intl. Inc., Wilmington, DE, 1983.

Nicholas, Anna Katherine, *The Book of the English Springer Spaniel*, T.F.H. Publications, Inc., Neptune City, NJ, 1983.

————. *The Book of the German Shepherd Dog*, T.F.H. Publications, Inc., Neptune City, NJ, 1983.

————. *The Book of the Miniature Schnauzer*, T.F.H. Publications, Inc., Neptune City, NJ, 1986.

————. *The Book of the Shetland Sheepdog*, T.F.H. Publications, Inc., Neptune City, NJ, 1984.

————. *The Boxer*, T.F.H. Publications, Inc., Neptune City, NJ, 1984.

————. *The Boston Terrier*, T.F.H. Publications, Inc., Neptune City, NJ, 1988.

————. *The Chihuahua*, T.F.H. Publications, Inc., Neptune City, NJ, 1988.

————. *The Chow Chow*, T.F.H. Publications, Inc., Neptune City, NJ, 1985.

————. *The Collie*, T.F.H. Publications, Inc., Neptune City, NJ, 1986.

————. "The Collie," *Dog Fancy*, 12/86, p. 36.

————. *The Dachshund*, T.F.H. Publications, Inc., Neptune City, NJ, 1987.

————. *The Dalmatian*, T.F.H. Publications, Inc., Neptune City, NJ, 1986.

————. *The Fox Terrier*, T.F.H. Publications, Inc., Neptune City, NJ, 1989.

————. *The German Pointer (Shorthaired and Wirehaired)*, T.F.H. Publications, Inc., Neptune City, NJ, 1985.

————. *The Great Dane*, T.F.H. Publications, Inc., Neptune City, NJ, 1988.

————. *The Keeshond*, T.F.H. Publications, Inc., Neptune City, NJ, 1985.

————. *The Lhasa Apso*, T.F.H. Publications, Inc., Neptune City, NJ, 1989.

————. *The Maltese*, T.F.H. Publications, Inc., Neptune City, NJ, 1984.

————. *The Pekingese*, T.F.H. Publications, Inc., Neptune City, NJ, 1989.

————. *The Poodle*, T.F.H. Publications, Inc., Neptune City, NJ, 1984.

————. *The Weimaraner*, T.F.H. Publications, Inc., Neptune City, NJ, 1986.

————. *The World of Doberman Pinschers*, T.F.H. Publications, Inc., Neptune City, NJ, 1986.

Norwegian Buhund Magazine of Great Britain, "The Buhund Nature," 1980.

Norwegian Lundehund Club, "The Lundehund."

Pagel, Adrienne, "Vive La Difference," *Pure-Bred Dogs/American Kennel Gazette*, 11/86, pp. 66-68.

Parsons, A.D., *The Working Kelpie*, Nelson Pub., Melbourne, Victoria, Australia, 1986.

Peterson, Clementione, *The Complete Keeshond*, Howell Book House, NY, NY.

Pielanen-Degenhardt, E., "De Saarloos Wolfhond," *De Hondenwereld*, Asten, Netherlands, November, 1985.

————. *Nederlandse Vereniging van Saarlooswolfhonden*, Oud-Beyerland, Netherlands.

Pugnetti, Gino, *Guide to Dogs*, ed., Elizabeth Meriwether Schuler, Simon & Schuster, NY, NY, 1980.

Pye, Roger F. F.S.A., *The Estrela Mountain Dog and Its Background*, Oporto, 1980.

Raber, Hans, *Die Schweizer Hunderassen*.

Rahn, Mike, "For Whom the Dog Tolls," *Fins and Feathers*, Vol. 14, No. 2, 2/85, pp. 48-49, 51-52.

Redditt, JoAnne, *The Chinese Shar Pei Puppy Book*.

Riddle, Maxwell, *Dogs in History*, Denliger's Ltd., Fairfax, VA, 1987.

————. "My Portuguese Castro Laboreiros," *Dog World*, 1/84, pp 20, 47, 48.

Rine, Josephine, *The World of Dogs*, Doubleday & Co., Garden City, NY, 1965, Dolphin Books Edition 1973.

Robinson, Jerome B., "Decoy Dogs," *Sports Afield*, 8/81, pp. 64, 106-109.

Rorem, Linda, "Three American Herding Breeds," *Dog Fancy*, 3/87, pp. 42-43.

Rutledge, Richard, "Skye Terrier Column - Vocabulary Lesson," *Pure-Bred Dogs/American Kennel Gazette*, 11/86, p. 140.

Sammon, Edy, "Pure-bred World. The Pit Bull Controversy," *Dog Fancy*, p. 54, 8/86.

Scott, Willie and Edwin, "The American Hairless Terrier, *Bloodlines*, 5-6/86, pp. 16-17.

Seiger, Herr H.F. and Dr. F. von Dewitz-Colpin, *The Complete German Shorthaired Pointer*, Howell Book House Inc., NY, NY, 1951.

Semencic, Carl, PhD, "The Canary Dog," *Dog World*, 11/86.

————. "Introducing the Dogo Argentino," *Dog World*, 11/85.

————. *Man-Stopping Guard Dogs*, T.F.H. Publications, Inc., Neptune City, NJ, 1989.

————. *The Tosa Ken*, Tosa Ken Assoc. of America.

————. *The World of Fighting Dogs*, TFH Publications, Neptune City, NJ, 1984.

Semencic, Carl, PhD and Don Fiorino, "A New Look at the Contribution of the Eastern Brachycephalic Breeds to 'Bull Breed' History," *Dog World*, 3/84.

Smith, A. Croxton, *Dogs Since 1900*, Andrew Dakers, Ltd., London, 1950.

Spencer, James B., "Newfies to the Rescue," *Dog Fancy*, 11/86.

————. "The Noble Newfoundland," *Dog Fancy*, 11/86, pp. 36, 41-43.

Steele, Ernie, "How St. Patrick and His Little Dogs Rid Ireland of Snakes," *Canine Chronicle*, 3/15/86, pp. 18, 22.

Stodghill, Tom D., *Stodghill's Animal Research Magazine*, issues fall '69, spring '66, fall-winter '72-'73.

Strang, Alison, "The Nova Scotia Duck Tolling Retriever, Canada's Own All-around Dog," *Show Ring*, 1978.

Strang, Paul D., ed., "The Pyrenean Shepherd Dog," Pyrenean Shepherd Dog Club of America Newsletter, 1981.

Stratton, Richard F., *The Rottweiler*, T.F.H. Publications, Inc., Neptune City, NJ, 1985.

————. *The World of the American Pit Bull Terrier*, T.F.H. Publications, Inc., Neptune City, NJ, 1983.

Sundqvist, Margareta, "Tibetan Terrier column—A Swedish View," *Pure-Bred Dogs/American Kennel Gazette*, 12/81, p. 173.

Sverdrup, Otto, *New Land: Four Years in the Arctic Regions*.

Swift, E.M., "The Mutt with a Touch of Class," *Sports Illustrated*, 11/81, pp. 92-102.

Tanner, Renee, "The Dynamic Dobermans," *Dog Fancy*, Oct. '86, pp 36.

The Telomian Dog Club of America official brochure, Grand Rapids, OH.

Thornton, Kim, "The American Eskimo Dog," *Dog Fancy*, 2/87, p. 59.

Tobias, John, "Singing Dogs of New Guinea," *Dog Fancy*, 5/87, pp. 33-35.

Topsell, Edward, *The Historie of the Foure-Footed Beastes*, Wm. Iaggard, London, 1607.

Treen, Esmeralda, "Where Are They Now?" *Pure-Bred Dogs/American Kennel Gazette*, 11/84, pp. 72--79.

Triebels, Dr. L.F., *De Hollandse Herder*, Nederlandse Herdershonden Club.

United Kennel Club, *American Pit Bull Terrier*, Kalamazoo, MI.

United Kennel Club, *Early Days of U.K.C. Registered Redbone Coonhound*, Kalamazoo, MI.

Vlanin, Nina, "Are There Dogs in Russia?" *Pure-Bred Dogs/American Kennel Gazette*, 7/87, pp. 28-31.

Walker, Tom T., Ed.D, "Introducing the Finnish Spitz," *Dog World*, 2/84, pp. 14, 42.

Walkowicz, Chris, *The Bearded Collie*, Denlinger's Ltd., 1987.

Walkowicz, Chris and Bonnie Wilcox DVM, *Successful Dog Breeding*, Arco, 1985.

Walsh, J.H., (Stonehenge) *The Dogs of the British Islands*, 1878.

Warwick, Helen, *The New Complete Labrador Retriever*, 3rd Edition, Howell Book House, NY, NY 1986.

White, H. Ellen DVM, "Catahoula Hog Dog Brings Back Memories of Home," *DVM Newsmagazine*, 3/85, pp. 36-37.

Williams, Jill, "What's a Pudelpointer?," *Dog Fancy*, 1/87, pp. 44-45.

Wolk, Bruce Harold, "Herr Essig and His Leonberger," *Dog World*, 3/84.

———. "The Spaniels of Joy," *Dog World*, 1/84, pp. 24, 49-51, 55.

Zilberman, Gisele, "Teamwork and Responsibility."

Contributors

Photographers

Isabelle Francais, as the principal photographer for this Atlas, has traveled throughout Europe and North America capturing the dogs of the world on film. Ms. Francais has focused her dedicated effort on this project over the past five years. The success of her efforts is evident: for the first time ever have over 400 breeds been assembled in full-color in one captivating, all-encompassing volume.

We also acknowledge the contribution of Vladimir Pcholkin who provided the outstanding photography of the dogs of the Soviet Union. Other contributing photographers include: Alton Anderson, John L. Ashbey, Maria Carlos, Bryna Comski, Jay Lorenz Corvallis, Lloyd Donner, Michael Gilroy, Rich Johnson, Ron Moat, M. Montoya, Robert Pearcy, Fritz Prenzel, Ron Reagan, A. & J. Riely, Joe R. Rinehart, Vincent Serbin, Robert Smith, Pete Souza (the White House), Sandra E. Tucker, Marianne von der Lanken, Ken Walters and Irene Weidler.

Translators

Lilianne Black; Taylor Ridge, Illinois. Lea Gut; Siglistorf, Switzerland. Kiyoko Kibble, Spring Valley, New York. Julie McFarland, Rock Island, Illinois. Elleka Mesdag; Normal, Illinois. Karen Pouder; Eli-Fran Cockers, Silvis, Illinois. Dr. Lars Scott; Augustana College, Rock Island, Illinois. Helga Steiner; Friendship Farm West, Milan, Illinois. Thomas Swegle; Sherrard High School, Sherrard, Illinois. Marsha Winters; Rockridge High School, Edgington, Illinois.

Dog Owners & Correspondents

The following compilation represents the owners of the dogs portrayed in this book as well as the authors' correspondents. The authors are deeply indebted to these persons who willingly shared first-hand experience and information. The editorial staff of T.F.H. congratulates all dog fanciers associated with this Atlas and extends a sincere apology to anyone who may have been accidentally excluded from this list. Much thanks to all!

Aboczky, Maria; Upper Saddle River, New Jersey. Abraham, Lee; New Jersey. Accrudo, Rafael; Zaragoza, Spain. Aceto, Gratia; Torino, Italy. Aigeldinger, Ingrid; Siglistorf, Switzerland. Albaronte, Juan A.C.; Madrid, Spain. Alderfer, J. Ralph; Souderton, Pennsylvania. Allen, Peggy; Centre, Alabama. Alstede, Joanne; Chester, New Jersey. Althaus, Fritz; Kirchberg, Switzerland. Amyot, Gilbert; Quebec, Canada. Andersen, Chickie; Brooklyn, New York. André, Pioc; Vilaine, France. Andrews, Bill & BJ; Ashville, North Carolina. Andrews, Gayle; St. Augustine, Florida. Andrews, Miss Valerie; Hampshire, England. Animals Unlimited; USA. Armor, Rallye; Plesidy, France. Ashbey, Janet; Stewartsville, New Jersey. Attalla, Anthony; Rutland, Massachusetts. Augustowski, Kaz & Betty; Severn, Maryland. Austin, B.M.; Leicester, England. Australian National Kennel Council; Victoria, Australia. Aveaux, Carpe; Paris, France. Avery, Sarah; Bristol, England. Ayza, Jose Drago; Peniscola, Spain. Back, Nancy; Hedgesville, West Virginia. Backa-Greeven, M.; Holland. Bailey, Eunice; Allendale, New Jersey. Bakelaar, D.C.; Amsterdam, Holland. Barger, Stephen W.; Old Chatham, New York. Barhammar, Bertil; Thorsby, Sweden. Barlow, Dianne; USA. Barth, Dr. Wolf-Eberhard; St. Andreasberg, Germany. Bayly, Judith A.; Ellsworth, Maine. Beakes, Louise D.; Quebec, Canada. Beaupre, Bob & Judy; Aliquippa, Pennsylvania. Bello, Hose; San Tander, Portugal. Belmont Jr., Peter; Kansas City, Kansas. Belson, Mr. & Mrs. G.J.; Norfolk, England. Benis, Les; Playa Del Ray, California. Benjamin, Carol Lea; New York City, New York. Berger, Jill; Speonk, New York. Bergeron, France; Quebec, Canada. Bergman, Hinda; Raleigh, North Carolina. Berkel, Mark J.; Floral Park, New York. Bernhardt, Valerie; Milford, Pennsylvania. Bessa, Joao; Peco d'Arcos, Portugal. Bett, Leta; Ashton, Ontario, Canada. Bickel, Elizabeth; Kansas City, Missouri. Bierwirth, Wolfgang; Wehretal, Germany. Bigot, Hubert; La Bourbonnaise, France. Blanck, Doris; Mainhardt-Hütten, Germany. Blankenagel, M.; Krefeld, Switzerland. Blankenship, John & Pauline; Christiana,

Tennessee. Blao, Robert; Dorylaton, New York. Blom-Meijer, Mrs. A.; Ede, Netherlands. Bloom, Robert; Douglastown, New York. Bodier, M.; Cosne d'Allier, France. Bodine, Nan; Lakewood, New Jersey. Boegli, A. Jean-Pierre; Delemont, Switzerland. Boel, D.V.; Holland. Boelte, P.; Valhalla, New York. Boerkamp, E.; Budapest, Hungary. Bolle, Frau; Kelsterbach, Germany. Bolzmann, Kurt; Witten, Germany. Book, Maureen; Havelock, North Carolina. Botega, Joann; Brooklyn, New York. Boxer, Shirley; Skillman, New Jersey. Braginton, Edith M.; Spotswood, New Jersey. Bramblett, Susan; New Jersey. Brandenburger, Dale; Millspadt, Illinois. Brasier, Rodger; Moreno Valley, California. Brennan, Mr. Sean; Kilkenny, Ireland. Breton, Denise; Quebec, Canada. Breum, Robert L.; Omaha, Nebraska. Brewster, Joy; Newtown, Connecticut. Brisbin Jr., Dr. I. Lehr; Aiken, South Carolina. Brody, Irene; Richmond, Texas. Brookes, Marjorie; Santa Rosa, California. Brown, Gerald & Patricia; Honeybrook, Pennsylvania. Brubaker, Joyce K.; Bernville, Pennsylvania. Brügger, Bernadette; Romanshorn, Finland. Bryan, C.; New South Wales, Australia. Bryant, Mildred; North Central Texas. Burg, C.; Amsterdam, Holland. Butterklee, Arlene; Nesconset, New York. Cabezas, Juan Antonio; Madrid, Spain. Cadwell, Julia; Santa Rosa, California. Cahill, Mr. & Mrs. George; Merseyside, England. Campagne, Dr. Y.; Sainte Maure, France. Canadian Kennel Club; Ontario, Canada. Caporale, Janet A.; Hammonton, New Jersey. Capstick, Beverly; USA. Carberry, Mary Jane; Pennington, New Jersey. Carnathan, Howard; Tupelo, Mississippi. Carpenter, Jim; Waxhaw, North Carolina. Caruso, Victoria; Cedar Grove, New Jersey. Casper, Ursula; Schwetzingen, Germany. Cavalchini, Dr.; Bergamo, Italy. Cawthera, Averi; Durham, England. Chalain, Nadine; Saint Gemmes, France. Chamberland, Mme. Louise; Quebec, Canada. Chaplain, Alain; Ste. Cernin, France. Chataigner, Jean. Chathos, Bobbie; Rutland, Massachusetts. Chorn, Donly; Deerfield, Illinois. Ciceri, Paolo; Milano, Italy. Cinofilla Italiana Ente Nazionale; Milan, Italy. Clark, Jean; Franklin, New Hampshire. Clark, Tom & Judy; Edmonds, Washington. Clarke, Robert N. & Bonnie S.; Ellington, Connecticut. Club for Native Moroccan Breeds. Cock 'N' Bull Kennels; Bloomington, California. Cocuzza, Patti; Jeffersonton, Virginia. Cohen, Dorothy; Las Vegas, Nevada. Coia, Arthur; Barrington, Rhode Island. Colburn, Mr. & Mrs. P.; Milton Keynes, England. Collins, Gerarda; Old Greenwich, Connecticut. Comski, Bryna; Hoffman Estates, Illinois. Cone, Susan; Livingston, New Jersey. Connelly, William; Dumont, New Jersey. Conner, Eileen & Wm.; Jerome, Idaho. Consolazio, Monique; Putnam Valley, New York. Coonhunters Assoc. Professional; Memphis, Tennessee. Coppinger, Lorna; Amherst, Massachusetts. Cornelissen, C.; West Germany. Cornwell, Sandy; Potomac, Illinois. Corrone, Susan; Bethany, Connecticut. Cottrell, Lynda; Pompano, Florida. Cowell, Robert P.; Bridgeport, Connecticut. Cruz, Hector; Humacao, Puerto Rico. Curley, Peter; Columbia, Missouri. Cynologique International Federation; Thuin,

Belgium. Cynologique Swisse Societe; Bern, Switzerland. Da Costa Botto, Hose Manuel; Sousel, Portugal. Danish Kennel Club; Solrodstrand, Denmark. Darkrooms Plus; USA. Davidson, Dr. & Mrs. John; Dunlap, Illinois. Davidson, Henry & Gabe; Annandale, Minnesota. Davis, Bob; San Diego, California. Davis, Helen T.; Hillside, New Jersey. Davis, Karla; Woodlake, California. De La Rochefoucauld, M.; Combreux, France. De Palma, Victoria K.; Milford, Connecticut. De Paula Bessa, A.; Voluntaris, Portugal. Dean, Mrs. P.A.; Hampshire, England. Deavers, Ruth A.; New York, New York. Defois, Aime; St. Armez, France. Dejaeger, Erik; Northwest Territories, Canada. Delhorne, C.; Bouc Bel Air, France. Demary, Allen; Valatic, New York. Derraugh, Mrs. C.; Orleans, Ontario, Canada. Dervin, Irene; Philadelphia. Deutsche Hunderassen e. V. Verband fur das; Dortmund, Germany. DeVore, Mrs. Pat; Birch Tree, Missouri. Dickson, Alice; Green Village, New Jersey. DiGiacomo, Kathy; Fair Lawn, New Jersey. Dijkmans, A.F.; Someren, Holland. Dixon, Alice; Green Village, New Jersey. Dobbyn, Mr. E.; County Cork, Ireland. Dobish, Denise; Garfield, New Jersey. Döbler, E.; Roesbenberg, Austria. Dokter, Kim; Stadskandal, Finland. Doniere, Pat & Judy; Holland, Ohio. Donyer, M.; Holland. Dremaux, Jacques; Gambersart, France. Dridrit, Klaus; Reukingen, West Germany. Droz, Paul; Switzerland. Duede, Daniel; St. Maurice, France. Dueker Schaffner, Nancy; Schwenksville, Pennsylvania. Duff, Robert; Davenport, California. Duryea, Carolyn S.; Riverside, New Jersey. Dusoux, Laurent; Douvaine, France. Eckes, Mrs. Charles R.; Denver, Colorado. Edwards, Alida; Frankville, Ontario, Canada. Eggers, Lynn; North Central Texas. Eichhorn, Richard; Simi Valley, California. Eisenberg, Nancy L.; Merrick, New York. Eisenolbe, J.; Riyswijk, Netherlands. El Yamani, M. Fatmi El Kadiri; Rabat, Morocco. Elitz, E.; Great Britain. Elly, Engleberu; Amsterdam, Holland. Equipage de Bramofam; Vienna, Austria. Erny, Andrew & Nancy; Mahwah, New Jersey. Ervin, Mercer Russo; Patterson, New York. Erwin, Florence; Scarborough, Ontario, Canada. Esteban, Julio & Isabel; Towson, Maryland. Evans, Mrs. J.; Purcell Bucks, England. Fairbanks, Mrs. Richmond; Greenville, South Carolina. Fajfar, Joze; Radovljica, Yugoslavia. Fargas Caribra, Miguel; La Margosta, Spain. Farley, John; Gig Harbor, Washington. Farr-Williams, Leah; Allentown, Pennsylvania. Farrar, P.; USA. Fasoli, Bruno; Tourville, Germany. Fassi-Fehri, Docteur Mahi; Rabat, Morocco. Fernandez, Amy & Mary; Forest Hills, New York. Field Sports Society; London, England. Fielder, Stephen (UKC); Kalamazoo, Michigan. Filiatrault, Raymond; Quebec, Canada. Fillenberg, Heinz; Roding, Germany. Filleul, M. Paul; Rochechouart, France. Findlay, Ann; Sussex, England. Fink, Wolfgang; Moers-Kapellen, Germany. Finkelstein, Barbara; Hewlett, New York. Finnegan, Edward J., Jr.; Monroe, New York. Fischer, Elyse; Port Washington, New York. Fisher, Betty; El Cajon, California. Fitt, Kevin; Marino Valley, California. Fonda, Cathy; Rialto, California. Fontaine, Mariette; Chassy, France. Ford, Judith E.; Wallkill, New York.

Fortin, Martin; Montreal, Quebec, Canada. Franzen, Christa; Rosrath, Germany. Fraser, Jocelyn; Cornwall, Ontario, Canada. Freeman, Edith L.; Ontario, Canada. French, Virginia, USA. Frenzel, Madame Edith; Riehen, Switzerland. Froats, Brad & Carol Ann; Ontario, Canada. From, Per-Alrik; Tarnaby, Sweden. Galera Ibanez, Albert; Spain. Galibois, Richard; Lauzon, Quebec, Canada. Gallantry Giant Schnauzers; Warminster, Pennsylvania. Gammons, David J.; White Plains, New York. Gannon, Dee; Wenonah, New Jersey. Garding, Dieter; Schiedsberg, Holland. Garrick, John; New York City, New York. Gascoigne, Mr. & Mrs. E.; Essex, England. Gaston, Daniel; Neuchâtel, Switzerland. Gebied in Nederland Raad v. Beheer op Kynologisch; Emmalaan, Netherlands. Genovese, Mary; Bristol, England. Genzález, Beatriz; San Tander, Portugal. Gerber, Fritz; Bretzwil, Switzerland. German Club for Pekes, Chins & Toy Spaniels. Getter, Lorraine; Old Tappan, New Jersey. Gettings, Ruth M.; Staten Island, New York. Gilat, Josette; Remasoble, France. Gioia, Margaret; Beechhurst, New York. Giuntini, Francesco; Firenze, Italy. Goby, Roger; Imphy, France. Goldsmith, Carol; Montpelier, Virginia. Gonzaga de Oliveira, Prof. Luiz; São Paulo, Brazil. Goodale, Dorothy; Montrose, Colorado. Gordon, Fred & Sandra; Ontario, Canada. Gormley, Mr. A. & Mrs. A.; County Dublin, Ireland. Goucher, Mary "Skeeter"; Bradley, Oklahoma. Grechko, Valerie; Wolcott, Connecticut. Green, Sheila; Mahwah, New Jersey. Greene, Forrest & Beverly; Houston, Texas. Greenwood, Nancy E.; Nashua, New Hampshire. Grey, Denise; USA. Grossenbacher, Evelyn; Bern, Switzerland. Grossman, Laura; Roeland Heights, California. Grouf, Joy; Dancer Poodles, New York. Gryzlo, Janet; Queens Village, New York. Guénolé, Patrick; Plougasnou, Switzerland. Guerin, Ana Filomena; Sesimbra, Portugal. Guerrini, Nadir; Vercelli, Italy. Guimard, M.; Lavardens, Belgium. Guinard, Maurice; Plourivo, France. Gunnell, Mrs. J.; Sussex, England. Guthier, Marie; Telford, Pennsylvania. Guyonard, Maurice; Berrien, France. Gyes, Nancy; San Jose, California. Haan, S.; Amsterdam, Holland. Haarlem, A.; Amsterdam, Holland. Haggkvist, Olle B.; Sveg, Sweden. Hagland, Rudolf; Haugesund, Norway. Haight, Judy; Lake Ronkonkoma, New York. Hailes, Helen; Ringoes, New Jersey. Hall, Robert & Laura; Aiken, South Carolina. Hamer, Sandra; Quebec, Canada. Hamilton Ed., Ferelith; Kent, England. Hampton, Suzanne H.; Fort Lee, New Jersey. Hansen, Dr. Jens; Bremervorde, Germany. Harmand, Daniel; Contreyeville, France. Harned, Quinn & Marilyn; Alpine, California. Harrison, J.C.; Mt. Horeb, Wisconsin. Hayden, Betty; Forestville, Connecticut. Healy, Leslie; San Angelo, Texas. Hecker, Heinrich; Wald-Michelbach, Germany. Heidenrijk, Ferry Bruhwiler & Marijke; Siegershausen, Switzerland. Heiderer, Fritz; Herzogenburg, Austria. Helbig, Maureen B.; Irvington, New York. Helén, Anne, Vantua, Finland. Helm, E.; Oranjewand, Poland. Henaff, Bruno; LaMontagne, France. Henderson, Karen Abbott; Duxbury, Massachusetts. Herschman, Patricia; Hewlett, New York. Hess, Irene; Wustenrot-Neulautern, Germany. Higgins,

Dorothy; Brooklyn, New York. Hodges, Shirley; New Jersey. Hoff, Graciela; Rio Grande, Puerto Rico. Hoffman, Mrs. J. Frederick; Lafayette, Indiana. Hofman, Nancy J.; Norwalk, California. Holler, Heinz; Alsdorf, Germany. Hollmann, Keistin; Aulendorf, Holland. Hood, Katherine; Altamont, Illinois. Houdou, Mr. & Mrs. Maurice; Lake Grove, New York. Hrabak, J. U. O.; Worms-Weinsheim, Germany. Huber, Dennis; USA. Hugo, Frank; Marlton, New Jersey. Huisman, J.; Leiden, Holland. Humphrey, Curtis; London, Ohio. Humphreys, Jim; Stuarts Draft, Virginia. Hunter, Mrs. Dorothy; Lincoln, England. Ibanez, Hugo J.; Charlotte, North Carolina. Impey, Gillian; Little Silver, New Jersey. Irish Kennel Club, Department of Publications; Dublin, Ireland. Irish Kennel Club; Dublin, Ireland. Irwin, Carroll Ann; North Hollywood, California. Israel, Edward; Atco, New Jersey. Jacques, Marie; Ontario, Canada. Jameson, Jean K.; Deep River, Connecticut. Jawzky, Tizsf; Budapest, Hungary. Jefferey, Richard C.; Frederick, Maryland. Jester, Carolyn; Stroud, Oklahoma. Joffe, Grace & Jeff; Ft. Lauderdale, Florida. Johle, Helmut; Vohrenbach, Switzerland. Johnson, John D.; Summerville, Georgia. Jones, Brenda; Tulsa, Oklahoma. Jones, Jacque & Ray; Coolville, Ohio. Jones, Kenneth C.; Adolphus, Kentucky. Joss, Helen; Hiuberbenzring, Switzerland. Joyal, Jeannine; St. Felix De Kingsley, Canada. Kaiser, Mrs. Henry J.; Alekai Kennels, USA. Karr, Diana; Arbutus, Maryland. Katz, Charlotte; Woodbine, Maryland. Kauen, Samuel; Lucerne, Switzerland. Keim, Margaret E.; Sacramento, California. Kellerman, Wendy L.; Glen Oaks, New York. Kennel Club, The; London, England. Kenyon, Dorothy; Devon, England. Kerkhof, E.P.; Vlaardingen, Switzerland. Kiaulenas, Laura; Farmingville, New York. Kiefer, Claus; Romerberg-Berghausen, Germany. King, Eileen J.; Philadelphia. Kirk, Mr. A.; Herfordshire, England. Klose, Ingeborg; St. Johann Tirol, Austria. Knight, James; Beeville, Texas. Knight, James H.; Hanna City, Illinois. Kolster-Reckman, Mrs. Th. F. M.; Emmer-Compascuum, Netherlands. Koppel, Robert A. Koul, C. Kerl; Austria. Kovakova M.V. Dr., Alzbeta; Kosice, Czechoslovakia. Kovalic, Virginia & Frank; Detroit, Michigan. Kristensen, Villy G.; Sonderborg, Denmark. Kroll, Kurt; Hawthorne, New Jersey. Krom, Esther C.; Clifton, New Jersey. Kruel, Clelia; Campinas, Brazil. Krukar, John & Linda; Bethlehem, Pennsylvania. Kuberski, Elaine B.; Englishtown, New Jersey. Kuczynski, Lynne; Emmaus, Pennsylvania. Kuehl, Elke; Juliustown, New Jersey. Kuenzle, Dr. Clive; Zurich, Switzerland. Kwait, Kathy; Fairlawn, New Jersey. Labaire, Beverly; Rutland, Massachusetts. Lacchia, Linda; Whitestone, New York. Laemmle, Cheryl; New York City, New York. Laflamme, Sandra; Manassas, Virginia. Lamoureus, Sarole; Sherbrooke, Canada. Lamphere, Al & Cindy; Sparta, New Jersey. Lang, Christen; Oslo, Norway. Langevin, Pauline; Sherbrooke, Quebec, Canada. Larsen, Poul; Skjern, Denmark. Lassagne, P.; Longpre Les Corps Saints, France. Lawler, Alice S.; Cream Ridge, New Jersey. Le Blanc, Joe; Telford, Pennsylvania. Le Fevre, Betty; Processieweg, Belgium. Le Pennec, Henry;

France. Lebris, Nane; Loudeac, France. Lecki, Irene & Tom; Philadelphia, Pennsylvania. Leclerc, Steve; Hampden, Massachusetts. Lee Jr., Donald T.O.; Honolulu, Hawaii. Lenz, Annette; Holland. Leone, Pat; Califon, New Jersey. Leroy, Jacques; Saint Chairsurelle, France. Les Loge Marchis; France. Leseigneur, Madame; Bernay, France. Leutenegger, A.; Eichtenstr, Holland. Lewis Jr., John R.; Natural Bridge, Virginia. Libson, Paul; Patchogue, New York. Linders, Ch.; Oudenbosch, Holland. Lindinger, Hans; Geroiering, Germany. Lingmont, Erik; Amsterdam, Holland. Link, Valerie; Pleasant Hill, California. Linn, Harriet; Concord, California. Little Mountain Kennels; Port Angeles, Washington. Liukkonen, Outi; Espoo, Finland. Ljungren, Doug & Penny; Kent, Washington. Llewellyn, Dick & Zella; Alvin, Texas. Lockquell, Lise; Quebec, Canada. Lopez, A.D.; Madrid, Spain. Loureiro Borges, Dr. J. M.; Lisbon, Portugal. Lowery, Dr. John C.; Muscle Shoals, Alabama. Luburich, Ms. Felicie E.H.; East Brunswick, New Jersey. Lucero, Michael; New York City, New York. Ludenberg, H.; Tilburg, Belgium. Lussion, R.A.; Wilberham, Massachusetts. Luttikhuis, Mr. K.G.M.; Rijn, Netherlands. Lyons, Joy; Pompano Beach, Florida. McCarthy, Sean & Elizabeth; USA. McCormack, Mary M.; Doylestown, Pennsylvania. McDuffie, J. Richard; Columbia, South Carolina. McGregor, Mrs. Freda; Kent, England. Machenaud, M.; Le Petit Bois, France. McKeever, M. Barbara; Malvern, Pennsylvania. McNeal, Jo Ann; Old Chatham, New York. McNeil, Germain; Richmond, Quebec. McNeil, Germaine; Quebec, Canada. Maggard, Stephen B.; Charlotte, North Carolina. Magowits, New York City, New York. Malloy, Mrs. Heidi; Bernardsville, New Jersey. Malone, Mary; Alliance, Ohio. Malone, Thomas Jr.; County Wicklow, Ireland. Mandarino, Sandy; Bergenfield, New Jersey. Mangold, Theodor; St. Leonhard, Austria. Mannings, Dr. Michael; Staten Island, New York. Mannlein, Stan & Sue; Staten Island, New York. Mansencal, Guy; Tarbes, France. Marburger, Sylvia; Truckee, California. Marcelle, Robin; Jonzic, France. Marks, Robert J.; Dundee, Illinois. Martin, Dawn; Windgap, Pennsylvania. Martin, Mona; Dover Plains, New York. Martin, Nancy; Spring House, Pennsylvania. Martinez, Antonio; Madrid, Spain. Martinez, Marie-Pierre; Chantoiseaux, France. Masse, Ives; Perpignan, France. Matalouge, Pepa; Barcelona, Spain. Matenaar, Frau Christa; Konigswinter, Germany. Matunas, Tom & Judy; New Jersey. Mauldin, Guy & Thelma; Richmond, Texas. Maus-Vickus, Elisabeth; Overath, Germany. Mazo, Hose; San Tander, Portugal. Mazurkiewicz, Linda; New Jersey. Mazzarella, Angelica C.; Syosset, New York. Merson, Shelly & Ron; New City, New York. Mertens, Joe & Jackie; Elgin, Illinois. Meyer, J. & J.; La Cibourg, Switzerland. Milliand, Claude; Yugoslavia. Mills-De Hoog, Mrs. W.H.; Kent, England. Milor, M.; Honfleur, France. Mitchell, Page; Ojai, California. Miyama, Tetsuo; Old Chatham, New York. Mohr, Terre, Newburgh, New York. Mollet, Janice; Holtsville, New York. Mollusky, Debbie; Staten Island, New York. Monadnock Kennels; Fitzwilliam, New

Hampshire. Monaghan, Kay; Woodlawn, Maryland. Moore, William E.; Trenton, New Jersey. Morneau, Louise; Quebec, Canada. Moron, Jean; St. Joachim, France. Morrissey, Michael J.; Middletown, Delaware. Moser, Silvia; Bigenthal, Switzerland. Mott, Margaret; Harris, New York. Mott, William J.; Glen Oaks, New York. Mousley, Greg; USA. Moyette, Gabriel; Ontario, Canada. Mulder, J.; Amsterdam, Holland. Mulder, Saskia; Haag, Netherlands. Munroe, Marilyn C.; Jeffersonville, New York. Munz, Ruth; Basel, Switzerland. Murphy, Pat; West Chicago, Illinois. Murray, Mignon; Jacksonville, Florida. Myre, Martha; Merrickville, Ontario, Canada. Nathan, Jody; Tulsa, Oklahoma. Nathanson, Amy; Lawrenceville, New Jersey. Navrotil, Huguette; Quebec, Canada. Nelinson, Leslie; Hackensack, New Jersey. Nelson, David & Judith; Chevy Chase, Maryland. Newhart Jr., Lee; Ithaca, New York. Nichol, Diana; Kent, England. Niederhauser, Mrs. Elizabeth; Mas Campiroi, Switzerland. Nijssen, Christina; Mallorca, Spain. Norden Laboratories; Lincoln, Nebraska. Normand, Claude; Dreuil, France. Norsk Kennel Klub; Oslo, Norway. Norstrom, Richard & Marjorie; Honolulu, Hawaii. Norton, Kirk & Anne; Herron, Michigan. Noyelle, Laureys; Edegem, Belgium. Noyelle, Rita; Paris, France. Nunez, Ojeda; Barcelona, Spain. Nysen, Willy; Brasschaat, Belgium. Obee, C.; Emmelwoord, Holland. Olciua, Manuel Maria; Alicante, Spain. O'Neil, George & Dorothy; Westwood, Massachusetts. O'Neill, Marie E.; Hewlett, New York. Oqueranza, R.; Alava, Spain. Orlik, Jo Ann; Jackson, New Jersey. Ostiguy, Louise; Montreal, Quebec, Canada. O'Weill Wagner, Beverly; Joppa, Maryland. Palmeiri, Frank; East Haven, Connecticut. Paludi, Gail & Carmen; Verona, New York. Pare, Mario; Fleurimont, France. Parker, Robert; Old Greenwich, Connecticut. Parkyns, Mrs. J.S.; Buckingham, England. Parr, Judith A.; West Islip, New York. Parrinha, Francisco; Barrvudo, Portugal. Paton, Jeanette; Kilmar Nock, Scotland. Pauciello, Rita A.; Hopatcong, New Jersey. Paule, Frances & Ruth; Riverton, Indiana. Paulsen, Patrick J.; New Jersey. Pedron, Jean; St. Brieu, France. Peek, Larry & Terri; Clearfield, Utah. Pellegrini, Melle; Le Puy, France. Perez, Ginette; Westbrookville, New York. Petersen, B. Kirkegaard; Vejenbrødvej, Denmark. Pfeister, Larry; Mt. Carmel, Illinois. Phillips, Mary; Little Silver, New Jersey. Pielanen-Degenhardt, E.; Beijerland, Netherlands. Pilat, Josette; Rémalard, France. Pinkus, Susan; West Orange, New Jersey. Pitts, Chuck & Marilyn; Lehi, Utah. Pober, Stacy; Roslyn, New York. Pohn, Hermann; Vöcklabruck, Austria. Pohoreau, B.; Lyon, France. Poisson, Anita; Katevale, Quebec, Canada. Pompeo, Patrick J. & Carol; Fairlawn, New Jersey. Pontois, Yves; Championne, France. Poole, Mrs. Jack A.; Johnstown, Pennsylvania. Porreca, Pat; Pleasanton, California. Pratt, Betty; Napa, California. Princehouse, Miss Patricia; Kent, Ohio. Purves, Mr. G. & Mrs. J.; Newcastle, England. Pye, Roger F.; Porto, Portugal. Quadri, Mario; Brescia, Italy. Quaintance, Judy; Lafayette, Indiana. Radonis, Virginia; Flushing Meadow, New York. Rafeio, F.A.; Faro-Allarve, Portugal.

Rahaman, Cheryl; New Paltz, New York. Ramalho, F.F.; Sintra, Portugal. Rancourt, Marcel; Quebec, Canada. Randall, Robert M.; USA. Rasch-Gründing, Fritz & Helga; Bramsche, Germany. Ratzlaff, Doris; Oakland, New Jersey. Rayner, Jacqueline; Hamilton, New Jersey. Rayner, Kenneth; Hopewell, New Jersey. Rector, Claas; Dornum, Germany. Redditt, JoAnn; Alexandria, Virginia. Reder, Marianne; Cuyahoga Falls, Ohio. Reed, Mauren L.; Baltimore, Maryland. Reed, Sharon D.; Bloomfield, New Jersey. Rees, W. Valerie; Doylestown, Pennsylvania. Regan, Martin; Richwood, New Jersey. Regelman, Kristin; Ridgewood, New Jersey. Reingold, Suzy A.; New York City, New York. Renaud, Danielle; Quebec, Canada. Resch, Helene; Piscataway, New Jersey. Ressa, Elaine; Neptune City, New Jersey. Reynolds, Richard L.; New York City, New York. Reyns, Frans; Olen, Belgium. Ricci, Dennis G. & Ruth Ann Freer-; Vincentown, New Jersey. Richter, Dr. Paul; Dreistetten, Austria. Ridgeway, Margaret; Haverford, Pennsylvania. Riederer, Rene & Sonja; Wila, Switzerland. Roadhouse, Donna; Aldergrove, British Columbia, Canada. Roberts Dumont, Karen; Quebec, Canada. Roberts, Dot; New City, New York. Roby, JC; Whitesville, Kentucky. Rodgers, Mary; Hamilton, Montana. Roeder-Thiede, Dr. M.; Munchen, Germany. Rogers, Amelia F.; Hampstead, Maryland. Roossien-Bruggink, Mrs. A.J.; Deventer, Netherlands. Roques, Cyrille; Aix-en Provence, France. Rosen, Betty & Herbert; Lutherville, Maryland. Roth R.Ph., Ann H.; Wilmington, North Carolina. Roth, Walter; Speonk, New York. Rowland, Mrs. B.; Surrey, England. Ruiz, Eduardo Benito; Madrid, Spain. Russell, J. Lewis; Marlton, New Jersey. Russell, Robert Jay; Torrance, California. Rutten, Andre; Veldwezelt, Austria. Ryan, James L.; Woodstown, New Jersey. Sachs, Lisa; Huntington, New York. Saint-Hubert Union Cynologique; Brussels, Belgium. Saint-Jean, Marcel; Simorre, France. Saintoingois, Rallye; La Treublade, France. Samson, Miss R.J.; Kent, England. San Diego Spuds; San Diego, California. Santiago, Rick & Brenda; Pearl River, New York. Sarret, Francoise; Ferrand, France. Sarttila, Reino; Helsinki, Finland. Saunders, Alex; Kingston, Ontario, Canada. Saunders, Ann; New Jersey. Saunders, Miss Jacky; Avon, England. Scagliotti, Patricia; Bergenfield, New Jersey. Scalzo, Gail; Nutley, New Jersey. Scheer, D.; Steenberger, West Germany. Schetters, C.; Laagboss, Holland. Schinz-Graf, Frau Dorothea; Gruningen, Switzerland. Schmid-Joggi, F. & L.; Wallbach, Switzerland. Schonheyder, Mrs. Sofie; Oslo, Norway. Schrage, Bill; Spokane, Washington. Schreurs, Joan A.; Edison, New Jersey. Schriber-Schar, Edy & Regina; Bern, Switzerland. Schultze, Ilse; Hamburg, Germany. Schutz, Pauline; Alvin, Texas. Schwartz, Barbara; Hollis, New Hampshire. Schwartz, Shirley; Little Neck, New York. Schwarz, Jane A.; Wyckoff, New Jersey. Scott, Edwin & Willie; Trout, Louisiana. Scott, Willie; Trout, Louisiana. Seiler, Regula Pales; Bern, Switzerland. Sellers, Monica; Lancester, California. Semencic, Carl; West Hempstead, New York. Sentis, Richard; Rouergue, France. Serman, Mrs. Chris; Erdington, England. Shannon, Ellen J.; Farmingdale, New York. Sherling, Kristina; Saugus, California. Shushunov, Sergey; Jacksonville, Florida. Siegenthaler-Eggiman, Dr. Margret; Zollbruck, Switzerland. Silkworth, Mary M.; Jackson, Michigan. Simard, H.; Agen, France. Simpson, Mrs. N.C.; New Plymouth, New Zealand. Sinnema, H.; Amsterdam, Holland. Skeen, Susan; Long Beach, California. Skilton, Donald & Louise; Weymouth, Massachusetts. Slater, Rachel; South Granby, Quebec, Canada. Slaughter, Bill; Land-O-Lakes, Florida. Smith, Mrs. M.M.; Watford, England. Smith, Susan & Daniel; Newtown, Connecticut. Snizer, Ed; Lincoln, New Jersey. Solarski, Diane E.; Wrightstown, New Jersey. Solinsky, Barbara; Nesco, New Jersey. Sombach, David E.; Schwenksville, Pennsylvania. Soriano, Pedro Pérez; Tarragona, Spain. Sorkin, Dr. Arthur; Los Gatos, California. Sorrentino, Diane; Bogota, New Jersey. Sottile, Michael; Bridgewater, New Jersey. Sousa Mendes, José; Portugal. Spannagl, Leopold; Zwettl, West Germany. Spesak, Barbara; Spring Valley, Ohio. Spies, K.; New Jersey. Spitz Club of Finland. Spurrell, Mrs. P.V.; Wiltshire, England. Squire, Karen; Valatie, New York. St. Onge, Jacqueline; Quebec, Canada. Stachel, Ernst; Franental, Austria. Stadler, W.; Germany. Stampe, Annelise Juul; Viborg, Denmark. Stanton, Kenneth & Charlotte; Westwood, Massachusetts. Starkweather; Patricia; Haverford, Pennsylvania. Steen, Mrs. Wiebke; Hamburg, Germany. Steghofer, Andreas; Vienna, Austria. Steidel, Kitty; Scottsdale, Arizona. Stein, Angela; New Jersey. Stein, Kathy & Louis; Icard, North Carolina. Stelql, Pia Maria; Wienfelden, Switzerland. Stephens, Jim; Beaver Dam, Kentucky. Stephens, Lorraine; Newcastle, Oklahoma. Stiles, Barbara; Newton, New Jersey. Stodghill, Tom; Quinlan, Texas. Stoeckli, Hans-Rudolf; Langenthal, Switzerland. Stone, Faye & Myrl; USA. Storace, Dr. Antonio; Genova, Italy. Storholm, Mr. Karl; Elverum, Norway. Strang, Alison & Roy; British Columbia, Canada. Streeter, Mrs. Elizabeth; Chester Springs, Pennsylvania. Stroink-Schreuder, Mrs. A.; Heerhugowaard, Netherlands. Strowe, Margaret & John; Sparta, New Jersey. Summons, Dr. Howard & Gretel; Sinking Spring, Pennsylvania. Sunzer, Ed; Lincoln Park, New Jersey. Sutter, Joseph; Waldkirch, Switzerland. Swanberg, Roberta; Stanfordville, New York. Tabor, Joan; Upper Montclair, New Jersey. Tapp, Susan; Washington, New Jersey. Tavernese, Yuan; D'Aigues, France. Terrada, Alejandro Malter; Argentina. Terry, Herb & Ruth; Weston, Connecticut. The Boykin Spaniel Society; Camden, South Carolina. Thiery, Michel; Puymirol, France. Thomas, Amanda; Clinton, New York. Thomas, Joan; Scarborough, Ontario, Canada. Thomas, Patricia A.; Lansing, Michigan. Thompson, Clarence E.; Macon, North Carolina. Thompson, Dottie; Bloomingdale, Illinois. Thompson, Robert; Brooklyn, New York. Thordsen, Carol; Andover, New Jersey. Thorp, Susan; Oskaloosa, Iowa. Tipoin, Albert; Beause, France. Tirry, R.; Hoboken, Belgium. Tomita, Rick Jacquet; Paramus, New Jersey. Touf, Alfonso; Barcelona, Spain. Toze, Zajtar; Radovljica, Yugoslavia. Trabiley, E.T. & L.J.; Brick Township, New Jersey. Trainor, William J.; Oxford,

Massachusetts. Trama, Noreen; Richmond, Texas. Travers, Garry & Lynn; Ontario, Canada. Traverse, E.S.; Castleton, Vermont. Trowbridge, Marjorie; Madison, Connecticut. Tschopp, Ilse E.; Forch, Switzerland. Tucker, Ron; Pennsburg, Pennsylvania. Tveter, Mr. Oddvar; Sarpsborg, Norway. Tyson, Miss Valerie; Coventry, England. Umlaas, Rod; Clinton, New York. Ungar, Kathy & Maurice; Valencia, California. United Kennel Club, USA. Vael, F.W.A.; Holland. Vallet, Alfred; Chevreuse, France. Van Abeelzoom Kennel; Kilburg, Holland. Van Benthem, Cees; Elst, West Germany. Van der Ende, H.; Mülheim-Ruhr, Germany. Van der Raadt, T.; Amsterdam, Holland. Van Elsbergen, Heimo; Bonn, Germany. Van Gelder, Ferdinand Nuyts & Lea; Averbode, Belgium. Van Huffel, Danny; Amsterdam, Holland. Van Vliet, Mr.; Connecticut. Vansteenkiste, Deleu; Klemskerke, Holland. Varese, Rosanna; Italy. Vasconcelos Pres., Señor; Lisbon, Portugal. Vaudo, Joseph & Mary; Newton, Connecticut. Verheugen, Mr. J.; Biezen-mortel, Netherlands. Vines, G.S.; Bretforton, England. Vittorio, Merigo; Issiglio, Italy. Vlanin, Nina; San Francisco, California. Voillot, Mr. Marcel; Montigny/Aube, France. Voorhees, Mr.; Edwardsburg, Michigan. Vooris, Donna; Shirley, New York. Vulvin, M.; La Geney Touse, France. Vutela, Paivi; Inkeroinen, Finland. Walker, Darlene; Kemah, Texas. Walschaerts, Mrs. A.; Lucca, Italy. Walters, Berenice; Bargo, Australia. Ward, Dr. Craig; Columbia, South Carolina. Ward, Jeanette & Joel; Wiscosville, Pennsylvania. Ward, Mrs. Janet; Suffolk, England. Wasserman, Ann; Pompton Lakes, New Jersey. Watson, Mrs. M.; Norwich, England. Wear, Mrs. W.P.; Cecilton, Maryland. Weber, Felix & Tina; Rickenbach, Switzerland. Weikel, John; Mt. Vernon, Indiana. Weiss, Jytte; Soro, Denmark. Werk, C.; Vlaardingen, Hungary. White, Lisa; Dickinson, Texas. Whitely, Dr. H. Ellen; Amarillo, Texas. Whitman, Janet & Marvin; Spring Valley, New Jersey. Wilkes, Paul & Pam; Hardwick, Massachusetts. Williams, Kenneth; Hempstead, Maryland. Wills, Angela; Spencer, Oklahoma. Wilson, Jeanne Kundell; Westford, Vermont. Wilson, Leon J.; Patterson, New Jersey. Wilson-Smith, Miss Kayte; Herfordshire, England. Winston, Ruth; Lido Beach, New York. Wöhry, Victor; Kapfenberg, Austria. Wojculewski, Stephen; Coram, New York. Wolforth, Gwendolyn; Icard, North Carolina. Wollpert, Neil & Marra; Kettering, Ohio. Wood, Barbara; Cranford, New Jersey. Wunsch, Nete; Naestved, Ontario, Canada. Wurgler, L.; Zollbruck, Switzerland. Wurtenberger, Heinz; Ludwigshafen-Oggersheim, Germany. Wuthrich, Hansruedi; Bernes Oberland, Switzerland. Yanoff, Arthur; Concord, New Hampshire. Yntema, R. & E.; British Columbia, Canada. Young, Fredricka; Fairfax Station, Virginia. Yrza, J.D.; Castellon, Portugal. Yuspa, Rochelle; Baltimore, Maryland. Zarko, Bengić; Pazin, Yugoslavia. Zarobinski, Karen M.; Dover, New Jersey. Zazempa, Daniel; Pontheirry, France. Zingler, Marcy; Fort Lee, New Jersey. Zollo, Michael; Bernardsville, New York.

Index

Page numbers in bold indicate major breed articles.